Teacher's Edition

Level 1 • Unit 1

Let's Read!

— PROGRAM AUTHORS —

Carl Bereiter
Ann Brown
Joe Campione
Iva Carruthers
Robbie Case
Jan Hirshberg
Marilyn Jager Adams
Anne McKeough
Michael Pressley
Marsha Roit
Marlene Scardamalia
Marcy Stein
Gerald H. Treadway, Jr.

A Division of The McGraw-Hill Companies

Columbus, Ohio

Acknowledgments

From WOLF!, by Becky Bloom, illustrated by Pascal Biet. Published by Orchard Books, an imprint of Scholastic, Inc. Copyright © 1999 by Siphano. Montpelier. Reprinted by permission of Scholastic, Inc. "Las hormiguitas*The Little Ants" by Jose Luis Orozco from DE COLORES AND OTHER LATIN AMERICAN FOLK SONGS FOR CHILDREN by Jose-Luis Orozco, copyright © 1994 by Jose-Luis Orozco. Used by permission of Dutton Children's Books, an imprint of Penguin Putnam Books For Young Readers, a division of Penguin Putnam Inc. "If I Were A Mouse" by Solveig Paulson Russell, reprinted from the September, Series III Issue of YOUR BIG BACKYARD magazine, with the permission of the publisher, the National Wildlife Federation. Copyright 1984 by the National Wildlife Federation. "There Was Once a Fish" by Arnold Lobel, from THE RANDOM HOUSE BOOK OF MOTHER GOOSE by Arnold Lobel. Copyright © 1986 by Arnold Lobel. Reprinted by permission of Random House Children's Books, a division of Random House, Inc. "Twinkle, Twinkle, Firefly" by kind permission of John Agard taken from No Hickory, No Dickory, No Dock (Viking 1990). THE CHASE by Beatrice Tanaka, Translation copyright © 1991 by Crown Publishers, Inc. Copyright © 1990 by Kaleidoscope, Paris. Published by arrangement with Random House Children's Books, a division of Random House, Inc., New York, New York. All rights reserved. MRS. GOOSE'S BABY. Copyright © 1989 Charlotte Voake. Reproduced by permission of Candlewick Press Inc., Cambridge, MA on behalf of Walker Books Ltd., London. "Babybuggy" copyright © 1991 by Jane Yolen. Reprinted by permission of Curtis Brown, Ltd.

Grateful acknowledgment is given to the preceding publishers and copyright owners for permissions granted to reprint selections from their publications. All possible care has been taken to trace ownership and secure permission for each selection included. In case of any errors or omissions, the Publisher will be pleased to make suitable acknowledgments in future editions.

www.sra4kids.com

SRA/McGraw-Hill

A Division of The ***McGraw-Hill*** *Companies*

Send all inquires to:
SRA/McGraw-Hill
8787 Orion Place
Columbus, OH 43240-4027

Printed in the United States of America.

ISBN 0-07-569613-4

1 2 3 4 5 6 7 8 9 WEB 07 06 05 04 03 02 01

Welcome to

Open Court Reading: The Most Complete, Effective Reading Program Available

Open Court Reading is the only reading program that provides:

- An **educational philosophy** based on scientific research and **nearly 40 years** of practical classroom experience
- A program that has been **proven successful in schools** nationwide
- A **well-defined plan of systematic, explicit instruction** for teaching the strategies and skills of reading
- A **partnership through training** that will help teachers and administrators successfully implement *Open Court Reading*

Open Court Reading is a **research-based** curriculum grounded in **systematic, explicit instruction** of:

- Phonemic awareness, phonics, and word knowledge
- Comprehension skills and strategies
- Inquiry skills and strategies
- Writing and language arts skills and strategies

The program creates a **literature-rich environment** that instills a passion for lifelong reading and a love of literature and the written word.

Our basic **philosophy** has remained consistent for nearly **40 years**. *Open Court Reading* has always contained the keys to teaching children how to read and read to learn.

Open Court Reading
Creates Confident Learners

Open Court Reading provides:

- Research-based instruction
- Strong authorship
- A systematic, explicit instructional plan
- Literature with a purpose
- Differentiating instruction for meeting students' individual needs

Research-Based Instruction

Open Court Reading is built on a solid foundation of nearly **40 years of research**. Test results repeatedly prove its effectiveness. Reading instruction trends may have changed; *Open Court Reading* has remained true to the fact that children learn best when taught using what has been researched and proven to work.

Open Court Reading is based on four types of research:

1. Academic
2. Most effective practices in education
3. Field testing
4. Learner verification results

Open Court Reading is the **only** program that guarantees all four.

Strong Authorship

The authors of *Open Court Reading* bring expertise in specific areas of educational research to our program. They are published widely; books, journal articles, and research studies are tributes to the respect they are given in the field of education.

Research in Action articles found throughout the program provide information showing how the work of our authors and others respected in the field of educational research have been incorporated into our program. These articles provide more information on how *Open Court Reading* works and why it is so successful.

Systematic, Explicit Instructional Plan

Students are most successful when they learn through a balance of systematic direct instruction in sound and word recognition, guided practice, and application of skills with extensive reading of decodable text and authentic literature.

Through systematic, explicit instruction, *Open Court Reading* has organized lessons in the most logical and efficient way possible for teaching children to read and write with skill and confidence. All strategies and skills are arranged from the simplest to the most complex. Because the skills build upon one another, children are able to grasp complex concepts more easily.

Open Court Reading provides more comprehensive Teacher Editions than any other program. The presentation of concepts, skills, and practice is detailed – all you need to do is follow the directions. Reading and writing strategies are delivered in a manner that has been proven through research to be the most effective.

Research in Action
Phonemic Awareness

The goal of phonemic awareness activities is to lead students to understand that spoken words are made up of chains of smaller sounds—the syllables and phonemes. Because students are accustomed to producing and hearing words as unbreakable wholes, this is not a natural insight. Nevertheless, for understanding an alphabetic language in which the letters and letter patterns represent the sub-sounds of words, it is a critical insight. After students have learned to think about words in terms of their component sounds, decoding will make sense and inventive spelling will come easily. Conversely, poorly developed phonemic awareness is believed to be the single greatest cause of reading disability. *(Marilyn J. Adams)*

Literature With a Purpose

Open Court Reading provides a **survey course of literature**, exposing students to a variety of different **writing styles** and **genres**. We guide students in understanding the strategies and skills necessary for reading text in the **real world**. Literature in *Open Court Reading* is found in:

- Big Books
- Anthologies
- Teacher Read Alouds
- Story Time Selections (Kindergarten)
- Online bibliography

In *Open Court Reading*, students are reading literature written by trade book authors by the middle of Grade 1. Our compilation of literature selections is so tightly woven that our students are involved in independent **Inquiry and Investigation** on complicated subjects much sooner and with more ease.

Differentiating Instruction for Meeting Individual Needs

Open Court Reading provides a variety of proven experiences for accommodating individual students' needs.

- Reteach
- Intervention
- Challenge
- English-Language Learners

Research and Results

Open Court Reading is The Most Thoroughly Researched Program Available

Research Shows:

Students who are early independent readers:

- Learn better throughout their school years
- Become motivated readers who typically read more than children who learn to read later
- Develop increased:
  - Vocabulary
  - Understanding of abstract concepts
  - Appreciation of a diverse array of literature and writing styles
  - General knowledge

While current educational standards call for students to be reading by the end of Grade 3, *Open Court Reading* is structured to ensure that students are reading fluently and comprehending what they read **by the end of Grade 1.**

The Open Court Response:

Open Court has always included those essential concepts that research has repeatedly shown are necessary for learning to read. By using established routines throughout the program, *Open Court Reading* systematically and explicitly teaches each of these essential concepts:

- The alphabetic principle
- Print awareness
- Phonemic awareness
- Systematic, explicit phonics
- Comprehension strategies and skills
- Inquiry techniques and strategies
- The writing process and writing skills
- Spelling and vocabulary
- Grammar, usage, and mechanics

A Success Story 40 Years in the Making

Since the early 1960s, Open Court has included the fundamental elements that research has shown are necessary for teaching children how to read.

For nearly 40 years, Open Court has monitored and learned from the research that experts in the field of reading have conducted, incorporating these important findings into the programs.

SRA is proud to note that many of those same researchers hold *Open Court Reading* in high esteem as a well-balanced program that teaches students not only how to read, but also how to comprehend and make the most of reading content.

A Reading Program Rooted In Research

Academic Research

Leaders in educational research, the authors of *Open Court Reading* are experts on how children learn to read and read to learn. Together, they have created *Open Court Reading* to most effectively help expand students' reading and learning capabilities.

- **Phonemic awareness and systematic, explicit phonics** instruction is based on the work of **Dr. Marilyn Jager Adams**, author of the most frequently cited book on beginning reading, *Learning to Read: Thinking and Learning about Print* (1990).
- **Comprehension skills and strategies** instruction is based on the work of **Dr. Ann Brown's** reciprocal teaching model and **Dr. Michael Pressley's** transactional strategy instruction model.
- **Dr. Marlene Scardamalia** lends the benefit of extensive research in the psychology of writing.
- Research conducted by **Dr. Carl Bereiter** is incorporated into the **Inquiry and Investigation** part of each lesson.
- A **Professional Development** plan has been developed and is expertly guided by **Dr. Marsha Roit**.
- The **Intervention** materials were created under the direction of **Dr. Marcy Stein**, who is widely published on the subject of special education, and **Dr. Marsha Roit** who, through her work in classrooms, brings a unique perspective to these materials.

Most Effective Practices in Education

- A comprehensive report by the **National Reading Panel** (2000) endorses the instructional model that *Open Court Reading* has used for nearly 40 years.
- Findings from studies being conducted by the **National Institute of Child Health and Human Development (NICHD)**, as well as conclusions from comprehensive reviews of beginning

reading research, all indicate that effective reading instruction should include the strategies found in *Open Court Reading* for teaching children how to read.

- The **American Federation of Teachers (AFT)** reviewed current reading programs and issued a statement called *What Works*. In this statement, Open Court was identified as a program that incorporates research-based instruction and has classroom data to support its effectiveness.
- The **U.S. Department of Education's** Reading Excellence Act has awarded state grants to improve reading achievement mandating that schools choose programs that show "scientifically based research and effective practices that have been replicated effectively." Open Court has been the program of choice for schools throughout the nation who are being awarded this grant.
- An independent study (**Educational Research Analysis**, 2000) states that "*Open Court Reading* has the highest decodability, comprehensiveness, intensiveness, and consistency of any reading program." It was ranked best of all programs reviewed.

Field Testing

A study conducted by Foorman, et al. (1996) compared the effectiveness of the explicit, systematic program, Open Court, to other approaches. Results of this study found that Open Court's direct instruction approach was more effective with students at risk of reading failure than the other approaches as measured by a variety of tests, including standardized measures.

Learner Verification Results

In a study conducted by Douglas J. McRae, educational measurement specialist, Stanford/9 test scores from the STAR program were analyzed. The results of that study indicate:

- Open Court schools had higher gain scores statewide.
- Open Court provided the largest gain scores for schools with high concentration of both LEP (Limited English Proficient) and Low-SES (Socio-Economic Status) students.
- Scores show cumulative advantage over the span of two years with Open Court.

The conclusion of this study was that using Open Court made a difference. These schools (a sampling of over 150,000 students) showed greater gains than either statewide gains or gains from a demographically matched set of schools.

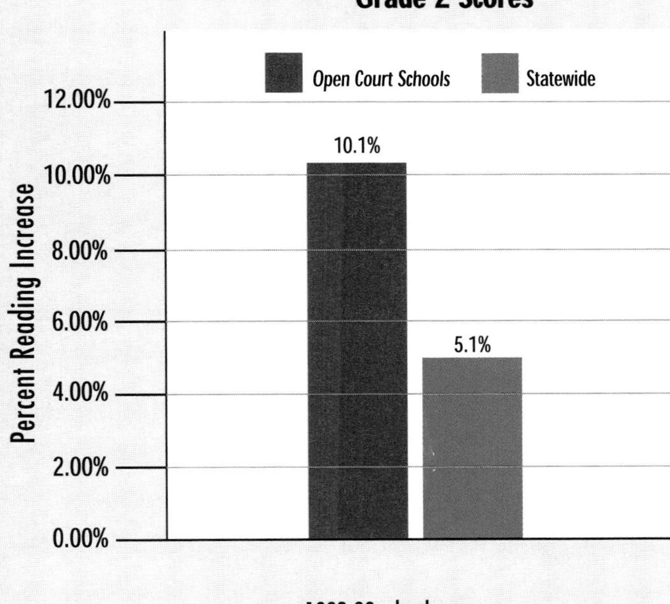

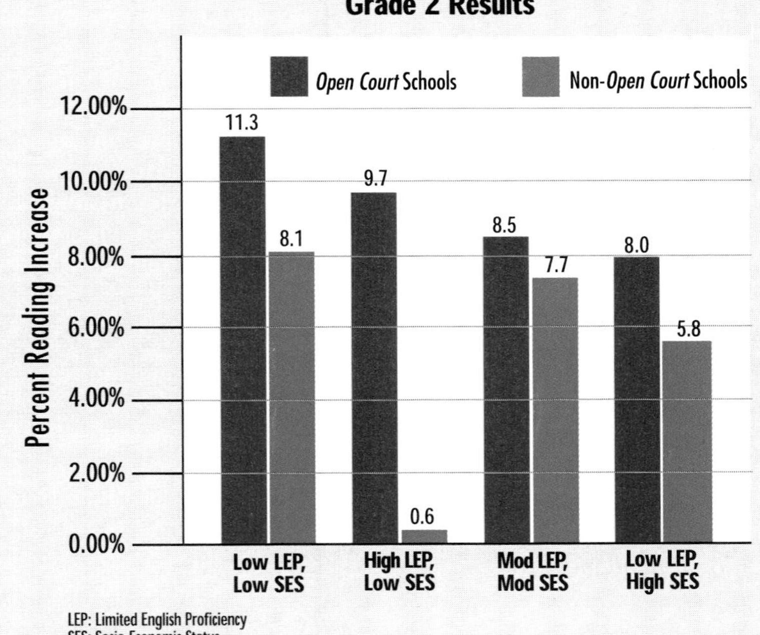

For a complete look at this study, please call 1-800-772-4543 and ask for Research Findings: The Research-Based Reading Materials You Choose May Have a Direct Impact on Your Students' Reading Performance, ISBN# R80000456.

Open Court Reading Authors

Bring Research Into Your Classroom

Marilyn Jager Adams, Ph.D.

Cited in the *2000 Politics of Education Yearbook* as one of the most influential people in the national reading policy arena, Dr. Adams has worked closely with a number of agencies to develop reading standards, policies, and staff development strategies.

- Author/co-author of:
  - *Beginning to Read: Thinking and Learning about Print*
  - *Preventing Reading Difficulties in Young Children*
  - *Fox in a Box* Assessment Program
  - *Phonemic Awareness in Young Children*
  - *Odyssey: A Curriculum for Thinking*
- Advisor to *Sesame Street* and *Between the Lions*

Carl Bereiter, Ph.D.

An accomplished author, researcher, and professor, Dr. Bereiter has published extensively on teaching and learning.

- Invented CSILE (Computer Supported Intentional Learning Environments), the first networked collaborative learning environment in schools, with Dr. Marlene Scardamalia; the current version, *Knowledge Forum®*, is in use in 12 countries
- Co-author of:
  - *The Psychology of Written Composition*
  - *Surpassing Ourselves: The Nature and Implications of Expertise*
- Author of *Education and the Mind of the Knowledge Age*
- Professor at Centre for Applied Cognitive Science, Ontario Institute for Studies in Education
- One of 100 people honored in the Routledge Great Thinkers in Education
- Member of the National Academy of Education

Joe Campione, Ph.D.

A leading researcher on cognitive development, individual differences, assessment, and the design of innovative learning environments, Dr. Campione is currently a Professor in the School of Education at University of California at Berkley.

- Most recent work has focused on methods to restructure elementary schools
- Has created curriculums that introduce students as early as Grade 1 to the research process

Iva Carruthers, Ph.D.

Equipped with both hands-on and academic experience, Dr. Carruthers serves as a consultant and lecturer in both educational technology and matters of multicultural inclusion.

- President of Nexus Unlimited, Inc., a human resources development and computer services consulting firm
- Consultant, U.S. Advisory Council on the National Information Infrastructure
- Former Chairperson and Professor of the Sociology Department at Northeastern Illinois University
- Has developed software for teaching African-American history and inter-disciplinary subjects
- Co-producer of *Know Your Heritage*, a televised academic quiz show
- Has also been an elementary school teacher, high school counselor, and research historian

Jan Hirshberg, Ed.D.

Focusing on how children learn to read and write and the logistics of teaching reading and writing in the early grades, Dr. Hirshberg is currently working as a language arts resource teacher and consultant in Alexandria, Virginia.

- Author/co-author of:
  - *Open Court 1989, Kindergarten and Grade 1 Reading and Writing Program*
  - *Collections for Young Scholars*
  - *Open Court 1995* and *2000*, reading, writing, and learning program
- Former teaching fellow, research assistant, instructor, and lecturer at the Graduate School of Education at Harvard University
- Former elementary school teacher and school district reading consultant

Anne McKeough, Ph.D.

A Professor in the Division of Applied Psychology and Chair of the Human Learning and Development program at the University of Calgary, Dr. McKeough has received a number of research awards and grants.

- Co-editor of several volumes, including:
  - *Toward the Practice of Theory Based Instruction: Current Cognitive Theories and Their Educational Promise*
  - *Teaching for Transfer: Fostering Generalization in Learning*
  - *Schools in Transition*
- Has authored numerous articles advocating the benefits of a continued and reflective partnership between teaching practices and child development research
- Current research focuses on cognitive development and developmentally based instruction

Michael Pressley, Ph.D.

Most recently honored by the National Reading Conference as the 2000 recipient of the Oscar Causey Award for career contributions to reading research, Dr. Pressley is the Academic Director of the Masters of Education Program and Professor of Psychology at the University of Notre Dame.

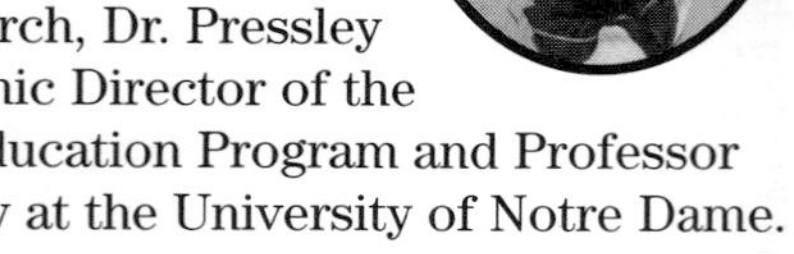

- Editor of *Journal of Educational Psychology*
- Author of *Reading Instruction That Works: The Case for Balanced Teaching* and co-author of *Learning to Read: Lessons from Exemplary First-Grade Classrooms*
- An expert in comprehension instruction and in the ethnographic study of the elementary classroom experience
- Author of more than 200 scientific articles

Marsha Roit, Ed.D.

The Director of Professional Development for SRA/McGraw-Hill, Dr. Roit spends considerable time in classrooms developing reading and writing curricula and training teachers and administrators in effective instructional practices.

- Works directly with school districts creating staff development models that support research-based instruction and its effectiveness
- Has focused research on strategy instruction with both mainstream and English-Language Learners
- Has published in a variety of professional journals, including:
  - *Exceptional Children*
  - *Journal of Learning Disabilities*
  - *The Elementary School Journal*

Marlene Scardamalia, Ph.D.

A Professor at Centre for Applied Cognitive Science and Department of Curriculum Teaching and Learning, Ontario Institute for Studies in Education, Dr. Scardamalia has conducted research and been published in the areas of cognitive development, psychology of writing, intentional learning, the nature of expertise, and educational uses of computers.

- Invented CSILE (Computer Supported Intentional Learning Environments), the first networked collaborative learning environment in schools, with Dr. Carl Bereiter; the current version, *Knowledge Forum*®, is in use in 12 countries
- Member of the U.S. National Academy of Education
- While a fellow at the Center for Advanced Study in Behavioral Sciences, headed "Cognitive Bases of Educational Reform," from which grew "Schools of Thought," a school reform program noted for its synthesis of major cognitive-based learning initiatives

Marcy Stein, Ph.D.

An Associate Professor and founding faculty member of the education program at the University of Washington, Dr. Stein currently coordinates At-Risk and Special Education graduate programs, and teaches in the teacher certification program. She has served as consultant to departments of education on the translation of reading research to instructional practice.

- She has published extensively on topics including:
  - Beginning and remedial reading instruction
  - Vocabulary acquisition
  - Curriculum and textbook analysis
- She has served on many national and local committees and in consultant positions, including:
  - Los Angeles Unified School District, Consultant
  - Washington State Special Education Improvement Grant Steering Committee, Invited Member
  - Effective School Practices, Reviewer

Gerald H. Treadway, Jr., Ph.D.

Professor at San Diego State University, Dr. Treadway teaches reading methods, balanced reading programs, and reading comprehension.

- Member of California's Reading Task Force and the Reading Credentials Task Force
- Member of California Academic Standards Commission
- Associate Director of the California Reading and Literature Project
- Contributing author to *Fox in a Box*, a diagnostic reading assessment for students in Grades K-2
- Former member and Chair of the California Curriculum Commission
- Former elementary school teacher

Ann Brown, Ph.D.

The Past President of the American Education Research Association, Dr. Brown conducted a great deal of research in the area of distributed expertise in the classroom.

- Worked as a professor of math, science, and technology in the Graduate School of Education at the University of California at Berkeley
- Served on the congressional panel to monitor National Assessment of Education Progress state-by-state assessments
- Received many honors and awards in both the United States and England for her contributions to educational research

Robbie Case, Ph.D.

Beginning in the mid-'70s, Dr. Case conducted research on the relationship between children's learning and their cognitive development during elementary school.

- Former Professor of Education at Stanford University
- Former Director of the Laidlaw-Centre at the Institute of Child Study, University of Toronto
- Authored books and scholarly articles on cognitive development that are sold throughout the world

Open Court Reading
Instructional Plan

Systematic and Explicit

Explicit instruction is teacher-directed identification of learning goals, specific presentation to students, teacher modeling, student practice, and assessment.

Systematic instruction outlines the logical sequence of skill presentation and research-based, effective learning routines.

2 Reading and Responding

Comprehension Skills and Strategies

Part 2 of every lesson teaches specific comprehension skills and strategies in conjunction with the excellent literature that forms the core of each lesson. Comprehension strategies, such as clarifying, summarizing, and predicting, are modeled, practiced, and reviewed in the first reading of the literature. Comprehension skills, including classifying and categorizing, and drawing conclusions are modeled, practiced, and reviewed in the second reading of the literature. This comprehensive development of skills and strategies builds life-long confidence.

Teacher Modeling

Teacher modeling is key to systematic, explicit instruction. Starting in Kindergarten, teachers model a repertoire of skills and strategies students learn to apply independently. Every lesson includes multiple opportunities to model the process that good readers use. Students then practice and apply the modeled strategies to work up to independent use of the strategies.

Open Court Reading provides systematic and explicit instruction for every skill throughout the program.

1 Preparing to Read

- Sounds and letters
- Phonemic awareness
- Phonics and fluency
- Word knowledge

In Kindergarten and Grade 1, Part 1 of every lesson carefully teaches letter names, sounds, and spellings in a carefully crafted sequence that enables students to begin reading real words as soon as possible. Phonemic awareness, phonics, and fluency skills are all presented using research-based strategies that include blending and segmentation. Students quickly, efficiently, and effectively learn the sound patterns that make up English words. Practice and review of these key skills are systematically built into the curriculum to ensure mastery. In later grades, word knowledge is presented with the same careful attention. At the same time, students increase vocabulary skills through careful presentation and practice using vocabulary from the literature selection.

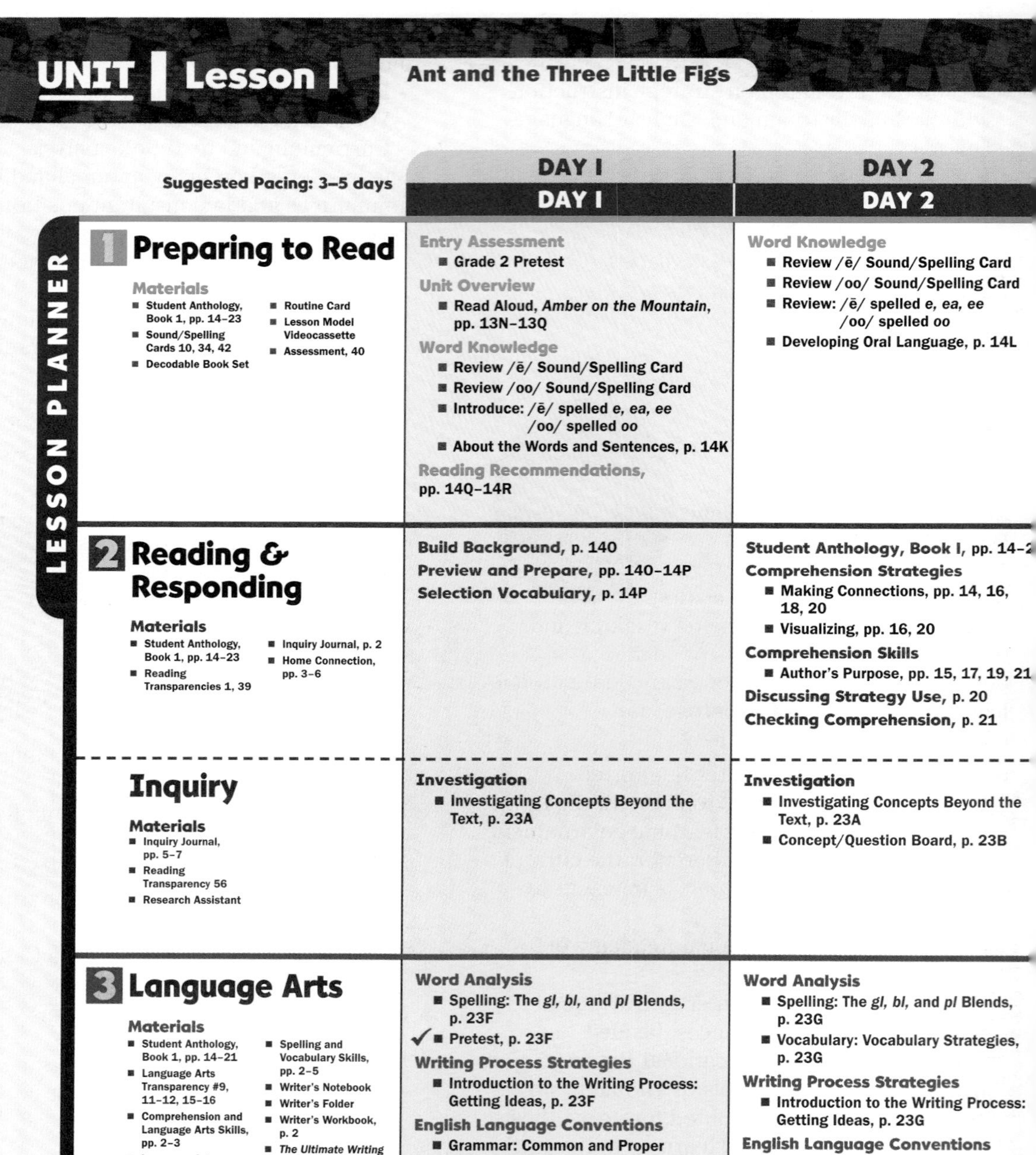

UNIT I Lesson I — Ant and the Three Little Figs

LESSON PLANNER

Suggested Pacing: 3–5 days	DAY I	DAY 2
1 Preparing to Read Materials ■ Student Anthology, Book 1, pp. 14–23 ■ Sound/Spelling Cards 10, 34, 42 ■ Decodable Book Set ■ Routine Card ■ Lesson Model Videocassette ■ Assessment, 40	**Entry Assessment** ■ Grade 2 Pretest **Unit Overview** ■ Read Aloud, *Amber on the Mountain*, pp. 13N–13Q **Word Knowledge** ■ Review /ē/ Sound/Spelling Card ■ Review /oo/ Sound/Spelling Card ■ Introduce: /ē/ spelled *e, ea, ee* /oo/ spelled *oo* ■ About the Words and Sentences, p. 14K **Reading Recommendations,** pp. 14Q–14R	**Word Knowledge** ■ Review /ē/ Sound/Spelling Card ■ Review /oo/ Sound/Spelling Card ■ Review: /ē/ spelled *e, ea, ee* /oo/ spelled *oo* ■ Developing Oral Language, p. 14L
2 Reading & Responding Materials ■ Student Anthology, Book 1, pp. 14–23 ■ Reading Transparencies 1, 39 ■ Inquiry Journal, p. 2 ■ Home Connection, pp. 3–6	**Build Background,** p. 14O **Preview and Prepare,** pp. 14O–14P **Selection Vocabulary,** p. 14P	**Student Anthology, Book I,** pp. 14–2[illegible] **Comprehension Strategies** ■ Making Connections, pp. 14, 16, 18, 20 ■ Visualizing, pp. 16, 20 **Comprehension Skills** ■ Author's Purpose, pp. 15, 17, 19, 21 **Discussing Strategy Use,** p. 20 **Checking Comprehension,** p. 21
Inquiry Materials ■ Inquiry Journal, pp. 5–7 ■ Reading Transparency 56 ■ Research Assistant	**Investigation** ■ Investigating Concepts Beyond the Text, p. 23A	**Investigation** ■ Investigating Concepts Beyond the Text, p. 23A ■ Concept/Question Board, p. 23B
3 Language Arts Materials ■ Student Anthology, Book 1, pp. 14–21 ■ Language Arts Transparency #9, 11–12, 15–16 ■ Comprehension and Language Arts Skills, pp. 2–3 ■ Language Arts Handbook ■ Spelling and Vocabulary Skills, pp. 2–5 ■ Writer's Notebook ■ Writer's Folder ■ Writer's Workbook, p. 2 ■ *The Ultimate Writing and Creativity Center* CD-ROM	**Word Analysis** ■ Spelling: The *gl, bl,* and *pl* Blends, p. 23F ✓■ Pretest, p. 23F **Writing Process Strategies** ■ Introduction to the Writing Process: Getting Ideas, p. 23F **English Language Conventions** ■ Grammar: Common and Proper Nouns, p. 23F	**Word Analysis** ■ Spelling: The *gl, bl,* and *pl* Blends, p. 23G ■ Vocabulary: Vocabulary Strategies, p. 23G **Writing Process Strategies** ■ Introduction to the Writing Process: Getting Ideas, p. 23G **English Language Conventions** ■ Grammar: Common and Proper Nouns, p. 23G

14E Unit I Lesson I

Ⓟ Phonics ✓Informal Assessment Available ✓Formal Assessment Ava[illegible]

Inquiry

Inquiry and investigation strategies are thoughtfully developed to teach students how to ask questions and find the answers to their questions. With Inquiry, students apply all of the reading, comprehension, and language arts skills they are learning in order to develop and present their investigations.

3 Language Arts

- Spelling
- Vocabulary
- Writing process strategies
- Writer's craft
- English language conventions
- Grammar, usage, and mechanics
- Listening, speaking, and viewing
- Penmanship
- Basic computer skills

Part 3 of every lesson includes systematic and explicit development of language arts skills, including the writing process, writing traits, writer's craft, and structures of writing in different genres. Each skill is explicitly taught using teacher models or models from the *Language Arts Handbook*, and practiced in reading and/or writing activities. These activities show how the skill is connected to the other parts of the lesson. Like the phonics and comprehension skills, the language arts skills are added to each student's knowledge toolbox, so that students can employ appropriate skills when developing their investigations, or in other contexts.

Theme: **Sharing Stories**

DAY 2 continued / DAY 3	DAY 3 / DAY 4	DAY 5
nics and Fluency Ⓟ Review /j/ Sound/Spelling Card Introduce: Short vowels /j/ spelled ■ *dge* Compound words About the Words and Sentences, p. 14M Developing Oral Language, p. 14N	Phonics and Fluency Ⓟ ■ Review /j/ Sound/Spelling Card ■ Review: Short vowels /j/ spelled ■ *dge* Compound words ■ Dictation, p. 14N Reading a Decodable Book ■ Decodable Book 15, p. 14N	Review Phonics and Fluency
dent Anthology, Book I, pp. 14–23 porting the Reading, p. 21C Making Connections et the Author/Illustrator, p. 22 me Connections, p. 23	Student Anthology, Book I, pp. 14–23 Discussing the Selection, p. 21A ■ Review the selection ■ Complete discussion Review Selection Vocabulary, p. 21B Literary Elements, p. 21D ■ Mood and Tone	Comprehension Test Home Connection, p. 21B Social Studies Connection, p. 21F ■ Sharing stories about different types of food
estigation Generating Questions to Investigate, p. 23C	Supporting the Investigation ■ Alphabetical Order, p. 23D	Investigation ■ Concept/Question Board
rd Analysis Spelling: The *gl*, *bl*, and *pl* Blends, p. 23H Vocabulary: Vocabulary Strategies, p. 23H iting Process Strategies Introduction to the Writing Process: Getting Ideas, p. 23H glish Language Conventions Grammar: Common and Proper Nouns, p. 23H	Word Analysis ■ Spelling: The *gl*, *bl*, and *pl* Blends, p. 23I ■ Vocabulary: Vocabulary Strategies, p. 23I Writing Process Strategies ■ Introduction to the Writing Process: Getting Ideas, p. 23I English Language Conventions ✓■ Listening, Speaking, Viewing Listening: Purposes of Listening, p. 23I	Word Analysis ■ Spelling: The *gl*, *bl*, and *pl* Blends, p. 23J ✓■ Final Test, p. 23J ✓■ Vocabulary: Strategies, p. 23J Writing Process Strategies ■ Introduction to the Writing Process: Getting Ideas, p. 23J English Language Conventions ✓■ Penmanship: Manuscript Letters *I* and *i*, p. 23J

Unit I Lesson I 14F

Assessment

Continuous assessment enables teachers to gauge the progress of their students so that no student misses needed instruction.

The assessment section of *Open Court Reading* contains:

- Program assessment
  - Teacher's Observation Log
  - Pretest
  - Midyear test
  - Posttest
- Unit assessments
  Includes assessments for all skills taught. Unit Assessments contain:
  - Oral Fluency Assessments
  - Writing assessments
  - Spelling assessments
  - Vocabulary assessments
  - Listening assessments
  - Grammar, usage, and mechanics assessments
  - Comprehension assessments
  - Literature assessments
  - Class assessment record
  - Student assessment record
- Diagnostic assessment
  Provides more focused assessment opportunities to aid in individualizing instruction.

Open Court Reading
Literature

In-Depth Literary Theme Perspectives

The goal of *Open Court Reading* is to efficiently and effectively teach children to decode then comprehend so that they can read a variety of literature types. All of the skills development throughout the program serves this purpose. From the very beginning, the program has emphasized the quality of the literature students read and the organization of that literature around big ideas to promote understanding and discussion.

Each unit throughout the program explores a comprehensive, interesting theme. The literature in each unit of *Open Court Reading* is organized around one of two types of themes:

- **Universal themes**, such as Keep Trying, Friendship, and Survival encourage in-depth and critical thinking.
- **Research themes**, such as Weather, Astronomy, and Ancient Civilizations, develop inquiry and research in science and social studies content areas.

Inquiry and Investigation

Throughout lessons in *Open Court Reading*, students do more than just read literature. They also ask questions, discuss, research, write about, and think about the concepts and ideas centered around the themes they read.

Quality Literature Organized into Unit Themes

	UNIT 1	UNIT 2	UNIT 3	UNIT 4
LEVEL K	BIG BOOKS			
	School	Shadows	Finding Friends	Wind
LEVEL 1	BIG BOOKS			
	Let's Read	Animals	Things That Go	Our Neighborhood at Work
LEVEL 2	STUDENT ANTHOLOGIES			
	Sharing Stories	Kindness	Look Again	Fossils
LEVEL 3	STUDENT ANTHOLOGIES			
	Friendship	City Wildlife	Imagination	Money
LEVEL 4	STUDENT ANTHOLOGY			
	Risks and Consequences	Dollars and Sense	From Mystery to Medicine	Survival
LEVEL 5	STUDENT ANTHOLOGY			
	Cooperation and Competition	Astronomy	Heritage	Making a New Nation
LEVEL 6	STUDENT ANTHOLOGY			
	Perseverance	Ancient Civilizations	Taking a Stand	Beyond the Notes

UNIT 5	UNIT 6	UNIT 7	UNIT 8	UNIT 9	UNIT 10
Stick to It	Red, White, and Blue	Teamwork	By the Sea		
STUDENT ANTHOLOGIES					
Weather	Journeys	Keep Trying	Games	Being Afraid	Homes
Courage	Our Country and Its People				
Storytelling	Country Life				
Communication	A Changing America				
Going West	Journeys and Quests				
Ecology	A Question of Value				

Focus Questions In what ways can we show kindness to nature? Have you ever had to "let go" of something you love because it was the kind thing to do?

Butterfly House

by Eve Bunting
illustrated by Greg Shed

When I was just a little girl
I saw a small black creature
like a tiny worm,
and saved it from a greedy jay
who wanted it
for lunch. 1

I carried it inside,
safe on its wide green leaf.
My grandpa said
it was a larva
and soon would be
a butterfly. 2

156

157

Open Court Reading Literature

Excellent Examples of a Variety of Literature

Interesting and high-quality literature is introduced in *Open Court Reading* as soon as students begin school. The literature provides the foundation of each lesson throughout the program. Comprehension skills and strategies, spelling and vocabulary, writing process strategies, and English language conventions all connect to the lesson selection.

Each literature selection in the Big Books and Anthologies was painstakingly selected with the following goals in mind:

- **Unique theme perspectives** encourage student inquiry. Each selection in a unit adds a new concept or idea about the theme.
- **A variety of literature** provides fiction and nonfiction genres, including novels, short stories, poems, essays, dramas, mysteries, and informational articles so students experience many different forms of literature.
- **Reading practice** includes grade-level appropriate literature.
- **Excellent examples of writing** in literature provide superior models for students' writing.
- **Classic and contemporary literature** works together to broaden students' perspectives.
- **Author Styles** offer award-winning works and different styles of writing so students develop a cultural literacy.

In addition to the literature in the Big Books and Anthologies, these components provide further exposure to literature in each unit:

- Teacher Read Alouds (K-6)
- Story Time Selections (K)
- Leveled Libraries (K-6)
- Online Bibliography (K-6)

Literature Selections Provide Foundation for Independent Inquiry and Investigation

Chart from Unit Overview found on the following page provides information on how the literature furthers theme-based study.

Focus Questions What information about Mars has been retrieved by the *Viking 1, Viking 2,* and *Pathfinder* landers? How is Mars like and unlike Earth? Is it possible that there ever was or will be life on Mars?

The Mystery of Mars

Sally Ride & Tam O'Shaughnessy

In 1976 *Viking 1* and *Viking 2* settled softly onto the surface of Mars. They were the first spacecraft from Earth ever to visit the Red Planet. Twenty-one years later, *Pathfinder* dropped out of the Martian sky to join them. A parachute opened to slow it down, then giant air bags inflated to cushion it during impact. *Pathfinder* bounced hard more than 15 times before it rolled to a stop on the red Martian soil.

Pathfinder *landed in Ares Vallis, an ancient floodplain. Many of the rocks*

140

Focus Questions How did Galileo contribute to what we know about our solar system? How did people react to his discoveries?

Galileo

from ***Pioneer Astronomers***
by Navin Sullivan
illustrated by Jim Roldan

One May evening in 1609, a carriage rattled briskly through the streets of Padua, in Italy. In it was Galileo Galilei, professor of mathematics, returning from a trip to Venice. While he was there, he had received news from a former pupil named Jacques Badovere—news that had sent him hurrying home.

"A marvelous tube is on sale here," wrote Badovere, who was now living in Paris. "This tube makes distant objects appear close. A man two miles away can be seen distinctly. ❶ People call these tubes 'Dutch perspectives' or 'Dutch cylinders.' Some say that they were invented by Hans Lippershey, an obscure maker of eyeglasses in Middleburg, Holland. What is sure is that they empl… convex and the other concave."

The carriage turned into the Borgo d… stopped outside Galileo's house. Pausin… his garden, Galileo hurried indoors and…

"One convex and one concave," he re… in a trance. He drew writing paper tow… a sharpened quill in the ink, and began…

"Suppose the convex lens is placed i… the light," he muttered. "Then if the co… is placed the right distance behind, it should magnify the gathered light."

102

Focus Questions What about humans might beings from other planets find strange? How might they react to objects that are ordinary to humans?

The Book That Saved the Earth

Claire Boiko
illustrated by Dennis Hockerman

❶ ***Characters***

Historian
Great and Mighty Think-Tank
Apprentice Noodle
Captain Omega
Sergeant Oop
Lieutenant Iota
Offstage Voice

❷ Time: 2543 A.D.

Before Rise: *Spotlight shines on* Historian, *who is sitting at table down right, on which there is a movie projector. A sign on an easel beside him reads:* MUSEUM OF ANCIENT HISTORY: DEPARTMENT OF THE TWENTIETH CENTURY. *He stands and bows to audience.*

Historian: Good afternoon. Welcome to our Museum of Ancient History, and to my department—curiosities of the good old, far-off twentieth century. The twentieth century was often called the Era of the Book. In those days, there were books about everything from anteaters to Zulus. Books taught people how to, and when to, and where to, and why to. They illustrated, educated, punctuated and even decorated. But the strangest thing a book ever did was to save the Earth.

166

	OVERVIEW OF SELECTION	LINK TO THE THEME	UNIT INVESTIGATIONS	SUPPORTING STUDENT INVESTIGATIONS
Lesson 1 *Galileo*	■ In this biographical selection, Galileo's telescope reveals things about the heavens that eventually put him at odds with church authorities.	■ Galileo introduced many people to the faraway planets, satellites, and stars studied in astronomy.	■ Generate questions and ideas to investigate	■ Investigation activities ■ Learn to use charts
Lesson 2 *Telescopes*	■ This nonfiction selection explains how different kinds of telescopes work, including the Hubble space telescope.	■ Telescopes, the basic tools of astronomy since the 1600s, have become more powerful and sophisticated.	■ Formulate questions and problems	■ Investigation activities ■ Learn to use diagrams
Lesson 3 *The Heavenly Zoo*	■ The origins of three astrological patterns are explained by ancient myths from different cultures.	■ Lacking scientific knowledge of the stars, ancient peoples created myths to give meaning to these phenomena. ■ Constellation myths helped ancient people remember, locate, and identify stars.	■ Make conjectures	■ Investigation activities ■ Learn to use card and computer catalogs
Lesson 4 *Circles, Squares, and Daggers*	■ This nonfiction selection illustrates how Native Americans of long ago created structures to mark the cycles of seasons and the passing of time.	■ Archaeoastronomy is a field of study that combines archaeology and astronomy.	■ Establish investigation needs	■ Investigation activities ■ Learn to use outlines
Lesson 5 *The Mystery of Mars*	■ This nonfiction selection illustrates how astronomers learned a great deal about Mars from the journeys of the *Viking 1*, *Viking 2*, and *Pathfinder* spacecraft.	■ Space missions to Mars have broadened our knowledge of the field of astronomy.	■ Establish investigation plans	■ Investigation activities ■ Learn to use indices
Lesson 6 *Stars*	■ This nonfiction selection provides an introduction to the different kinds of distant objects and systems that modern astronomers investigate.	■ Nebulas, supernovas, and quasars are some of the types of stars in the universe that have been discovered through astronomy.	■ Continue investigation ■ Make informal presentations	■ Investigation activities ■ Learn note-taking skills
Lesson 7 *The Book That Saved the Earth*	■ This humorous science fiction play suggests that some aliens may not be as intelligent as we think.	■ The study of astronomy leads some to wonder what alien life-forms would think of our culture if they should discover us first.	■ Present investigation findings	■ Investigation activities ■ Self-evaluate investigations

Open Court Reading

Adheres to California State Standards

Aligns With California Reading/Language Arts Requirements

Open Court Reading aligns with critical elements for teaching reading and language arts that have been adopted by the California Board of Education:

- *The English-Language Arts Content Standards for California Public Schools*
- *The Reading/Language Arts Framework for California Public Schools*
- California criteria for 2002 Language Arts Adoption
- The statewide assessment system

The instructional models in *Open Court Reading* ensure that every child has the benefit of the best reading instruction available, and California teachers are provided the support they need to meet the requirements of the state of California and implement our program successfully.

Program Organization

The instructional materials included in *Open Court Reading* are designed for the following minimal daily time periods:

- Kindergarten: one hour of instruction
- Grades 1-3: two-and-a-half hours of instruction
- Grades 4-6: two hours of instruction

Assessment

Assessments found in *Open Court Reading* provide a cumulative and spiraling review of skills. Assessments are designed to inform instruction so that teachers may evaluate the progress of their students before altering instruction.

Universal Access: Differentiating Instruction Meets Individual Needs

By making no assumptions about prior knowledge, *Open Court Reading* provides a variety of proven experiences that accommodate different student needs:

- **Reteach** lessons are available for all skills for students who need extra support with a particular phonics, comprehension, or language arts skill.
- **Intervention** lessons are for students who are working below grade level and need more intense support. Intervention includes controlled vocabulary selections based on unit themes and specific skill lessons to bring students up to grade level.
- **Challenge** activities are included to provide accelerated instruction for those students working above level and beyond the capabilities of the average readers in the class.
- **English-Language Development** lessons address the needs of today's increasingly diverse classrooms. This instructional support complements the *Open Court Reading* lessons. Also, Home Connections Blackline Masters include parent letters in both Spanish and English to communicate classroom progress, including unit themes and activities.

Instructional Planning and Support

Whole Group Instruction

Every lesson begins with whole-group, teacher-directed lessons so that all children have access to the same models and information.

Connection to Science/Social Studies Standards

Open Court Reading Science/Social Studies Connections Center packages and Blackline Masters have been specifically created to align with the California content standards for these subject areas. True learning can never be in isolation, and reading across the curriculum is a must for life-long learning. Through icons within the Teacher Edition, we have provided an easy way to incorporate the concepts into classrooms.

Differentiating Instruction: Workshop

Workshop is a period of time devoted to collaborating on investigations of unit concepts, working independently, or meeting individual needs. Workshop items and procedures are introduced to the whole group through direct-teaching sessions. Then students are released gradually from directed-teaching to work independently or in collaborative groups. Teachers work with individuals or small groups as needed.

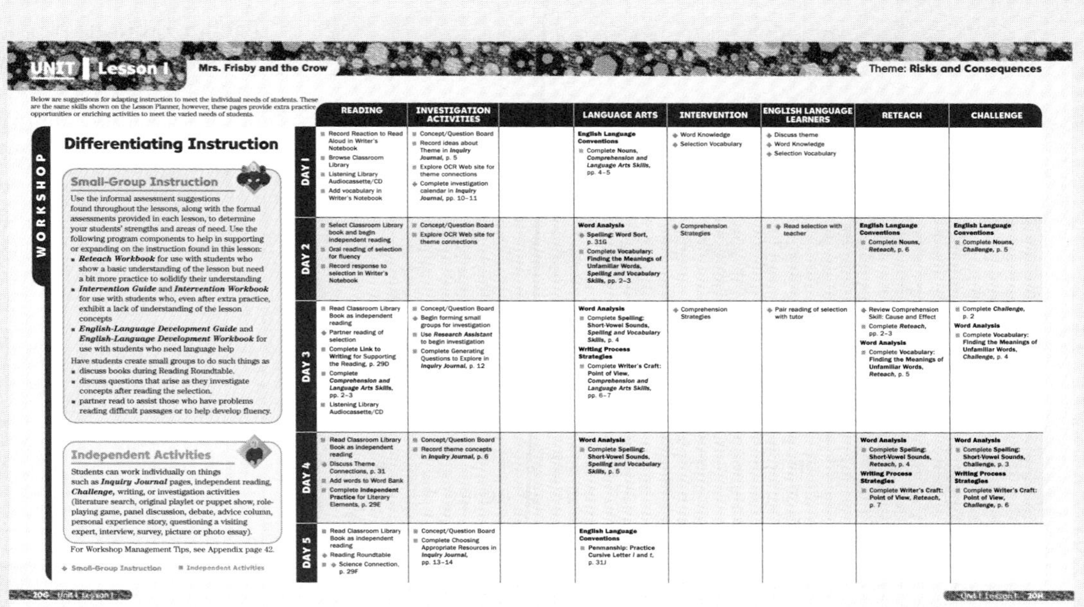

UNIT | Lesson 1 — Mrs. Frisby and the Crow — Theme: Risks and Consequences

Below are suggestions for adapting instruction to meet the individual needs of students. These are the same skills shown on the Lesson Planner, however, these pages provide extra practice opportunities or enriching activities to meet the varied needs of students.

WORKSHOP

Differentiating Instruction

Small-Group Instruction

Use the informal assessment suggestions found throughout the lessons, along with the formal assessments provided in each lesson, to determine your students' strengths and areas of need. Use the following program components to help in supporting or expanding on the instruction found in this lesson:

- ***Reteach Workbook*** for use with students who show a basic understanding of the lesson but need a bit more practice to solidify their understanding
- ***Intervention Guide*** and ***Intervention Workbook*** for use with students who, even after extra practice, exhibit a lack of understanding of the lesson concepts
- ***English-Language Development Guide*** and ***English-Language Development Workbook*** for use with students who need language help

Have students create small groups to do such things as

- discuss books during Reading Roundtable.
- discuss questions that arise as they investigate concepts after reading the selection.
- partner read to assist those who have problems reading difficult passages or to help develop fluency.

Independent Activities

Students can work individually on things such as ***Inquiry Journal*** pages, independent reading, ***Challenge,*** writing, or investigation activities (literature search, original playlet or puppet show, role-playing game, panel discussion, debate, advice column, personal experience story, questioning a visiting expert, interview, survey, picture or photo essay).

For Workshop Management Tips, see Appendix page 42.

◆ Small-Group Instruction ■ Independent Activities

	READING	INVESTIGATION ACTIVITIES		LANGUAGE ARTS	INTERVENTION	ENGLISH LANGUAGE LEARNERS	RETEACH	CHALLENGE
DAY 1	■ Record Reaction to Read Aloud in Writer's Notebook ■ Browse Classroom Library ■ Listening Library Audiocassette/CD ■ Add vocabulary in Writer's Notebook	■ Concept/Question Board ■ Record ideas about Theme in *Inquiry Journal,* p. 5 ■ Explore OCR Web site for theme connections ◆ Complete investigation calendar in *Inquiry Journal,* pp. 10–11		**English Language Conventions** ■ Complete Nouns, *Comprehension and Language Arts Skills,* pp. 4–5	◆ Word Knowledge ◆ Selection Vocabulary	◆ Discuss theme ◆ Word Knowledge ◆ Selection Vocabulary		
DAY 2	■ Select Classroom Library book and begin independent reading ■ Oral reading of selection for fluency ■ Record response to selection in Writer's Notebook	■ Concept/Question Board ■ Explore OCR Web site for theme connections		**Word Analysis** ◆ Spelling: Word Sort, p. 31G ■ Complete Vocabulary: Finding the Meanings of Unfamiliar Words, *Spelling and Vocabulary Skills,* pp. 2–3	◆ Comprehension Strategies	■ ◆ Read selection with teacher	**English Language Conventions** ■ Complete Nouns, *Reteach,* p. 6	**English Language Conventions** ■ Complete Nouns, *Challenge,* p. 5
DAY 3	■ Read Classroom Library Book as independent reading ◆ Partner reading of selection ■ Complete Link to Writing for Supporting the Reading, p. 29D ■ Complete *Comprehension and Language Arts Skills,* pp. 2–3 ■ Listening Library Audiocassette/CD	■ Concept/Question Board ◆ Begin forming small groups for investigation ■ Use *Research Assistant* to begin investigation ■ Complete Generating Questions to Explore in *Inquiry Journal,* p. 12		**Word Analysis** ■ Complete Spelling: Short-Vowel Sounds, *Spelling and Vocabulary Skills,* p. 4 **Writing Process Strategies** ■ Complete Writer's Craft: Point of View, *Comprehension and Language Arts Skills,* pp. 6–7	◆ Comprehension Strategies	◆ Pair reading of selection with tutor	◆ Review Comprehension Skill: Cause and Effect ■ Complete *Reteach,* pp. 2–3 **Word Analysis** ■ Complete Vocabulary: Finding the Meanings of Unfamiliar Words, *Reteach,* p. 5	■ Complete *Challenge,* p. 2 **Word Analysis** ■ Complete Vocabulary: Finding the Meanings of Unfamiliar Words, *Challenge,* p. 4
DAY 4	■ Read Classroom Library Book as independent reading ◆ Discuss Theme Connections, p. 31 ■ Add words to Word Bank ■ Complete Independent Practice for Literary Elements, p. 29E	■ Concept/Question Board ■ Record theme concepts in *Inquiry Journal,* p. 6		**Word Analysis** ■ Complete Spelling: Short-Vowel Sounds, *Spelling and Vocabulary Skills,* p. 5			**Word Analysis** ■ Complete Spelling: Short-Vowel Sounds, *Reteach,* p. 4 **Writing Process Strategies** ■ Complete Writer's Craft: Point of View, *Reteach,* p. 7	**Word Analysis** ■ Complete Spelling: Short-Vowel Sounds, Challenge, p. 3 **Writing Process Strategies** ■ Complete Writer's Craft: Point of View, *Challenge,* p. 6
DAY 5	■ Read Classroom Library Book as independent reading ◆ Reading Roundtable ■ ◆ Science Connection, p. 29F	■ Concept/Question Board ■ Complete Choosing Appropriate Resources in *Inquiry Journal,* pp. 13–14		**English Language Conventions** ■ Penmanship: Practice Cursive Letter *l* and *t,* p. 31J				

20G Unit 1 Lesson 1 — Unit 1 Lesson 1 20H

Concept/Question Board

A second grade Concept/Question Board from Karen Hansill in Georgia

Inquiry and Investigation

As part of the Inquiry strand, the Concept/Question Board is a place for students to ask questions and find answers that will give them a better understanding of the unit theme. It is also a place to publish the results of their investigations.

Program Components

Teacher Support (K-6)
(Teacher Editions, Online Support, Training Video Collection, Professional Development Guides)

Teacher Editions provide the information necessary for teaching systematic, explicit skills instruction centered around quality literature selections. Professional Development Guides and Lesson Model Videos offer a deepened understanding of the program, how it works, and why.

Big Books and Little Big Books (K-1)
Contain multiple literature selections and fine art to promote reading and shared reading experiences.

Story Time Selections
Trade books used to support each unit in kindergarten.

First Reader (2)
This reader for review and reinforcement of skills is used during the Getting Started Lessons at the beginning of Grade 2.

Blackline Masters and Workbooks
Sounds and Letters Skills (K)
Language Arts Skills (K)
Phonics Skills (1)
Comprehension and Language Arts Skills (1-6), Inquiry Journal (2-6), Spelling and Vocabulary Skills (1-6), Writer's Workbook are used to help reinforce and practice skills taught.

Student Anthologies (1-6)
Collections of literature based on themes. Each selection is chosen for the content it adds to the theme.

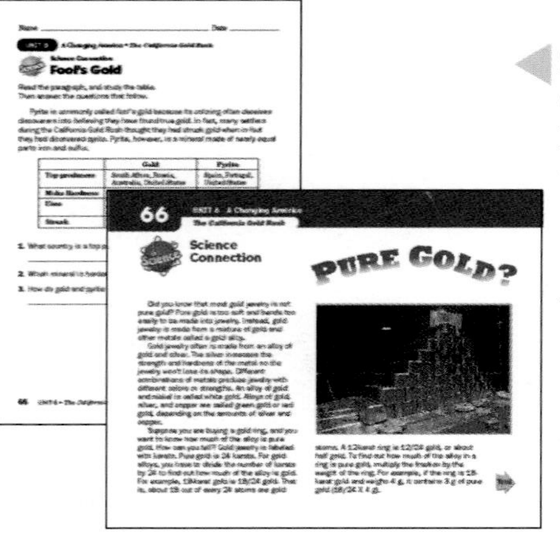

Science/Social Studies Connection Centers (K-6)
Reinforce reading across the curriculum by linking science and social studies content to the *Open Court Reading* lessons.

Technology
Alphabet Book Activities (K), Decodable Book Activities (1-3, K-3), Spelling (1-6), Writing (K-3, 4-6), Assessment (K-6), Research Assistant (2-6), and Management (K-6) CD ROMs, Audiocassette or CD Listening Libraries (K-6), Alphabet Sound Card Stories Audiocassette or CD (K), Sound/Spelling Card Stories (1-3), Lesson Models Video Collection (K-6), Online Bibliography (K-6), Online Teacher Support (K-6) Leap into Phonics (K-3)

Decodable Text (K-3)
(Pre-Decodable and Decodable Books and Takehomes)

Gives students the opportunity to practice the blending strategies and high-frequency words they are learning during Part 1 of the lesson. Individual (1 copy of each book) and Classroom Sets (6 copies of each book) are available. These also come in a tear-out Takehome format in which books are made by students to use during class or to take home to practice with parents. Takehomes are available in 4-color or black & white versions.

Assessment Blackline Masters or Workbooks (K-6)
Diagnostic, Program, Unit, Standardized Test specific assessments help evaluate the progress of each student using various types of formal assessment.

First Reader, Second Reader (1)
These readers help transition students from reading decodable text and high-frequency sight words to reading authentic trade-book literature in the Anthologies and Leveled Libraries. Although still somewhat controlled, the text in these engaging readers provides students with more of the challenges found in completely uncontrolled trade-book text. They provide the perfect step between the completely controlled Decodable Text and the text found in the Anthologies.

Phonics Packages (K-3)
Contain the manipulatives necessary for teaching the phonemic awareness and phonics instruction. The Story Crafting components can also be found in the Kindergarten Reading, Phonemic Awareness, and Phonics Package.

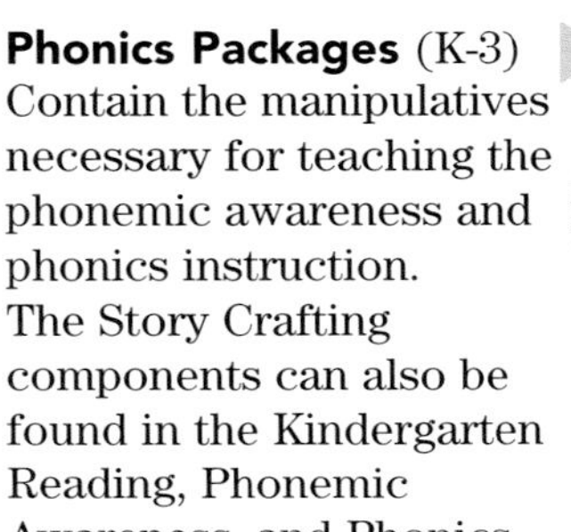

Additional Literature
Teacher Read Aloud Selections, Leveled Classroom Libraries, Online Bibliography (K-6)

Selections chosen to supplement the literature found in the Big Books and Anthologies. Leveled Libraries contain trade book selections that are leveled easy, average, and advanced.

Language Arts Handbook (2-6)
Language Arts Big Book (K-1)

Contains models of the writing process, writing traits, writer's craft, and structures of writing.

Practice Books (K-6)
(Challenge, Reteach, Intervention, English-Language Development)

For use during Differentiating Instruction: Workshop. These practice books remediate, reinforce, and extend lessons for meeting the needs of all learners in your classroom. They are available in both workbook and blackline master formats.

Every Child a Reader, Every Teacher a Success

Every Child Deserves to Read

According to educational researchers:

- Children who learn to read by the end of Grade 1 perform better in school and beyond.
- Children who enjoy reading learn more quickly and read more.

Literacy in today's society means more than simply being able to read the billboards stretched along the interstates, sign a name to a bank account, or read a newspaper article. In today's workplaces, literacy means being able to pursue multiple tasks at one time, being able to understand written and spoken language, and even knowing how to research and solve problems.

All children, regardless of background, deserve an equal opportunity to excel. Children should be invigorated and excited about having the opportunity to acquire knowledge. This will only happen if all children are given equal access to those practices that are proven to work in the classroom.

***Open Court Reading* is *the* proven curriculum for teaching children how to read, comprehend, and gain knowledge from what they read.** The instructional plan found in *Open Court Reading* prepares our children for the reality of a literate future. The research and results that support *Open Court Reading* have shown this to be true.

When children are given the structure they need from the beginning, they move beyond that which any program or teacher can provide. Equal access is the right of every child that we are asked to educate. Every child must be taught to read fluently and independently by the end of Grade 1. With *Open Court Reading*, this is a reality, not a chance.

Every Teacher Deserves the Best Program and Support for Teaching It

The Best Program

According to the latest research, the classrooms of the most effective teachers are characterized by:

- High academic engagement
- Excellent classroom management
- Positive reinforcement and cooperation
- Explicit teaching of skills
- An emphasis on literature
- Plenty of reading and writing practice
- Matching of task demands to student competence
- Encouragement of student self-regulation
- Strong cross-curricular connections

(CELA Report Number 11007)

Only a reading program such as *Open Court Reading* can help you accomplish such a daunting list of tasks.

***Open Court Reading* is the only reading program that provides:**

- **An educational philosophy based on scientific research and nearly 40 years of practical classroom experience**
- **A program that has been successful in classrooms nationwide**
- **A partnership through training that will help you not only successfully implement *Open Court Reading*, but also understand solid reading instruction**

What does this mean to you? **Success**, and the added assurance that the children in your classroom are getting **the best program available**.

What Open Court Means to Me

"Personally, I find your program very helpful for teaching my students. I teach at a high-risk school, and this series is not just for accelerated readers."

– Ryan Williams, Teacher

"Open Court is the most complete program that I have seen in my career."

– Linda LaMarre, Superintendent

"Open Court is not just phonics-oriented, but it includes phonics, comprehension, and writing...It is important to consider all aspects of reading instruction. If a school chooses a program that relies on phonics alone, teachers will abandon the program when they realize it does not offer the balanced instruction that Open Court does."

– Marge Thompson, Principal

"In 26 years of work in education, I have never experienced the high level of support we received from SRA. It's really amazing!"

– Lois Zercher, Assistant Superintendent

"People are always looking for quick fixes to education problems in this country and there aren't any. Open Court requires a lot of work on the part of the teacher and students, but we're happy to work hard if we're going to keep getting such great results."

– Diane Yules, Reading Specialist

For more Open Court Success Stories, call 1-800-SRA-4543 or visit SRA's web site at www.sra4kids.com.

Support for Teaching

One component of the success of *Open Court Reading* is SRA's strong commitment to professional development. SRA is dedicated not only to the education of students, but of educators as well.

During one of our many training events, you learn not only how to successfully implement *Open Court Reading*, but also how to successfully implement the best educational practices in your classroom. Our professional team of consultants are former classroom and Open Court teachers who know our program intimately. They continuously participate in professional development training in order to make sure that the information they share with you is the best and the most current.

We provide support through:

- In-service training
- On-site follow-up
- Weekend seminars
- Online training
- Summer institutes
- Professional development guides
- Training video collection

Teachers and administrators may get information about training sessions by calling the Teacher Learning Exchange at 1-800-382-7670 or by visiting www.tlexchange.com.

UNIT 1

Table of Contents

Let's Read!

Lesson Skills

Letter Recognition	Comprehension	Language Arts
• *Aa, Bb* • *Cc, Dd* • *Ee, Ff, Gg* • *Hh, Ii, Jj* • *Kk, Ll, Mm*	Strategies: • Visualizing • Asking Questions	• Vocabulary: Classification • Introduction to the Writing Process • Grammar: Capital Letters—Names and I • Listening: Listening Attentively • Penmanship: Letter Are Lines

Lessons 6–10

Letter Recognition	Comprehension	Language Arts	Lesson Skills
• *Nn, Oo, Pp* • *Qq, Rr, Ss* • *Tt, Uu, Vv* • *Ww, Xx, Yy, Zz* • *Alphabet*	**Strategies:** • Monitoring and Clarifying • Visualizing • Asking Questions	• Vocabulary: Rhyming Words • Introduction to the Writing Process: Planning • Grammar: Capital Letters—Cities and States; Days and Months • Speaking: Speaking Clearly • Penmanship: Letters Are Lines	

Lessons 11–15

Phonics	Comprehension	Language Arts	Lesson Skills
• /s/ Spelled *s* • /m/ Spelled *m* • /a/ Spelled *a* • /t/ Spelled *t* • /h/ Spelled *h*	**Strategies:** • Monitoring and Clarifying • Visualizing • Predicting • Asking Questions **Skills:** • Reality and Fantasy • Comparing and Contrasting	• Vocabulary: Context Clues • Introduction to the Writing Process: Writing • Grammar: Capital Letters—Beginning of Sentences • Language: Informal and Formal Language • Penmanship: Letters Are Lines	

California Advisory Board

Arlene Amodei
Curriculum Coordinator
Sierraville, CA

Pam Barrett
Teacher
Murrietta, CA

Jennifer Charles
Teacher
Irvine, CA

Beverly Chernoff
Teacher
Freemont, CA

Karen Cooksey
Director of Curriculum
Santa Barbara, CA

Susan Drew
Teacher
Lemoore, CA

Nancy Hanssen
Reading Specialist
San Diego, CA

Ann Harvey
Reading Specialist
San Diego, CA

Barbara Johnson
Curriculum Coordinator
Salinas, CA

Mickey Manning
Reading Coordinator
Santa Barbara, CA

Sharon Massingill
Teacher
Lemoore, CA

Jennifer O'Donnell
Teacher
San Diego, CA

Elaine Wiener
Teacher
Villa Park, CA

Contributing Author

Michael Milone
Assessment Specialist
Placitas, NM

Literature Consultants

Dr. Sylvia Hutchinson
Professor, University of Georgia
Athens, GA

Dr. Helen Foster James
Lecturer, San Diego State University
San Diego, CA

Program Reviewers

Ann Adams
Chair, Teacher Education
Mobile, AL

Judy Alexander
Teacher
Grand Ridge, FL

Charlotte Bennett
Reading Coordinator K-5
Sweeny, TX

Mita Bhattacharya
Teacher
Inglewood, CA

Charlene Bigelow
Teacher
West Valley City, UT

Carol Bishop
Principal
Tallahassee, FL

Virginia Blount
Principal
Sneads, FL

Mary Brandenburg
Teacher
Gainesville, FL

Jennifer Bray
Teacher
Jefferson, GA

Frances Brown
Teacher
Shalimar, FL

Shayla Brown
Teacher
Long Beach, CA

Sheree Bryant
Curriculum Director
Covington, GA

Angela Burkard
Teacher
Dallas, TX

Carolyn Cappleman
Headmaster
Windermere, FL

Linda Carle
Teacher
Roanoke, VA

Kris Charlton
Head of School
Coral Gables, FL

Susan Clarabut
Principal
Grass Valley, CA

Kathy Degi
Reading Specialist
Denver, CO

Suzanne Delaware
Assistant Superintendent
Atwater, CA

Court DeSpain
Principal
Salt Lake City, UT

Kerri Doyle
Teacher
Charlotte, NC

Joan Draper
Teacher
Ogden, UT

Dr. Mary Fritz
Principal
Westbury, NY

Diane Garland
Teacher
Cartersville, GA

Stuart Greenberg
Director, Broward County Schools
Ft. Lauderdale, FL

Karen Hansill
Teacher
Savannah, GA

Victoria Holland
Teacher
Santa Ana, CA

Michelle Holman
Teacher
Sonora, CA

Judy Hughes
Teacher
Media, PA

Georgana Johnston
Consultant
Hatteras, NC

Barbara Jones
Teacher
Baltimore, MD

Linda Kehe
Teacher
Tualatin, OR

Ray King
Principal
Tallahassee, FL

Lucy Kozak
Teacher
Bradenton, FL

Linda Kramer
Teacher
Grass Valley, CA

Sandy Loose
Consultant
Media, PA

David Maresh
Teacher
Yucca Valley, CA

Mary McAdoo
Consultant
Fenwick Island, DE

Anne McKee
Teacher
Tualatin, OR

Karen McKenna
Reading Coordinator
Cloquet, MN

Ann McMillen
Teacher
Ringgold, GA

Barbara Miles
Teacher
North Tonawanda, NY

Nancy Mitchell
Consultant
Grass Valley, CA

Jeff Ohmer
Teacher
Baltimore, MD

Bethany Payne
Consultant
Ft. Lauderdale, FL

Becky Player
Teacher
Grand Ridge, FL

Sharon Preston
Teacher
Hortonville, WI

Joyce Pulley
Principal
Jackson, MS

Billie Reeves
Principal
Perris, CA

Dolores M. Roberts
Teacher
Monterey, CA

Gretchen Rogers
Teacher
Lakeland, FL

Kathryn Scozzari
Teacher
Union Springs, NY

Aundrea Sellars
Teacher
Marianna, FL

Suzanne Slaughter
Teacher
Ocala, FL

Cherry Mae Smith
Teacher
Rupert, ID

Heather Stephens
Teacher
Marianna, FL

Jill Strange
Teacher
Lawrenceville, GA

Vicki Thomas
Teacher
Los Angeles, CA

Margaret Tomko
Teacher
Johnstown, NY

Dr. Sandy Trinca
Director of Professional Development
Ft. Lauderdale, FL

Tricia Trucker
Teacher
Monmouth Beach, NJ

Sharon Van Vleck
Principal
Sacramento, CA

Maria Wentworth
Educational Consultant
Union, NH

Brenda Williams
Teacher
Ft. Lauderdale, FL

Lois Zercher
Assistant Superintendant/Curriculum
Lemoore, CA

Robin A. Zimmerman
Teacher
Grass Valley, CA

Preparing to Use

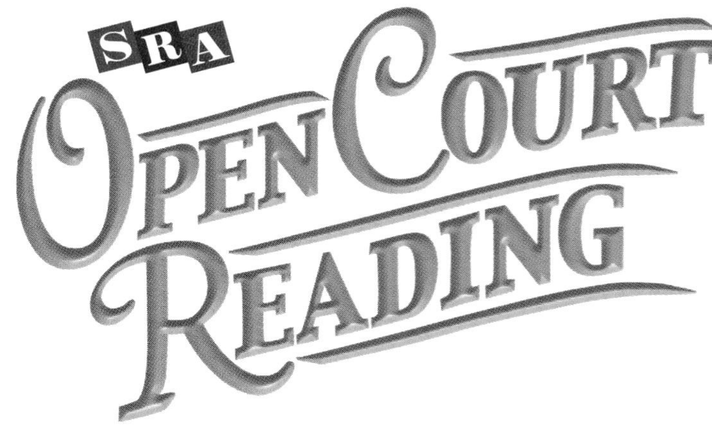

This section provides an overview of classroom management issues and introductory activities that explain the function of the ***SRA/Open Court Reading*** program elements and how to use them.

Organizing Your Classroom

Phonemic Awareness and Phonics Instruction

In the ***SRA/Open Court Reading*** program, early reading instruction does not assume that students already have the ability to consciously attend to, discriminate, and manipulate the sounds of words—phonemic awareness or knowledge of the alphabetic principle. Although speaking and understanding the English language do not require a conscious understanding of or ability in either of these, reading and writing do. Instruction involves the systematic, explicit teaching of the relationship of individual sounds to spoken language, sound/spellings, the blending of sounds into words, and the application of this knowledge to reading and writing.

Sound/Spelling Cards

The **Sound/Spelling Cards** are used to introduce or review sound/spellings. Each card contains the common spelling or spellings of a sound. With the exception of the long vowel **Sound/Spelling Cards,** each card depicts both an action-sound association and a picture of something whose name includes the sound. The **Sound/Spelling Cards** are numbered and should be displayed in order. Place them in a prominent place in the classroom so that all students can see them and use them for reference. As you proceed through the **Getting Started** activities and through the first three units of regular instruction, you and your students will need to point out specific cards. Therefore, the cards should be placed low enough to make this possible but high enough for all students to have an unobstructed view of them.

Although they are not specifically referenced in the final three units, the **Sound/Spelling Cards** should remain on display for the entire school year. They are an invaluable tool for the students in both their reading and writing.

Reading

For students to become more than competent decoders, they must become strategic readers. That is, they must learn how to think about what they read and to use specific reading strategies and behaviors. Teachers help students become strategic readers by modeling the key reading strategies used by expert readers and by providing them with multiple opportunities to read fine literature. First-rate reading selections illustrate for students the best possible use of language and stimulates them to think about, write about, and discuss important ideas and concepts.

Oral Reading

Reading aloud is one of the best ways for students to develop their reading skills. In the course of the daily lessons, there are two opportunities for oral reading: the oral/choral reading of Student Anthology selections and the reading of the Decodable books.

A third opportunity for oral reading arises at the beginning of each unit with the Read Aloud selection. The Read Aloud selection introduces the unit theme to students and prepares them for the other selections in the unit. To promote students' reading growth, you will want to multiply oral reading opportunities. For example, you may:

- ask students to reread in pairs the anthology selections.
- set aside a period of time each day for oral reading of trade books.
- set up a home reading log, asking parents to read with their children.
- have students partner-read content area texts from other subjects your class is studying.

However you do it, you will find that every minute of oral reading by students pays off in terms of reading growth.

On a regular basis, take time to listen to students as they read favorite stories and books aloud. Listening to students read from an anthology selection provides you with information about their ability to manage the vocabulary and concepts of the text, as well as to gauge their reading fluency. Listening to students read ***Decodable Books*** allows you to evaluate their developing fluency more closely and to identify particular decoding challenges that they have conquered or with which they need more work. To complement these activities, you may also want to listen to students read books they have selected for themselves. This will give you insights into their taste in reading materials, their own opinion of their reading ability, as well as their reading progress.

Decodable Books

As students are introduced to the sound/spelling relationships, they are given ***Decodable Books*** to read. These stories are designed to help students practice reading in connected text the sound/spelling relationships they are learning. With the introduction of each new sound/spelling there are two decodable stories that emphasize that particular sound/spelling. In addition, there are ***Decodable Books*** that review previously taught sound/spellings.

Students should be encouraged to read and reread these stories to help them gain the fluency they will need in order to be comfortable and confident readers. Although the books are introduced and used first during the lessons, students should partner-read these stories over and over again during Workshop, and take copies home to read to their families.

The more the students read these little, engaging, decodable stories, the faster they will become proficient at recognizing the different sound/spellings and the more comfortable they will be when they are asked to apply this knowledge to any story they want to read.

These stories should be read daily. You may want to make a chart for each student with the titles of the ***Decodable Books*** and a place to check off how many times the student has read the story.

	First Reading	Second Reading	Third Reading	Fourth Reading	Fifth Reading
Decodable 1 Title	**X**	**X**	**X**		
Decodable 2 Title	**X**	**X**			

Reading Area

Provide as many books as possible for your classroom Reading Area. During the course of the year the students will be asked to do much reading on specific subjects. Prepare your classroom ahead of time by bringing in books on the concepts or themes the students will be studying. You may choose to order the **Leveled Classroom Library** that accompanies the program or you may decide to provide your own library. In either case, you should encourage students to bring in books that they have enjoyed and want to share with their classmates.

Word Bank

Create and maintain a Word Bank in your classroom. The students will be introduced to many new sight words. They will see these in their ***Decodable Books*** as well as in the ***Big Books.*** Most of these words are very familiar to the students as they hear them every day. They need to start recognizing these words in print.

You may want to start by asking the children if there are any words they can read. Print on index cards the words the students offer. Start your word wall with these words. As you introduce ***Decodable Books*** and as you work with the ***Big Books,*** encourage the students to point out words that they recognize. As they do this, print the words on index cards and place them on the Word Bank. Encourage the students to spend extra time each day reading the words on the Word Bank to each other. Students will be thrilled as they see their Word Bank growing and growing throughout the year.

Listening Area

Each selection in the Student Anthology is recorded on audiocassette and compact disc for use in your classroom. As you read each selection, encourage students to listen to the recording during Workshop. Provide one or two tape recorders or CD players that work both with and without earphones. In this way, individual students may listen to selections without disturbing the rest of the class. You will also be able to play the selections for the whole class if you choose.

You should also encourage students to record their own stories, then share these stories with their classmates.

Discussion

Discussion is an integral part of learning. Through discussion, students are exposed to different points of view and reactions to text. Also, it is through discussion that students learn to express their thoughts and opinions coherently as well as to respect the ideas and opinions of others.

Listening and responding to each other's ideas and questions is fundamental to learning. Throughout the program students are expected to listen and respond to each other—during Writing Seminar, collaborative activities, investigation of the unit concepts—not just in a discussion about a story.

Talk to the students about what a discussion is and what is expected of participants during a discussion. Students must listen to what others are saying and respond to what is being said. Students should:

- not interrupt.
- raise their hands when they want to say something.
- ask questions of each other.
- not talk while others are speaking.
- take turns.
- respond directly to each other's questions or ideas rather than going off on a different or unrelated thought or tangent.

Handing Off

Through a process called handing off, students learn to take the primary responsibility for holding and controlling discussions. Handing off simply means that each student who responds in a discussion is responsible for drawing another student into the discussion.

This is a skill students will build on throughout their experience with the ***SRA/Open Court Reading*** program. You can start the process with your first grade students by having them get used to calling on one other classmate as they complete a response. For example, if the students are discussing their favorite stories, as one student completes his or her response, he or she can point to another student and say, "Tell us about your favorite story, Jan."

In order for discussions and handing off to work effectively, a seating arrangement that allows students to see one another is important just as in a real conversation or discussion. A circle or a semi-circle is effective.

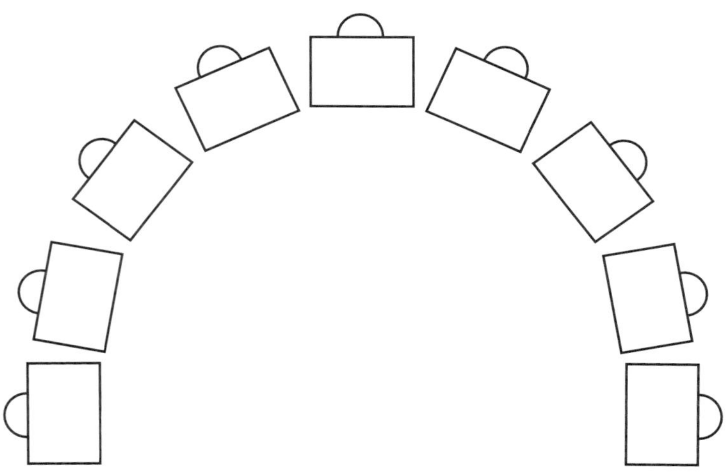

Writing

Reading and writing are interwoven processes, and each helps build and strengthen the other. Throughout the year, students do a tremendous amount of writing, both independently and collaboratively. They write for an array of purposes and audiences. Extended writing includes stories and various nonfiction pieces such as research reports, biographies, persuasive papers, and letters. In addition, they write daily in the form of note taking, making lists, labeling pictures, and making journal entries.

To assure success in writing, the students will need:

- **A Writer's Notebook**

  Each student should provide his or her own Writer's Notebook. This notebook can be a three-ring binder with different sections; however, a spiral notebook with sections will work also.

- **A Writing Portfolio**

  An artist's portfolio contains pieces that the artist considers the best of his or her work. Help students to develop a similar portfolio of their writing. From time to time, hold conferences with individual students so that they can show you the work they have put in their portfolios and explain what they particularly like about the pieces they have chosen to keep.

  You should keep your own portfolio for each student in which you place samples of written work that show the student's progress throughout the year.

- **A Writing Folder**

  Students should be encouraged continually to revise and edit their writing. Each student should have a folder in which they keep this writing-in-progress. Any pocket folder will work for this purpose; however, you may choose to order the **Writing Folders** that accompany the ***SRA/Open Court Reading*** program. In addition to pockets to hold student writing, these folders contain a list of proofreading marks and tips for revising that students will find useful.

Writing Area

The Writing Area should contain materials students can use to write and illustrate their work and to facilitate students' efforts as they work together on unit investigations, including:

- pencils, crayons, or pens
- white paper
- colored paper
- old magazines they can cut up
- scissors
- staplers
- reference books such as dictionaries and encyclopedias
- computers—preferably with Internet access. The SRA Home Page (see http://www.SRA4kids.com) includes materials specifically related to the themes the students are studying.
- books on the themes the students are studying. You may choose to order the **Leveled Classroom Library** that accompanies the program. In addition, bibliographies of additional related books can be found following each unit in the Unit Overviews of the ***Teacher's Editions.***

Writing Seminar

Seminar is a time when students will be able to share their work with each other. This is a time when two or three students will share their work with the class, and then their classmates will have time to give feedback. Seminar participants must listen carefully and politely, just as they do during discussion and handing off. When the author is finished reading, the other students should say something positive about what the author wrote. They can tell what they liked and why, how the author's story made them feel good, and what the author's story reminded them of. You may need to model this in the beginning by telling what you liked about the story and why.

At first, students will be sharing drawings that they have done to show stories. As the year progresses, they will write simple captions. The purpose of seminar is to help students see that they can get valuable help with their writing from their peers. It also is an invaluable tool for teaching the students how to give constructive, positive feedback.

Inquiry and Investigation

In ***SRA/Open Court Reading,*** lessons are integrated through extensive reading, writing, and discussion. In turn, the lessons are organized into learning units, with each selection in a unit adding more information or a different perspective to the students' growing knowledge of a theme or concept.

Some units allow students to expand their perspectives on universal themes such as kindness, courage, perseverance, and friendship by relating what they read to their own experience. Other units involve students in the research process, giving them the tools they need to discover and learn on their own and as part of a collaborative group. Inquiry activities provide students with a systematic structure for exploration that is driven by their own interests and conjectures.

All units are designed to help students:

- deepen their comprehension by enabling them to apply the skills they are learning to texts and activities of their own choosing.
- synthesize and organize what they are learning in order to present their findings to their classmates.
- determine suitable avenues of inquiry and methods of presentation.
- become more independent and responsible about their time and efforts.
- work efficiently in collaborative groups.

Concept/Question Board

One of the primary goals of ***SRA/Open Court Reading*** is to help you and your students form a community of learners. To do this, sharing information is essential. The **Concept/Question Board** is a bulletin board or chart. The students can share their growing knowledge about a unit theme or concept by posting on the Board newspaper clippings, magazine articles, information taken from the Internet, photographs, and other items that might be of interest to or help for their classmates. As the class progresses through a unit, the Board serves as the place where common interests become evident. As these interests emerge, the students can use them as the basis for forming collaborative groups to explore ideas in greater depth.

In addition, the Board gives students an outlet for questions that arise as they read on their own. The questions can be written directly on a sheet of paper attached to the Board, or they can be written on separate slips of paper and pinned to it. Self-sticking notepads can also be used. The **Concept/Question Board** lets students know that questions are not problems but a way of learning. Questions thus become a springboard to further exploration. Collaborative groups can be formed around common questions.

The Board should change constantly, reflecting the developing and changing interests of the class. For the **Getting Started** section and for Unit 1, you may use one **Concept/Question Board**. If you choose, you can give the Board a title, such as "Reading and Writing."

Workshop

Workshop is integral to ***SRA/Open Court Reading***. It is during this time, which you designate as a part of each class day, that students gain the experience of managing their own learning process. In Workshop, students work on their own or collaboratively to practice and review material taught in the lessons or to complete projects of their own choosing. As students gradually take more responsibility for their work, they learn to set learning goals, to make decisions about the use of time and materials, and to collaborate with classmates. Of equal importance, Workshop gives you a designated time each day to work with students one-on-one or in small groups.

During Workshop, your students can:

- read to each other for pleasure and to increase fluency.
- work independently and in small collaborative groups on their investigation projects.
- work on unfinished writing projects.
- work on any unfinished projects or assignments they have.
- assess what projects they have that need work, prioritize their time, and direct their own efforts.

During Workshop, you can:

- work with individuals and small groups who have shown a need for additional instruction.
- listen to individuals read in order to assess informally their progress and help them gain fluency.
- conduct writing conferences with individual students to discuss their progress as writers.

The Reading, Listening, and Writing Areas will be used extensively during Workshop. If possible, equip these areas with furniture that is easy to move and will allow for both independent work and small group work.

Getting Started Checklist

This checklist will help you be prepared for the school year. Look back over the Getting Started section if you have any questions about these program elements.

- ◯ **Display Sound/Spelling Cards**
- ◯ **Organize Big Books, Decodables, and Student Anthologies**
- ◯ **Set Up Reading Area**
- ◯ **Create Word Bank**
- ◯ **Establish Listening Area**
- ◯ **Plan for Discussions**
- ◯ **Plan for Writer's Notebook**
- ◯ **Establish Writing Folder**
- ◯ **Establish Writing Area**
- ◯ **Plan for Writing Seminar**
- ◯ **Develop Concept/Question Board**
- ◯ **Plan for Workshop**

Grade 1 Overview

Grade 1 reading instruction is explicit and systematic. It takes into account the individual needs of students, and includes a great deal of practice with engaging yet predictable reading materials. The goal of instruction is to ensure that by December or January of the Grade 1 year, students have acquired the skills to read, with fluency and comprehension, the many different kinds of literature they encounter in their ***Student Anthologies*** and in trade books.

To accomplish this goal, instruction in the first part of Grade 1—the six ***Big Book*** units—focuses on

- Phonemic Awareness
- Sounds and Spellings
- Blending
- Dictation and Spelling
- Reading ***Big Books***
- Writing
- Workshop

Phonemic Awareness, which begins in ***Big Book*** Unit 1 and concludes in ***Big Book*** Unit 2, gives students practice in discriminating the sounds that make up words. It is taught by two complementary techniques: oral blending and segmentation. Students use oral blending to put sounds together to make words, and they use segmentation to separate words into sounds. The phonemic awareness activities are purely oral and do not involve the teaching of sound/spelling relationships.

Sounds and Spellings are introduced to students at the rate of about one a lesson in the ***Big Book*** units. The introduction follows a see, hear, say, write sequence: Students see the spelling on the ***Sound/Spelling Cards***; they hear the sound used in words and in isolation in a brief, alliterative story related to the picture on the card and to associated sound; they say the sound, both during the story and in isolation; and they write the spelling of the sound.

Blending is the key strategy in phonics instruction. Beginning in Lesson 13 of ***Big Book*** Unit 1, blending becomes a daily activity. To reinforce the connection between the sounds students are blending and the words they know, you write the spelling for each sound in a word; students say the sound, relying on the associations they have learned from the ***Sound/Spelling Cards***; they blend the sounds into a word; and finally, they use the word in a sentence.

Dictation and Spelling, which also begins at the end of ***Big Book*** Unit 1, shows students that reading and writing are interrelated. Just as blending gives them a strategy for figuring out unfamiliar words, dictation gives them a strategy for spelling them.

Reading Big Books engages students in hearing and reading literature from all genres. It introduces them both to print and book conventions and to the behaviors and strategies that good readers use to get meaning from what they read.

Writing includes a variety of personal, expository, narrative, descriptive, and persuasive writing, as well as poetry.

Workshop is integral to the success of ***Open Court Reading.*** Workshop gives students an early experience of managing their own learning process. For this reason, you should designate a time each day for students to work independently, with partners, in small groups, or with you to reinforce learning. Workshop is also the time for you to provide extra help for those students who need it and to assess and monitor the progress of individuals or of the class. At this point in the school year, you will take the lead in directing Workshop, reinforcing and reviewing learning for students or providing extra help to those students who need it.

Lesson Format

Each ***Big Book*** unit contains fifteen daily lessons. The lessons of each ***Anthology*** unit vary from one to five days. Program Resources, a five-day Lesson Planner, a five-day Workshop chart, and Assessment Options are provided before every five days of lessons in both ***Big Book*** units and ***Anthology*** units. Activities in all lessons are presented in three major divisions.

1 Preparing to Read

- **Warming Up** activities in Units 1–6 bring students together and focus their attention for the learning that follows. In the later lessons, these activities offer opportunities to review.
- **Phonemic Awareness** activities in Units 1–2 focus on taking words apart sound by sound and putting the sounds of words together.
- **Letter Knowledge** is reviewed in the first 10 lessons of Unit 1, along with print awareness using games, songs, the ***Alphabet Flash Cards,*** and ***Sound/ Spelling Cards.***
- Beginning in Unit 1, Lesson 11, the program introduces the ***Sound/Spelling Cards*** at the rate of about one per lesson through Unit 6. Direct instruction in blending sound/spellings also begins in this lesson and continues through grade 1.
- Students will read ***Pre-Decodable*** and ***Decodable Books*** to reinforce what students are learning and provide practice with high-frequency words.
- **Dictation and Spelling** is introduced to students in Unit 1, Lesson 13. In the ***Anthology*** units, Dictation will remain in Part 1, but Spelling skills will move to Part 3.
- **Phonics and Fluency** begins in Unit 7, which has become a phonics review. All the sound/spellings have been introduced, and blending continues. Students will read a ***Decodable Book*** in the last lesson of each unit. This provides a continuing opportunity to gauge students' increasing fluency.

2 Reading & Responding

- In this section of the lesson, you will read the ***Big Books*** in Units 1–6, and students will read the ***Student Anthology*** selections in Units 7–10. In the ***Big Book*** units, model comprehension strategies and help students develop comprehension skills. Continue to model these strategies along with the students in the ***Anthology*** lessons.
- After-reading activities heighten students' appreciation of literature, build selection vocabulary, and connect reading to the theme.
- In this section of the lesson, students view and discuss fine art, learning that the same ideas may be expressed in both visual and printed media.
- This part is concluded by theme-related activities, which invite students to investigate the unit theme in depth and to do independent writing and research.

3 Language Arts

Part 3 of each lesson contains an array of language arts activities, including independent and collaborative writing exercises; vocabulary skills, grammar, usage, and mechanics; listening, speaking, and viewing skills; and penmanship.

Writing Process Strategies lessons appear in each lesson, with the writing process steps applied over a five-day span: Lesson 1, Getting Ideas; Lesson 2, Plan; Lesson 3, Write; Lesson 4, Revise; and Lesson 5, Check and Share. Writer's Craft lessons act as a supplement to the skills that students are learning.

The English Language Conventions strand can be broken down into Word Analysis; Grammar, Usage, and Mechanics; Listening, Speaking, Viewing; and Penmanship. Word Analysis includes Vocabulary and Spelling and occurs in every lesson. Spelling skills appear in Part 1 for Units 1–6, then Part 3 for Units 7–10. Grammar, Usage, and Mechanics occur in the first three days of the week. The last week in a unit review that unit's skills, and Units 9–10 are devoted to a complete skills review. Listening, Speaking, Viewing lessons occur during the fourth day of each week, and Penmanship lessons occur during the last day of each week.

Level 1 • Unit 1

Let's Read!

Exploring the Theme

Introduction

This ***Big Book*** *Let's Read!* is a collection of poems, rhymes, and stories that encourages students to explore the foundations of literacy: sounds, letters, and the conventions of print and meaning.

By exploring sounds, letters, and spellings (the letters and combinations of letters that represent spoken sounds), the students begin to reflect on the sounds of our language, how these sounds are represented by letters, and how letters are combined to write the words we speak. Students come to appreciate the conventions of our written language—that sentences begin with capital letters and end with some form of punctuation, that spaces separate words, and that a particular word is spelled the same way every time it's written. They also will realize that all of the words and sentences combine to create stories and poems that spark our curiosity and open our minds to the ideas of the world.

Investigation Goals

The investigation goals of this unit are

- To develop the students' awareness of how the sounds of the language work together.
- To enable the students to understand that written English is a code system.
- To develop the tools to break that code so that all students have access to print.
- To provide the students with exposure to good literature even before they can read on their own.
- To introduce the students to the reading behaviors used by skilled readers to get meaning from text.

Learning Goals

The learning goals of this unit are

- To develop the students' awareness of sounds.
- To expand the students' understanding of print and book concepts.
- To help the students understand that sounds are represented by spellings.
- To help the students learn to blend sounds and spellings to read.

California Theme Connections

Reading is a skill that is fundamental to a child being able to reason and think. Reading entertains and allows children the ability to imagine and visualize. In 1999, **READ California** was established to promote the involvement of all Californians in encouraging children to read. READ California combines a multi-media approach using advertising, special events and publicity to promote reading.

Look for the California Theme Connections throughout the Unit.

Lesson 5 **Reading/Language Arts:** Readapalooza Reader Program.

Lesson 10 **Reading/Language Arts:** Tip of the Month, Make a time and place for reading.

Lesson 15 **Reading/Language Arts:** READ California Cheer!

Teacher Tip **COGNITIVE SKILLS** Learning to read involves the successful integration of a number of cognitive skills. Young readers need to understand

- ✔ How print works.
- ✔ The connection between sounds and letters.
- ✔ How to use sounds and letters to read and spell.
- ✔ How to get meaning from text.

Exploring the Theme

Supporting Student Investigations

Because students are just learning to write, they will need much help and support from you and their classmates in these first attempts at literacy. Start most of the activities as large-group activities and provide models for the student to follow. Some activities that can help with these projects include the following:

- Encourage students to draw and write responses to the stories they share in class. Their Writer's Notebooks are their place to put their private responses to the work they are doing in class.
- Keep your own Writer's Notebook and make sure students see you making entries. Keeping a Writer's Notebook is a habit that many professional writers have developed to help them get and keep ideas for their writing.
- Be sure to have magazines on hand for students to use in making their Alphabet Books.
- Discussing this project as a group will help students become familiar with their classmates' ideas about writing and help them see that they are all just learning and that the learning is fun.

Unit Investigations

Throughout this unit the students will be working on several different activities that range from the beginnings of experimenting with print to making a book. The purpose of all of these activities is to encourage students to become interested in and excited about the processes of reading and writing. The following unit activities will help students learn to be authors, and through these activities learn about the parts of a book, different purposes for writing, and the joys of reading and writing.

- Making a Writer's Notebook and learning to use it from the beginning will help students see how writing can be an outlet for their reactions to reading and the characters they meet in their reading.
- The ***Big Book*** selections in this unit are primarily poetry. The students are exposed to old classic rhymes and poems along with more modern pieces. Using these pieces to compose their own rhymes and poems will encourage a sense of the fun of reading and writing.
- One of the first and favorite types of books students encounter is alphabet books. Creating their own Alphabet Books will be fun for the students and will solidify their knowledge about the alphabet.

	OVERVIEW OF SELECTION	LINK TO THE THEME	UNIT INVESTIGATIONS	SUPPORTING STUDENT INVESTIGATIONS
Lesson 1 **Unit Introduction**	A fantasy about a wolf who is so fascinated when he sees animals reading that he goes to school and learns to read.	Reading takes a lot of hard work, and we have to put in a lot of effort and practice before we succeed.	■ Tell the students about the unit project, an alphabet book.	
Lesson 2 ***The Purple Cow***	A poem about a make-believe animal, a purple cow.	The students are introduced to poetry through a short, entertaining, rhyming poem.	■ Introduce the students to the purpose of alphabet books, and discuss different alphabet books with them.	■ Provide examples of alphabet books. ■ Read them to the class, and have them discuss their similarities and differences.
Lesson 3 ***Las hormiguitas***	A poem about ants.	The students are introduced to repeated words or phrases that are common to poetry.	■ Continue introducing the students to new alphabet books.	■ Read more alphabet books and discuss them.
Lesson 4 ***If I Were a Mouse***	A poem about what it would be like to be a mouse.	The students can put themselves in the place of a character in the poem.	■ As a class, create a sample page for the class alphabet book.	■ Discuss the different designs of alphabet books.
Lesson 5 ***Hey, Diddle, Diddle***	A nursery rhyme that may be familiar to most students.	The students may be able to recite a familiar nursery rhyme.	■ Create alphabet book pages for the letters *a*, *b*, *c*, and *d*.	■ Provide materials for the class alphabet book. ■ Discuss with the students designs for their pages.
Lesson 6 ***There Was Once a Fish***	A rhyming poem about fish.	This poem introduces the students to the structures of questions and dialogue.	■ Complete alphabet book pages for the letters *e*, *f*, *g*, and *h*.	■ Discuss with the students the possibilities for designing their next set of pages.
Lesson 7 ***Rain***	A poem about where rain falls.	This short poem uses rhyming words and classic poetry structure.	■ Complete alphabet book pages for the letters *i*, *j*, *k*, and *l*.	■ Discuss with the students the possibilities for designing their next set of pages.
Lesson 8 ***Rhyme Stew***	A poem that uses rhyming words to concoct a rhyme stew.	This poem gives the students the opportunity to use illustrations with rhyming words.	■ Complete alphabet book pages for the letters *m*, *n*, *o*, and *p*.	■ Discuss with the students the possibilities for designing their next set of pages.
Lesson 9 ***Rags***	A poem about a pet dog.	This poem uses the elements of rhyme, repetition, and describing words to convey the message of the poem.	■ Complete alphabet book pages for the letters *q*, *r*, *s*, and *t*.	■ Discuss with the students the possibilities for designing their next set of pages.
Lesson 10 ***Twinkle Twinkle Firefly***	A poem about fireflies.	This poem uses the elements of rhyme and repetition, as well as broken lines.	■ Complete alphabet book pages for the letters *u*, *v*, *w*, *x*, *y*, and *z*.	■ Discuss with the students the possibilities for designing their next set of pages.
Lessons 11–12 ***The Chase***	A folktale about animals who see other animals running, and think they should be running, although they don't know why.	The students are introduced to a humorous cumulative story.	■ Share the pages from the class alphabet book.	■ Explain how to share a page from the class alphabet book.
Lessons 13–14 ***Mrs. Goose's Baby***	A fantasy about a goose and her baby.	The students use the story to compare and contrast a mother and her baby.	■ Continue to share pages from the class alphabet book. ■ Add to the class alphabet book.	■ Assist the students as they share their pages in the class alphabet book.
Lesson 15 ***Babybuggy***	A poem about ladybugs.	This poem includes rhyming words that are compound words.	■ Create a poem to add to the class alphabet book.	■ Write the poem on the board for the students to copy. ■ Assist the students as they add the poem to their book.

PROGRAM RESOURCES

Student Materials

Little Big Book, *Let's Read!*
Pages 1–56

Phonics Skills
Pages 2–23

Pre-Decodable Books 1–4

Decodable Books Core Set 5–7 Practice Set 1–2

Language Arts Big Book

Comprehension and Language Arts Skills
Pages 2–15

Writer's Workbook
Pages 2–3

Additional Materials

- Listening Library Audiocassette/CD
- Program Assessment
- Units 1–6 Assessment
- Decodable Takehome Books
- Sound/Spelling Card Stories Audiocassette/CD
- Sound/Spelling Card Strips
- Writing Folder

UNIVERSAL ACCESS:
Meeting Individual Needs

- ELD Workbook
- Intervention Workbook
- Reteach: Phonics Skills
- Challenge: Phonics Skills
- Reteach: Comprehension and Language Arts Skills
- Challenge: Comprehension and Language Arts Skills

Teacher Materials

Teacher's Edition, Book 1

Big Book, *Let's Read!*

Pages 1–56

Read Aloud *Wolf!*

Phonics Skills Teacher's Edition

Pages 2–23

Comprehension and Language Arts Skills Teacher's Edition

Pages 2–15

Writer's Workbook Teacher's Edition

Pages 2–3

Home Connection

Pages 1–8

Additional Materials

- Language Arts Big Book
- Teacher's Professional Guides
- Program Assessment Teacher's Edition
- Units 1–6 Assessment Teacher's Edition
- Alphabet Flash Cards, Letter Cards
- High-Frequency Word Cards
- Lion Puppet
- Reading Transparencies, 39, 49
- Language Arts Transparencies 1–3

Sound/Spelling Cards

Universal Access:

Meeting Individual Needs

- ELD Guide
- ELD Glossary
- Intervention Guide
- Intervention Annotated Bibliography
- Reteach Teacher's Editions
- Challenge Teacher's Editions

PROGRAM RESOURCES

Leveled Classroom Library*

Easy	Average	Challenge

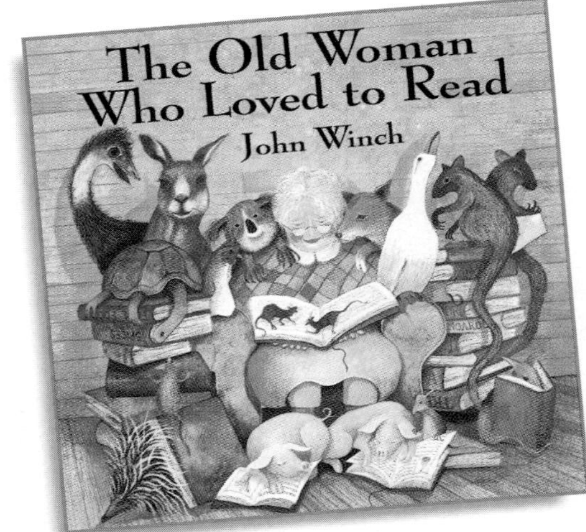

Bibliography**

A Weed Is a Seed **by Ferida Wolff**

Jack's Tale **by Ellen Stoll Walsh**

Mop's Treasure Hunt **by Martine Schaap**

Stella Louella's Runaway Book **by Lisa Campbell Ernst**

Note: Teachers should preview any trade books and videos for appropriateness in their classrooms before recommending them to students.

* These books, which support the unit theme *Let's Read!*, are part of a 60-book ***Leveled Classroom Library*** available for purchase from SRA/McGraw-Hill.

** These books may go out of print. Check libraries or bookstores for availability.

TECHNOLOGY

Web Connections

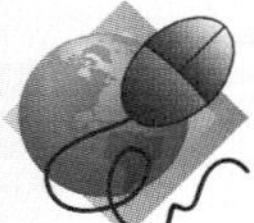

www.sra4kids.com

***Let's Read!* Web Sites**

Information about *Let's Read!* and links to sites concerning *Let's Read!* can be found at SRA's Web site.

CD-ROMs

Leap Into Phonics

LEAP INTO LEARNING, 2001

Use this software to practice identifying sounds and blending words.

*** *The Ultimate Writing and Creativity Center***

THE LEARNING COMPANY

Students can use this word processing software to get ideas, draft, revise, edit, and publish their Writing Process Strategies activities in this unit.

Children's Treasury of Stories, Nursery Rhymes, and Songs

QUEUE

These nursery rhymes and classic songs, accompanied by beautiful music and graphics, will enchant beginning readers.

My First Amazing Words and Pictures

DK MULTIMEDIA

This CD-ROM activity pack includes more than 1,000 words and pictures that beginning readers encounter every day.

Computer Skills

*** Basic Computer Skills**

SRA Basic Computer Skills can be used to help students develop computer skills within the context of the unit theme.

Videocassettes

*** Lesson Model Videocassette**

SRA/MCGRAW-HILL

Use the Lesson Model Videocassette as a model for teaching phonics.

*** *Fables***

Arnold Lobel's delightful collection of fables will amuse students as well as provide some practical advice. Available in English and Spanish. 18 min.

*** *Leo Lionni's Caldecotts***

Three of Lionni's charming stories—*Alexander and the Windup Mouse*, *Swimmy*, and *Frederick*—are included in this award-winning collection. 16 min.

*** *A Visit to William Blake's Inn: Poems for Innocent and Experienced Travelers***

In a playful parody of William Blake's *Songs of Innocence and Experience*, these magical poems describe life in an imaginary inn whose proprietor is William Blake.

Audiocassettes/CDs

*** Listening Library: *Let's Read!***

SRA/MCGRAW-HILL, 2002

Students will enjoy listening to the selections they have read. Encourage them to use the ***Listening Library*** during Workshop.

*** Sound Spelling Card Stories**

SRA/MCGRAW-HILL, 2002

Students can listen to the sound/spelling stories for each ***Sound/Spelling Card.*** Encourage them to listen to them during Workshop.

Titles preceded by an asterisk (*) are available through SRA/McGraw-Hill. Other titles can be obtained by contacting the publisher listed with the title.

UNIT | OVERVIEW

UNIT SKILLS OVERVIEW

	PHONEMIC AWARENESS & PHONICS	COMPREHENSION	PRINT AND BOOK AWARENESS
Lesson 1 **Unit Introduction** *Wolf* **Genre: Fantasy**	**Oral Blending:** Syllables and Word Parts **Segmentation:** Clapping Syllables in Names		
Lesson 2 *The Purple Cow* **Genre: Poetry**	**Oral Blending:** Syllables and Word Parts **Segmentation:** Clapping Syllables in Names and Words; Onsets and Rimes	**Strategies** ■ Visualizing	■ Book Covers, Titles, and Table of Contents
Lesson 3 *Las hormiguitas* **Genre: Poetry**	**Oral Blending:** Blending Initial Consonant Sounds; Comparing Word Length **Segmentation:** Onsets and Rimes	**Strategies** ■ Asking Questions	■ Left-to-Right Directionality of Print
Lesson 4 *If I Were a Mouse* **Genre: Poetry**	**Oral Blending:** Initial Consonant Sounds **Segmentation:** Onsets and Rimes	**Strategies** ■ Visualizing	■ Word Boundaries
Lesson 5 *Hey, Diddle, Diddle* **Genre: Poetry**	**Oral Blending:** Initial Consonant Sounds; Initial Consonant Restoration	**Strategies** ■ Asking Questions	■ Print Directionality
Lesson 6 *There Was Once a Fish* **Genre: Poetry**	**Oral Blending:** Initial Consonant **Segmentation:** Initial Phoneme Segmentaion	**Strategies** ■ Monitoring and Clarifying	■ Word Boundaries
Lesson 7 *Rain* **Genre: Poetry**	**Oral Blending:** Final Consonant Sounds **Segmentation:** Segmenting Initial Phonemes **"Did you Ever?" Song**	**Strategies** ■ Visualizing	
Lesson 8 *Rhyme Stew* **Genre: Poetry**	**Oral Blending:** Final Consonant Sounds **Segmentation:** Initial Phoneme Segmentation; Final Phoneme Segmentation	**Strategies** ■ Asking Questions	■ Table of Contents
Lesson 9 *Rags* **Genre: Poetry**	**Listening for Vowel Sounds** **Segmentation:** Blending Initial Consonants	**Strategies** ■ Monitoring and Clarifying	
Lesson 10 *Twinkle Twinkle Firefly* **Genre: Poetry**	**Oral Blending:** Blending Initial Consonant Sounds **Segmentation:** Final Consonant Segmentation	**Strategies** ■ Visualizing	■ Authors and Illustrators
Lessons 11–12 *The Chase* **Genre: Folktale**	**Oral Blending:** Blending Initial Consonant Sounds **Segmentation:** Final Phoneme Segmentation	**Strategies** ■ Monitoring and Clarifying ■ Visualizing **Skills** ■ Reality and Fantasy	■ Word Boundaries ■ Illustration/Text Relationship
Lessons 13–14 *Mrs. Goose's Baby* **Genre: Fantasy**	**Oral Blending:** Initial Consonant Sounds **Segmentation:** Dropping Final Consonants	**Strategies** ■ Predicting ■ Visualizing **Skills** ■ Comparing and Contrasting	■ Speech Balloons
Lesson 15 *Babybuggy* **Genre: Poetry**	**Oral Blending:** One Syllable Words **Segmentation:** Restoring Final Consonant Sounds	**Strategies** ■ Asking Questions	■ Illustration/Text Relationship

INQUIRY	WORD ANALYSIS	WRITING PROCESS STRATEGIES	ENGLISH-LANGUAGE CONVENTIONS
Previewing the Unit ■ Introduce Unit Investigation ■ Concept/Question Board	**Vocabulary** ■ Introduction to Vocabulary	**Introduction to the Writing Process** ■ Purposes for Writing	**Grammar, Usage, and Mechanics** ■ Capital Letters: Names and I
Supporting Student Investigations ■ Investigating Concepts Beyond the Text ■ Art Connection: Imaginary Animals	**Vocabulary** ■ Introduction to Classification: Colors	**Introduction to the Writing Process** ■ What Writers Do **Writer's Craft** ■ Writing Words	**Grammar, Usage, and Mechanics** ■ Capital Letters: Names
Supporting Student Investigations ■ Investigating Concepts Beyond the Text ■ Math Connection: Graphing Names	**Vocabulary** ■ Introduction to Classification: Animals	**Introduction to the Writing Process** ■ The Steps of the Writing Process	**Grammar, Usage, and Mechanics** ■ Capital Letters: Names
Supporting Student Investigations ■ Investigating Concepts Beyond the Text ■ Art Connection: Illustrating Poems	**Vocabulary** ■ Introduction to Classification: Animals	**Introduction to the Writing Process** ■ Getting Ideas	**Listening, Speaking, Viewing** ■ Listening: Listening Attentively
Supporting Student Investigations ■ Investigating Concepts Beyond the Text ■ Math Connection: Alphabet Counting	**Vocabulary** ■ Classification: Animals	**Introduction to the Writing Process** ■ Getting Ideas for Autobiography	**Penmanship** ■ Letters Are Lines
Supporting Student Investigations ■ Investigating Concepts Beyond the Text ■Science Connection: Life in the Water	**Vocabulary** ■ Introduction to Rhyming Words	**Introduction to the Writing Process** ■ Plan	**Grammar, Usage, and Mechanics** ■ Capital Letters: Cities and States
Supporting Student Investigations ■ Investigating Concepts Beyond the Text ■ Science Connection: Weather Words	**Vocabulary** ■ Introduction to Rhyming Words	**Introduction to the Writing Process** ■ Plan	**Grammar, Usage, and Mechanics** ■ Capital Letters: Cities and States
Supporting Student Investigations ■ Investigating Concepts Beyond the Text ■ Music Connection: Stew Chant	**Vocabulary** ■ Introduction to Rhyming Words	**Introduction to the Writing Process** ■ Plan **Writer's Craft** ■ Time and Order Words	**Grammar, Usage, and Mechanics** ■ Capital Letters: Days and Months
Supporting Student Investigations ■ Investigating Concepts Beyond the Text ■ Math Connection: Finish the Pattern	**Vocabulary** ■ Introduction to Rhyming Words	**Introduction to the Writing Process** ■ Plan	**Listening, Speaking, Viewing** ■ Speaking: Speaking Clearly
Supporting Student Investigations ■ Investigating Concepts Beyond the Text ■ Music Connection: Clapping to a Beat	**Vocabulary** ■ Rhyming Words	**Introduction to the Writing Process** ■ Plan for Autobiography	**Penmanship** ■ Letters Are Lines
Supporting Student Investigations ■ Investigating Concepts Beyond the Text ■ Social Studies Connection: Seasons ■ Music Connection: Cumulative Rhymes	**Vocabulary** ■ Introduction to Context Clues	**Introduction to the Writing Process** ■ Write **Writer's Craft** ■Sentences	**Grammar, Usage, and Mechanics** ■ Capital Letters: Sentences ■ End Marks: Periods
Supporting Student Investigations ■ Investigating Concepts Beyond the Text ■ Math Connection: Alike and Different ■ Drama Connection: Talk Without Speaking	**Vocabulary** ■ Introduction to Context Clues	**Introduction to the Writing Process** ■ Write	**Grammar, Usage, and Mechanics** ■ Capital Letters: Sentences **Listening, Speaking, Viewing** ■ Language: Informal and Formal Language
Supporting Student Investigations ■ Investigating Concepts Beyond the Text ■ Language Arts Connection: Making Rhymes	**Vocabulary** ■ Context Clues	**Introduction to the Writing Process** ■ Write for Autobiography	**Penmanship** ■ Letters Are Lines

Differentiating Instruction Workshop

Explain to students that there will be a time every day that they will be expected to work on activities. This time, called Workshop, will be devoted to collaborating on their investigations of unit concepts, working independently to meeting each of their individual needs. Students will work on their own, in pairs, or in small groups independently.

Workshop is a means of leading students to make good use of free time. It assures that the needs of all students will be met, from those who require extra help to the advanced learners. During this time, encourage them to become independent, self-motivated learners. During this time, students will learn to make good use of their time; make decisions about activities, materials, and work; understand organization and care of materials; share and cooperate with others; and adapt skills learned from direct teaching in self-teaching situations.

Students can make the best use of Workshop when the following takes place:

- A set of rules, such as be polite, share, and whisper, is posted and observed.
- A set of classroom materials necessary for the various activities is available.
- The physical organization of the classroom facilitates both independent and group activities.
- The teacher closely supervises this time.

Because students will be working on a variety of activities, you will be afforded time and opportunity to differentiate instruction to address the special needs of all students. At this time, you may want to have students preread or listen to tomorrow's story; read a favorite ***Decodable Book*** (or ***Pre-Decodable***); review ***Sound/Spelling Cards*** by playing What Do You Hear? in small groups; and find words in the selection that connect with the Phonics lesson.

Universal Access:
Meeting Individual Needs

The following are examples of the types of activities that you might have going on during Workshop:

Collaborating on Investigation Students will meet in small groups with you to formulate questions about the unit concept. They may make assignments that can be investigated individually in order to answer the questions. During this time students may also share and evaluate materials for their investigations. In addition to their investigations, students may choose other activities to engage in, including practicing skills and independent reading.

Preteaching/Reteaching The time you set aside for Workshop will also allow you to help individuals or small groups of students who have exhibited a need in any area.

Use the ***Reteach*** workbooks for sudents who show a basic understanding of the lesson but need more practice. Use ***Intervention*** for students who, even after extra practice, exhibit a lack of understanding of the lesson concepts.

Independent Reading Students may wish to read or peruse the books listed in the ***Leveled Classroom Library.*** Students should also be reading or looking at books for at least 20 minutes daily outside the classroom.

Partner Reading Provide time every day for students who are able to read with a partner. This is a time for students to practice reading ***Decodable Books*** to increase fluency.

Reading Roundtable During this time students may share information about additional books they have read independently and discuss how they support the unit theme or simply what they thought of them

Writing Seminar This is a time when students can share their writing with you. You may model by doing your own writing as the students do theirs.

For more information on Workshop, see the Appendix, pages 40–42.

Setting Up the Classroom

Setting up your classroom to accommodate different activities will help assure that Workshop progresses smoothly and effectively. While setting up your classroom, keep in mind the primary activities of Workshop. Because students will be doing both independent and collaborative reading and writing, it is suggested that you provide the following space and materials:

- A reading area supplied with books and magazines.
- A writing and publishing area supplied with paper, pencils, rulers, colored markers, crayons, tape, string,and scissors.
- A listening area that includes a tape recorder (or CD-player) and audiocassettes (or CDs) of stories, poems, and songs for students to hear. You might also want to provide blank tapes and encourage the students to use them for writing projects or for other investigations.
- The ***Sound/Spelling Cards*** should line the front wall above the board so that students can easily see the cards.

Students work much better independently when there is adequate space and a sense of order. The room arrangement below is one possibility, but is not the only way to arrange your classroom, especially if space is an issue. The proposed arrangement provides for easy movement of the students, leaves a large open space on the floor for whole-class and individual activities, facilitates easy access for the teacher, and organizes the class into manageable sections. It also allows the placement of those with visual, auditory, and other impairments in advantageous positions near the front of the room. However, students should not be grouped at desks or tables according to ability. They should be heterogeneously grouped.

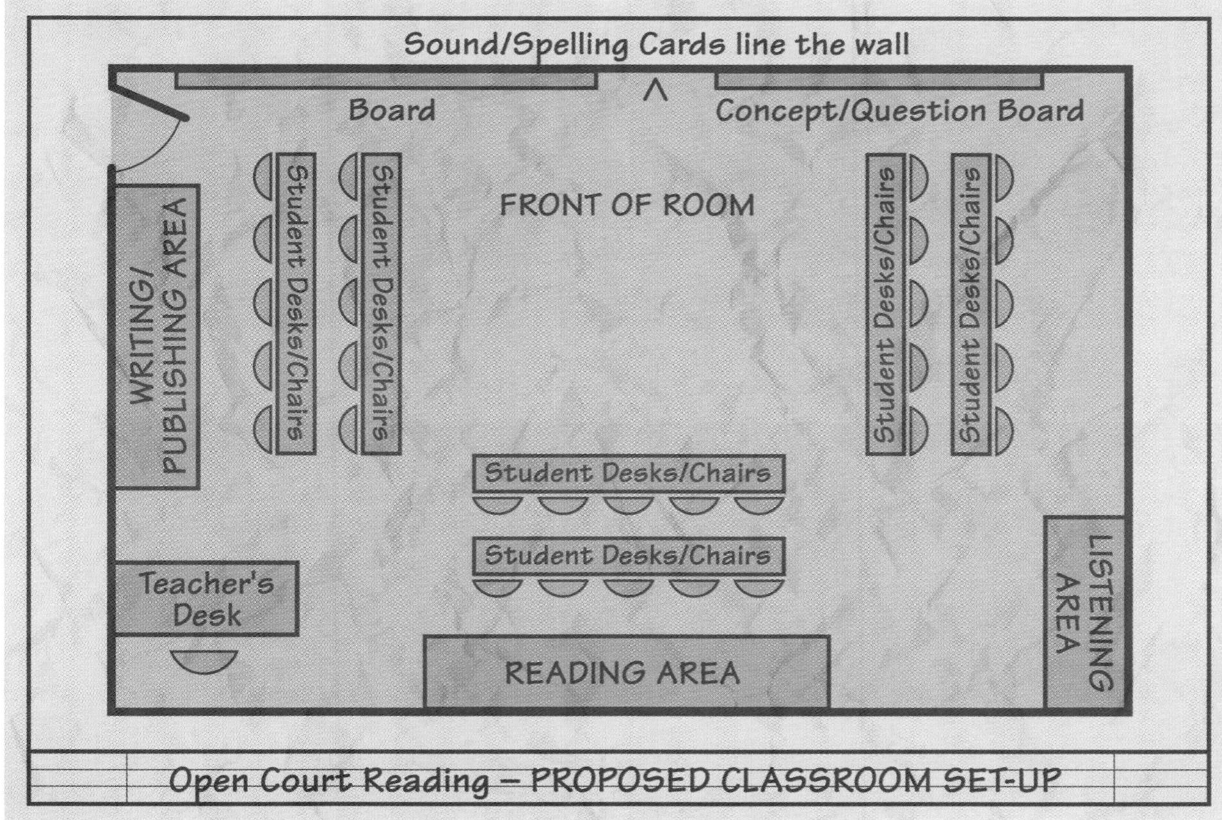

UNIT 1 OVERVIEW

Universal Access: Meeting Individual Needs

UNIVERSAL ACCESS: MEETING INDIVIDUAL NEEDS

	Reteach	ELL	Challenge	Intervention
Lesson 1 **Unit Introduction**	**Preparing to Read:** Letter Formation, *Aa, Bb* **Language Arts:** Mechanics, Capital Letters	**Preparing to Read:** Phonemic Awareness **Reading and Responding:** Selection Vocabulary **Language Arts:** Grammar and Usage	**Preparing to Read:** Letter Formation, Aa, Bb **Language Arts:** Mechanics, Capital Letters	**Preparing to Read:** Phonemc Awareness; Letters; Letter Practice **Reading and Responding:** Selection Vocabulary, Comprehension **Language Arts:** Vocabulary, Mechanics
Lesson 2 ***The Purple Cow***	**Preparing to Read:** Letter Formation, *Cc, Dd* **Language Arts:** Writer's Craft, Writing Words	**Preparing to Read:** Phonemic Awareness; Word Meaning **Reading and Responding:** Selection Vocabulary; Poetry; Preteach Selection; Word Meaning **Language Arts:** Vocabulary, Mechanics	**Preparing to Read:** Letter Formation, Cc, Dd **Language Arts:** Writer's Craft, Writing Words	**Preparing to Read:** Phonemic Awareness; Letter Formation **Reading and Responding:** Selection Vocabulary, Comprehension Language Arts: Vocabulary, Mechanics
Lesson 3 ***Las hormiguitas***	**Preparing to Read:** Letter Formation, *Ee, Ff, Gg* **Reading and Responding:** High-Frequency Words; Letter Recognition	**Preparing to Read:** Phonemic Awareness; Word Meaning **Reading and Responding:** Selection Vocabulary **Language Arts:** Mechanics	**Preparing to Read:** Letter Formation, *Ee, Ff, Gg*	**Preparing to Read:** Phonemic Awareness; Letter Recognition **Reading and Responding:** Selection Vocabulary, Comprehension; Repetition; Letter Recognition **Language Arts:** Vocabulary, Mechanics
Lesson 4 ***If I Were a Mouse***	**Preparing to Read:** Letter Formation, *Hh, Ii, Jj*	**Preparing to Read:** Phonemic Awareness; Word Meaning **Reading and Responding:** Selection Vocabulary **Language Arts:** Vocabulary	**Preparing to Read:** Letter Formation, *Hh, Ii, Jj*	**Preparing to Read:** Phonemic Awareness; Forming Letters **Reading and Responding:** Selection Vocabulary, Comprehension; Repetition **Language Arts:** Vocabulary
Lesson 5 ***Hey, Diddle, Diddle***	**Preparing to Read:** Letter Formation, *Kk, Ll, Mm* **Reading and Responding:** Reading the Poem; Alphabet Practice	**Preparing to Read:** Phonemic Awareness; Word Meaning; Pictures; Dramatize the Poem **Reading and Responding:** Selection Vocabulary **Language Arts:** Vocabulary	**Preparing to Read:** Letter Formation, *Kk, Ll, Mm*; Exploring Nursery Rhymes	**Preparing to Read:** Phonemic Awareness; Letter Recognition **Reading and Responding:** Selection Vocabulary; Comprehension; Letter Recognition; Alphabet Game **Language Arts:** Vocabulary
Lesson 6 ***There Was Once a Fish***	**Preparing to Read:** Oral Blending; Letter Formation, *Nn, Oo, Pp* **Language Arts:** Mechanics, Capital Letters	**Preparing to Read:** Phonemic Awareness **Reading and Responding:** Selection Vocabulary; Preteach; Using Pictures **Language Arts:** Vocabulary	**Preparing to Read:** Letter Formation, *Nn, Oo, Pp* **Language Arts:** Mechanics, Capital Letters	**Preparing to Read:** Phonemic Awareness; Oral Blending; Letter Recognition **Reading and Responding:** Selection Vocabulary; Comprehension; Word Boundaries **Language Arts:** Vocabulary
Lesson 7 ***Rain***	**Preparing to Read:** Letter Formation, *Qq, Rr, Ss*	**Preparing to Read:** Phonemic Awareness; Word Meanings **Reading and Responding:** Selection Vocabulary; Picture Story, Sharing **Language Arts:** Vocabulary	**Preparing to Read:** Letter Formation, *Qq, Rr, Ss*	**Preparing to Read:** Phonemic Awareness; Letter Recognition **Reading and Responding:** Selection Vocabulary; Comprehension **Language Arts:** Vocabulary, Mechanics
Lesson 8 ***Rhyme Stew***	**Preparing to Read:** Phonemic Awareness; Letter Formation, *Tt, Uu, Vv* **Reading and Responding:** Big Books; Nursery Rhymes **Language Arts:** Writer's Craft, Order Words	**Preparing to Read:** Phonemic Awareness; Word Meaning **Reading and Responding:** Selection Vocabulary; Preteach; Rhyming Words **Language Arts:** Vocabulary	**Preparing to Read:** Letter Formation, *Tt, Uu, Vv* **Language Arts:** Writer's Craft, Order Words	**Preparing to Read:** Phonemic Awareness; Rhyming Words; Letter Recognition; Letter Formation **Reading and Responding:** Selection Vocabulary; Comprehension; Rhyming Words **Language Arts:** Vocabulary
Lesson 9 ***Rags***	**Preparing to Read:** Oral Blending and Segmentation; Letter Formation, *Ww, Xx, Yy, Zz* **Reading and Responding:** Rhyming Dictionary; Rhyming Dictionary	**Preparing to Read:** Phonemic Awareness; Word Meaning **Reading and Responding:** Selection Vocabulary; Using Illustrations; Preteach; Picture Story **Language Arts:** Vocabulary, Listening, Speaking, Viewing	**Preparing to Read:** Letter Formation, *Ww, Xx, Yy, Zz*	**Preparing to Read:** Phonemic Awareness; Letter Recognition **Reading and Responding:** Selection Vocabulary; Comprehension; Letter Recognition **Language Arts:** Vocabulary; Listening, Speaking, Viewing
Lesson 10 ***Twinkle Twinkle Firefly***	**Preparing to Read:** Letter Recognition; Letter Recognition: Letters; High-Frequency Words	**Preparing to Read:** Phonemic Awareness **Reading and Responding:** Selection Vocabulary; Preteach **Language Arts:** Vocabulary	**Preparing to Read:** Letter Recognition	**Preparing to Read:** Phonemic Awareness **Reading and Responding:** Selection Vocabulary; Comprehension; Rhythm **Language Arts:** Vocabulary
Lessons 11–12 ***The Chase***	**Preparing to Read:** Oral Blending; /s/ Spelled *s*; Initial Consonants; Phonics; /m/ Spelled *m* **Reading and Responding:** Reread; Reality and Fantasy; Using Illustrations **Language Arts:** Mechanics, Capital Letters; Writer's Craft, Sentences	**Preparing to Read:** Phonemic Awareness; *s* Blends in Spanish; Inflectional Endings; /m/ Sound; Activities **Reading and Responding:** Selection Vocabulary; Using Illustrations; Preteach; Read Aloud **Language Arts:** Mechanics	**Preparing to Read:** /s/ Spelled *s*; /m/ Spelled *m* **Language Arts:** Mechanics, Capital Letters; Writer's Craft, Sentences	**Preparing to Read:** Phonemic Awareness; *s* Sounds; Initial Consonant Sounds; /m/ Sound **Reading and Responding:** Selection Vocabulary; Comprehension; Reality and Fantasy **Language Arts:** Vocabulary, Mechanics
Lessons 13–14 ***Mrs. Goose's Baby***	**Preparing to Read:** Oral Blending; /a/ Spelled *a*; Initial Consonant Sounds; /t/ Spelled *t* **Reading and Responding:** Comparing and Contrasting	**Preparing to Read:** Phonemic Awareness; Word Meaning; Vowel Sounds for Arabic Speakers; /a/ in Asian Languages; /t/ Sound **Reading and Responding:** Selection Vocabulary; Preteach **Language Arts:** Mechanics, Penmanship	**Preparing to Read:** /a/ Spelled *a*; /t/ Spelled *t* **Reading and Responding:** Comparing and Contrasting	**Preparing to Read:** Phonemic Awareness; Vowel/Consonant/Vowel **Reading and Responding:** Selection Vocabulary; Comprehension; Contrasting **Language Arts:** Vocabulary; Listening, Speaking, Viewing
Lesson 15 ***Babybuggy***	**Preparing to Read:** Phonemic Awareness; /h/ Spelled *h*	**Preparing to Read:** Phonemic Awareness; Vocabulary; /h/ Sound; Silent *h* in Spanish **Reading and Responding:** Selection Vocabulary	**Preparing to Read:** /h/ Spelled *h*	**Preparing to Read:** Phonemic Awareness; Blending **Reading and Responding:** Selection Vocabulary; Comprehension **Language Arts:** Vocabulary

Above are suggestions for Workshop to meet the individual needs of students. These are the same skills shown on Unit Skills Overview, however, these pages provide extra practice opportunities or enriching activities to meet the varied needs of students.

ASSESSMENT

Lesson	Informal Assessment	Progress Assessment	Formal Assessment
Lesson 1	*Phonemic Awareness, p. T26 *Letter Recognition, pp. T27, T31	Phonics Skills, p. 2 Reteach: Phonics Skills, p. 2 Challenge: Phonics Skills, p. 1 Comprehension and Language Arts Skills, pp. 2–3 Reteach: Comprehension and Language Arts Skills, p. 2 Challenge: Comprehension and Language Arts Skills, p. 2	
Lesson 2	*Phonemic Awareness, p. T43 *Letter Recognition, p. T45	Phonics Skills, p. 3 Reteach: Phonics Skills, p. 3 Challenge: Phonics Skills, p. 2 Comprehension and Language Arts Skills, pp. 4–5 Reteach: Comprehension and Language Arts Skills, p. 3 Challenge: Comprehension and Language Arts Skills, p. 3	
Lesson 3	*Phonemic Awareness, p. T61 *Dictation, p. T65 *Reading a Pre-Decodable Book, p. T66 *Mechanics: Capital Letters, p. T79	Phonics Skills, p. 4 Reteach: Phonics Skills, p. 4 Challenge: Phonics Skills, p. 3	
Lesson 4	*Phonemic Awareness, p. T81 *Reviewing Sounds and Letters, p. T85 *Letter Recognition, p. T91 *Listening, Speaking, Viewing: Listening Attentively, p. T97	Phonics Skills, p. 5 Reteach: Phonics Skills, p. 5 Challenge: Phonics Skills, p. 4	
Lesson 5	*Phonemic Awareness, p. T99 *Reading a Pre-Decodable Book, p. T103 *Vocabulary: Classification, p. T115 *Penmanship: Letters are Lines, p. T115	Phonics Skills, p. 6 Reteach: Phonics Skills, p. 6 Challenge: Phonics Skills, p. 5 Writer's Workbook, p. 2	Units 1–6 Assessment ■ Syllables, p. 3 ■ Rhyme Building, p. 4
Lesson 6	*Phonemic Awareness, pp. T125 *Dictation, p. T129 *Letter Recognition, p. T135	Phonics Skills, p. 7 Reteach: Phonics Skills, p. 7 Challenge: Phonics Skills, p. 6 Comprehension and Language Arts Skills, pp. 6–7 Reteach: Comprehension and Language Arts Skills, p. 4 Challenge: Comprehension and Language Arts Skills, p. 4	
Lesson 7	*Reading a Pre-Decodable Book, p. T149	Phonics Skills, p. 8 Reteach: Phonics Skills, p. 8 Challenge: Phonics Skills, p. 7	
Lesson 8	*Reviewing Sounds and Letters, p. T166 *Dictation, p. T167 *Letter Recognition, p. T176 *Mechanics: Capital Letters, p. T179	Phonics Skills, p. 9 Reteach: Phonics Skills, p. 9 Challenge: Phonics Skills, p. 8 Comprehension and Language Arts Skills, pp. 8–9 Reteach: Comprehension and Language Arts Skills, p. 5 Challenge: Comprehension and Language Arts Skills, p. 5	
Lesson 9	*Letter Recognition, p. T183 *Reading a Pre-Decodable Book, p. T187 *Listening, Speaking, Viewing: Speaking Clearly, p. T199	Phonics Skills, pp. 10–11 Reteach: Phonics Skills, pp. 10–11 Challenge: Phonics Skills, pp. 9–10	
Lesson 10	*Phonemic Awareness, p. 201 *Dictation, p. T203 *Vocabulary: Rhyming Words, p. T215 *Penmanship: Letters Are Lines, p. T215	Phonics Skills, pp. 12–13 Reteach: Phonics Skills, pp. 12–13 Challenge: Phonics Skills, p. 11 Writer's Workbook, p. 3	Units 1–6 Assessment ■ Initial Consonants, p. 5 ■ Dropping Final Sounds, p. 6
Lessons 11–12	*Phonemic Awareness, pp. T224, T245 *Phonics, pp. T229, T251	Phonics Skills, pp. 14–17 Reteach: Phonics Skills, pp. 14–17 Challenge: Phonics Skills, pp. 12–13 Comprehension and Language Arts Skills, pp. 10–13 Reteach: Comprehension and Language Arts Skills, pp. 6–7 Challenge: Comprehension and Language Arts Skills, pp. 6–7	
Lessons 13–14	*Phonemic Awareness, pp. T263, T268, T283 *Phonics, pp. T284, T291 *Mechanics: Capital Letters and Periods, p. T281 *Listening, Speaking, Viewing: Informal and Formal Language, p. T303	Phonics Skills, pp. 18–21 Reteach: Phonics Skills, pp. 18–21 Challenge: Phonics Skills, pp. 14–15 Comprehension and Language Arts Skills, pp. 14–15 Reteach: Comprehension and Language Arts Skills, pp. 14–15 Challenge: Comprehension and Language Arts Skills, pp. 14–15	
Lesson 15	*Phonics, pp. T307, T311 *Vocabulary: Context Clues, p. T323 *Penmanship: Letters are Lines, p. T323	Phonics Skills, pp. 22–23 Reteach: Phonics Skills, pp. 22–23 Challenge: Phonics Skills, p. 16	Units 1–6 Assessment ■ *Phonemic Awareness, pp. 7A–7B ■ Sound Blending, p. 7 End of Unit 1 Assessment ■ Word Boundaries, p. 8 ■ Selection Vocabulary, p. 10 ■ Print and Book Awareness, pp. 9A–9B ■ Vocabulary, p. 11 ■ High-Frequency Words, p. 9 ■ *Writing Prompt, p. 12A ■ Grammar, Usage and Mechanics, p. 12

**Teacher's Edition* page reference

California

Professional Resources

The resources listed here are intended to help you develop the concepts and organize information to share with the students in whatever way you choose.

Reading Instruction

Adams, M.J. (1990). Beginning to Read: Thinking and learning about print. Cambridge, MA: MIT Press.

California State Board of Education. (1998), *Learning to Read.* Sacramento, CA: California State Board of Education.

Phonemic Awareness/Phonics

Carnine, D., & Silbert, J. (1970). *Direct instruction reading.* Columbus, OH: Merrill.

Consortium on Reading Excellence, (1999). *CORE teaching reading sourcebook.* Novato, CA: Consortium on Reading Excellence.

Literature

Helbig, Alethea and Perkins, Agnes Regan. *Many Peoples, One Land: A Guide to New Multicultural Literature for Children and Young Adults.* Greenwood Publishing Group, 2000. Fiction, oral tradition, and poetry from four U.S. ethnic groups: African-American, Asian American, Hispanic, and Native American. The authors evaluate 500 multicultural books published between 1994–1999.

Lima, Carolyn W. and Lima, John A. *A to Zoo: Subject Access to Children's Picture Books.* R.R. Bowker, 1998. Comprehensive subject listing for more than 18,000 picture book titles under 1,000 subjects. Also indexed by author and illustrator.

Professional Checkpoints

As you proceed through the unit with your class, you may find it useful to think about the following questions:

- Do you remember learning to read? How did you feel while you were learning?
- Which elements of both reading and learning in general do you find enjoyable?
- Which elements do you find challenging?
- How might you share your enthusiasm for reading with students?
- Why might learning to read seem a bit overwhelming? What exercises might be used to help someone overcome this feeling?

Concept/Question Board

The Concept/Question Board is a place for students to ask questions and find answers in order to have a better understanding of the unit theme.

This board could be a standard bulletin board or a large, three-sided board placed in the front or to the side of the classroom. The board will be a permanent place for students to ask questions, post articles or objects, and so on throughout the study of each unit theme. Students should have easy access to the Concept/Question Board, as they will need it to be able to attach items on their own.

Have a large supply of self-stick notepads or index cards and thumbtacks available. Or you could have construction paper cut in various shapes to represent each story available for the students to write on. For example, you could cut purple construction paper in the shape of a cow to represent the poem "The Purple Cow." These cut-out shapes, which would easily identify the poem in the unit, would be used to write questions or words pertaining to the story.

To begin using your Concept/Question Board, ask the students to formulate statements about what they know about the unit theme or what they believe to be important about the theme after listening to the Read Aloud *Wolf!* Write these statements and attach them to the Concept side of the Board. Then, write any preliminary questions they have about the unit theme and attach those to the Question side of the Board.

Another idea to help get the students started is to put up a chart or web that they can add to throughout the unit. For example, you might put up a list of books students like and add to it as you go through the unit.

As the students progress through the unit, they can refer to the Board often to learn which classmates have similar interests. This information can be used to form groups to investigate questions and ideas about the unit theme.

Throughout the unit, you should reread and reflect on the contributions listed on the Concept/Question Board with the students. Discuss whether reading selections have provided information that might be added or that might revise existing postings. Have the students note, in their Writer's Notebooks, the contributions that mean the most to them by adding their own articles, pictures, and so on.

Research in Reading

Marilyn Jager Adams
Phonemic Awareness

Awareness that spoken words are made up of sounds, or phonemes, is an extremely important predictor of success in reading. Faced with an alphabetic script, students' level of phonemic awareness on entering school might be the single most powerful determinant of their success, or failure, in learning to read. The goal of phonemic awareness activities is to help students understand that words are made up of chains of smaller sounds/syllables and phonemes. This critical insight is necessary to understanding the alphabetic principle of written English: Letters and their associated sounds work together in a systematic way to create words.

Phonemic awareness involves more than rhyming activities. Through gamelike activities, students explore and manipulate the sounds of the English language. They learn to blend sounds into words, to segment words into their component sounds, and to listen for sounds at the beginning, middle, and end of words.

Because phonemic awareness activities require the students to simply listen to, reproduce, and manipulate sounds, the activities work equally well with all students. The gamelike nature of the activities encourages all students to participate, enjoy, and succeed.

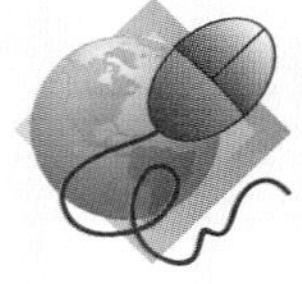

www.sra4kids.com
Web Connection
Check the Reading link of the SRA Web page for more information on Research in Reading.

Leveled Practice

Reteach: Phonics Skills
Pages 2–6

Challenge: Phonics Skills
Pages 1–5

Reteach: Comprehension and Language Arts Skills
Pages 2–3

Challenge: Comprehension and Language Arts Skills
Pages 2–3

ELD Workbook

Intervention Workbook

Additional Materials

- Pre-Decodable Books 1, 2

Leveled Classroom Library*

Students are encouraged to read for 20 minutes daily outside of class. The ***Leveled Classroom Library*** is a great source for reading material that supports the unit theme and helps students develop their vocabulary by reading independently.

I Read Signs

BY TANA HOBAN. MULBERRY BOOKS, 1983.

This book has common signs found around neighborhoods that children may readily recognize. **(Easy)**

Miss Malarkey Doesn't Live in Room 10

BY JUDY FINCHLER. WALKER AND COMPANY, 1995.

Don't teachers live at school. This story will help clarify children's notions about teachers. **(Average)**

A Cake for Herbie

BY PETRA MATHERS. ATHENEUM BOOKS FOR YOUNG READERS, 2000.

Herbie decides to enter a poetry contest, and he teaches us that not all people will like the poems we write, but some people will. **(Advanced)**

* These books, which support the unit theme Let's Read!, are part of a 60-book ***Leveled Classroom Library*** available for purchase from SRA/McGraw-Hill.
Note: Teachers should preview any trade books for appropriateness in their classrooms before recommending them to students.

TECHNOLOGY

Web Connections

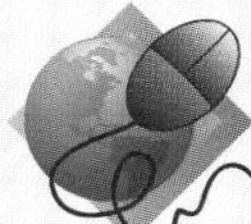

www.sra4kids.com
***Let's Read!* Web Site**

CD-ROMs

*** Leap Into Phonics**
LEAP INTO LEARNING, 2001

**** The Ultimate Writing and Creativity Center***
THE LEARNING COMPANY

Computer Skills

*** Basic Computer Skills**

Audiocassettes/CDs

*** Listening Library: *Let's Read!***
SRA/MCGRAW-HILL, 2002

*** Sound Spelling Card Stories**
SRA/MCGRAW-HILL, 2002

Titles preceded by an asterisk (*) are available through SRA/McGraw-Hill. Other titles can be obtained by contacting the publisher listed with the title.

LESSON PLANNER

	DAY 1	DAY 2
1 Preparing to Read **Materials** ■ Sound/Spelling Cards ■ Pre-Decodable Books ■ Decodable Books ■ Phonics Skills ■ ELD Workbook ■ Intervention Workbook	**Warming Up,** p. T24 **Phonemic Awareness,** pp. T25–T26 **Letter Recognition,** pp. T27–T31 **Reviewing Sounds and Letters** ■ Listening for Vowel Sounds, p. T32 ■ Introducing Consonant Sounds, p. T33 **Dictation,** p. T33	**Warming Up,** p. T42 **Phonemic Awareness,** pp. T43–T44 **Letter Recognition,** p. T45 **Reviewing Sounds and Letters** ■ Introducing Consonant Sounds, p. T46 **Dictation,** p. T47
2 Reading & Responding **Materials** ■ Read Aloud *Wolf!* ■ Big Book *Let's Read!* ■ Teacher Observation Log ■ Home Connection ■ Comprehension and Language Arts Skills ■ ELD Workbook ■ Intervention Workbook	**Previewing the Unit** ■ Read Aloud *Wolf!* pp. T34–T37 ■ Introduce Unit Investigation, p. T38 ■ Concept/Question Board, p. T38 ■ Setting Reading Goals, p. T39 ■ Browsing the Unit, p. T39 ■ Home Connection, p. T39	**Build Background,** p. T50 **Preview and Prepare,** p. T50 **Selection Vocabulary,** p. T51 **Reading Recommendations,** p. T51 **Big Book *Let's Read!*,** pp. 6–7 **Comprehension Strategies,** p. T52 **Discussing the Selection,** p. T54 **Letter Recognition,** p. T53 **Review Selection Vocabulary,** p. T54 **Print and Book Awareness,** p. T55 **Supporting the Reading,** p. T55
Inquiry **Materials** ■ sample Alphabet Books		**Investigating Concepts Beyond the Text,** p. T56 **Art Connection** ■ Imaginary Animals, p. T57
3 Language Arts **Materials** ■ Big Book, *Let's Read!*, pp. 7–15 ■ Language Arts Big Book ■ Comprehension and Language Arts Skills, pp. 2–5 ■ The Ultimate Writing and Creativity Center CD-ROM ■ Writer's Workbook, p. 2 ■ Read Aloud *Wolf!*	**Word Analysis** **Vocabulary** ■ Introduction to Vocabulary, p. T41 **Writing Process Strategies** ■ Introduction to the Writing Process: Purposes for Writing, p. T41 **English Language Conventions** ■ Mechanics: Capital Letters, Names, p. T41	**Word Analysis** **Vocabulary** ■ Introduction to Classification, p. T59 **Writing Process Strategies** ■ Introduction to the Writing Process: What Writers Do, p. T59 ■ Writer's Craft: Writing Words, p. 59 **English Language Conventions** ■ Mechanics: Capital Letters, Names, p. T59

P Phonics ✓ Informal Assessment Available ✓ Formal Assessment Available

DAY 3	DAY 4	DAY 5
Warming Up, p. T60 **Phonemic Awareness,** pp. T61–T62 **Letter Recognition,** pp. T62–T63 **Reviewing Sounds and Letters** ■ Listening for Vowel Sounds, p. T64 **Dictation,** p. T65 **Reading a Pre-Decodable Book** ■ *Book 1, A Table,* pp. T66–T67	**Warming Up,** p. T80 **Phonemic Awareness,** p. T81 **Letter Recognition,** pp. T82–T83 **Reviewing Sounds and Letters** ■ Introducing Consonant Sounds, p. T84 ■ Listening for Vowel Sounds, p. T84 ■ Vowel Chant, p. T85 **Dictation,** p. T85	**Warming Up,** p. T98 **Phonemic Awareness,** p. T99 **Letter Recognition,** p. T100 **Reviewing Sounds and Letters** ■ Silly Senences, p. T101 **Dictation,** p. T101 **Reading a Pre-Decodable Book** ■ *Book 2, The Egg,* pp. T102–T103
Build Background, p. T70 **Preview and Prepare,** p. T70 **Selection Vocabulary,** p. T71 **Reading Recommendations,** p. T71 **Big Book *Let's Read!*,** pp. 8–11 **Comprehension Strategies,** p. T72 **Discussing the Selection,** p. T74 **Letter Recognition,** p. T73 **Review Selection Vocabulary,** p. T74 **Print and Book Awareness,** p. T75 **Supporting the Reading,** p. T75	**Build Background,** p. T88 **Preview and Prepare,** p. T88 **Selection Vocabulary,** p. T89 **Reading Recommendations,** p. T89 **Big Book *Let's Read!*,** pp. 12–13 **Comprehension Strategies** p. T90 **Discussing the Selection,** p. T92 **Letter Recognition,** p. T91 **Review Selection Vocabulary,** p. T92 **Print and Book Awareness,** p. T93 **Supporting the Reading,** p. T93	**Build Background,** p. T106 **Preview and Prepare,** p. T106 **Selection Vocabulary,** p. T107 **Reading Recommendations,** p. T107 **Big Book *Let's Read!*,** pp. 14–15 **Comprehension Strategies,** p. T108 **Discussing the Selection,** p. T110 **Letter Recognition,** p. T109 **Review Selection Vocabulary,** p. T110 **Print and Book Awareness,** p. T111 **Supporting the Reading,** p. T111 **Home Connection,** p. T111
Investigating Concepts Beyond the Text, p. T76 **Math Connection** ■ Graphing Names, p. T77	**Investigating Concepts Beyond the Text,** p. T94 **Art Connection** ■ Illustrating Poems, p. T95	**Investigating Concepts Beyond the Text,** p. T112 **Math Connection** ■ Alphabet Counting, p. T113
Word Analysis **Vocabulary** ■ Introduction to Classification, p. T79 **Writing Process Strategies** ■ Introduction to the Writing Process: The Steps of the Writing Process, p. T79 **English Language Conventions** ✓ ■ Mechanics: Capital Letters, names, p. T79	**Word Analysis** **Vocabulary** ■ Introduction to Classification, p. T97 **Writing Process Strategies** ■ Introduction to the Writing Process: Getting Ideas, p. T97 **English Language Conventions** ■ Listening, Speaking, Viewing. Listening: Listening Attentively, p. T97	**Word Analysis** **Vocabulary** ■ Classification, p. T115 **Writing Process Strategies** ■ Introduction to the Writing Process: Getting Ideas for Autobiography, p. T115 **English Language Conventions** ■ Penmanship: Letters Are Lines, p. T115

Below are suggestions for Workshop to meet the individual needs of students. These are the same skills shown in the Lesson Planner; however, these pages provide extra practice opportunities or enriching activities to meet the varied needs of students.

WORKSHOP

Differentiating Instruction

Small-Group Instruction

Use the informal assessment suggestions found throughout the lesson along with the formal assessment provided to determine your students' strengths and areas of need. Use the following program components to help in supporting or expanding on the instruction found in these lessons:

- ***Reteach: Phonics Skills*** and ***Reteach: Comprehension and Language Arts Skills*** workbooks for use with those students who show a basic understanding of the lesson but need a bit more practice to solidify their understanding
- ***Intervention Guide*** and ***Workbook*** for use with those students who even after extra practice exhibit a lack of understanding of the lesson concepts
- ***English-Language Development Guide*** and ***Workbook*** for use with those students who need language assistance

Have students create small groups to do such things as:

- Discuss books during Reading Roundtable.
- Discuss questions that arise as they investigate concepts after reading the selection.
- Partner read to assist those who have problems reading difficult passages or to help develop fluency.

Independent Activities

Students can work individually on such things as:

- Independent reading
- Challenge
- Writing
- Investigation activities

For Workshop Management Tips, see Appendix page 42.

◆ Small-Group Instruction ■ Independent Activities

	READING	INVESTIGATION ACTIVITIES
DAY 1	◆ Browse ***Leveled Classroom Library*** selections	
DAY 2	◆ Reread selection ◆ Listen to selection in ***Listening Library*** ■ Choose ***Leveled Classroom Library Book***	**Investigating Concepts Beyond the Text** ◆ Discuss class alphabet book
DAY 3	◆ Reread selection ◆ Listen to selection in ***Listening Library*** ◆ Choose ***Leveled Classroom Library Book*** ◆ Reread ***Decodable Book***	**Investigating Concepts Beyond the Text** ◆ Discuss class alphabet book
DAY 4	◆ Reread selection ◆ Listen to selection in ***Listening Library*** ◆ Choose ***Leveled Classroom Library Book*** ◆ Reread ***Decodable Book***	**Investigating Concepts Beyond the Text** ◆ Work on class alphabet book
DAY 5	◆ Reread selection ◆ Listen to selection in ***Listening Library*** ◆ Choose ***Leveled Classroom Library Book*** ◆ Reread ***Decodable Book***	**Investigating Concepts Beyond the Text** ◆ Work on class alphabet book

LANGUAGE ARTS	INTERVENTION	ENGLISH-LANGUAGE LEARNERS	RETEACH	CHALLENGE
English Language Conventions ◆ Complete Capital Letters, ***Comprehension and Language Arts Skills,*** pp. 2–3	◆ **Phonics,** p. T24 ◆ **Letters,** p. T28 ◆ **Letter Practice,** p. T30 ◆ **English Language Conventions,** p. T40	◆ **Phonics,** p. T24 ◆ **English Language Conventions,** p. T40	◆ **Phonics:** p. T31 **Phonics:** *Aa/Bb* ◆ ***Reteach: Phonics Skills,*** p. 2	◆ **Phonics:** p. T31 **Phonics:** *Aa/Bb* ◆ ***Challenge: Phonics Skills,*** p. 1
Writing Process Strategies ◆ Complete **Writer's Craft: Writing Words, *Comprehension and Language Arts Skills,*** p. 3	◆ **Phonics,** p. T42 ◆ **Letter Formation,** p. T45 ◆ **Selection Vocabulary and Comprehension Skills,** p. T50 ◆ **English Language Conventions,** p. T58	◆ **Phonics,** p. T42 ◆ **Word Meaning,** p. T43 ◆ **Selection Vocabulary,** p. T50 ◆ **Understanding the Selection,** p. T54 ◆ **English Language Conventions,** p. T58	◆ **Letter Formation,** p. T46 **Phonics:** *Cc/Dd* ◆ ***Reteach: Phonics Skills,*** p. 3 ◆ Complete **Capital Letters, *Reteach: Comprehension and Language Arts Skills,*** p. 2	◆ **Phonics,** p. T46 ◆ **Independent Reading,** p. T53 **Phonics:** *Cc/Dd* ◆ ***Challenge: Phonics Skills,*** p. 2 ◆ Complete **Capital Letters, *Challenge: Comprehension and Language Arts Skills,*** p. 2
	◆ **Phonics,** p. T60 ◆ **Letter Recognition,** p. T63 ◆ **Selection Vocabulary and Comprehension Skills,** p. T70 ◆ **Repetition,** p. T71 ◆ **English Language Conventions,** p. T78	◆ **Phonics,** p. T60 ◆ **Word Meaning,** p. T61 ◆ **Selection Vocabulary,** p. T70 ◆ **English Language Conventions,** p. T78	◆ **Letter Formation,** p. T63 ◆ **High-Frequency Words,** p. T71 **Phonics:** *Ee/Ff/Gg* ◆ ***Reteach: Phonics Skills,*** p. 4	◆ **Phonics,** p. T63 ◆ **Read Aloud,** p. T71 **Phonics:** *Ee/Ff/Gg* ◆ ***Challenge: Phonics Skills,*** p. 3
	◆ **Phonics,** p. T80 ◆ **Forming Letters,** p. T83 ◆ **Selection Vocabulary and Comprehension Skills,** p. T88 ◆ **Repetition,** p. T90 ◆ **English Language Conventions,** p. T96	◆ **Phonics,** p. T80 ◆ **Word Meaning,** p. T80 ◆ **Selection Vocabulary,** p. T88 ◆ **English Language Conventions,** p. T96	◆ **Phonics,** p. T83 **Phonics:** *Hh/Ii/Jj* ◆ ***Reteach: Phonics Skills,*** p. 5	◆ **Phonics,** p. T83 ◆ **Writing,** p. T92 **Phonics:** *Hh/Ii/Jj* ◆ ***Challenge: Phonics Skills,*** p. 4
Writing Process Strategies ■ **Seminar: Getting Ideas for Autobiography,** p. T115 **English Language Conventions** ◆ **Penmanship:** Letters Are Lines, p. T115	◆ **Letter Recognition,** p. T101 ◆ **English Language Conventions,** p. T114	◆ **Word Meaning,** p. T99 ◆ **English Language Conventions,** p. T114	**Phonics:** *Kk/Ll/Mm* ◆ ***Reteach: Phonics Skills,*** p. 6 **Writing Process Strategies** ◆ Complete **Writing Words, *Reteach: Comprehension and Language Arts Skills,*** p. 3	**Phonics:** *Kk/Ll/Mm* ◆ ***Challenge: Phonics Skills,*** p. 5 **Writing Process Strategies** ◆ Complete **Writing Words, *Challenge: Comprehension and Language Arts Skills,*** p. 3

Formal Assessment Options

Use these summative assessments along with your informal observations to assess student progress.

Written Assessment

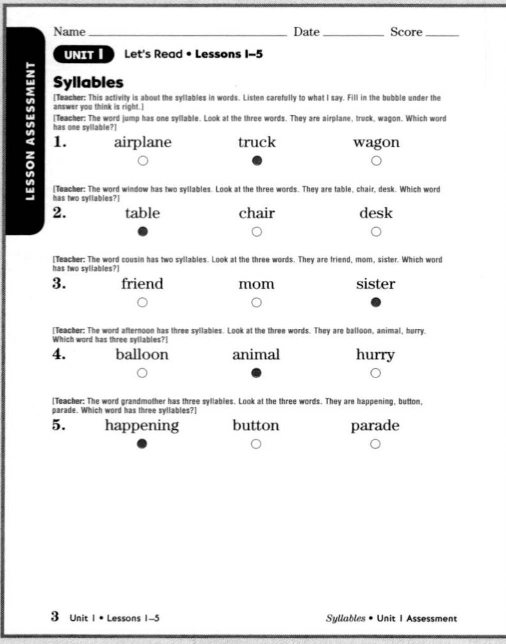

LESSON ASSESSMENT

Name ______ Date ______ Score ______

UNIT 1 Let's Read • **Lessons 1–5**

Syllables

[**Teacher:** This activity is about the syllables in words. Listen carefully to what I say. Fill in the bubble under the answer you think is right.]

[**Teacher:** The word jump has one syllable. Look at the three words. They are airplane, truck, wagon. Which word has one syllable?]

1. airplane ○ truck ● wagon ○

[**Teacher:** The word window has two syllables. Look at the three words. They are table, chair, desk. Which word has two syllables?]

2. table ● chair ○ desk ○

[**Teacher:** The word cousin has two syllables. Look at the three words. They are friend, mom, sister. Which word has two syllables?]

3. friend ○ mom ○ sister ●

[**Teacher:** The word afternoon has three syllables. Look at the three words. They are balloon, animal, hurry. Which word has three syllables?]

4. balloon ○ animal ● hurry ○

[**Teacher:** The word grandmother has three syllables. Look at the three words. They are happening, button, parade. Which word has three syllables?]

5. happening ● button ○ parade ○

3 Unit 1 • Lessons 1–5 *Syllables* • Unit 1 Assessment

Units 1–6 Assessment, p. 3

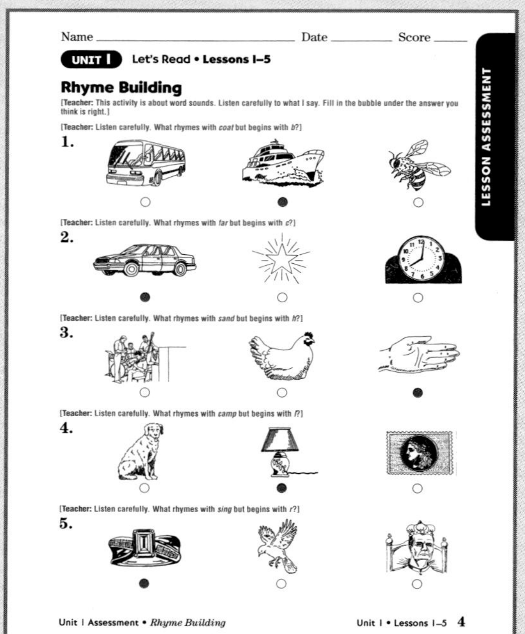

LESSON ASSESSMENT

Name ______ Date ______ Score ______

UNIT 1 Let's Read • **Lessons 1–5**

Rhyme Building

[**Teacher:** This activity is about word sounds. Listen carefully to what I say. Fill in the bubble under the answer you think is right.]

[**Teacher:** Listen carefully. What rhymes with *coat* but begins with *b*?]

1. ○ ● ○

[**Teacher:** Listen carefully. What rhymes with *far* but begins with *c*?]

2. ● ○ ○

[**Teacher:** Listen carefully. What rhymes with *sand* but begins with *h*?]

3. ○ ○ ●

[**Teacher:** Listen carefully. What rhymes with *camp* but begins with *l*?]

4. ○ ● ○

[**Teacher:** Listen carefully. What rhymes with *sing* but begins with *r*?]

5. ● ○ ○

Unit 1 Assessment • *Rhyme Building* Unit 1 • Lessons 1–5 4

Units 1–6 Assessment, p. 4

California

Informal Assessment

The Teacher Observation Log, found in the ***Program Assessment Teacher's Edition,*** is a vehicle for recording anecdotal information about individual student performance on an ongoing basis. Information such as students' strengths and weaknesses can be recorded at any time the occasion warrants. It is recommended that you maintain a Cumulative Folder for each student in which you can store the logs for purposes of comparison and analysis as the school year progresses. You will gradually build up a comprehensive file that reveals which students are progressing smoothly and which students need additional help.

Tips for using the Teacher Observation Log:

- Keep Observation Logs available so you can easily record your informal observations. A clipboard or other similar device might be helpful.
- Decide which aspect of the student's learning you want to monitor on the log.
- Record your observations. It might take four to five days to observe and record the performance of each student.
- If you need more information on some of your students, you might want to observe them more than once, either during the lesson, during Workshop, or at other times during the day.

Teacher's Observation Log

Student ____________________

Date __________ **Unit** __________

Activity ____________________

General Comprehension

Concepts Discussed ____________________

Behavior Within a Group

Articulates, expresses ideas ____________________

Joins discussions ____________________

Collaboration (such as works with other students, works alone) ____________________

Role in Group

Role (such as leader, summarizer, questioner, recorder, critic, observer, non-participant)

Flexibility (changes roles when necessary) ____________________

Use of Reading Strategies

Uses strategies when needed (either those taught or student's own)/Describe strategies used

Changes strategies when appropriate ____________________

Changes Since Last Observation

If more space is needed, write on the back or use another sheet.

32 **Program Assessment**

Program Assessment Teacher's Edition, p. 32

ASSESSMENT

Objectives

- Students will attend to the sounds through word play.
- Students will blend words orally.
- Students will segment words into syllables.
- Students will write letters of the alphabet.
- Students will associate sounds with letters.

Materials

- Lion Puppet
- Sound/Spelling Cards
- one index card for each student
- Phonic Skills, p. 2
- Letter Cards
- yarn
- paper

Universal Access: Meeting Individual Needs

ELL Support

For ELD strategies, use the ***English-Language Development Guide,*** Unit 1, Lesson 1.

Intervention Support

For intervention strategies, use the ***Intervention Guide,*** Unit 1, Lesson 1.

Teacher Tip STUDENTS' NAMES
You may want to create a Word Bank on a bulletin board or on a section of a wall, of all the students' names.

Teacher Tip PREPARE AHEAD
When preparing to make the Name Necklaces, you should do the following:

- ✔ Print each student's name on an index card. You may want to write both their first and last names.
- ✔ Attach each index card to a length of yarn to make a necklace.

Note: Have the students wear their name necklaces as they move around the room. When working at their desks, students should place the card in front of them to help them spell their names.

LESSON MODELS VIDEOCASSETTE
Use the ***Lesson Models Videocassette*** at this time for a Warming Up lesson model.

Warming Up

Throughout the program, Warming Up activities are used to focus students' attention and to review and reinforce what they have learned in previous lessons. These first Warming Up lessons also will be used to help the teacher and students get to know each other.

How Are You? Game Listen/Speak 2.1

- Have the students sit in a circle and tell them you are going to give each of them a "name necklace."
- Hold up the necklaces one at a time, allowing the students to recognize their own names and claim their necklaces. Read the name if a student doesn't readily recognize it.
- Teach the students to play the How Are You? Game. Point to one student and say the following rhyme, using the name of student you point to:

  Michael Murphy
  How are you?
  Who's that sitting
  Next to you?

- Have the students recite the rhyme with you, then point to the next student and ask his or her name. Lead the students in saying the rhyme with the new name. Continue around the circle.
- Collect the necklaces at the end of the day. Distribute them each day through the first week of school, or longer if you wish.

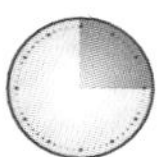

Phonemic Awareness

Oral Blending Reading 1.3; Listen/Speak 1.1

Syllables and Word Parts

- Tell the students that they're already good at listening and speaking: They understand words they hear and they say words that others can understand. But, to be good readers and writers, they must listen for the sounds that make up a word.
- Explain that to help them learn to do this, you have a listening game for the class to play. Introduce the Lion Puppet to the students and let them know that he will be playing the listening game with them. Tell them that the puppet will say a word in two parts. They must listen carefully to both parts of each word to figure out what it is.
- To give the students a moment to think about their answers, establish a response signal such as thumbs-up, and tell them not to respond until you give the signal.
- Using the puppet read each word, pronouncing each part distinctly and pausing at the breaks indicated. Then have the students tell what the word is.

Puppet: Ap . . . ple. What's the word?
Students: Apple

Continue with the following words:

air . . . plane	teach . . . er	pen . . . cil
whis . . . per	pa . . . per	pho . . . to
ba . . . by	bas . . . ket	air . . . port

Teacher Tip PHONEMIC AWARENESS ACTIVITIES These activities should be quick and snappy, taking only 15 minutes of class time. The activities should not drag, despite the fact that some students may not master these activities before moving on to the day's next activity. Over the course of these activities, you will notice that the ability to master phonemic awareness varies greatly among students, regardless of their experience with language and literacy. This is normal, and many students who do not catch on at first will learn how to respond by observing their fellow students. Do not slow or abandon the activities, as insights are more likely to come through repeated encounters than through prolonged drill. Watch carefully for those who are having difficulty so you can give them extra guidance and encouragement during Workshop.

Research in Action
Phonemic Awareness

The goal of phonemic awareness activities is to lead students to understand that spoken words are made up of chains of smaller sounds—the syllables and phonemes. Because students are accustomed to producing and hearing words as unbreakable wholes, this is not a natural insight. Nevertheless, for understanding an alphabetic language in which the letters and letter patterns represent the sub-sounds of words, it is a critical insight. After students have learned to think about words in terms of their component sounds, decoding will make sense and inventive spelling will come easily. Conversely, poorly developed phonemic awareness is believed to be the single greatest cause of reading disability. *(Marilyn J. Adams)*

LESSON MODELS VIDEOCASSETTE
Use the ***Lesson Models Videocassette*** at this time for Oral Blending lesson model.

Informal Assessment

SEGMENTING Watch for students who are having difficulty. As you work with these students, determine whether the problem is with differentiating syllables or with counting.

Teacher Tip GAMES All games that require students to focus on the sounds of words are harder if the words are unfamiliar. When a word in these activities is beyond your students' comfortable vocabulary, substitute it or take a small amout of time to make it familiar through discussion and use.

Research in Action
Blending and Segmentation

Blending and segmentation are complementary processes in developing phonemic awareness and in learning to read and write. While learning to blend syllables and phonemes into familiar words is essential to decoding, learning to segment (divide up) familiar words into syllables and phonemes is essential to independent spelling. Both activities contribute vitally to phonemic awareness in general. *(Marilyn J. Adams)*

LESSON MODELS VIDEOCASSETTE
Use the ***Lesson Models Videocassette*** at this time for a Segmentation lesson model.

PHONEMIC AWARENESS

Segmentation Reading 1.9

Clapping Syllables in Names

- Tell the students that now it's their turn to divide words into parts.
- Choose a student's name and say, for example, "Let's clap out Jennifer's name. Here we go. Jen-ni-fer." Have the students clap and say the syllables along with you.
- Use a few more polysyllabic names to help students quickly understand the kind of units they are listening for. Then mix in one-syllable names.
- Repeat with other names until the students are clapping the right number of times. Point out, if necessary, that some names get only one clap, while others get more.
- Tell the students that the word parts they've been clapping out are called *syllables*.
- Clap out a few more names and ask "How many syllables?" after each.

Letter Recognition

Sound/Spelling Cards

The ***Sound/Spelling Cards*** are an essential part of phonics instruction, which begins in Lesson 11 of this unit. For the first ten lessons, the first 26 ***Sound/Spelling Cards*** should be mounted on the wall with the *back* of each card facing out, displaying the alphabet. In order not to confuse letter names with the sounds the letters make, the front of the card (with the picture) is kept facing the wall until its sound is introduced.

Throughout this guide, letter names are written as the letters themselves; for example: lowercase *a*, or just *a*, capital *R*, or just *R*. Letter sounds are enclosed in slashes; for example: /a/, /ā/, /g/, /r/, /s/.

"Alphabet Song" Reading 1.3; Listen/Speak 2.1

- Focus the students' attention on the ***Sound/Spelling Cards.***
- Call attention to the display and ask the students to tell you what we call this group of letters. Explain that sounds and letters are divided into two groups, and the red letters are called *vowels*. Tell them that vowels are special letters. Then tell them that the black letters are called *consonants*.
- Teach the following version of the "Alphabet Song." In this version of the "Alphabet Song," all letters except *W* are sung slowly, making it easier for students to remember and to recognize all the letters. The best way to teach this version, particularly if the students already know the traditional version, is to teach it through the letter *G*, then through *N*, through *Q*, through *T*, through *W*, and finally to *Z* and the ending.

  A B C D E F G (clap or pause)
  H I J K L M N (clap or pause)
  O P Q (clap or pause)
  R S T (clap or pause)
  U V W (clap or pause)
  X Y Z (clap or pause)
  Now I never will forget
  How to say the alphabet.
- After singing the song for students, have them recite all of it together.
- Have the students talk about how this version is different than other versions they've learned.

Teacher Tip RHYTHM Many teachers suggest that the students clap when they come to the letters *G, N, Q, T, W,* and *Z.* Point to the cards as you sing the song. You may want to have a student point. Reading 1.3

Informal Assessment

ALPHABET Many students will know the alphabet already. To check quickly what students know, point to the letters on the backs of the ***Sound/Spelling Cards*** one by one and ask the students to name the letters. Run through the alphabet in order and then point to the letters out of order. To get a more accurate assessment—use the ***Letter Cards*** to flash to individual students. At this time, do not be concerned about the designation "capital" or "lowercase." Record your observations on the Teacher Observation Log in the ***Program Assessment Teacher's Edition,*** particularly noting those students who do not seem to know the letters. Work with those students during Workshop by having them identify letters on the ***Letter Cards.*** Also, mix up the ***Letter Cards*** and have the students put them in order. Reading 1.3

LESSON MODELS VIDEOCASSETTE
Use the ***Lesson Models Videocassette*** at this time for an Alphabet Song lesson model

LETTER RECOGNITION

Exploring *Aa*

Capital *A* Reading 1.3; Writing 1.3

Introduce the letter *A* to the students, calling it capital *A* and either writing it on the board or pointing to it on the back of the ***Sound/Spelling Card.***

- Ask the students to repeat the letter name. Explain that capital letters are used to begin important words, such as people's names and the first word of a sentence. Ask if anyone's name begins with A. Write it on the board.
- Write a capital *A* on the board, describing each stroke as you do so. (You can use the handwriting system outlined here or the writing system that is standard in your school.) Have the students say the strokes outloud with you as you write the letter.

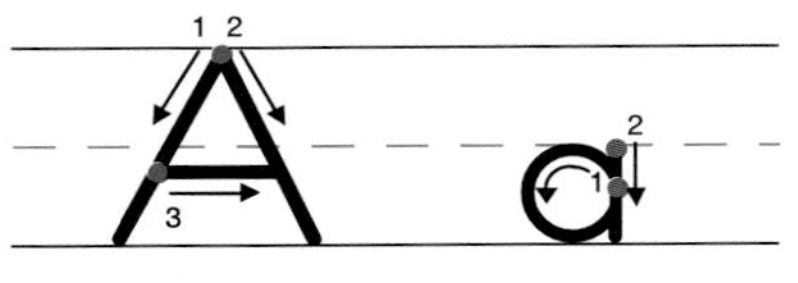

A Starting point, slanting down left
Starting point, slanting down right
Starting point, across the middle: capital *A*

a Starting point, around left all the way
Starting point, straight down touching the circle: small *a*

- Have the students say the strokes as they are writing. Trace over the *A* several times and have students write the letter with their fingers on a surface in front of them.
- Write several *A*'s on the board. As you do, point out that you leave some space between letters. Encourage the students to space letters one width of a finger. Then have several students come up and write a couple capital *A*'s, while the rest of the class writes the letter several times on paper at their seats.

Proofreading Writing 1.3

After the students at the board have written their *A*'s, use their work to introduce proofreading. Explain that the purpose of proofreading is to make written work better. Model think alouds about the letter that students have written on the board to show how to self-check your work. Be sure to comment on the spacing between the letters.

A a

a

1 Lamb

Universal Access: Reading 1.3
Meeting Individual Needs

Intervention Tip

LETTERS Some students will not yet know the letters of the alphabet automatically. During Workshop, spend time with those students who do not yet know the alphabet to help them learn it. If students need help forming the letters, encourage them to say the strokes to themselves as they form the letters. Have the students trace letters in different materials such as sand or salt.

Teacher Tip PROOFREADING Be sure to use the term *proofreading* with students ("Let's proofread these capital *A*'s.") and encourage them to use the term. Students will also be using this term in Dictation and Spelling.

LESSON MODELS VIDEOCASSETTE
Use the ***Lesson Models Videocassette*** at this time for a Writing and Proofreading lesson model.

- Praise each student's work and encourage the class to do so by asking, *Of the* A's *on the board, which do you think are very good?*
- For the others, ask what might be made better and allow the student whose work you are proofreading to answer before the rest of the class chimes in.
- If the students agree that something might be done better, say *This is a good capital A, but it can be made better. I'm not going to erase it. I'm going to circle it and write a better capital A above this one.*
- Ask the students to box their best *A*'s on their papers and/or to add new ones. Without taking any extra time, walk amidst them offering praise or assistance.

Remind the students that the purpose of proofreading is to correct their own work, rather than having the teacher correct it. In addition, be sure to explain that not all letters need correction because some are fine just the way they are. Tell them that they are proofreading their *letters* today, but that as they learn to write words and sentences, they will proofread those as well. A full explanation of the proofreading procedure is in the Program Appendix on page 18.

Lowercase *a* Writing 1.3

Teach the lowercase *a* as you did capital *A*. Call it lowercase *a*, point to it on the ***Sound/Spelling Card***, write it on the board, and have the students repeat its name.

- Write a lowercase *a* on the board, describing each stroke as you do so.
- Trace over the *a* several times and have the students write the letter with their fingers on a surface in front of them saying the strokes as they write.
- Write several *a*'s on the board and have several students come up and write letter *a*'s, while others write them on paper or a small board.
- Tell the students that lowercase *a* is used when it is not at the beginning of a sentence or a name. Tell them that they will use lowercase letters most of the time.
- Have the students proofread the letters on the board, and then their lowercase letters on their papers.

LETTER RECOGNITION

Research in Action

Proofreading

Students learn self-reliance if they can correct their own work rather than expecting someone else to tell them whether they are right. Proofreading encourages each student to evaluate his or her work and to correct mistakes independently. The process of examining one's work, which you will model, is important in all stages of the writing process and will be used by students when they share their written pieces later this year and in years to come.
(Michael Pressley)

Research in Action
Letter Formation

Helping students develop a fixed sequence of strokes for each letter is important because letter formation is ultimately mastered kinesthetically—as a muscle habit. Students who instead treat letter writing like drawing (start anywhere but make it look right) have far more trouble remembering the letter shapes and orientation. *(Marsha Roit)*

UNIVERSAL ACCESS: MEETING INDIVIDUAL NEEDS

Intervention Tip

LETTER PRACTICE During Workshop, have students practice making their letters in a sand tray or with finger paints. Reading 1.3

Investigating *Bb*

Capital *B* and Lowercase *b* Reading 1.3

Introduce capital *B* and lowercase *b* as you did *Aa*. One at a time, call them capital *B* and lowercase *b*, point to each letter on the ***Sound/Spelling Card,*** write each on the board, and have the students repeat its name. Ask whether anyone's name begins with capital *B* and write the name(s) on the board. Have those students circle the letter *B* in their names.

- Draw students' attention to the fact that the *B* and *b* on the ***Sound/Spelling Card*** are not the same as the *A* and *a* and ask how they are different. *(The* A *and* a *are red.)*
- Tell them that the *A* and *a* are red because *a* is a special letter, a *vowel.*
- Tell the students that they will learn more about vowels soon.
- Proofread the students' work after they have written the capital *B*'s and again after they have written the lowercase *b*'s. Writing 1.3

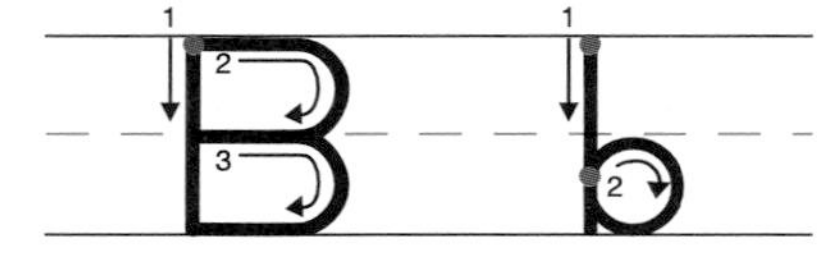

B Starting point, straight down
Starting point, around right and in at the middle, around right and in at the bottom: capital *B*

b Starting point, straight down, back up, around right all the way: small *b*

Phonics Skills Reading 1.3; Writing 1.3

Phonics Skills page 2 provides practice with writing the letters *Aa* and *Bb*. Work with students to complete the page. They should write the letter *B* as a class, say the strokes together, and space them appropriately on each line of the page.

***Phonics Skills* p. 2**

LETTER RECOGNITION

Universal Access: Meeting Individual Needs

Reteach

PHONICS For additional practice, have students use ***Reteach: Phonics Skills*** page 2.

Challenge

PHONICS Use ***Challenge: Phonics Skills*** page 1 with students who are ready for a challenge.

Informal Assessment

WRITING LETTERS Review students' papers to find out who is still uncomfortable writing letters. Watch these students carefully so that you can provide extra support and practice as soon as possible, perhaps during Workshop.

Teacher Tip PRACTICE PAGES Reading and writing always should be the goal. Students who are able to read and write should do so rather than complete worksheets. During this first lesson, circulate to give individuals help. In later lessons, as students become familiar with independent work procedures, you might want to work with small groups to reinforce what has been taught during a previous lesson; for example, identification of letter names and shapes.

LESSON MODELS VIDEOCASSETTE Use the ***Lesson Models Videocassette*** at this time for a ***Phonics Skills*** lesson model.

REVIEW SOUNDS & LETTERS

Reviewing Sounds and Letters

Listening for Vowel Sounds: /ā/ Reading 1.3; Listen/Speak 1.1

The primary focus of these activities is to reinforce students' knowledge of letters. Many students, however, have had earlier instruction in connecting letters to sounds. You will begin sound/letter instruction in detail in Lesson 11 of this unit.

- Remind the students that the red letters, the *vowels*, are special letters. Explain that one of the reasons that vowels are special is that they can say their own names in words. They can hear this sound in words they know.
- Write the letters *Aa* on the board and tell students that you will read a list of words aloud. They must listen carefully to find out whether they can hear the /ā/ sound in each word. These words are meant to be heard by the students but not seen. They should not be written on the board.
- If they do, they should repeat the /ā/ sound and point to the *Aa* on the board; if they do not, they should put their hands down and remain silent.

day	**say**	so	bow	**bay**
bake	**cake**	cute	**case**	**face**
chase	choose	**lace**	lose	**made**
mood	**raid**	rude	clue	**clay**

Research in Action
Action in Activities

The actions that accompany these games are recommended for two reasons. First, such multisensory activities help students maintain focus. Second, they give you a means of identifying individuals who might be having trouble even during whole-group activities. *(Marsha Roit)*

Teacher Tip PHONEMIC AWARENESS Remember to leave ample wait time before signaling for a response.

LESSON MODELS VIDEOCASSETTE
Use the ***Lesson Models Videocassette*** at this time for a Listening for Vowel Sounds lesson model.

Introducing Consonant Sounds Reading 1.3, 1.4

- Explain to the students that each of the consonants makes a sound, too.
- Write the following sentence on the board:

  Baby Bobby blows big bubbles.
- Read the sentence aloud, orally exaggerating each /b/ sound and underlining each *b* as you read it.
- Ask the students to tell you the sound of the letter *b*, confirming that it is /b/.
- Ask them to repeat the sentence several times with you, emphasizing each /b/ sound orally and by touching each *b* as it is said.
- Encourage the students to think of words that begin with the letter *b*, writing their suggestions in a list on the board.
- Every now and then, add a word of your own to stimulate students' imaginations and to increase the variety of words and word lengths on the board.
- If students suggest a word that does not begin with the /b/ sound, write it to the side on the board, taking the opportunity to contrast its initial sound with the /b/ sound and to compare its initial spelling with the spelling for *b*.
- At the end of the activity, read the list of words with the /b/ sound on the board, underlining each *b* as you do.

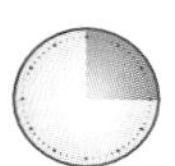

Dictation

Dictation: Letter Dictation Reading 1.3; Writing 1.3

Ask the students to write as many letters of the alphabet as they can. Tell them that if they can write only capital letters, that's fine. If they can write lowercase letters, that's fine too. Say that if they can write the alphabet both ways, that's even better.

Explain to students that you do not expect them to know all their letters at this point. The purpose today is simply to show what they do know. The goal for them is to write as many letters as they can. You may want to put these papers in students' folders to compare with a similar exercise done mid-year and at the end of the year.

REVIEW SOUNDS & LETTERS

Research in Action
Letter Dictation

Collect and review these papers carefully. They offer an efficient way for you to establish how comfortable each of your students is with the letters of the alphabet. This is very important to the extent that if students cannot quickly and accurately discern one letter from another, they cannot profit from their phonics or reading lessons.

Entering first graders generally fall into one of several distinct categories on this challenge, corresponding to whether they recognizably write: (1) 12 or fewer letters; (2) more than 18 letters; (3) all of the letters; or (4) all letters in both upper- and lowercase. The letter review work in the present lessons is aimed at students in the middle categories. Students who write fewer than 18 letters need urgently to receive extra attention and practice with letter recognition and writing activities at school *and* at home. *(Marilyn J. Adams)*

Teacher Tip CONSONANT SOUNDS You may want to write the suggestions the students make for words that begin with *b* on chart paper. The papers can then be saved and put together to make a class Big Book of words. The students can create a cover, number the pages, and bind it together with you.

Teacher Tip BASELINE Date the sheet of paper for dictation. Save it as a baseline to share with parents and students later on.

PREVIEWING THE UNIT

Read Aloud *Wolf!*

Objectives

- Students will listen attentively to a story being read aloud.
- Students will discuss the story to develop comprehension.
- Students will browse the unit stories to set reading goals.

Materials

- Read Aloud *Wolf!*
- Big Book *Let's Read*
- Home Connection, p. 1

Teacher Tip ACTIVATE PRIOR KNOWLEDGE Inform the students that good readers typically activate what they already know about a topic before reading something new about the topic. Tell students that they should get in the habit of thinking about the topic of an upcoming selection and activating relevant background knowledge.

UNIVERSAL ACCESS:
MEETING INDIVIDUAL NEEDS

ELL Support

For ELD strategies, use the ***English-Language Development Guide,*** Unit 1, Lesson 1.

Intervention Support

For intervention strategies, use the ***Intervention Guide,*** Unit 1, Lesson 1.

Activate Prior Knowledge

Tell students that they are about to begin a unit called *Let's Read!* Tell them that in this unit you will share many poems and stories, and that they will have to listen carefully as the poems and selections are read. Tell the students that the first story you will share is called *Wolf!*

Ask the students to tell about, or describe, a wolf. Ask them questions, such as: *What is a wolf? What does a wolf look like? What does a wolf eat?*

About the Author

Prior to reading *Wolf!*, provide students with the following background information about the author, **BECKY BLOOM.**

BECKY BLOOM was born in Greece, and has lived in many countries, including the United States. She aims to publish books that both children and adults enjoy. Ms. Bloom recognizes that children enjoy many books, "but a child is especially delighted when the adult, reading aloud, enjoys the books just as much." She lives in Athens, Greece, with her husband, three children and many animals.

About the Illustrator

Prior to reading *Wolf!*, provide students with the following background information about the illustrator, **PASCAL BIET.**

PASCAL BIET was born in northern France. He studied illustration and visual communication and began illustrating children's books in 1998. His work has been shown around the world, including twice at the Bologna Exhibition of Illustration. He currently lives in Paris, France.

Read Aloud

Tell students that they should listen carefully as you read *Wolf!* aloud. Encourage them to listen to the story and find out what the wolf learns to do.

Then read the Focus Questions (at the top of the next page). Discuss these questions with the students. Display the cover of the book and have the students describe the wolf on the cover.

It is important for you as the teacher to let your students know that you use the comprehension strategies being taught in the program when you read. Thus, before you read "Wolf!," make some predictions aloud as to what the selection might be about. As you are reading, let students know what questions are occurring to you, what images pop up in your mind as you are reading, and how point made in the reading relate to ideas you already know.

Toward the end of the reading, sum up for students. If you cannot sum up the selection well, let students see you go back and reread to fill in the gaps in your summary. The selection does contain some reminders for you to use these processes, because one of the most powerful ways to get students to use comprehension strategies is for them to see you using them.

READ ALOUD

Focus Questions Do you know any stories about wolves or that have a wolf in them? Do wolves know how to read?

WOLF!

by Becky Bloom

After walking for many days, a wolf wandered into a quiet little town. He was tired and hungry, his feet ached, and he had only a little money that he kept for emergencies.

Then he remembered. There's a farm outside this village, he thought. I'll find some food there. . . .

As he peered over the farm fence, he saw a pig, a duck, and a cow reading in the sun.

The wolf had never seen animals read before. "I'm so hungry that my eyes are playing tricks on me," he said to himself. But he really was very hungry and didn't stop to think about it for long.

The wolf stood up tall, took a deep breath . . . and leaped at the animals with a howl—"AaaOOOOOooo!"

Chickens and rabbits ran for their lives, but the duck, the pig, and the cow didn't budge. "What is that awful noise?" complained the cow. "I can't concentrate on my book."

"Just ignore it," said the duck.

The wolf did not like to be ignored. "What's wrong with you?" growled the wolf. "Can't you see I'm a big and dangerous wolf?"

"I'm sure you are," replied the pig. "But couldn't you be big and dangerous somewhere else? We're trying to read. This is a farm for educated animals. Now be a good wolf and go away," said the pig, giving him a push.

The wolf had never been treated like this before. "Educated animals . . . educated animals!" the wolf repeated to himself. "This is something new. Well then! I'll learn how to read too." And off he went to school.

Teacher Tip READING ALOUD Good readers are also good listeners. Reading aloud to students provides an opportunity to teach the reader responses and problem-solving strategies that good readers employ. In addition to reading aloud with expression and enthusiasm, model your own reading strategies while reading aloud to students. This makes the use of strategies "real" for students and encourages them to begin to respond to text similarly.

PREVIEWING THE UNIT

The students found it strange to have a wolf in their class, but since he didn't try to eat anyone, they soon got used to him. The wolf was serious and hardworking, and after much effort he learned to read and write. Soon he became the best in the class.

Feeling quite satisfied, the wolf went back to the farm and jumped over the fence. I'll show them, he thought. He opened his book and began to read:

"Run, wolf! Run!
See wolf run."

You've got a long way to go," said the duck, without even bothering to look up. And the pig, the duck, and the cow went on reading their own books, not the least impressed.

The wolf jumped back over the fence and ran straight to the public library. He studied long and hard, reading lots of dusty old books, and he practiced and practiced until he could read without stopping.

"They'll be impressed with my reading now," he said to himself.

The wolf walked up to the farm gate and knocked. He opened *The Three Little Pigs* and began to read:

"Onceuponatimetherewerethreelittlepigsonedaytheirmothercalledthemand toldthem—"

"Stop that racket," interrupted the duck.

"You have improved," remarked the pig, "but you still need to work on your style."

The wolf tucked his tail between his legs and slunk away.

But the wolf wasn't about to give up. He counted the little money he had left, went to the bookshop, and bought a splendid new storybook. His first very own book!

READ ALOUD

He was going to read it day and night, every letter and every line. He would read so well that the farm animals would admire him.

Ding-dong, rang the wolf at the farm gate.

He lay down on the grass, made himself comfortable, took out his new book, and began to read.

He read with confidence and passion, and the pig, the cow, and the duck all listened and said not one word.

Each time he finished a story, the pig, the duck, and the cow asked if he would please read them another.

So the wolf read on, story after story. One minute he was Little Red Riding Hood, the next a genie emerging from a lamp, and then a swashbuckling pirate.

"This is so much fun!" said the duck.

"He's a master," said the pig.

"Why don't you join us on our picnic today?" offered the cow.

And so they all had a picnic—the pig, the duck, the cow, and the wolf. They lay in the tall grass and told stories all the afternoon long.

"We should all become storytellers," said the cow suddenly.

"We could travel around the world," added the duck.

"We can start tomorrow morning," said the pig.

The wolf stretched in the grass. He was happy to have such wonderful friends.

Discussing the Read Aloud Reading 2.2

After you have read the Read Aloud, ensure that the students have understood the selection by asking these questions:

- What did the wolf learn to do? *(He learned to read.)*
- Who can remember what the wolf did to learn to read? *(He went to school, read library books, and bought and read his own book.)*
- Why did the wolf want to learn to read? *(Because he wanted to be educated, like the animals he met. He hadn't met educated animals before, and he wanted to be educated, so he wanted to learn to read.)*
- Was it easy for the wolf to learn to read? *(No, but he did it because he worked at it and he wanted to learn to read.)*
- Is this a real story? How do you know? *(It is not a real story because animals can't read.)*

Introduce Unit Investigations

Tell the students that they will work on and complete a unit project over the next few weeks. They will make a class alphabet book that includes a page(s) for each letter of the alphabet.

Concept/Question Board

Begin a bulletin board that is easily accessible by students (at their height). Tell them that this is their Concept/Question Board. Explain that concepts are ideas or information. Tell the students that throughout the unit they will be using it to display all their questions, information, and ideas about the theme *Let's Read!* Explain that it's a place for them to put their ideas, thoughts, and feelings about reading and writing and a place for their questions, too. Tell them that in addition to the information they learn in this unit, they also can place their own original writing and poems on the Board. Ensure that the students know that the Board is a place they can go to find information as well as display what they have learned. If possible, ask for their input in designing the Board. Ask them to describe the kind of background and border they would like to see on the Board. Let them know that it will change as they progress through the unit.

Teacher Tip CONCEPT/QUESTION BOARD At this time, you may want to add something to the board to get it started. You may post a question for students to think about, such as *Do you have a favorite book* or *What kinds of books do you like?*

Setting Reading Goals Listen/Speak 2.1

Tell the students that many of the selections in this book are poems. Ask them to identify anything they may already know about poems, such as form, the use of rhyming words, the different use of punctuation, and so on. Make sure students know that it is all right if they do not know much about poems at this point. Tell them that as you read the book, they will become more familiar with poems and poetry. Tell the students that they may be familiar with some of the selections in this unit. Ask the students if they know the poem "Hey, Diddle, Diddle." Encourage them to recite it if they do. Then point out that there are also some unfamiliar selections in this unit. Take a minute to read through the Table of Contents and identify some of the less familiar selections.

Browsing the Unit

Display the cover of the ***Big Book*** *Let's Read!* Point out the cover illustration and the title. Invite students to make any observations about what the cover tells them.

Turn to the Table of Contents and explain that it lists all the reading selections in the book and shows on which page each starts. Read through the list of the selections, pointing to each title as you do so, and pointing to the page number each one starts on. Point out that the Table of Contents lists the selections in the order that they appear. For instance, "The Purple Cow" is the first selection on the Table of Contents and it is the first selection in the book. Fine Art is the last entry on the Table of Contents and the last entry in the book.

Flip through the first pages of the book. Encourage the students to look at the text and illustrations on the pages and tell what they see. Have them point out anything they find interesting.

Home Connection

Distribute page 1 of ***Home Connection*** to the students. ***Home Connection*** also is available in Spanish on page 2. Encourage the students to take this home and share it with their families.

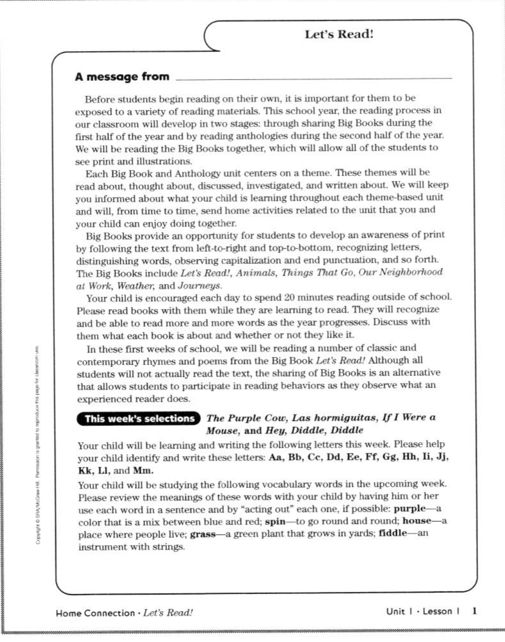

Let's Read!

A message from ____________________

Before students begin reading on their own, it is important for them to be exposed to a variety of reading materials. This school year, the reading process in our classroom will develop in two stages: through sharing Big Books during the first half of the year and by reading anthologies during the second half of the year. We will be reading the Big Books together, which will allow all of the students to see print and illustrations.

Each Big Book and Anthology unit centers on a theme. These themes will be read about, thought about, discussed, investigated, and written about. We will keep you informed about what your child is learning throughout each theme-based unit and will, from time to time, send home activities related to the unit that you and your child can enjoy doing together.

Big Books provide an opportunity for students to develop an awareness of print by following the text from left-to-right and top-to-bottom, recognizing letters, distinguishing words, observing capitalization and end punctuation, and so forth. The Big Books include *Let's Read!*, *Animals*, *Things That Go*, *Our Neighborhood at Work*, *Weather*, and *Journeys*.

Your child is encouraged each day to spend 20 minutes reading outside of school. Please read books with them while they are learning to read. They will recognize and be able to read more and more words as the year progresses. Discuss with them what each book is about and whether or not they like it.

In these first weeks of school, we will be reading a number of classic and contemporary rhymes and poems from the Big Book *Let's Read!* Although all students will not actually read the text, the sharing of Big Books is an alternative that allows students to participate in reading behaviors as they observe what an experienced reader does.

This week's selections ***The Purple Cow*, *Las hormiguitas*, *If I Were a Mouse*, and *Hey, Diddle, Diddle***

Your child will be learning and writing the following letters this week. Please help your child identify and write these letters: **Aa, Bb, Cc, Dd, Ee, Ff, Gg, Hh, Ii, Jj, Kk, Ll,** and **Mm.**

Your child will be studying the following vocabulary words in the upcoming week. Please review the meanings of these words with your child by having him or her use each word in a sentence and by "acting out" each one, if possible: **purple**—a color that is a mix between blue and red; **spin**—to go round and round; **house**—a place where people live; **grass**—a green plant that grows in yards; **fiddle**—an instrument with strings.

Home Connection · *Let's Read!* Unit 1 · Lesson 1 1

***Home Connection* p. 1**

Objectives

Word Analysis

Vocabulary

- **Strategy Introduction** Using words from "WOLF!," introduce strategies for learning vocabulary.

Writing Process Strategies

- **Introduction to the Writing Process** Building on the theme Let's Read!, understand that writing is a process and that writers write for many reasons.

English Language Conventions

- **Mechanics: Capital Letters** Using their own names, understand that names and the pronoun *I* begin with capital letters.

Materials

- Language Arts Big Book pp. 5–6
- Comprehension and Language Arts Skills pp. 2–3

UNIVERSAL ACCESS:
MEETING INDIVIDUAL NEEDS

Reteach, Challenge, English-Language Development and ***Intervention*** lessons are available to support the language arts instruction in this lesson.

Research in Action
Writing

The objective of writing lessons at this point is to stimulate thinking about writing and how it is used. Students' attention will be directed to the nature and function of the many kinds of print they encounter daily at home and in the community—newspapers, newsletters, magazines, books, signs in stores, street signs, mail, and grocery lists. They will be encouraged to consider the importance of communicating in print.

When asked, first graders often will say they know how to write. Capitalize on this confidence and have them write, write, write! *(Marsha Roit)*

OVERVIEW

Language Arts Overview

Word Analysis

Vocabulary This lesson introduces students to strategies for learning new words. The Vocabulary activity focuses on vocabulary from "WOLF!" to understand meaning classification. Classification is a vocabulary strategy for developing a deeper understanding of words that the student might have heard but does not know well. Comparing and contrasting an unfamiliar word to others in the same classification *(llama, cow, horse, donkey)* develops word meaning of unfamiliar words.

Vocabulary Skill Words

animals **wolf** **dogs** **coyotes** **fox**

Writing Process Strategies

The Writing Process Strategies lesson introduces students to the writing process by providing an overview of why people write.

Basic Computer Skills: To introduce students to the computer as a writing tool, teach them about the parts of a computer and how to care for computer equipment. ***SRA Basic Computer Skills*** Level 1 Lessons 1–2 teach these basic computer skills.

English Language Conventions

Grammar, Usage, and Mechanics **Capital Letters.** The English Language Conventions support the reading and writing skills development in this lesson. This lesson introduces students to capital letters.

Word Analysis

Vocabulary

Classification Reading 1.17

Teach

- Ask the students what they do when they don't know what a word means. *(Answers might include asking someone else or thinking of another word.)*
- Explain that when students know the meanings of a lot of words, they can pick the best ones to use.
- Explain that you will be teaching the students strategies for learning new words.
- Explain that many words are names of things that are part of groups. For example, in "WOLF!" a wolf is an animal.

Guided Practice

- As an example of what you will be doing, write *Animals* as a column heading on the board or chart paper.
- Write *wolf* under the heading and have students suggest different animals as you write the words. Encourage students to suggest animals that are like wolves; for example, dogs, coyotes, and foxes.
- Discuss characteristics of animals listed and how they are the same and different; for example
  - How many legs does each animal have?
  - Does each animal have fur, feathers, scales, or a shell? Science 2.a
  - Where does each animal live? Science 2.a
  - Which animal is most like a wolf?
- Encourage students to describe any animals that others are unfamiliar with by comparing them to animals they know.
- Conclude by emphasizing that by comparing words, students can learn more about each word.

Writing Process Strategies

Introduction to the Writing Process

Purposes for Writing Writing 1.0

Teach

- Introduce purposes for writing by reading ***Language Arts Big Book*** pages 5–6. Discuss each page.
- Everyone is a writer. Point out that everyone has to write.
- Why do people write?
  - to tell other people something
  - to entertain other people
  - to make notes to yourself to help you remember
  - to keep records
- What do people write?
  - books
  - letters
  - lists
  - newspaper articles
  - advertisements
  - menus

Guided Practice

- Have the students help you make a list of the reasons people write. Write them on the board or chart paper. Point out that a list, like this one, is also a form of writing.
  - People write things they want others to know. Books, newspapers, magazines, signs, letters, and labels are examples of things people write.
  - People write things they want to remember—shopping lists, phone numbers, addresses and dates.
  - People write things they want to share with others including stories, plays, and poems.

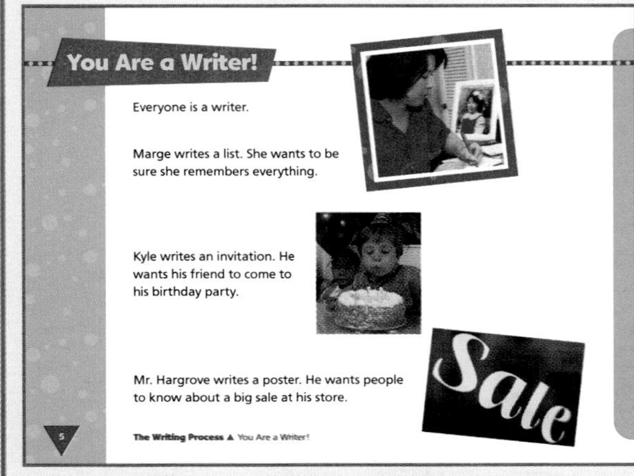

***Language Arts Big Book* p. 5**

English Language Conventions

Grammar, Usage, and Mechanics

Capital Letters Eng. Lang. Conv. 1.7

Teach

- Review from the Phonemic Awareness lesson on page T8 that each letter, *Aa*, *Bb*, and *Cc*, has a capital and a lowercase form.
- Have each student spell his or her name aloud, if possible, as you write it on the board or chart paper.
- **Teacher Model:** Model that when you write a person's name, you start with a capital letter.
- Explain that the word *I* is always capitalized, too, because it refers to a special person.

Independent Practice

Have the students complete pages 2 and 3 in ***Comprehension and Language Arts Skills*** to practice capitalizing the first letters of their names.

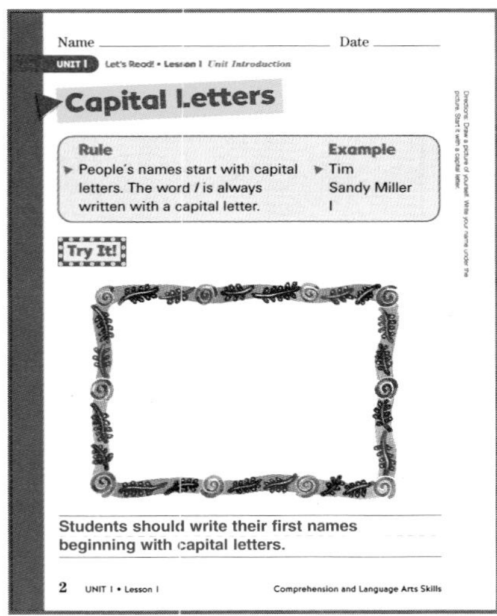

Name ______ Date ______

UNIT 1 Let's Read! • Lesson 1 Unit Introduction

Capital Letters

Rule	Example
▸ People's names start with capital letters. The word *I* is always written with a capital letter.	▸ Tim Sandy Miller I

Try It!

Students should write their first names beginning with capital letters.

2 UNIT 1 • Lesson 1 Comprehension and Language Arts Skills

***Comprehension and Language Arts Skills* p. 2**

1 Preparing to Read

The Purple Cow

Objectives

- Students will segment words into syllables.
- Students will say the rimes, or endings, of words.
- Students will write letters of the alphabet.
- Students will associate sounds with letters.

Materials

- Lion Puppet
- Sound/Spelling Cards
- Phonics Skills, p. 3
- Letter Cards
- High Frequency Word Cards

Reading 1.3

Teacher Tip NAME NECKLACES Have students wear their name necklaces at the start of each day until everyone knows the names of all the students in the class.

Universal Access: Meeting Individual Needs

ELL Support

For ELD strategies, use the ***English-Language Development Guide,*** Unit 1, Lesson 2.

Intervention Support

For intervention strategies, use the ***Intervention Guide,*** Unit 1, Lesson 2.

Teacher Tip PREPARE AHEAD Prepare a chart containing the first names of all your students.

Warming Up

Use one or both of the following activities to focus the students' attention for the learning that follows.

How Are You? Game Listen/Speak 2.1

- Have the students sit in a circle wearing their name necklaces. Remind them of the How Are You? Game they played earlier. Invite volunteers to review the way the game is played.
- Play the How Are You? Game until everyone has been included at least once.

I Spy Reading 1.3, 1.4; Listen/Speak 2.1

Play I Spy with the letter *b*.

> "I spy with my little eye,
> Something with the letter *b*."

To discover the word you have in mind, ask students to point out words in the classroom that have the letter *b*. Have the students recite the rhyme when they answer.

Phonemic Awareness

Oral Blending

Syllables and Word Parts
Reading 1.3; Listen/Speak 1.1

- Reintroduce the Lion Puppet to the students and tell them that he will be playing a listening game with them. Tell the students that the puppet will say a word in two parts. They will put the two parts back together and say the word.
- Remind the students to listen attentively to both parts and not to respond until you give the signal.

Puppet: Di . . . nosaur What's the word?
Students: dinosaur

Continue with the following words. Alternate between having all the students respond in unison and calling on individuals:

re . . . member	sum . . . mer	ba . . . nana
car . . . toon	let . . . ter	let . . . tuce
le . . . mon	pur . . . ple	per . . . fume

Segmentation

Clapping Syllables in Names and Words
Reading 1.9

- Tell the students that it's their turn again to divide words into parts.
- Proceed as in Lesson 1, beginning with students' names that haven't been used yet.
- Then say the word *television.*
- Have students repeat the word and then clap the syllables.
- Ask "How many syllables did you hear and clap?"
- Repeat with the following words:

button	newspaper	package	cinnamon
ambulance	cake	zebra	rocket
alligator	principal	teacher	friend

- Have the students work with partners and figure out the number of syllables in each partner's first and last names. Encourage the partners to tell the number of syllables in each name and in both names together. As a class, make a chart identifying the number of syllables in each name. It might be helpful to have the names on a chart in advance. Next, have the students write the number of syllables for his/her name.

PHONEMIC AWARENESS

Listen/Speak 1.1

Teacher Tip **LISTENING** The words used in this exercise are somewhat harder to guess from just the first part of the word, so tell the students that they will have to listen carefully.

Teacher Tip **RESPONDING** When playing oral games, switch unpredictably between requesting the response from the group and from individuals that you choose. This serves two purposes. First, it helps to maintain the students' attention and engagement. Second, it gives you an invaluable means of assessing progress and difficulty in the course of the activity.

UNIVERSAL ACCESS: MEETING INDIVIDUAL NEEDS

ELL Support

WORD MEANING Make sure the English-language learners know the meanings of the words in the oral blending activities. During Workshop, use pictures, photos, objects, stick drawings, or the ***English-Language Development Glossary*** to assist students.

Teacher Tip **SYLLABLES** With multisyllabic words, many students have trouble clapping and counting the number of syllables at the same time. Some students need to put up a finger for each syllable as they clap.

Informal Assessment

BLENDING INITIAL CONSONANTS Remember to monitor six or seven students per day on their ability to blend initial consonant sounds orally. Record your observation Log in the ***Program Assessment Teacher's Edition.***

Teacher Tip RESPONSES Remind the students not to call out their responses until you give the signal, and don't forget to shift unpredictably between requesting the response from the group or from individuals. This game should be quite easy for most, but it is extremely important that you discover and make time to help any who do not catch on.

Teacher Tip ONSETS AND RIMES In this activity, the Lion Puppet repeats only the last part of the syllable, which is called the *rime.* The first part of the syllable is called the *onset.*

PHONEMIC AWARENESS

Onsets and Rimes Reading 1.4

- Tell the students that it is important to listen for the end sound of words.
- Use the Lion Puppet and explain that he loves to play games with words.
- Explain that the game the puppet wants to play today is like a copycat game, except that he will repeat only the *end* of each word.
- Look the puppet in the eye and say the word *zoo*, exaggerating the /z/ sound.
- Then have the puppet repeat /o͞o/, omitting the first phoneme of the word.
- After a few more demonstrations, continue the game by asking the students to respond *for* the puppet. Give the class a signal for when to respond.

Teacher: moo
Puppet: oo
Teacher: say
Puppet: ay
Teacher: see
Students: ee

- Continue the game with the following list:

sigh	say	so	soap	seal
new	no	nose	nice	neat
my	may	make	mouse	mouth
cheese	cheer	cheap	cheek	chief

Letter Recognition

"Alphabet Song" Reading 1.3; Listen/Speak 2.1

- Sing the "Alphabet Song" once or twice with the students.
- Briefly review *Aa* and *Bb*, asking the students "What letter is this?" as you point to the letters on the ***Sound/Spelling Cards.*** Challenge the students to find these letters on print materials elsewhere in the classroom. If necessary, remind them to look at the name necklaces of the students near them.

Exploring *Cc* and *Dd* Reading 1.3; Writing 1.3

- Introduce the letters *Cc* and *Dd*, following the same steps as in Lesson 1.
- Call on a volunteer to tell what special words always begin with a capital letter. Then have students look at their name necklaces and raise their hands if their names begin with either *C* or *D*.
- Ask the students whether they see these letters anywhere else in the classroom. Have volunteers touch the letters they have identified.
- Write *C* on the board, identifying the starting point and describing the stroke. Ask the students to notice the shape of the letter.
- Trace over the letter several times while having the students write the letter with their fingers in the air. Then have them write it with their fingers on the tops of their desks or tables.
- Invite several volunteers to write the letter on the board while the others write it several times on paper at their seats saying the strokes as they write.
- Ask the students to proofread the letters they wrote and to choose the best one. Ask what can be done to make it better. Have them circle the letter and write a better one above it. Box the best letter.
- Repeat with *c*, *D*, and *d*.

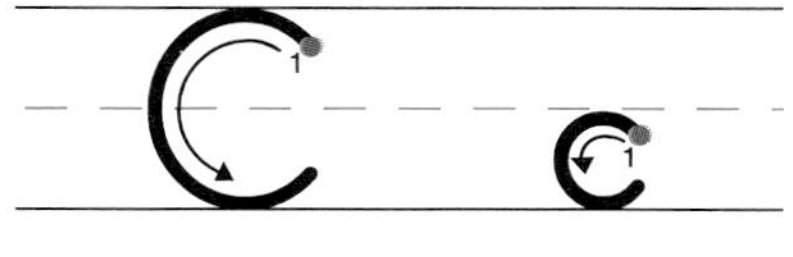

C Starting point, around left to stopping place: capital *C*

c Starting point, around left to stopping place: small *c*

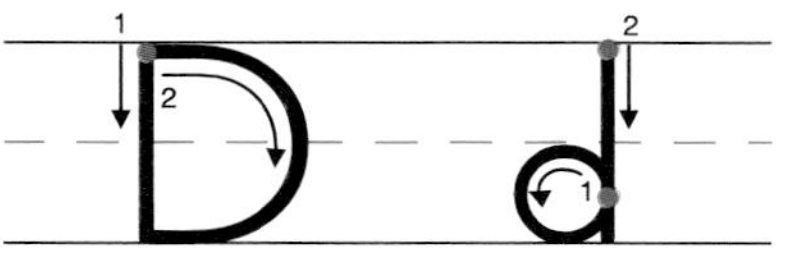

D Starting point, straight down
Starting point, around right and in at the bottom: capital *D*

d Starting point, around left all the way
Starting point, straight down, touching the circle: small *d*

LETTER RECOGNITION

Teacher Tip ALPHABET SONG Write the "Alphabet Song" on chart paper for students to see the letters as they say them (see page T27 for a copy of the Song). Students may also enjoy using different voices as they sing the "Alphabet Song," such as soft voices, loud voices, baby voices, and so on. Listen/Speak 2.1

Teacher Tip PRINT AWARENESS A letter might appear more than once in a student's name, and the same letters will appear in more than one name. This activity develops the students' print awareness by making the point that letters are symbols and are considered identical although they appear in different words.

Informal Assessment

LETTER ORIENTATION Frequent letter orientation errors are often a sign that students are ignoring the starting point and stroke sequence for the letters. Encourage the students to always find the correct starting point and follow the correct stroke sequence for each letter when they write. Writing 1.3

Reading 1.3, 1.4

Teacher Tip SENTENCES
Encourage the students to come up with their own sentences in which all words begin with either *c* or *d*.

Reading 1.3

UNIVERSAL ACCESS: MEETING INDIVIDUAL NEEDS

Reteach

LETTER FORMATION Use ***Reteach: Phonics Skills*** page 3 to provide additional practice writing capital and lowercase letters.

Challenge

PHONICS Use ***Challenge: Phonics Skills*** page 2 with students who are ready for a challenge.

Intervention Tip

LETTER FORMATION During Workshop, work with students who are having difficulty recognizing or forming letters. Students can write the letters on the board or on unlined paper with crayons. Encourage the students to say the strokes as they form the letters. Gradually get the students to use pencils and guidelines. Use flash cards and letter arrays to help the students recognize the letters that have been introduced. Using individual ***Letter Cards,*** have the students find the target letter.

REVIEW SOUNDS & LETTERS

Phonics Skills Writing 1.3

Phonics Skills page 3 provides practice writing the letters *Cc* and *Dd*. Help students complete the page. Encourage them to write legibly and space between letters.

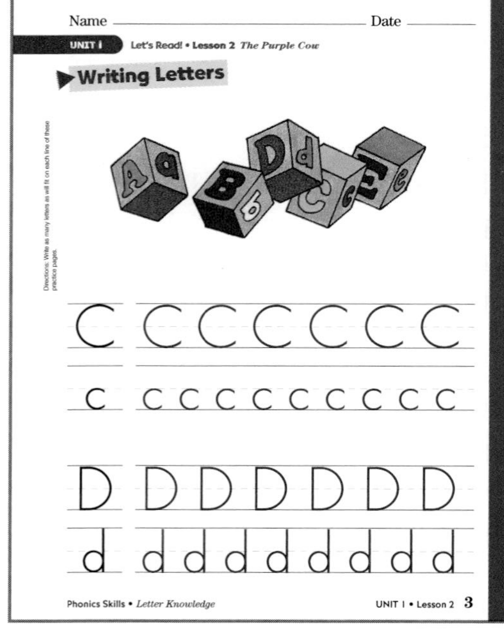

Phonics Skills p. 3

Reviewing Sounds and Letters

Introducing Consonant Sounds Reading 1.3, 1.4

- Write the following sentence on the board:

  Carl cuddles creepy, crawly caterpillars.

- Read the sentence aloud, orally exaggerating and underlining each *c* as you read it.
- Ask the students to tell you the sound of the letter *c*, confirming that it is the /k/ sound.
- Ask the students to repeat the sentence several times with you, emphasizing each /k/ sound, orally and by touching each *c* as it is said. Be sure the sound is /k/ and not /kw/ as the sound is emphasized.
- Ask the students to think of words that begin with the /k/ sound, repeating their suggestions and asking the others whether they agree and, if so, writing the suggestions on the board.
- Because this is a phonemic awareness activity, suggestions that begin with *Kk* should be praised. On the board, make a separate list of such words, pointing out that the sound for the letter *Kk* is also /k/.
- Repeat for the letter *d:*

  Dizzy Dan digs dandy dinosaurs.

- Again, be sure to say /d/ and not /du/ as the sound is spoken.

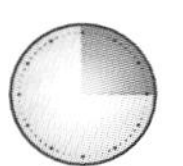

Dictation

Dictation Reading 1.3

- Ask the students to take out writing materials. Dictate the following letters, giving the students time to write each before dictating the next:

  A a B b C c D d

- If students need help, refer to the letters on the ***Sound/Spelling Cards.***
- Remind the students to proofread their work.
- Collect the papers to see how students are progressing.

Pages 6–7 of *Let's Read!*

SELECTION INTRODUCTION

About the Author Reading 3.2

Gelett Burgess was an American humorist and illustrator who began his writing career as the editor of *Wave* magazine. He was also editor of *Lark* magazine, a monthly publication that made him well known for his humor.

Burgess's humor is evident in his collection of poems about "the goops."

Other Books by Gelett Burgess

Goops and How to Be Them, The Little Father

About the Illustrator Reading 3.2

Luis de Horna was born in Salamanca, Spain, in the summer of 1942. For Luis de Horna, drawing is something as natural as breathing. He has felt this way ever since he was very young. On vacation in 1954, his mother encouraged him to paint. Ever since then, he has been hooked on illustrating. Over the years, he has won many prizes and awards, including the 1981 National Childhood Literature Award for best illustration in a children's book. He also received this award in the book *Sing, Faraway Bird*, written by Juan Ramón Jiménez, and for the books *Would You Like Me to Teach You How to Make Bread?* and *Call Me Friend!*, written by Luis de Horna himself.

Objectives

- Students will discuss rhyme.
- Students will begin a list of color words.
- Students will consider the importance of imagination.
- Students will learn about the parts of a book.

Materials

- Big Book *Let's Read!*, p. 6

Selection Summary

Genre: Poetry

This famous rhyme about an imaginary cow should make the students laugh.

The elements of poetry are listed below. Poetry may have one or more of these elements:

- Sentences are sometimes broken into parts. Each part is a line of its own.
- Words that rhyme are often used.
- The lines of a poem often have rhythm or meter.
- Some words may be repeated.

Inquiry Connections

In the first selection of the ***Big Book,*** the students listen to a simple poem about an imaginary animal, a purple cow.

Key concepts to be explored are

- The elements of poetry may include rhyming words.
- Poetry often has a rhythm, or a beat.
- Visualization is a comprehension strategy in which readers picture in their minds what happens in a selection.

Remind the students of your discussion about the Concept/Question Board and have them tell what they remember about that discussion. Encourage the students to post on the Concept/Question Board any questions they have about poems or rhymes. They may know a poem or rhyme by heart, and may want to draw a picture that represents that poem. Or, you may want to make a list of poems the students know and enjoy, and post the list on the Board.

Concept/Question Board

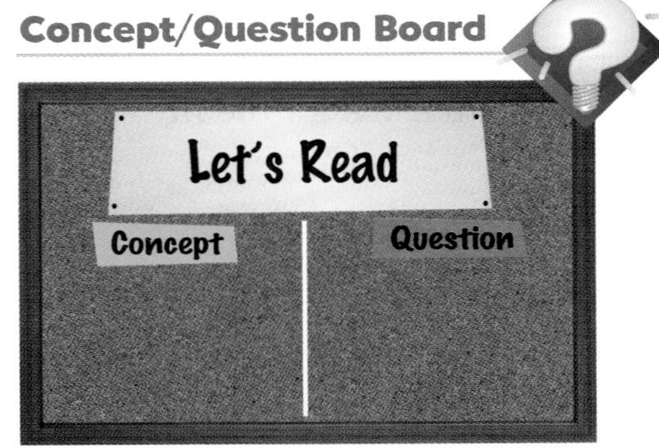

- Tell the students to put their name or initials on everything they post on the Board. It will help them identify students in the class who have similar interests.
- If students aren't ready to put anything on the Board at this time, tell them they can post something at any time during the unit.

Research in Action
Reading Big Books

The goals when reading ***Big Books*** are to engage students in unlocking the books' messages and to begin to understand how the author conveys that message (i.e., the craft of writing). The teacher models what a good reader does—remarking on the illustrations and the title, wondering about the content and what might happen, making predictions, and commenting on events and how the author tells about the events. *(Michael Pressley)* Recognizing basic literary techniques (such as contrasting characters—good guys and bad guys) helps children understand what they are reading. In other words, knowledge of form contributes to understanding content.

Universal Access: Meeting Individual Needs

ELL Tip

POETRY Encourage English-language learners to recite poems in their native languages and post a picture or a title on the Board describing their poems.

Teacher Tip BIG BOOKS Shared reading of rhyming or repetitive text such as that in the first *Big Book, Let's Read!* reinforces the correspondence between spoken and written words, and allows the students to participate in the "reading" of memorizable or predictable parts.

UNIVERSAL ACCESS:
MEETING INDIVIDUAL NEEDS

ELL Support

For ELD strategies, use the ***English-Language Development Guide,*** Unit 1, Lesson 2.

Intervention Support

For intervention strategies, use the ***Intervention Guide,*** Unit 1, Lesson 2.

Teacher Tip BROWSE Remind the students that good readers browse before reading. Tell them that they should be getting in the habit of browsing before they read, and that doing so can help them activate prior knowledge relevant to the selection.

Routine Card Refer to ***Routine 11*** for the procedure for reading the selection.

Build Background

Activate Prior Knowledge Reading 2.6

Tell the students that you are going to read them a poem about an unusual cow. Ask whether anyone has seen a cow or has seen pictures of cows. Have volunteers tell what a cow looks like, how big it is, and the colors it might be.

Preview and Prepare

Browse Reading 1.2

- Open the ***Big Book*** *Let's Read!* to the Table of Contents. Point to the title of the selection, "The Purple Cow." Tell them that it is the first selection in the ***Big Book.*** Remind them that besides listing the titles of the selections, the Table of Contents gives the page number on which each selection begins. Point to the "6" next to "The Purple Cow" and tell the students that this poem begins on page 6. Turn to page 6, and point to and read the names of the author and illustrator, explaining that the *author* is the person who wrote the poem and the *illustrator* is the person who drew the pictures.
- Have the students look at the illustration. Ask a volunteer to explain why a purple cow is funny. *(There are no purple cows in real life.)*
- Before reading the selection to the students, read the Focus Questions on the first page of the selection together. Briefly discuss the questions, and tell the students to keep these questions in mind as you read.

Set Purposes

Explain that readers often read poems or stories for many reasons. Because the illustration is funny, suggest that the purpose of reading this poem is for fun and entertainment. Also point out that many poems have rhyming words. Encourage the students to listen for the rhyming words in this poem.

Selection Vocabulary

Reading 1.17

- Write the following word on the board and read it:

  purple

- Point out to the students that this is a color word. Tell them that one way we can put things into groups is by their color. Ask them to look around the classroom and name things that are the color purple. Ask them to name other things that are purple. *(Things they may mention include flowers such as violets, grapes, and so on.)*
- Use the students' responses to use the word in a sentence. For instance, if a student suggests that she is wearing a purple sweater, say *Jennifer is wearing a purple sweater.*
- Call on volunteers to name other color words. If a student says *red*, ask him or her to point to something red in the classroom. Repeat with several other colors.

Reading Recommendations

Read Aloud

- Read the rhyme through without pausing. Then reread the poem, pointing to each word to show the students that when we read we go from the left side of the page to the right. Also point out that when you get to the end of a line, you go to the beginning of the next line, and you continue in this way until the end. Invite the students to say the words along with you.

Using Comprehension Strategies

Students will be introduced to a number of comprehension strategies in this unit. Comprehension strategy instruction allows students to become aware of what good readers do when they read. Good readers constantly check their understanding as they are reading and ask themselves questions. Skilled readers also recognize when they are having problems understanding a selection and stop to use various comprehension strategies to help them make sense of what they are reading.

Students are exposed to the comprehension strategies through teacher modeling given on the left pages next to the reduced ***Student Edition*** pages. As the students become familiar with the comprehension strategies, encourage them to apply any strategy that helps them comprehend the selection.

During the reading of "The Purple Cow," you will introduce and model the following comprehension strategy:

- **Visualizing** helps readers picture in their minds what is going on in a selection to gain a clearer understanding.

Teacher Tip COLOR WORDS Begin a list of color words. Continue to add words to this list throughout the year. Reading 1.17

Routine Card
Refer to ***Routine 10*** for the Selection Vocabulary procedure.

Universal Access: Meeting Individual Needs

ELL Support

PRETEACH THE SELECTION Be aware of English-language learners and other students who might have difficulty with any reading selection. You might wish to read the selection with the students before it is read with the class. As you read, give them the opportunity to discuss the selection and to clarify any problems they have with it. When they read the selection with the class, they might feel more comfortable asking questions. Use the ***English-Language Development Guide*** as needed.

Teacher Tip VISUALIZING An extended lesson on Visualizing can be found on page T55. This lesson is intended to give extra practice with visualizing.

COMPREHENSION

Comprehension Strategies

Introducing Strategy Use

Introduce the word *visualizing* to the students. Tell them that *visualizing* is imagining in their minds what something or someone looks like. As they read or listen to a selection, they can better understand it by picturing in their minds such things as the setting, characters, and actions. Often there are illustrations that help readers visualize what is happening in a selection.

Teacher Modeling

Visualizing *I wonder what a purple cow would look like. On page 7, I can see the thought balloon that shows what the boy thinks a purple cow looks like. If I close my eyes, I can imagine a cow that is purple. Close your eyes and imagine the cow. What do you see? Good readers are always getting images in their heads about what they read. If you get a good one, tell the class about it.*

Phonemic Awareness

SYLLABLES Remind the students how they clapped out the syllables in names in the Preparing to Read section. Tell the students that now you are going to point to each word in the poem and read it. Ask them to give a thumbs-up signal each time they hear a word with more than one syllable. The words with more than one syllable are *never, purple, anyhow,* and *rather.*

Teacher Tip READING Encourage the students to spend at least 20 minutes reading after school.

UNIVERSAL ACCESS: MEETING INDIVIDUAL NEEDS

ELL Support

WORD MEANING Check that English-language learners know the meaning of *hope (that you want something to happen).* Reread the first two lines of the poem. Ask, "Does the boy want to see a purple cow? Does he think that he will see a purple cow? Does he *hope* that he will see a purple cow?" See the ***English-Language Development Glossary*** for additional suggestions.

Letter Recognition

Reading 1.3

C, c, D, or *d*

Remind the students of the letters they learned to identify and write in Preparing to Read. Point to these letters on the ***Sound/Spelling Cards Aa, Bb, Cc,*** and ***Dd.*** Review with the students that the bigger letters are called *capital letters*, and the smaller letters are called *Lowercase* letters. Explain that these letters are in some of the words in "The Purple Cow." To practice, point to the word *Cow* in the title. Tell the students that this is a word, and words are made up of letters. The letters in *Cow* are *c*, *o*, and *w*.

Ask students to look for the letters *A, a, B, b, C, c, D,* or *d* in the words of the selection. Call on volunteers to go to the ***Big Book*** and point to each letter, identify it, and tell whether it is a capital or lowercase letter *(illustrated, Horna, saw, a, can, anyhow, rather, than, Burgess, by, But, be).*

(Aa *words include Illustrated, Horna, saw, a, anyhow, rather, than;* Bb *words include Burgess, But;* Cc *words include Cow (2 times), can;* Dd *words include Illustrated, I'd.*)

Writing Words
Read the first line of the poem to the class. Point out each word in the line, noting that words are made up of letters and are separated by spaces. Explain that the author wrote each word to help him tell about his idea. They read the words to know what the writer is saying. Explain to students that they too write words to express their ideas.

Teacher Tip LETTER RECOGNITION Encourage the students to look at the ***Sound/Spelling Cards,*** and to find a pattern on the cards regarding capital and lowercase letters (the first letter is always the capital letter). Reading 1.3

UNIVERSAL ACCESS:
MEETING INDIVIDUAL NEEDS

Challenge

INDEPENDENT READING Invite volunteers to go to the ***Big Book*** and point to any word they can read. If no one volunteers, reread the selection, pointing to each word. Then encourage them to volunteer.

UNIVERSAL ACCESS:
MEETING INDIVIDUAL NEEDS

ELL Tip

UNDERSTANDING THE SELECTION During Workshop, provide the opportunity for English-language learners to clarify their understanding of the idea of the poem and to express their ideas about it. Reread with them the title of the poem and ask them to look at the illustration again. Have them try to explain the idea of the poem to themselves. Then pair English-language learners with native English-speaking partners. Encourage partners to talk about the poem. Informally monitor the students' conversations to assess their understanding and check that each student is participating. Reading 2.4

Teacher Tip COMPREHENSION Good readers constantly evaluate their understanding of what they read. Stop often to make sure you and the students are doing this.

Discussing the Selection Reading 1.3; Listen/Speak 1.2

- Ask the students whether they liked "The Purple Cow" and why or why not. Ask them what they found funny about it. If the students don't mention the illustrations, ask them what they think of them.
- Ask a volunteer to read the title of the book the boy in the illustration is holding. If necessary, point to each word as you read the title. Ask the students why this is a good title for the book in the illustration. *(Reading a purple book, or a book about purple might cause the reader to see other objects as purple in color.)*
- Ask the students whether they noticed the circles leading from the boy's head to the cloud around the cow. Ask the students whether anyone can explain what this means. If necessary, explain that this is called a *thought cloud. Thought clouds* are part of the illustrations, and they are a way for an author to show what someone or something is thinking. Discuss how a thought cloud can help the reader in this selection. *(The thought clouds let the reader see the purple cow the boy is imaging.)*
- Ask the students how imagination helps the person in "The Purple Cow." *(He can imagine, or visualize, what a purple cow looks like and then decide that he doesn't want to be one.)*
- Tell the students that poems often have rhyming words. Ask the students to name the rhyming words in the poem. *(Cow, anyhow)*
- With the students, refer back to the Focus Questions for the selection. Have all the questions been answered? If not, answer them now.

Ask the students to bring in a spiral notebook or a three-ring binder that they will label Writer's Notebook. Let them know that their notebook will be divided into at least five different sections. These sections should include the following:

- Partner Reading List—students should keep track of when they partner read a ***Decodable Book*** with another student, what they read, and the name of the student they read with
- Vocabulary Words—selection vocabulary words and their definitions
- Response Journal—notes about selections or literary responses to the selections
- Personal Dictionary—words that are hard to spell or any interesting words that students find in their reading
- Writing Ideas—notes, observations, and other prewriting for writing assignments
- Investigation Ideas—notes and ideas for investigations

Feel free during the year to add new sections that you and your students find useful. Tell students that as they work on different ideas for writing, vocabulary words, or literary techniques, they will keep their notes in their Writer's Notebooks.

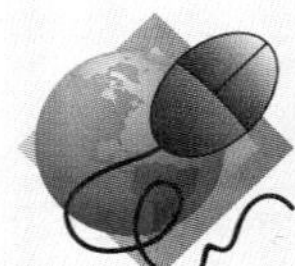

www.sra4kids.com
Web Connection
Remind the students to look for additional funny poems by using Web connections that are available at the Reading link of the SRA Web page.

Review Selection Vocabulary

Have students review the selection vocabulary word for this lesson. Remind them that they discussed the meaning of this word at the beginning of the lesson. Have them write this word and any other interesting words that they clarified while reading to the Vocabulary Words section of their Writer's Notebooks.

The word from this selection is:

purple

- Have the students use the word in oral sentences.
- Ask the students to draw a picture that represents the word.

Encourage students to refer to the vocabulary words throughout the unit.

Print and Book Awareness

Book Covers, Titles, and Tables of Contents Reading 1.2

- Invite a volunteer to come up to the ***Big Book***, identify the front cover, and point to the title of the book.
- Ask who remembers the title of the ***Big Book*** and encourage the students to say the title, *Let's Read!*, together.
- Open the ***Big Book*** to the Table of Contents. Explain that this part of a book shows the names of the selections in the book, the names of the authors, and the page number where each selection begins.
- Call on volunteers to find "The Purple Cow" on the Table of Contents, point to the author's name, and point to the page number on which "The Purple Cow" begins *(page 6)*.

Supporting the Reading

Comprehension Strategy: Visualizing

Ask the students if they remember what *visualizing* is *(imagining in your mind what something or someone looks like)*. Remind them that when you read "The Purple Cow," they visualized what the purple cow looked like. Reread the poem, encouraging students to close their eyes as you do, and have them visualize the cow again. Discuss their visualizations, noting whether the students visualized a cow like the one in the illustration or a different cow.

Purposes for Reading Reading 3.2

Remind students that before reading the poem the class discussed that the author's purpose for writing this selection was to entertain. Ask the students if the author's writing was funny and entertaining. Have them explain their answers.

Objectives

- Students will become familiar with the format of alphabet books.
- Students will review alphabet books during Workshop.
- Students will understand how poems and rhyme can be used in their alphabet books.

Materials

- alphabet books

Teacher Tip INVESTIGATION You may, if you prefer, have the students make group alphabet books rather than one class alphabet book.

INVESTIGATION

Supporting the Investigation

Investigating Concepts Beyond the Text Reading 1.3

In Lesson 1, the students were introduced to the unit activity, making an alphabet book. Point to the (backs of the) *Aa–Zz* ***Sound/Spelling Cards,*** and tell the students that these make up the alphabet. Ask the students if they've seen books that have the alphabet in them. Then show the students one or more alphabet books. Some good examples include:

Alligator Arrived with Apples: A Potluck Alphabet Feast by Crescent Dragonwagon

Alphabears: An ABC Book by Kathleen Hague

Crazy Alphabet by Lynn Cox

- Point out the title and title page of one of the books, and then browse the book together. Ask the students to describe what they see on each page. Then ask what they think the purpose of an alphabet book is. Guide the students to conclude that an alphabet book helps a person become familiar with the letters of the alphabet.
- Make available a number of alphabet books for the students to look at during Workshop. Suggest that they look through these books in the classroom or at home for more ideas. Encourage the students to bring in alphabet books from home to share with the class.
- Remind the students that "The Purple Cow" is a rhyme, or short poem. Ask them to pay attention to each poem as they go through the unit. They can use these rhymes and poems as models for dictating their own rhymes and poems for the class alphabet book.

Unit 1 Investigation Management

Lessons 1–5	**Collaborative Investigation** **Discuss the letters of the alphabet. Work together to come up with concepts for the class alphabet book. Create class alphabet book pages.** **Supporting Activities** **Look at and compare various alphabet books. Provide the students with the materials necessary to create their alphabet pages.**
Lessons 6–10	Continue to create and share class alphabet book pages.
Lessons 11–15	Share class alphabet book pages, and create a class poem to add to the alphabet book.

Art Connection

Imaginary Animals Reading 3.2

Purpose: To increase students' understanding that using imagination can help authors when they write

Tell the students that authors often use their vivid imaginations to create unusual people, places, and things that are different than the people, places, and things most people would be familiar with. Explain to the students that they will use their imaginations to create some unusual, imaginary animals just as Gelett Burgess might have done before he wrote "The Purple Cow."

- Ask the students to recall what colors cows are in real life. Then ask them to tell you other animals they know that are also black, white, shades of brown, or some combination of those colors.
- Write the names of the animals they suggest on the board. Then tell them to use their imaginations to picture those animals in different colors.
- Distribute drawing paper. Ask the students to pick at least one animal and to draw it in any color or colors that they think are funny, like a purple cow.
- Write the following on the board, and have the students copy it on their papers: "I never saw ___________.
- Tell the students to write their names on their papers. Encourage them to use their Name Necklaces or name tags if necessary.
- Give the students an opportunity to share their work with classmates. Have the students show their picture and read the caption, filling in the blank with the color(s) and name of their animal. Display the drawings around the classroom.

Teacher Tip ASSISTANCE Some students may need assistance copying the phrase on their papers. Assist as necessary.

Teacher Tip MATERIALS You will need the following materials for this activity: drawing paper and crayons or markers.

Science/Social Studies Connection Center

Refer to the ***Science/Social Studies Connection Center*** for a science activity about why plants and animals need water and food.

Objectives

Word Analysis Vocabulary
- **Vocabulary Strategies: Classification** Using words from "The Purple Cow," develop the understanding that knowing a group of words in a category allows students to more fully develop an understanding of the meaning of each word.

Writing Process Strategies
- **Introduction to the Writing Process** Building on the theme Let's Read!, understand that writing is a process and that writers write words.

English Language Conventions
- **Mechanics: Capital Letters** Look for people's names to understand that names begin with capital letters.

Materials

- Language Arts Big Book pp. 7–8
- Big Book *Let's Read!*, pp. 6–7

OVERVIEW

Language Arts Overview

Word Analysis

Vocabulary The Vocabulary activity focuses on color vocabulary from "The Purple Cow" to develop understanding of the vocabulary strategy of classification. Classification is useful for learning words that one may have heard but does not know. Comparing and contrasting an unfamiliar word to others

in the same classification expands vocabulary.

Vocabulary Skill Words

purple* **colors** **blue** **red** **green** **yellow** **white**

**Also Selection Vocabulary*

Writing Process Strategies

The Writing Process Strategies lesson introduces students to the writing process by providing an overview of how and where writers get ideas.

English Language Conventions

Grammar, Usage, and Mechanics **Capital Letters.** The English Language Conventions support the reading and writing skills development from Part 1 of this lesson. This lesson reinforces the use of capital letters in names and the pronoun *I* in writing.

Universal Access: Meeting Individual Needs

Reteach, Challenge, English-Language Development and ***Intervention*** lessons are available to support the language arts instruction in this lesson.

Research in Action
Vocabulary

Students have a natural tendency to create simple compare-and-contrast categories. Expanding on this natural tendency to sort and classify can be an effective way to help kindergarten and first-grade students develop word consciousness and build vocabulary.

Word Analysis

Vocabulary

Classification: Colors Reading 1.17

Teach

Explain that many words are names of things that are parts of groups. For example, in "The Purple Cow," purple is a color.

Guided Practice

- Write *Colors* as a column heading on the board or chart paper.
- Write *purple* under the heading and have students suggest different colors as you write the words.
- Discuss characteristics of each color listed and how they are the same and different; for example:
  - What other colors are most like purple? *(blue, violet, red)*
  - What colors are most unlike purple? *(yellow, green, white)*
  - Encourage students to describe any colors that others are unfamiliar with by comparing them to colors they know. For example, variations of purple include violet, plum, magenta, amethyst, and lilac.
- Conclude by emphasizing that by comparing words, students can learn more about each word.

Writing Process Strategies

Introduction to the Writing Process

What Writers Do Writing 1.0

Teach

- Read pages 7–8 of ***Language Arts Big Book*** to provide an overview of where people get ideas to write. These include looking, thinking, talking, and listening. Ideas also come from reading, drawing, journal writing, familiar objects, events, and experiences.

Writer's Craft

Writing Words

- Review the letters students have learned so far in Phonics. Explain that letters are used to make words: bad, cab, dad. Point out that writers put letters together to write words that other people can read. Use ***Comprehension and Language Arts Skills*** pages 4 and 5 to challenge students to put individual letters together to write as many words as they can.

Guided Practice

- Have students help you make a list of where people get ideas for writing. Write them on the board or chart paper.
- Ask the students where they think the author got the idea for writing "The Purple Cow" *(from his imagination)*. Ask them to imagine silly animals and share descriptions of them. Write their ideas on the board.

***Language Arts Big Book* p. 7**

English Language Conventions

Grammar, Usage, and Mechanics

Capital Letters Eng. Lang. Conv. 1.7

Teach

- Review that students' names begin with a capital letter.
- Write your name on the board. Point out that when you write a person's first or last name, you start with a capital letter.

Guided Practice in Reading

- Have the students look at "The Purple Cow" in the ***Big Book*** *Let's Read!* and find the name of the poet, Gelett Burgess. Have the students identify the capital letters in the name, noting that both the first name and the last name begin with a capital letter. You may want to point out that the illustrator's name, Luis de Horna, has two parts that make up his last name. His first name begins with a capital letter and the main part of his last name begins with a capital letter.
- Read the poem and look for the word *I*, which appears four times. Point out that it is always capitalized.
- Summarize that people's names start with capital letters.

1 Preparing to Read

Las hormiguitas

Objectives

- Students will orally blend initial consonant sounds.
- Students will distinguish long words from short words.
- Students will segment words into onsets and rimes.
- Students will write letters of the alphabet.
- Students will associate sounds with letters.
- Students will read a ***Pre-Decodable Book.***

Materials

- Lion Puppet
- Sound/Spelling Cards
- Phonics Skills, p. 4
- Routine Card 5
- Letter Cards
- High-Frequency Word Cards
- Pre-Decodable Book 1

Universal Access: Meeting Individual Needs

ELL Support

For ELD strategies, use the ***English-Language Development Guide,*** Unit 1, Lesson 3.

Intervention Support

For intervention strategies, use the ***Intervention Guide,*** Unit 1, Lesson 3.

Warming Up

Use one or both of the following activities to focus students' attention for the learning that follows.

How Are You? Game Listen/Speak 2.1

Play the How Are You? Game. Have the students sit in a circle and start the game with a student who has not yet had a chance to participate. Continue through five or six names.

I Spy Reading 1.3, 1.4; Listen/Speak 2.1

Play I Spy with the letters *a* and *c*.

> "I spy with my little eye,
> Something with the letter ____."

To discover the word you have in mind, students must point out words in the classroom that have the appropriate letter. Have the students recite the rhyme when they answer.

Phonemic Awareness

Oral Blending Reading 1.4

Blending Initial Consonant Sounds

Tell the students that you are going to ask them to put some sounds together to make words. Explain that you will say just the very beginning sound and then the Lion Puppet will say the rest of the word. Tell them to listen carefully so they can be ready to put the whole word together. Give a signal for the class to respond. Demonstrate as necessary.

Teacher: /s/ . . .
Puppet: plash What's the word?
Students: splash
Teacher: /f/ . . .
Puppet: lour What's the word?
Students: flour

Continue with the following words. From time to time, ask individual students to respond instead of the whole class.

/t/ . . . rampoline	/k/ . . . rystal	/p/ . . . rincipal
/b/ . . . reakfast	/s/ . . . weater	/s/ . . . taircase
/d/ . . . rugstore	/d/ . . . ragonfly	/p/ . . . resident

Comparing Word Length Reading 1.9

- Choose two students' names that begin with the same sound—one a short name and the other a long name (for example, *Ann* and *Anthony*).
- Write the names on the board one above the other so the difference in length is obvious.
- Tell the students that one says *Ann* and the other says *Anthony.* Clap the number of syllables for both and ask which says *Anthony.* Ask the class, "How do we know this is Anthony?"
- After the students have chosen, ask them to clap and say each name, syllable by syllable, as you move your finger beneath the printed letters.
- Repeat with the following pairs:

basketball / ball	family / fly
dog / dragonfly	mow / motorcycle
boy / apatosaurus	umbrella / up
carnival / car	hip / hippopotamus
elf / elephant	rag / rectangle
dime / dinosaur	Mars / Mississippi

- Ask the students what they found out about the length of words, and help them conclude that, in general, the words that look longer also sound longer, take longer to say, and have more syllables.

UNIVERSAL ACCESS:
MEETING INDIVIDUAL NEEDS

ELL Support

WORD MEANING During Workshop, meet with English-language learners to make sure they know the meanings of the words in the oral blending and word length vocabularies. Use pictures, photos, objects, stick drawings, or the ***English-Language Development Guide.***

Informal Assessment

OBSERVE During the lesson, observe six or seven students per day by calling on them individually to determine if they can blend initial consonant sounds orally. Do this each day until you have checked every student. Record your observations in the Teacher Observation Log in the ***Program Assessment Teacher's Edition.***

Teacher Tip TEXT MARKINGS Slash marks denote phonemes. Where a letter is surrounded by slash marks, you should pronounce the letter's sound, not its name. For example, /m/ denotes the *mmmm* sound.

Reading 1.3

Teacher Tip FINDING CLUES Students are so good at finding clues that, if you are not careful, some surely will find the wrong one. With this in mind,

- ✔ sometimes write the longer word above the shorter one, sometimes write the shorter word above the longer.
- ✔ sometimes ask for the shorter word, and sometimes ask for the longer word.
- ✔ sometimes ask for the top word, and sometimes ask for the bottom word.
- ✔ sometimes ask them to point to the word you have named; sometimes ask them to name the word to which you have pointed.
- ✔ use some pairs in which the short word names the bigger object and some in which it names the smaller object.

Teacher Tip SIGNALING Tell the students not to call out their responses until you give the signal and don't forget to shift unpredictably between requesting the response from the group or from individuals. This game should be easy for most, but it is extremely important that you discover and make time to help any students who do not catch on.

Teacher Tip SYLLABLES In this activity, the Lion Puppet repeats only the last part of the syllable, which is called the *rime*. The first part of the syllable is called the *onset*.

PHONEMIC AWARENESS

Segmentation Reading 1.4

Onsets and Rimes

- Reintroduce the Lion Puppet and explain that the game he wants to play today is like a copycat game, except that he will repeat only the *end* of each word.
- Look the puppet in the eye and say the word *buy*, exaggerating the /b/ sound.
- Then have the puppet repeat the /ī/ sound, omitting the first phoneme of the word.
- After a few more demonstrations, continue the game by asking the students to respond *for* the puppet. Give them a signal to respond.

Teacher:	buy
Puppet:	/ī/
Teacher:	go
Puppet:	/ō/
Teacher:	key
Students:	/ē/

- Continue the game with the following list:

say	same	soon	seek	seat
bone	bow	bay	bake	bike
tea	tie	toe	toad	toast
now	knee	neat	night	nice

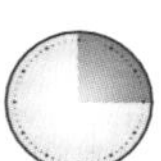

Letter Recognition Reading 1.3; Listen/Speak 2.1

- Review the letters learned so far using the ***Sound/Spelling Cards*** and asking students to name them.
- Recite the "Alphabet Song" learned in Lesson 1 with students.

Exploring *Ee, Ff,* and *Gg* Reading 1.3; Writing 1.3

- For each letter, *Ee*, *Ff*, and *Gg*, touch the ***Sound/Spelling Card*** and name the letter.
- Write each letter on the board, explaining how each one is made.
- Have students write the letters on paper and proofread their letters. (See the Appendix on page 18 for the steps of proofreading.)
- Ask the students why the letter *Ee* is red on the ***Sound/Spelling Card.*** If necessary, tell them that *Ee* is red because it is a special kind of letter, a *vowel.* Ask them to name other vowels using the ***Sound/Spelling Cards.***

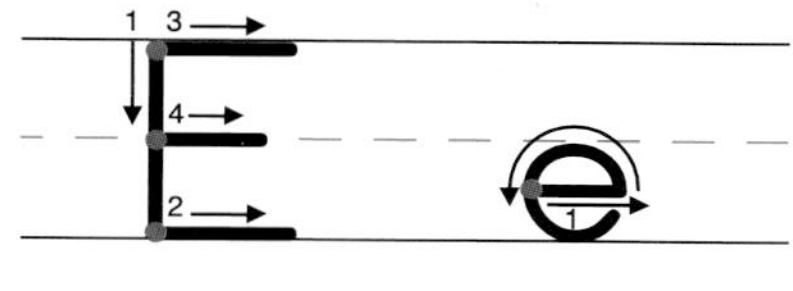

E Starting point, straight down
Starting point, straight out
Starting point, straight out
Starting point, straight out: capital *E*

e Starting point, straight out up and around to the left, curving down and around to the right: small *e*

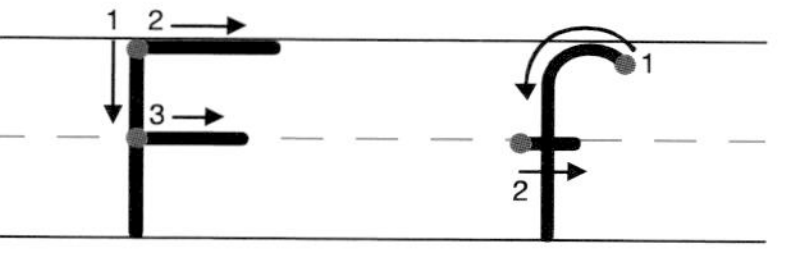

F Starting point, straight down
Starting point, straight out
Starting point, straight out: capital *F*

f Starting point, around left and straight down
Starting point, straight across: small *f*

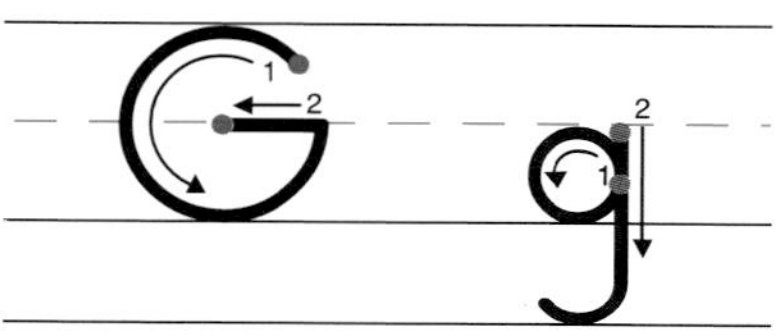

G Starting point, around left, curving up and around
Straight in: capital *G*

g Starting point, around left all the way
Starting point, straight down, touching the circle, around left to stopping place: small *g*

Phonics Skills Writing 1.3

Phonics Skills page 4 provides practice in writing the letters *Ee, Ff,* and *Gg*. Work with students to complete the page. Remind them to print legibly.

Name Date
UNIT 1 Let's Read! • Lesson 3 *Las hormiguitas*
Writing Letters
E E E E E E E
e e e e e e e e e e
F F F F F F F
f f f f f f f f f f f f f f f
G G G G G G G
g g g g g g g g g
4 UNIT 1 • Lesson 3 *Letter Knowledge* • Phonics Skills

Phonics Skills p. 4

LETTER RECOGNITION

Reading 1.3

UNIVERSAL ACCESS: MEETING INDIVIDUAL NEEDS

Reteach

LETTER FORMATION For additional practice in letter formation, use ***Reteach: Phonics Skills*** page 4.

Challenge

PHONICS Use ***Challenge: Phonics Skills*** page 3 with students who are ready for a challenge.

Intervention Tip

LETTER RECOGNITION Check students who were unable to write the alphabet in yesterday's lesson to make sure they can recognize the capital letters and lowercase letters introduced so far *(Aa–Gg)*. If not, make sure they spend Workshop on related activities, or send home an alphabet practice sheet or flash cards for parents and students to work with.

Research in Action
Alphabetic Knowledge

Until children can identify the shape of each letter and discriminate one letter from another, there is no point in introducing them to the alphabetic principle. Unless children can recognize letters quickly and with ease, they cannot begin to appreciate that all words are made up of letters and spelling patterns. On the other hand, once children are able to identify letters quickly, they have little difficulty learning letter sounds and word spellings.
(Marilyn Jager Adams)

Adams, Marilyn J. 1990. *Beginning to read: Thinking and learning about print.* Cambridge, MA: The MIT Press.

Reading 1.3

Teacher Tip LETTER CARDS
Students may use *a* and *e* ***Letter Cards*** as they listen for the /ā/ and /ē/ sounds, by raising the one used in each word.

REVIEW SOUNDS & LETTERS

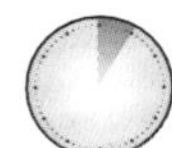

Reviewing Sounds and Letters

Listening for Vowel Sounds: /ā/ and /ē/ Reading 1.3, 1.5

- Remind the students that one of the reasons that vowels are special is that they can say their own names in words.
- Write the letters *Aa* on the extreme left side of the board and the letters *Ee* on the extreme right.
- Tell the students that you will read a list of words aloud. They must listen carefully and decide whether they hear the /ā/ sound or the /ē/ sound in each word.
- If they hear the /ā/ sound, they should say /ā/ and point to the *Aa* on the board; if they hear the /ē/ sound, they should say /ē/ and point to the *Ee* on the board. Use the following list of words:

see	say	may	me	he
hay	way	we	week	wake
flea	tree	tray	play	place
bee	bay	keys	cheese	sneeze

Introducing Consonant Sounds Reading 1.3, 1.4

- Write the following sentence on the board:

  Fearless Fred found five fat frogs.
- Read the sentence aloud, orally exaggerating and underlining each *f* as you read it.
- Ask the students to tell you the sound of the letter *f*, confirming that it is /f/.
- Ask students to repeat the sentence several times with you as you emphasize each /f/ sound orally and touch each letter *f*.
- Ask students to think of words that begin with the letter *f*, writing their suggestions in a list on the board. Ask whether anyone's name begins with the letter *f*. If they happen to suggest a word that begins with *ph*, write that word in a different column. Point out that sometimes the /f/ sound is spelled *ph* and that they'll learn about that spelling later.
- Repeat this sequence for the letters *Gg*, beginning with the sentence:

  Gordon gobbles gobs of gooey gumdrops.

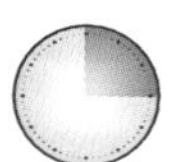

Dictation

Dictation Reading 1.11; Eng. Lang. Conv. 1.8

- Ask the student to take out writing materials. Dictate the following letters, giving the students time to write each before dictating the next:

  b d E e F f G g

- If students need help, refer to the letters on the ***Sound/Spelling Cards***.
- Remind students to proofread their work.
- Collect the papers to see how students are progressing.

Informal Assessment

WRITING This is a good opportunity to assess informally the way students approach this first structured writing task. Note those who still have trouble writing their name without copying. Note also those who are attempting to write more. Plan to meet these differing needs during Workshop.

Reading a Pre-Decodable Book

Core Set, Book 1: *A Table*

See Program Appendix pages 3–4 for more information about using ***Decodable Books.***

High-Frequency Words Reading 1.1, 1.3, 1.11

The high-frequency words in this book are *is*, *on*, *a*, and *the*. Before reading the story, write these words on the board, pointing to each one as you read it. Reread the list slowly. Encourage students to read with you. Then point to words randomly and have students read them.

Note: As students are introduced to sound/spellings and high-frequency sight words become decodable, the high-frequency sight words will not be listed.

Reading Recommendations Reading 1.1, 1.3

- The nondecodable words in this story are *table* and *zzz*. Introduce these words to students before reading Pre-Decodable Book 1. Use the same procedure as introducing the high-frequency words.
- Ask the students to look through the book and point out anything they notice about the pictures or the words.
- Make sure that everyone understands the concept of a rebus and knows how to read the rebus for *table.*
- Read the title aloud. Then have students read the first page of the story to themselves.
- Have the students read each page silently, then have a volunteer read it aloud.
- Have the class reread the story aloud together. Discuss what is happening on each page and how the pictures connect with the text.

Teacher Tip HIGH-FREQUENCY WORD BANK Place the high-frequency words from this book in the Word Bank.

a the is on

Informal Assessment

RESPONDING Ask students to extend their arms fully when they point; this way it will be easy for you to spot those who are confused.

Pre-Decodable Book 1

Research in Action

High-Frequency Words

Before asking children to read, teachers should familiarize them with any high-frequency words in the text, so that such words will not distract them from focusing on the words that they are able to decode. *Marilyn Jager Adams*

Adams, Marilyn J. 1990. *Beginning to read: thinking and learning about print.* Cambridge, MA: The MIT Press.

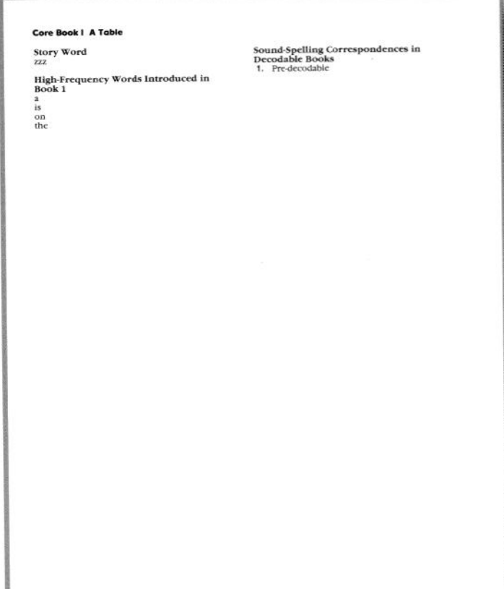

Core Book 1 A Table

Story Word
zzz

High-Frequency Words Introduced in Book 1
a
is
on
the

Sound-Spelling Correspondences in Decodable Books
1. Pre-decodable

Responding

Reading 1.1, 1.3, 1.11; Listen/Speak 1.2

- Invite the students to ask any questions they have about the story.
- Ask students to tell what happened in the story. Encourage them by asking "Anything more?" or saying "Tell me more."
- Read the words *a*, *the*, *is*, and *on*. Have students find these words and point to them in the story.

Building Fluency

- Encourage students to reread the book with a partner.

Reading 1.11

Research in Action

Pre-Decodable Books

Each ***Pre-Decodable Book*** contains several high-frequency words that most students already have in their spoken vocabularies and that are a basic part of all meaningful stories. Learning to identify high-frequency words quickly, accurately, and effortlessly is a critical part of students' development as fluent, independent readers.

Teacher Tip TAKEHOME The ***Decodable Takehome Book*** includes versions of the ***Pre-Decodable*** and ***Decodable*** stories that can be sent home with students. Send a story home after it has been read several times in class. Also, have students copy the high-frequency words onto 3 × 5 cards and send them home to practice.

Routine Card
Refer to ***Routine 5*** for reading ***Decodable Books***.

Pages 8–11 of *Let's Read!*

Focus Questions What is an ant? Where have you seen ants? What does a group of ants look like when they move together?

Las hormiguitas
(The Little Ants)

José-Luis Orozco ● *illustrated by Doug Roy*

Por los cerritos
y vereditas
van caminando
las hormiguitas.

Las hormiguitas,
las hormiguitas,
van caminando
las hormiguitas.

8

SELECTION INTRODUCTION

About the Author

José Luis Orozco has dedicated his life's work to sharing Latin American culture and language through music. He has made many musical recordings about Latin American folklore and folk songs. He believes music is an exceptional learning tool because it allows children to learn as they play.

About the Illustrator

Doug Roy loved to draw when he was a child growing up in Ironwood, Michigan. He lives with his wife, two daughters, four cats, and a pond full of fish.

Objectives

- Students will use the Table of Contents.
- Students will practice saying *the* and *on*.
- Students will discuss the content of the selection.
- Students will practice reading from left to right.
- Students will show knowledge of the parts of a book.
- Students will complete a graph.
- Students will complete sums up to 7.

Materials

- Big Book *Let's Read!*, pp. 8–11
- Listening Library Audiocassette/CD
- Letter Cards
- Home Connection, p. 3

Selection Summary

Genre: Poetry

This poem focuses on tiny creatures that, though ordinary and easy to overlook, are really quite special and extraordinary.

The elements of poetry are listed below. Poetry may have one or more of these elements:

- Sentences are sometimes broken into parts. Each part is on a line of its own.
- Words that rhyme are often used.
- The lines of a poem often have rhythm or meter.
- Some words may be repeated.

Inquiry Connections

In the first selection of the ***Big Book*** *Let's Read!*, the students listened to a short poem, or rhyme, about an imaginary animal. In this next selection, they will listen to a longer poem about real animals, ants.

Key concepts investigated are

- the elements of poetry
- matching oral words to printed words
- print and book awareness

Direct the students to the Concept/Question Board. Encourage them to post any questions or ideas they have about the unit. They may want to include a picture of an ant or another poem about ants. You may want to make a list of Spanish words that the class knows and place it on the Board.

- Make sure the students put their names or initials on anything they post on the Board.
- Tell them that they can post something on the Board any day. Be sure to have students discuss what they put on the Board with the class.

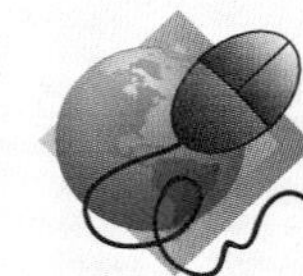

www.sra4kids.com
Web Connection
Help students look for additional information about ants by using the Web connections that are available at the Reading link of the SRA Web page.

Teacher Tip RESPONDING TO TEXTS Below are some responses thay you can model while you read aloud. Model two or three of these by "thinking aloud" as you read to students. Choose responses that fit the text you are reading. Invite students to offer their responses by thinking aloud as you do.

- ✔ React emotionally by showing joy, sadness, amusement, or surprise.
- ✔ Wonder about ideas in the text by posing questions that you really do wonder about.
- ✔ Relate the text to something that happened to you or to something you already know.
- ✔ Show interest in the text ideas.
- ✔ Clarify the meanings of words and ideas in the text.

Universal Access:
Meeting Individual Needs

ELL Support

For ELD strategies, use the ***English-Language Development Guide,*** Unit 1, Lesson 3.

Intervention Support

For intervention strategies, use the ***Intervention Guide,*** Unit 1, Lesson 3.

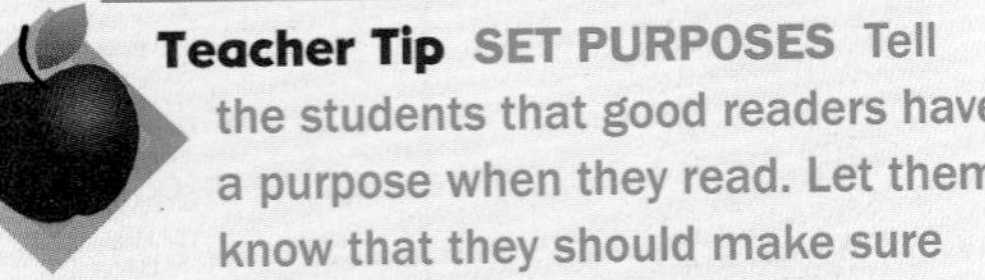

Teacher Tip SET PURPOSES Tell the students that good readers have a purpose when they read. Let them know that they should make sure they know the purpose for reading whenever they read.

Routine Card Refer to ***Routine 11*** for the procedure for reading the selection.

Teacher Tip HIGH-FREQUENCY WORDS The following high-frequency words appear in the selection: *the* and *on.* Point to these words in the High-Frequency Word Bank, have students read them, and encourage them to read these words with you when you encounter them in the reading.

Build Background

Activate Prior Knowledge Reading 2.6

- Tell the students that you are going to read them a poem called "Las hormiguitas." If you have Spanish-speaking students in your class, have them tell what language uses the words *las hormiguitas* and what the phrase means in English. Otherwise, explain that it means "the little ants."
- Ask the students what they know about ants. Ask them what ants look like, where they live, and how they move.

Background Information

Tell the students that there are many kinds of ants. They are different colors, eat different things, and live in different places. They all live in groups, however some ants live with about 20–30 ants, and others live with thousands of other ants. Some kinds of ants travel in long lines, as shown in the poem.

Tell the students that sometimes poems repeat words for emphasis. They will notice in "Las hormiguitas" that the words "las hormiguitas" or "the little ants" are repeated.

Preview and Prepare

Browse Reading 1.2

- Open the ***Big Book*** *Let's Read!* to the Table of Contents. Call on a volunteer to tell what information is found on this page. Point to the poem title, "Las hormiguitas," and invite volunteers to tell on what page the poem begins.
- Turn to page 8. Read the title of the poem and the names of the author and illustrator, pointing to each as you do.
- Invite a volunteer to explain what the ants in the illustration are doing. *(walking in a line)*
- Before reading the selection to the students, read the Focus Questions on the first page of the selection together. Briefly discuss the questions and tell the students to keep these questions in mind as you read.

Set Purposes

Suggest to the students that this poem is intended to tell them about ants. By using words like *ants, line,* and *on and on* repeatedly, the author tells readers that ants move together, and in the same direction.

Selection Vocabulary

- Write the following word on the board and pronounce it:

  spin

- Use the word in a sentence such as, When we spin a top, it goes round and round.
- Ask a volunteer to tell what *spin* means. Invite one or two students to demonstrate the meaning, either by spinning a ball or by spinning around. Encourage another student to use the word *spin* in a sentence, describing what the other student demonstrated. *(For example: Tom spins the ball.)*

Reading Recommendations Reading 1.11

Read Aloud

- Read the poem through in English without pausing. Then read it verse by verse, moving your finger or pointer under each word. Remind the students that when you get to the end of a line, you go to the beginning of the next line (or return sweep).
- On a third reading, invite the students to say the words they know.
- Find out whether any Spanish-speaking student knows this poem and would like to recite it in Spanish. If not, read the Spanish version yourself or play the ***Listening Library Audiocassette.***
- Have students find and say the words *the* and *on*.

Using Comprehension Strategies Listen/Speak 2.1

Comprehension strategy instruction allows students to become aware of what good readers do when they read. Good readers constantly check their understanding as they are reading and ask themselves questions. Skilled readers also recognize when they are having problems understanding a selection and stop to use various comprehension strategies to help them make sense of what they are reading.

In the previous lesson, the students were introduced to the comprehension strategy, Visualizing. In this lesson, they will be introduced to another strategy. You will model the use of the following comprehension strategy:

- **Asking Questions** helps readers focus their attention on what they are reading, and engages them in deeper understanding of themes, concepts, and ideas.

Students should not be limited to using only the strategy suggested, but be encouraged to use any strategy they know to better understand a selection. You may wish to encourage your students to visualize the ants and what they are doing in the poem.

Routine Card
Refer to ***Routine 10*** for the Selection Vocabulary procedure.

Reading 1.3, 1.11

UNIVERSAL ACCESS:
MEETING INDIVIDUAL NEEDS

Reteach

HIGH-FREQUENCY WORDS Use this poem to reteach the high-frequency words *the* and *on,* which are repeated several times in this selection. Read the words and point to the high-frequency words so that the students may say them with you.

Challenge

READ-ALOUD Have students who can read the poem read it with a partner or to the class.

Intervention Tip

REPETITION Meet with students who are not participating in reading during Workshop. Point out the repetition in the poem. For example, point to the word *little* and have students point to the word in other places. Then reread the poem, having students "read" each instance of the word. The goal is to focus their attention on these words so that they can participate.

Teacher Tip COMPREHENSION
Good readers constantly evaluate their understanding of what they read. Stop often to make sure you and the students are doing this.

Teacher Tip ASKING QUESTIONS
An extended lesson on Asking Questions can be found on page T75. This lesson is intended to give extra practice with asking questions.

COMPREHENSION

Comprehension Strategies

Introducing Strategy Use

Tell the students that as they read or listen to a selection, they can ask themselves questions. Then as they continue to read or listen, their questions may be answered. This will help them better understand what is happening. Tell the students that sometimes the questions they ask may not be answered in the text, and they may need to seek answers elsewhere.

Teacher Modeling

Asking Questions *We can ask questions about a poem or selection to help us better understand it. As I look at pages 8 and 9, I see a long, curvy line of ants. Where are they going? Maybe we will find out when we read the poem.*

[After reading]

We found out that the little ants went over hills and roads, but it didn't tell us where they were going.

Phonemic Awareness Reading 1.4

INITIAL CONSONANTS Remind the students how they put sounds together to make words in the Preparing to Read section. Tell the students that now you are going to say just the beginning sound of a word from the poem and then the rest of the word. Ask them to listen carefully so they can be ready to say the whole word from the poem. Use the following words:

/h/ . . . ills	/r/ . . . oads
/l/ . . . ine	/l/ . . . ittle

Teacher Tip **READING FOR ENJOYMENT** Remind students that they should spend at least 20 minutes reading after school.

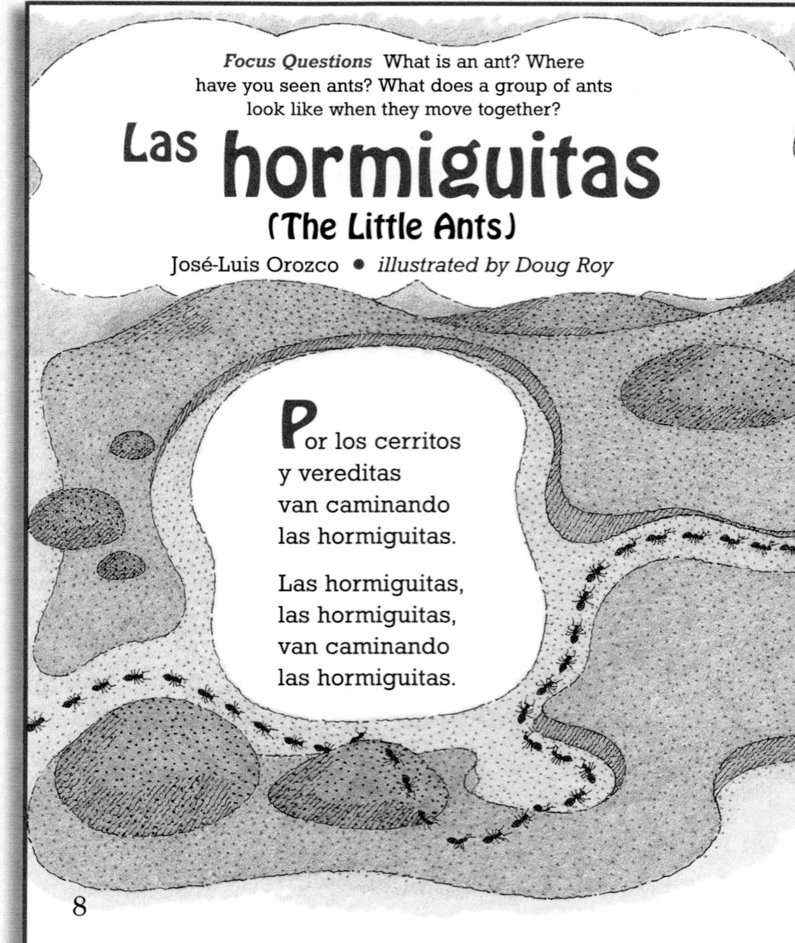

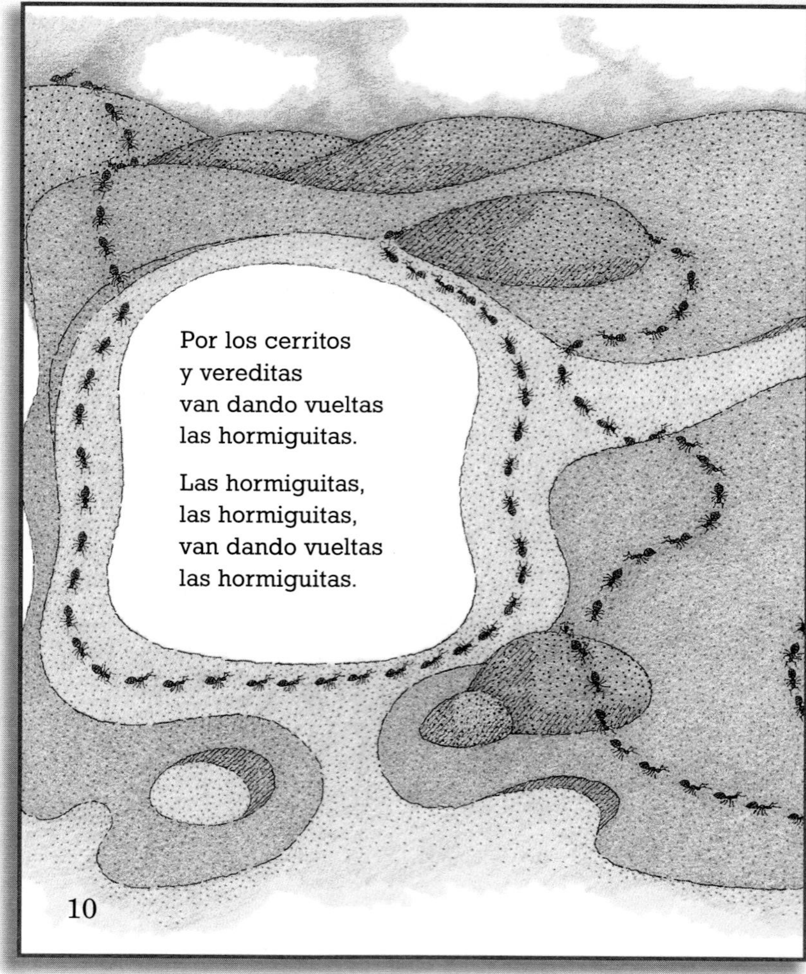

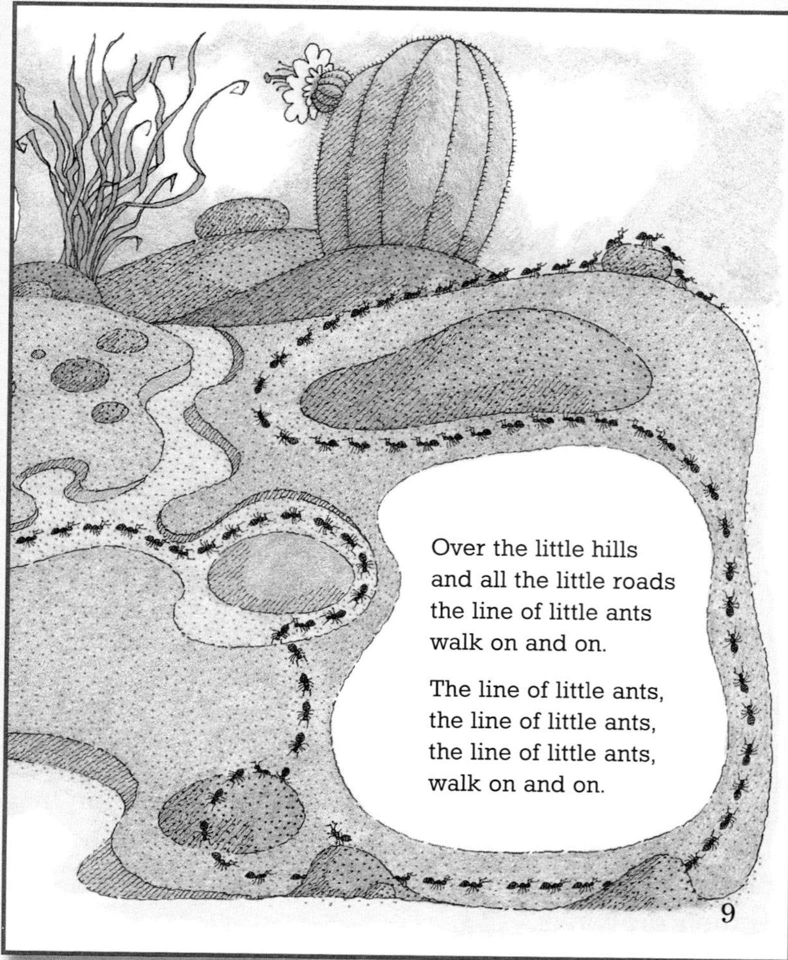

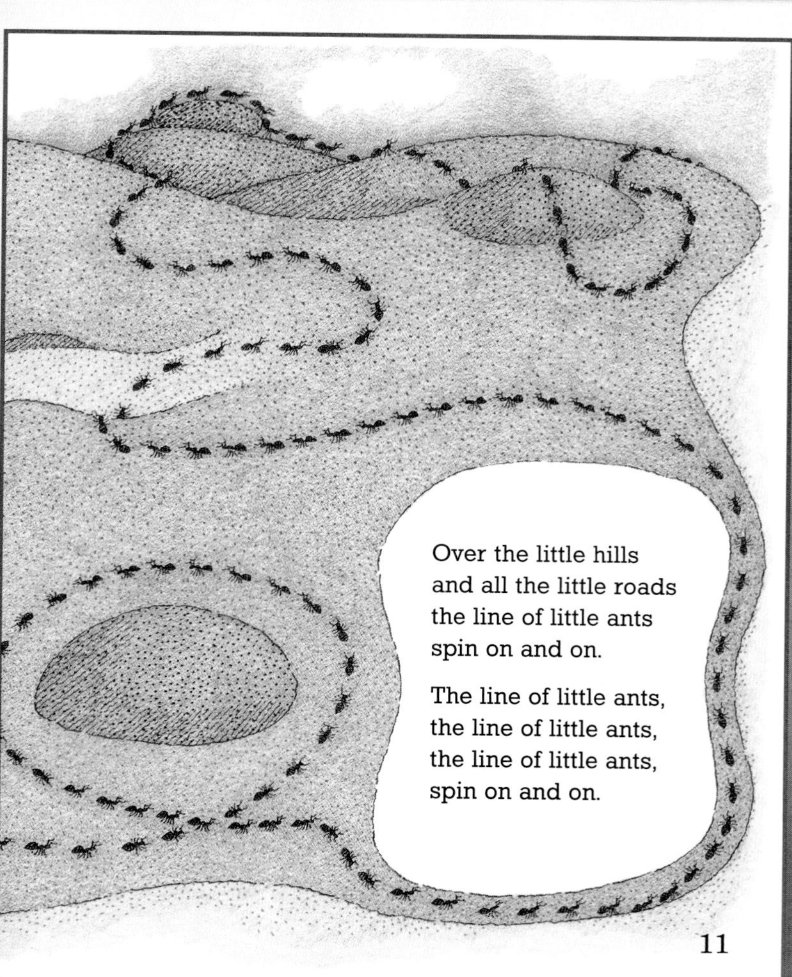

Letter Recognition Reading 1.3

Ee, Ff, Gg

- Have the ***Big Book*** *Let's Read!* open to pages 8–9. Ask the students to look for the word on that page that *ends* with the letter *f. (of)*
- Invite volunteers to go to the ***Big Book*** and point out a word that contains the letter *e. (over, the, little, line)*
- Then have them point to a word containing the letter *g. (hormiguitas)*
- If time permits, have students look for other letters they have learned: *a, b, c,* and *d. (and, all, roads, ants, walk)*

COMPREHENSION

Universal Access: Meeting Individual Needs Reading 1.3

Reteach

LETTER RECOGNITION Students who still are having difficulty with letter recognition should be given the ***Letter Cards*** for *f, e,* and *g* and be asked to match the cards to letters in the poem. Review other letters in the same way.

Intervention Tip

LETTER RECOGNITION Cut out large sandpaper letters. With markers, draw stroke arrows and number the strokes. Let the students trace the letters with their finger and then with a pencil.

UNIVERSAL ACCESS:
MEETING INDIVIDUAL NEEDS

Challenge

EXTENDING THE POEM Some students will enjoy creating other verses using the pattern of the poem, for example:

march on and on
dance on and on, and so forth.

Listen/Speak 1.4

Teacher Tip STAYING ON TOPIC If the students begin to talk about another topic, remind them that the topic they should be discussing is ants.

Discussing the Selection

- Point to the illustrations and have the students notice that the ants all look much the same. Draw their attention to the words that are repeated in the poem (*the line of little ants*). Explain that repeating words is a way writers can show readers that events are repeated.
- Ask the students what words in this poem helped them imagine, or visualize, the ants' movements.
- Encourage the students to speculate why ants sometimes walk in lines. Show what you mean by pointing to the illustrations. Point out that the ants may be following a trail to a place where one of them has found food.
- Have the students discuss parts of the poem they liked. Ask what they learned from the poem about ants, besides how they move.
- Take a moment to ask the students how they think this poem compares to "The Purple Cow."
- With the students, refer back to the Focus Questions for the selection. Have all the questions been answered? If not, answer them now.

Have students record their responses to the selection in the Response Journal section of their Writer's Notebooks by drawing pictures featuring ants. Help the students label their drawings.

Review Selection Vocabulary

Have students review the selection vocabulary word for this lesson. Remind them that they discussed the meaning of this word at the beginning of the lesson. Have them add this and any other interesting words that they clarified while reading to the Vocabulary Words section of their Writer's Notebooks.
The word from this selection is

spin

- Ask the students how the word spin was used in the poem. *(to describe the way the ants moved)*
- Ask the students to use the word in oral sentences. Help the students expand their sentences by asking who, what, where, why, when, and how questions.
- Ask the students to draw a picture that represents the word.

Encourage students to refer to the vocabulary words throughout the unit.

Print and Book Awareness

Left-to-Right Directionality of Print

- Ask the students whether they've noticed that we always begin reading the lines in a book from the same side. Invite a volunteer to go up to the ***Big Book*** and point to the side on which we start reading.
- Then have another volunteer point to the words in the first line to show the order in which the words should be read. Ask him or her what we do when we finish reading a line *(sweep to the next line)*.

Supporting the Reading

Comprehension Strategy: Asking Questions Listen/Speak 1.2

Remind the students that you used the Asking Questions comprehension skill when you read the poem "Las hormiguitas." Tell them that by asking questions as people read, they can better understand what they are reading. Turn back to "The Purple Cow" on pages 6 and 7 of the ***Big Book.*** Encourage the students to ask questions about the poem and/or illustrations.

Purposes for Reading

Earlier in the lesson, the class discussed that the purpose of the poem is to tell readers about ants. Ask students whether they can think of any other purpose for the poem.

View Fine Art

- Show the students page 56 of Let's Read! Big Book, and point out *The Libraries Are Appreciated.* Ask the students whether they like the painting. Why or why not?
- Ask the students to name all the objects pictured, and have them describe or comment on the colors, lines, and shapes in the piece.
- Ask the students how they think the people in the painting feel about reading; do they seem interested in their books?
- Have students tell the rest of the class what they like best or appreciate most about libraries.

Fine Art Let's Read!

Untitled. August 6, 1988. **Keith Haring.** Sumi ink on paper.

The Libraries Are Appreciated. 1943. **Jacob Lawrence.** Gouache and watercolor on paper. Philadelphia Museum of Art.

Layla and Majnum at School. 1524–1525. **Artist unknown,** style of Shaykh Zadeh. Persian (Herat) miniature; ink, colors, and gold on paper. The Metropolitan Museum of Art, New York.

56

Big Book Lets Read! p. 56

Teacher Tip **COMPREHENSION** Skilled readers are active readers. They interact with the text as they read—by emoting, reacting, responding, and problem solving in their efforts to construct and maintain meaning.

Objectives

- Students will continue learning about alphabet books.
- Students will apply concepts and ideas through a curricular connection.

Materials

- Reading Transparency 49

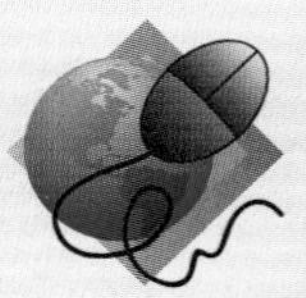

www.sra4kids.com
Web Connection
Help the students look for additional information about poems and rhymes by using the Web connections that are available at the Reading link of the SRA Web page.

INVESTIGATION

Supporting the Investigation Reading 1.3

Investigating Concepts Beyond the Text

- Remind the students about the unit project. They will make a class alphabet book.
- Display several alphabet books for the students. Then read several pages from one book. Point out how each page is set up.
- Share several alphabet books and point out any that are developed around a single theme. Help the students see that entire alphabet books can have one theme, or each page can have an independent theme.
- After sharing several books, remind the students that they will be making their own class alphabet book. Ask what kinds of things they might like to include. Accept any suggestions they offer, which might include ways to make the letters, types of themes, or how to make the pictures. List the suggestions on chart paper.

Math Connection

Graphing Names Science 4b, 4c

Purpose: To give students practice in counting syllables up to 7 and showing that number on a graph

Draw a graph with five columns and nine rows. Number the rows 1 to 7 from the bottom up in the first column. Write the label *Syllables* at the top of the first column. Under each of the columns two through five, write the last name of a student.

Have students whose last names are on the board come up and fill in the graph to indicate how many syllables are in their names. Ask students to use counters to show the syllables on the graph. As they fill the graph, have students tell you the sum. Have them say their names out loud, clapping out the syllables.

When the graph is complete, ask questions such as: "Whose name has the most syllables? The fewest syllables?" Ask students, "How did you know how many times to clap?"

Counting Syllables

Syllables				
7				
6				
5				
4				
3				
2				
1				
Last Names of Students	Lee	Finnegan	Payton Smith	DiCaprio

INVESTIGATION

Teacher Tip MATERIALS You will need chart paper or *Reading Transparency 49.*

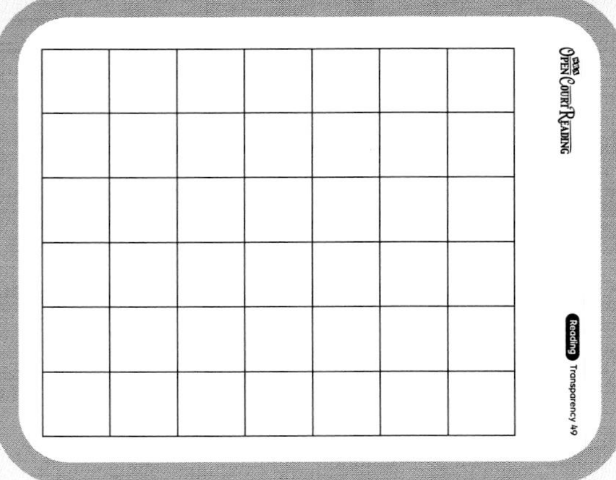

Reading Transparency 49

Objectives

Word Analysis Vocabulary
- **Classification** Using words from "Las hormiguitas," develop an understanding that knowing a group of words in a category allows students to more fully develop an understanding of the meaning of each word.

Writing Process Strategies
- **Introduction to the Writing Process** Develop an initial understanding that writing is a process that involves several steps.

English Language Conventions
- **Mechanics: Capital Letters** By writing their own names, understand that names begin with capital letters.

Materials

- Language Arts Big Book, pp. 10–11
- Writer's Notebook

UNIVERSAL ACCESS:
MEETING INDIVIDUAL NEEDS

Reteach, Challenge, English-Language Development, and ***Intervention*** lessons are available to support the language arts instruction in this lesson.

Research in Action
Vocabulary

Research has shown that students need to encounter a word about 12 times before they know it well enough to improve their comprehension. *(Michael Pressley)*

OVERVIEW

Language Arts Overview

Word Analysis

Vocabulary The Vocabulary activity focuses on vocabulary from "Las hormiguitas" to understand classification. Comparing and contrasting an unfamiliar word with others in the same category develops word meaning of unfamiliar words.

Vocabulary Skill Words

ants **birds** **insects** **reptiles** **amphibians** **mammals**

Writing Process Strategies

The Writing Process Strategies lesson introduces students to the steps of the writing process: prewriting (Plan), drafting (Write), revising (Revise), editing (Check), and publishing (Share). Many students struggle so much with handwriting that they often do not realize they are proceeding through several thought processes as they plan, draft, and complete their written work. By starting the writing as a process concept early on, they will be more inclined to think about the planning, revising, and editing stages of the process as well as the drafting stage.

English Language Conventions

Grammar, Usage, and Mechanics **Capital Letters.** The English Language Conventions support the reading and writing skills development in Part 1 of this lesson. This lesson encourages practice of writing names with capital letters.

Word Analysis

Vocabulary

Classification: Animals

Teach Reading 1.17

- Explain that many words are names of things that are part of groups. For example, in "Las hormiguitas," an ant is an animal.
- Explain that there are several different types of animals, such as birds, insects (ants and bees), reptiles (snakes and turtles), amphibians (frogs), and mammals (dogs, cats, cows, and wolves).

Guided Practice

- Write *Animals* at the top center of the board or chart paper.
- Write or draw pictures of birds, insects, reptiles, amphibians, and mammals under the heading and have students suggest different animals as you write the words.
- Discuss characteristics of the animals listed and how they are the same and different; for example
  - Birds have feathers.
  - Amphibians can live in water and on land.
  - Reptiles have scales or shells.
  - Mammals have fur.
  - Insects have six legs.
- Conclude by emphasizing that by comparing words, students can learn more about each word.

Writing Process Strategies

Introduction to the Writing Process

The Steps of the Writing Process

Teach Writing 1.0

- Explain the writing process by reading pages 10–11 of ***Language Arts Big Book***—Plan, Write, Revise, Check, and Share.
- **Teacher Model:** Model the steps of the writing process. *I think I will write a story about myself. First, I will list some things I want to tell about me. Then, I will organize my ideas. Next, I will write them. After that I will read it to make sure I said everything I want to say in the way I want to say it. After I make changes, I will read it one more time to make sure I don't have any mistakes. Last, I will copy it neatly and maybe draw a picture, and I will let you read it.*

Guided Practice

Using the words *first, next, then,* and *last,* outline the steps of the writing process together as a class on the board or chart paper.

Language Arts Big Book p. 10

English Language Conventions

Grammar, Usage, and Mechanics

Capital Letters

Teach Eng. Lang. Conv. 1.7

- Write the alphabet across the board.
- Have each student spell his or her last name aloud, if possible, as you write it on the board under the letter that is the first letter in each name.
- **Teacher Model:** Model that when you write a person's last name, you start with a capital letter.

Practice in Writing

- Help students write their first and last names in their Writer's Notebooks.
- Have them proofread to make sure the first letter in each word is capitalized.

Informal Assessment

Take note of students who can and cannot write their names with ease. Help students who are having difficulty focus on the first letters of their first and last names.

Objectives

- Students will blend initial consonant sounds.
- Students will segment words into onsets and rimes.
- Students will write letters of the alphabet.
- Students will associate sounds with letters.
- Students will distinguish between two distinct long-vowel sounds.
- Students will identify consonant sounds.

Materials

- Lion Puppet
- Sound/Spelling Cards
- Phonics Skills, p. 5
- Letter Cards
- High-Frequency Word Cards

Universal Access: Meeting Individual Needs

ELL Support

For ELD strategies, use the ***English-Language Development Guide,*** Unit 1, Lesson 4.

Intervention Support

For intervention strategies, use the ***Intervention Guide,*** Unit 1, Lesson 4.

ELL Support

WORD MEANING Make sure the English-language learners know the meanings of the words used in the activities. During Workshop, use pictures or photos, objects, drawings, pantomime, or the ***English-Language Development Guide*** to assist students.

Warming Up

Choose one or both of the following activities to focus students' attention and to reinforce the concepts they have been working on.

Syllable Blending Reading 1.3

Tell students that you will be saying some words in parts called syllables. As before, have them listen carefully to both parts and blend the word.

base . . . ball	base . . . ment	ba . . . by
mon . . . key	ba . . . boon	wa . . . ter
win . . . dow	win . . . ner	

I Spy Reading 1.3, 1.4; Listen/Speak 2.1

Play I Spy with the letters *f* and *g*.

"I spy with my little eye,

Something with the letter _______."

To discover the word you have in mind, students must point out a word in the classroom that has the appropriate letter. Have the students recite the rhyme when they answer.

Phonemic Awareness

Oral Blending Reading 1.3, 1.4

Initial Consonant Sounds

- Tell the students that you will help them practice putting the beginning sound with the rest of a word to make a whole word.

  Teacher: /m/ . . . otorcycle. What's the word?

  Students: motorcycle

- Continue with the following words:

/l/ . . . ibrary	/s/ . . . upper	/s/ . . . andwich
/m/ . . . eatball	/f/ . . . urniture	/m/ . . . orning
/l/ . . . etter	/p/ . . . opsicle	/m/ . . . usic
/sh/ . . . adow	/s/ . . . oda	/f/ . . . eather

Segmentation Reading 1.3, 1.4

Onsets and Rimes

- Bring out the Lion Puppet and remind the students that he is a special puppet who loves to play games with the words he hears. The puppet always does something a little strange with the words.
- Invite the students to find out what game the puppet is playing today. Look at the puppet and say the word *zoo*, exaggerating the /z/ sound as you do so. Then have the puppet copy you but omit the first phoneme of the word the puppet should say. Write *zoo* on the board and cover *z* as the puppet says /o͞o/. Tell the class that the word you've written is *zoo*.
- Repeat the demonstration with a few more words:

  Teacher: moo

  Puppet: oo

  Teacher: say

  Puppet ay

  Teacher: seat

  Puppet eat

- Ask the students to tell what the puppet is doing. Help them understand that the puppet is leaving off the first sound of the word.
- Continue the game and have the students taking the role of the puppet. You can use these words or words of your own that begin with single consonants. Write each word on the board to show the initial and end sounds.

sigh	lay	say	so	real
low	me	pie	pay	night
my	no	zoo	two	face

PHONEMIC AWARENESS

Reading 1.3

Teacher Tip ONSETS AND RIMES In this activity, the Lion Puppet repeats only the last part of the syllable, which is called the *rime*. The first part of the syllable is called the onset.

Teacher Tip WORD SELECTION If you use your own words, be sure to use only words with single initial consonant phonemes (no blends). In addition, the game will be easier to understand if you first use words with consonants that are continuants (*f, l, m, s, n, r, z*), such as *feel, lap, meet, see, nose, rain,* or *zip.*

Informal Assessment

MONITORING You should be completing the monitoring of students' ability to blend initial consonant sounds. Because students will start blending the sounds in written words in Lesson 13 of this unit, it is important that if students need extra help, you provide it during Workshop.

LESSON MODELS VIDEOCASSETTE
Use the ***Lesson Models Videocassette*** at this time for a Segmentation lesson model.

Reading 1.3

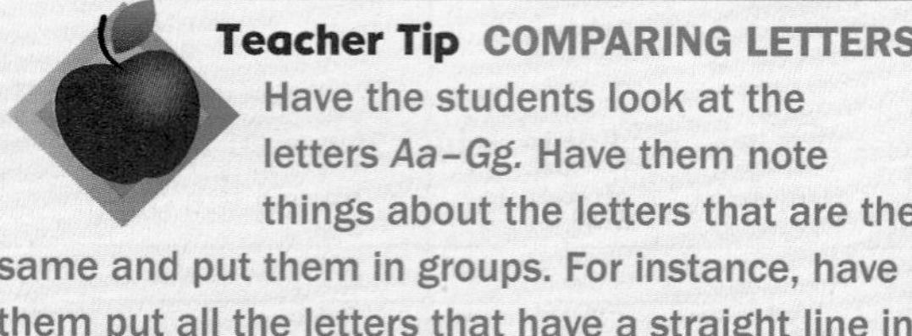

Teacher Tip COMPARING LETTERS Have the students look at the letters *Aa–Gg*. Have them note things about the letters that are the same and put them in groups. For instance, have them put all the letters that have a straight line in them in a group *(A, a, B, b, D, d, E, e, F, f)*.

Research in Action

Naming Letters

Although the ability to name letters is important, it is not enough. To become successful readers, children must be able to name the letters with ease and speed. (*Keith E. Stanovich, Anne E. Cunningham, and B. B. Cramer*)

Stanovich, Keith E., Cunningham, Anne E., & Cramer, B. B. 1984. Assessing phonological awareness in kindergarten children: Issue of task comparability. *Journal of Experimental Child Psychology, 38,* 175–190.

LETTER RECOGNITION

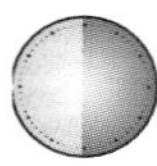

Letter Recognition

Reviewing Letters *Aa–Gg* Reading 1.3

- Review the letters learned so far, using the ***Letter Cards*** to practice quick recognition. Have the students call out the letter names when you give the signal. For a few letters, call on individual students.
- Ask the students to tell you which of the letters that they have learned so far are vowels and point out (if the students do not do so) that vowels are red on the ***Sound/Spelling Cards.*** Tell the students that vowels are special because they are the only letters whose sounds are the same as their name.
- Write *tmts* on the board and ask the students to listen carefully as you pronounce the whole thing several times: /t/-/m/-/t/-/s/. Your pronunciation of this string necessarily will be relatively quiet, because it contains no vowels. Then ask the students if what you have pronounced sounds like a word. Explain that the string *tmts* can't be a word because it contains no vowels.
- Explain that one reason that vowels are special letters is because every syllable has to have at least one vowel. It is the vowels that let our voices sing. Rewrite the word on the board, adding the vowels, and read it aloud, *tomatoes*.

Exploring *Hh, Ii,* and *Jj* Reading 1.3; Writing 1.3

- Introduce the letters *Hh*, *Ii*, and *Jj*, following the same procedure as in the previous lessons.
- Touch the ***Sound/Spelling Card*** and name each letter.
- Write the letter on the board, explaining how the letter is made. Be sure to indicate the starting point for each part of the letters and to describe the direction in which students should make any curves or other motions.

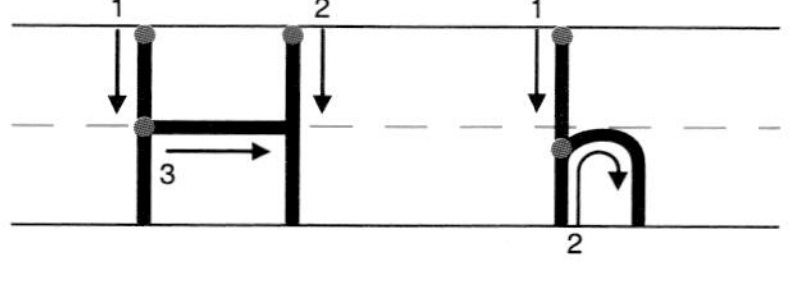

H Starting point, straight down
Starting point, straight down
Starting point, across the middle: capital *H*

h Starting point, straight down, back up, around right, and straight down: small *h*

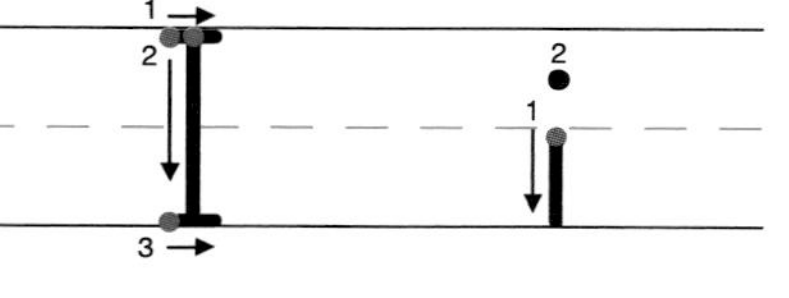

I Starting point, across
Starting point, straight down
Starting point, across: capital *I*

i Starting point, straight down
Dot exactly above: small *i*

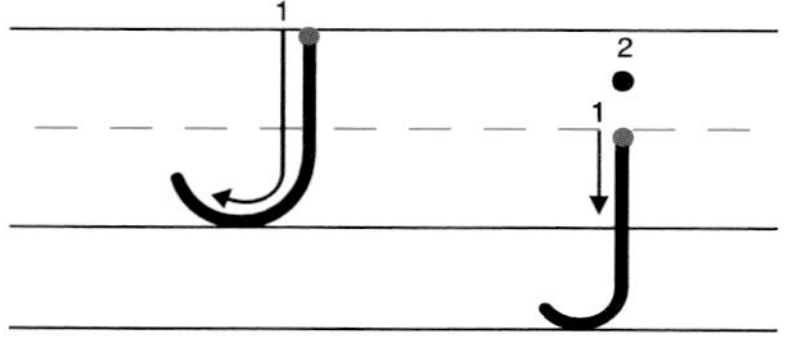

J Starting point, straight down
Around left to stopping place: capital *J*

j Starting point, straight down
Around left to stopping place
Dot exactly above: small *j*

- After the students have traced the shapes of the letters in the air and on their desks, have them write the letters on paper. Remind them to proofread the shape of each letter.
- Point to the ***Sound/Spelling Card*** for each letter again. Then ask a volunteer to explain why the letter *I* is red on the card.

Phonics Skills

Phonics Skills page 5 provides practice in writing the letters *Hh*, *Ii*, and *Jj*. Work with students to complete the page. Remind them to write legibly.

LETTER RECOGNITION

Reading 1.3

Universal Access: Meeting Individual Needs

Reteach

PHONICS Use ***Reteach: Phonics Skills*** page 5 to provide additional practice with *Hh, Ii,* and *Jj.*

Challenge

PHONICS Use ***Challenge: Phonics Skills*** page 4 with students who are ready for a challenge.

Intervention Tip

FORMING LETTERS During Workshop, continue providing individual or small-group attention to students who still have trouble recognizing and forming letters. Hold up a ***Letter Card*** or point to a ***Sound/Spelling Card.*** Have students name the letter and then write it as they say the strokes.

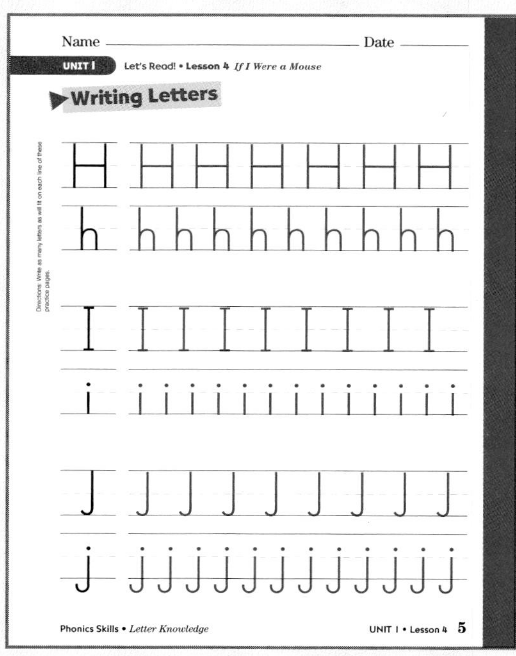

***Phonics Skills* p. 5**

Teacher Tip LETTER CARDS
Students may use ***Letter Cards*** *e* and *i* as they do the Listening for Vowel Sounds activity.

REVIEW SOUNDS & LETTERS

Reviewing Sounds and Letters

Introducing Consonant Sounds Reading 1.3, 1.4

- Write the following sentence on the board:
  Handsome Harry hugs happy hyenas.
- Read the sentence aloud, orally exaggerating and underlining each *h* as you read it.
- Ask students to tell you the sound of the letter *h*, confirming that it is /h/.
- Ask students to repeat the sentence several times with you, emphasizing each /h/ sound orally as you touch each one.
- Ask students whether any of their names begin with the letter *H*. Write them on the board.
- Ask students to think of words that begin with the letter *h*, writing their suggestions in a list on the board.
- Repeat this sequence for the letters *Jj*, beginning with the sentence
  Jolly Joe juggles Jenny's jewels.

Listening for Vowel Sounds: /ē/ and /ī/ Reading 1.3, 1.5

- Remind the students that one of the reasons vowels are special is that they can say their own names in words.
- Write the letters *Ee* on the extreme left side of the board and the letters *Ii* on the extreme right.
- Tell the students that you will read a list of words aloud. They must listen carefully to tell whether they hear the /ē/ sound or the /ī/ sound in each word.
- If they hear the /ē/ sound, they should say /ē/ and point to the *Ee* on the board. If they hear the /ī/ sound, they should say /ī/ and point to the *Ii* on the board.

see	sigh	bee	buy	die
tree	try	fry	free	freeze
key	me	my	mice	rice
why	we	week	wheat	white

Vowel Chant
Reading 1.3, 1.11; Listen/Speak 2.1

Teach the students the vowel chant as follows:

A [clap] E [clap] I O U, [clap]

I can name the vowels for you. [clap]

A [clap] E [clap] I O U, [clap]

you can name them, too! [clap, clap]

- Remind the students that the letter *Ii* is a vowel and write capital *I* and lowercase *i* on the board.
- Have the students repeat the vowel chant as you point to the words and letters on the board.
- The second time through, have students recite the poem in soft voices, speaking up only on the letter *I*.
- When they come to *I*, have them clap twice. Ask students how many times they hear *I* in the chant.
- Have the students recite the chant in small groups.

Dictation

Dictation
Reading 1.11; Eng. Lang. Conv. 1.8

- Ask the students to take out writing materials. Dictate the following letters, giving the students time to write each before dictating the next:

  e g H h I i J j
- If students need help, refer to the letters on the ***Sound/Spelling Cards.***
- Remind students to proofread their work.
- Dictate the high-frequency words below. Use each word in a sentence and remind students to look in the High-Frequency Word Bank for guidance and confirmation of their spelling.

  is, on, the
- Collect the papers to see how students are progressing.

REVIEW SOUNDS & LETTERS

Reading 1.3

Informal Assessment

SOUND/SPELLING CARDS Have students put out the ***Letter Cards a–j.*** Name a letter and have students show you the letter. Point to a letter on the ***Sound/Spelling Cards.*** Have students hold up the matching card and say the letter name.

Pages 12–13 of *Let's Read!*

Focus Questions In what ways would your life be different if you were a mouse? In what ways would your life be the same if you were a mouse?

If I Were a Mouse

Solveig Paulson Russell
illustrated by Charmie Curran

If I were a mouse,
a mouse, a mouse,
I'd never live in
a house, a house;
I'd live outside
where grass
grows tall,
With other
mouse friends,
big and small.

12

SELECTION INTRODUCTION

About the Author Reading 3.2

Solveig Paulson Russell was born in Salt Lake City, Utah. She lived in the city, on a farm, and on a cattle and sheep ranch. After moving to a farm in Oregon, Ms. Russell became a junior high school teacher. Her writing career began after the birth of her daughter, whom she stayed home to raise. She has contributed more than 3,400 short stories, poems, and articles to children's publications.

Other Books by Solveig Paulson Russell
What's the Time, Starling?, *The Big Ditch Waterways*, *Teeny Teeny Tiny Giraffe*

About the Illustrator Reading 3.2

Charmie Curran always liked to draw. She studied art in college and works out of her studio in Bow, New Hampshire. She sometimes collaborates on projects with her husband.

Objectives

- Students will use the Table of Contents.
- Students will discuss selection vocabulary.
- Students will demonstrate that written words are made up of letters.
- Students will ask and answer questions about the poem.
- Students will demonstrate knowledge of spacing between words.
- Students will describe the job of an illustrator.

Materials

- Big Book *Let's Read!*, pp. 12–13

Selection Summary

Genre: Poetry

Rhyme and repetition team up in this enjoyable poem that invites readers to imagine life as a mouse.

The elements of poetry are listed below. Poetry may have one or more of these elements:

- Sentences are sometimes broken into parts. Each part is a line of its own.
- Words that rhyme are often used.
- The lines of a poem often have rhythm or meter.
- Some words may be repeated.

Inquiry Connections

In this selection of the ***Big Book*** the students will listen to a poem about a mouse.

Key concepts investigated are

- the elements of poetry
- matching oral words to printed words
- print and book awareness

Direct the students to the Concept/Question Board. Encourage them to post any questions or ideas they have about the unit. They may want to include a picture or poem about a mouse. If a student has a pet mouse, encourage him or her to bring in a photograph of it.

- Make sure the students put their names or initials on anything they post on the Board.
- Tell them that they can post something on the Board any day. Be sure to have students discuss what they put on the Board with the class.

Concept/Question Board

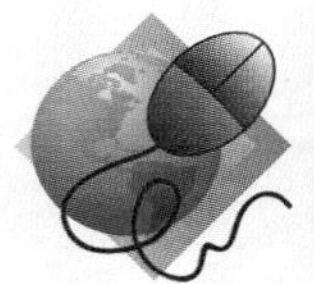

www.sra4kids.com
Web Connection
Help the students look for additional information about mice by using the Web connections that are available at the Reading link of the SRA Web page.

Teacher Tip **CONCEPT/QUESTION BOARD** Remind the students that when working on a unit, they will have questions that they will want answered. New questions will arise as the unit proceeds. Tell them that good readers continue to generate questions as they get deeper into a topic.

Universal Access:
Meeting Individual Needs

ELL Support

For ELD strategies, use the ***English-Language Development Guide,*** Unit 1, Lesson 4.

Intervention Support

For intervention strategies, use the ***Intervention Guide,*** Unit 1, Lesson 4.

Reading 2.6

Teacher Tip ACTIVATE PRIOR KNOWLEDGE Tell the students that good readers think about what they already know that relates to the selection they are reading. Remind the students that whenever they read, they should think about what they already know that might relate to the ideas in the reading.

Teacher Tip Good readers constantly evaluate their understanding of what they read. Stop often to make sure you and the students are doing this.

Routine Card
Refer to ***Routine 11*** for the procedure for reading the selection.

Build Background

Activate Prior Knowledge Reading 2.6; Eng. Lang. Conv. 1.1

- Tell the students that you are going to read them a poem called "If I Were a Mouse." If any students have mice as pets, encourage them to share information about their care in a simple sentence.
- If any students mention the computer *mouse,* let them speculate about why it was given this name. Tell the students that some words can have multiple meanings.

Preview and Prepare

Browse Reading 1.2

- Open the ***Big Book*** *Let's Read!* to the Table of Contents. Point to and read the title of "If I Were a Mouse." Call on a volunteer to point to the name of the author, and then read the author's name to the class.
- Ask the students what other information they can find in the Table of Contents. If necessary, remind them that they can find the page number where the selection begins. Call on a volunteer to point to the page number. Have another volunteer open the ***Big Book*** to pages 12–13 and point to the page numbers as you say them.
- Read the title, tracking each word with your finger or a pointer.
- Invite the students to look at the picture on pages 12–13 and comment on what they notice.
- Before reading the selection to the students, read the Focus Questions on the first page together. Briefly discuss the questions, and tell the students to keep these questions in mind as you read.

Set Purposes

Explain to the students that readers gain knowledge when they read. Because the title of this poem is "If I Were a Mouse," the purpose of reading it will be to find out what it might be like to be a mouse.

Selection Vocabulary Eng. Lang. Conv. 1.1

- Write the following words on the board and say each one out loud:

  house **grass**

- Use each word in a sentence. Ask the students to tell what each word means.
- Then ask the students to use each word in a complete sentence.

Reading Recommendations

Read Aloud

- Have the students listen as you read the poem.
- Reread the poem, pointing to each word as you read.
- Then read the poem once more, inviting the students to join in on "a mouse, a mouse, a mouse" and "a house, a house."

Using Comprehension Strategies

Comprehension strategy instruction allows students to become aware of what good readers do when they read. Good readers constantly check their understanding as they are reading and ask themselves questions. Skilled readers also recognize when they are having problems understanding a selection and stop to use various comprehension strategies to help them make sense of what they are reading.

During the reading of "If I Were a Mouse," you will model the use of the following comprehension strategy:

- **Visualizing** helps readers picture in their minds what is going on in a selection to gain a clearer understanding.

Routine Card
Refer to ***Routine 10*** for the Selection Vocabulary procedure.

Teacher Tip HIGH-FREQUENCY WORDS The following high-frequency words appears in the selection: *a*. Point to this word in the High-Frequency Word Bank, have students read it, and encourage them to read *a* with you when you encounter it in the reading.

Teacher Tip MOVEMENT Encourage the students to create motions to go with the poem. If possible, audiotape or videotape them and let them listen/watch their performances.

Teacher Tip COMPREHENSION STRATEGIES Good readers are also good listeners. Reading aloud to students provides an opportunity to teach the reader responses and problem-solving strategies that good readers employ. In addition to reading aloud with expression and enthusiasm, model your own comprehension strategies while reading aloud to students. This makes the use of strategies real for students and encourages them to begin to respond to text similarly.

Teacher Tip VISUALIZING An extended lesson on Visualizing can be found on page T93. This lesson is intended to give extra practice with visualizing.

COMPREHENSION

Comprehension Strategies

Visualizing Listen/Speak 2.4

Teacher Modeling

Visualizing *If I close my eyes I can picture a mouse scampering in tall grass surrounded by other big and small gray mice. What do you picture?*

Reading 1.4

Phonemic Awareness

ONSETS AND RIMES Remind the students how, in the previous section, they said words but left off the first sound. Tell the students that now you are going to say a word from the poem.
Ask them to repeat the word and then say it again, leaving off the first sound. Use the following words: *mouse, house, tall,* and *big.* Students will say *ouse, ouse, all,* and *ig.*

Teacher Tip **READING FOR ENJOYMENT** Remind the students that they should spend at least 20 minutes reading after school.

Universal Access: Meeting Individual Needs

ELL Tip

IDENTIFYING RHYMES Check that the English-language learners know which words rhyme in the poem. Read the poem aloud, pointing to the words. Have students point out which words have the same sound. Have the students illustrate the words. Say the rhyming words aloud, and have students say them back to you. When they are finished drawing, have them find other students who have drawn illustrations for the same word or a rhyming word.

Intervention Tip

REPETITION Meet with students who are not participating in reading during Workshop. Point out the repeated words. Have students "read" the repetitions so that they can participate more readily.

Focus Questions In what ways would your life be different if you were a mouse? In what ways would your life be the same if you were a mouse?

If I Were a Mouse

Solveig Paulson Russell
illustrated by Charmie Curran

If I were a mouse,
a mouse, a mouse,
I'd never live in
a house, a house;
I'd live outside
where grass
grows tall,
With other
mouse friends,
big and small.

12

Letter Recognition Reading 1.3

Word/Letter Differentiation

Review with the students the difference between letters and words *(words are made up of letters)*. Point to the word *house* on page 12. Tell the students that *house* is a word, and the letters in *house* include *h*, *o*, *u*, *s*, and *e*. Tell the students that words mean something, and that most letters by themselves do not. Ask them what *house* means. Point to another word, such as *grass.* Ask them what letters make up the word *grass (g, r, a,* and *s).*

- Ask the students whether they notice anything different about two of the words in the first line of the poem.
- Let them know that *I* and *a* are unusual because they are spelled with only one letter each—a vowel. This is a good place to reinforce the idea that in English, every word and syllable must have a vowel.

Informal Assessment

WORDS AND LETTERS On a sheet of paper, write words and individual letters to assess students' abilities to differentiate between words and letters. Have students point to words versus letters. Using the ***Big Book,*** have students frame individual words and letters with their hands.

Writing 1.1

UNIVERSAL ACCESS: MEETING INDIVIDUAL NEEDS

Challenge

WRITING Write individual "If I were an (animal)" poems, using "If I Were a Mouse" as a model.

Listen/Speak 1.4

Teacher Tip **STAYING ON TASK** If students are having conversations about other subjects, remind them that they are supposed to talk only about the poem.

Discussing the Selection Listen/Speak 1.2

- Have volunteers retell the poem.
- Let a few students share what they liked about the poem. Then ask whether anyone has questions about it. You also could have the students ask each other questions about the poem.
- Have the students look at the illustration. Ask them how they can tell that the mouse is outside. *The boy and the mouse are on opposite sides of a window. The mouse is outside because behind him are grass hills, flowers, and other mice playing outside. The boy is inside sitting on his bed.*
- Ask the students what they think the mouse would say to the poet about what it is like to be a mouse. Encourage the students to imagine a conversation between the poet and the mouse.
- Have them discuss whether this poem made them think differently about mice. They also could talk about what it would be like to be another animal.
- Draw the students' attention to the rhyme and rhythm of the selection. Have them compare the rhyme and rhythm of this poem with those of the previous selections.
- With the students, refer back to the Focus Questions for the selection. Have all the questions been answered? If not, answer them now.

Have students record their responses to the selection in the Response Journal section of their Writer's Notebooks by drawing pictures of themselves as animals of their choice. Help the students label their drawings.

Review Selection Vocabulary

Have students review the selection vocabulary words for this lesson. Remind them that they discussed the meanings of these words at the beginning of the lesson. Have them add these and any other interesting words that they clarified while reading to the Vocabulary Words section of their Writer's Notebooks. The words from this selection are

house **grass**

- Have the students use the words in oral sentences. Help them expand their sentences by asking who, what, where, when, why, and how questions as needed.
- Ask the students to draw pictures that represent the words.

Encourage students to refer to the vocabulary words throughout the unit.

Print and Book Awareness

Word Boundaries Reading 1.3

- Ask the students how they can tell when a word begins or ends. Let them explain that the spaces separate the words.
- Have a volunteer come to the ***Big Book*** and point out the spaces between the words in the first line.
- Have the students look at the first line of the poem. Ask a volunteer to count the words in the line. If they have any difficulty, say each word as you point to it and have the students count aloud.
- Then write the first line of the poem on the board, leaving out the spaces between words, such as

  IfIwereamouse,
- Tell the students that if we didn't have spaces we wouldn't know where each word begins and ends.

Supporting the Reading

Comprehension Strategy: Visualizing

Remind the students that you modeled the use of the comprehension strategy Visualizing when you shared "If I Were a Mouse." Reread the poem, and this time have the students close their eyes and visualize what the mouse in the poem looks like. Encourage the students to describe what they visualized.

Purposes for Reading

Remind students that before they read the poem, the class discussed that the purpose of the poem was to explain to readers what it would be like to be a mouse. Ask students what the poem taught them about where mice live. Having read the poem, ask them what they think it would be like to be a mouse.

Objectives

- Students will begin working on their alphabet book.
- Students will apply concepts and ideas through a curricular connection.

Materials

- Class alphabet book

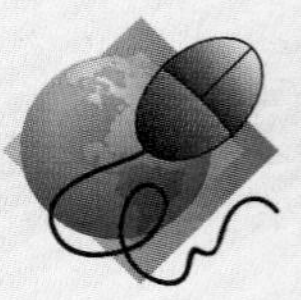

www.sra4kids.com
Web Connection
Help the students look for additional information about poems and rhymes by using the Web connections that are available at the Reading link of the SRA Web page.

Teacher Tip ALPHABET BOOKS
You have the option to make one class alphabet book in which everyone contributes something to a page, each student makes his or her own, or groups of students make their own books.

INVESTIGATION

Supporting the Investigation Reading 1.3

Investigating Concepts Beyond the Text

Tell the students they will continue with their unit project, the alphabet book, today.

- Display any alphabet books that you have available, and briefly discuss with students the ways the authors display the letters of the alphabet. If students brought books from home, give them time to share them. Comment on how the books are alike or different. Add any new ideas to the list you began on chart paper.
- Work with the students to create a sample page of an alphabet book on chart paper. Tell them that you want to make a page for the letter *a* and ask them what they would like to include on this page. Guide students to suggest that the page should include the capital *A* and the lowercase *a*. Write the letters on the page, or have a student do the writing.
- Ask the students to suggest other things to show on the page. If the students are reluctant to answer, you might ask whether any of their names begin with *A* or whether anyone knows a word that begins with the /a/ sound.
- Have the students work in groups for a few minutes to think of other words to include. Follow their suggestions to complete the sample page.

Concept/Question Board

After reading the selection, students should use the Concept/Question Board with or without your help to

- post any questions they asked about the selection before reading that they haven't answered yet.
- continue to post articles, pictures, or other items they have found during their investigations.
- read and think about posted questions, articles, pictures, or concepts that interest them and provide answers to their questions.

Art Connection

Illustrating Poems Reading 3.2

Purpose: To learn about the job of an illustrator

- Explain to the students than an illustrator's job is to help the readers visualize the author's ideas.
- Ask the students to pretend that this poem will need a new drawing to go with it. Tell them that they will be the illustrators.
- Ask the students to choose an animal they like and illustrate it.
- Encourage them to put whatever they want in their illustration to help others see what they are imagining. They may look back to previous poems and look at these illustrations for ideas.
- Encourage the students to describe their finished work and to tell how it illustrates their imagination.
- Write captions on the illustrations for students and display their work. Revisit these poems and illustrations on other days for students' enjoyment.

INVESTIGATION

Teacher Tip MATERIALS For this Art Connection, you will need the following materials: drawing paper and markers or crayons.

Objectives

Word Analysis Vocabulary

- **Classification** Using words from "If I Were a Mouse," develop the understanding that knowing a group of words in a category helps students more fully develop an understanding of the meaning of each word.

Writing Process Strategies

- **Introduction to the Writing Process** Building on the theme of Let's Read!, understand that prewriting involves getting ideas.

English Language Conventions

Listening, Speaking, Viewing

- Listening: Listening Attentively. Discuss and practice good listening skills.

Materials

- Writing Folder
- Language Arts Big Book, pp. 12–13

UNIVERSAL ACCESS:
MEETING INDIVIDUAL NEEDS

Reteach, Challenge, English-Language Development, and ***Intervention*** lessons are available to support the language arts instruction in this lesson.

Research in Action
Vocabulary

"Many types of vocabulary instruction have resulted in reliable gains in reading comprehension. Vocabulary instruction that does improve comprehension generally has some of the following characteristics: multiple exposures to instructed words, exposure to words in meaningful contexts, rich or varied information about each word, the establishment of ties between instructed words and students' own experience and prior knowledge, and an active role by students in the word-learning process."— *William E. Nagy and Patricia A. Herman.* 1987. "Breadth and Depth of Vocabulary Knowledge: Implications for Acquisition and Instruction" in *The Nature of Vocabulary Acquisition.*

OVERVIEW

Language Arts Overview

Word Analysis

Vocabulary The Vocabulary activity focuses on vocabulary from "If I Were a Mouse" to understand that words can be classified in different categories.

Vocabulary Skill Words

mouse **cat** **cow** **dog** **fish**

Writing Process Strategies

The Writing Process Strategies lesson introduces students to sharing to get ideas to write as they develop an understanding of prewriting.

English Language Conventions

Listening, Speaking, Viewing **Listening: Listening Attentively.** This lesson introduces students to the importance of good listening skills. Of the language processes—speaking, listening, reading, and writing—that make up language arts, listening is the one students use the most. In primary classrooms, where students are not yet fluent readers, almost all interactions take place orally. Listening involves the various skills of self-control, maintaining attention, and critical evaluation. It is an extremely important social skill, as well.

Word Analysis

Vocabulary

Classification: Animals Reading 1.17

Teach

- Explain that words can be part of different categories and those categories aid in the understanding of a word. For example, a mouse is an animal. In the animal category, it is a mammal. In the mammal category, it is one of the smaller mammals.

Guided Practice

- Write the words *ant, cat, cow, dog, fish, mouse,* and *wolf* in alphabetical order in a column on the board or chart paper.
- In another column have the students order the animals from big to small as you write them on the board. *(cow, wolf, dog, cat, fish, mouse, ant)*
- In another column have the students order the animals from the most number of legs to the least with the four-legged animals in any order. *(ant, cat, cow, dog, mouse, wolf, fish)*
- Conclude by emphasizing that by comparing words, students can learn more about each word.

Writing Process Strategies

Introduction to the Writing Process

Getting Ideas Writing 1.0, 1.1

Teach

- Introduce getting ideas for writing by reading ***Language Arts Big Book*** pages 12–13.
- Explain that after writers decide to write something, they start to generate a list of ideas.
- As a class, begin to generate a list of ideas to write about. These might include the following:
  - people I know
  - things at home
  - where I live

Guided Practice

- Have the students list or indicate by pictures things that they might want to write about. Start by listing people students know and where they live. Encourage them to consider things they see, things they read, or things they hear from other people. Have students keep their lists in their ***Writing Folders.***
- Review the lists and make a class list on chart paper of topics for writing. You might want to add to this list throughout the year. Students can use it when they can't think of anything to write about.

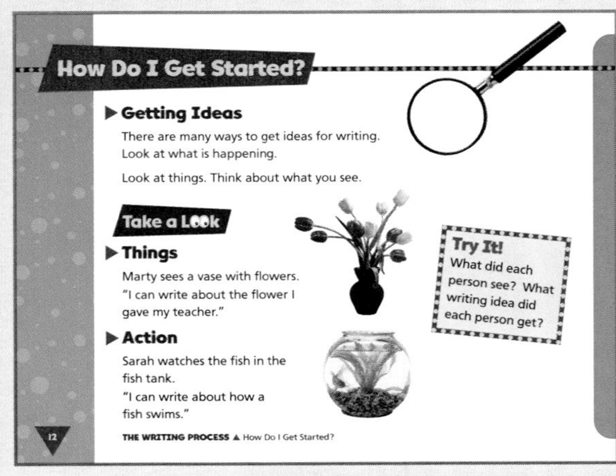
How Do I Get Started?

Getting Ideas

There are many ways to get ideas for writing. Look at what is happening.

Look at things. Think about what you see.

Take a Look

Things

Marty sees a vase with flowers. "I can write about the flower I gave my teacher."

Action

Sarah watches the fish in the fish tank. "I can write about how a fish swims."

Try It! What did each person see? What writing idea did each person get?

12

THE WRITING PROCESS ▲ How Do I Get Started?

***Language Arts Big Book* p. 12**

English Language Conventions

Listening, Speaking, Viewing

Listening: Listening Attentively

Teach Listen/Speak 1.1, 1.3

- Explain to students that every week they will be learning and practicing listening, speaking, and viewing skills. This week they are going to practice listening.
- Ask students why they might want to practice good listening in school. Discuss their responses. *(Good listeners can hear what they are supposed to do; can make friends more easily; don't always leap to conclusions.)*
- Explain that being a good listener takes practice and self-control.

Guided Practice

- Play a short, five-minute simple game of Simon Says to practice listening skills. Explain that students should do what you say if if your sentence begins with the words "Simon Says." Students should do nothing if you do not say, "Simon Says" before your command.
- **Teacher Model:**
  - Simon Says, look at the ceiling.
  - Simon Says, put your finger on your chin.
  - Simon Says, close your eyes.
  - Open your eyes.
- Have the students raise their hands if they opened their eyes without listening for "Simon Says."
- Close by explaining that listening is an important skill that will help students throughout their lives.

Informal Assessment

Note which students could follow most group directions and which students could not follow even simple directions without individual instruction.

Objectives

- Students will blend word parts orally to form words.
- Students will supply initial consonant sounds to complete words.
- Students will write letters of the alphabet.
- Students will associate sounds with letters.
- Students will read a *Pre-Decodable Book.*

Materials

- Lion Puppet
- Sound/Spelling Cards
- Routine Card 5
- Phonics Skills, p. 6
- Letter Cards
- High-Frequency Word Cards
- Pre-Decodable Book 2

Universal Access: Meeting Individual Needs

ELL Support

For ELD strategies, use the ***English-Language Development Guide,*** Unit 1, Lesson 5.

Intervention Support

For intervention strategies, use the ***Intervention Guide,*** Unit 1, Lesson 5.

Warming Up

Choose one or all of the following activities to focus the students' attention and to reinforce some of the concepts they have been working on.

"Alphabet Song" Listen/Speak 2.1

Sing the "Alphabet Song" with the students. Refer to page 61 in the Appendix for the words.

Syllable Blending and Counting Reading 1.3

- Say the following words, pausing briefly between syllables.
- Ask the students to put the words back together.

al . . . phabet	ca . . . mera	he . . . licopter
ba . . . by	pe . . . ppermint	

- Have the students say the words again, clapping along with each syllable. After each word, ask them to tell how many syllables the word has.

I Spy Reading 1.3, 1.4; Listen/Speak 2.1

- Play I Spy with the letters *h* and *j*.
  "I spy with my little eye,
  Something with the letter _______."
- To discover the word you have in mind, the students must point to a word in the classroom that has the appropriate letter. Have students recite the rhyme when they answer.

Phonemic Awareness

Oral Blending

Initial Consonant Sounds Reading 1.3, 1.4

- Tell the students that they will be putting some sounds together to make words.
- Have the students listen carefully. Use the following sounds and word parts: Tell them that they will hear a sound and a part of a word and they will make it into a whole word. Have students respond on your signal.

/t/ . . . oothache	/d/ . . . inosaur	/d/ . . . aytime
/m/ . . . idnight	/t/ . . . uesday	/t/ . . . omorrow
/b/ . . . eetle	/n/ . . . eedle	/n/ . . . oodle
/p/ . . . oodle	/p/ . . . each	/t/ . . . each

Initial Consonant Restoration Reading 1.3, 1.4

Tell the students that today the Lion Puppet wants to repeat their names instead of regular words. Tell them that if he makes any mistakes or leaves off any sounds, they should tell him exactly what to say.

Choosing students whose names begin with consonants, demonstrate a few turns before asking the students to play.

Teacher:	Susan
Puppet:	Usan
Teacher:	Usan? What is her name really? What sound did the puppet leave off?
Students:	Susan /s/!
Teacher:	Mary
Puppet:	Ary
Teacher:	Help the puppet. What did he forget?
Students:	Mary, /mmm/!

Continue playing with the names of different students. It is very important that the students isolate the initial phoneme vocally, for that is the value of the game.

PHONEMIC AWARENESS

Reading 1.10

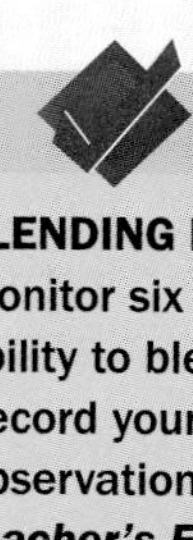

Informal Assessment

BLENDING INITIAL CONSONANTS Remember to monitor six or seven students per day on their ability to blend initial consonant sounds orally. Record your observations in the Teacher Observation Log in the ***Program Assessment Teacher's Edition.***

Teacher Tip BLENDING Be careful not to distort the initial consonant sound by stretching it out or trying to make it louder.

Teacher Tip INDIVIDUAL RESPONSES To make sure that every student is thinking on every turn, you might want to switch unpredictably from asking for a group response to asking for individual responses.

UNIVERSAL ACCESS: MEETING INDIVIDUAL NEEDS

ELL Support

WORD MEANING Make sure the English-language learners know the meanings of the words in the activities. During Workshop, use pictures, photos, objects, drawings, pantomime, or the ***English-Language Development Glossary*** to assist students.

LESSON MODELS VIDEOCASSETTE Use the ***Lesson Models Videocassette*** at this time for an Oral Blending lesson model.

Teacher Tip WRITING LETTERS As you introduce the letters, have the students write the letters in the air or on the surface in front of them.

LETTER RECOGNITION

Letter Recognition

Exploring *Kk, Ll,* and *Mm* Reading 1.3; Writing 1.3

Introduce the names and shapes of the letters *Kk*, *Ll*, and *Mm*, following the same procedures as used in previous lessons.

- Touch the ***Sound/Spelling Card*** and name the letter.
- Write the letter on the board or on the overhead, explaining how the letter is made.
- Have the students write and proofread the letters.

Kk

k
c
ck

Camera

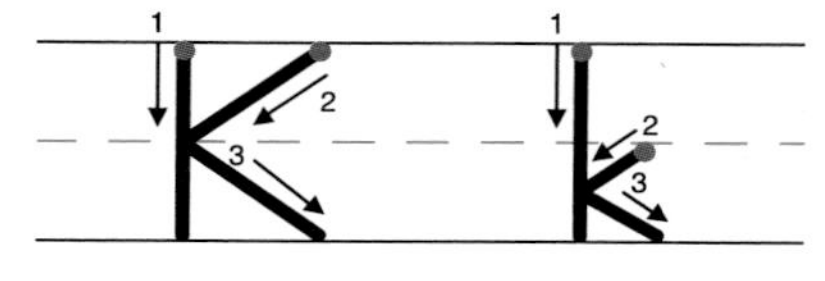

K Starting point, straight down
Starting point, slanting down left
touching the line,
slanting down right: capital *K*

k Starting point, straight down
Starting point, slanting down left,
touching the line,
slanting down right: small *k*

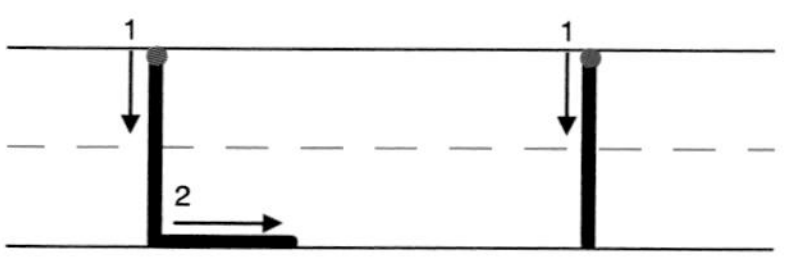

L Starting point, straight down,
straight right: capital *L*

l Starting point, straight down: small *l*

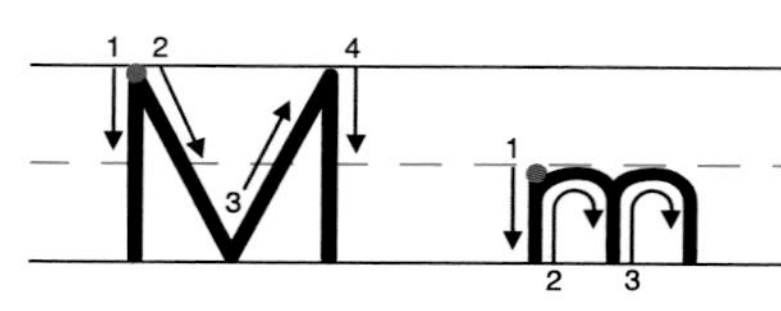

M Starting point, straight down
Starting point, slanting down right to the point, slanting back up to the right,
straight down: capital *M*

m Starting point, straight down, back up,
around right, straight down, back up,
around right, straight down: small *m*

Research in Action
Learning About Letters

Children appear to learn about letters by first learning letter names, then letter shapes, and finally letter sounds. For many children, this learning begins long before they enter school. At home, they learn letter names by singing songs and reciting rhymes, which provides them with the necessary background for learning letter shapes. Later, this familiarity with letter names and shapes may protect children from confusing letters with sounds as they learn sound-letter correspondences. Children who enter school with little knowledge about letter names and shapes are more likely to confuse letter names with letter sounds. *(Marilyn Jager Adams)*

Adams, Marilyn J. 1990. *Beginning to read: Thinking and learning about print.* Cambridge, MA: The MIT Press.

Reviewing Sounds and Letters

Introducing Consonant Sounds Reading 1.3, 1.4

- Write silly sentences on the board using *Kk*, *Ll*, and *Mm*. For example; write this sentence:

  Kind Katie kisses kicking kangaroos.

- Read the sentence aloud, pointing to the key letter each time you say it. Then have volunteers come up and underline all the key letters in the sentence. Read the sentence again as a class, having the students exaggerate the letter's sound with you.
- Ask volunteers to tell why *Kind* and *Katie* begin with capital *K*.
- Ask whether any of their names begin with /k/. Write their names on the board.
- Ask the students to think of and say other words that begin with *Kk*. Because students read orally, suggestions that begin with *Cc* should be praised. On the board, make a separate list of such words, pointing out that sometimes the sound for the letter *Cc* is also /k/.
- Repeat with *Ll* and *Mm*, using sentences such as

  Little Lizzy loves lemon lollipops.
  Max makes messy, mushy meatballs.

- Reread each sentence, framing each word. Have the students repeat each word and identify the beginning letter. Explain that all the words together form a sentence.

Phonics Skills Writing 1.3

Help the students complete ***Phonics Skills*** page 6. Have the students write the letters as a class, saying the words together. Remind them to space appropriately on each line of the page.

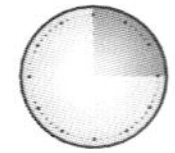

Dictation Reading 1.3

Dictation Reading 1.3, 1.11; Eng. Lang. Conv. 1.8

- Ask the students to take out writing materials. Dictate the following letters, giving the students time to rewrite each before dictating the next:

  g c C K k M m L l f

- Dictate the high-frequency words below. Use each word in a sentence and remind the students to look in the High-Frequency Word Bank for guidance and confirmation of their spelling. Encourage them to say each word after you, use it in a sentence, and then write it.

  the, a, on, is

- Collect the papers to see how the students are progressing.

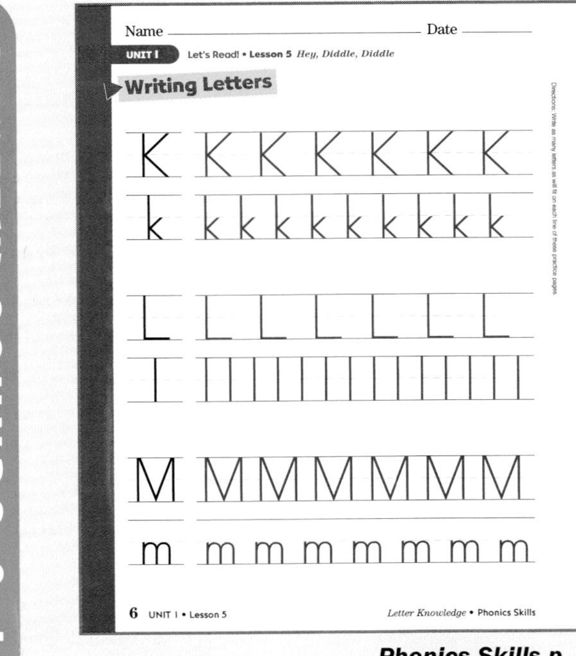

Name ____ Date ____

UNIT 1 Let's Read! • Lesson 5 *Hey, Diddle, Diddle*

Writing Letters

K K K K K K K

k k k k k k k k k k

L L L L L L L

l l l l l l l l l l l l

M M M M M M M

m m m m m m m m

6 UNIT 1 • Lesson 5 *Letter Knowledge* • Phonics Skills

***Phonics Skills* p. 6**

Reading 1.3; Writing 1.3

UNIVERSAL ACCESS:
MEETING INDIVIDUAL NEEDS

Reteach

LETTER FORMATION For additional practice with letter formation, use ***Reteach: Phonics Skills*** page 6 during Workshop.

Challenge

PHONICS Use ***Challenge: Phonics Skills*** page 5 with students who are ready for a challenge.

Intervention Tip

LETTER RECOGNITION During Workshop, provide help for students who still are having difficulty recognizing letters. Write an array of letters on the board, and have the students find letters you say, then reverse. Point to a letter and ask for a name. Also provide extra practice for students who are experiencing difficulty with letter formation.

Reading a Pre-Decodable Book

Core Set, Book 2: *The Egg*

High-Frequency Words Reading 1.3

The high-frequency words introduced in this book are *an*, *is*, and *was*. Write each word individually on the board and ask students to say the word. Pronounce them, have the students repeat them, spell them together, and have them say the words again. Then have volunteers use *an*, *is*, and *was* in sentences. Review the high-frequency words already in the High-Frequency Word Bank. Have students volunteer to read the ones they recognize.

Reading Recommendations Reading 1.1, 1.2, 1.3, 1.8

- The nondecodable word in the book is *egg*. Write *egg* on the board. Ask the students to say the word. Pronounce it, have the students repeat it, spell it together, and have them say it again. Then have volunteers use *egg* in sentences.
- Have the students read the title and browse the story.
- Have students read a page silently, then read the page aloud. Repeat this procedure for each page.
- Have another student reread the page before going on.
- Reread the story at least twice, calling on different students to read. Then have the entire group do a choral reading of the story.

Teacher Tip **HIGH-FREQUENCY WORD BANK** Add the high-frequency words from this book to the Word Bank. Have students write the words on 3X5 cards to take home to practice or add to their ring of words.

is **was** **an**

Pre-Decodable Book 2

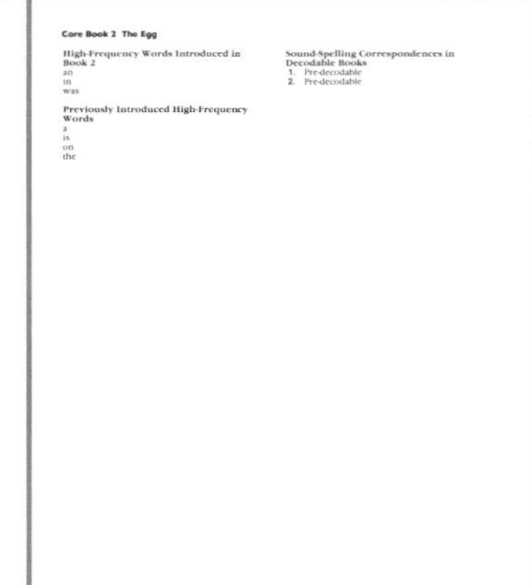

Core Book 2 The Egg

High-Frequency Words Introduced in Book 2
an
in
was

Previously Introduced High-Frequency Words
a
is
on
the

Sound-Spelling Correspondences in Decodable Books
1. Pre-decodable
2. Pre-decodable

Responding Reading 2.2; Listen/Speak 1.2, 2.2

- Invite the students to discuss any hard words they encountered in *The Egg* and how they figured out these words. Call on volunteers to retell the story.
- To make sure the students are focusing on the story, ask the following questions, having the students answer by pointing to and reading aloud the words:

  What is on the island? *(On an island is a forest.)*

  What is on the branch? *(On the branch is a nest.)*

  What is in the nest? *(In the nest is an egg.)*

  What was in the egg? *(In the egg was a bird.)*

Building Fluency Reading 1.16

Encourage partners to build fluency rereading ***Decodable Book 2,*** *The Egg*, of the Core Set. The first time through, one partner should read the odd-numbered pages and the other the even-numbered pages. Review the difference between odd and even if students need clarification. For the second reading, the partners should switch pages. After the second reading, the partners should reread ***Decodable Book 1,*** *A Table*, and continue to read to each other.

Universal Access: Meeting Individual Needs

ELL Tip

PICTURES Make sure English-language learners can name each rebus before reading the book.

Reading 1.11, 1.16

Informal Assessment

PRE-DECODABLES Have individual students or small groups read the story to you. Note which students know the high-frequency words. Note also which students are reading the rebus stories in a fluent manner. Finally, have students retell the story to assess comprehension.

Teacher Tip NONDECODABLE WORDS Always refer to the inside back cover of the *Decodable Book* for the words that need to be taught before the students read the book.

Routine Card
Refer to *Routine 5* for reading *Decodable Books.*

Pages 14–15 of *Let's Read!*

SELECTION INTRODUCTION

About the Illustrator Reading 3.2

BONNIE MACKAIN spent a lot of time reading library books when she was a child. She would copy and trace the pictures in the books. Her style of art also has been influenced by the physical humor of silent film stars and cartoon characters. Bonnie lives in Southern California and enjoys singing, crossword puzzles, and the Internet.

Other Books Illustrated by Bonnie MacKain

One Hundred Hungry Ants, *A Remainder of One*

Objectives

- Students will use the Table of Contents.
- Students will discuss selection vocabulary.
- Students will identify words with the letters *Ll* and *Mm*.
- Students will identify left and right directionality.
- Students will review counting by using the alphabet.

Materials

- Big Book *Let's Read!*
- Home Connection, p.3
- Letter Cards

Selection Summary

Genre: Poetry

For generations, students have found this rhyme wonderfully silly, and Bonnie MacKain's illustrations add to the humor.

The elements of poetry are listed below. Poetry may have one or more of these elements.

- Sentences are sometimes broken into parts. Each part is on a line of its own.
- Words that rhyme are often used.
- The lines of a poem often have rhythm, or meter.
- Some words may be repeated.

Inquiry Connections

In this selection of the ***Big Book*** the students will listen to "Hey, Diddle, Diddle."

Key concepts to be investigated are

- the elements of poetry
- matching oral words to printed words
- becoming more aware of print

Direct the students to the Concept/Question Board. Encourage them to post any questions or ideas they have about the unit.

- Make sure the students put their names or initials on anything they post on the Board.
- Tell them that they can post something on the Board any day. Be sure to have students discuss what they put on the Board with the class.

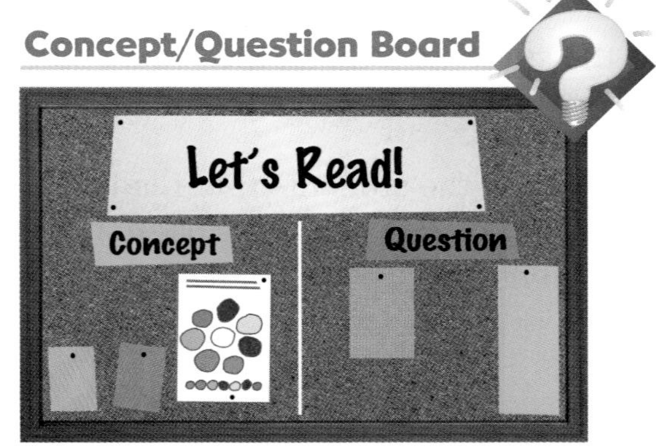

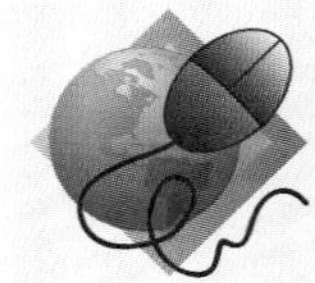

www.sra4kids.com
Web Connection
Help the students look for additional information about nursery rhymes by using the Web connections that are available at the Reading link of the SRA Web page.

Teacher Tip **CONCEPT/QUESTION BOARD** Remind the students that when working on a unit, they will have questions that they will want answered. New questions will arise as the unit proceeds. Tell them that good readers continue to generate questions as they get deeper into a topic.

Build Background

Activate Prior Knowledge

- Ask the students how high they think a cow can jump, and invite the students to try jumping like a cow.
- Then invite them to tell about any stories or rhymes they know that are about things that just couldn't happen.

Preview and Prepare

Browse Listen/Speak 2.1

- Open the ***Big Book*** *Let's Read!* to the Table of Contents. Tell the students to help you find the page that the rhyme "Hey, Diddle, Diddle" begins on. Have a volunteer point to the page number. Help the student find and turn to page 14.
- Invite the students to look at the illustrations and comment on what they notice.
- Because "Hey, Diddle, Diddle" is well known, the students might figure out which rhyme this is from the pictures. Ask if anyone knows the rhyme. Invite those who do to recite it together.
- Point out that no author is listed for this rhyme because it was written long ago, and no one knows who wrote it. Then read the illustrator's name.
- Before reading the selection to the students, read through the Focus Questions on the first page of the selection together. Briefly discuss the questions, and tell the students to keep these questions in mind as you read.

Set Purposes

Explain to the students that readers read poems for many reasons. Suggest that the reason for reading this poem might be to enjoy the rhyme and the silly situations.

Universal Access: Meeting Individual Needs

ELL Support

For ELD strategies, use the ***English-Language Development Guide,*** Unit 1, Lesson 5.

Intervention Support

For intervention strategies, use the ***Intervention Guide,*** Unit 1, Lesson 5.

Teacher Tip BROWSE Remind the students that good readers browse before reading. Tell them that they should be getting in the habit of browsing before they read, and that doing so can help them activate prior knowledge relevant to the selection.

Routine Card
Refer to ***Routine 11*** for the procedure for reading the selection.

Selection Vocabulary Reading 1.7

- Write the following word on the board and read it out loud.

  fiddle

- Open the ***Big Book*** *Let's Read!* to pages 14 and 15, and call attention to the fiddle in the first drawing. Ask the students to name this instrument. *(violin, fiddle)*
- Explain that the expression "hey, diddle, diddle" is a silly expression. It is funny to say and *diddle* rhymes with *fiddle*. Ask whether anyone can make a silly rhyme for *violin* by changing the first sound. *(hey, diolin, diolin)*

Reading Recommendations

Read Aloud

- Read the poem in a quick and spirited manner, without pausing.
- Tell students that the question word *who* refers to the characters in a selection. The characters might be people or animals or made-up creatures. Tell students to listen for the characters in the poem.
- During rereadings, invite the students to join in as you point to each word.

Using Comprehension Strategies Listen/Speak 1.2

Comprehension strategy instruction allows the students to become aware of what good readers do when they read. Good readers constantly check their understanding as they are reading and ask themselves questions. Skilled readers also recognize when they are having problems understanding a selection and stop to use various comprehension strategies to help them make sense of what they are reading.

During the reading of this selection, you will model the use of the following comprehension strategy:

- **Asking Questions** helps readers focus their attention on what they are reading, and engages them in deeper understanding of themes, concepts, and ideas.

Teacher Tip HIGH-FREQUENCY WORDS The following high-frequency word appears in the selection: *the.* Point to this word in the High-Frequency Word Bank, have students read it, and encourage them to read *the* with you when you encounter it in the reading.

Routine Card
Refer to ***Routine 10*** for the Selection Vocabulary procedure.

Teacher Tip RHYME Because many students will be familiar with the rhyme, more students than usual should be able to read the rhyme along with you. Have the students identify the words that repeat and the words that rhyme in "Hey, Diddle, Diddle."

Universal Access: Meeting Individual Needs

ELL Support

WORD MEANING Using the suggestion in the ***English-Language Development Guide,*** preteach key vocabulary words.

Teacher Tip ASKING QUESTIONS An extended lesson on Asking Questions can be found on page T111. This lesson is intended to give extra practice with asking questions.

COMPREHENSION

Comprehension Strategies

Teacher Modeling

Asking Questions *When we read, we can better understand what we are reading if we ask questions. Look at the illustrations on pages 14–15. Is this poem realistic?*

Reading 1.4

Phonemic Awareness

Initial Consonant Sounds

Remind the students that they put together sounds to make words when they did the previous section. Tell the students that now you are going to say just the beginning sound of a word from the poem and then the rest of the word. Ask the students to be ready to say the whole word. Use the following words:

/d/ . . . iddle	/k/ . . . ow	/l/ . . . ittle
/k/ . . . at	/j/ . . . umped	/d/ . . . og
/f/ . . . iddle	/m/ . . . oon	/d/ . . . ish

Teacher Tip COMPREHENSION Good readers constantly evaluate their understanding of what they read. Stop often to make sure you and the students are doing this.

Universal Access: Listen/Speak 2.1

Meeting Individual Needs

ELL Tip

DRAMATIZE THE POEM Read the poem to the English-language learners and tell them that it is a poem written for them to have fun with. Have the students look at the pictures for the poem. Divide the class into four groups and assign each a line of the poem to dramatize. While the students are working in their groups, remind them to use an appropriate volume level. After they have practiced their routines, have the students chant the poem with you while each group acts out its line in turn.

Reteach

READING THE POEM Divide the students into two groups and help them say the rhyme as a call-response: One group says the first part of each phrase and the other group says the second part.

Focus Questions What nursery rhymes do you know? What words rhyme with fiddle?

illustrated by Bonnie MacKain

Hey, diddle, diddle!
The cat and the fiddle,
The cow jumped over the moon;

14

California Theme Connection
Reading/Language Arts

One of READ California's programs is the Readapalooza Reader Program. In this program the child first finds a sponsor. Then with his or her sponsors, they decide how many pages to read to earn a reward and what the reward will be. Every time the child reaches his or her goal, the sponsor marks or punches the child's Readapalooza Reader Bookmark. When the book mark is completely full, the child earns the reward. Discuss with students how the Readapalooza Reader Program encourages them to read more.

Letter Recognition Reading 1.3

l, m

- Ask the students to look for words in the selection that begin with either *l* or *m*. Have volunteers go to the ***Big Book*** and point to those letters. *(little, laughed, moon)*
- If time permits, have the students look for words that begin with the other letters that they have learned: *a, b, c, d, e, f, g, h, i, j,* and *k*.

Universal Access: Meeting Individual Needs

Intervention Tip

LETTER RECOGNITION If the students are having difficulty recognizing the letters *Ll* and *Mm,* help them find those letters in previous poems.

Informal Assessment

LETTER KNOWLEDGE Continue assessing the students' letter knowledge using letter arrays or individual ***Letter Cards A–M.*** Name the letter and have the students point to the letter in the array or hold up the appropriate ***Letter Card.*** Then point to a letter and have the students name the letter.

Teacher Tip READING FOR ENJOYMENT Remind the students to spend about 20 minutes reading after school.

Teacher Tip DISCUSSION Encourage all students to participate in class discussions. Be careful not to let a few students dominate class discussions.

UNIVERSAL ACCESS: Reading 2.6
MEETING INDIVIDUAL NEEDS

Challenge

EXPLORING NURSERY RHYMES Explain that "Hey, Diddle, Diddle" is an old rhyme that many different people have illustrated over the years. Show the students the poem in your own favorite nursery rhyme collection and have them compare the illustrations and topics with those in the ***Big Book*** *Let's Read!* Let them say what they like about each. Discuss the ways in which the poem uses rhyme and repetition.

Science/Social Studies Connection Center
Refer to the ***Science/Social Studies Connection Center*** for a descriptive drawing activity.

Discussing the Selection Reading 2.2; Listen/Speak 1.5

- Ask the students to tell who the characters are in "Hey, Diddle, Diddle" *(cat, cow, dog, dish, and spoon).*
- Ask the students to think about all the things in the poem that couldn't really happen.
- Ask them why they think the cow is wearing a space suit.
- Suggest to the students that they should think of other silly things that the author might have included in the poem. What if there were a table in the poem? A duck? What might they do?
- Have the students discuss their reactions to the rhyme. Did they think it was funny? Confusing? Was anything difficult to understand?
- How would the students compare the cow in this poem to the cow in "The Purple Cow"?
- With the students, refer to the Focus Questions for the selection. Have all the questions been answered? If not, answer them now.

Have the students record their responses to the selection in the Response Journal section of their Writer's Notebooks by drawing pictures of other silly events that the selection brought to mind. Help the students label their drawings.

Review Selection Vocabulary

Have students review the selection vocabulary word for this lesson. Remind them that they discussed the meaning of this word at the beginning of the lesson. Have them add this and any other interesting words that they clarified while reading to the Vocabulary Words section of their Writer's Notebooks. The word from this selection is

fiddle

- Have the students use the word in oral sentences. Help the students expand their sentences by asking who, what, where, when, why, and how questions.
- Ask the students to draw a picture that represents the word.

Encourage students to refer to the vocabulary words throughout the unit.

Print and Book Awareness

Print Directionality

- Observe that "Hey, Diddle, Diddle" is printed on two pages and ask a volunteer to go to the ***Big Book*** and point to the page that should be read first.
- Introduce the terms *left* and *right* and help the students identify and raise their left and right hands in turn. Remind them that we begin reading on the left-hand page—the page on the same side as our left hand when we hold the book.
- As you discuss the left-to-right and top-to-bottom directionality of reading print, be sure to let the students know that we also write in the same manner. Remind them that as they write in their Writer's Notebooks or complete the Independent and Collaborative Writing projects, they should be aware that they are writing from left to right and top to bottom.
- Ask volunteers to point to the beginnings of various lines and remind the students that we begin reading each line on the left side of the page.

Supporting the Reading

Comprehension Strategy: Asking Questions Listen/Speak 1.2

Remind the students that you modeled the use of the comprehension strategy Asking Questions when you read "Hey, Diddle, Diddle." Display the ***Big Book*** *Let's Read!* pages 14 and 15. Invite the students to ask any other questions they might have about the poem. Asking questions can help students better understand a reading selection.

Purposes for Reading

Remind students that before reading the poem, they talked about enjoying the poem and the silly situations in the poem. Ask the students to describe their favorite silly situations.

Home Connection

Distribute ***Home Connection*** page 3. Encourage the students to discuss the poems that were read this week with their families. ***Home Connection*** is also available in Spanish on page 4.

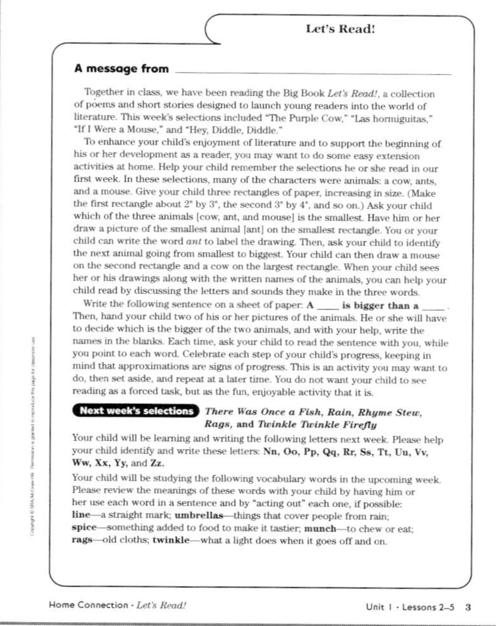

Let's Read!

A message from ______________________

Together in class, we have been reading the Big Book *Let's Read!*, a collection of poems and short stories designed to launch young readers into the world of literature. This week's selections included "The Purple Cow," "Las hormiguitas," "If I Were a Mouse," and "Hey, Diddle, Diddle."

To enhance your child's enjoyment of literature and to support the beginning of his or her development as a reader, you may want to do some easy extension activities at home. Help your child remember the selections he or she read in our first week. In these selections, many of the characters were animals: a cow, ants, and a mouse. Give your child three rectangles of paper, increasing in size. (Make the first rectangle about 2" by 3", the second 3" by 4", and so on.) Ask your child which of the three animals [cow, ant, and mouse] is the smallest. Have him or her draw a picture of the smallest animal [ant] on the smallest rectangle. You or your child can write the word *ant* to label the drawing. Then, ask your child to identify the next animal going from smallest to biggest. Your child can then draw a mouse on the second rectangle and a cow on the largest rectangle. When your child sees her or his drawings along with the written names of the animals, you can help your child read by discussing the letters and sounds they make in the three words.

Write the following sentence on a sheet of paper: **A ____ is bigger than a ____**. Then, hand your child two of his or her pictures of the animals. He or she will have to decide which is the bigger of the two animals, and with your help, write the names in the blanks. Each time, ask your child to read the sentence with you, while you point to each word. Celebrate each step of your child's progress, keeping in mind that approximations are signs of progress. This is an activity you may want to do, then set aside, and repeat at a later time. You do not want your child to see reading as a forced task, but as the fun, enjoyable activity that it is.

Next week's selections ***There Was Once a Fish*, *Rain*, *Rhyme Stew*, *Rags*, and *Twinkle Twinkle Firefly***

Your child will be learning and writing the following letters next week. Please help your child identify and write these letters: **Nn, Oo, Pp, Qq, Rr, Ss, Tt, Uu, Vv, Ww, Xx, Yy,** and **Zz.**

Your child will be studying the following vocabulary words in the upcoming week. Please review the meanings of these words with your child by having him or her use each word in a sentence and by "acting out" each one, if possible: **line**—a straight mark; **umbrellas**—things that cover people from rain; **spice**—something added to food to make it tastier; **munch**—to chew or eat; **rags**—old cloths; **twinkle**—what a light does when it goes off and on.

Home Connection · *Let's Read!* Unit 1 · Lessons 2–5 3

***Home Connection* p. 3**

Teacher Tip COMPREHENSION STRATEGIES Tell students that skilled readers think about the questions that come up about the topic they are reading about, and they keep coming back to those questions. As they read, tell the students to keep in mind the questions on the Concept/Question Board. Have them make notes to themselves in the Response Journal section of their Writer's Notebooks about which questions seem important and about what information in the selections seems most important. Tell them that skilled readers always think about what is important in selections, and they try to remember this important information.

Objectives

- Students will continue working on their Alphabet Books.
- Students will apply concepts and ideas through a curricular connection.

Materials

- Class alphabet book

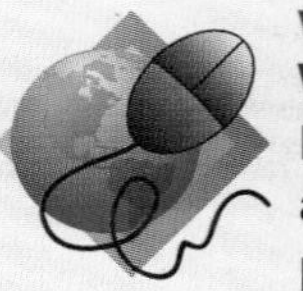

www.sra4kids.com
Web Connection
Help the students look for additional information about poems and rhymes by using the Web connections that are available at the Reading link of the SRA Web page.

INVESTIGATION

Supporting the Investigation

Investigating Concepts Beyond the Text Reading 1.3

Tell the students that they will continue working on the class alphabet book.

- Refer back to the list of suggestions made by the students. Review their ideas. Tell the students that they are going to begin working on their own pages for the class alphabet book.
- Distribute drawing paper or story paper and discuss with the students what they might include on their pages. Encourage a variety of suggestions. For example, they might want to draw the pictures or cut them from magazines. Emphasize that they can decide for themselves what they want to include. Have supplies such as crayons, markers, scissors, paste, and old magazines or catalogs available.
- Remind the students to plan before they begin to write on or design their pages. Assign the letters *a*, *b*, *c*, and *d*.

Concept/Question Board

Encourage the students to add something to the Concept/Question Board at this time. You may also want to discuss anything that the students posted recently.

Math Connections

Alphabet Counting Listen/Speak 2.1

Purpose: To review counting by using the alphabet

On the board, write the letters *A*, *B*, and *C*. Ask which letter is in the middle. Now add the letters *D* and *E* and ask the same thing. Show the students how to find the middle by counting in from each end. Place one hand over the *A* and the other over the *E* and count in—*1*, *2*. Tell the students that your hands meet over the letter in the middle. Add the letter *F* and do the same thing. Point out that sometimes no one letter is in the middle.

Add the rest of the letters of the alphabet, keeping all letters on the same row across the board. Lead the class in reciting the "Alphabet Song" learned in Lesson 1.

UNIVERSAL ACCESS: Reading 1.3

MEETING INDIVIDUAL NEEDS

Reteach

ALPHABET PRACTICE Pin an alphabet letter to each student in the group, beginning with A and going as far as you can. Then do the Alphabet Counting activity with the students.

Challenge

ALPHABET GAME Make four sets of ***Letter Cards*** (or any 12 letters) and teach the students to play Old Maid using the ***Letter Cards*** instead of regular playing cards.

Teacher Tip MATERIALS You will need the "Alphabet Song" for this activity.

Objectives

Word Analysis Vocabulary

- **Classification.** Using animal words from the first five selections, develop the understanding that knowing a group of words in a category helps students more fully develop an understanding of the meaning of each word.

Writing Process Strategies

- **Introduction to the Writing Process.** Building on the theme Let's Read!, practice making a list to generate ideas to write an autobiography.

English Language Conventions

- **Penmanship: Letters Are Lines.** To extend the letter formation instruction in Phonics and Fluency and understand that letters are made of different types of lines.

Materials

- Language Arts Big Book, pp. 10–12
- Writer's Workbook, p. 2
- Writer's Notebook
- Language Arts Transparency 1

Universal Access: Meeting Individual Needs

Reteach, Challenge, English-Language Development, and ***Intervention*** lessons are available to support the language arts instruction in this lesson.

OVERVIEW

Language Arts Overview

Word Analysis

Vocabulary The first five selections provide a bank of animal vocabulary words that can help students develop an understanding of word classifications to build vocabulary.

Vocabulary Skill Words

cat **cow** **dog** **list** **words** **names**

Writing Process Strategies

The Writing Process Strategies lesson involves students in generating ideas for an autobiography. Many students have difficulty generating writing ideas and will complain that they can't think of anything to write. Practice in brainstorming ideas and stimulating ideas through experiences can help them take responsibility for idea generation.

English Language Conventions

Penmanship **Letters Are Lines** This lesson reinforces the letter formation instruction in Phonics and Fluency by teaching students that letters are made of vertical, horizontal, curved, and slanted lines. The instruction in this lesson presents a ball-and-stick model of manuscript handwriting. Continuous stroke models are available in the Appendix of this ***Teacher's Edition.***

Word Analysis

Vocabulary

Classification: Animals Reading 1.17

Teach

- Make a list of the animal words from the first five sections in a column on the board. *(ant, cat, cow, dog, fish, mouse, wolf)*
- Next, play a word association game, asking each student to take turns suggesting a similar type of animal or a type of the given animal. *(ant—fly, cat—lion, cow—goat, dog—German shepherd, fish—trout, mouse—chipmunk, wolf—fox)*

Guided Practice

- Continue taking turns suggesting animal words as you write them on the board.
- Close by counting the number of different vocabulary words you have written and commenting on how many different animal words students know.

Informal Assessment

Take note of students who are not contributing animal names to the discussion. For those students who do not contribute, consider whether it is a vocabulary, speaking, or social concern.

Writing Process Strategies

Introduction to the Writing Process Writing 1.0, 1.1

Getting Ideas for Autobiography

Teach

- Introduce getting ideas for an autobiography by reading ***Language Arts Big Book*** pages 14–17.
- **Teacher Model:** Model inspiration for writing. *I want to write a little story about me so you can know me better. This is called an autobiography. I need to think of some things that will tell about me.*
- Then as a class, make a list of ideas that students can write about themselves. Use ***Language Arts Transparency 1*** to make a web organizer with the word *Me* in the middle. These could include the following:
  - what I look like
  - my age
  - what I like to do
  - my favorite animal
  - my favorite food
  - my family
  - my pets
  - my home
  - my favorite game

Independent Practice

- Have students use ***Writer's Workbook*** page 2 to draw or record their personal list of ideas.

Name ______________________ Date __________

UNIT 1 Let's Read! • Lesson 5 *Hey Diddle, Diddle*

Autobiography

Draw pictures about you.
Write words about you.

1. 2.

3. 4.

Review to see that students have drawn and written words about themselves.

2 UNIT 1 • Lesson 5 *Autobiography* • Writer's Workbook

***Writer's Workbook* p. 2**

English Language Conventions

Penmanship Writing 1.3

Letters Are Lines

Teach

- Explain to the students that every week they will be learning how to write letters of the alphabet, and that we call this Penmanship or Handwriting.
- Tell the students to think about the letters they practiced in Phonics and Fluency. Explain that all those letters are made up of four lines: curved lines, vertical lines, horizontal lines, and slanted lines.
- **Teacher Model:** Model the formation of these lines on the board.

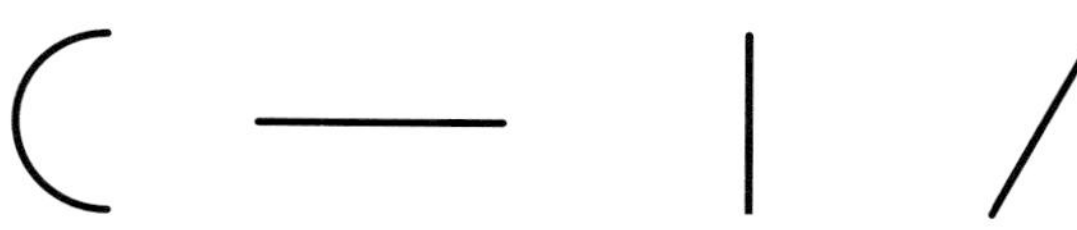

Guided Practice

- Write the letters *A*, *B*, *C*, and *D* on the board.
- Explain that the letter *C* is made out of a curved line. Invite a student to come to the board and trace the curved line in *C*.
- Tell the students that there also are curves in *B* and *D*. Invite another student to come to the board and trace the curves in *B* and *D*.
- Tell the students that *B* and *D* also have vertical lines. Invite another student to trace the vertical lines in *B* and *D*.
- Have another student trace the two slanted lines in *A*. Invite a student to the board to trace the horizontal line in *A*.
- Have the students practice drawing curved, vertical, horizontal, and slanted lines on a sheet of first-grade paper.

Informal Assessment

As students practice writing different types of lines, observe how they hold their pencils and how much control they have in making each stroke.

Leveled Practice

Reteach: Phonics Skills
Pages 7–13

Challenge: Phonics Skills
Pages 6–11

Reteach: Comprehension and Language Arts Skills
Pages 4–5

Challenge: Comprehension and Language Arts Skills
Pages 4–5

ELD Workbook

Intervention Workbook

Additional Materials
Pre-Decodable Book 3

Leveled Classroom Library*

Encourage students to read for at least 20 minutes daily outside of class. Have them read books in the ***Leveled Classroom Library,*** which supports the unit theme and helps students develop their vocabulary by reading independently.

America

BY W. NIKOLA-LISA. LEE AND LOW BOOKS, INC., 1997.

This book about America describes its features through opposites. The work of fourteen American artists is featured. **(Easy)**

The Old Woman Who Loved to Read

BY JOHN WINCH. HOLIDAY HOUSE, 1996.

The old woman in this story loves to read, but must endure many obstacles until she is able to do so. **(Average)**

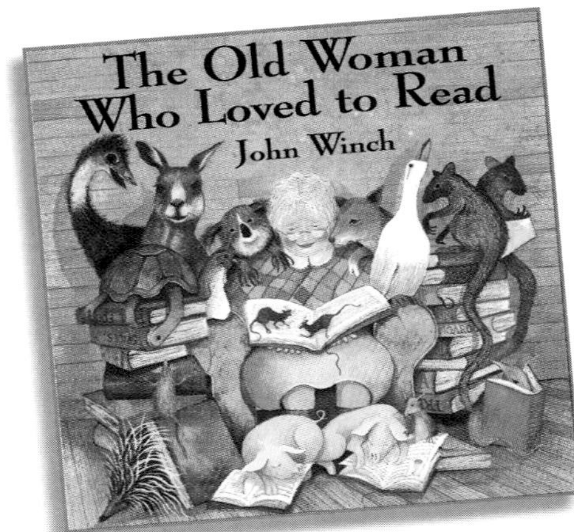

More Than Anything Else

BY MARIE BRADBY. ORCHARD BOOKS, 1995.

More than anything else, Booker wants to learn to read. This is a fictionalized account of the life of Booker T. Washington. **(Advanced)**

* These books, which support the unit theme Let's Read!, are part of a 60-book ***Leveled Classroom Library*** available for purchase from SRA/McGraw-Hill. **Note:** Teachers should preview any trade books for appropriateness in their classrooms before recommending them to students.

TECHNOLOGY

Web Connections

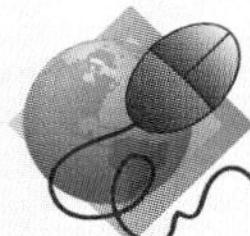

www.sra4kids.com
Let's Read! Web Site

CD-ROM

* ***The Ultimate Writing and Creativity Center***
THE LEARNING COMPANY

Videocassette

* **Lesson Model Videocassette**
SRA/MCGRAW-HILL, 2002

Computer Skills

* **Basic Computer Skills**

Audiocassettes/CDs

* **Listening Library Let's Read!**
SRA/MCGRAW-HILL, 2002

* **Sound Spelling Card Stories**
SRA/MCGRAW-HILL, 2002

Titles preceded by an asterisk (*) are available through SRA/McGraw-Hill. Other titles can be obtained by contacting the publisher listed with the title.

LESSON PLANNER

	DAY 1	DAY 2
1 Preparing to Read Materials ■ Sound/Spelling Cards ■ Pre-Decodable Books ■ Decodable Books ■ Phonics Skills ■ ELD Workbook ■ Intervention Workbook	Warming Up, p. T124 Phonemic Awareness, p. T125 Letter Recognition, p. T126 Reviewing Sounds and Letters ■ Listening for Vowel Sounds, p. T128 ■ Introducing Consonant Sounds, p. T128 Dictation and Spelling, p. T129	Warming Up, p. T142 Phonemic Awareness, pp. T143–T144 Letter Recognition, pp. T145–T146 Reviewing Sounds and Letters ■ Introducing Consonant Sounds, p. T146 Dictation and Spelling, p. T147 Reading a Pre-Decodable Book ■ *Book 3, The Baby,* "The Cake," pp. T148–T149
2 Reading & Responding Materials ■ Big Book *Let's Read!* ■ Teacher Observation Log ■ Home Connection ■ Comprehension and Language Arts Skills ■ ELD Workbook ■ Intervention Workbook	Build Background, p. T132 Preview and Prepare, p. T132 Selection Vocabulary, p. T133 Reading Recommendations, p. T133 Big Book *Let's Read!*, pp. 16–17 Comprehension Strategies, p. T134 Discussing the Selection, p. T136 Letter Recognition, p. T135 Review Selection Vocabulary, p. T136 Print and Book Awareness, p. T137 Supporting the Reading, p. T137	Build Background, p. T152 Preview and Prepare, p. T152 Selection Vocabulary, p. T153 Reading Recommendations, p. T153 Big Book *Let's Read!*, pp. 18–19 Comprehension Strategies, p. T154 Discussing the Selection, p. T156 Letter Recognition, p. T157 Review Selection Vocabulary, p. T156 Print and Book Awareness, p. T157 Supporting the Reading, p. T157 View Fine Art, p. T157
Inquiry Materials ■ Class Alphabet Book	Investigating Concepts Beyond the Text, p. T138 Science Connection ■ Life in the Water, p. T139	Investigating Concepts Beyond the Text, p. T158 ■ Science Connection, p. T159
3 Language Arts Materials ■ Big Book *Let's Read!*, pp. 16–29 ■ Language Arts Big Book ■ Writer's Workbook ■ Writer's Notebook ■ Comprehension and Language Arts Skills, pp. 6–9 ■ The Ultimate Writing and Creativity Center CD-ROM	Word Analysis ■ Introduction to Rhyming Words, p. T141 Writing Process Strategies ■ Introduction to the Writing Process: Plan—web, p. T141 English-Language Conventions ■ Mechanics: Capital Letters, Cities and States, p. T141	Word Analysis ■ Introduction to Rhyming Words, p. T161 Writing Process Strategies ■ Introduction to the Writing Process: Plan—list, p. T161 English-Language Conventions ■ Mechanics: Capital Letters, Cities and States, p. T161

P Phonics ✓ Informal Assessment Available ✓ Formal Assessment Available

DAY 3	DAY 4	DAY 5
Warming Up, p. T162 **Phonemic Awareness,** pp. T163–T164 **Letter Recognition,** pp. T165–T166 **Reviewing Sounds and Letters** ■ Listening for Vowel Sounds, p. T166 ■ Introducing Consonant Sounds, p. T166 **Dictation,** p. T167	**Warming Up,** p. T180 **Phonemic Awareness,** pp. T181–T182 **Letter Recognition,** pp. T183–T184 ■ Exploring *Ww, Xx, Yy, Zz* **Reviewing Sounds and Letters** ■ Introducing Consonant Sounds, p. T184 **Dictation,** p. T185 **Reading a Pre-Decodable Book** ■ *Book 3, The Baby,* "The Shirt," pp. T186–T187	**Warming Up,** p. T200 **Phonemic Awareness** ■ Oral Blending, p. T201 ■ Segmentation, p. T201 **Letter Recognition** ■ Celebrate the Alphabet, p. T202 **Dictation,** p. T203
Build Background, p. T170 **Preview and Prepare,** p. T170 **Selection Vocabulary,** p. T171 **Reading Recommendations,** p. T171 **Big Book *Let's Read!*,** pp. 20–21 **Comprehension Strategies,** p. T172 **Discussing the Selection,** p. T174 **Letter Recognition,** p. T173 **Review Selection Vocabulary,** p. T174 **Print and Book Awareness,** p. T175 **Supporting the Reading,** p. T175	**Build Background,** p. T190 **Preview and Prepare,** p. T190 **Selection Vocabulary,** p. T191 **Reading Recommendations,** p. T191 **Big Book *Let's Read!*,** pp. 24–27 **Comprehension Strategies,** p. T192 **Discussing the Selection,** p. T194 **Letter Recognition,** p. T193 **Review Selection Vocabulary,** p. T194 **Print and Book Awareness,** p. T195 **Supporting the Reading,** p. T195	**Build Background,** p. T206 **Preview and Prepare,** p. T06 **Selection Vocabulary,** p. T207 **Reading Recommendations,** p. T207 **Big Book *Let's Read!*,** pp. 28–29 **Comprehension Strategies,** p. T208 **Discussing the Selection,** p. T210 **Letter Recognition,** p. T209 **Review Selection Vocabulary,** p. T210 **Print and Book Awareness,** p. T211 **Supporting the Reading,** p. T211 **Home Connection,** p. T211
Investigating Concepts Beyond the Text, p. T176 **Music Connection** ■ Stew Chant, p. T177	**Investigating Concepts Beyond the Text,** p. T196 **Math Connection** ■ Finish the Pattern, p. T197	**Investigating Concepts Beyond the Text,** p. T212 **Music Connection** ■ Clapping to a Beat, p. T213
Word Analysis ■ Introduction to Rhyming Words, p. T179 **Writing Process Strategies** ■ Introduction to the Writing Process: Plan—grouping, p. T179 ■ Writer's Craft: Order Words, p. T179 **English Language Conventions** ✓■ Mechanics: Capital Letters, Days and Months, p. T179	**Word Analysis** ■ Introduction to Rhyming Words, p. T199 **Writing Process Strategies** ■ Introduction to the Writing Process: Plan—grouping, p. T199 **English Language Conventions** ■ Listening, Speaking, Viewing. Speaking: Speaking Clearly, p. T199	**Word Analysis** ■ Rhyming Words, p. T215 **Writing Process Strategies** ■ Introduction to the Writing Process: Plan for Autobiography, p. T215 **English Language Conventions** ■ Penmanship: Letters are Lines, p. T215

Below are suggestions for Workshop to meet the individual needs of students. These are the same skills shown in the Lesson Planner; however, these pages provide extra practice opportunities or enriching activities to meet the varied needs of students.

WORKSHOP

Differentiating Instruction Workshop

Small-Group Instruction

Use the informal assessment suggestions found throughout the lesson along with the formal assessments provided to determine your student's strengths and areas of need. Use the following program components to help in supporting or expanding on the instruction found in these lessons:

- ***Reteach: Phonics Skills*** and ***Reteach: Comprehension and Language Arts Skills*** workbooks for use with those students who show a basic understanding of the lesson but need a bit more practice to solidify their understanding.
- ***Intervention Guide*** and ***Workbook*** for use with those students who even after extra practice exhibit a lack of understanding of the lesson concepts.
- ***English-Language Development Guide*** and ***Workbook*** for use with those students who need language assistance.

Have students create small groups to do such things as:

- Discuss books during Reading Roundtable.
- Discuss questions that arise as they investigate concepts after reading the selection.
- Partner read to assist those who have problems reading difficult passages or to help develop fluency.

Independent Activities

Students can work individually on such things as:

- Independent reading
- Challenge
- Writing
- Investigation activities

For Workshop Management Tips see Appendix, page 42.

◆ **Small-Group Instruction** ■ **Independent Activities**

	READING	INVESTIGATION ACTIVITIES
DAY 1	◆ Reread selection ◆ Listen to selection in ***Listening Library*** ◆ Choose ***Leveled Classroom Library Book*** Reread ***Decodable Book***	**Investigating Concepts Beyond the Text** ◆ Work on class alphabet book
DAY 2	◆ Reread selection ◆ Listen to selection in ***Listening Library*** ◆ Choose ***Leveled Classroom Library Book*** Reread ***Decodable Book***	**Investigating Concepts Beyond the Text** ◆ Work on class alphabet book
DAY 3	◆ Reread selection ◆ Listen to selection in ***Listening Library*** ◆ Choose ***Leveled Classroom Library Book*** Reread ***Decodable Book***	**Investigating Concepts Beyond the Text** ◆ Work on class alphabet book
DAY 4	◆ Reread selection ◆ Listen to selection in ***Listening Library*** ◆ Choose ***Leveled Classroom Library Book*** Reread ***Decodable Book***	**Investigating Concepts Beyond the Text** ◆ Work on class alphabet book
DAY 5	◆ Reread selection ◆ Listen to selection in ***Listening Library*** ◆ Choose ***Leveled Classroom Library Book*** Reread ***Decodable Book***	**Investigating Concepts Beyond the Text** ◆ Work on class alphabet book

LANGUAGE ARTS	INTERVENTION	ENGLISH-LANGUAGE LEARNERS	RETEACH	CHALLENGE
English Language Conventions ◆ Complete **Capital Letters, *Comprehension and Language Arts Skills,*** pp. 6-7	◆ Oral Blending, p. T125 ◆ Letter Recognition, p. T127 ◆ English Language Conventions, p. T140	◆ English Language Conventions, p. T140	◆ Oral Blending, p. T125 **Phonics:** *Nn/Oo/Pp* ◆ ***Reteach: Phonics Skills,*** p. 7	**Phonics:** *Nn/Oo/Pp* ■ ***Challenge: Phonics Skills,*** p. 6
Word Analysis ■ **Spelling** ◆ ***Spelling and Vocabulary Skills*** **Writing Process Strategies**	◆ Letter Recognition, p. T146 ◆ Selection Vocabulary and Comprehension Strategies, p. T152 ◆ English Language Conventions, p. T160	◆ Word Meaning, p. T142 ◆ Selection Vocabulary, p. T152 ◆ Picture Story, p. T153 ◆ Sharing, p. T154 ◆ English Language Conventions, p. T160	**Phonics:** *Qq/Rr/Ss* ◆ ***Reteach: Phonics Skills,*** p. 8 ◆ Complete **Capital Letters, *Reteach: Comprehension and Language Arts Skills,*** p. 4	**Phonics:** *Qq/Rr/Ss* ■ ***Challenge: Phonics Skills,*** p. 7 ◆ Complete **Capital Letters, *Challenge: Comprehension and Language Arts Skills,*** p. 4
Word Analysis ◆ ***Spelling and Vocabulary Skills*** ◆ ***Comprehension and Language Arts Skills*** **Writing Process Strategies** ◆ Complete **Writer's Craft: Order Words, *Comprehension and Language Arts Skills,*** pp.8-9	◆ Letters Recognition, pp. T165, T166 ◆ Vocabulary and Comprehension, p. T170 ◆ Rhyming Words, p. T175 ◆ English Language Conventions, p. T178	◆ Word Meaning, p. T163 ◆ Selection Vocabulary, p. T170 ◆ Preteach, p. T171 ◆ English Language Conventions, p. T178	◆ Phonemic Awareness, p. T163 ◆ Big Books, p. T175 **Phonics:** *Tt/Uu/Vv* ◆ ***Reteach: Phonics Skills,*** p. 8	**Phonics:** *Tt/Uu/Vv* ■ ***Challenge: Phonics Skills,*** p. 8
Word Analysis ◆ ***Vocabulary Skills***	◆ Letter Recognition, p. T184 ◆ Selection Vocabulary and Comprehension Strategies, p. T190 ◆ Letter Recognition, p. T193 ◆ English Language Conventions, p. T198	◆ Selection Vocabulary, p. T190 ◆ Using Illustrations, p. T191 ◆ Preteach, p. T192 ◆ Picture Story, p. T194 ◆ English Language Conventions, p. T198	◆ Oral Blending and Segmentation, p. T183 **Phonics:** *Ww/Xx/Yy/Zz* ◆ ***Reteach: Phonics Skills,*** pp. 10–11	**Phonics:** *Ww/Xx/Yy/Zz* ■ ***Challenge: Phonics Skills,*** pp. 9–10
Writing Process Strategies ■ **Seminar:** Plan an Autobiography, p. T215 **English Language Conventions** ◆ **Penmanship:** Letters are Lines, p. T215	◆ Selection Vocabulary and Comprehension Strategies, p. T206 ◆ English Language Conventions, p. T214	◆ Selection Vocabulary, p. T206 ◆ Preteach, p. T207 ◆ English Language Conventions, p. T214	◆ ***Reteach: Phonics Skills,*** pp. 12–13 **Writing Process Strategies** ◆ Complete **Writer's Craft, *Reteach: Comprehension and Language Arts Skills,*** p.5	■ ***Challenge: Phonics Skills,*** p. 11 **Writing Process Strategies** ◆ Complete **Writer's Craft: Order Words, *Challenge: Comprehension and Language Arts Skills,*** p.5

ASSESSMENT

Formal Assessment

Use these summative assessments along with your informal observation to assess student progress.

Written Assessments

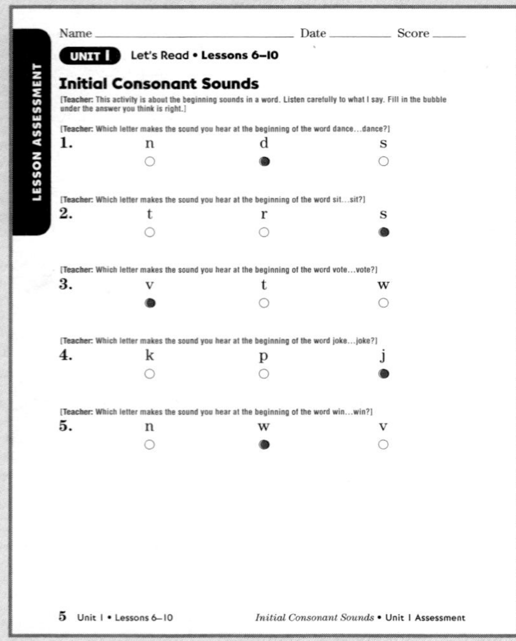

Name ______ Date ______ Score ______

UNIT 1 Let's Read • **Lessons 6–10**

LESSON ASSESSMENT

Initial Consonant Sounds

[**Teacher:** This activity is about the beginning sounds in a word. Listen carefully to what I say. Fill in the bubble under the answer you think is right.]

[**Teacher:** Which letter makes the sound you hear at the beginning of the word dance…dance?]

1. n d s

[**Teacher:** Which letter makes the sound you hear at the beginning of the word sit…sit?]

2. t r s

[**Teacher:** Which letter makes the sound you hear at the beginning of the word vote…vote?]

3. v t w

[**Teacher:** Which letter makes the sound you hear at the beginning of the word joke…joke?]

4. k p j

[**Teacher:** Which letter makes the sound you hear at the beginning of the word win…win?]

5. n w v

5 Unit 1 • Lessons 6–10 *Initial Consonant Sounds* • Unit 1 Assessment

Units 1–6 Assessment p. 5

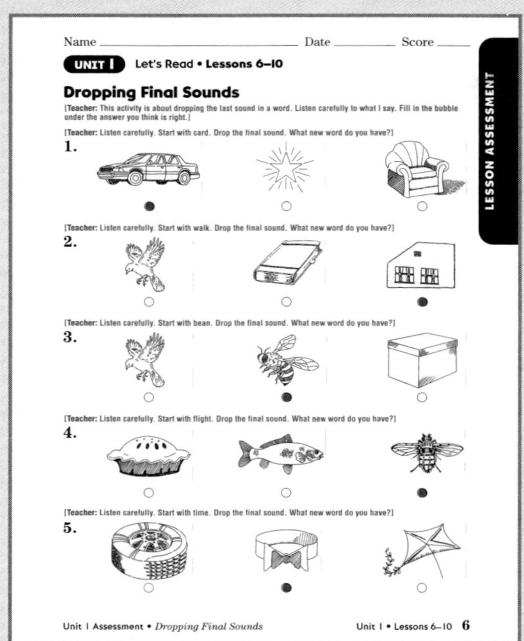

Name ______ Date ______ Score ______

UNIT 1 Let's Read • **Lessons 6–10**

LESSON ASSESSMENT

Dropping Final Sounds

[**Teacher:** This activity is about dropping the last sound in a word. Listen carefully to what I say. Fill in the bubble under the answer you think is right.]

[**Teacher:** Listen carefully. Start with card. Drop the final sound. What new word do you have?]

1.

[**Teacher:** Listen carefully. Start with walk. Drop the final sound. What new word do you have?]

2.

[**Teacher:** Listen carefully. Start with bean. Drop the final sound. What new word do you have?]

3.

[**Teacher:** Listen carefully. Start with flight. Drop the final sound. What new word do you have?]

4.

[**Teacher:** Listen carefully. Start with time. Drop the final sound. What new word do you have?]

5.

Unit 1 Assessment • *Dropping Final Sounds* Unit 1 • Lessons 6–10 6

Units 1–6 Assessment p. 6

Informal Assessment

The Teacher Observation Log, found in the ***Program Assessment Teacher's Edition,*** is a vehicle for recording anecdotal information about individual student performance on an ongoing basis. Information such as students' strengths and weaknesses can be recorded at any time the occasion warrants. It is recommended that you maintain a Cumulative Folder for each student in which you can store the logs for purposes of comparison and analysis as the school year progresses. You will gradually build up a comprehensive file that reveals which students are progressing smoothly and which students need additional help.

Tips for using the Teacher Observation Log:

- Keep Observation Logs available so you can easily record your informal observations. A clipboard or other similar device might be helpful.
- Decide which aspect of the student's learning you want to monitor on the log.
- Record your observations. It might take four to five days to observe and record the performance of each student.
- If you need more information on some of your students, you might want to observe them more than once, either during the lesson, during Workshop, or at other times during the day.

Teacher's Observation Log

Student ______

Date ______ Unit ______

Activity ______

General Comprehension

Concepts Discussed ______

Behavior Within a Group

Articulates, expresses ideas ______

Joins discussions ______

Collaboration (such as works with other students, works alone) ______

Role in Group

Role (such as leader, summarizer, questioner, recorder, critic, observer, non-participant) ______

Flexibility (changes roles when necessary) ______

Use of Reading Strategies

Uses strategies when needed (either those taught or student's own)/Describe strategies used ______

Changes strategies when appropriate ______

Changes Since Last Observation

______

If more space is needed, write on the back or use another sheet.

32 **Program Assessment**

Program Assessment Teacher's Edition p. 32

1 Preparing to Read

Objectives

- Students will attend to initial sounds of words through oral blending and segmentation.
- Students will write letters of the alphabet.
- Students will discriminate between distinct long-vowel sounds.
- Students will associate letters with sounds.

Materials

- Lion Puppet
- Sound/Spelling Cards
- Phonics Skills, p. 7
- Letter Cards
- High-Frequency Word Cards

Warming Up

Use one or both of the following activities to focus students' attention and to reinforce some of the concepts they have been learning.

Comparing Word Length Reading 1.3

- Write each pair of words on the board one at a time.

foot	treetop	bird	sailboat
football	tree	birdhouse	sail

- Read each pair and ask students which word is longer.
- Have the students clap out syllables. Help the students recognize that the longer words have more syllables.
- If the students are doing well with the first few pairs, switch to writing the words side by side rather than one word below the other.
- Erase each pair before you write the next one.

I Spy Reading 1.3, 1.4; Listen/Speak 2.1

- Play I Spy with the letters *l* and *m*.

  "I spy with my little eye,
  Something with the letter _____."

- To discover the word you see, students point out words in the classroom that have the appropriate letter.

Universal Access: Meeting Individual Needs

ELL Support

For ELD strategies, use the ***English-Language Development Guide,*** Unit 1, Lesson 6.

Intervention Support

For intervention strategies, use the ***Intervention Guide,*** Unit 1, Lesson 6.

Reading 1.3, 1.4

Teacher Tip **INVESTIGATORS** Teach the students to be investigators. Have them walk around the room and search for objects that begin with *l* and *m*.

Phonemic Awareness

Oral Blending Reading 1.4, 1.8

Initial Consonant Sounds

- Read the following words clearly and ask students to blend the parts into a whole word.
- Tell students to listen carefully to both parts of the word.

/p/ . . . aper	/t/ . . . able	/d/ . . . octor
/m/ . . . eat	/s/ . . . ong	/l/ . . . ake
/m/ . . . ean	/s/ . . . ee	/z/ . . . oo
/b/ . . . ean	/l/ . . . ove	/p/ . . . et

Segmentation Reading 1.4

Initial Phoneme

- In today's lesson, students are asked to correct the puppet by saying the sound that it has omitted. In this way, students are introduced to the challenge of *segmenting* or isolating the initial phonemes of words.
- Tell the students that now the puppet wants them to say only the *first sound* of each word. First, he'll show students how, then he wants them to play.

Teacher:	chair
Puppet:	/ch/
Teacher:	sail
Puppet:	/s/
Teacher:	soup
Students:	/s/

- Continue with the following words:

face	lace	race	chase	base
sight	fight	height	right	might
vine	line	shine	fine	mine
rose	nose	hose	goes	shows

PHONEMIC AWARENESS

Reading 1.4, 1.8, 1.9

Universal Access: Meeting Individual Needs

Reteach

ORAL BLENDING During Workshop, reteach the oral blending lesson to students who had difficulty. Remind students to say the initial sound and the rest of the word before blending the word. For extra practice use the following words: /s/at, /c/ane, /c/amel, /b/it, /t/ape, /m/ake.

Intervention Tip

ORAL BLENDING Since Lesson 3, students have been orally blending the initial consonant with the rest of the word. By now, they should be able to do this easily. If they are not, they will have trouble with sound-symbol blending, which begins in Lesson 13 of this unit. You should spend some time during Workshop with students who find oral blending and segmentation exercises difficult. Start with blending syllables and word parts. Then move on to initial consonant blending. If they have difficulty with the transition, use the puppet to help them segment the initial sound.

Reading 1.4, 1.8

Informal Assessment

MONITORING You should be completing the monitoring of students' ability to blend initial consonant sounds. Because students will start blending the sounds in written words in Lesson 13 of this unit, it is important that if students need extra help, you provide it during Workshop.

Reading 1.3

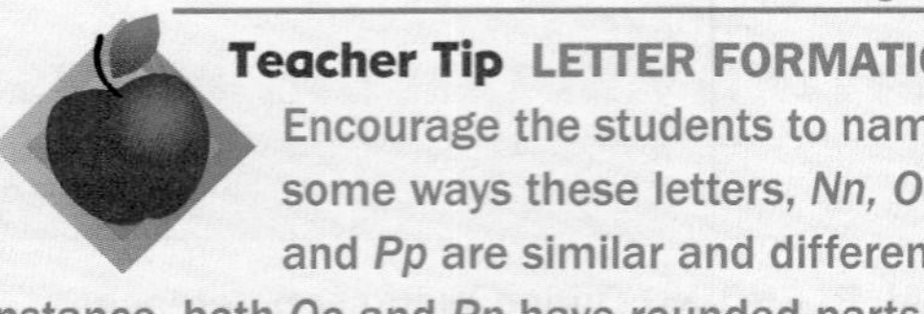

Teacher Tip LETTER FORMATION
Encourage the students to name some ways these letters, *Nn, Oo,* and *Pp* are similar and different. For instance, both *Oo* and *Pp* have rounded parts.

LETTER RECOGNITION

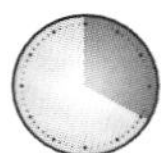

Letter Recognition

Exploring *Nn, Oo,* and *Pp* Reading 1.3; Writing 1.3

- Introduce the letters *Nn*, *Oo*, and *Pp*.
- Point to the ***Sound/Spelling Cards*** for each of the three letters. Ask students which of these letters is a vowel and have them explain how they know.
- Review the vowels students have learned so far. Remind the class that vowels are special (which is why they are red on the cards) because they are vital in making words—no word can exist without a vowel.
- Demonstrate how to make a capital *N* on the board, pointing out all the starting points. Have the students copy your motions in the air and then have them trace the letter with their fingers on their desktops or tables. Repeat the procedure with lowercase *n*.
- After the students have practiced a few times, have them write their letters on paper. Have the students say the strokes with you for *all* letters.
- Then repeat the process with the letters *Oo* and *Pp*.
- Remind students to proofread their work, making sure it is legible and spaced appropriately.

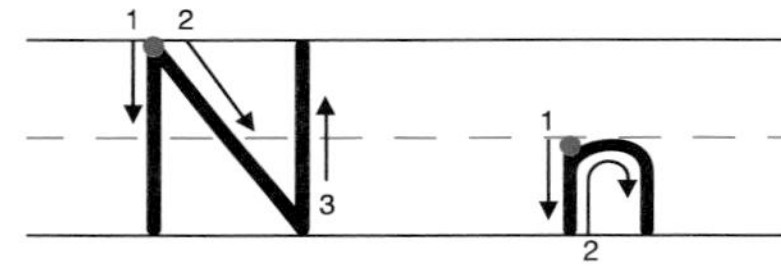

N Starting point, straight down
Starting point, slanting down right; straight back up: capital *N*

n Starting point, straight down, back up, around right, straight down: small *n*

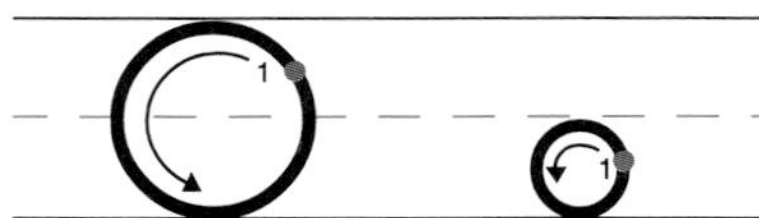

O Starting point, around left all the way: capital *O*

o Starting point, around left all the way: small *o*

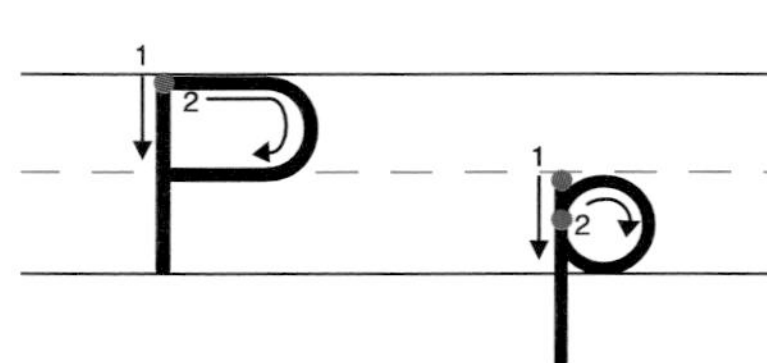

P Starting point, straight down
Starting point, around right and in at the middle: capital *P*

p Starting point, straight down
Starting point, around right all the way, touching the line: small *p*

Phonics Skills Writing 1.3

Work with students to complete ***Phonics Skills*** page 7. Have the students write the letters as a class saying the words together. Remind them to space appropriately on each line of the page.

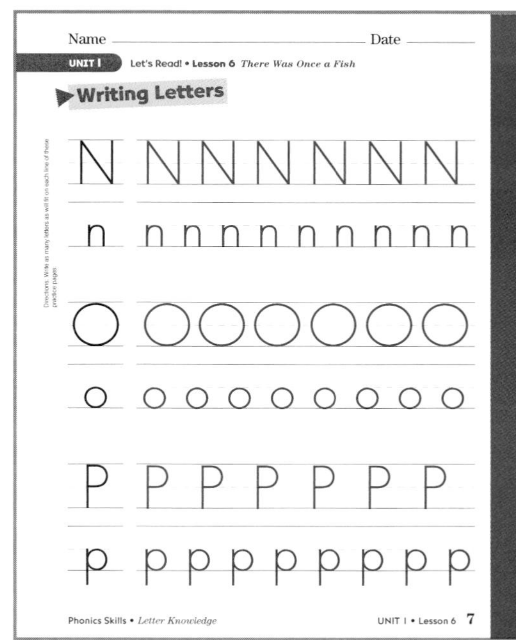
Name ____________ Date ________
UNIT 1 Let's Read! • Lesson 6 *There Was Once a Fish*
Writing Letters
N N N N N N N
n n n n n n n n n
O O O O O O O
o o o o o o o o o
P P P P P P P
p p p p p p p p p
Phonics Skills • *Letter Knowledge* UNIT 1 • Lesson 6 7

***Phonics Skills* p. 7**

LETTER RECOGNITION

Reading 1.3; Writing 1.3

Universal Access: Meeting Individual Needs

Reteach

LETTER FORMATION For additional practice with letter formation, use ***Reteach: Phonics Skills*** page 7.

Challenge

For students who are ready for a challenge, use ***Challenge: Phonics Skills*** page 6.

Intervention Tip

LETTER RECOGNITION During Workshop, work with students who are having difficulty with letter recognition. Encourage students to put ***Letter Cards A–P*** in alphabetical order. They can sing the "Alphabet Song" and use the ***Sound/Spelling Cards*** to help them.

Reading 1.3

Teacher Tip PRINT AWARENESS Having the students count the words in the sentences will help them identify words and the beginnings and ends of sentences.

REVIEW SOUNDS & LETTERS

Reviewing Sounds and Letters

Listening for Vowel Sounds: /ā/ and /ō/ Reading 1.3, 1.5

- Write the letters *Aa* on the extreme left side of the board and the letters *Oo* on the extreme right.
- Tell the students that they must listen carefully to hear the /ō/ sound or the /ā/ sound in each word you say.
- If they hear the /ā/ sound, they should say /ā/ and point to the letters *Aa* on the board; if they hear the /ō/ sound, they should say /ō/ and point to the letters *Oo* on the board.

no	so	say	lay	low
grow	gray	race	rose	nose
blow	slow	snow	snake	rake
go	goat	gate	ate	oat

Introducing Consonant Sounds Reading 1.1, 1.3, 1.4

- Write an alliterative sentence on the board for each of the consonants, such as

  Nellie nibbled nine nutty noodles.

  Pretty Patty picks purple pansies.
- Read the sentence aloud, underlining the key letter each time you say it.
- After challenging students to tell you the sound of the key letter, ask them to recite the sentence several times with you, exaggerating its sound.
- Ask the students whether any of their names begin with /N/ or /P/. Write them on the board.
- Ask the students to think of other words that begin with the key letter.
- Call on students to frame each complete sentence. Then have volunteers count the words in each sentence.

Dictation
Reading 1.3, 1.11; Writing 1.3; Eng. Lang. Conv. 1.8

Dictation

- Ask students to take out writing materials.
- Dictate the high-frequency words below. Use each word in a sentence and remind students to look in the High-Frequency Word Bank for guidance and confirmation of their spelling. Encourage them to write neatly and space the words appropriately.

  is, was
- Collect the papers to see how students are progressing.

Informal Assessment

LETTER ORIENTATION Frequent letter orientation errors are often a symptom that students are not respecting the starting point and stroke sequence for the letters.

Pages 16–17 of *Let's Read!*

SELECTION INTRODUCTION

Objectives

- Students will use the Table of Contents to find information.
- Students will listen and respond to "There Was Once a Fish."
- Students will identify words with the letters *Nn* and *Oo*.
- Students will retell "There Was Once a Fish."
- Students will identify beginnings and endings of words and spaces between words.
- Students will classify animals by habitat.

Materials

- Big Book *Let's Read!*, pp. 16–17

About the Illustrator

ARNOLD LOBEL was a talented and prolific writer as well as an illustrator. As a youth he was ill much of the time, but he used his isolation to develop his creative skills. He wrote more than 70 works, which are well known for their wit and charm.

Other Books Illustrated or Written by Arnold Lobel

Frog and Toad Are Friends (Caldecott Honor), *Frog and Toad Together* (Newbery Honor Book), *Fables* (Caldecott Medal)

Selection Summary

Genre: Poetry

A simple tale of catching a fish becomes an amusing poem.

The elements of poetry are listed below. Poetry may have one or more of these elements.

- Sentences are sometimes broken into parts. Each part is on a line of its own.
- Words that rhyme are often used.
- The lines of a poem often have rhythm, or meter.
- Some words may be repeated.

Inquiry Connections

In this selection of the ***Big Book*** the students will listen to a poem about a fish.

Key concepts investigated are

- the elements of poetry
- matching oral words to printed words
- becoming more aware of print

Direct the students to the Concept/Question Board. Encourage them to post any questions or ideas they have about the unit. They may want to include a drawing or poem about a fish. If any students have a pet fish at home, encourage them to bring in a photograph of it.

- Make sure the students put their names or initials on anything they post on the Board.
- Tell them that they can post something on the Board any day. Be sure to have students discuss what they put on the Board with the class.

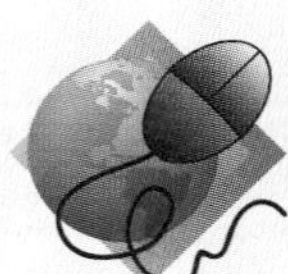

www.sra4kids.com
Web Connection
Help the students look for additional information about poems and rhymes by using the Web connections that are available at the Reading link of the SRA Web page.

UNIVERSAL ACCESS:
MEETING INDIVIDUAL NEEDS

ELL Support

For ELD strategies, use the ***English-Language Development Guide,*** Unit 1, Lesson 6.

Intervention Support

For intervention strategies, use the ***Intervention Guide,*** Unit 1, Lesson 6.

Teacher Tip SET PURPOSES
Remind the students that good readers have a purpose when they read. Let them know that they should make sure they know the purpose for reading whenever they read.

Routine Card
Refer to ***Routine 11*** for the procedure for reading selection.

Build Background

Activate Prior Knowledge Reading 2.6

Tell the students that you are going to read them a poem about a fish. Invite volunteers to tell about their experiences fishing or perhaps visiting an aquarium. Have them tell about the kinds of places fish live.

Preview and Prepare

Browse Reading 1.2

- Open *Let's Read!* to the Table of Contents and find "There Was Once a Fish." Ask a student to point to the page number. Say the number and turn to that page. Read the title of the poem and the name of the illustrator.
- Before reading the selection to the students, read the Focus Questions on the first page of the selection together. Briefly discuss the questions, and tell the students to keep the questions in mind as you read.

Set Purposes

Explain to the students that people read poems for many different reasons. The poem they are about to read will tell about fishing. The rhymes like "fish" and "wish" or "sea" and "be" will add to the enjoyment of reading the poem.

Selection Vocabulary

- Write the following word on the board and pronounce it.

    line

- Invite a few volunteers to draw some straight lines on the board. Then discuss the different meaning of the word line, such as what is between two points, a fishing line, and so on. Tell the students that some words mean many different things.
- Open the ***Big Book*** to any poem you already have read, and call on volunteers to point to the first line of the poem, then the last line. Have students discuss how the line of words is like the line on the board.

Reading Recommendations Reading 1.3

Read Aloud

- Read the poem through without pausing.
- Read it again, more slowly, pointing to the words.
- Ask students to read the first line of each verse with you, while you read the parenthetical statements.
- Reverse the procedure, signaling students at first and then having them read without cue.
- Tell students that the question word *what* refers to a thing or event and *where* refers to a place. Tell students to listen for the character in the poem (who), what happens to it, and where it lives.

Using Comprehension Strategies

Comprehension strategy instruction allows students to become aware of what good readers do when they read. Good readers constantly check their understanding as they are reading and ask themselves questions. Skilled readers also recognize when they are having problems understanding a selection and stop to use various comprehension strategies to help them make sense of what they are reading.

During the reading of this selection, you will introduce and model the use of the following comprehension strategy:

- **Monitoring and Clarifying** helps readers understand the meaning of words and difficult ideas or passages.

Teacher Tip HIGH-FREQUENCY WORDS The following high-frequency words appear in the selection: *was, a, in, the,* and *on.* Point to these words in the High-Frequency Word Bank, have students read them, and encourage them to read these words with you when you encounter them in the reading.

Routine Card
Refer to ***Routine 10*** for the Selection Vocabulary procedure.

UNIVERSAL ACCESS: MEETING INDIVIDUAL NEEDS

ELL Support

PRETEACH Read the selection to the English-language learners before you read it to the class. As you read, give students the opportunity to ask questions to clarify what they don't understand. Model the strategy so that they can feel more comfortable asking questions when the selection is read to the class. Use the ***English-Language Development Guide*** as needed.

Teacher Tip TRACKING TEXT If students are using the small version of *Let's Read!,* invite them to point to the words as you do so.

Teacher Tip MONITORING AND CLARIFYING An extended lesson on Monitoring and Clarifying can be found on page T137. This lesson is intended to give extra practice with monitoring and clarifying text.

COMPREHENSION

Comprehension Strategies

Introducing Strategy Use

Monitoring and Clarifying This poem offers an opportunity to introduce students to the reading strategy Clarifying. Explain that when good readers read, they do various things, such as rereading, looking at pictures, or using a dictionary to help them figure out or clarify something that confuses them. Point out the text in parentheses and explain that the curved lines show that the poem has two parts. Invite volunteers to clarify how the two parts are different. *(One part is the main story line. The part in parentheses is really just funny questions to the reader.)*

Teacher Modeling

Clarifying *If you are not sure about something when you read, try to figure it out or clarify. One way to do this is to reread the line you are not sure about. I'm not exactly sure whether the writer caught the fish. I'll clarify this by rereading the line "So I brought him to you." Now I know the writer did.*

Reading 1.4

Phonemic Awareness

Initial Consonant Sounds

Remind students that they said the first sounds in words you named when they completed the previous section. Tell students that now you are going to say some words from the poem. Ask students to listen carefully and then say the first sound of each word. Use the following words:

fish, lived, sea, be, line, caught

UNIVERSAL ACCESS:
MEETING INDIVIDUAL NEEDS

ELL Tip

USING PICTURES Before reading a selection, talk to the English-language learners about the illustrations in it. Ask them how the illustrations support the humor in the poem. Associating the words in the text with the illustrations helps the English-language learners learn to think of English words before translating them first from their native languages.

Letter Recognition

Reading 1.3

Nn, Oo, Pp

Ask students to look for the letters *Nn*, *Oo*, and *Pp* in words in the selection *(once, more, could, you, in, would, on, line, whose, not, mine, So, brought, to, you, should, do)*. Invite volunteers to point out these letters on the ***Big Book*** page. Students should soon notice that the letters *Pp* do not appear in the selection. If they do not, help them notice this.

Teacher Tip READING FOR ENJOYMENT Remind students that they should spend at least 20 minutes reading after school.

Reading 1.3

Informal Assessment

LETTER RECOGNITION Continue assessing students' letter knowledge using letter arrays or individual ***Letter Cards (A–P).*** Name the letter and have students point to the letter in the array or hold up the appropriate ***Letter Card***. Then point to a letter and have students name it.

Discussing the Selection Reading 2.2, 3.1

- Ask volunteers to retell the story about the fish in their own words.
- Ask students to tell who this poem is about *(a fish).* Then have them tell where the fish lives *(the sea)* and what happened to it *(it got caught in a line).*
- Point to the illustrations in the ***Big Book*** and ask which part of the story is shown by each picture.
- If the students want to know more about a part of the story, have them ask questions about it. Remind them to take turns by raising their hands before they speak. Remind them that they can post their questions on the Concept/Question Board, too.
- Look at the text again. Point out, or have a student point out, the text in parentheses. Remind the students that authors use parentheses when they want to say something that is not really a part of the story.
- Read the poem without the parenthetical lines to show the main story line. Ask the students if they feel the parenthetical lines are necessary.
- Ask students whether this poem made them want to go fishing or whether it made them feel differently about fish. Ask them which selections have made them feel differently about the animals featured in them.
- With the students, refer back to the Focus Questions for the selection. Have all the questions been answered? If not, answer them now.

Have the students record their responses to the selection in the Response Journal section of their Writer's Notebooks by drawing pictures. Help the students label their drawings.

Review Selection Vocabulary

Have students review the selection vocabulary word for this lesson. Remind them that they discussed the meaning of this word at the beginning of the lesson. Have them add this and any other interesting words that they clarified while reading to the Vocabulary Words section of their Writer's Notebooks. The word from this selection is

line

- Have the students use the word in oral sentences. Help the students expand their sentences by asking who, what, where, when, why, and how questions.
- Ask the students to draw a picture that represents the word.
- Add this word to the *Let's Read!* Word Bank.

Encourage students to refer to the vocabulary words throughout the unit.

Print and Book Awareness

Word Boundaries

- Review the concept of word boundaries with students. Let volunteers go to the ***Big Book*** *Let's Read!* and point to the beginnings and endings of words and to the spaces between them.
- Help the students decode words by looking at sentence boundaries. Remind students that the first word of any sentence begins with a capital letter. Ask volunteers to point to the beginning of each sentence in "There Was Once a Fish."
- Write the following on the board:

  Therewasonceafish.

Ask the students to describe what is wrong with the word spacing. Have a volunteer rewrite the sentence using correct letter and word spacing. Writing 1.3

Supporting the Reading

Comprehension Strategy: Clarifying

Remind the students that you modeled the use of the comprehension strategy Clarifying when you read the selection. Review the previous selection, "Hey, Diddle, Diddle," and ask the students if there is anything they would like to clarify.

Listening to Rhyme and Rhythm Listen/Speak 2.1

- Discuss with the students the rhymes and poems that they have been listening to during the past few days.
- Ask volunteers to explain how they know which words rhyme. Say the following pair of words aloud. have students tell whether or not they rhyme: *yawn, dawn; hot, pot; stew, you; cook, munch;* and *hole, bowl.*
- Continue with other selections, inviting volunteers to take turns leading the class in clapping out the rhythm.

Purposes for Reading

Remind the students that before they read the poem the class discussed that the purposes for reading were to learn about fishing and to enjoy the poet's use of rhyme. Ask students whether they enjoyed this rhyme and why. Have them share what they learned about fishing.

UNIVERSAL ACCESS:
MEETING INDIVIDUAL NEEDS

Intervention Tip

WORD BOUNDARIES Meet with students during Workshop. Write several crowded sentences, and have the students rewrite them correctly using proper letter and word spacing.

Teacher Tip COMPREHENSION Skilled readers constantly evaluate their understanding of what they read. Stop often to make sure you and the students are doing this.

Objectives

- Students will continue working on their alphabet book.
- Students will apply concepts and ideas through a curricular connection.

Materials

- Class alphabet book

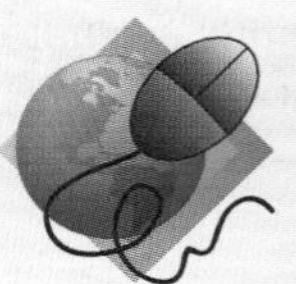

www.sra4kids.com
Web Connection
Help the students look for additional information about poems and rhymes by using the Web connections that are available at the Reading link of the SRA Web page.

INVESTIGATION

Supporting the Investigation

Investigating Concepts Beyond the Text Reading 1.3

Remind the students about the alphabet books they are working on for this unit.

- Begin by sharing the completed pages of the alphabet book that students created for the letters *a*, *b*, *c*, and *d*. Point out similarities and differences on the pages. Call attention to the capital and lowercase letters written in large print on each page.
- Distribute drawing paper or story paper and discuss with students what they might include on their pages. Encourage a variety of suggestions and emphasize that they can decide for themselves what they want to include. They might want to draw the pictures or cut them from magazines. Have supplies such as crayons, markers, scissors, paste, and old magazines or catalogs available.
- Remind the students to plan before they begin to write on or design their pages. Assign the letters *e*, *f*, *g*, and *h*.

Unit 1 Investigation Management

Lessons 1–5	Discuss the class alphabet book. Create and share class alphabet book pages.
Lessons 6–10	Collaborative Investigation **Create and share class alphabet book pages for the letters e to z.** Supplementary Activities **Provide the students with the materials necessary to create their alphabet pages. Discuss different ideas for designing their alphabet pages with the students. Help the students complete their pages.**
Lessons 11–15	Share the class alphabet book pages, and create a class poem to add to the alphabet book.

Science Connection Science 2a

Life in the Water

Purpose: To classify animals according to the environments they live in

Tell students that the fish in the poem is one example of an animal that lives in water. Many other animals live there, too. Other animals live on land, and others live in the air.

- Draw a wavy line across the lower third of the board to represent the surface of water. Draw a straight line in the middle third of the board, and add a tree or two to represent land. In the upper third, draw a circle to represent the sun and add a few clouds. Ask students to tell you the names of animals and whether they live in the water, on land, or in the air. Write the names on the appropriate section of the board.
- Have the students draw an outdoor scene including one of the animals from the list or any other they wish to draw. On the bulletin board place the title *Animals* and three captions: *In the Water*, *On Land*, and *In the Air*.
- As students finish, have them place their drawings on the bulletin board under the appropriate caption.

INVESTIGATION

Teacher Tip MATERIALS For this Science Connection, you will need the following materials: drawing paper and crayons or colored pencils. You could also use butcher paper instead of writing on the board.

Science/Social Studies Connection Center

Refer to the ***Science/Social Studies Connection Center*** for an activity about the habitats and adaptations of animals.

Objectives

Word Analysis Vocabulary

- **Vocabulary Strategies: Rhyming Words.** Using words from "There Was Once a Fish," distinguish between nonsense words and common English words.

Writing Process Strategies

- **Introduction to the Writing Process.** Building on the theme of Let's Read!, understand that writing is a process and prewriting involves organizing for writing.

English Language Conventions

- **Mechanics: Capital Letters.** Building on Letter Recognition in the Phonemic Awareness lesson, develop understanding that names of cities and states begin with capital letters.

Materials

- Language Arts Big Book, pp. 13–14
- Language Arts Transparency 1
- Comprehension and Language Arts Skills, pp. 6–7

Universal Access: Meeting Individual Needs

Reteach, Challenge, English-Language Development, and ***Intervention*** lessons are available to support the language arts instruction in this lesson.

OVERVIEW

Language Arts Overview

Word Analysis

Vocabulary The Vocabulary activity focuses on rhyming vocabulary from "There Was Once a Fish" to understand the difference between common English words and nonsense words. For example, *fish, wish, dish, swish,* are all words, but *bish, lish,* and *sish* are not. This reinforces the concept that sounds and letters have meaning, but not all sounds and letters are meaningful.

Vocabulary Skill Words

fish **wish** **line***

Also Selection Vocabulary

Writing Process Strategies

The Writing Process Strategies lesson introduces students to the writing process by providing an overview of the prewriting skill of organizing their ideas. Many students do not consider this crucial step in the writing process.

Basic Computer Skills To introduce students to the computer as a writing tool, teach students how to use a mouse to point, click, and drag; explain to students that they can use the mouse to tell the computer what to do. Help students key their first names. ***Basic Computer Skills*** Level 1 Lessons 3–4 teach these basic computer skills.

English Language Conventions

Grammar, Usage, and Mechanics **Capital Letters** The English Language Conventions support the reading and writing skills development in this lesson. This lesson introduces students to the conventions of capitalizing names of cities and states.

Word Analysis

Vocabulary

Rhyming Words Reading 1.6

Teach

- Write the following words on the board and say them to emphasize their rhymes: *fish, wish.* Explain that words that have the same ending sounds are rhyming words.
- Have the students suggest other words that rhyme with *fish (dish, swish)* as you write them on the board. Discuss the meaning of each word.
- When the students or you suggest nonsense words, explain that even though those words rhyme with *fish*, they have no meaning. Some words, like *Tish*, might have meaning only as a person's name.

Guided Practice

- Write *Line* as a column heading on the board or chart paper.
- Have the students suggest other words that rhyme with *line* as you write them on the board *(fine, mine, sign, dine, whine, nine).* They might notice that not all words with rhyming sounds have the same spelling. Discuss the meaning of each word.
- Have the students suggest nonsense words that rhyme with *line.* Emphasize that these words have no meaning.

Writing Process Strategies

Introduction to the Writing Process

Plan Writing 1.0, 1.1

Teach

- Introduce the idea of organizing ideas by reading ***Language Arts Big Book*** pages 18–19. Discuss each page.
- Explain that after writers have ideas, they have to think about the best way to organize them.

Guided Practice

- Using the selection "There Was Once a Fish" as a basis for ideas, write the word *fish* on the board or chart paper.
- As a class, brainstorm some ideas about fish as you make a list. These can include:
  - live in water Science 2.a
  - eat plants or other fish Science 2.c
  - have fins and scales Science 2.a
- Use ***Language Arts Transparency 1*** to make a web of the three top ideas with *fish* at the center of the web.
- Explain to the students that a web can be used to plan ideas to write about any topic, including themselves.
- Conclude by emphasizing the importance of thinking of ideas and then organizing them before writing.

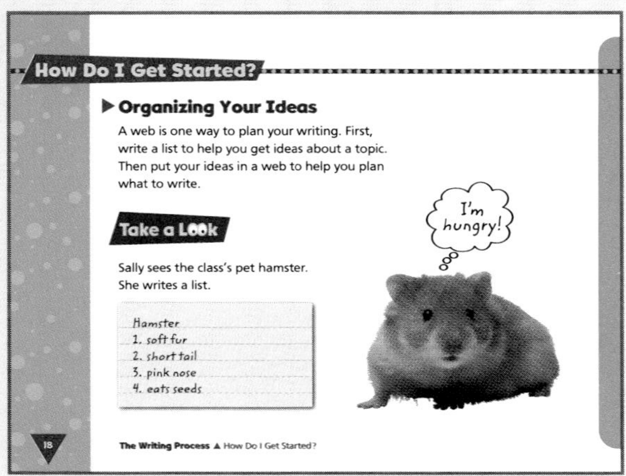
How Do I Get Started?

▶ Organizing Your Ideas

A web is one way to plan your writing. First, write a list to help you get ideas about a topic. Then put your ideas in a web to help you plan what to write.

Take a Look

Sally sees the class's pet hamster. She writes a list.

Hamster
1. soft fur
2. short tail
3. pink nose
4. eats seeds

18 The Writing Process ▲ How Do I Get Started?

Language Arts Big Book p. 18

English Language Conventions

Grammar, Usage, and Mechanics

Capital Letters Eng. Lang. Conv. 1.6

Teach

- Review the capital and lowercase letters that students have explored thus far *(A–P)*.
- Review that people's names start with capital letters.
- Explain that cities and states start with capital letters, too.
- Write the name of your city and state on the board and point to the capital letter in each word.

Independent Practice

Have the students complete pages 6–7 in ***Comprehension and Language Arts Skills*** to practice capitalizing the first letter of cities and states.

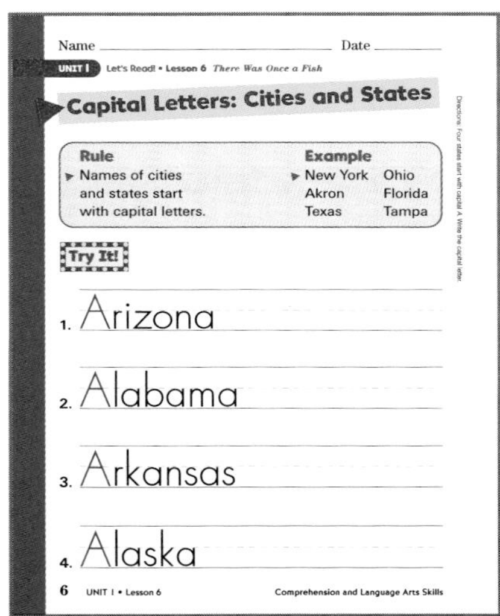
Name ______ Date ______

UNIT 1 Let's Read! • Lesson 6 *There Was Once a Fish*

Capital Letters: Cities and States

Rule	Example	
▸ Names of cities and states start with capital letters.	▸ New York Akron Texas	Ohio Florida Tampa

Try It!

1. Arizona
2. Alabama
3. Arkansas
4. Alaska

6 UNIT 1 • Lesson 6 Comprehension and Language Arts Skills

Comprehension and Language Arts Skills p. 6

Preparing to Read

Objectives

- Students will attend to phonemes through segmenting sounds.
- Students will write letters of the alphabet.
- Students will associate letters with sounds.
- Students will read a ***Pre-Decodable Book.***

Materials

- Lion Puppet
- Routine Card 5
- Sound/Spelling Cards
- Phonics Skills, p. 8
- Letter Cards
- High-Frequency Word Cards
- Pre-Decodable Book 3

Universal Access: Meeting Individual Needs

ELL Support

For ELD strategies, use the ***English-Language Development Guide,*** Unit 1, Lesson7.

Intervention Support

For intervention strategies, use the ***Intervention Guide,*** Unit 1, Lesson 7.

ELL Support

WORD MEANINGS Make sure the English-language learners know the meanings of the words. During Workshop, use pictures, photos, objects, drawings, pantomime, or the ***English-Language Development Guide*** to assist them.

Teacher Tip RIDDLES Encourage the students to come up with their own riddles.

Warming Up

Use one or both of the following activities to focus students' attention and to reinforce some of the concepts they have been learning.

I Spy Reading 1.3, 1.4; Listen/Speak 2.1

- Play I Spy with the letters *n* and *p*.

  "I spy with my little eye,
  Something with the letter ________."

- To discover the word you see, students must point out words in the classroom that have the appropriate letter.

Consonant Riddle Game Reading 1.4

This activity focuses students' awareness on initial consonant sounds and reinforces sound segmentation. Ask students

What starts with /k/? /b/? /r/? /f/? /s/ and rhymes with *hat?*
What starts with /n/? /t/? /z/? /g/? /ch/ and rhymes with *you?*
What starts with /t/? /m/? /r/? /b/ and rhymes with *post?*
What starts with /n/? /r/? /b/? /s/? /l/ and rhymes with *might?*

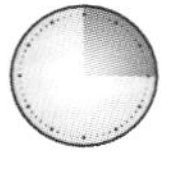

Phonemic Awareness

Oral Blending

Final Consonant Sounds Reading 1.3

In this variation of word blending, separate the final consonant from the first part of the word. The examples are easy to blend because the words are recognized easily even before the final consonant is pronounced.

superma . . . /n/	astronau . . . /t/	elephan . . . /t/
sailboa . . . /t/	tremendou . . . /s/	telepho . . . /n/
doorkno . . . /b/	acroba . . . /t/	lighthou . . . /s/
workboo . . . /k/	pocke . . . /t/	ketchu . . . /p/

Briefly discuss meanings of these words if any of them are unfamiliar to students.

Segmentation

Segmenting Initial Phonemes Reading 1.4, 1.9

Present the Lion Puppet and tell students that today he is saying only the beginning sound when he repeats a word. Ask them to help the puppet by saying the initial phoneme of each word.

- Demonstrate, as follows:

  Teacher: moose
  Puppet: /m/

  Teacher: sign
  Puppet: /s/

- Continue with the following words, first saying the word, then having the students speak for the puppet:

bee	sea	we	say	low
see	sigh	hoe	boat	take
lake	meet	my	tie	toll

Teacher Tip ROUNDS You may want to repeat this song in a round, having a teacher's aide or a capable student(s) recite the song starting when others say, *Back to my Home.*

Listen/Speak 2.1

PHONEMIC AWARENESS

"Did You Ever?" Song Reading 1.6, 1.7; Listen/Speak 2.1

- Teach the following song to students. (Music is provided in the Appendix on page 61.). Tell students that they will be substituting or replacing sounds in words. The two lines in quotation marks change with each repetition. Pause when you come to this verse and call out the lines, then sing them together with students. On a second singing, invite students to make a gesture to demonstrate how they might feel to see the named action.

  Down by the sea
  Where the watermelons grow.
  Back to my home
  I dare not go.
  For if I do
  My mother will say,
  "Did you ever see a *frog*
  Kissing a *dog?*"
  Down by the sea.

- In further verses, the lines in quotation marks become:

  "Did you ever see a *goose*
  Riding a *moose?*"
  "Did you ever see a *cat*
  Wearing a *hat?*"
  "Did you ever see a *duck*
  Driving a *truck?*"
  "Did you ever see a *bear*
  Curling her *hair?*"

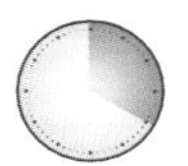

Letter Recognition

LETTER RECOGNITION

Reviewing *Aa–Pp* Reading 1.3

Review the "Alphabet Song" and the letters learned so far. Point out instances of the letters in the classroom and in students' names. You might want to use ***Letter Cards*** to do a quick recognition drill with cards for letters *Aa* through *Pp*. Have students pull letters *A* through *P* and spread them across their desks. Say a letter and have the students hold up the correct card on your signal. Be sure to have your set of ***Letter Cards*** to hold up or point to the ***Sound/Spelling Cards.***

Exploring *Qq, Rr,* and *Ss* Reading 1.3; Writing 1.3

- Introduce the letters *Qq*, *Rr*, and *Ss*.
- Begin by writing the capital *Q* on the board. Be sure to indicate the starting point and the placement of the "tail."
- Have the students imitate your movements by tracing the letter in the air. Then have them use their fingers to trace the letter on their desks saying the strokes with you.
- When you introduce capital *S*, demonstrate writing the letter a few times, emphasizing the starting point and stressing the left-right-left order of the curves.
- After the students have written all their letters, have them proofread their work against the letters you have written. You might invite volunteers to the board to demonstrate writing one or two letters.

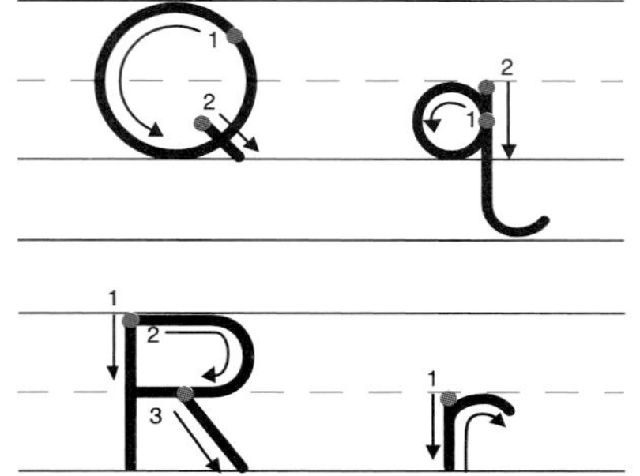

Q Starting point, around left all the way
Starting point, slanting down right: capital *Q*

q Starting point, around left all the way
Starting point, straight down, touching the circle, curving up right to stopping place: small *q*

R Starting point, straight down
Starting point, around right and in at the middle, touching the line
Starting point, slanting down right: capital *R*

r Starting point, straight down, back up, curving around right to stopping place: small *r*

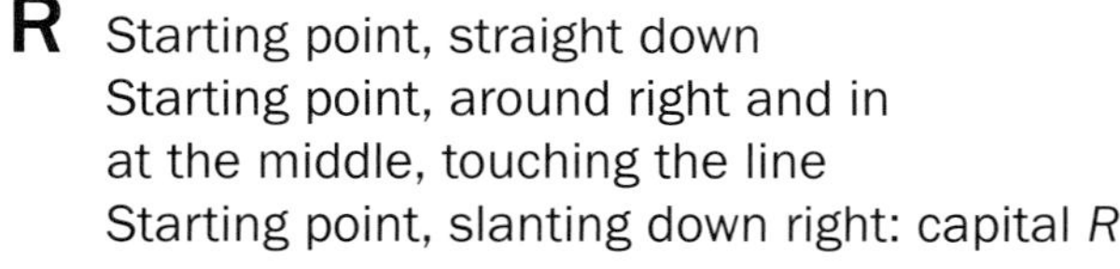

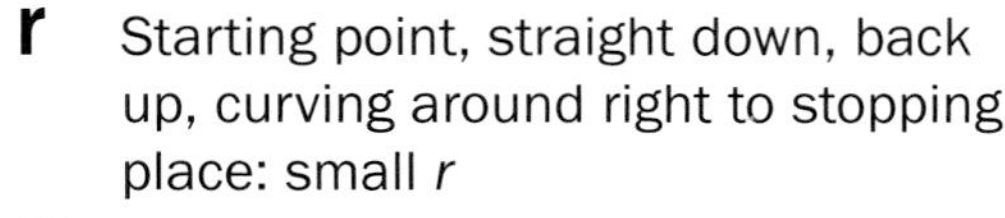

S Starting point, around left, curving right and down around right,curving left and up: capital *S*

s Starting point, around left, curving right and down around right, curving left and up: small s

Informal Assessment

LETTER ORIENTATION Frequent letter orientation errors are often a symptom that students are not respecting the starting point and stroke sequence for the letters.

Reading 1.3; Writing 1.3

UNIVERSAL ACCESS: MEETING INDIVIDUAL NEEDS

Reteach

LETTER FORMATION Students who need more help with letter formation can complete ***Reteach: Phonics Skills*** page 8 during Workshop.

Challenge

PHONICS For students who are ready for a challenge, use ***Challenge: Phonics Skills*** page 7.

Intervention Support

LETTER RECOGNITION During Workshop, shuffle ***Letter Cards A–S*** and place them in a container. Students should work with a partner to put the cards in alphabetical order, using the "Alphabet Song" as a reference. This could also be a game to put on the Phonics Game Shelf.

LETTER RECOGNITION

Phonics Skills Writing 1.3

Phonics Skills page 8 provides practice writing the letters *Qq*, *Rr*, and *Ss*. Help students write the letters as a class, saying the words together. Remind them to space appropriately on each line of the page.

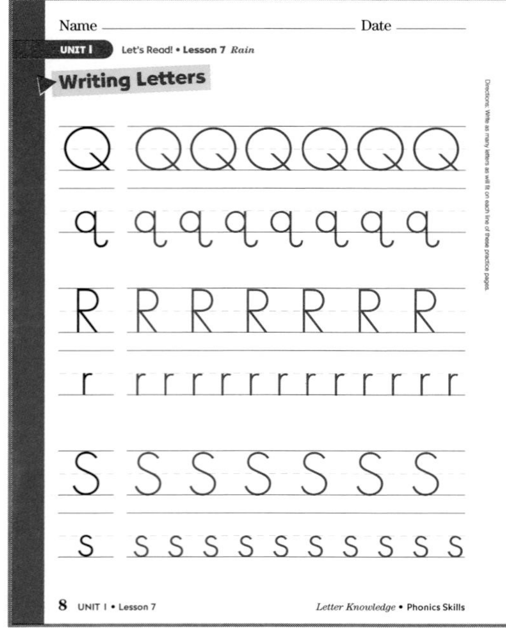
Name Date
UNIT 1 Let's Read! • Lesson 7 *Rain*
Writing Letters
Q Q Q Q Q Q Q
q q q q q q q q
R R R R R R R
r r r r r r r r r r r r r
S S S S S S S
s s s s s s s s s s s
8 UNIT 1 • Lesson 7 *Letter Knowledge* • Phonics Skills

***Phonics Skills* p. 8**

REVIEW SOUNDS & LETTERS

Reviewing Sounds and Letters

Introducing Consonant Sounds Reading 1.3, 1.4

- Write an alliterative sentence on the board for each of the consonants, such as

  The queen quietly questions Quincy.
  Rude Ricky raises rotten rattlesnakes.
  Susie's sister sings silly songs.

- Read the sentence aloud, underlining the key letter each time you say it.
- After challenging students to tell you the sound of the key letter, ask them to recite the sentence several times with you, exaggerating its sound.
- Tell the students a few other words that begin with *q*, such as *quack*, *quilt*, *quick*, and *quit*. Ask whether anyone's name begins with target letters and write them on the board or chart paper.
- Ask them to think of other words that begin with *Rr* and *Ss* and to confirm each other's suggestions.

Dictation

Dictation Reading 1.3; Eng. Lang. Conv. 1.8

- Have the students take out writing materials. Dictate the following letters, giving students time to write each letter before dictating the next:

  s q Q O S R r m n h

- Dictate the high-frequency words below. Use each word in a sentence and remind students to look in the High-Frequency Word Bank for guidance and confirmation on their spelling.

  a, on

- Collect the papers to see how the students are progressing.

Teacher Tip **HIGH-FREQUENCY WORDS** Encourage the students to use high-frequency words in sentences. Reading 1.3

Pre-Decodable Book 3

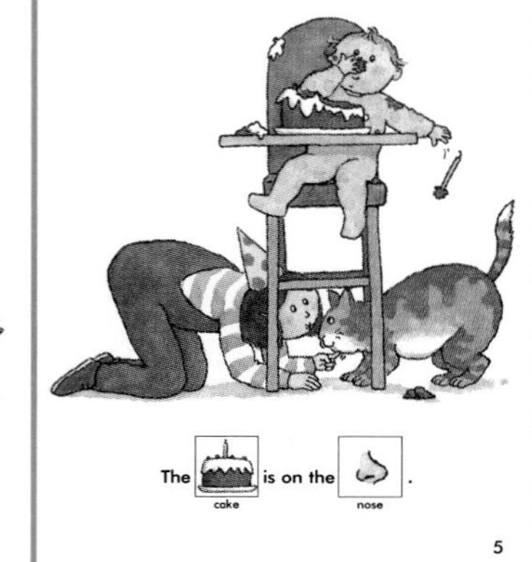

Reading a Pre-Decodable Book

Core Set, Book 3: *The Baby,* Story 1: "The Cake"

High-Frequency Words Reading 1.3

The high-frequency word introduced in this book is *are.* Write *are* on the board and ask students to say the word. Pronounce it, have the students repeat it, spell it together, and say it again. Then have volunteers use *are* in sentences. Review the high-frequency words already in the High-Frequency Word Bank. Have students volunteer to read the ones they recognize.

Reading Recommendations Reading 1.1, 1.2, 1.3, 1.8

- The nondecodable words in this book are *baby* and *cake.* Write each word on the board. Ask the students to say the word. Pronounce it, have the students repeat it, spell it together, and have them say it again. Then have volunteers use *baby* and *cake* in sentences.
- Read the title and credit lines on the front cover. Then open to the title page, which is also the Table of Contents. Point out that there are two stories in this book and that today they will read "The Cake." Point out that "The Cake" begins on page 3. Then have the students turn to page 3 and read the title, "The Cake" again.
- Briefly discuss the rebus pictures, telling the students what each represents, if necessary.
- Have the students read a page silently, then read the page aloud. Repeat this procedure for each page.
- Have another student reread the page before going on.
- Reread the story at least twice, calling on different students to read. Then have the entire group do a choral reading of the story.

Teacher Tip HIGH-FREQUENCY WORD BANK Review the high-frequency word *are* from this book in the Word Bank. Have students write the new word on a 3 x 5 card to take home to practice or add to their ring of words.

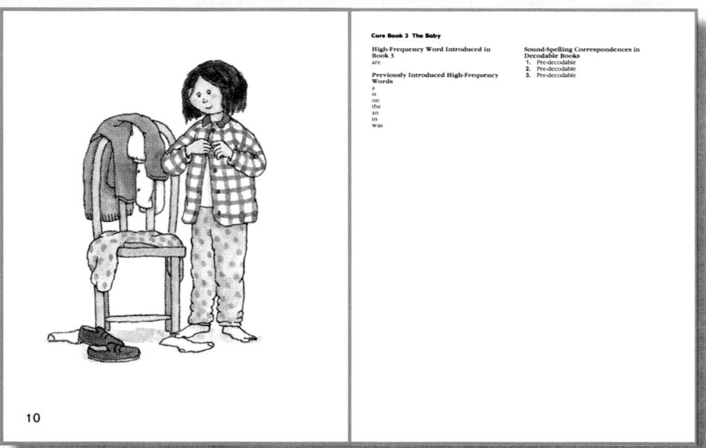

Responding Reading 2.2; Listen/Speak 1.2, 2.2

- Invite the students to discuss any hard words they encountered in *The Baby* and how they figured out these words. Call on volunteers to retell the story.
- To make sure the students are focusing on the story, ask questions such as the following, having the students answer by pointing to and reading aloud the words:

  Who is on the chair? *(The baby is on the chair.)*
  What is on the ear? *(The cake is on the ear.)*
  What is on the nose? *(The cake is on the nose.)*
  What is on the girl? *(The cake is on the girl.)*

Building Fluency Reading 1.16

Encourage partners to build fluency rereading ***Decodable Book 2,*** *The Egg*, of the Core Set. The first time through, one partner should read the odd-numbered pages and the other the even-numbered pages. For the second reading, the partners should switch pages. After the second reading, the partners should choose other ***Decodable Books*** from previous lessons and continue to read to each other.

Informal Assessment

MONITORING Have individual students or partners read "The Cake" to you. Note which students recognize the high-frequency words, and which do not. Also note which students are reading the rebus stories in a fluent manner. Finally, have the students retell the story to assess comprehension.

Routine Card
Refer to ***Routine 5*** for reading **Decodable Books.**

Pages 18–19 of *Let's Read!*

SELECTION INTRODUCTION

About the Author Reading 3.2

Robert Louis Stevenson is probably most widely remembered for his adventure stories. However, in *A Child's Garden of Verses*, a collection of 63 poems, he explores the world and expresses his observations from a child's point of view.

Other Books by Robert Louis Stevenson

Treasure Island, Kidnapped!

About the Illustrator Reading 3.2

Ann Trainor Domingue knew she wanted to become an artist when she was five years old. While attending college, she decided the field of graphic design best combined her interests and skills. She has since created everything from ads to billboards to posters and computer-generated illustrations. Domingue has received numerous awards for her designs and illustrations. She continues her work as a watercolorist in her spare time at her home in New Hampshire, where she resides with her husband, children, and pets.

Objectives

- Students will use the Table of Contents to locate information.
- Students will listen and respond to "Rain."
- Students will tell what they liked about the selection.
- Students will discuss the images in the selection after reflection.
- Students will look at artwork.
- Students will practice rhyming words.

Materials

- Big Book *Let's Read!*, pp. 18–19

Selection Summary

Genre: Poetry

Using simple but eloquent language, this little poem looks at rain from a child's point of view. The strong rhythm, alliteration, and repetition of words make the poem an ideal choice for reading aloud to students.

The elements of poetry are listed below. Poetry may have one or more of these elements.

- Sentences are sometimes broken into parts. Each part is on a line of its own.
- Words that rhyme are often used.
- The lines of a poem often have rhythm, or meter.
- Some words may be repeated.

Inquiry Connections

In this selection of the ***Big Book*** the students will listen to a poem about rain.

Key concepts investigated are:

- The elements of poetry.
- Matching oral words to printed words.
- Becoming more aware of print.

Direct the students to the Concept/Question Board. Encourage them to post any questions or ideas they have about the unit. They may want to include a drawing or poem about a rainy day.

- Make sure the students put their names or initials on anything they post on the Board.
- Tell them that they can post anything on the Board any day. Be sure to have students discuss what they put on the Board with the class.

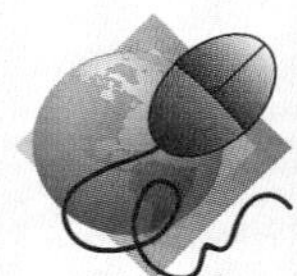

www.sra4kids.com
Web Connection
Help the students look for additional information about poems and rhymes by using the Web connections that are available at the Reading link of the SRA Web page.

Universal Access: Meeting Individual Needs

ELL Support

For ELD strategies, use the ***English-Language Development Guide,*** Unit 1, Lesson 7.

Intervention Support

For intervention strategies, use the ***Intervention Guide,*** Unit 1, Lesson 7.

Teacher Tip ACTIVATE PRIOR KNOWLEDGE Tell the students that good readers think about what they already know that relates to the selection they are reading. Remind the students that whenever they read, they should think about what they already know that might relate to the ideas in the reading. Reading 2.6

Routine Card
Refer to ***Routine 11*** for the procedure for reading the selection.

Build Background

Activate Prior Knowledge Listen/Speak 2.3

Ask the students what they know or think about rain. Perhaps they could tell what happened the last time it rained. Have them share in a simple sentence any funny experiences, such as getting soaked, very wet, or having an umbrella turn inside out.

Preview and Prepare

Browse Reading 1.2

- Open *Let's Read!* to the Table of Contents. Tell students that you are going to read them a poem called "Rain." Call on volunteers to find the poem in the Table of Contents and to point to the page number where it can be found.
- Ask the students why they should browse before they read and what they might do when they browse.
- Display page 18 of the ***Big Book.*** Point out the title, author, and illustrator and read the names aloud. Then have students look at the illustration and predict what they think the main idea is in the poem. Tell students that illustrations give us hints about the meaning of the words in the poem.
- Before reading the selection to the students, read the Focus Questions on the first page of the selection together. Briefly discuss the questions, and tell the students to keep these questions in mind as you read.

Set Purposes

Explain to students that the purpose for reading this poem is to share the poet's idea about all the places rain falls.

Selection Vocabulary

- Write the following word on the board and read it:

  umbrellas

- Read the word again, and ask the students to repeat it after you.
- Ask the students to tell what an umbrella is used for.
- Then have them use the word in a sentence.
- Invite the students to enjoy the rhyme and rhythm of this poem.
- If you choose, point out the alliteration, and explain that by using words that contain the same sound, poets help create a rhythm and a mood.

Reading Recommendations

Read Aloud Listen/Speak 2.1

- Read the poem through once without pausing.
- Ask the students to look at the poem and to say any words they think they know.
- Reread the poem one line at a time. Have students recite each line as you say it.

Using Comprehension Strategies

Comprehension strategy instruction allows students to become aware of what good readers do when they read. Good readers constantly check their understanding as they are reading and asking themselves questions. Skilled readers also recognize when they are having problems understanding a selection and stop to use various comprehension strategies to help them make sense of what they are reading.

During the reading of this selection, you will model the use of the following comprehension strategy:

- **Visualizing** helps readers picture in their minds what is going on in a selection to gain a clearer understanding.

Teacher Tip HIGH-FREQUENCY WORDS The following high-frequency words appear in the selection *the, is,* and *on.* Point to these words in the High-Frequency Word Bank, have students read them, and encourage them to read these words with you when you encounter them in the reading.

Routine Card
Refer to ***Routine 10*** for the Selection Vocabulary procedure.

UNIVERSAL ACCESS: MEETING INDIVIDUAL NEEDS

ELL Tip

PICTURE STORY Read the poem "Rain" to the English-language learners ahead of time. Ask them to tell you what it is about and answer any questions they have. Ask them to draw pictures that illustrate the poem. Help them write labels for their pictures.

Teacher Tip COMPREHENSION Good readers constantly evaluate their understanding of what they read. Stop often to make sure you and the students are doing this.

Teacher Tip VISUALIZING An extended lesson on Visualizing can be found on page T157. This lesson is intended to give extra practice with visualizing.

COMPREHENSION

Comprehension Strategies Listen/Speak 1.5, 2.4

Visualizing *This poem offers an excellent opportunity for students to use the visualizing strategy. Invite them to discuss the images that come to mind as they hear the poem. Remind them to use descriptive words and to pay attention to sensory detail. You can help students use strategies by modeling Visualizing with them.*

Teacher Modeling

Visualizing *When I read about the rain on umbrellas, I imagine a street filled with students carrying red umbrellas. What did you picture?*

Phonemic Awareness Reading 1.4

FINAL CONSONANT SOUNDS Remind students that they have had the experience of saying the first sound of a word you named. Tell students that now you are going to say some familiar words and leave off the end sound. After you say a word without its final sound, ask a volunteer to think of the missing sound, say it aloud, and then say the completed word. For example: when you say "rai," the student says "/n/, rain." Use these words: *boat, ship, sail, drip, cloud, drop,* and *field.*

Universal Access: Meeting Individual Needs

ELL Tip

SHARING Encourage English-language learners to share short poems or rhymes in their native languages. After reciting the poem one or more times, invite the other students to participate by clapping to keep time with the rhythm.

Teacher Tip **COMPREHENSION STRATEGIES** Tell students that good readers think about the questions that come up about the topic they are reading about, and they keep coming back to those questions. As they read, tell them to keep in mind the questions on the Concept/Question Board. Have them make notes to themselves in the Response Journal section of their Writer's Notebooks about which questions seem really important and what information in the selections seems most important. Tell them that good readers always think about what is important in selections, and they try to remember this important information.

Letter Recognition

Qq, Rr, Ss Reading 1.3

Ask the students to look for the letters *Qq*, *Rr*, and *Ss* in words in the selection. Invite volunteers to point out these letters on the ***Big Book*** pages.

Teacher Tip READING FOR ENJOYMENT Remind students that they should spend at least 20 minutes reading after school.

Teacher Tip SPEAKING When the students are speaking to the class about the poem, remind them to make eye contact with their classmates and to stay on topic. Remind students that when you call on one of them, it is his or her turn to speak. Tell students that they should not speak when it is another student's turn. Make sure that students speak loudly and clearly when they are addressing the class. Listen/Speak 1.1, 1.4

Discussing the Selection Reading 2.2; Listen/Speak 1.4, 1.5

- Invite the students to share what they like about the poem.
- Ask students if there are any characters in this poem *(no)*. Then ask them to tell what this poem is about *(rain)*.
- Have the students find the ship in the illustration. Ask them how this illustration helps them understand the poem.
- Ask the students to think about what the words of the poem convey. Call on a volunteer. If necessary, call on other students to offer help and clarification.
- Ask the students what interested them about this poem. Have students discuss what images this poem created in their minds. How is this poem similar to or different from the other poems they have read?
- With the students, refer back to the Focus Questions for the selection. Have all the questions been answered? If not, answer them now.

Have the students record their responses to the selection in the Response Journal section of their Writer's Notebooks by drawing pictures of what they like to do when it rains. Help the students label their drawings.

Review Selection Vocabulary

Have students review the selection vocabulary word for this lesson. Remind them that they discussed the meanings of this word at the beginning of the lesson. Have them add this and any other interesting words that they clarified while reading to the Vocabulary Words section of their Writer's Notebooks. The word from this selection is:

umbrellas

- Have the students use the word in oral sentences. Help the students expand their sentences by asking who, what, where, when, why, and how questions.
- Ask the students to draw a picture that represents the word.
- Read all the words in the *Let's Read!* Word Bank, and encourage the students to review what they mean by using the words in sentences or using actions to describe them.

Encourage the students to refer to the vocabulary words throughout the unit.

Print and Book Awareness

Directionality

Remind students that people read from the left side of the page to the right side of the page. When readers finish a line, they move to the line below it, and they keep reading from left to right until they reach the end of the page.

Match Oral and Printed Words Reading 1.1

Display the title page of "Rain." Reminding students about the direction in which people read, ask volunteers to come up and point to the title and the author's name as you read them aloud.

Supporting the Reading

Comprehension Strategy: Visualizing

Remind the students that they have already visualized what happened in the poem once. Reread the poem, having the students close their eyes as you read, and visualize the poem again. Discuss what they imagined.

Purposes for Reading

Remind students that before they read this poem, they discussed the purpose for reading and determined that it was to share ideas about where rain falls. Ask students to name places where rain falls. They may name those places mentioned in the poem and add to that list based on their own knowledge.

View Fine Art

- Display page 56 of *Let's Read!* and have students look at the untitled art piece. Point out that this art piece looks more like a cartoon than a painting. Ask the students to describe the lines, shapes, and colors in the piece. Ask volunteers to decribe the scene pictured here.
- Invite the students to talk about a time when they sat with someone to listen to a story. Ask the students whether they enjoyed listening to the stories and whether they remember the stories well enough to retell them.

Fine Art **Let's Read!**

Untitled. August 6, 1988. **Keith Haring.** Sumi ink on paper.

Layla and Majnum at School. 1524–1525. **Artist unknown,** style of Shaykh Zadeh. Persian (Herat) miniature; ink, colors, and gold on paper. The Metropolitan Museum of Art, New York.

The Libraries Are Appreciated. 1943. **Jacob Lawrence.** Gouache and watercolor on paper. Philadelphia Museum of Art.

56

Objectives

- Students will continue working on their alphabet books.
- Students will apply concepts and ideas through a curricular connection.

Materials

- Class alphabet book

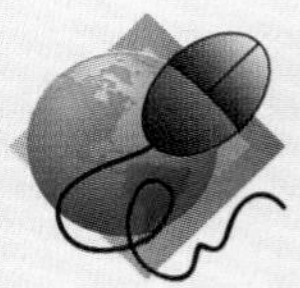

www.sra4kids.com
Web Connection
Help the students look for additional information about poems and rhymes by using the Web connections that are available at the Reading link of the SRA Web page.

INVESTIGATION

Supporting the Investigation

Investigating Concepts Beyond the Text Reading 1.3

Remind students about the alphabet books they are working on for this unit.

- Begin by spending a few minutes sharing the completed pages of the alphabet book that students created for the letters *e*, *f*, *g*, and *h*. Point out interesting approaches. For example, one student might have a page of all animals whose names begin with *e*—*elephant*, *eel*, *eagle*, and *egret*. Another might have a page of foods that begin with *f*—*fish*, *fudge*, *French fries*, and *figs*.
- Distribute drawing paper or story paper, and discuss with students what they might include on their next set of pages. Encourage a variety of suggestions, emphasizing that they can decide for themselves what they want to include. Have supplies such as crayons, markers, scissors, paste, and old magazines or catalogs available.
- Remind students to plan before they begin to write on or design their pages. Assign the letters *i*, *j*, *k*, and *l*.

INVESTIGATION

Concept/Question Board

- Encourage the students to add to the Concept/Question Board at this time.
- Discuss questions, articles, pictures, or other items already posted.

Science Connection

Science

Weather Words Reading 1.17; Writing 1.1

Purpose: To create a Weather Word Bank

- Post some sheets of chart paper on the board. Then begin a discussion about weather. Ask students what the weather is like today, and write down key words as they say them. Then have students continue supplying all the weather words they can think of. Prompt them as necessary by asking about different seasons, such as "What is the weather like where you live at Thanksgiving?"
- Write each dictated weather word on the chart paper. Then use the oaktag strips and have volunteers help you write a weather word on each strip.
- Distribute strips to all students and help them identify their words. Then invite students to decorate their weather words with appropriate pictures.
- Place the strips on the wall and review the words with students. Every day, when you discuss the day's weather, have students go to the wall and identify the appropriate words for the day.

Teacher Tip MATERIALS For this Science Connection, you will need chart paper, markers, and oaktag strips

Objectives

Word Analysis Vocabulary

- **Vocabulary Strategies: Rhyming Words.** Using words from "Rain," build vocabulary from rhyming word games and introduce finding definitions through dictionary use.

Writing Process Strategies

- **Introduction to the Writing Process.** Building on the theme Let's Read!, understand that writing is a process and prewriting involves organizing for writing.

English Language Conventions

- **Mechanics: Capital Letters.** Building on Letter Recognition in the Phonemic Awareness lesson, develop understanding that names of cities and states and other names of specific places or things begin with capital letters.

Materials

- Language Arts Transparency 2
- Big Book *Let's Read!* pp. 18–19

UNIVERSAL ACCESS:
MEETING INDIVIDUAL NEEDS

Reteach, Challenge, English-Language Development and ***Intervention*** lessons are available to support the language arts instruction in this lesson.

OVERVIEW

Language Arts Overview

Word Analysis

Vocabulary The Vocabulary lesson focuses on rhyming as a strategy for expanding vocabulary. Building on vocabulary from "Rain," students will generate lists of rhyming words and investigate the meanings of any unknown words, including using a dictionary. This form of word play provides an enjoyable way to develop interest in vocabulary study.

Vocabulary Skill Words

rain **sea** **tree** **gain** **pain**

Writing Process Strategies

The Writing Process Strategies lesson continues the introduction of the prewriting skill of organizing for drafting. Many inexperienced writers do not organize before they start writing. Experienced writers, however, spend a great deal of time in the prewriting phase, getting ideas and then organizing them before they start writing.

English Language Conventions

Grammar, Usage, and Mechanics **Capital Letters** The English Language Conventions support the reading and writing skills development in this lesson. This lesson introduces students to the conventions of capitalizing names of cities and states and other proper nouns.

Word Analysis

Vocabulary

Rhyming Words Reading 1.6

Teach

- Write the following words on the board and say them to emphasize their rhymes: *rain, gain, pain.* Explain that words that have the same ending sounds are rhyming words.
- Have the students suggest words that rhyme with *tree (bee, flea, fee, glee, he, knee, me, pea, she, see, sea, we)* as you write them on the board. Discuss how they could learn the meaning of any unfamiliar word. *(Ideas could include asking someone or looking the word up in a dictionary.)*
- **Teacher Model:** Model use of a classroom dictionary to look up the word *sea.* Read the dictionary definition *(a great body of salty water that covers much of Earth)* and use the word in a sentence, such as, *Whales live in the sea.* Explain that using a new word in a sentence helps students remember it.

Guided Practice

- Write *Rain* as a column heading on the board or chart paper.
- Have the students suggest other words that rhyme with *rain* as you write them on the board *(Jane, Maine, mane, main, Wayne, wane).* Discuss the meaning of each word. When the class doesn't know a word, model using a dictionary to look it up. Explain that you will teach students how to use a dictionary this year, but for right now, all they need to know is that there is a source of information for finding definitions of unknown words.
- Encourage each student to use the word in an oral sentence.
- Conclude by explaining that playing rhyming games can lead students to learn new words.

Writing Process Strategies

Introduction to the Writing Process

Plan Writing 1.0, 1.1

Teach

- Review the web students made about fish on Day 1.
- Explain that after writers have ideas, they have to think about the best way to organize them.

Guided Practice

- Reread or recite the poem "Rain." Write the word *Rain* on the board or chart paper.
- As a class, brainstorm some ideas to write about rain. Use ***Language Arts Transparency 2*** to make a list. Ideas might include:
  - falls from the sky
  - is wet
  - makes plants grow
- With students' help, identify three ideas students would want to write about rain and star them.
- Order the ideas as to which you could write about first, second, and third.
- Remind students that lists can be used to plan ideas about any topic. Review the class list that was made in Lesson 5 to generate ideas for their autobiographies.
- Follow up by having students identify three ideas from the list in Lesson 5 that they would want to write about. Then have them order the ideas according to how they would want to write about them.

English Language Conventions

Grammar, Usage, and Mechanics

Capital Letters Eng. Lang. Conv. 1.6

Teach

- Review the capital and lowercase letters that students have explored thus far *(A–P).*
- Review that people's names start with capital letters.
- Explain that cities and states start with capital letters, too.
- Write the names of some states and their state capitals on the board and point to the capital letter in each word: *Richmond, Virginia; Columbus, Ohio; Boston, Massachusetts; Sacramento, California; Albany, New York.*

Guided Practice in Reading

- Write the name of your school on the board and point out the capital letters. Have students look for the name of your school on newsletters or school stationery and point out the capital letters.
- Ask the students to tell the name of the street where they live. Write the names of local streets on the board and point to each capital letter. Have students look in a phone book or student directory to see that names of streets are capitalized.
- Explain that we all live in the United States of America and write that on the board, pointing to each capital letter. On the copyright page of the ***Big Book Let's Read!***, point out the capital letters in *United States of America* in the copyright.
- Encourage students to name other countries *(Mexico, Canada, France, China)* as you write them on the board. Explain that all countries start with a capital letter.
- Conclude by explaining that special or specific places start with capital letters.

Objectives

- Students will attend to phonemes through blending and segmentation.
- Students will write letters of the alphabet.
- Students will associate letters with sounds.

Materials

- Lion Puppet
- Sound/Spelling Cards
- Phonics Skills, p. 9
- Letter Cards
- High-Frequency Word Cards

Warming Up

Use one or both of the following activities to focus students' attention and to reinforce some of the concepts they have been learning.

I Spy Reading 1.3, 1.4; Listen/Speak 2.1

- Play I Spy with the letters *r* and *s*.

  "I spy with my little eye,

  Something with the letter _____."

- To discover the word you see, students must point out words in the classroom that have the appropriate letter.

Initial Consonant Blending Reading 1.4, 1.8

Read the following words, asking the students to blend the initial consonant with the rest into a whole word.

/t/ . . . ortoise	/t/ . . . iptoe	/p/ . . . ark	/d/ . . . ark
/d/ . . . octor	/d/ . . . esk	/p/ . . . art	/h/ . . . eart
/t/ . . . ank	/m/ . . . ark	/k/ . . . oat	/g/ . . . oat
/s/ . . . it	/s/ . . . ip	/d/ . . . ip	/d/ . . . id

Universal Access: Meeting Individual Needs

ELL Support

For ELD strategies, use the ***English-Language Development Guide,*** Unit 1, Lesson 8.

Intervention Support

For intervention strategies, use the ***Intervention Guide,*** Unit 1, Lesson 8.

Teacher Tip **CONSONANT BLENDING** You may want to call on individuals to blend words, and then have the other students signal whether they were corrrect.

Reading 1.8

Phonemic Awareness

Oral Blending

Final Consonant Sounds Reading 1.4, 1.8

As in yesterday's blending activity, pause before the final consonant of each of the following words. Today's list is a little harder to blend because the first part of each word does not give such a strong clue to the final consonant as yesterday's words did.

cabba . . . /j/	mushroo . . . /m/	bathro . . . /b/	lollipo . . . /p/
liqui . . . /d/	panca . . . /k/	carpe . . . /t/	plasti . . . /k/
chee . . . /z/	chea . . . /p/	tru . . . /th/	troo . . . /p/
mou . . . /th/	mou . . . /s/	pea . . . /ch/	pee . . . /k/

Segmentation

Initial Phoneme Segmentation Reading 1.4

Tell the students that the puppet wants them to repeat only the *first sound* of each word.

Teacher: chair
Puppet: /ch/

Teacher: sail
Puppet: /s/

Teacher: soup
Students: /s/

Continue with the following words:

zoo	moo	chew	too	boo
buy	sigh	lie	pie	high
me	see	seed	feed	bead
ship	rip	tip	lip	zip

Reading 1.6, 1.8, 1.9

UNIVERSAL ACCESS: MEETING INDIVIDUAL NEEDS

Reteach

PHONEMIC AWARENESS Be sure to spend some time during Workshop with students who find oral blending and segmentation exercises difficult. Start with syllable blending, then move on to initial consonant blending. If they have difficulty with the transition, use the puppet to help them segment initial sounds.

ELL Tip

WORD MEANING Make sure the English-language learners know the meanings of the words before doing the activities with the class. Use pictures, photos, objects, stick drawings, pantomime, or the ***English-Language Development Glossary***.

Intervention Tip

RHYMING WORDS If the students still are having difficulty, use groups of one-syllable rhyming words: *troop, scoop, droop; room, zoom, loom; cheap, sleep, peep;* and *mouse, house, louse.*

Teacher Tip PHRASES Have the students describe each of the phrases to make sure all students understand what each one is.

PHONEMIC AWARENESS

Final Phoneme Segmentation Reading 1.4

- Tell the students that the puppet now has a new game. When he repeats words, he leaves off the last sound. Tell the students to listen carefully so that they can tell the puppet the sound he forgets.

Teacher:	Peanut butter sandwich
Puppet:	Peanut butter sandwiiiiii . . .
Teacher:	Listen again. Peanut butter sandwiCH
Puppet:	Peanut butter sandwiiiiii . . .
Teacher:	He forgot something. What sound did he forget?
Students:	/ch/
Teacher:	Chicken noodle soup
Puppet:	Chicken noodle sou . . .
Teacher:	What's the missing sound?
Students:	/p/

- Continue with:

chocolate mil /k/	Frosty the Snowma /n/
a glass of orange jui /s/	hamburger bu /n/
mustard and ketchu /p/	comb and bru /sh/
crackers and chee /z/	Go fly a ki /t/

LETTER RECOGNITION

Letter Recognition

Exploring *Tt, Uu,* and *Vv* Reading 1.3; Writing 1.3

- Introduce the letters *Tt, Uu,* and *Vv*.
- Begin by writing a capital *T* on the board. Be sure to indicate the starting point and remind the students that the line that goes across rests on top of the line that goes down.
- Have the students imitate your movements by tracing the letter in the air and saying the strokes as you write them. Then have them use their fingers to trace the letter on their desks.
- After a few tracings, have them write the letter on paper.
- Repeat the process with lowercase *t*. Then continue with the letters *Uu* and *Vv*.
- When you introduce capital *U*, demonstrate writing the letter a few times, and point out that the letter should end across from where it started.
- Invite volunteers to the board to demonstrate writing one or two letters.
- After the students have written all their letters, have them proofread their work.

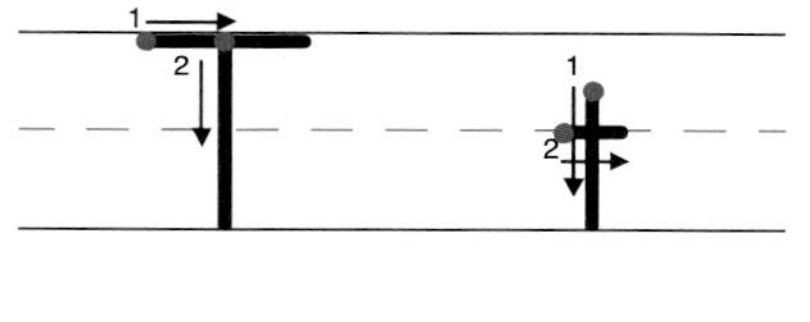

T Starting point, straight across
Starting point, straight down: capital *T*

t Starting point, straight down
Starting point, across short: small *t*

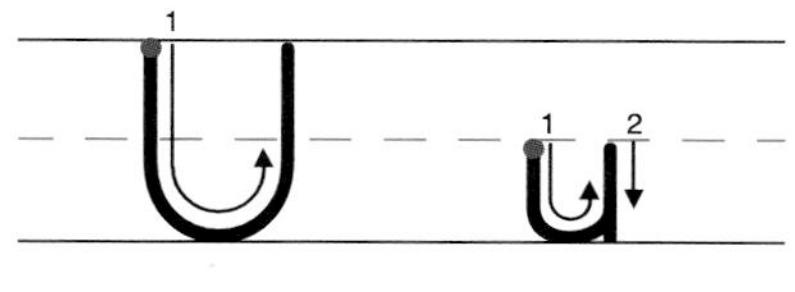

U Starting point, straight down,
curving around right and up,
straight up: capital *U*

u Starting point, straight down,
curving around right and up,
straight up, straight back down: small *u*

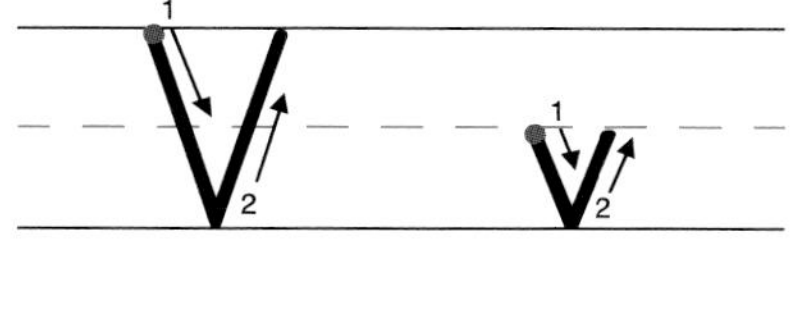

V Starting point, slanting down right,
slanting up right: capital *V*

v Starting point, slanting down right,
slanting up right: small *v*

UNIVERSAL ACCESS:
MEETING INDIVIDUAL NEEDS

Intervention Tip

LETTER RECOGNITION During Workshop, provide extra help with letter formation and recognition, such as having students put ***Letter Cards*** in order, match capital and lowercase letters, or practice forming letters. Or, you could write the words on the board or a sheet of paper and have the students trace them before writing them independently.

Reading 1.3; Writing 1.3

Writing 1.3

Universal Access: Meeting Individual Needs

Reteach

LETTER FORMATION Students who need more help with letter formation can complete ***Reteach: Phonics Skills*** page 9 during Workshop.

Challenge

LETTER FORMATION For students who are ready for a challenge, use ***Challenge: Phonics Skills*** page 8.

Intervention Tip

LETTER FORMATION During Workshop, have the students practice making their letters in a sand tray or with finger paints. You can also have the students use water and a paintbrush to "paint" their letters on a chalkboard. This will help them get a better feel for the letters.

Teacher Tip LETTER CARDS It may be helpful to have students use the *i* and *u* ***Letter Cards.*** Have them raise the *i* card if the word contains /ī/ or the *u* card if the word contains /ū/.

Reading 1.5

Informal Assessment

WRITING LETTERS Review students' papers to find out who is still uncomfortable writing letters. Watch these students carefully so that you can provide extra support and practice as soon as possible, perhaps during Workshop.

Reading 1.3; Writing 1.3

LETTER RECOGNITION

Phonics Skills Writing 1.3

Help the students complete ***Phonics Skills*** page 9. Have students write as many letters as will fit on each line of the practice page, reminding students to be sure to leave enough space between the letters so the letters can be distinguished from each other.

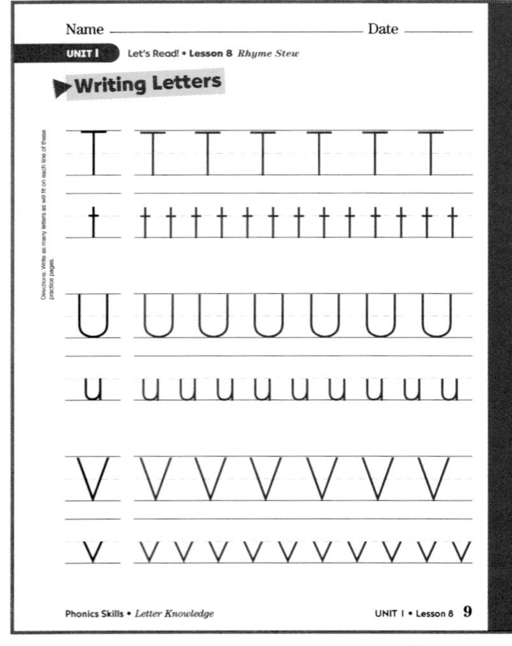

Name Date

UNIT 1 Let's Read! • Lesson 8 *Rhyme Stew*

Writing Letters

T T T T T T T

t t t t t t t t t t t t t

U U U U U U U

u u u u u u u u u

V V V V V V V

v v v v v v v v v v v

Phonics Skills • *Letter Knowledge* UNIT 1 • Lesson 8 9

***Phonics Skills* p. 9**

REVIEW SOUNDS & LETTERS

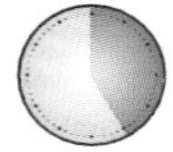

Reviewing Sounds and Letters

Listening for Vowel Sounds: /ī/ and /ū/ Reading 1.3, 1.5

- Write the letters *Ii* on the extreme left side of the board and the letters *Uu* on the extreme right side.
- Tell the students they must listen carefully to hear the /ī/ sound or the /ū/ sound in each word you say.
- If they hear the /ī/ sound, they should say /ī/ and point to the letter *Ii* on the board; if they hear the /ū/ sound, they should say /ū/ and point to the letter *Uu* on the board on your cue or signal.

cube	few	use	sigh	my
pew	try	mute	fly	fry
hide	ride	usual	huge	pupil
unit	sight	kite	cute	puny

Introducing Consonant Sounds Reading 1.3, 1.4

- Write an alliterative sentence on the board for each of the consonants, such as:

  Tricky Tony tickles turtle tummies.
  Vicky vacuums velvet valentines.
- Read the sentence aloud, underlining the key letter each time you say it.
- After challenging the students to tell you the sound of the key letter, ask them to recite the sentence several times with you, exaggerating its sound.
- Ask the students whether any of their names begin with the target letters. Write the names on the board.
- Ask the students to think of other words that begin with the key letter.

Dictation

Dictation Reading 1.1, 1.3, 1.9; Eng. Lang. Conv. 1.8

- Ask the students to take out writing materials. Dictate the following letters, giving the students time to write each letter before dictating the next:

  T L P U V t u v r s

- Dictate the high-frequency words below. Use each word in a sentence and remind the students to look in the High-Frequency Word Bank for guidance and confirmation of their spellings.

  is, was, the

- Collect the papers to see how the students are progressing.

Informal Assessment

MONITORING Continue to monitor students' letter knowledge by assessing their ability to name and recognize the shapes of letters.

Reading 1.3

Pages 20–23 of *Let's Read!*

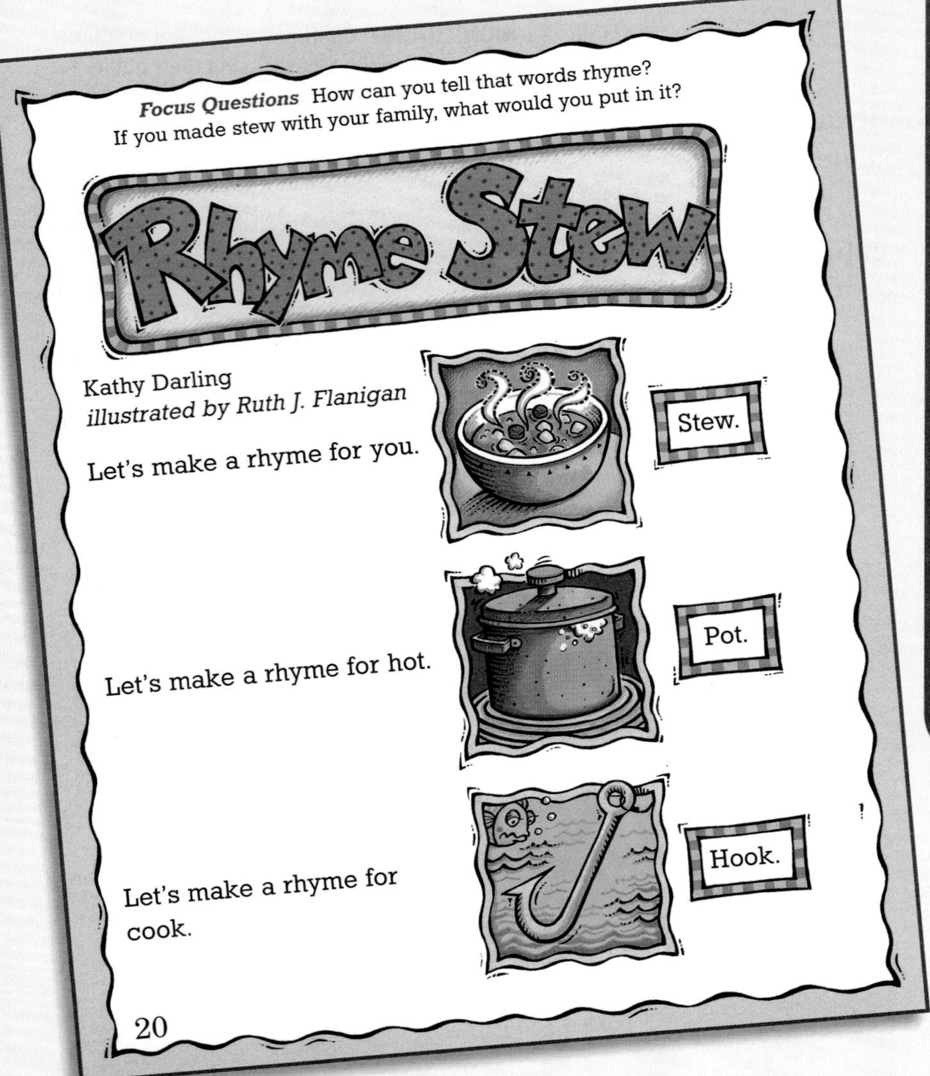

SELECTION INTRODUCTION

About the Author Reading 3.2

KATHY DARLING was a children's book editor and promotion director before turning her hand to writing. In addition to her earlier imaginative tales, she has written many fine nonfiction books about science and animals.

Other Books by Kathy Darling
Jack Frost and the Magic Paint Brush, *Pecos Bill Finds a Horse*, *Bet You Can't! Science Impossibilities to Fool You* (with Vicki Cobb)

About the Illustrator Reading 3.2

RUTH FLANIGAN knew that she wanted to be an artist at age 6. She now works as an illustrator for publishers all over the country. Her encouragement to young people is that they should "*not be afraid to pursue an unusual profession. If you're willing to work hard enough to make your dream come true, your hobby may well become your life's work.*" She lives in Rhode Island with her husband and little blue parakeet, Baby, who sits on her shoulder and pen while she works.

Objectives

- Students will recognize words that rhyme.
- Students will identify words in the selection with the letters *Rs* and *Ss*.
- Students will use a Table of Contents to locate information.
- Students will discuss how words and pictures go together.
- Students will clap rhythms.
- Students will recognize patterns of sounds and rhythms in a chant.

Materials

- Big Book *Let's Read!*, pp. 20–23

Selection Summary

Genre: Rhyming Fiction

This rhyme contains lots of ingredients for a hearty stew—and a generous mixture of rhymes to make a "rhyme stew," as well.

The elements of rhyming fiction are listed below. Rhyming fiction may have one or more of these elements.

- Rhyming fiction presents a made-up story.
- Its primary purpose is to entertain.
- Words that rhyme are used to make the work of fiction more amusing.
- Some words that rhyme are used to help the reader more easily remember the work of fiction.

Inquiry Connections

In this selection of the ***Big Book*** the students will listen to "Rhyme Stew."

Key concepts investigated are

- the elements of poetry.
- matching oral words to printed words.
- becoming more aware of print.

Direct the students to the Concept/Question Board. Encourage them to post any questions or ideas they have about the unit. Have the students generate a list of rhyming words and post it on the Board.

- Make sure the students put their names or initials on anything they post on the Board.
- Tell them that they can post something on the Board any day. Be sure to have students discuss what they put on the Board with the class.

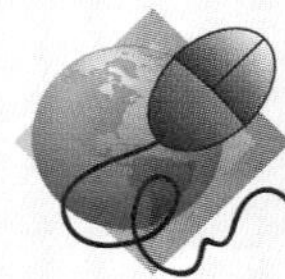

www.sra4kids.com
Web Connection
Help the students look for additional information about poems and rhymes by using the Web connections that are available at the Reading link of the SRA Web page.

Universal Access: Meeting Individual Needs

ELL Support

For ELD strategies, use the ***English-Language Development Guide,*** Unit 1, Lesson 8.

Intervention Support

For intervention strategies, use the ***Intervention Guide,*** Unit 1, Lesson 8.

Teacher Tip BROWSE Remind the students that good readers browse before reading. Tell them that they should be getting in the habit of browsing before they read, and that doing so can help them activate prior knowledge relevant to the selection.

Routine Card
Refer to ***Routine 11*** for the procedure for reading the selection.

Build Background

Activate Prior Knowledge Reading 2.6

Ask someone to tell what a *stew* is and have them discuss when they have eaten it or even helped make one. Help the students understand that stews tend to have lots of ingredients, probably several vegetables and perhaps some meat, that are all stirred up and cooked together.

Preview and Prepare

Browse

Open *Let's Read!* to the Table of Contents. Read the previous titles with the students. Name two and discuss how they are alike. Find the titles that have animals named in them. Then find "Rhyme Stew." Ask whether anyone can tell what page number the poem is on, and then turn to that page.

Before reading the selection to the students, read the Focus Questions on the first page of the selection together. Briefly discuss the questions, and tell the students to keep these questions in mind as you read.

Set Purposes

Explain that readers have many reasons for reading. Because the title is "Rhyme Stew," suggest that the purpose for reading might be to listen for rhymes that are all mixed together.

Selection Vocabulary

- Write the following words on the board, then pronounce them.

  spice **munch**

- Tell the students that a *spice* is something you add to food to make it tastier. Salt, pepper, and cinnamon are spices they might know. Use the word *spice* in a sentence. Then ask the students to think of a sentence with the word *spice.* Invite volunteers to say their sentences out loud.
- Ask what the word *munch* means. Explain that it means "to chew" or "to eat something with enjoyment."

Reading Recommendations

Read Aloud

- Read the poem once without pausing.
- Read the poem again, reviewing the rhyming words in each line.
- Point to the pictures and ask students to find the pictures that go with the rhyming words.
- Read the poem one more time, encouraging the students to join in when they can.
- Point out to the students that in this selection, the art is an important part of the poem.

Using Comprehension Strategies Listen/Speak 1.2

Comprehension strategy instruction allows students to become aware of what good readers do when they read. Good readers constantly check their understanding as they are reading and ask themselves questions. Skilled readers also recognize when they are having problems understanding a selection and stop to use various comprehension strategies to help them make sense of what they are reading.

During the reading of this selection, you will model the use of the following comprehension strategy:

- **Asking Questions** helps readers focus their attention on what they are reading, and engages them in deeper understanding of themes, concepts, and ideas.

Teacher Tip HIGH-FREQUENCY WORDS The following high-frequency word appears in the selection: *a.* Point to this word in the High-Frequency Word Bank, have students read it, and encourage them to read *a* with you when you encounter it in the reading.

Routine Card
Refer to ***Routine 10*** for the Selection Vocabulary procedure.

Teacher Tip FOODS Begin a list of words that name students' favorite foods. Add to the list as students develop new favorites. Reading 1.17

Universal Access: Meeting Individual Needs

ELL Support

PRETEACH Read the selection to the English-language learners before you read it to the class. As you read, give the students the opportunity to ask questions to clarify what they don't understand. Model the Asking Questions strategy so they can feel more comfortable asking questions when the selection is read to the class. Listen/Speak 1.2

Teacher Tip ASKING QUESTIONS An extended lesson on Asking Questions can be found on page T175. This lesson is intended to give extra practice with asking questions.

Teacher Tip COMPREHENSION STRATEGIES Good readers are also good listeners. Reading aloud to students provides an opportunity to teach the reader responses and problem-solving strategies that good readers employ. In addition to reading aloud with expression and enthusiasm, model your own comprehension strategies while reading aloud to students. This makes the use of strategies real for students and encourages them to begin to respond to text similarly.

COMPREHENSION

Comprehension Strategies

Teacher Modeling

Asking Questions *We can ask questions when we read to help us better understand a selection. Looking at the title and illustrations on pages 20 and 21, we can ask,* What kind of stew is Rhyme Stew?

Phonemic Awareness Reading 1.4

INITIAL PHONEMES Remind the students how they listened for and then said the beginning sound in a word. Tell students that now you will say a word from the poem. Ask the students to say the beginning sound after you say it. Use the following words from the poem: *hot, pot, peas, hook, munch, for, let's.*

Teacher Tip READING FOR ENJOYMENT Remind students that they should spend at least 20 minutes reading after school.

Universal Access: Meeting Individual Needs

ELL Tip

RHYMING WORDS Ask English-language learners to use the rebuses to help them figure out the rhyming word that precedes each one.

Teacher Tip COMPREHENSION Good readers constantly evaluate their understanding of what they read. Stop often to make sure you and the students are doing this.

Focus Questions How can you tell that words rhyme? If you made stew with your family, what would you put in it?

Rhyme Stew

Kathy Darling
illustrated by Ruth J. Flanigan

Let's make a rhyme for you. Stew.

Let's make a rhyme for hot. Pot.

Let's make a rhyme for cook. Hook.

20

Let's make a rhyme for peas. Sneeze.

Let's make a rhyme for tomatoes. Potatoes.

Let's make a rhyme for noodle. Doodle.

22

Letter Recognition

Rr, Ss Reading 1.3, 1.6

- Tell the students to look for a word that begins with capital *R*, and let volunteers go to the ***Big Book*** and point to it. *(Rhyme)*
- Repeat for small *r*, capital *S*, then small *s*. *(rhyme, stir, Stew, Sneeze, spoon)*
- Invite the students to make rhymes for each word they find.

COMPREHENSION

Discussing the Selection

- Invite volunteers to explain the title of the poem. *(Students might suggest that the poem has lots of rhymes and that it is also about making a stew. They also might see that each thing needed to make the stew is a rhyming word. The stew is actually a stew of words, rather than food.)*
- Ask the students whether they have any questions or comments about the poem. Remind the students to raise their hands, wait to be called on, and ask their questions or share ideas.
- Have the students come up with additional rhymes.
- Encourage the students to think about the following question:

  How is the poem like a real recipe? How is it different? *(A real recipe has lists of ingredients and gives instructions; real recipes don't rhyme. Real recipes have edible ingredients.)*
- Ask the students to tell which illustration they liked best and why.
- With the students, refer back to the Focus Questions for the selection. Have all the questions been answered? If not, answer them now.

Have the students record their responses to the selection in the Response Journal section of their Writer's Notebooks by drawing pictures. Help the students label their drawings.

Review Selection Vocabulary

Have students review the selection vocabulary words for this lesson. Remind them that they discussed the meanings of these words at the beginning of the lesson. Have them add these and any other interesting words that they clarified while reading to the Vocabulary Words section of their Writer's Notebooks. The words from this selection are

spice **munch**

- Have the students use the words in oral sentences. Help the students expand their sentences by asking who, what, where, when, why, and how questions.
- Ask the students to draw pictures that represent the words.

Encourage the students to refer to the vocabulary words throughout the unit.

Print and Book Awareness

Illustration/Text Relationship Reading 1.2

- Remind the students that sometimes readers need pictures to understand everything a writer is writing about. Remind them of the rebus pictures in their ***Pre-Decodable Books*** and point out how important those pictures are. Ask the students how the pictures helped them read "Rhyme Stew." Help the students understand that the pictures convey the main idea or common theme.
- Establish that each picture goes with just one word, so the pictures are very useful in helping readers understand those words.

Supporting the Reading

Comprehension Strategy: Asking Questions Listen/Speak 1.2

Remind the students that you modeled Asking Questions while you read the selection. Review "Rhyme Stew," and ask the students whether they have any questions they'd like to find answers for.

Purposes for Reading

Remind students that before reading the poem, the class discussed that the purpose for reading was to listen for rhymes. Ask the students to share their favorite rhymes from the poem.

Listening/Speaking/Viewing

Listening Attentively Listen/Speak 1.1

Here's a poem just for fun. It has such a catchy rhythm and natural rhyme that students will be able to say it with you after hearing it a couple of times. It will also inspire your budding poets.

Did You Ever Go Fishing?
Did you ever go fishing on a bright, sunny day—
Sit on a fence and have the fence give way?
Slide off the fence and rip your pants,
And see the little fishes do the hootchy-kootchy dance?
Anonymous

- Find out students' preferences by asking whether they liked listening to this poem better than listening to "There Was Once a Fish." Review "There Was Once a Fish" if necessary.
- During one reading of the poem, play music in the background. On the next reading, leave the music off. Discuss with students whether they understood the poem better with or without music. Suggest that they will enjoy and understand what they read more easily when noise is not distracting them.
- Students may enjoy adding their own actions to go with the poem. Encourage all of the students to participate and create a routine of movements.

UNIVERSAL ACCESS: MEETING INDIVIDUAL NEEDS

Reteach

BIG BOOKS Small groups of students might look at the student versions of the ***Big Books.*** They can talk about words they know, recite the rhymes, and discuss what they remember about the selections.

Intervention Tip

RHYMING WORDS If students have difficulty identifying rhyming words, try singing rhymes. Make sure that you choose pure rhymes, such as "Jack and Jill," "Mary, Mary," and "Little Miss Muffet."

Teacher Tip WRITING Help the students recognize the rhyme pattern in "Rhyme Stew." Tell the students that the class can write a poem of their own, using "Rhyme Stew" as a model. Tell them to begin their lines with "Let's make a rhyme for. . . ." Then they should make up different rhyming words. Explain that one student should complete the sentence "Let's make a rhyme for. . . ." Then another student should respond orally with a rhyming word. If no one can think of a rhyme, that line does not go in the poem. Write the poem as the class dictates it to you. Then have students identify the rhymes. Remind the students that they can write about this poem in their Writer's Notebooks if they like, or they can choose a word from the poem and make a list of words that rhyme with it. Reading 1.6; Writing 1.1

Objectives

- Students will continue working on their alphabet books.
- Students will apply concepts and ideas through a curricular connection.

Materials

- Class alphabet book

Universal Access: Meeting Individual Needs

Reteach

NURSERY RHYMES Select an audiocassette of nursery rhymes set to music, and allow the students to listen to it in small groups. Remind them to keep the volume low so they do not disturb others during Workshop.

Informal Assessment

LETTER FORMATION Frequent letter orientation errors are often a sign that students are ignoring the starting point and stroke sequence for the letters.

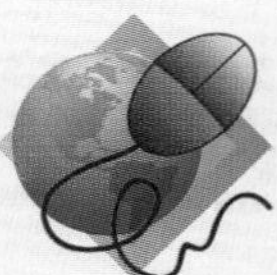

www.sra4kids.com
Web Connection
Remind the students to look for additional information about poetry by using Web connections that are available at the Reading link on the SRA Web page.

INVESTIGATION

Supporting the Investigation

Investigating Concepts Beyond the Text Reading 1.3

Remind the students about the alphabet book they are working on for this unit.

- Begin by sharing the completed pages of the alphabet book that the students created for the letters *i*, *j*, *k*, and *l*. Note the capital and lowercase letters on each page. Ask the students to share any problems they may have encountered while doing the work.
- Distribute drawing paper or story paper, and discuss with the students what they might include on their new set of pages. Emphasize that they can decide for themselves what they want to include. Have supplies such as crayons, markers, scissors, paste, and old magazines or catalogs available.
- Remind the students to plan before they begin to write on or design their pages. Assign the letters *m*, *n*, *o*, and *p*.

INVESTIGATION

Music Connection

Stew Chant Listen/Speak 2.1

Purpose: To recognize and enjoy the patterns and rhythms of a new version of a familiar chant

- Tell the students they will listen to a new version of a chant they might know called "Who Stole the Cookie?"
- Using the tune and format of "Who Stole the Cookie from the Cookie Jar?", teach the students this chant:

  Who put the carrots in the big stew pot?
  Sara put the carrots in the big stew pot.
  Who, me?
  Yes, you!
  Couldn't be!

  Then who?
  Peter put the carrots in the big stew pot . . .

- Encourage the students to clap or stamp their feet to the rhythm.
- From time to time, substitute the names of specific vegetables or other foods for *carrots*—potatoes, parsnips, celery, turnips, and so on.

Objectives

Word Analysis Vocabulary

- **Vocabulary Strategies: Rhyming Words.** Using words from "Rhyme Stew," build vocabulary from rhyming word play.

Writing Process Strategies

- **Introduction to the Writing Process.** Building on the theme Let's Read! and ideas from "Rhyme Stew," develop the understanding that writing is a process and prewriting involves organizing for writing.

English Language Conventions

- **Mechanics: Capital Letters.** Building on Letter Recognition in the Phonemic Awareness lesson, develop the understanding that names of specific people, places, and dates begin with capital letters.

Materials

- Big Book Let's Read!, pp. 20–23
- Comprehension and Language Arts Skills, pp. 8–9

UNIVERSAL ACCESS:
MEETING INDIVIDUAL NEEDS

Reteach, Challenge, English-Language Development and ***Intervention*** lessons are available to support the language arts instruction in this lesson.

OVERVIEW

Language Arts Overview

Word Analysis

Vocabulary The Vocabulary lesson focuses on rhyming as a strategy for expanding vocabulary. Building on vocabulary from "Rhyme Stew" students will generate lists of rhyming words and investigate the meanings of any unknown words. This lesson introduces the idea of asking someone else the meaning of a word. This form of word play provides an enjoyable way to develop interest in vocabulary study.

Vocabulary Skill Words

you	**hot**	**cook**	**spoon**	**meat**	**rice**	**beans**
stew	**pot**	**hook**	**moon**	**feet**	**spice***	**jeans**
peas	**tomatoes**	**noodle**	**bowl**	**stir**	**lunch**	
sneeze	**potatoes**	**doodle**	**hole**	**fur**	**munch***	

**Also Selection Vocabulary*

Writing Process Strategies

The Writing Process Strategies lesson continues the introduction of the prewriting skill of organizing using ideas from "Rhyme Stew." This skill will be practiced in the Writing Process Strategy activities throughout the year. Many inexperienced writers do not organize before they start writing. Experienced writers, however, spend a great deal of time in the prewriting phase, getting ideas and then organizing them before they start writing. That is an observable difference between inexperienced and experienced writers.

English Language Conventions

Grammar, Usage, and Mechanics **Capital Letters** The English Language Conventions support the reading and writing skills development in this lesson. This lesson continues the introduction of students to the conventions of capitalizing proper nouns. Students are introduced to capital and lowercase letters in the Preparing to Read part of the lesson and can begin to understand when capital letters are used. This introduction to capitalization provides a context for when to use capital and lowercase letters. Students will review capitalization rules throughout the year and in subsequent years.

Word Analysis

Vocabulary

Rhyming Words Reading 1.6

Teach

- Write the following words on the board and say them to emphasize their rhymes: *you, stew.*
- Have students direct you to list all of the rhyming pairs in "Rhyme Stew" as you write them on the board: *you/stew, hot/pot, cook/hook, spoon/moon, meat/feet, rice/spice, beans/jeans, peas/sneeze, tomatoes/potatoes, noodle/doodle, bowl/hole, stir/fur, lunch/munch.*
- For each pair of rhyming words, have students suggest an additional rhyming word or words as you write them on the board. These could include *true, dot, book, tune, beat, nice, means, fleas, poodle, mole, purr,* and *crunch.*

Guided Practice

- Ask students these questions about the rhyming words:
  - Are there any words you have never heard before?
  - Which words have you heard, but you don't know the meanings of?
  - What is a word you know for sure?
- For each word that students are unsure of, give them a minute to discuss it with a friend and suggest the definition.
- Conclude by explaining that asking someone else is a strategy for learning words you do not know.
- Have students copy any new words into the vocabulary section of their Writer's Notebooks.

Writing Process Strategies

Introduction to the Writing Process Writing 1.0, 1.1

Plan

Teach

- Discuss the web and list that students made. Explain that they thought of ideas about the topic, chose the best ideas, and organized them to get ready to write.
- Explain that you are going to plan to write about Favorite Foods after reading "Rhyme Stew." This will add to the ideas for their autobiographies.
- Write the words *Favorite Foods* on the board. Under the heading, make a class list of everyone's favorite food.

Writer's Craft

Order Words

- Review counting to five. Explain that in writing or speaking certain words help us understand the order in which things happen. These are order words, such as *first, second, next, then, last,* and *finally.*
- **Teacher Model:** Model using order words by explaining how to do a simple task such as cleaning the board. *First, I find the eraser. Second, I make sure I don't want to save anything. Next, I wipe the board. Finally, I put the eraser away.*
- Use ***Comprehension and Language Arts Skills*** pages 8–9 to reinforce the concept of order words.

Guided Practice

- Review the class list of favorite foods together. Identify all duplicates and group them together.
- Organize the list by grouping the foods into breakfast, lunch, dinner, and snack.
- Apply the order words by reciting which foods you would eat first in the day, second, third, and so on.
- Explain that one way to organize your ideas for writing is to group them before you write.

English Language Conventions

Grammar, Usage, and Mechanics

Capital Letters Eng. Lang. Conv. 1.6

Teach

- Review the capital and lowercase letters that students have explored thus far.
- Review that people's names, your school name, streets, cities, states, and countries all start with capital letters. Find the "Rhyme Stew" author and illustrator names in the ***Big Book*** *Let's Read!* on page 20 and point out that they start with capital letters.
- Explain that days and months start with capital letters, too. Write today's date on the board. Circle the capital letters in the day and month.

Guided Practice in Writing

- As students suggest them, write the days of the week and the months of the year on the board or chart paper. Point out the capital letters.
- Help students write the date including day and month, and their names and addresses including street, city, and state in their Writer's Notebooks. Have them check to make sure they used capital letters appropriately.
- Conclude by reviewing that special or specific people, places, and times start with a capital letter.

Informal Assessment

Read students' writing to make sure they began each word with a capital letter. If necessary, review the examples you wrote on the board circling the first letter in each word.

1 Preparing to Read

Rags

Objectives

- Students will manipulate vowel sounds to change words.
- Students will attend to consonant sounds.
- Students will write letters of the alphabet.
- Students will read a ***Pre-Decodable Book.***

Materials

- Lion Puppet
- Sound/Spelling Cards
- Routine Card 5
- Phonics Skills, pp. 10–11
- Letter Cards
- High-Frequency Word Cards
- Pre-Decodable Book 3

Universal Access: Meeting Individual Needs

ELL Support

For ELD strategies, use the ***English-Language Development Guide,*** Unit 1, Lesson 9.

Intervention Support

For intervention strategies, use the ***Intervention Guide,*** Unit 1, Lesson 9.

Warming Up

Use one or both of the following activities to focus students' attention and to reinforce some of the concepts they have been learning.

I Spy Reading 1.3, 1.4; Listen/Speak 2.1

- Play I Spy with the letters *t* and *v*.
- Tell the students that they are going to play a game using a rhyme. Ask if anyone can tell you what a rhyme is *(words whose ending sounds are alike).* Recite the rhyme for students using an example.

  "I spy with my little eye,
  Something with the letter _____."
- To discover the word you see, students must point out words in the classroom that have the appropriate letter. After the student who is "it" tells the letter the object starts with, he or she will call on other students to guess the object.
- The student who is guessing will express what he or she knows by asking a question relating to the senses; for example, "Can I hold it in my hand?" or "Is it furry?" Encourage the students to use a complete sentence.
- The person who is "it" should answer the questions being asked.

"Did You Ever?" Song Reading 1.3, 1.7

- Tell the students that one way we express ourselves or find new information is by asking questions.
- Sing the "Did You Ever?" song found on pages 61–63 of the Appendix, having students supply the last word of the silly question.

  Did you ever see a pig wearing a /w/_____?
  Did you ever see a snake baking a /k/_____?
  Did you ever see a bug buying a /r/_____?
  Did you ever see a rat wearing a /h/_____?
  Did you ever take a nap on top of a /m/_____?

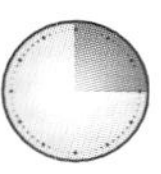

Phonemic Awareness

Listening for Vowel Sounds Reading 1.5; Listen/Speak 2.1

- Pointing to the ***Sound/Spelling Cards,*** review with students the long-vowel sounds that they have heard. Explain that vowel sounds are an important part of every word, because you need them to make words.
- Tell the students that you will teach them a new song, "Apples and Bananas." Explain that in the song, the vowel sounds change and the new words can be silly words. (The music is found on page 63 of the Appendix.)

  I like to eat, eat, eat
  Apples and bananas,
  I like to eat, eat, eat
  Apples and bananas.

- For each verse, key vowels are replaced with one of the long vowels.
- Point to the replacement vowel before beginning each verse.

  (ā)
  I like to ate, ate, ate
  āpples and bānānās.

  (ē)
  I like to eat, eat, eat
  ēples and bēnēnēs.

  (ī)
  I like to ite, ite, ite
  īples and bīnīnīs.

  (ō)
  I like to oat, oat, oat
  ōpples and bōnōnōs.

  (ū)
  I like to oot, oot, oot
  ooples and boonoonoos.

- Have the students join in singing after you go through it once with them.

Teacher Tip VOWEL REPLACEMENT This vowel-replacement activity demonstrates the role that vowels play in syllables. However, this activity is purely oral and does *not* involve sound spellings. Its focus is to distinguish and play with the vowel sounds in the words of the song.

"Apples and Bananas" is ideal for this purpose because it is a vowel-replacement song. The song requires students to consciously control vowel sounds in words while leaving the consonants unchanged. "Apples and Bananas" provides strong support for students in using the same vowel sound in different consonant contexts.

If you sing slowly, it is easy to make these vowel replacements. If you sing the new verse, students will join you. Announce each new verse (for example, "and now /ō/".)

Reading 1.5; Listen/Speak 2.1

Teacher Tip WORD MEANINGS If students are unfamiliar with any of the words used, have students who do understand describe the meanings of the words for the student(s).

PHONEMIC AWARENESS

Segmentation

Blending Initial Consonants Reading 1.4; Listen/Speak 1.1

- Present the Lion Puppet. Remind students that you will say a word and the puppet will say only part of each word. Today the puppet will say only the initial consonant. Then tell the students to listen carefully and add the missing sound.
- Begin with this example:

Teacher:	zoo
Puppet:	/z/
Teacher:	me
Puppet:	/m/

- As in previous lessons, demonstrate the switch in the game by speaking to and for the puppet at first. When students have caught on, have them speak for the puppet.
- Continue with the following words:

see	knee	she	show	go
goat	boat	lay	day	sigh
my	pie	right	light	fight
kite	feet	neat	room	boom

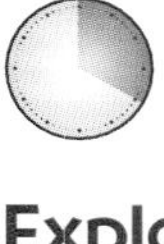

Letter Recognition

Exploring *Ww, Xx, Yy,* and *Zz* Reading 1.3; Writing 1.3

- Introduce the letters *Ww*, *Xx*, *Yy*, and *Zz* in the usual manner.
- Have students observe as you write capital *W* on the board. Clearly indicate each of the starting points.
- Then tell the students to imitate your movements by tracing the letter in the air and then on their desktops while saying the strokes with you.
- Then have students write their *W*'s on paper.
- Continue with the other letters, each time stressing the starting points for each part of the letter.
- Invite volunteers to come up and write their letters on the board.
- When students have finished their letters, have them proofread the shape against those on the board.

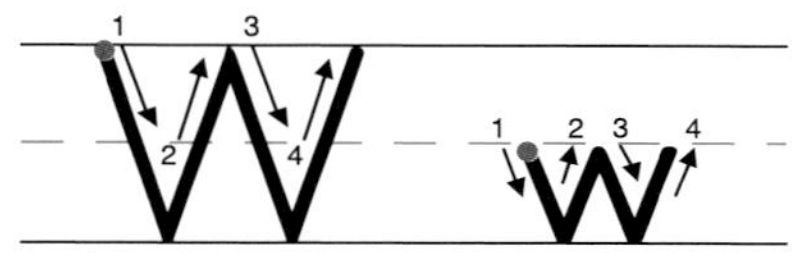

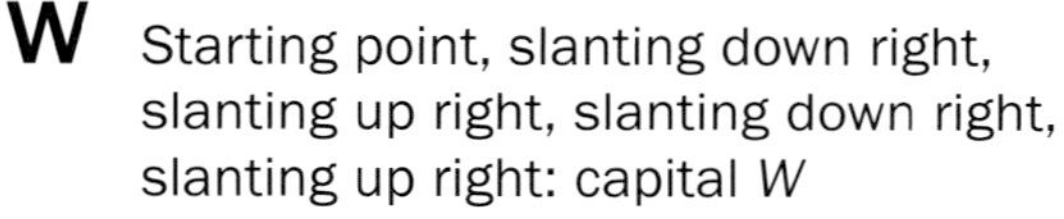

W Starting point, slanting down right, slanting up right, slanting down right, slanting up right: capital *W*

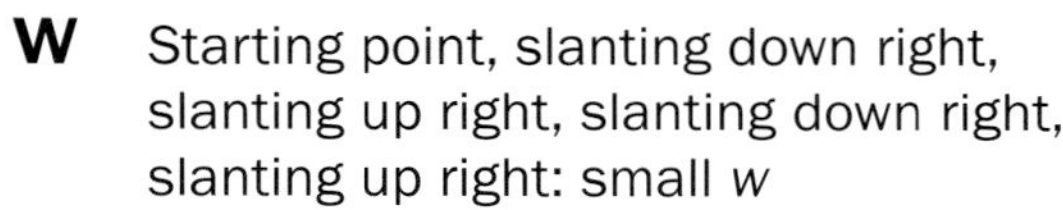

w Starting point, slanting down right, slanting up right, slanting down right, slanting up right: small *w*

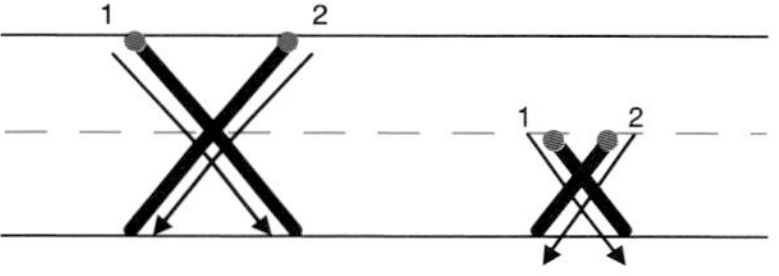

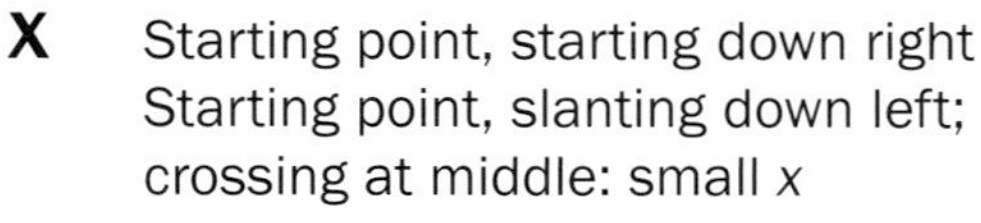

X Starting point, slanting down right Starting point, slanting down left; crossing at middle: capital *X*

x Starting point, starting down right Starting point, slanting down left; crossing at middle: small *x*

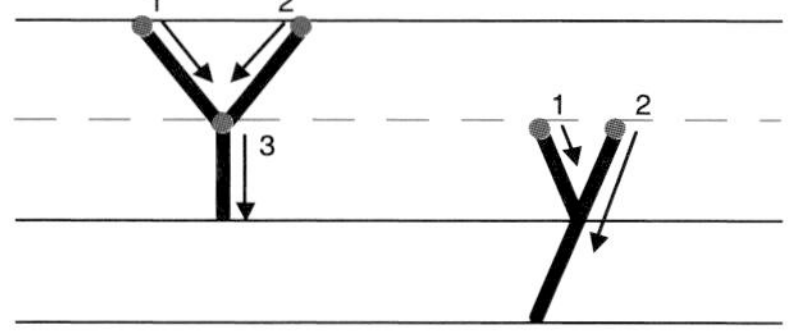

Y Starting point, slanting down right, stop Starting point, slanting down left, stop Starting point, straight down: capital *Y*

y Starting point, slanting down right Starting point, slanting down left, connecting the lines: small *y*

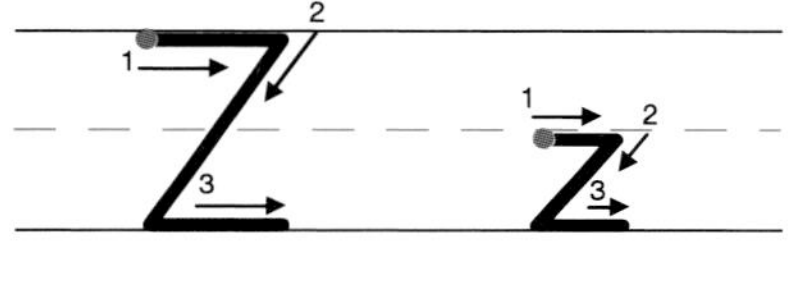

Z Starting point, straight across slanting down left, straight across: capital *Z*

z Starting point, straight across, slanting down left, straight across: small *z*

LETTER RECOGNITION

Universal Access: Meeting Individual Needs

Reteach

ORAL BLENDING AND SEGMENTATION
During Workshop, review oral blending or segmentation activities with students identified earlier as needing additional practice. If they have problems with blending initial consonants orally, start at the beginning with syllable and word-part blending. Students who have difficulty with these activities will face greater problems with sound-symbol blending in Lesson 13 and thereafter. Reading 1.4, 1.8, 1.9

Informal Assessment

Monitoring Continue to monitor students' letter knowledge by assessing their ability to name and recognize the shapes of letters. Reading 1.3

Reading 1.3; Writing 1.3

UNIVERSAL ACCESS: MEETING INDIVIDUAL NEEDS

Reteach

LETTER FORMATION For additional practice with letter formation, use ***Reteach: Phonics Skills*** pages 10–11 during Workshop.

Challenge

Use ***Challenge: Phonics Skills*** pages 9–10 with students who are ready for a challenge.

Intervention Support

LETTER RECOGNITION During Workshop, pairs of students can use ***Letter Cards*** to play a flash card game. When one partner has named the letters, the two should reverse roles.

REVIEW SOUNDS & LETTERS

Phonics Skills

Help the students practice the letters *Ww*, *Xx*, *Yy*, and *Zz* by guiding them through ***Phonics Skills*** pages 10 and 11.

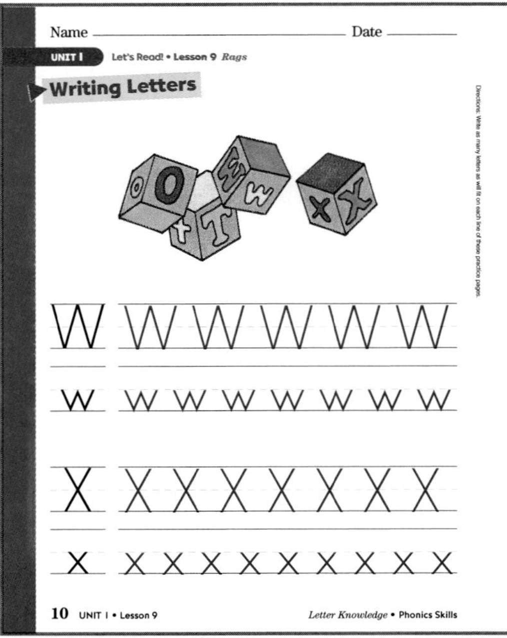

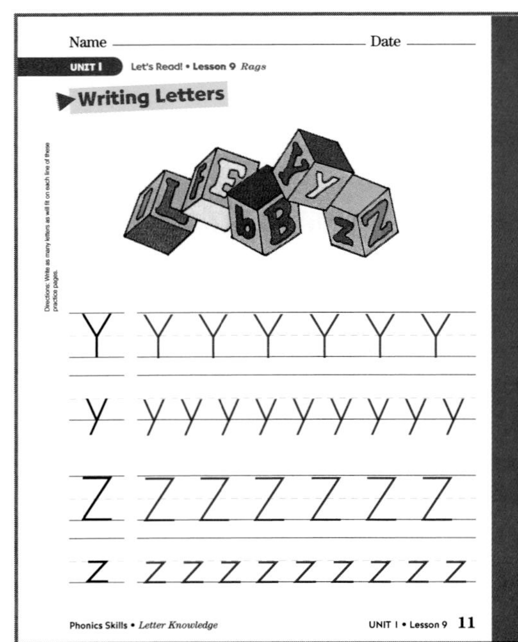

***Phonics Skills* pp. 10–11**

Reviewing Sounds and Letters

Reading 1.1, 1.3, 1.4

Introducing Consonant Sounds

- Write a sentence on the board for each of the consonants, explaining that words almost never begin with the letter *Xx*, so the *x* will be at the end of the words.

  Willie wants wiggly worms.

  Fix a box for the fox.

  Yetta's yaks yell yippee-yi-yo.

  Zack's zoo has zillions of zebras.

- Read the sentence aloud, underlining the key letter each time you say it.
- After challenging students to tell you the sound of the key letter, ask them to recite the sentence several times with you, exaggerating its sound.
- Ask the students whether any of their names begin with the target letters.
- Ask the students to think of other words that begin with the letter sounds *Ww*, *Yy*, and *Zz*.

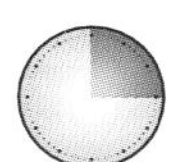

Dictation

Dictation Reading 1.1, 1.3, 1.9; Writing 1.3; Eng. Lang. Conv. 1.8

- Dictate the high-frequency words below. Use each word in a sentence and remind students to look in the High-Frequency Word Bank for guidance and confirmation of their spelling. Encourage them to write neatly and space their letters appropriately.

  an, was, are

- Collect the papers to see how students are progressing.

Teacher Tip HIGH-FREQUENCY WORDS Have the students use the high-frequency words orally in sentences. Reading 1.3

PHONICS

Reading a Pre-Decodable Book

Core Set, Book 3: *The Baby,* Story 2: "The Shirt"

High-Frequency Words Reading 1.3

No high-frequency words are introduced in this book. Review the high-frequency words already in the High-Frequency Word Bank. Have students volunteer to read the ones they recognize.

Reading Recommendations Reading 1.1, 1.2, 1.3, 1.8

- The nondecodable word in this book is *shirt.* Write the word on the board. Ask the students to say the word. Pronounce it, have the students repeat it, spell it together, and have them say it again. Then have volunteers use *shirt* in sentences.
- Hold the book so the students can see the cover. Ask them what the title of this book is. Recall with the students that the book *The Baby* contains two stories, and ask them what happened in "The Cake." Explain that they will now read the second story, "The Shirt."
- Have students read a page silently and then read the page aloud. Repeat this procedure for each page.
- Have another student reread the page before going on.
- Reread the story at least twice, calling on different students to read. Then have the entire group do c choral reading of the story.

UNIVERSAL ACCESS:
MEETING INDIVIDUAL NEEDS

ELL Tip

WORD MEANING Make sure English-language learners can name each rebus before reading the book.

Pre-Decodable Book 2

The shirt is on the arms.

14

The pants are on the legs.

15

The socks are on the feet.

16

Core Book 3 The Baby

High-Frequency Word Introduced in Book 3
are

Previously Introduced High-Frequency Words
a
is
on
the
an
in
was

Sound-Spelling Correspondences in Decodable Books
1. Pre-decodable
2. Pre-decodable
3. Pre-decodable

PHONICS

Responding Reading 2.2; Listen/Speak 1.2, 2.2

- Invite the students to discuss any hard words they encountered in *The Baby* and how they figured out these words. Call on volunteers to retell the story.
- To make sure the students are focusing on the story, ask questions such as the following, having the students answer by pointing to and reading aloud the words:

  Where is the shirt? *(The shirt is on the head.)*

  Where are the socks? *(The socks are on the hands.)*

  Where are the pants? *(The pants are on the legs.)*

Building Fluency Reading 1.16

Encourage partners to build fluency rereading ***Decodable Book 3,*** *The Baby,* of the Core Set. The first time through, one partner should read the odd-numbered pages and the other the even-numbered pages. For the second reading, the partners should switch pages. After the second reading, the partners should choose one of the ***Decodable Books*** from previous lessons and continue to read to each other.

Reading 1.11

Informal Assessment

MONITORING Monitor students' knowledge of high-frequency words by having them read ***Pre-Decodable Books*** to you. Note students who may need extra help learning these words.

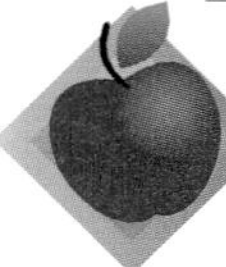

Teacher Tip READING PRE-DECODABLE BOOKS

During the time you set aside each day for individual and small-group work, encourage students to choose previous ***Pre-Decodable Books*** to reread with a partner. This provides important practice reading high-frequency words.

Routine Card

Refer to ***Routine 5*** for the reading ***Decodable Books.***

SELECTION INTRODUCTION

Pages 24–27 *Let's Read!*

Focus Questions What pets do you have? How do your pets move?

Rags

Anonymous • *illustrated by Anne Kennedy*

I have a dog and his name is Rags.
He eats so much that his tummy sags.
His ears flip-flop,
And his tail wig-wags,
And when he walks he goes zig-zag.

24

About the Illustrator

Reading 3.2

ANNE KENNEDY was a teacher of vocal music for years before becoming an author and illustrator. She has always had a love for the arts and for animals, which have become the inspiration for her work. She resides in Columbus, Ohio, with her husband Jack, their dog Brody, and horse Sitka.

Objectives

- Students will use a Table of Contents to locate information.
- Students will listen and respond to "Rags."
- Students will practice rhyming words.
- Students will identify words with the letters *Ww, Yy.*
- Students will discuss what they liked about the selection.
- Students will identify and draw shape patterns.

Materials

- Big Book *Let's Read!,* pp. 24–27

Selection Summary

Genre: Poetry

This poem about a wayward but lovable dog employs amusing compound words such as *flip-flop* for added enjoyment.

The elements of poetry are listed below. Poetry may have one or more of these elements.

- Sentences are sometimes broken into parts. Each part is a line of its own.
- Words that rhyme are often used.
- The lines of a poem often have rhythm, or meter.
- Some words may be repeated.

Inquiry Connections

In this selection of the ***Big Book,*** the students will listen to a poem about a dog named Rags.

Key concepts investigated are

- the elements of poetry.
- matching oral words to printed words.
- becoming more aware of print.

Direct the students to the Concept/Question Board. Encourage them to post any questions or ideas they have about the unit. They may want to include a drawing or poem about a dog. If any of the students have a pet dog at home, encourage them to bring in a photograph of it.

- Make sure the students put their names or initials on anything they post on the Board.
- Tell them that they can post something on the Board any day. Be sure to have students discuss what they put on the Board with the class.

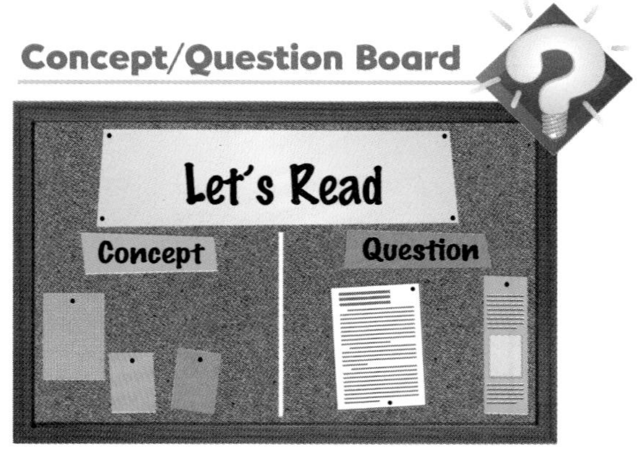

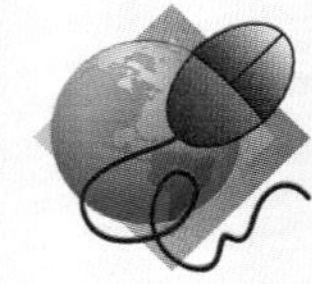

www.sra4kids.com
Web Connection
Help the students look for additional information about poems and rhymes by using the Web connections that are available at the Reading link of the SRA Web page.

Universal Access: Meeting Individual Needs

ELL Support

For ELD strategies, use the ***English-Language Development Guide,*** Unit 1, Lesson 9.

Intervention Support

For intervention strategies, use the ***Intervention Guide,*** Unit 1, Lesson 9.

Teacher Tip SET PURPOSES Remind the students that good readers have a purpose when they read. Let them know that they should make sure they know the purpose for reading whenever they read.

Routine Card Refer to ***Routine 11*** for the procedure for reading the selection.

Build Background

Activate Prior Knowledge Reading 2.6

Tell the students that they are going to read a funny poem about a pet dog. Ask students what they already know about dogs that might help them understand the poem.

Preview and Prepare

Browse Reading 1.2

Invite students to use the Table of Contents of *Let's Read!* to find the poem "Rags" and the page on which it begins *(page 24)*.

- Read the title and the illustrator's name. Explain that the term *anonymous* means that the author of "Rags" is not known.
- Let the students look at the illustrations on these pages and the following two pages.
- Ask what they notice about the illustrations and what clues the illustrations may provide about what kind of dog Rags is.
- Before reading the selection to the students, read the Focus Questions on the first page of the selection together. Briefly discuss the questions, and tell the students to keep these questions in mind as you read.

Set Purposes

Explain to students that the purpose of the poem they are about to read is to show that Rags is a lovable dog. Tell them that the poem describes Rags with silly words like *tummy* and *zig-zag* that will be fun to read.

Selection Vocabulary

- Write the following word on the board and invite volunteers to read it.

  rags
- Ask what a rag is and let a volunteer explain.
- Call on volunteers to explain what a dog named Rags might look like.

Reading Recommendations

Read Aloud

- Give the poem a quick, lively reading through to the end.
- Reread the poem, pointing to the words and letting students join in on words such as *flip-flop* and *wig-wag*.

Using Comprehension Strategies Reading 2.4

Comprehension strategy instruction allows students to become aware of what good readers do when they read. Good readers constantly check their understanding as they are reading and ask themselves questions. Skilled readers also recognize when they are having problems understanding a selection and stop to use various comprehension strategies to help them make sense of what they are reading.

During the reading of this selection, you will model the use of the following comprehension strategy:

- **Monitoring and Clarifying** helps readers understand the meaning of words and difficult ideas or passages.

Routine Card Refer to ***Routine 10*** for the Selection Vocabulary procedure.

Teacher Tip HIGH-FREQUENCY WORDS The following high-frequency words appear in the selection: *a, is, and, the,* and *in.* Point to these words in the High-Frequency Word Bank, have students read them, and encourage them to read these words with you when you encounter them in the reading.

UNIVERSAL ACCESS: MEETING INDIVIDUAL NEEDS

ELL Support

USING ILLUSTRATIONS Before reading a selection, talk to the English-language learners about the illustrations in it. Associating the words in the text with the illustrations can help the English-language learners learn to think of English words before translating them first from their native languages. Use the ***English-Language Development Guide*** as needed.

Teacher Tip COMPREHENSION Good readers constantly evaluate their understanding of what they read. Stop often to make sure you and the students are doing this.

Teacher Tip MONITORING AND CLARIFYING An extended lesson on Monitoring and Clarifying can be found on page T195. This lesson is intended to give extra practice with asking monitoring and clarifying text.

COMPREHENSION

Comprehension Strategies

Teacher Modeling

Monitoring and Clarifying *When I read this poem, I wonder what it means to say "his tummy sags." Let me clarify by reading carefully. I see "He eats so much" right before "his tummy sags." This tells me that Rags's tummy is so full it sags, or droops, to the ground. If you don't understand something when you read, you need to try to figure out, or clarify, what is going on.*

Teacher Tip **READING FOR ENJOYMENT** Remind students that they should spend at least 20 minutes reading after school.

Phonemic Awareness

Reading 1.4, 1.8

FINAL CONSONANT SOUNDS Remind the students how they put sounds together to make words. Tell the students to listen carefully as you say words from the poem so they can blend the final sound and say the whole word. Use the following words:

do . . . /g/	zi . . . /g/	za . . . /g/
tai . . . /l/	fli . . . /p/	hi . . . /z/
wi . . . /g/	wa . . . /g/	mu . . . /d/

UNIVERSAL ACCESS: MEETING INDIVIDUAL NEEDS

Reading 1.6

Reteach

RHYME Invite students to create a rhyming dictionary. Help them spell any words they don't know. They can use the poem in *Let's Read!* to help them get started.

ELL Tip

PRETEACH Read the selection to the English-language learners before you read it to the class. As you read, give students the opportunity to ask questions to clarify what they don't understand. Model the Asking Questions strategy so that they can feel more comfortable asking questions when the selection is read to the class.

Focus Questions What pets do you have? How do your pets move?

Anonymous • *illustrated by Anne Kennedy*

I have a dog and his name is Rags.
He eats so much that his tummy sags.
His ears flip-flop,
And his tail wig-wags,
And when he walks he goes zig-zag.

24

My dog Rags he loves to play.
He rolls around in the mud all day.
I whistle but he won't obey,
He always runs the other way.

26

Letter Recognition

Ww, Yy Reading 1.3

- Tell the students to look for words that begin with the letter *w*, and let volunteers go to the ***Big Book*** and point out the words. Help them say each of the words they find. *(wig-wag, wig-wags, walks, when, way, whistle, won't)*
- Ask the students to find all the words they can that end with the letter *y*. Again, help them say the words they find. *(tummy, play, day, obey, way)*
- If time permits, have students find and say words that begin with the following:

capital *H*	capital *M*
lowercase *h*	lowercase *r*
capital *A*	lowercase *l*
lowercase *z*	lowercase *g*

(He, His, have, his, he, And, zig-zag, My, rolls, runs, love, loves, goes)

Universal Access:
Meeting Individual Needs

Intervention Tip

LETTER RECOGNITION If students are having difficulty recognizing specific letters, help them find those letters in environmental print.

Universal Access: Meeting Individual Needs

ELL Tip

PICTURE STORY Ask the English-language learners to tell you what the poem is about. Answer any questions they have. Ask them to draw pictures that illustrate the poem. Help them write labels for their pictures.

Discussing the Selection Reading 2.2

- Let the students comment in general on the poem and ask any questions that they have about it. Remind students to raise their hands before they ask questions and to take turns speaking.
- Ask students to tell who the characters in the poem are *(Rags the dog and Rag's owner)*. Then ask them what Rags does all day. *(Rags rolls around in the mud all day)*.
- Have the students look at the illustrations. Ask what Rags is doing in each picture. Then ask what line in the poem each drawing matches.
- Ask the students how they feel about Rags after reading the poem. Also, ask what parts of the poem they found funny. Ask them which poem in the unit they think has been the funniest so far.
- With the students, refer back to the Focus Questions for the selection. Have all the questions been answered? If not, answer them now.

Have students record their responses to the selection in the Response Journal Section of the Writer's Notebooks by drawing pictures of Rags. Help the students label their drawings.

Review Selection Vocabulary

Have students review the selection vocabulary word for this lesson. Remind them that they discussed the meaning of this word at the beginning of the lesson. Have them add this and any other interesting words that they clarified while reading to the Vocabulary Words section of the Writer's Notebooks.

The word from this selection is

rags

- Have the students use the word in oral sentences. Help the students expand their sentence by asking who, what, where, when, why, and how questions.
- Ask the students to draw a picture that represents the word.

Encourage students to refer to the vocabulary words throughout the unit.

Supporting the Reading

Comprehension Strategy: Monitoring and Clarifying Reading 2.4

Remind the students that you modeled the Monitoring and Clarifying strategy while reading "Rags" in order to understand what the word *sags* means. Have the students look at the previous selection, "Rhyme Stew," and encourage them to discuss anything they still need clarified.

Purposes for Reading

Remind students that before they read this poem, it was suggested that the purpose for reading would be to learn how lovable Rags was. Discuss with students how the poem makes Rags seem like a lovable pet. Also, ask which words students thought were fun to read.

Listening/Speaking/Viewing

Listening Attentively

Here's a poem just for fun. It has such a catchy rhythm and natural rhyme that students will be able to say it with you after hearing it a couple of times. It will also inspire your budding poets.

Did You Ever Go Fishing?
Did you ever go fishing on a bright, sunny day—
Sit on a fence and have the fence give way?
Slide off the fence and rip your pants,
And see the little fishes do the hootchy-kootchy dance?
Anonymous

- Find out students' preferences by asking whether they liked listening to this poem better than listening to "There Was Once a Fish." Review "There Was Once a Fish" if necessary.
- During one reading of the poem, play music in the background. On the next reading, leave the music off. Discuss with students whether they understood the poem better with or without music. Suggest that they will enjoy and understand what they read more easily when noise is not distracting them.
- Students may enjoy adding their own actions to go with the poem. Encourage all of the students to participate and create a routine of movements to do as they recite the poem.

Teacher Tip USING MOTIONS Discuss with the students how they can use their hands to show the meaning of the funny "double" words in the poem. For example, they could show flip-flop by holding one hand palm-side up and one hand palm-side down and then reversing positions. Let students practice each motion a few times. Tell the students that you are going to reread the poem. When you come to one of these humorous words, they should say the word and act out the motion.

Teacher Tip WRITING Remind the students that they can write about this poem in the Response section of their Writer's Notebooks if they like. To help students select a focus, suggest that they also might like to write about their own pets or a pet they would like to have.

Objectives

- Students will continue working on their alphabet books.
- Students will apply concepts and ideas through a curricular connection.

Materials

- Class alphabet book

Writing 1.1

Universal Access: Meeting Individual Needs

Reteach

RHYMING DICTIONARY Invite the students to create a rhyming dictionary. Help them spell any words they don't know. They can use the poems in *Let's Read!* to help them get started.

Challenge

FUNNY WORDS Invite students to start a Word Bank of funny words. They can write the words on index cards and keep them in a plastic bag or create a special glossary of funny words in their Writer's Notebooks.

Intervention Tip

LETTER RECOGNITION If students are having difficulty recognizing specific letters, help them find those letters in environmental print.

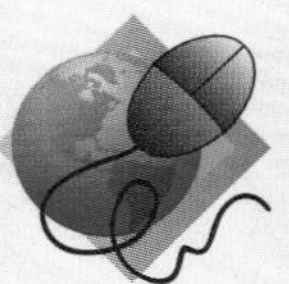

www.sra4kids.com
Web Connection
Help the students look for additional information about poems and rhymes by using the Web connections that are available at the Reading link of the SRA Web page.

INVESTIGATION

Supporting the Investigation

Investigating Concepts Beyond the Text Reading 1.3

Remind students about the alphabet books they are working on for this unit.

- Begin by sharing the completed pages of the alphabet book that students created for the letters *m*, *n*, *o*, and *p*. Point out interesting approaches. For example, one student might have a page of all animals whose names begin with *p*—*pig*, *penguin*, *parrot*, and *panther*. Invite students to add to any pages that might need more pictures.
- Ask the students to suggest other materials they might want to use for today's alphabet book pages. Distribute materials. Have supplies such as crayons, markers, scissors, paste, and old magazines or catalogs available. Discuss what the students might like to put on their pages. Encourage students to decide for themselves what to include.
- Remind students to plan before they begin to write on or design their pages. Assign the letters *q*, *r*, *s*, and *t*.

Concept/Question Board

Ask students to look at the Concept/Question Board.

- Are there any questions on the board that they can answer now?
- Help them write or post any additional questions.
- Encourage the students to consult the Concept/Question Board periodically to answer questions that are posted, to look for ideas for investigations, or to find out who has similar ideas so they can exchange ideas or information with them.

Mathematics Connection

Finish the Patterns

Purpose: To identify and give students an understanding of patterns; to help students in making predictions about how to complete patterns or arrange items in sequence

- Reread the poem "Rags" and invite students to "read" along with you. Point out to students how the lines of the poem make a pattern.
- Ask them to recall their earlier discussion of rhyming words. Read the third stanza again, and call on volunteers to identify the end rhymes that were previously discussed *(play, day, obey, way)*.
- Explain to the students that those rhyming words make a pattern in the poem because they can tell what the last word in each sentence will sound like.
- Then tell students that patterns also can be made with shapes. Draw the following on the board: a circle, a square, and then another circle.
- Have volunteers come up to the board and add a shape to the shapes to continue the pattern.
- Have the students make their own pattern on a sheet of paper. Then, have them trade patterns with a friend.
- Ask students to describe how they completed the pattern. Ask students to make the other person's pattern.

INVESTIGATION

Universal Access: Meeting Individual Needs

Reteach

PATTERNS If students are having difficulty drawing patterns, let them make patterns with beads or geometric forms.

Teacher Tip MATERIALS For this Mathematics Connection, you will need paper and pencils.

Objectives

Word Analysis Vocabulary
- **Vocabulary Strategies: Rhyming Words.** Using words from "Rags," build vocabulary from rhyming word play.

Writing Process Strategies
- **Introduction to the Writing Process.** Building on the theme of Let's Read!, develop the understanding that writing is a process and prewriting involves organizing for writing.

English-Language Conventions
Listening, Speaking, Viewing
- **Speaking: Speaking Clearly** Use the selection "Rags" to practice speaking in clear sentences at appropriate volume.

Materials

- Big Book *Let's Read!*, pp. 24–27
- Language Arts Transparency 3

OVERVIEW

Universal Access: Meeting Individual Needs

Reteach, Challenge, English-Language Development and ***Intervention*** lessons are available to support the language arts instruction in this lesson.

Research in Action
Speaking

Oral language forms the basis of children's literacy. It is the primary way they communicate both before and after they have learned to read and write, and whatever will be learned and mastered in print is based on this foundation *(Charles Temple and Jean Wallace Gillet.* Language Arts: Learning Processes and Teaching Practices)

Language Arts Overview

Word Analysis

Vocabulary The Vocabulary lesson focuses on rhyming as a strategy for expanding vocabulary. Building on vocabulary from "Rags" students will generate lists of rhyming words and investigate the meanings of any unknown words. This lesson introduces them to the idea of developing mnemonic clues to remember vocabulary. This form of word play provides an enjoyable way to develop interest in vocabulary study.

Vocabulary Skill Words

Rags* **sags** **wags**

play **day** **obey** **way**

**Also Selection Vocabulary*

Writing Process Strategies

The Writing Process Strategies lesson continues the introduction of the prewriting skill of organizing ideas. This skill will be practiced in the Writing Process Strategy activities throughout the year. Time spent introducing and modeling this process will help students consider prewriting as a vital part of the writing process.

English Language Conventions

Listening, Speaking, Viewing **Speaking: Speaking Clearly.** This lesson introduces students to the importance of speaking clearly with appropriate volume. Many young children have great difficulty controlling their voices. Some children speak very softly. Some children always appear to be shouting. This lesson provides an opportunity to review classroom rules for indoor and outdoor voices, raising hands, and interruptions.

Word Analysis

Vocabulary

Rhyming Words Reading 1.6

Teach

- Have the students direct you to list all the rhyming words in "Rags" as you write them on the board. *(Rags/sags/wags, play/day/obey/way)*
- **Teacher Model:** Model using a rhyming mnemonic clue for unknown words. *If I don't know what the word* sags *means, I can ask somebody or look it up in the dictionary. To remember it, I can use it in a sentence, or I can make up a poem to help me remember it. For example, I found out that* sag *means "to droop, or hang down." My little rhyming clue is* Wet Bags Sag. *If I think about a wet bag, I can remember what* sag *means.*

Guided Practice

- Have the students name other words that rhyme with *play* as you write them on the board. *(gray, jay, hay, May, bay, day, way, hay, Kay, say)*
- Ask students the following questions about the rhyming words:
  - Are there any words you have never heard before?
  - Which words have you heard but you don't know the meanings of?
  - Which is a word you know for sure?
- Give students a minute to come up with a way to remember any words they are unsure of by using a rhyming clue.
- Review the clues with the entire class.
- Conclude by explaining that thinking of a rhyming clue is a good strategy for remembering words students do not know.

Writing Process Strategies

Introduction to the Writing Process Writing.1.0, 1.1

Plan

Teach

- Discuss the three organizations students made about fish, rain, and favorite foods on previous days. Explain that they thought of ideas about the topic and then chose the best ideas and organized them to get ready to write.
- Explain that today you are going to plan to write about pets, like the dog Rags in the poem "Rags."

Guided Practice

- Write the word *Pets* on the board.
- Under the heading, make a class list of everyone's pets.
- Review the list together. Identify all duplicates and group them together.
- Identify all pets that were mentioned only once.
- **Teacher Model:** Model organizing the list by grouping the pets into dogs, cats, birds, fish, and so on. Use ***Language Arts Transparency 3*** to demonstrate how to group items in a list.
- Explain that if you were going to write about everyone's pets, one way to organize your ideas for writing is to group them before you write.

English Language Conventions

Listening, Speaking, Viewing

Speaking: Speaking Clearly Eng. Lang. Conv. 1.1

Teach

- Explain to students that today they are going to practice different voices.
- Explain that sometimes it is right to speak loudly, as when you are outside and need to get someone's attention. Other times it is necessary to speak softly so that only the person next to you can hear you. There is also a volume that is appropriate when you speak to a group of people.
- The important thing is to choose the volume you need to make sure you are heard clearly.
- **Teacher Model:** Model demonstrating a loud voice as you read the first stanza of "Rags." Demonstrate a soft voice as you read the second stanza. Demonstrate a group voice as you read the third stanza.
- Discuss when each type of voice would be appropriate. *(outside, asking your friend for a pencil, sharing with the whole class)*

Guided Practice

- Invite the students to chant the chorus "Rags" in the three different types of voices: loud, soft, group: "He goes flip-flop, wig-wag, zig-zag."
- Say the last two lines together in soft voices: "I love Rags and he loves me."
- Close by explaining that speaking clearly is an important skill that will help students all through their lives.

Informal Assessment

Note which students appear to have control over their speech and which students you will need to work with to increase volume to appropriate levels.

Objectives

- Students will blend sounds orally to form words.
- Students will associate sounds with letters.
- Students will segment final consonant sounds.

Materials

- Lion Puppet
- Sound/Spelling Cards
- Phonics Skills, pp. 12–13
- Letter Cards
- Alphabet Flash Cards

UNIVERSAL ACCESS:
MEETING INDIVIDUAL NEEDS

ELL Support

For ELD strategies, use the ***English-Language Development Guide,*** Unit 1, Lesson 10.

Intervention Support

For intervention strategies, use the ***Intervention Guide,*** Unit 1, Lesson 10.

Teacher Tip "APPLES AND BANANAS" Divide the students into groups and have them each sing one verse of the song.

Listen/Speak 2.1

Warming Up

Use the following activity to focus the students' attention and to reinforce some of the concepts they have been learning.

"Apples and Bananas" Song Reading 1.5; Listen/Speak 2.1

- Sing "Apples and Bananas" with students. Review the main verse with them. Write the five vowels on the board, and then have the students sing each verse changing the sound for /ā/, /ē/, /ī/, /ō/, and /ū/, depending on the vowel to which you point. Refer to page 63 of the Appendix for a copy of the entire song.

  I like to eat, eat, eat,
  Apples and bananas.
  I like to eat, eat, eat,
  Apples and bananas.

- As an example, use the verse below using the /ō/ sound.

  I like to oat, oat, oat,
  opples and bononoes.
  I like to oat, oat, oat,
  opples and bononoes.

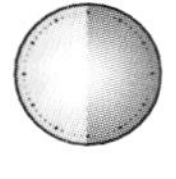

Phonemic Awareness

Oral Blending

Blending Initial Consonant Sounds   Reading 1.3, 1.7

- Tell the students that you will show them how changing just one sound can make a whole new word.
- The activity should go something like this:

Teacher:	[Write *dinosaur* on the board.] This word is *dinosaur.* What is it?
Students:	Dinosaur.
Teacher:	Now I'm going to change it. [Erase *d.*] Now it's going to start with /m/. What's the new word?
Students:	Minosaur.
Teacher:	[Write *m.*] That's right, *minosaur.* Now I'm going to change it again.

- Continue erasing the initial letter and telling the students which new sound you will put at the beginning, asking them to tell what the new word will be before writing the letter in place.
- Repeat the exercise with the words *butterfly*, *television*, *ladybug*, *doorbell*, *baseball*, *rainbow*, and *saddlebag*, replacing the initial consonant with a series of consonant sounds such as /p/, /f/, /k/, /g/, /n/, /m/, and /sh/.
- The students should not be expected to read the words. Tell them the word and the new sound that will be added.

Segmentation

Final Consonant Segmentaton   Reading 1.4, 1.9

- Present the Lion Puppet and tell the students that he is going to do something different today. Remind them that he often says only part of a word. Tell the students to listen closely to see which part he says.
- Talk to the puppet, and respond for him as follows:

Teacher:	peach
Puppet:	/ch/
Teacher:	make
Puppet:	/k/

- Ask the students which part of the words the puppet is saying *(the end sound)*. Then have the students take the part of the puppet as you say these words. Periodically ask for individual responses rather than group responses.

soap	lake	bake	mean	seat
bean	pour	feast	touch	meat
love	fate	road	mash	nest
ran	with	push	nice	seed

PHONEMIC AWARENESS

Reading 1.7

Research in Action
Initial Consonant Sounds

This oral blending activity further develops awareness of initial consonant sounds by building on the initial consonant segmentation and blending activities and on the Alliterative Word game. The activity starts with a common word whose initial consonant sound is then rapidly changed. The students produce the new words (for instance, *rabbit* becomes *babbit*, then *nabbit*, then *tabbit*, and so on). Most of these are nonsense words, of course, but this serves to focus attention on the sound of the word itself. Writing the word on the board helps make the connection between sounds and writing.

Remember that at this stage you are *not* teaching letter-sound correspondences. You're just getting across the idea that such correspondences exist.
(Marilyn J. Adams)

Informal Assessment

INITIAL CONSONANT SOUNDS Begin observation of five or six students during the Initial Consonant Sounds activity. You might want to ask for class response to some of these words, then call on individuals to respond to specific words. Try to observe all the students over the next several days. Record your observations in your Teacher Observation Log in the ***Program Assessment Teacher's Edition.*** Reading 1.3, 1.7

UNIVERSAL ACCESS:
MEETING INDIVIDUAL NEEDS

Reteach

LETTER RECOGNITION For Workshop, divide a set of the ***Letter Cards*** among four containers and place the containers on a table. Four students can work together to put the cards from the four containers in alphabetical order. They can check their completed alphabet against the ***Sound/ Spelling Cards.*** When they are finished, they should mix up the cards and divide them among the containers for the next group of students. Reading 1.3

Teacher Tip ALPHABET CHEER Students can also walk around the room in a train formation and replace the *booms* with stomps of their feet; i.e, [stomp, stomp, clap]! [stomp, stomp, clap]! ABCD and so on.

LETTER RECOGNITION

Letter Recognition

Celebrate the Alphabet Reading 1.3; Listen/Speak 2.1

- Briefly review the alphabet by flipping through the ***Alphabet Flash Cards*** in order for class response. Then choose a few cards randomly and call on individual students.
- Congratulate the students for having learned all the letters, and have them sing the "Alphabet Song." After they finish the song, invite them to go on a celebration march around the classroom.
- Provide rhythm instruments and teach the students the Alphabet Cheer. Encourage them to drum out the booms, patting their desks or using the rhythm instruments.

Boom, boom [clap]! Boom, boom [clap]! A B C D
Boom, boom [clap]! Boom, boom [clap]! E F G H
Boom, boom [clap]! Boom, boom [clap]! I J K L
Boom, boom [clap]! Boom, boom [clap]! M N O P
Boom, boom [clap]! Boom, boom [clap]! Q R S T
Boom, boom [clap]! Boom, boom [clap]! U V W X
Boom, boom [clap]! Boom, boom [clap]! Y AND Z
Boom, boom [clap, clap] boom!

Phonics Skills Reading 1.3

Have the students complete ***Phonics Skills*** pages 12 and 13. Help them practice recognizing capital and lowercase letters by connecting the dots in alphabetical order. Demonstrate for the students how to connect the dots.

***Phonics Skills* pp. 12–13**

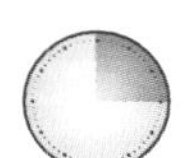

Dictation

Dictation Reading 1.1, 1.3, 1.9; Eng. Lang. Conv. 1.8

- Dictate the high-frequency words below. Use each word in a sentence and remind the students to look in the High-Frequency Word Bank for guidance and confirmation of their spelling.

  is, a, are

- Collect the papers so you can see how the students are progressing.

Universal Access: Meeting Individual Needs

Reteach

LETTER RECOGNITION For additional practice, have students use ***Reteach: Phonics Skills*** pages 12–13.

Challenge

LETTER RECOGNITION Use ***Challenge: Phonics Skills*** page 11 with students who are ready for a challenge.

Informal Assessment

LETTER ORIENTATION Frequent letter orientation errors are often a sign that students are ignoring the starting point and stroke sequence for the letters. Encourage the students to always find the correct starting point and follow the correct stroke sequence for each letter when they write. Writing 1.3

Universal Access: Meeting Individual Needs

Reteach

HIGH-FREQUENCY WORDS Make each student a set of cards with the high-frequency words they have learned so far. Show a card, say the word, and ask the students to find the word in their stack. Then have the students say the word. Continue with the other words. Then show the words again in random order. Continue with the activity, getting faster each time. Do this activity often during Workshop.

Reading 1.11

SELECTION INTRODUCTION

Pages 28–29 of *Let's Read!*

What animals do you see at night? What do fireflies do at night?

Twinkle Twinkle Firefly

John Agard
illustrated by Lyn Martin

Twinkle
Twinkle
Firefly
In the dark
It's you I spy.

28

Objectives

- Students will listen and respond to the selection.
- Students will read the selection along with teacher.
- Students will substitute target sounds to create new words.
- Students will use basic conversation strategies.
- Students will discuss specific details about Visualizing.
- Students will recognize rhythm through music.

Materials

- Big Book *Let's Read!* pp. 28–29
- Home Connection, p.5

About the Author

Reading 3.2

John Agard was born in British Guiana (now Guyana). Much of his imagery is derived from the Caribbean and Britain, but the catchy rhythms and word play in his work have wide appeal. He also has worked as a professional actor and a jazz musician.

Other Books by John Agard

The Emperor's Dan-Dan, *Laughter Is an Egg*, *The Calypso Alphabet*

About the Illustrator

Reading 3.2

Growing up in Chattanooga, Tennessee, **Lyn Martin** learned about colors and how to mix them while working in her father's paint store. That experience, combined with her love of drawing and reading, led her to attend the Ringling School of Art and Design in Florida. Lyn says of her profession, *"Creating pictures of . . . places and . . . things that really only exist in my imagination can be hard sometimes, but it's also a lot of fun."*

Selection Summary

Genre: Rhyme

This lovely poem evokes a pastoral scene that sparkles with the light of fireflies on a warm summer night.

The elements of poetry are listed below. Poetry may have one or more of these elements.

- Sentences are sometimes broken into parts. Each part is on a line of its own.
- Words that rhyme are often used.
- The lines of a poem often have rhythm, or meter.
- Some words may be repeated.

Inquiry Connections

In this selection of the ***Big Book,*** the students will listen to "Twinkle Twinkle Firefly".

Key concepts investigated are

- the elements of poetry, in particular, the use of repeated words or phrases.
- matching oral words to printed words.
- becoming more aware of print.

Direct the students to the Concept/Question Board. Encourage them to post any questions or ideas they have about the unit. They may want to include a picture or poem about fireflies.

- Make sure the students put their names or initials on anything they post on the Board.
- Tell them that they can post something on the Board any day. Be sure to have students discuss what they put on the Board with the class.

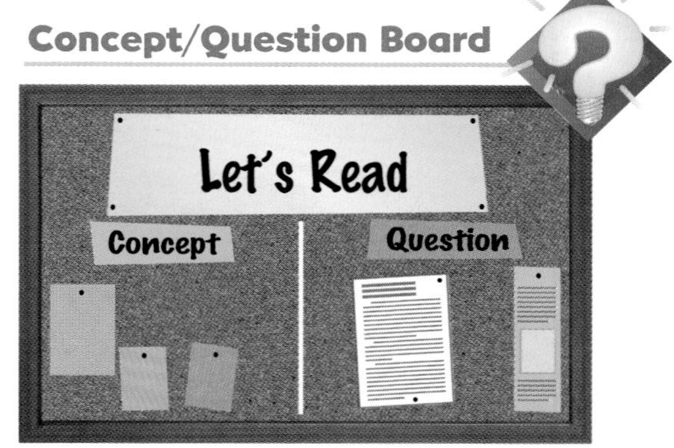

www.sra4kids.com
Web Connection
Help the students look for additional information about poems and rhymes by using the Web connections that are available at the Reading link of the SRA Web page.

UNIVERSAL ACCESS:
MEETING INDIVIDUAL NEEDS

ELL Support

For ELD strategies, use the ***English-Language Development Guide,*** Unit 1, Lesson 10.

Intervention Support

For intervention strategies, use the ***Intervention Guide,*** Unit 1, Lesson 10.

Teacher Tip ACTIVATE PRIOR KNOWLEDGE Tell the students that good readers typically activate what they already know about a topic before reading something new about the topic.

Reading 2.6

Routine Card
Refer to ***Routine 11*** for the procedure for reading the selection.

Build Background

Activate Prior Knowledge Listen/Speak 2.3

- Tell the students that the next poem you will read together is about a firefly or lightning bug.
- If they have never seen one, ask if they can guess something special about it from its name. Ask the students to describe a firefly, or lightning bug. Tell them to describe their personal experience in a simple sentence.

Preview and Prepare

Browse

- Open the ***Big Book*** to the Table of Contents pages 4 and 5, and read the names of the author and illustrator. Let the students look at the illustration.
- Ask them what they can tell you about the place in the picture.
- Before reading the selection to the students, read through the Focus Questions on the first page of the selection together. Briefly discuss the questions, and tell students to keep these questions in mind as you read.

Set Purposes

Readers like to read poems for many reasons. Suggest to students that a reader might like to read "Twinkle Twinkle Firefly" as a way to understand what nighttime is like in the country.

Selection Vocabulary

- Write the following word on the board and pronounce it.

  twinkle

- Tell the students that we use this word to describe how some lights behave, and ask whether anyone can think of a light that twinkles. Accept examples such as stars and holiday lights. Establish that when a light seems to go on and off quickly, we say it *twinkles*.

Reading Recommendations

Read Aloud

- Read the poem without pausing.
- Ask the students to close their eyes and imagine the scene described in the poem as you read it to them.
- Have them open their eyes and follow along as you reread the poem and point to the words.
- Tell students that the question word *when* refers to the time. Tell students to listen for the character (who) in the poem, what the poem is about, where it takes place, and what time of day it takes place.

Using Comprehension Strategies

Comprehension strategy instruction allows students to become aware of what good readers do when they read. Good readers constantly check their understanding as they are reading and ask themselves questions. Skilled readers also recognize when they are having problems understanding a selection and stop to use various comprehension strategies to help them make sense of what they are reading.

During the reading of this selection, you will model the use of the following comprehension strategy:

- **Visualizing** helps readers picture in their minds what is going on in a selection to gain a clearer understanding.

Routine Card
Refer to ***Routine 10*** for the Selection Vocabulary procedure.

Teacher Tip HIGH-FREQUENCY WORDS The following high-frequency words appear in the selection: *in* and *the.* Point to these words in the High-Frequency Word Bank, have students read them, and encourage them to read these words with you when you encounter them in the reading.

UNIVERSAL ACCESS: MEETING INDIVIDUAL NEEDS

ELL TIP

PRETEACH Before reading a selection, talk to the English-language learners about the illustrations in it. Associating the words in the text with the illustrations helps the English-language learners learn to think of English words before translating them from their native languages.

Teacher Tip COMPREHENSION Good readers constantly evaluate their understanding of what they read. Stop often to make sure you and the students are doing this.

Teacher Tip VISUALIZING An extended lesson on Visualizing can be found on page T211. This lesson is intended to give extra practice with visualizing.

COMPREHENSION

Comprehension Strategies

Visualizing

This poem is an excellent place for the students to practice the *Visualizing* reading strategy. This strategy was introduced before. Although the students will not be using formal reading strategies as they read the simple rhymes and poems of this unit, you might want to model the Visualizing strategy.

Teacher Modeling

Visualizing

I close my eyes and visualize, or imagine, what the dark country night looks like. Then I imagine fireflies lighting up the night and helping me see my way through the dark. Close your eyes and picture the night. How do you think the fireflies might help them find their way in the dark?

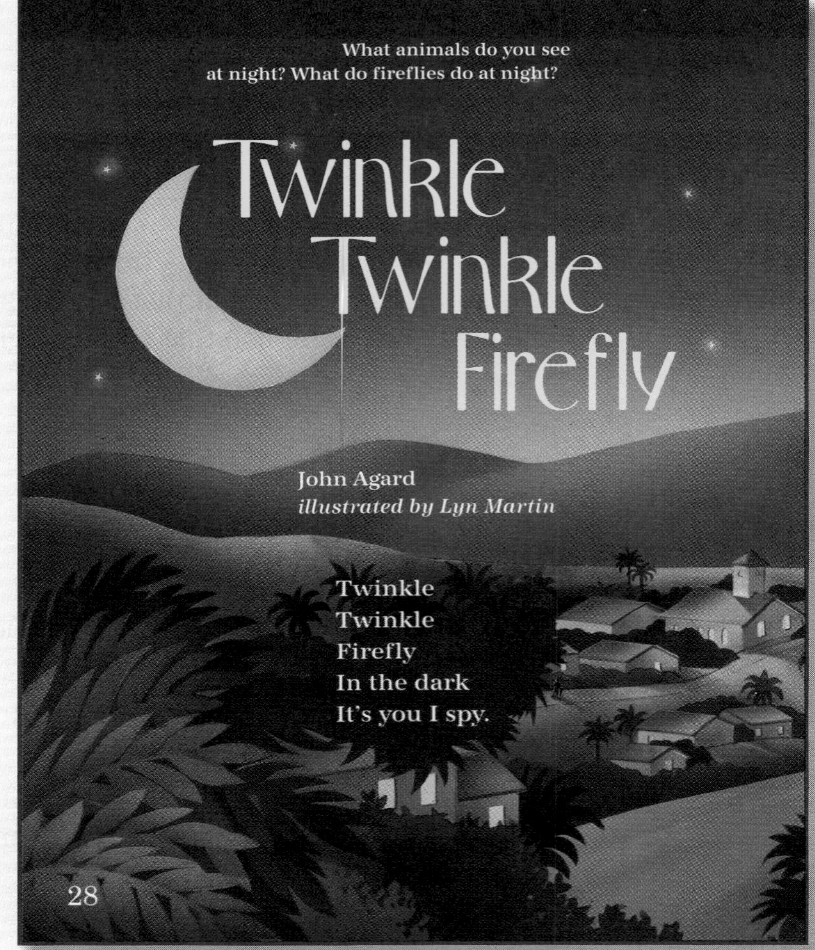

Phonemic Awareness Reading 1.4, 1.7

INITIAL CONSONANT SOUNDS Remind the students how changing just one sound can make a whole new word. Invite the students to join you in making new words from several words in the poem. Have the students take turns replacing initial sounds with other consonants that you suggest. Explain that the new words might be nonsense words. Use the following words: *twinkle, dark, for, lend,* and *river.*

Teacher Tip FOR ENJOYMENT READING Remind students to spend at least 20 minutes reading after school.

Teacher Tip COMPREHENSION Good readers are active readers. They interact with the text as they read—by emoting, reacting, responding, and problem solving in their efforts to construct and maintain meaning.

California Theme Connection
Reading/Language Arts

Each month READ California has a Tip of the Month to help parents encourage their children to read. One month the tip was "Make a time and place for reading." One idea was for the parent and child to read a story together before bedtime.

Discuss with students what some of their ideas would be for "Make a time and place for reading."

Letter Recognition

Invite the students to point out the letters in the poem that are capitals. Then have them identify the lowercase letters. Next, have them identify capital and lowercase pairs.

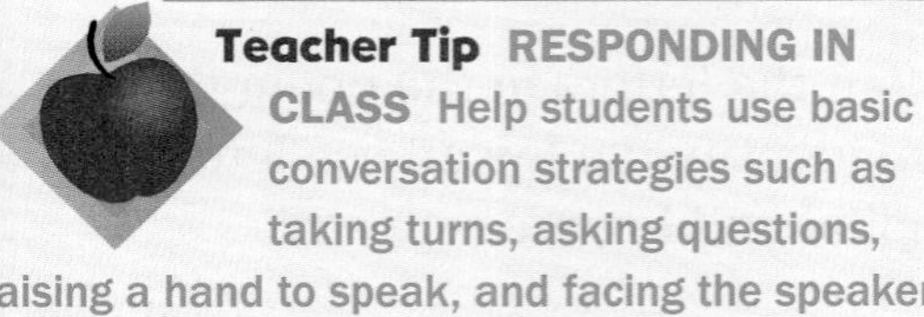

Teacher Tip RESPONDING IN CLASS Help students use basic conversation strategies such as taking turns, asking questions, raising a hand to speak, and facing the speaker.

Discussing the Selection Listen/Speak 1.2, 1.5, 2.4

- Ask students to tell who this poem is about *(a firefly)*, what the poem is about *(the firefly's twinkle)*, where it takes place *(by a river)*, and when it takes place *(at night)*.
- Ask whether the students have any questions, and then let them discuss their reactions to the poem.
- Look at the illustration of the countryside at night. What is missing? Why might the fireflies be a big help to a traveler during the night?
- Turn back to page 6, and reread "The Purple Cow" with the class. Ask them how their imaginary pictures of the purple cow are different from their pictures of the fireflies. Students should provide specific details about their images.
- Explain to the students that using the word *twinkle* two times (i.e., Twinkle Twinkle Firefly) is like the repeated blinking of the firefly's light. Tell them that authors sometimes use words in a way that imitates the object or idea they are writing about. Tell them that the same process was used in "Las hormiguitas" in Lesson 3. Ask them what words were repeated in the poem "Twinkle Twinkle Firefly." Then ask the students whether they are familiar with the poem, "Twinkle, Twinkle, Little Star." Recite the poem, and ask the students which words are repeated *(twinkle, twinkle)* and what this might mean. *(It might imitate the repeated twinkling or sparkling of the stars.)*
- With the students, refer back to the Focus Questions for the selection. Have all the questions been answered? If not, answer them now.

Have the students record their responses to the selection in the Response Journal Section of their Writer's Notebooks by drawing pictures. Help the students label the drawings.

Review Selection Vocabulary

Have students review the selection vocabulary word for this lesson. Remind them that they discussed the meaning of this word at the beginning of the lesson. Have them add this and any other interesting words that they clarified while reading to the Vocabulary Words section of the Writer's Notebooks.

The word from this selection is

twinkle

- Have the students use the word in oral sentences. Help the students expand their sentence by asking who, what, where, when, why, and how questions.
- Ask the students to draw a picture that represents the word.

Encourage students to refer to the vocabulary words throughout the unit.

Print and Book Awareness

Author and Illustrator Reading 1.2, 3.2

- Review the concept of credit lines, and invite volunteers to point out the line that tells who wrote the poem and the line that tells who illustrated it. Read each credit line as a student points to it.
- Ask the students to think about how the illustrator of "Twinkle Twinkle Firefly" knew what to put in her pictures. Perhaps the illustrator used the words of the poem and formed pictures in her mind. Then the illustrator would have created the pictures.

Supporting the Reading

Comprehension Strategy: Visualizing

Ask the students what it means to visualize something *(to imagine or picture it in your mind).* Reread the poem, having the students close their eyes and visualize what is happening. Encourage the students to discuss their mental pictures.

Purposes for Reading

Remind students that before reading the poem, they talked about what nighttime might be like in the country. Ask students to describe their images of the countryside at night, paying careful attention to sensory detail.

Home Connection

Distribute ***Home Connection*** page 5. Encourage the students to discuss the poems that were read in school this week with their families. This letter is also available in Spanish on page 6.

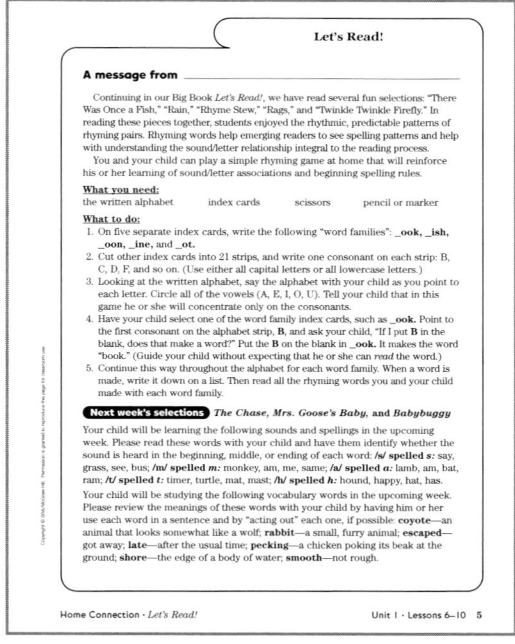

Let's Read!

A message from ______________________

Continuing in our Big Book *Let's Read!*, we have read several fun selections: "There Was Once a Fish," "Rain," "Rhyme Stew," "Rags," and "Twinkle Twinkle Firefly." In reading these pieces together, students enjoyed the rhythmic, predictable patterns of rhyming pairs. Rhyming words help emerging readers to see spelling patterns and help with understanding the sound/letter relationship integral to the reading process.

You and your child can play a simple rhyming game at home that will reinforce his or her learning of sound/letter associations and beginning spelling rules.

What you need:

the written alphabet index cards scissors pencil or marker

What to do:

1. On five separate index cards, write the following "word families": **_ook, _ish, _oon, _ine,** and **_ot.**
2. Cut other index cards into 21 strips, and write one consonant on each strip: B, C, D, F, and so on. (Use either all capital letters or all lowercase letters.)
3. Looking at the written alphabet, say the alphabet with your child as you point to each letter. Circle all of the vowels (A, E, I, O, U). Tell your child that in this game he or she will concentrate only on the consonants.
4. Have your child select one of the word family index cards, such as **_ook.** Point to the first consonant on the alphabet strip, **B**, and ask your child, "If I put **B** in the blank, does that make a word?" Put the **B** on the blank in **_ook.** It makes the word "book." (Guide your child without expecting that he or she can *read* the word.)
5. Continue this way throughout the alphabet for each word family. When a word is made, write it down on a list. Then read all the rhyming words you and your child made with each word family.

Next week's selections ***The Chase, Mrs. Goose's Baby,*** **and** ***Babybuggy***

Your child will be learning the following sounds and spellings in the upcoming week. Please read these words with your child and have them identify whether the sound is heard in the beginning, middle, or ending of each word: **/s/ spelled *s:*** say, grass, see, bus; **/m/ spelled *m:*** monkey, am, me, same; **/a/ spelled *a:*** lamb, am, bat, ram; **/t/ spelled *t:*** timer, turtle, mat, mast; **/h/ spelled *h:*** hound, happy, hat, has.

Your child will be studying the following vocabulary words in the upcoming week. Please review the meanings of these words with your child by having him or her use each word in a sentence and by "acting out" each one, if possible: **coyote**—an animal that looks somewhat like a wolf; **rabbit**—a small, furry animal; **escaped**—got away; **late**—after the usual time; **pecking**—a chicken poking its beak at the ground; **shore**—the edge of a body of water; **smooth**—not rough.

Home Connection · *Let's Read!* Unit 1 · Lessons 6–10 5

Home Connection p. 5

Objectives

- Students will continue working on their alphabet books.
- Students will apply concepts and ideas through a curricular connection.

Materials

- Class alphabet book

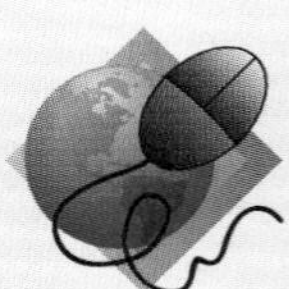

www.sra4kids.com
Web Connection
Help the students look for additional information about poems and rhymes by using the Web connections that are available at the Reading link of the SRA Web page.

INVESTIGATION

Supporting the Investigation

Investigating Concepts Beyond the Text Reading 1.3

Remind the students about the alphabet book they are working on for this unit.

- Begin by sharing the completed pages of the alphabet book that the students created for the letters *q*, *r*, *s*, and *t*. Note the capital and lowercase letters on each page. Recall the letters of the alphabet with the students. Tell students that today they will complete the alphabet book with letters *u*, *v*, *w*, *x*, *y*, and *z*.
- Ask the students to suggest other materials they might want to use for today's alphabet book pages. Distribute materials. Have crayons, markers, scissors, paste, and old magazines or catalogs available. Discuss what to put on the pages; you could suggest that students draw pictures of animals that begin with these letters. Encourage students to choose for themselves.
- Some of the letters in this group can be particularly difficult for students. Plan ahead with examples for each of the letters to help the students along.
- Remind the students to plan before they begin to write on or design their pages. Assign the letters *u*, *v*, *w*, *x*, *y*, and *z*.

Music Connection

Clapping to a Beat Listen/Speak 2.1

Purpose: To have the students recognize rhythm

- Write the words *butterfly*, *television*, *ladybug*, *rainbow*, and *saddlebag* on the board.
- Read each word and have the students clap the rhythm of each word by breaking the words into syllables and listening to the sounds. *(but-ter-fly, tel-e-vi-sion, la-dy-bug, rain-bow, sad-dle-bag)*
- Then write some one-syllable words on the board: *soap*, *bean*, *ran*, *cat*, *nice*, and *seat*.
- Read them and have the students clap out the rhythm of those words as well.
- Randomly point to the words on the board; for example, *butterfly*, *television*, *soap*, *bean*, *ran*, and *saddlebag*. As the class claps out the syllables, write the number of syllables they clapped under each word.
- Help the students identify repetition, rhyme, and rhythm in oral and written texts. Help them distinguish between rhyming and non-rhyming words in the poem.
- Say

  firefly, by

  firefly, eye

  river, bush
- Then give them other word pairs

  dark, spark

  twinkle, sprinkle

  your, sure

  traveler, passing

  firefly, butterfly

INVESTIGATION

UNIVERSAL ACCESS:
MEETING INDIVIDUAL NEEDS

Intervention Tip

RHYTHM Clap out nursery rhymes with the students. For variety, let them tap their feet.

Objectives

Word Analysis Vocabulary

- **Vocabulary Strategies: Rhyming Words.** Using words from "Twinkle Twinkle Firefly," build vocabulary from rhyming word play.

Writing Process Strategies

- **Introduction to the Writing Process.** Students organize ideas for their autobiographies to review prewriting strategies that build on the theme Let's Read!

English Language Conventions

- **Penmanship: Letters Are Lines.** To extend the letter formation instruction in Phonics and Fluency and understand that letters are made of different types of lines.

Materials

- Big Book Lets Read, pp.28–29
- Writer's Workbook, p. 3

Universal Access: Meeting Individual Needs

Reteach, Challenge, English-Language Development and ***Intervention*** lessons are available to support the language arts instruction in this lesson.

Research in Action
Penmanship

The goal of teaching handwriting is to help children write *legibly* and *comfortably.* Effective writing must be readable in order to convey a message, but it must be done without frustrating or fatiguing the writer . . . handwriting instruction should be deliberate, systematic, and well organized as well as humane. *(Charles Temple and Jean Wallace Gillet.* Language Arts: Learning Processes and Teaching Practices.)

OVERVIEW

Language Arts Overview

Word Analysis

Vocabulary **Rhyming Words.** The Vocabulary activity in this lesson reviews the concepts of recognizing rhyming words and using different strategies to investigate meanings of unfamiliar words. Students should have a basic understanding of what rhyming words are and how they can determine word meaning by asking someone, by referencing a dictionary, or by making a mnemonic clue. Remind students that knowledge of these concepts will be helpful to them as they experiment with word choices in their speech and, eventually, in their written work.

Vocabulary Skill Words

firefly **spy** **by** **eye**

Writing Process Strategies

The Writing Process Strategies lesson applies the prewriting skill of organizing for drafting as students organize their ideas for their autobiographies.

English Language Conventions

Penmanship **Letters Are Lines.** This lesson reinforces the letter formation instruction in Phonics and Fluency by teaching students that letters are made of vertical, horizontal, curved, and slanted lines. The instruction in this lesson presents a ball-and-stick model of manuscript handwriting. Continuous stroke models are available in the Appendix of this ***Teacher's Edition.***

Word Analysis

Vocabulary

Rhyming Words Reading 1.6

Teach

- Have students direct you to list all of the rhyming words in "Twinkle Twinkle Firefly" as you write them on the board. *(Firefly, spy, by, eye)*
- Ask the class to generate as many words as possible that rhyme with *fly*, as you write them on the board. *(bye, cry, die, dye, guy, hi, I, lie, my, rye, sigh, tie, why)*
- Discuss the definitions of each word. Identify those words that students do not know with certainty.

Guided Practice

- Review strategies for learning new words that have been introduced so far: ask someone, use a dictionary, make a rhyming clue.
- As a class, tackle each unfamiliar word, using one of the strategies.
  - Ask whether anyone has ever eaten *rye* bread and explain that rye is a grain.
  - Look up the word *dye* in a dictionary and find that it means "to stain with color."
  - Demonstrate a *sigh.* Then make a mnemonic such as *I sigh when we say good-bye.*
- Conclude by explaining that thinking of rhyming words can introduce students to many different words they might or might not know. Vocabulary strategies that students will practice throughout the year will help them learn many new words.

Informal Assessment

Periodically check to see if students are able to identify words ending in the same sound, such as *did, lid, kid.* Offer encouragement and praise as needed.

Writing Process Strategies

Introduction to the Writing Process

Plan Writing 1.1, 2.1

Teach

- Review the prewriting organizations students made about favorite foods and pets on previous days. Explain that they thought of ideas about the topic and then chose the best ideas and organized them to get ready to write.
- Explain that today students are going to make a plan for writing about themselves.
- Have them review the ideas they drew and wrote about themselves on page 2 of ***Writer's Workbook.***

Guided Practice

- Use page 2 of ***Writer's Workbook*** to help students organize their ideas to plan their autobiographies.
- Have them write the word *Me* in the center of the web on page 3. In each of the circles, have each of them include an idea about themselves. Suggest that they include ideas they had listed previously such as favorite foods and pets, as well as ideas the class generated in Lessons 4 and 5 (pages T97 and T115).
- As a way of organizing before drafting, have them put a star next to the two ideas that they think tell the most about them.

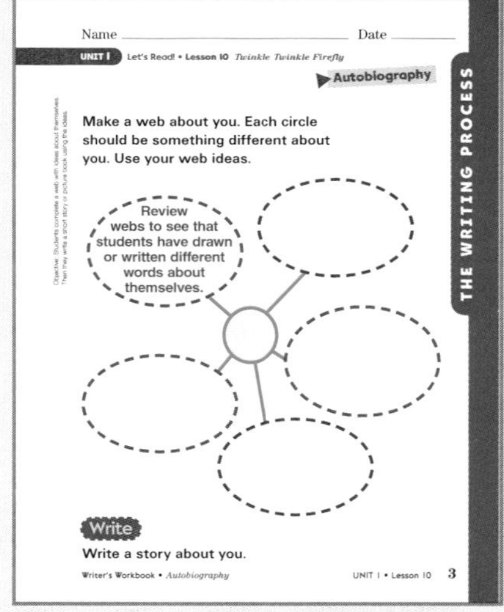
Name ____ Date ____
UNIT 1 Let's Read! • Lesson 10 Twinkle Twinkle Firefly
Autobiography
THE WRITING PROCESS
Make a web about you. Each circle should be something different about you. Use your web ideas.
Review webs to see that students have drawn or written different words about themselves.
Write
Write a story about you.
Writer's Workbook • Autobiography UNIT 1 • Lesson 10 3

Writer's Workbook p. 3

English Language Conventions

Penmanship Writing.1.3

Letters Are Lines

Teach

- Tell the students again how we use different types of lines to write letters of the alphabet. Ask if anyone can name these four lines. The four lines are curved lines, vertical lines, horizontal lines, and slanted lines.
- Ask the students to think about the letters they learned in Phonics and Fluency. Tell them that those letters are made of the four types of lines, and we are going to look at those letters today.
- **Teacher Model:** Model the formation of the four lines on the board.

Guided Practice

- Write the letters *E, F, G,* and *H* on the board. Tell the students someone has stolen all the lines and that you need their help to find the missing lines. Tell them they now are all detectives on a case to find the missing lines that have been hidden in these letters.
- Ask the students if there are vertical lines in any of the letters. Invite a student to come to the board to find and trace the vertical lines (in *E, F,* and *H*).
- Tell the students you need to find the horizontal lines next. Invite another student to come to the board to find and trace the horizontal lines (in *E, F,* and *H*).
- Tell the students that you see a curved line somewhere in the letters. Invite another student to find and trace a curved line (in *G*).
- Tell the students that they have solved the mystery and that they should put their clues on paper. Have the students practice drawing curved lines on a sheet of first-grade paper.

Informal Assessment

As students practice writing curved lines, observe how they hold their pencils and how much control they have in making each stroke.

Leveled Practice

Reteach: Phonics Skills
Pages 12–23

Challenge: Phonics Skills
Pages 12–16

Reteach: Comprehension and Language Arts Skills
Pages 6–9

Challenge: Comprehension and Language Arts Skills
Pages 6–8

ELD Workbook

Intervention Workbook

Decodable Books
Core Set, Books 5–7
Practice Set, Books 1–2

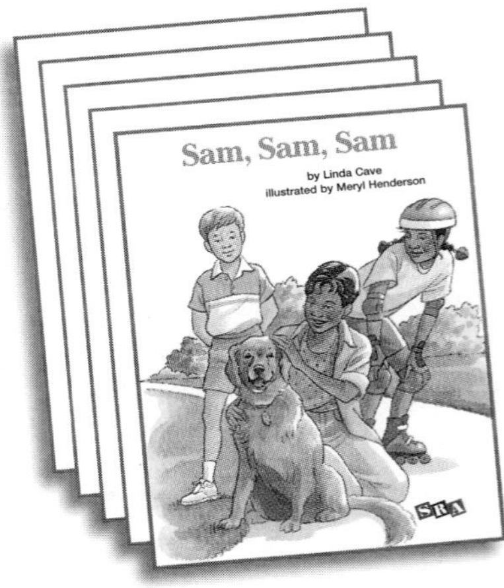

Additional Materials
Pre-Decodable Book 4

Leveled Classroom Library*

Encourage the students to read for at least 20 minutes daily outside of class. Have them read books in the ***Leveled Classroom Library,*** which supports the unit theme and helps students develop their vocabulary by reading independently.

America

BY W. NIKOLA-LISA.
LEE AND LOW BOOKS, INC., 1997.

This book about America describes its features through opposites. The work of 14 American artists is featured. **(Easy)**

Miss Malarkey Doesn't Live in Room 10

BY JUDY FINCHLER.
WALKER AND COMPANY, 1995.

Don't teachers live at school? This story will help clarify children's notions about teachers. **(Average)**

A Cake for Herbie

BY PETRA MATHERS.
ATHENEUM BOOKS FOR YOUNG READERS, 2000.

Herbie decides to enter a poetry contest, and he teaches us that not all people will like the poems we write, but some people will. **(Advanced)**

* These books, which support the unit theme Let's Read!, are part of a 60-book ***Leveled Classroom Library*** available for purchase from SRA/McGraw-Hill.
Note: Teachers should preview any trade books for appropriateness in their classrooms before recommending them to students.

TECHNOLOGY

Web Connections

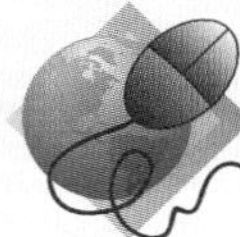

www.sra4kids.com
Let's Read! Web Site

CD-ROMs

Leap Into Phonics
LEAP INTO LEARNING, 2001

*** The Ultimate Writing and Creativity Center**
THE LEARNING COMPANY, 2001

Computer Skills

*** Basic Computer Skills**

Audiocassettes/CDs

*** Listening Library: Let's Read!**
SRA/MCGRAW-HILL, 2002

Sound Spelling Card Stories
SRA/MCGRAW-HILL, 2002

Titles preceded by an asterisk (*) are available through SRA/McGraw-Hill. Other titles can be obtained by contacting the publisher listed with the title.

LESSON PLANNER

	DAY 1	DAY 2
1 Preparing to Read **Materials** ■ Sound/Spelling Cards ■ Pre-Decodable Books ■ Decodable Books ■ Phonics Skills ■ ELD Workbook ■ Intervention Workbook	**Warming Up,** p. T224 **Phonemic Awareness,** p. T225 **Phonics** Ⓟ ■ Introduce the Sound/Spelling Cards, p. T226 ■ Introduce /s/ Spelled s, p. T226–228 **Dictation,** p. T229	**Warming Up,** p. T244 **Phonemic Awareness,** p. T245 **Phonics** Ⓟ ■ Introduce /m/ Spelled *m*, pp. T246–248 **Dictation,** p. T249 **Reading a Pre-Decodable Book** ■ *Book 4, Mom and I,* pp. T250–T251
2 Reading & Responding **Materials** ■ Big Book *Let's Read!* ■ Teacher Observation Log ■ Home Connection ■ Comprehension and Language Arts Skills ■ ELD Workbook ■ Intervention Workbook	**Build Background,** p. T232 **Preview and Prepare,** p. T232 **Selection Vocabulary,** p. T233 **Reading Recommendations,** p. T233 **Big Book *Let's Read!*,** pp. 30–37 **Comprehension Strategies,** pp. T234, T236 **Discussing the Selection,** p. T238 **Big Book *Let's Read!*,** pp. 30–37 **Comprehension Skills,** p. T237 **Review Selection Vocabulary,** p. T238 **Print and Book Awareness,** p. T239 **Supporting the Reading,** p. T239	**Build Background,** p. T252 **Preview and Prepare,** p. T252 **Selection Vocabulary,** p. T253 **Reading Recommendations,** p. T253 **Big Book *Let's Read!*,** pp. 38–41 **Comprehension Strategies,** p. T254 **Discussing the Selection,** p. T256 **Big Book *Let's Read!*,** pp. 38–41 **Comprehension Skills,** p. T255 **Review Selection Vocabulary,** p. T256 **Print and Book Awareness,** p. T257 **Supporting the Reading,** p. T257
Inquiry **Materials** ■ Class Alphabet Books	**Investigating Concepts Beyond the Text,** p. T240 **Social Studies Connection** ■ Seasons, p. T241	**Investigating Concepts Beyond the Text,** p. T258 **Music Connection** ■ Cumulative Rhymes, p. T259
3 Language Arts **Materials** ■ Big Book, *Let's Read!*, pp. 7–53 ■ Comprehension and Language Arts Skills, pp. 10–13 ■ Writer's Workbook, p. 3 ■ Language Arts Big Book ■ The Ultimate Writing and Creativity Center CD-ROM ■ Writer's Notebook	**Word Analysis** ■ Introduction to Context Clues, p. T243 **Writing Process Strategies** ■ Introduction to the Writing Process: Write, p. T243 **English Language Conventions** ■ Mechanics: Capital Letters and End Marks, p. T243	**Word Analysis** ■ Introduction to Context Clues, p. T261 **Writing Process Strategies** ■ Introduction to the Writing Process: Write, p. T261 ■ Writer's Craft: Sentences **English Language Conventions** ■ Mechanics: Sentences, p. T261

Interactive Lesson Planner Ⓟ Phonics ✓Informal Assessment Available ✓Formal Assessment Available

DAY 3	DAY 4	DAY 5
Warming Up, p. T262 Phonemic Awareness, p. T263 Phonics (P) ■ Introduce /a/ Spelled *a*, p. T264 ■ Initial *a*, p. T264 ■ Listening for /a/ and /ā/, p. T265 ■ Sing the "Short-Vowel" Song, p. T265 ■ Introducing Blending, p. T266 Dictation and Spelling, p. T267 ■ Introduction to Blending, p. T266 Reading a Decodable Book ■ *Book 5, Sam, Sam, Sam,* pp. T268–T269	Warming Up, p. T282 Phonemic Awareness, p. T283 Phonics (P) ■ Introduce /t/ Spelled *t*, pp. T284–T285 ■ Blending, pp. T286–T288 Dictation and Spelling, p. T289 Reading a Decodable Book ■ *Book 6, Matt and Sam,* pp. T290–T291	Warming Up, p. T304 Phonemic Awareness, p. T305 Phonics (P) ■ Introduce /h/ Spelled *h*, p. T306 ■ Blending, pp. T307–T308 Dictation and Spelling, p. T309 Reading a Decodable Book ■ *Book 7, A Hat,* pp. T310–T311
Build Background, p. T272 Preview and Prepare, p. T272 Selection Vocabulary, p. T273 Reading Recommendations, p. T273 Big Book *Let's Read!,* pp. 42–45 Comprehension Strategies, p. T274 Discussing the Selection, p. T276 Big Book *Let's Read!,* pp. 42–45 Comprehension Skills, p. T275 Review Selection Vocabulary, p. T276 Print and Book Awareness, p. T277 Supporting the Reading, p. T277	Build Background, p. T292 Preview and Prepare, p. T292 Selection Vocabulary, p. T293 Reading Recommendations, p. T293 Big Book *Let's Read!,* pp. 46–53 Comprehension Strategies, pp. T294, T296 Discussing the Selection, p. T298 Big Book *Let's Read!,* pp. 46–53 Comprehension Skills, pp. T295, T297 Review Selection Vocabulary, p. T298 Print and Book Awareness, p. T299 Supporting the Reading, p. T299	Build Background, p. T314 Preview and Prepare, p. T314 Selection Vocabulary, p. T315 Reading Recommendations, p. T315 Big Book *Let's Read!,* pp. 54–55 Comprehension Strategies, p. T2316 Discussing the Selection, p. T318 Letter Recognition, p. T317 Review Selection Vocabulary, p. T318 Print and Book Awareness, p. T319 Supporting the Reading, p. T319 Home Connection, p. T319
Investigating Concepts Beyond the Text, p. T278 Math Connection ■ Alike and Different, p. T279	Investigating Concepts Beyond the Text, p. T300 Drama Connection ■ Talk Without Speaking, p. T301	Investigating Concepts Beyond the Text, p. T320 Language Arts Connection ■ Making Rhymes, p. T321
Word Analysis ■ Introduction to Context Clues, p. T281 Writing Process Strategies ■ Introduction to the Writing Process, Drafting: Write, p. T281 English Language Conventions ✓■ Mechanics: Sentences, Capital Letters, and End Marks, p. T281	Word Analysis ■ Introduction to Context Clues, p. T303 Writing Process Strategies ■ Introduction to the Writing Process, Drafting: Write for Autobiography, p. T303 English-Language Conventions ■ Listening, Speaking, Viewing. Language: Informal and Formal Language, p. T303	Word Analysis ■ Context Clues, p. T323 Writing Process Strategies ■ Introduction to the Writing Process, Drafting: Write for Autobiography, p. T323 English Language Conventions ■ Penmanship: Letters Are Lines, p. T323

Below are suggestions for Workshop to meet the individual needs of students. These are the same skills shown in the Lesson Planner; however, these pages provide extra practice opportunities or enriching activities to meet the varied needs of students.

WORKSHOP

Differentiating Instruction Workshop

Small-Group Instruction

Use the informal assessment suggestions found throughout the lesson along with the formal assessments provided to determine your students' strengths and areas of need. Use the following program components to help in supporting or expanding on the instruction found in these lessons:

- ***Reteach: Phonics Skills*** and ***Reteach: Comprehension and Language Arts Skills*** workbooks for use with those students who show a basic understanding of the lesson but need a bit more practice to solidify their understanding
- ***Intervention Guide*** and ***Workbook*** for use with those students who even after extra practice exhibit a lack of understanding of the lesson concepts
- ***English Language Development Guide*** and ***Workbook*** for use with those students who need language assistance

Have students create small groups to do such things as:

- Discuss books during Reading Roundtable.
- Discuss questions that arise as they investigate concepts after reading the selection.
- Partner read to assist those who have problems reading difficult passages or to help develop fluency.

Independent Activities

Students can work individually on such things as:

- Independent reading
- Challenge
- Writing
- Investigation activities

For Workshop Management Tips, see Appendix page 42.

◆ **Small-Group Instruction** ■ **Independent Activities**

	READING	INVESTIGATION ACTIVITIES
DAY 1	◆ Reread selection ◆ Listen to selection in ***Listening Library*** ◆ Choose ***Leveled Classroom Library Book*** Reread ***Decodable Book***	**Investigating Concepts Beyond the Text** ◆ Work on class alphabet book
DAY 2	◆ Reread selection ◆ Listen to selection in ***Listening Library*** ◆ Choose ***Leveled Classroom Library Book*** Reread ***Decodable Book***	**Investigating Concepts Beyond the Text** ◆ Work on class alphabet book
DAY 3	◆ Reread selection ◆ Listen to selection in ***Listening Library*** ◆ Choose ***Leveled Classroom Library Book*** Reread ***Decodable Book***	**Investigating Concepts Beyond the Text** ◆ Work on class alphabet book
DAY 4	◆ Reread selection ◆ Listen to selection in ***Listening Library*** ◆ Choose ***Leveled Classroom Library Book*** Reread ***Decodable Book***	**Investigating Concepts Beyond the Text**
DAY 5	◆ Reread selection ◆ Listen to selection in ***Listening Library*** ◆ Choose ***Leveled Classroom Library Book*** Reread ***Decodable Book***	**Investigating Concepts Beyond the Text**

LANGUAGE ARTS	INTERVENTION	ENGLISH-LANGUAGE LEARNERS	RETEACH	CHALLENGE
English Language Conventions ◆ Complete **Sentences,** ***Comprehension and Language Arts Skills,*** pp. 10–11	◆ Selection Vocabulary and Comprehension Strategies, p. T232 ◆ English Language Conventions, p. T242	◆ s Blends in Spanish, p. T227 ◆ Selection Vocabulary, p. T232 ◆ Preteach, p. T233 ◆ English Language Conventions, p. T242	◆ Reread, p. T233 ◆ Reread, p. T236 **Phonics:** *Ss* ◆ ***Reteach: Phonics Skills,*** pp. 14–15	**Phonics:** *Ss* ■ ***Challenge: Phonics Skills,*** p. 12
Word Analysis ■ **Spelling** ◆ ***Spelling and Vocabulary Skills*** **Writing Process Strategies** ◆ Complete **Writer's Craft: Sentences,** ***Comprehension and Language Arts Skills,*** pp. 12–13	◆ Initial Consonants, p. T245 ◆ Initial /m/ Sound, p. T246 ◆ Selection Vocabulary and Comprehension Strategies, p. T253 ◆ Reread, p. T254 ◆ English Language Conventions, p. T260	◆ Selection Vocabulary, p. T253 ◆ English Language Conventions, p. T260	◆ Initial Consonants, p. T245 **Phonics:** *Mm* ◆ ***Reteach: Phonics Skills,*** pp. 16–17	**Phonics:** *Mm* ■ ***Challenge: Phonics Skills,*** p. 13
Word Analysis ◆ ***Spelling and Vocabulary Skills***	◆ Selection Vocabulary and Comprehension Strategies, p. T272 ◆ English Language Conventions, p. T280	◆ Word Meaning, p. T263 ◆ Selection Vocabulary, p. T272 ◆ Using Illustrations, p. T272 ◆ Preteach, p. T273 ◆ English Language Conventions, p. T280	◆ Oral Blending, p. T263 **Phonics:** *Aa* ◆ ***Reteach: Phonics Skills,*** pp. 18–19	**Phonics:** *Aa* ■ ***Challenge: Phonics Skills,*** p. 14
Word Analysis ◆ ***Spelling and Vocabulary Skills***	◆ Selection Vocabulary and Comprehension Strategies, p. T293 ◆ Compare and Contrast, p. T295 ◆ English Language Conventions, p. T302	◆ Word Meaning, p. T286 ◆ Reading Aloud, p. T292 ◆ Selection Vocabulary, p. T293 ◆ English Language Conventions, p. T302	◆ Initial Consonant Sounds, p. T283 ◆ Compare and Contrast, p. T299 **Phonics:** *Tt* ◆ ***Reteach: Phonics Skills,*** pp. 20–21	■ Compare and Contrast, p. T299 **Phonics:** *Tt* ■ ***Challenge: Phonics Skills,*** p. 15
Writing Process Strategies ■ **Seminar:** Draft an Autobiography, p. T323 **English Language Conventions** ◆ **Penmanship:** Letters are Lines, p. T323	◆ Blending, p. T307 ◆ Selection Vocabulary and Comprehension Strategies, p. T314 ◆ English Language Conventions, p. T323	◆ Vocabulary, p. T306 ◆ Selection Vocabulary, p. T314 ◆ Preteach, p. T315 ◆ English Language Conventions, p. T323	◆ Phonemic Awareness, p. T305 **Phonics:** *Hh* ◆ ***Reteach: Phonics Skills,*** pp. 22–23 **Writing Process Strategies** ◆ Complete **Writer's Craft: Sentences,** ***Reteach: Comprehension and Language Arts Skills,*** p. 7	■ Independent Reading, p. T317 **Phonics:** *Hh* ◆ ***Challenge: Phonics Skills,*** p. 16 **Writing Process Strategies** ◆ Complete **Writer's Craft: Sentences,** ***Challenge: Comprehension and Language Arts Skills,*** p. 7

ASSESSMENT

Formal Assessment

Use these summative assessments along with your informal observations to assess student progress.

Written Assessment

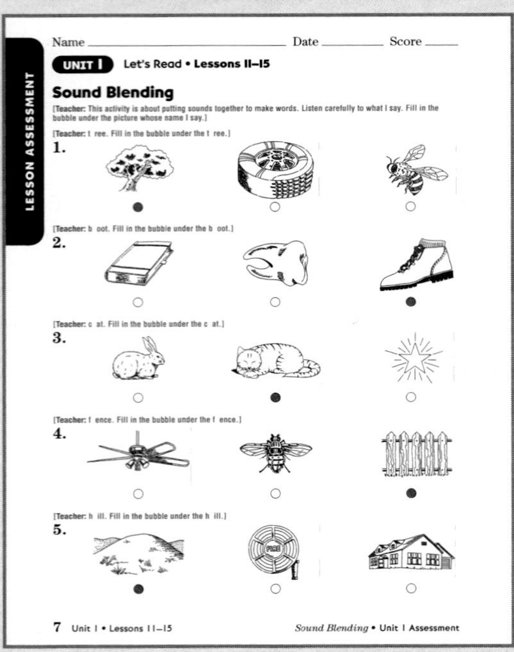

LESSON ASSESSMENT

Name ______________ Date ________ Score _____

UNIT 1 Let's Read • **Lessons 11–15**

Sound Blending

[**Teacher:** This activity is about putting sounds together to make words. Listen carefully to what I say. Fill in the bubble under the picture whose name I say.]

[**Teacher:** t ree. Fill in the bubble under the t ree.]
1.

[**Teacher:** b oot. Fill in the bubble under the b oot.]
2.

[**Teacher:** c at. Fill in the bubble under the c at.]
3.

[**Teacher:** f ence. Fill in the bubble under the f ence.]
4.

[**Teacher:** h ill. Fill in the bubble under the h ill.]
5.

7 Unit 1 • Lessons 11–15 *Sound Blending* • Unit 1 Assessment

Units 1–6 Assessment p. 7

Oral Assessments

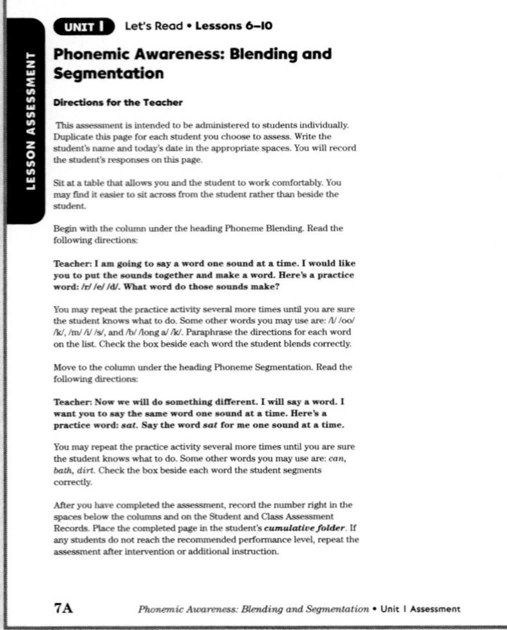

LESSON ASSESSMENT

UNIT 1 Let's Read • **Lessons 6–10**

Phonemic Awareness: Blending and Segmentation

Directions for the Teacher

This assessment is intended to be administered to students individually. Duplicate this page for each student you choose to assess. Write the student's name and today's date in the appropriate spaces. You will record the student's responses on this page.

Sit at a table that allows you and the student to work comfortably. You may find it easier to sit across from the student rather than beside the student.

Begin with the column under the heading Phoneme Blending. Read the following directions:

Teacher: I am going to say a word one sound at a time. I would like you to put the sounds together and make a word. Here's a practice word: /r/ /e/ /d/. What word do those sounds make?

You may repeat the practice activity several more times until you are sure the student knows what to do. Some other words you may use are: /l/ /oo/ /k/, /m/ /i/ /s/, and /b/ /long a/ /k/. Paraphrase the directions for each word on the list. Check the box beside each word the student blends correctly.

Move to the column under the heading Phoneme Segmentation. Read the following directions:

Teacher: Now we will do something different. I will say a word. I want you to say the same word one sound at a time. Here's a practice word: *sat*. Say the word *sat* for me one sound at a time.

You may repeat the practice activity several more times until you are sure the student knows what to do. Some other words you may use are: *can*, *bath*, *dirt*. Check the box beside each word the student segments correctly.

After you have completed the assessment, record the number right in the spaces below the columns and on the Student and Class Assessment Records. Place the completed page in the student's ***cumulative folder***. If any students do not reach the recommended performance level, repeat the assessment after intervention or additional instruction.

7A *Phonemic Awareness: Blending and Segmentation* • Unit 1 Assessment

Units 1–6 Assessment, Teacher's Edition, p. 7A

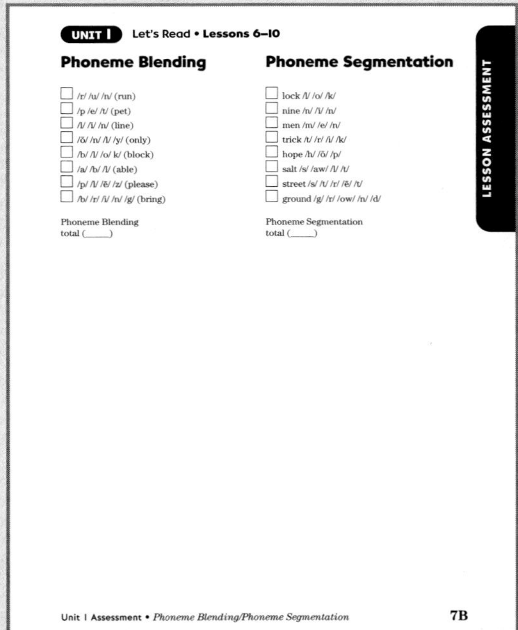

UNIT 1 Let's Read • **Lessons 6–10**

LESSON ASSESSMENT

Phoneme Blending	Phoneme Segmentation
☐ /r/ /u/ /n/ (run)	☐ lock /l/ /o/ /k/
☐ /p /e/ /t/ (pet)	☐ nine /n/ /i/ /n/
☐ /l/ /i/ /n/ (line)	☐ men /m/ /e/ /n/
☐ /ō/ /n/ /l/ /y/ (only)	☐ trick /t/ /r/ /i/ /k/
☐ /b/ /l/ /o/ k/ (block)	☐ hope /h/ /ō/ /p/
☐ /a/ /b/ /l/ (able)	☐ salt /s/ /aw/ /l/ /t/
☐ /p/ /l/ /ē/ /z/ (please)	☐ street /s/ /t/ /r/ /ē/ /t/
☐ /b/ /r/ /i/ /n/ /g/ (bring)	☐ ground /g/ /r/ /ow/ /n/ /d/
Phoneme Blending total (_____)	Phoneme Segmentation total (_____)

Unit 1 Assessment • *Phoneme Blending/Phoneme Segmentation* 7B

Units 1–6 Assessment, Teacher's Edition, p. 7B

Informal Assessment

The Teacher Observation Log, found in the ***Program Assessment Teacher's Edition,*** is a vehicle for recording anecdotal information about individual student performance on an ongoing basis. Information such as students' strengths and weaknesses can be recorded at any time the occasion warrants. It is recommended that you maintain a Cumulative Folder for each student in which you can store the logs for purposes of comparison and analysis as the school year progresses. You will gradually build up a comprehensive file that reveals which students are progressing smoothly and which students need additional help.

Tips for using the Teacher Observation Log:

- Keep Observation Logs available so you can easily record your informal observations. A clipboard or other similar device might be helpful.
- Decide which aspect of the student's learning you want to monitor on the log.
- Record your observations. It might take four to five days to observe and record the performance of each student.
- If you need more information on some of your students, you might want to observe them more than once, either during the lesson, during Workshop, or at other times during the day.

Teacher's Observation Log

Student ______

Date ______ Unit ______

Activity ______

General Comprehension

Concepts Discussed ______

Behavior Within a Group

Articulates, expresses ideas ______

Joins discussions ______

Collaboration (such as works with other students, works alone) ______

Role in Group

Role (such as leader, summarizer, questioner, recorder, critic, observer, non-participant)

Flexibility (changes roles when necessary) ______

Use of Reading Strategies

Uses strategies when needed (either those taught or student's own)/Describe strategies used

Changes strategies when appropriate ______

Changes Since Last Observation

If more space is needed, write on the back or use another sheet.

32 **Program Assessment**

Program Assessment Teacher's Edition p. 32

ASSESSMENT

Objectives

- Students will blend sounds orally to form words.
- Students will attend to final sounds in words.
- Students will associate the /s/ sound with the letter *s* in words.

Materials

- Lion Puppet
- Sound/Spelling Cards
- Sound/Spelling Card Audiocassette/CD
- Routine Card 1
- Letter Cards
- Phonics Skills, pp. 14–15

Teacher Tip PREPARE AHEAD Write the "Apples and Bananas" song on chart paper. This will allow the students to visualize the words they are singing. Reading 1.1

UNIVERSAL ACCESS: MEETING INDIVIDUAL NEEDS

ELL Support

For ELD strategies, use the ***English-Language Development Guide,*** Unit 1, Lesson 11.

Intervention Support

For intervention strategies, use the ***Intervention Guide,*** Unit 1, Lesson 11.

Informal Assessment

INITIAL CONSONANT SOUNDS Begin observation of five and six students during the Consonant Riddle Game. You might want to ask for class response to some of these words, then call on individuals to respond to specific words. Try to observe all the students over the next several days. Record your observations in your Teacher Observation Log in the ***Program Assessment Teacher's Edition.*** Reading 1.4

LESSON MODELS VIDEOCASSETTE Use the ***Lesson Models Videocassette*** at this time for a Warming Up lesson model with Apples and Bananas and the Consonant Riddle Game.

Warming Up

Use one or both of the following activities to focus students' attention on the repetition, rhyme, and rhythm. This activity will help students review concepts they have been learning.

"Apples and Bananas" Song Reading 1.5; Listen/Speak 2.1

Sing "Apples and Bananas." Post the song in the classroom so that everyone can see it. Encourage the students to follow the words on the chart paper as they sing. Review the main verse with students and then have them change the sound for /ā/, /ē/, /ī/, /ō/, and /ū/. Ask the students to listen carefully to determine which sound to use next. Before each verse, pronounce the vowel sound you will be using.

I like to eat, eat, eat,
Apples and bananas.
I like to eat, eat, eat,
Apples and bananas.

Consonant Riddle Game Reading 1.4, 1.6, 1.7

Tell the students they can blend sounds you will give them to make new words. Then have students solve the following riddles:

What starts with /b/? /t/? /h/? /m/? /k/? and rhymes with *fall?*

What starts with /k/? /sh/? /w/? /l/? /b/? and rhymes with *deep?*

What starts with /m/? /h/? /sh/? /w/? /s/? /b/? and rhymes with *knee?*

What starts with /t/? /ch/? /sh/? /h/? /p/? and rhymes with *mop?*

What starts with /k/? /b/? /r/? /f/? /t/? /sh/? and rhymes with *make?*

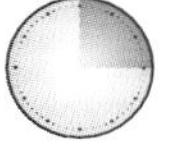

Phonemic Awareness

Oral Blending

Initial Consonant Sounds Reading 1.7

- Write *hamburger* on the board. Touch the word, and tell students that this word is *hamburger*. Have them say the word.
- Then tell the students that you will change the word by changing the first sound.
- Erase the *h* and tell them that now the word will begin with /s/. Ask what the new word is *(samburger)*. Have the students say the new word.
- Continue by erasing the first letter and substituting with other consonant sounds, such as /b/, /g/, /k/, /sh/, and /t/. Pronounce each sound. Then write the letters. Ask the students what each new word is.
- Other words that can be used for this activity include *visitor, cinnamon, railroad, building, sailboat,* and *garbage.*

Segmentation

Final Phoneme Segmentation Reading 1.4

Tell the students that for today's game, the puppet wants them to repeat only the very *last sound* of each word you say. After a few demonstrations, let students speak for the puppet, repeating only the last phoneme of each word you say.

Teacher: beach
Puppet: /ch/
Teacher: race
Puppet: /s/

After giving students their cue to speak, invite students to speak in place of the puppet with the following words:

mouse	mouth	cheese	cheap	cheek
cave	case	cage	came	cake
mash	math	man	map	mad
him	hiss	hip	mug	much

Universal Access: Meeting Individual Needs

Reteach

ORAL BLENDING If any students still have problems with blending initial consonants orally, review oral blending at the beginning with syllable and word-part blending. Students who have difficulty with these activities will face greater problems in sound blending in Lesson 13 and thereafter. Reading 1.8

Research in Action

Initial Consonant Sounds

This activity develops fluency with blending initial consonant sounds. Starting with a common word, the initial sound is changed rapidly, with students producing the resulting changes in pronunciation. Most of the new pronunciations will be nonsense words. The point of the activity is to make students conscious of sounds and to give them some skill in manipulating the sounds. *(Marilyn J. Adams)*

SOUND/SPELLING CARD STORIES Use the ***Sound/Spelling Card Stories*** for practice with the /s/ sound. Have students respond by saying the words with the /s/ sound in their heads.

Teacher Tip INTRODUCING SOUNDS AND SPELLINGS Many teachers use tape or other materials to cover the *ce* and *ci_* spellings on the card until they are introduced in a later lesson.

Teacher Tip BODY MOVEMENT Some teachers find it helpful to encourage the students to use physical actions as an aid in remembering the sounds of some spellings. For example, you might have the students make a slithering motion with their arms and /s/ like a snake. To remember the /s/ sound, have the students move their hands as if holding a spatula and rolling sausages over in a hot pan.

Teacher Tip REPETITION For some students it is helpful to repeat the word after the teacher says it. Have the student(s) give a thumbs-up if they hear the sound.

Routine Card Refer to ***Routine 1*** for an introduction to the sounds and spellings procedure.

LESSON MODELS VIDEOCASSETTE Use the ***Lesson Models Videocassette*** at this time for a lesson model introducing /s/ spelled *s*.

PHONICS

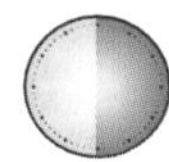

Phonics

Introduce the Sound/Spelling Cards

- Tell the students that when people read, they use the sounds that letters make to figure out the words. Tell them they are now going to begin learning about sounds and spellings.
- As you turn the letter *s* card and display the picture, point out the capital and small letters at the top of the card and point out the picture. Explain that each card has a picture that will help them remember the sounds. Explain that the way we write or "spell" the sounds is listed on the bottom of the card.
- See page 15 of the Program Appendix for a more detailed description of the ***Sound/Spelling Cards*** and the procedure for introducing and using them.

Introduce /s/ Spelled s Reading 1.3, 1.4, 1.10

S s

s
ce
ci_

19 Sausages

- Turn ***Sound/Spelling Card 19—Sausages*** around to show the picture, and have a volunteer identify the capital *S* and lowercase *s* at the top of the card. Remind the students that the letter *s* is a consonant and is written in black.
- Explain that each card has a picture that will help them remember the sound of the spelling(s) listed on the bottom of the card. Ask the students what this picture shows, and tell them that this is the ***Sausages Card.***
- Point to the letter *s* at the bottom of the card. Explain that this part of the card shows how this sound is spelled when it is in a word. We refer to these letters as "spellings."
- Tell the students that you will read them a story that will help them remember how to read and write the /s/ sound. Then read the Sausage story:

  Sue and Sammy had a nice place in the city.
  On Saturday, Sue and Sammy decided to have sausages for supper.
  Sam put seven sausages in a skillet /s/ /s/ /s/ /s/ /s/ /s/ /s/.
  Soon the smell of sausages filled the air.
  /s/ /s/ /s/ /s/ /s/, sizzled the sausages.
  "Pull up a seat, Sue," said Sammy. "The sausages are almost ready to serve."
  /s/ /s/ /s/ /s/ /s/, sizzled the sausages.
  Sue and Sammy ate the delicious sausages. Soon they wanted more, so Sam put six more sausages in the frying pan.
  /s/ /s/ /s/ /s/ /s/, sizzled the sausages.

- If you were cooking sausages with Sammy and Sue, what sound would the sausages make as they sizzled? (Have the students join in.) /s/ /s/ /s/ /s/ /s/
- Write the letter *s* on the board, reminding students of the proper stroke sequences. Touch the letter and say the /s/ sound.
- Have the students write the letter *s* several times, either on paper or with their finger on a surface, saying the /s/ sound each time they form the letter.
- Tell the students that you are going to say some words. Make sure that they understand the established signal, and tell them to signal thumbs-up when they hear the /s/ sound at the beginning of a word and to do nothing when they do not hear the sound. Some words are:

say	**see**	kite	**sun**
sit	time	**suit**	**sight**
boot	**song**	**soap**	note

- Ask the students to suggest other words that begin with /s/.
- Then have the students listen for /s/ at the end of the words and use the established signal when they hear it. Some words are:

less	toad	fake	**pass**	road
like	**dress**	**fuss**	drip	**grass**
fun	night	**mess**	nine	**bus**

- Conclude the activity by reviewing that *s* is one of the spellings for the /s/ sound in words. Explain to students that whenever they look at the ***Sausage Card,*** they can remember that *sausage* starts with /s/, and they can think of the sound the sausage makes when it's sizzling in the frying pan: /s/ /s/ /s/ /s/.

PHONICS

Teacher Tip HEARING /S/ It may be helpful for the students to repeat each word after you and then give the signal. Reading 1.3

Universal Access: Meeting Individual Needs

ELL Tip

S BLENDS IN SPANISH In Spanish, there are no words that begin with *s* blends. In Spanish, a vowel always comes before an *s* blend so there may be a tendency for students to add a vowel sound at the beginning of words that begin with *sc, st, str,* and so on. Take time to review *s* blends sound by sound to focus on the /s/ sound of *s*.

ELL Tip

INFLECTIONAL ENDINGS The English inflectional ending for plurals might cause problems. In English, the pronunciation of the final *s* varies. It can be pronounced /s/ or /z/.

UNIVERSAL ACCESS: MEETING INDIVIDUAL NEEDS
Reading 1.4

Reteach

/S/ SPELLED S Students should complete ***Reteach: Phonics Skills*** pages 14–15 for additional practice with the /s/ sound spelled *s*.

Challenge

/S/ SPELLED S Use ***Challenge: Phonics Skills*** page 12 with students who are ready for a challenge.

Intervention Tip

/S/ SOUNDS Teach students /s/ tongue twisters; for example, sister Susie sips soda at the seashore; or Sidney sees seven snakes sneaking some sausages.

PHONICS

Phonics Skills
Reading 1.3

Phonics Skills pages 14–15 provide additional practice with /s/ spelled *s*. Students practice forming the letter *s* and listen for the /s/ sound in words. Have the students say the sound as they write each letter. The names of the pictures at the bottom of page 14 are: *sun*, *sand*, and *soup*. On page 15, the names of the pictures are: *saw*, *seal*, *pail*, *salt*, *six*, *duck*, *sock*, and *snail*.

Name ______ Date ______
UNIT 1 Let's Read! • Lesson 11 *The Chase*
Sounds and Spellings
s
s s s s s s s s s s
S S S S S S S
Listening for Consonants
s s s
14 UNIT 1 • Lesson 11 *Consonant Sounds and Spellings* • Phonics Skills

Name ______ Date ______
UNIT 1 Let's Read! • Lesson 11 *The Chase*
Listening for Consonants
s s
s
s
s s
Phonics Skills • *Consonant Sounds and Spellings* UNIT 1 • Lesson 11 15

***Phonics Skills* pp. 14–15**

Dictation

Dictation Reading 1.3

- Have the students write the whole alphabet independently. For today, ask them to use capital letters only. Remind them to proofread their letters.
- Review these papers to identify any students who are in need of extra practice.
- Return the papers to the students to insert in the letter book they are making.

PHONICS

Teacher Tip DICTATION You may wish to dictate the alphabet for the students. Reading 1.3

Informal Assessment

MONITORING Continue to monitor students' letter knowledge by assessing their ability to name and recognize the shapes of letters.

Reading 1.3

Pages 30–37 of *Let's Read!*

First of two lessons.

Focus Questions Why are people in a hurry sometimes? Have you ever done something just because someone else was doing it?

The Chase

told by Béatrice Tanaka • *illustrated by Michel Gay*

Coyote was sitting peacefully in the meadow when he saw Rabbit run past, quick as an arrow. **1**

"If Rabbit's running that fast, there must be hunters after him," Coyote said to himself. "I'd better run too."

30

Objectives

- Students will share prior knowledge about folktales.
- Students will use the Table of Contents to locate information.
- Students will discuss selection vocabulary.
- Students will listen and respond to the first part of the selection.
- Students will discuss reality and fantasy.
- Students will make predictions.
- Students will identify word boundaries.
- Students will discuss the impact of the seasons.

Materials

- Big Book *Let's Read!*, pp. 30–37

SELECTION INTRODUCTION

About the Author Reading 3.2

BÉATRICE TANAKA Born in Romania, Ms. Tanaka lived in Brazil where she became an award-winning set and costume designer. She began her writing career when she was looking for books for her own children. Since that time, she has focused on folktales from African, Asian, and Native American cultures.

Other Books by Béatrice Tanaka

Seaside Treasures, *The Tortoise and the Sword: A Vietnamese Legend*, *Green Tales*

About the Illustrator Reading 3.2

MICHEL GAY was born in Lyon, France, to a family of musicians. His grandfather encouraged young Michel to become a musician, but Michel was more interested in drawing.

Other Books Illustrated by Michel Gay

Rabbit Express, *The Christmas Wolf*, *White Owl and Blue Mouse*

Selection Summary

Genre: Folktale

Students will enjoy this cumulative Native American folktale that presents the mystery: Why is Rabbit running? None of the animals know, but that doesn't stop them from running, too. The humorous ending is a big surprise to all.

The elements of a folktale are listed below. A folktale may have one or more of these elements.

- A folktale is a story that has been told and retold from one generation to the next over many years.
- People from different parts of the world tell folktales that are similar.
- Folktales often begin with the words, "Once upon a time" or "Long ago and far away."
- The characters can be animals or inanimate objects that speak.
- The story often teaches a lesson or moral.
- Characters who are good or smart win out over those who are evil or not as smart.
- The story is told using the words *he*, *she*, or *it*—rather than *I*—to talk about the characters.
- Actions and words are often repeated.
- The story has an exciting high point at the end.

Inquiry Connections

In this selection of the ***Big Book*** the students will listen to a folktale in which all the animals chase another animal.

Key concepts investigated are

- the elements of a folktale.
- matching oral words to printed words.
- becoming more aware of print.

Direct the students to the Concept/Question Board. Encourage them to post any questions or ideas they have about the unit. They may want to include a drawing that tells about the folktale. As a class, make a list of folktales the students are familiar with and post on the Board.

- Make sure the students put their names or initials on anything they post on the Board.
- Tell them that they can post something on the Board any day. Be sure to have students discuss what they put on the Board with the class.

Concept/Question Board

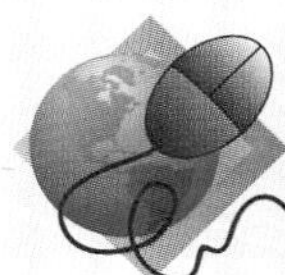

www.sra4kids.com
Web Connection
Help the students look for additional information about folktales by using the Web connections that are available at the Reading link of the SRA Web page.

Universal Access: Meeting Individual Needs

ELL Support

For ELD strategies, use the ***English-Language Development Guide,*** Unit 1, Lesson 11.

Intervention Support

For intervention strategies, use the ***Intervention Guide,*** Unit 1, Lesson 11.

Routine Card
Refer to ***Routine 11*** for the procedure for reading the selection.

Teacher Tip BROWSE Remind the students that good readers browse before reading. Tell them that they should be getting in the habit of browsing before they read, and that doing so can help them activate prior knowledge relevant to the selection.

Research in Action
Comprehension and Skillful Reading

Skilled readers are good comprehenders. They differ from unskilled readers in their use of general world knowledge to comprehend text literally as well as to draw valid inferences from texts, in their comprehension of words, and in their use of comprehension monitoring and repair strategies.
Catherine E. Snow, M. Susan Burns, and Peg Griffin

Snow, Catherine E., Burns, M. Susan, and Griffin, Peg (Eds.). 1998. *Preventing reading difficulties in young children.* Washington, DC: National Academy Press.

Build Background

Activate Prior Knowledge Reading 2.6

- Tell students that you are going to read a folktale about animals in a chase. Help students recall other folktales they are familiar with that have animal characters, for example, "The Three Little Pigs," "The Three Bears," and "The Three Billy Goats Gruff."
- Ask the students what a chase is. Ask them whether they've ever seen animals chase one another before. Why would animals chase one another?

Preview and Prepare

Browse

- Open *Let's Read!* to the Table of Contents and find "The Chase." Ask whether anyone can tell what page number the story is on and then turn to the page.
- Have the students look at the cover illustration. Ask a volunteer to tell what Coyote is looking at. Then have students browse several pages and name the other animals they see.
- Before reading the selection to the students, read through the Focus Questions on the first page of the selection together. Briefly discuss the questions, and tell the students to keep these questions in mind as you read.

Set Purposes

Explain that readers often read stories to find out what happens to the characters. Because the title of this story is "The Chase," the purpose for reading this story might be to find out which characters are in the chase and why.

Selection Vocabulary Reading 3.1

- Write the following words on the board and pronounce them.

  Coyote **Rabbit**

- Point out to students that these words name animals. Ask students to name other animals they will meet in the story. Then talk about other animal characters students have met in stories and poems.

Reading Recommendations

Read Aloud

- Read pages 30–37 aloud to the students. As you read, point to each word. Also apply the comprehension strategy instruction when you see a number on the reduced student page. This number refers to instruction on the left page.
- When you reread pages 30–37, apply the comprehension skill instruction to the right of the reduced student pages.
- Tell students that the question word *why* refers to a reason something happens. Tell students to listen for the characters (who) in the selection, what the poem is about, where it takes place, what time it takes place, and why the animals are chasing another animal.

Using Comprehension Strategies  Reading 2.4

Comprehension strategy instruction allows students to become aware of what good readers do when they read. Good readers constantly check their understanding as they are reading and ask themselves questions. Skilled readers also recognize when they are having problems understanding a selection and stop to use various comprehension strategies to help them make sense of what they are reading.

During the reading of this selection, you will model the use of the following comprehension strategies:

- **Monitoring and Clarifying** helps readers understand the meaning of words and difficult ideas or passages.
- **Visualizing** helps readers picture in their minds what is going on in a selection to gain a clearer understanding.

Building Comprehension Skills Second Read

Beginning in this lesson, on the right pages next to the reduced student pages, comprehension skill instruction will be given.

When you read "The Chase," you will apply the following comprehension skill:

- Distinguishing **Reality from Fantasy** helps readers identify characters, settings, and/or events that do not exist in the real world. It helps readers evaluate what they are reading.

Routine Card
Refer to ***Routine 10*** for the Selection Vocabulary procedure.

Teacher Tip HIGH-FREQUENCY WORDS The following high-frequency words appear in the selection: *was, in, the an, is, on,* and *a.* Point to these words in the High-Frequency Word Bank, have students read them, and encourage them to read these words with you when you encounter them in the reading.

Listen/Speak 1.2

UNIVERSAL ACCESS:
MEETING INDIVIDUAL NEEDS

ELL Tip

VOCABULARY Encourage English-language learners to offer vocabulary words in their own languages. Invite them to talk about their experience or knowledge of what the words mean in their home countries.

PRETEACH Read the selection to the English-language learners before you read it to the class. As you read, give students the opportunity to ask questions to clarify what they don't understand. Discuss the differences between real and make-believe.

Teacher Tip REALITY AND FANTASY An extended lesson on Reality and Fantasy can be found on page T239. This lesson is intended to give extra practice with distinguishing reality from fantasy.

COMPREHENSION

Comprehension Strategies

Teacher Modeling

1 Monitoring and Clarifying *We know that good readers clarify while they read to check their understanding. I don't know what* quick as an arrow *means. Let's keep reading and look for story clues to help us figure this out. Coyote says "If Rabbit's running that fast, there must be hunters after him." That helps us understand that* quick as an arrow *means "to run very fast."*

Phonemic Awareness

Remind the students that they learned /s/ spelled s in the Preparing to Read section. Reread pages 30–33, and have the students signal when they hear /s/ and see that it is spelled s. *(Words with /s/ spelled* s *include chase, sitting, saw, past, Rabbit's, fast, must, said, himself, Moose, swamp, herself, footsteps, forest, stream, speed, situation, and serious.)*

Reading 3.1

Universal Access: Meeting Individual Needs

Reteach

REREAD Encourage students to reread small sections of the story and identify what each of the story characters does. Write their answers on the board in list form.

Challenge

PREDICTING Invite students to predict the ending of the story. Will the other animals catch up with Rabbit? Why was Rabbit running?

Focus Questions Why are people in a hurry sometimes? Have you ever done something just because someone else was doing it?

The Chase

told by Béatrice Tanaka • *illustrated by Michel Gay*

Coyote was sitting peacefully in the meadow when he saw Rabbit run past, quick as an arrow. 1

"If Rabbit's running that fast, there must be hunters after him," Coyote said to himself. "I'd better run too."

30

Wolf, who had been lazily napping in his den, was awakened by the galloping footsteps of the three runners.

"If Moose is running that fast, the forest must be on fire," said Wolf to himself. "I'd better put off my nap until later."

32

Moose, who was quietly grazing in the swamp, noticed her two friends running by.

"If Coyote's running that fast, the river must be flooding," Moose said to herself. "I'd better be off too."

31

Bear, who was calmly fishing in the stream, saw the four runners racing by at top speed. He recognized his friend Wolf.

"If Wolf is running that fast, the situation must be serious, very serious," thought bear, and he lumbered off after them.

33

Comprehension Skills

Beginning in this lesson, you will introduce students to simple comprehension skills that are used by good readers. The first skill is distinguishing Reality from Fantasy.

Reality and Fantasy Reading 3.1

Explain to students that a fantasy story is a make-believe story about something that could not happen in real life. However, a more realistic story tells about something that could happen in real life, even though the characters might be made up.

Review with students the story events on pages 30–33. Ask them to identify the story characters and what they do and say.

Encourage the students to identify the ways in which the animal characters are like people. Then ask students to explain what happens in this story to make them think that it could not happen in real life. *(The animals talk and have thoughts like people do.)* This means the story is a fantasy.

Universal Access: Meeting Individual Needs

Reteach

REALITY AND FANTASY Give examples of things that are real and things that are make-believe.

COMPREHENSION

Comprehension Strategies

Teacher Modeling

2 Visualizing *When I've been running for awhile, I get very tired. I can see how tired Bear must be.*

Phonemic Awareness

Reread pages 34–37, and have students signal when they hear /s/ and see that it is spelled *s*.

Teacher Tip READING FOR ENJOYMENT Remind students that they should spend 20 minutes reading after school.

Universal Access: Meeting Individual Needs

Reteach

REREAD Ask the students to reread small sections of the story on pages 34–37. Then ask them why each of the story characters began to run.

Challenge

DRAMATIZATION Encourage the students to dramatize favorite scenes from the story by taking the parts of different story characters and reading the dialogue aloud.

Teacher Tip RESPONDING TO TEXT Below are some responses that you can model while you read aloud. Model two to three of these by "thinking aloud" as you read to students. Choose responses that fit the text you are reading. Invite students to offer their responses by thinking aloud as you do.

- ✔ React emotionally by showing joy, sadness, amusement, or surprise.
- ✔ Wonder about ideas in the text by posing questions that you really do wonder about.
- ✔ Relate the text to something that happened to you or to something you already know.
- ✔ Show interest in the text ideas.
- ✔ Clarify the meanings of words and ideas in the text.

After running a good while, Bear caught up with Wolf, who was crouched in a clearing, exhausted and panting. 2

34

"I have no idea," said Wolf. "It's Moose we should ask. When I saw her running so fast, I decided I'd better put off my nap and follow her."

"Tell us, Moose, why were you running?"

36

"What's going on?" demanded Bear. "I know someone as brave as you wouldn't run unless there was real danger."

35

"I have no idea," said Moose. "It's Coyote we should ask. When I saw him run by so fast, I thought I'd better be off too."

"Say, Coyote, why were you running?"

37

Comprehension Skills

Reality and Fantasy Reading 3.1

Ask the students to identify what the story characters do and say that proves this story is a fantasy.

Universal Access: Meeting Individual Needs

Reteach

REALITY AND FANTASY Remind students that a fantasy is a story in which characters that are not human do human things, like talk.

Intervention Tip

REALITY AND FANTASY Reinforce the concept by having students look at other stories in the ***Big Book*** and decide which category the stories belong in.

Discussing the Selection Reading 3.1

- Ask students whether they are enjoying "The Chase" and what they like about it. Ask them to name the animals who were in the chase so far.
- Ask students to identify story details that indicate that the story could not really happen.
- Invite the students to make predictions about what will happen next in the story and suggest reasons for why the first animal, Rabbit, began to run.
- Have the students discuss their reactions to the story so far. What was surprising? Why might someone want to read the rest of the story?
- Ask the students whether the story, which is a folktale, reminds them of other folktales they have read particularly those in which the characters are animals.

Review Selection Vocabulary

Have students review the selection vocabulary words for this lesson. Remind them that they discussed the meanings of these words at the beginning of the lesson. Have them add these and any other interesting words that they clarified while reading to the Vocabulary Words section of their Writer's Notebooks. The words from this lesson are

Coyote **Rabbit**

- Have the students use the words in oral sentences. Help the students expand their sentences by asking who, what, where, when, why, and how questions.
- Ask the students to draw pictures that represent the words.

Encourage students to refer to the vocabulary words throughout the unit.

Print and Book Awareness

Word Boundaries

- Write this crowded sentence on the board:

  Coyotewasinthemeadow.

- Tell the students that this is a sentence about the story they just read, and ask a volunteer to read it. Then ask students why it is so difficult to read the sentence.
- Ask the students to suggest ways to show where each word begins and ends. Rewrite the sentence using each suggestion. Finally, let the students decide which version of the sentence they think is best. You might need to help them figure out some of the problems their suggestions pose.

Teacher Tip COMPREHENSION Skilled readers constantly evaluate their understanding of what they read. Stop often to make sure you and the students are doing this.

Supporting the Reading

Comprehension Skill: Reality and Fantasy

Remind the students that readers can use comprehension skills to find out more about a selection. In "The Chase" the class is finding clues and details that help them determine whether this story could really happen or not. Review with the students reasons why this story could not really happen. *(Animals cannot talk; in the real world, some of these animals would eat each other rather than talk to each other.)*

Purposes for Reading

Remind the students that before reading the story, the class discussed that the purpose for reading this selection was to find out why the animals are running. Ask the students to suggest reasons for why they are running. Explain that when you finish reading, they might have their answers.

Objectives

- Students will continue working on their alphabet books.
- Students will apply concepts and ideas through a curricular connection.

Materials

- Class alphabet book

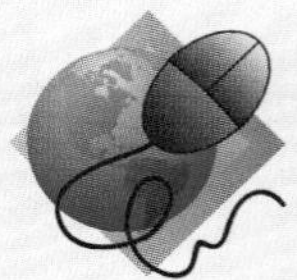

www.sra4kids.com
Web Connection
Help the students look for additional information about folktales by using the Web connections that are available at the Reading link of the SRA Web page.

INVESTIGATION

Supporting the Investigation

Investigating Concepts Beyond the Text

Remind the students about the alphabet book they are working on for this unit.

- Begin by sharing the completed pages of the alphabet book that students created for the letters *v*, *w*, *x*, *y*, and *z*.
- Explain to students that for the next few days, they will be sharing the class alphabet book. Tell students that they might find pages that are missing something or decide that they want to add to the book. Encourage them to do so as you come to each page.
- Comment on any words used and on how students have organized their pages.
- Suggest that the class give their alphabet book a title. For example, *Our Alphabet Book, Room 150.* In addition, you will probably want to give credit to the authors. You can either list each student's name individually or write, for example, "Mrs. Brown's 1st Grade Class."

Unit 1 Investigation Management	
Lessons 1–5	Discuss the class alphabet book. Create and share class alphabet book pages.
Lessons 6–10	Continue to create and share class alphabet book pages.
Lessons 11–15	**Collaborative Investigation** **Share pages from the class alphabet book. Add to the class alphabet book pages, if necessary. Create a poem to add to the class alphabet book.** **Supplementary Activities** **Explain how to share the class alphabet book pages. Assist the students as they share their pages in the class alphabet book. Write the class poem on the board, and assist the students in copying the poem into the book.**

Social Studies Connection

INVESTIGATION

Nonsense Seasons Reading 2.2; Soc. St. 1.2.4

Purpose: To describe how seasons change and the impact of such changes on people in the local community

- Tell the students that the animals in the story were frightened of different things. Sometimes seasons and weather can be dangerous for animals as well as for people. For example, summer rains might cause flooding, or summer dry spells may cause fire.
- Ask the students to think about what happens each season. Ask students the following questions, listing their answers on the board.
    - **Rain falls. Grass turns green. What else happens in spring?**
    - **Summer days are long and hot. What else happens in summer?**
    - **Leaves turn yellow, orange, and red. What else happens in autumn?**
    - **Winter days are short and cold. What else happens in winter?**
- Using the list that students have created, have them think of their favorite seasonal activity, such as swimming in summer or building a snowman in winter.
- Then have each student draw a picture on the construction paper of his or her favorite seasonal activity being done in a different season; for example, trying to build a snowman in summer or swim in a pond in winter.
- Encourage them to notice how such simple changes as these can create funny and entertaining images.

Teacher Tip MATERIALS for this Social Studies Connection you will need colored chalk and black construction paper

Objectives

Word Analysis Vocabulary

- **Vocabulary Strategies: Context Clues.** Using words from "The Chase," identify helpful context clues as a way to infer meaning of unfamiliar vocabulary.

Writing Process Strategies

- **Introduction to the Writing Process.** Building on the theme Let's Read!, learn strategies for drafting and understand that writing is a process that involves drafting.

English Language Conventions

- **Mechanics: Capital Letters.** Building on the Phonics lesson, develop understanding that sentences begin with capital letters and end with periods.

Materials

- Big Book Let's Read!, pp. 30–37
- Language Arts Big Book, pp. 20–21
- Sound/Spelling Cards
- Comprehension and Language Arts Skills, pp. 10–11

UNIVERSAL ACCESS:
MEETING INDIVIDUAL NEEDS

Reteach, Challenge, English-Language Development and ***Intervention*** lessons are available to support the language arts instruction in this lesson.

Research in Action
Vocabulary

. . . meaningful experiences with words are important to the acquisition of their spelling, as well as their usage and interpretation. The best way to build children's visual vocabulary is to have them read meaningful words in meaningful contexts. (*Marilyn Jager Adams.* Beginning to Read: Thinking and Learning About Print.)

OVERVIEW

Language Arts Overview

Word Analysis

Vocabulary The Vocabulary activity focuses on vocabulary from "The Chase" to learn how to use context clues to infer meaning as a way of understanding vocabulary. Context clues are hints to meaning embedded in other words in a sentence. Although context clues are not always available, context is the only feasible method of word learning for a majority of vocabulary building skills. Context clues can include setting, description, and/or synonyms for unknown words.

Vocabulary Skill Words

sitting	**grazing**	**napping**	**fishing**
peacefully	**quietly**	**lazily**	**calmly**

To introduce students to the computer as a writing tool, teach students how to open a word processing program and a new file, key their names, save and name the file, close the file, and quit the program. ***Basic Computer Skills*** Level 1 Lessons 5–6 support these basic computer skills.

Writing Process Strategies

The Writing Process Strategies lesson introduces students to the writing process by providing an overview of drafting. Many inexperienced writers consider drafting to be the only part of the writing process and neglect planning before drafting or revising or editing afterwards. Young students might have so much trouble with handwriting that getting anything on paper is an accomplishment. The purpose of drafting is to let words pour out onto the paper and to express ideas quickly.

English Language Conventions

Grammar, Usage, and Mechanics **Capital Letters** The English Language Conventions support the reading and writing skills development in this lesson. This lesson introduces students to the conventions of capitalizing and punctuating sentences, which will be useful in all writing activities.

Word Analysis

Vocabulary

Context Clues Reading 2.4, 3.2

Teach

- Write the following sentence on the board: *We had to chase the dog all the way down the street before we caught her.*
- Explain that if students don't know the word *chase*, they have some clues in the sentence that could tell you something about it. For example, *chase* is something you can do down a street. The sentence clues also tell students that *chase* must have something to do with trying to catch a dog.
- Have the students suggest other clues that the sentence might give the reader for the word *chase*.

Guided Practice

- Read the first part of "The Chase" and ask students to stop when you read the words that describe what the animals were doing when they saw the other animals run by. *(sitting peacefully, quietly grazing, lazily napping, calmly fishing)*
- Discuss how these descriptions are alike and different. Ask students to infer what the words *grazing* and *napping* mean based on their use in context.
- Conclude by explaining that context clues help students understand the meanings of unknown words.

Writing Process Strategies

Introduction to the Writing Process

Write Writing 1.0

Teach

- Introduce the idea of drafting ideas by reading ***Language Arts Big Book*** pages 20–21. Read and discuss each page. First Sean thought of some ideas, then he organized his ideas by making a web, and then he used the words in his web to write sentences.
- Explain that after writers have a plan, it is time to write their ideas in a draft. Writers need to get their ideas written without worrying too much about making mistakes. They don't stop to look up the spellings of words or write in their neatest handwriting. Good writers write a draft, read what they have written, and then make changes. The purpose of drafting is to let words pour out on paper and to express ideas quickly.

Guided Practice

- **Teacher Model:** Model drafting by referring to the prewriting exercise you did about fish or another simple prewriting plan.
- Ideas might have included
  - live in water Science 2.a
  - eat plants or other fish Science 2.c
  - have fins and scales Science 2.a
- Turn each idea into a sentence, thinking aloud as you write. Stress that you are not concerned with handwriting or spelling right now but want to concentrate on your ideas. An example is: *I won a gold fish at the fair. It lives in fresh water in a bowl. I feed it every day. It has gold scales.*
- Conclude by emphasizing the importance of getting your ideas down on paper.

English Language Conventions

Grammar, Usage, and Mechanics

Capital Letters Eng. Lang. Conv. 1.1, 1.5, 1.6, 1.7

Teach

- Review the capital and lowercase letters that students have explored thus far by pointing to the ***Sound/Spelling Cards.***
- Review that people's names, the pronoun *I*, cities, states, months, and days start with capital letters.
- To reinforce sentence blending and dictation in the Phonics exercises, explain that sentences begin with capital letters, too. Many sentences end with periods.
- Write this sentence on the board: *Big fish eat smaller fish.* Point out the capital letter at the beginning of the sentence and the period at the end.

Independent Practice

Have students complete pages 10–11 in ***Comprehension and Language Arts Skills*** to practice capitalizing and punctuating sentences.

Name ______ Date ______

UNIT 1 Let's Read! • Lesson 11 *The Chase*

Sentences

Rule	Example
Sentences start with capital letters. Many sentences end with periods.	Frogs leap.

Try It!

1. Birds fly.
2. Dogs run.
3. Fish swim.
4. We have fun.

10 UNIT 1 • Lesson 11 Comprehension and Language Arts Skills

Comprehension and Language Arts Skills p. 10

Objectives

- Students will blend words orally by manipulating initial consonant sounds.
- Students will identify and isolate final consonant sounds.
- Students will associate the /m/ sound with the letter *m* in words.
- Students will read a ***Pre-Decodable Book***.

Materials

- Lion Puppet
- Sound/Spelling Cards
- Sound/Spelling Card Stories Audiocassette CD
- Routine Card 1, 5
- Phonics Skills, pp. 16–17
- Letter Cards
- Pre-Decodable Book 4

Teacher Tip SENTENCE EXTENSION Encourage the students to extend the sentences using more words that begin with the target sound. Reading 1.3

Universal Access: Meeting Individual Needs

ELL Support

For ELD strategies, use the ***English-Language Development Guide,*** Unit 1, Lesson 12.

Intervention Support

For intervention strategies, use the ***Intervention Guide,*** Unit 1, Lesson 12.

Warming Up

Use one or both of the following activities to focus the students' attention and to reinforce some of the concepts they have been learning.

Silly Sentences Reading 1.4, 1.7

Engage the students in playing with initial consonant sounds by having them substitute sounds in an alliterative sentence. Help them understand how to use alliteration.

- Say the sentence *Tom tickled ten turtles* and have the students repeat it after you. Tell the students that you will change the sentence by changing the beginning sound to the /s/ sound.
- Say *Som sickled sen surtles* and have the students repeat it. Ask them to change the beginning sound to /p/, /m/, and then /z/.
- If time and interest permit, you can use other alliterative sentences, such as:

  Mom made mushy muffins.
  Daffy dinosaurs dance.

Initial Consonant Substitutions Reading 1.7

The puppet's game today involves replacing the initial phonemes of the students' names.

- Write the letter *s* on the board.
- Have the puppet replace the initial phoneme of several students' first names with /b/ (e.g., *Savid, Soward, Satie, Sennifer*).
- Repeat with several more consonants, but now invite the students to make the substitutions in their names.

Phonemic Awareness

Oral Blending

Initial Consonant Sounds Reading 1.3, 1.4, 1.7

- The students might notice that many of the words they make in this activity are not nonsense words. You might wish to discuss this with them briefly. Ask them why they think this is so *(because there are many, many short words in English)*. Although this is an interesting point, do not emphasize it by choosing consonant replacements so only real words result. Again, the purpose of this activity is to help the students understand that when letters change, the word sounds different.
- Have the students replace the initial consonants in words to make nonsense words, following the procedure as in Lessons 10 and 11.
- Start with the word *seem*. Tell the students that this word is *seem*. Then tell them that you are going to change the word by replacing the /s/ sound with the /f/ sound. Do not write the new letter until the students have identified the new word, using the initial sound that you give them. Erase the *s* and tell the students that you are going to change the word by replacing the /s/ sound with the /f/ sound. Then write the letter *f*.
- Urge them to listen carefully to the original word and to the replacement consonant. Use the following words: *melt*, *sag*, *sent*, *tip*, *fill*, *tap*, and *rat*.

Segmentation

Final Phoneme Segmentation Reading 1.4

- Tell the students that for today's game, the puppet wants them to repeat only the very last sound of each word you say. After a few demonstrations, let the students speak for the puppet, repeating only the last phoneme of each word you say.

Teacher:	beach
Puppet:	/ch/
Teacher:	race
Puppet:	/s/

- Invite the students to speak in place of the puppet with the following words:

peach	peace	peas	speak	speed
tease	teeth	team	beach	beat
moon	moose	mood	move	room
him	hiss	hip	hid	have

PHONEMIC AWARENESS

Reading 1.4, 1.8

Universal Access: Meeting Individual Needs

Reteach

INITIAL CONSONANTS If the students are having trouble orally blending the initial consonant with the rest of the word, work with them in small groups during Workshop on syllable and initial consonant blending.

Intervention Tip

INITIAL CONSONANT SOUNDS During Workshop, review segmenting initial sounds with the students. Say, *I'm thinking of something that begins with /m/* and make a list with the students. Challenge the students to come up with ten or more words.

Informal Assessment

PHONEMIC AWARENESS Continue observing five or six students during the Initial Consonant Sounds activity that you started in Lesson 10. Record your observations in the Teacher Observation Log in the ***Program Assessment Teacher's Edition.*** Reading 1.4

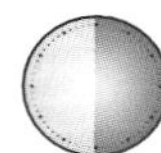

Phonics

PHONICS

Introduce /m/ Spelled *m* Reading 1.3, 1.4

- Turn ***Sound/Spelling Card 13—Monkey*** around and show the picture.
- Ask the students what they know about the card. If necessary, point out the capital and lowercase letters at the top of the card, and tell the students that the letter *m* is a consonant.
- Remind the students that each card has a picture that will help them remember the sound of the spelling(s) listed on the bottom of the card. Ask the students what this picture shows, and tell them that this is the ***Monkey Card.***
- Point to the letter *m* at the bottom of the card, and remind the students that this part of the card shows the spelling of this sound when it is in a word. Tell the students that we call the letters the spelling for /m/.
- Tell the students that you are going to read them a story that will help them remember how to read and write the /m/ sound. Then read the Monkey story:

  For Muzzy the Monkey, bananas are yummy,
  She munches so many, they fill up her tummy.
  When she eats, she says /m/ /m/ /m/ /m/ /m/!

  Bananas for breakfast, bananas for lunch.
  Mash them up, mush them up.
  Munch, munch, munch, munch.
  What does Muzzy the Monkey say?
  (Have the students say) /m/ /m/ /m/ /m/ /m/!

  Bananas at bedtime? I have a hunch
  Muzzy will mash them up, mush them up,
  Munch, munch, munch, munch.
  Then what will Muzzy the Monkey say?
  (Have the students say) /m/ /m/ /m/ /m/ /m/!

- Write the letter *m* on the board. Touch the letter and say /m/.
- Have the students write the letter *m* several times, either on paper or with their finger on a surface, saying /m/ each time they form the letter.

Universal Access: Meeting Individual Needs

ELL Tip

/M/ SOUND /m/ is a voiced sound. Students can feel the vibration in their throat when they make the /m/ sound. Have the children look at you when you make the /m/ sound. The sound is made with your lips together. This sound comes through the nose. Have children say the sound and then hold their noses as they say the sound again. The sound stops.

Universal Access: Meeting Individual Needs

Intervention Tip

/M/ SOUND Read the Monkey story with small groups in Workshop and have them listen for words with the /m/ sound. Reading 1.3

SOUND/SPELLING CARD STORIES
Use the ***Sound/Spelling Card Stories*** for practice with the /m/ sound. Have the students respond by saying words with the /m/ sound.

Teacher Tip PHYSICAL ACTIONS
You might want to encourage the students to use physical actions to remember the /m/ sound. For example, you might have the students rub their tummies as they say /m/ /m/ /m/ /m/. You could also have the students rub their tummy as a signal instead of raising their hand.

Routine Card
Refer to ***Routine 1*** to review the procedure for introducing sounds and spellings.

Initial M

- Tell the students to listen for the /m/ sound in the words you are about to say. Tell them to signal by raising their hand when they hear /m/ at the beginning of a word and to remain silent when they do not.

me	see	**my**	sigh	**meal**
marble	beat	**meet**	soup	feel
moon	**minute**	pickle	**mountain**	**map**
rabbit	**moose**	cookie	**muffin**	**maybe**

- Ask the students to suggest other words that begin with /m/.

Final M

- Then have the students listen for the /m/ sound at the end of words and signal by raising their hand when they hear it. Some words are

am	**aim**	ace	**tame**	take
time	**rhyme**	right	**lime**	bus
gas	**scream**	**dream**	shake	**come**
came	rice	**same**	**name**	**hum**

- Conclude the activity by reviewing that *m* is the spelling for the /m/ sound in words. Explain to the students that when they look at the ***Monkey Card,*** they can remember that *monkey* starts with /m/, and they can think of the sound the *monkey* makes when she eats a banana: /m/ /m/ /m/ /m/.

PHONICS

Teacher Tip DISTINGUISHING /m/ You may also wish to have the students close their eyes as they listen for the initial and final /m/ sounds in these activities. Reading 1.4

UNIVERSAL ACCESS: MEETING INDIVIDUAL NEEDS

ELL Tip

ACTIVITIES Repeat activities often so English-language learners come to feel comfortable with them. Encourage them to participate in class activities. Watch for students who are not responding and work with them separately in small groups.

Universal Access:
Meeting Individual Needs

Reteach

/M/ SPELLED M For additional practice, use ***Reteach: Phonics Skills*** pages 16 and 17.

Challenge

/M/ SPELLED M Use ***Challenge: Phonics Skills*** page 13 with the students who are ready for a challenge.

PHONICS

Phonics Skills Reading 1.3, 1.4; Writing 1.3; Listen/Speak 1.1

- ***Phonics Skills*** pages 16–17 provide additional practice with the /m/ sound spelled *m*. Review the purpose of the picture at the top of the page, and ask which letter stands for the /m/ sound. Then have the students write the letter *m* on the top line, saying /m/ as they write each one. Repeat in the same way with the line of capital *M*'s.
- Ask the students to look at the pictures on the bottom of page 16. Tell the students to say the name of the object in each picture aloud. If they hear the /m/ sound when they say the name aloud, they should write *m* in the space provided. *(The pictures include: mop, swing, and mouse.)*
- On page 17, the students should look again at the pictures and say each name aloud. Tell them that each of these words will have an /m/ sound in it. They should listen carefully to hear whether the /m/ sound is at the beginning or end of each word. They should write the letter *m* in the first space if the /m/ sound is at the beginning and in the second space if the /m/ sound is at the end. On this and subsequent pages, review proper letter formation. *(The pictures include: mouse, monkey, ham, milk, gum, money, broom, and mirror.)*

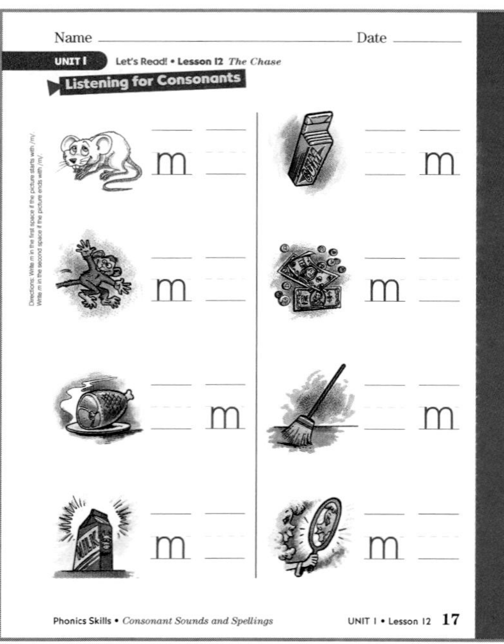

***Phonics Skills* pp. 16–17**

Dictation

Dictation Reading 1.3; Writing 1.3

- Ask the students to write the whole alphabet independently. For today, ask them to use lowercase letters only.
- Review these papers to identify any students or letters that are in need of extra attention.
- Return them to the students to insert in the letter book they will make in the next few lessons.

PHONICS

Teacher Tip WRITING Encourage the students to write neatly and space their letters appropriately.

Writing 1.3

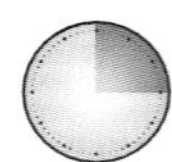

Reading a Pre-Decodable Book

Core Set, Book 4: *Mom and I*
Phonics Focus: /S/ Spelled s

Reading 1.1

High-Frequency Words

Reading 1.3

The high-frequency words introduced in this book are: *and*, *I*, and *make(s)*. Write *know* on the board and ask students to say the word. Pronounce it, have the students repeat it, spell it together, and have them say it again. Follow this same procedure for *I*, and *make(s)*. Then have volunteers use *and*, *I*, and *make(s)* in sentences. Review the high-frequency words already in the High-Frequency Word Bank. Have students volunteer to read the ones they recognize.

Reading Recommendations

Reading 1.1, 1.2, 1.3, 1.8

- The nondecobale word in this book is *Mom*. Write *Mom* on the board. Ask the students to say the word. Pronounce it, have the students repeat it, spell it together, and have them say it again. Then have volunteers use *Mom* in sentences.
- Have the students read the title and browse the story.
- Have students read a page silently, then read the page aloud. Repeat this procedure for each page.
- Have another student reread the page before going on.
- Reread the story at least twice, calling on different students to read. Then have the entire group do a choral reading of the story.

Teacher Tip HIGH-FREQUENCY WORD BANK Add the high-frequency words from this selection to the Word Bank. Have students write words on 3 x 5 cards to take home to practice or add to their ring of words.

and I make

Pre-Decodable Book 4

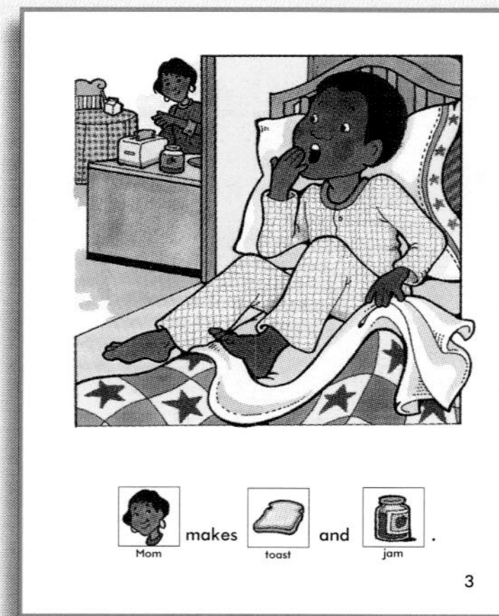

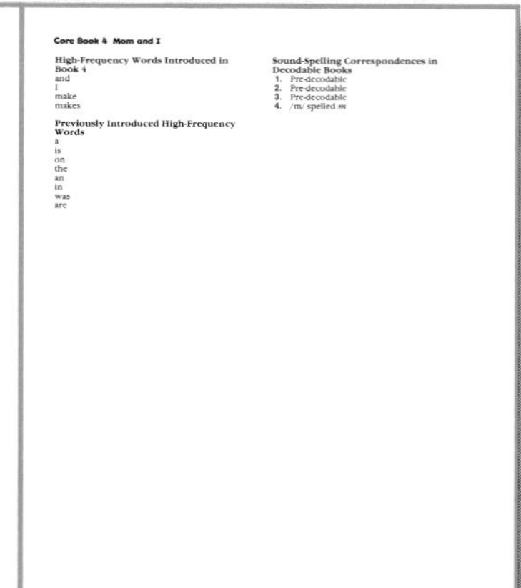

Core Book 4 Mom and I

High-Frequency Words Introduced in Book 4
and
I
make
makes

Previously Introduced High-Frequency Words
a
is
on
the
an
in
was
are

Sound-Spelling Correspondences in Decodable Books
1. Pre-decodable
2. Pre-decodable
3. Pre-decodable
4. /m/ spelled *m*

Responding Reading 2.2; Listen/Speak 1.2, 2.2

- Invite the students to discuss any hard words they encountered in *Mom and I* and how they figured out these words. Call on volunteers to retell the story.
- To make sure the students are focusing on the words in the story, ask the following questions, having the students answer by pointing to and reading aloud the words:

  What does mom make? *(Mom makes toast and jam.)*

  What does Mom make after school? *(After school, Mom makes cookies and milk.)*

  What does the boy make for his mom? *(He makes a card for Mom.)*

Building Fluency Reading 1.16

Encourage partners to build fluency rereading ***Decodable Book 4***, *Mom and I*, of the Core Set. The first time through, one partner should read the odd-numbered pages and the other the even-numbered pages. For the second reading, the partners should switch pages. After the second reading, the partners should choose one of the ***Decodable Books*** from previous lessons and continue to read to each other.

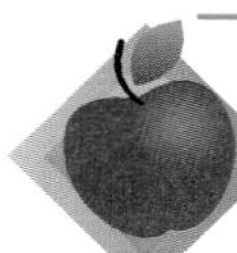

Teacher Tip RESPONDING Watch for students who can't find the answers and work with them during Workshop.

Informal Assessment

READING PROGRESS While the students are reading to each other, use the time to invite several individuals to read with you so that you can assess their reading growth.

Routine Card
Refer to ***Routine 5*** for reading ***Decodable Books.***

Pages 38–41 of *Let's Read!*

Second of two lessons.

Focus Questions Why are people in a hurry sometimes? Have you ever done something just because someone else was doing it?

The Chase

told by Béatrice Tanaka • *illustrated by Michel Gay*

Coyote was sitting peacefully in the meadow when he saw Rabbit run past, quick as an arrow. 1

"If Rabbit's running that fast, there must be hunters after him," Coyote said to himself. "I'd better run too."

30

Objectives

- Students will share prior knowledge about the story.
- Students will identify the author and illustrator.
- Students will discuss whether this story could really happen or not.
- Students will look at text and illustration format.
- Students will dramatize a story in sequence.
- Students will learn a cumulative rhyme.

Materials

- Big Book *Let's Read!*, pp. 38–41

Routine Card
Refer to ***Routine 11*** for the procedure for reading the selection.

Teacher Tip SET PURPOSES
Remind the students that good readers have a purpose when they read. Let them know that they should make sure they know the purpose for reading whenever they read.

Build Background

Activate Prior Knowledge

Have the students retell what they remember from reading the first part of this selection.

Preview and Prepare

Browse Reading 1.2, 2.1

- Open the ***Big Book*** *Let's Read!* to the Table of Contents. Call on a volunteer to point to the author's name and the illustrator's name. Read the names aloud.
- Review the pages already read and recall the sequence of events.

Set Purposes

- Remind the students that they will be reading to find out why Rabbit began the chase.

Selection Vocabulary

Discuss the following words and their meanings before reading pages 38–41 of the selection. Write the words on the board and say them. Use each word in a sentence.

escaped **late**

- Explain that *escaped* means "to get out or get away."
- Explain that *late* means "to arrive at a time after one was supposed to." Relate to the students what time would be considered late for school.
- Encourage the students to use these words in sentences.

Reading Recommendations

Read Aloud

- Read pages 38–41 of the story, pausing only to model simple reading strategies.
- Invite the students to discuss each page and the illustration.

Using Comprehension Strategies

During the first reading of these pages, you will model the use of the following comprehension strategy:

- **Visualizing** helps readers picture in their minds what is going on in a selection to gain a clearer understanding.

As you read these pages, pause to remind the students how good readers use this strategy to help them better understand what they read.

Building Comprehension Skills

Rereading a selection allows readers to apply skills that give them a more complete understanding of what they read. Some of these follow-up comprehension skills, such as Classifying and Categorizing, Cause and Effect, Sequence, and Compare and Contrast, help readers organize the information in a selection. Other skills, such as Drawing Conclusions, lead them to a deeper understanding of the selection.

As you reread the selection, the students will be using the following comprehension skill:

- **Reality and Fantasy** helps readers understand what can really happen and what is imaginary.

Routine Card
Refer to ***Routine 10*** for the Selection Vocabulary procedure.

Teacher Tip HIGH-FREQUENCY WORDS The following high-frequency word appears in the selection: *was.* Point to this word in the High-Frequency Word Bank, have students read it, and encourage them to read this word with you when you encounter it in the reading.

UNIVERSAL ACCESS:
MEETING INDIVIDUAL NEEDS

ELL Support

For ELD strategies, use the ***English-Language Development Guide,*** Unit 1, Lesson 12.

Intervention Support

For intervention strategies, use the ***Intervention Guide,*** Unit 1, Lesson 12.

Teacher Tip REALITY AND FANTASY An extended lesson on Reality and Fantasy can be found on page T257. This lesson is intended to give extra practice with distinguishing reality from fantasy.

COMPREHENSION

Comprehension Strategies

First Read

Teacher Modeling

3 Visualizing *We can better understand what we read if we visualize what is happening. We can use the illustrations on the pages to help us visualize, or we might imagine in our own minds what is happening. After reading pages 38 and 39, I can imagine Bear, Wolf, Moose, and Coyote calling Rabbit at the same time. What do you visualize?*

Phonemic Awareness

Remind the students that in the Preparing to Read section, they learned the /m/ sound spelled *m.* Reread these pages, having the students listen for /m/ and checking to see that it is spelled *m.*

Teacher Tip COMPREHENSION STRATEGIES Although you are modeling the use of Visualizing above, as you read pages 38–41, stop to clarify anything that may be confusing to your students.

Universal Access: Meeting Individual Needs

Intervention Tip

REREAD Reread the story. Be sure to model and discuss strategies during the rereading.

"I have no idea," said Coyote. "It's Rabbit we should ask. When I saw how fast he was running, I thought I'd better run too. When he stopped, so did I. He'll know what terrible danger we've escaped."

38

"Why were *you* running?" said Rabbit.

40

"Hey, Rabbit!" cried Bear, Wolf, Moose, and Coyote together. "Why were we running?" 3

39

"I have no idea. But *me*—I was late for dinner!"

41

Comprehension Skills

Reality and Fantasy

Write the words *Reality* and *Fantasy* on the board. Encourage students to provide examples of other fantasy stories they have read. Then, ask them to identify story details in support of their judgment that the story is a fantasy.

- Ask the students to tell how they think the animals feel when they find out why Rabbit was running so fast.
- Ask the students to identify story details that show that the story could not really happen.

Teacher Tip READING FOR ENJOYMENT Remind the students that they should spend at least 20 minutes reading after school.

Sentences

Point out the sentences in this story. Each one tells who and what. Each one starts with a capital letter and ends with a period. Explain that students can use this model in their own writing. See *Writer's Craft* page T261.

COMPREHENSION

Teacher Tip CHARACTERS
Encourage the students to describe each character in the story.

Reading 3.1

Discussing the Selection Reading 2.2, 3.1

- Ask students the following questions:

  Who are the characters in the story? *(Coyote, Rabbit, Moose, Wolf, and Bear)*
  What are the characters doing? *(Coyote, Moose, Wolf, and Bear are chasing one another.)*
  Where does this story take place? *(in a meadow, swamp, and forest)*
  When does the story take place? *(dinnertime)*
  Why does Coyote chase Rabbit? *(He thinks there are hunters.)*
  Why does Moose chase Coyote? *(She thinks the river is flooding.)*
  Why does Wolf chase Rabbit, Coyote, and Moose? *(He thinks the forest is on fire.)*
  Why does Bear chase the other animals? *(He recognizes Wolf and thinks the situation must be serious.)*
  Why was Rabbit running? *(He was late for dinner.)*
- Have the students discuss their reactions to the story. Ask them to share whether or not they guessed the ending.
- Ask the students to describe the ways the characters in this folktale seem like people the students know or like the students themselves.
- Ask the students to explain how this selection is different from the other selections in this unit.
- With the students, refer back to the Focus Questions for the selection. Have all the questions been answered? It not, answer them now.

Have the students record their responses to the selection in the Response Journal section of their Writer's Notebooks by drawing pictures. Help the students label their drawings.

Review Selection Vocabulary

Have students review the definition of the selection vocabulary words for this lesson. Remind them that they discussed the meaning of this word at the beginning of the lesson. Have them add these and any other interesting words that they clarified while reading to the Vocabulary Words section of their Writer's Notebooks. The words from this lesson are

late **escaped**

- Have the students use these words in oral sentences. Help the students expand their sentences by asking who, what, where, when, why, and how questions.
- Ask the students to draw a picture that represents each word.

Encourage students to refer to the vocabulary words throughout the unit.

Print and Book Awareness

Illustration/Text Relationship Reading 3.1

- Ask the students what they notice about how the story pages are organized. Help them understand that a new animal character is introduced on each new page.
- Point out the way the illustrator shows the animal character and one or more of the animals already in the chase.

Supporting the Reading

Comprehension Skill: Reality and Fantasy Reading 2.1, 2.7

Tell the students that by figuring out whether a selection could really happen or not, readers may understand more about it. Review with the students the details or clues in the story that indicate that it could not really happen.

Turn back to previous selections in the ***Big Book*** *Let's Read!* Have the students decide whether these selections could really happen or not.

Purposes for Reading

Remind the students that before reading the story, they discussed that the purpose for reading this selection was to find out why the animals are running. Ask the students whether the author's ending surprised them. How did the answer in the selection compare with their suggestions?

View Fine Art

- Open the ***Big Book*** *Let's Read!* to page 56 and show the students the piece *Layla and Majnum at School.* Explain to the students that this piece shows students at school in Persia (now Iran).
- Ask the students to comment on the colors, lines, and shapes in the piece. Have them discuss how these students and this school are alike and different from them and their school.
- If possible, take a moment to show the students where Iran is located on a world map or a globe. Explain that the country's name was changed from Persia to Iran.

Fine Art **Let's Read!**

Untitled. August 6, 1988. **Keith Haring.** Sumi ink on paper.

Layla and Majnum at School. 1524–1525. **Artist unknown,** style of Shaykh Zadeh. Persian (Herat) miniature; ink, colors, and gold on paper. The Metropolitan Museum of Art, New York.

The Libraries Are Appreciated. 1943. **Jacob Lawrence.** Gouache and watercolor on paper. Philadelphia Museum of Art.

56

Big Book Let's Read! p. 56

UNIVERSAL ACCESS:
MEETING INDIVIDUAL NEEDS

Reteach

USING ILLUSTRATIONS Encourage students to review the story by explaining what is happening in each illustration.

Objectives

- Students will share their alphabet books.
- Students will apply concepts and ideas through a curricular connection.

Materials

- Student alphabet book

www.sra4kids.com
Web Connection
Help the students look for additional information about poems and rhymes by using the Web connections that are available at the Reading link of the SRA Web page.

INVESTIGATION

Supporting the Investigation

Investigating Concepts Beyond the Text

Remind the students about the alphabet book they are working on for this unit.

- Before having students share their pages, show them how to share by using the book, holding it up in front of the class, and describing what is on each page.
- Invite students to share their pages in the alphabet book. Begin with *Aa* and continue for several pages.
- Comment on any words used and on how the students have organized their pages.

Concept/Question Board

After reading the selection, the students should use the Concept/Question Board with or without your help to

- post any questions they asked before reading that still need to be answered.
- post general statements formulated while studying the selection.
- continue to post articles, pictures, or other items they find that pertain to the unit.
- read and think about posted questions, articles, pictures, or concepts that interest them.
- provide answers to posted questions.

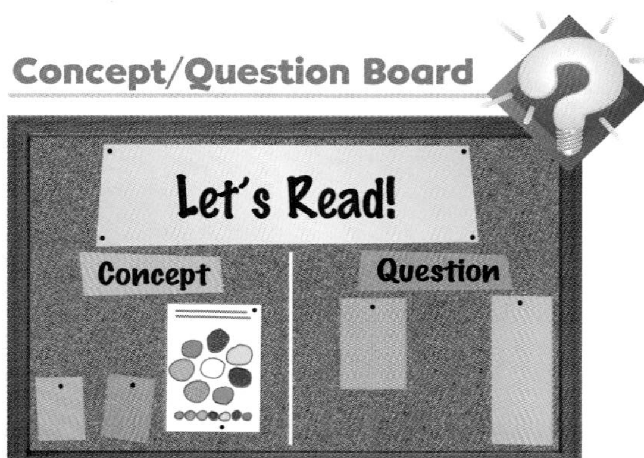

Music Connection

Cumulative Rhymes Listen/Speak 2.1

Purpose: To learn a cumulative rhyme set to music

- Teach the students the song "I Know an Old Woman Who Swallowed a Fly." Play a recording of the song, if possible. Tell the students that this song is like "The Chase" because more and more things are added to the story. In "The Chase," more and more animals begin chasing Rabbit. In this song, the Old Woman keeps eating more and more things.
- Repeat the singing several times.
- Point out that the order of the song is logical; each time the Old Woman is swallowing something bigger.
- Ask the students why the song is fun to sing. Help them conclude that the repeated verses make it fun.

INVESTIGATION

Teacher Tip MATERIALS For this Music Connection, if available, you might wish to use a recording of "I Know an Old Woman Who Swallowed a Fly."

Objectives

Word Analysis Vocabulary

- **Vocabulary Strategies: Context Clues.** Using words from "The Chase," identify helpful context clues as a way to infer meaning of unfamiliar vocabulary.

Writing Process Strategies

- **Introduction to the Writing Process.** Building on the theme Let's Read!, learn strategies for drafting and understand that writing is a process that involves drafting.

English Language Conventions

- **Mechanics: Capital Letters.** Building on the Phonics lesson, develop the understanding that sentences begin with capital letters and many end with periods.

Materials

- Big Book Let's Read!, pp. 30–41
- Comprehension and Language Arts Skills, pp. 12–13

OVERVIEW

Language Arts Overview

Word Analysis

Vocabulary The Vocabulary activity focuses on vocabulary from "The Chase" to learn how to use context clues to infer meaning as a way of understanding vocabulary. Most vocabulary is acquired from context, because only a few words can be taught explicitly. Teaching students how to "decontextualize" words and practice this skill will help them teach themselves new vocabulary. Context has limitations for teaching specific vocabulary definitions because word definitions are rarely part of context in most forms of writing.

Vocabulary Skill Words

running **galloped** **racing** **lumbered**

Writing Process Strategies

The Writing Process Strategies lesson introduces students to the writing process by providing an overview of drafting. Many inexperienced writers consider drafting to be the only part of the writing process and neglect planning before drafting or revising or editing afterwards. Experienced writers plan their writing and then use the drafting stage to put their ideas together.

English Language Conventions

Grammar, Usage, and Mechanics **Capital Letters** The English Language Conventions support the reading and writing skills development in this lesson. This lesson points out the conventions of capitalizing and punctuating sentences in student reading materials.

Universal Access: Meeting Individual Needs

Reteach, Challenge, English-Language Development and ***Intervention*** lessons are available to support the language arts instruction in this lesson.

Word Analysis

Vocabulary

Context Clues Reading 2.4, 3.2

Teach

- Write the following sentences on the board: *The cat chased the mouse. The dog pursued the cat. The boy ran after the dog.*
- Explain that if students didn't know the word *pursued*, they have some clues in the other sentences that could tell them something about it. In these sentences the words *chased* and *ran after* mean almost the same as *pursued*. Ask students what they think the word *pursued* means. For example, *chase* is something you can do down a street.
- Have students suggest other clues that the sentence might give the reader for the word *pursued*.

Guided Practice

- Read "The Chase" in the ***Big Book*** *Let's Read!* pages 30–41. Have them stop you every time you come to a word that tells how the animals moved. *(running, galloping, racing, lumbered)*
- Have students explain as if to a younger person what the words *galloping* and *lumbered* mean based on the context clues in the story. *(They must mean "to move fast" because all the animals were in a hurry.)*
- Have students suggest sentences that use the words.
- Conclude by explaining that context clues help students understand the meanings of unknown words.

Writing Process Strategies

Introduction to the Writing Process

Write Writing 1.0, 2.1; Eng. Lang. Conv. 1.1

Teach

Writer's Craft
Sentences

- Explain that a sentence is a group of words that go together to state an idea. Sentences can be short *(Dogs bark.)* or long *(My dog makes a lot of noise when she barks at night.)*.
- Explain that sentences have two parts. One part tells *what* or *who*. The other part tells *what happened*.
- Have students make sentences out of the following words. Write their sentences on the board:
  - wolves   chirp
  - crickets   howl
  - frogs   croak
- Use ***Comprehension and Language Arts Skills*** pages 12–13 to reinforce the concept of sentences.

Guided Practice

- Explain that after writers have a plan, they write their ideas into sentences.
- Review the plan that students made in Lesson 8 about their favorite foods for breakfast, lunch, dinner, and snack.
- Have the class dictate sentences to you for each of the ideas in the prewriting plan.
- Turn each idea into a sentence, thinking aloud as you write. Stress that you are not concerned with handwriting or spelling right now but want to concentrate on your ideas. An example might be: *Our favorite food for lunch is pizza.*

English Language Conventions

Grammar, Usage, and Mechanics

Capital Letters Eng. Lang. Conv. 1.1, 1.5, 1.7

Teach

- Review that sentences begin with capital letters and many end with periods.
- Have students dictate complete, coherent sentences, identifying where the capital letter and period belong. Write their sentences on the board.

Guided Practice in Reading

Read "The Chase" on ***Big Book*** *Let's Read!* pages 30–41 aloud with students, pointing out sentences with capital letters and periods.

Objectives

- Students will blend words orally by manipulating initial consonant sounds.
- Students will attend to final consonant sounds by segmenting.
- Students will associate the /a/ sound with the letter *a* in words.
- Students will blend sounds to read words.
- Students will read a ***Decodable Book***

Materials

- Lion Puppet
- Sound/Spelling Cards
- Sound/Spelling Card Stories Audiocassette/CD
- Routine Cards 1, 2, 3, 4, 5
- Phonics Skills, pp. 18–19
- Letter Cards
- Decodable Book 5
- High-Frequency Word Cards

Teacher Tip MEANING Have the students describe what each word means.

Universal Access: Meeting Individual Needs

ELL Support

For ELD strategies, use the ***English-Language Development Guide,*** Unit 1, Lesson 13.

Intervention Support

For intervention strategies, use the ***Intervention Guide,*** Unit 1, Lesson 13.

Warming Up

Use one or both of the following activities to focus students' attention for the lessons that follow.

Alliterative Word Game Reading 1.4

- Say the following phrase to students: "My mom makes me drink milk." Ask students what sound is repeated. After they identify that the letter /m/ is repeated, tell them that this is called alliteration.
- Start with a series of words beginning with /m/ and have students join in with their own words. You might start with some of the following:

monkey	mom	maybe	Monica
maple	make	man	milk

- Then have students suggest words beginning with /s/. Start them off and help them if they get stuck with any of the following:

sausage	Sammy	soon	supper
sizzle	silly	Saturday	Sue

Initial Consonant Blending Reading 1.8

Make a game of oral blending by telling students that you're going on a pretend walk in the jungle.

- Ask them to blend some words to guess what you see. Use these words:

  /m/ . . . onkey
  /l/ . . . ion
  /t/ . . . iger
  /ch/ . . . imp
  /b/ . . . utterflies
  /v/ . . . ines

- If the students seem comfortable with the activity, you might ask them to give words for the class to blend.

Phonemic Awareness

Oral Blending

Initial Consonant Sounds Reading 1.4, 1.7

- Have the students make new words by replacing the initial consonant with a new one.
- Write the word *mend* on the board, touch it, and tell the students that this is the word *mend*. Erase the *m* and write *s* in its place. Tell them the word now begins with the /s/ sound and ask what the new word is.
- Allow for wait time and remind students to listen carefully.
- Use any single initial consonants in any order. Remember to tell the students the word and the new sound before asking what the new word is. You can continue the activity with any of the following words:

ban tag had tip
mail rain seed song

Segmentation

Dropping Final Consonants Reading 1.4, 1.9

- Tell the students that you're going to talk to the puppet, and they should listen to find out which word game he's playing today. Have the puppet delete the final consonant of a word. Have the students give the consonant sound, then say the complete word. Tell the students that they are going to help the puppet by correcting him.

Teacher: soon
Puppet: soo
Students: /n/, soon
Teacher: grab
Puppet: gra
Students: /b/, grab

- Ask the students to speak for the puppet. Use the following words:

soup loop leap beep
bake bike like lake
lace lame late laid
nine nice night knife

Universal Access: Meeting Individual Needs Reading 1.9

ELL Tip

WORD MEANING Make sure the English-language learners know the meanings of the words used in the activities. Use pictures, photos, objects, stick drawings, pantomime, or the ***English-Language Development Glossary.***

Reteach

ORAL BLENDING During workshop, review oral blending or segmenting with groups of students who might need additional practice. Students who are having difficulty might benefit from reviewing earlier forms of blending and segmentation activities.

Reading 1.4

Informal Assessment

FINAL CONSONANT SOUNDS Observe five or six students for their ability to segment final consonant sounds. Do this monitoring for the next five lessons until you have observed all students. Record your observations in the Teacher Observation Log in the ***Program Assessment Teacher's Edition.***

SOUND/SPELLING CARD STORIES PHONICS Use the ***Sound/Spelling Card Stories*** for practice with the /a/ sound. Have students respond by saying the /a/ sound in their head.

Routine Card
See ***Routine 1*** to review the procedure for introducing sounds and spellings.

UNIVERSAL ACCESS:
MEETING INDIVIDUAL NEEDS

ELL

VOWEL SOUNDS FOR ARABIC SPEAKERS Vowels may be problematic for some Arabic speakers. For example, they may substitute /u/ for /a/. Have students make the two sounds. There are subtle differences. Remind them to check the ***Lamb Sound/Spelling Card*** when they see the /a/ spelling *a*. The sound the lamb makes is /a/, /a/, /a/.

ELL

SHORT *A* IN ASIAN LANGUAGES The short *a* sound does not exist in many Asian languages. Give students the opportunity to practice the sound the lamb makes—/a/ /a/ /a/. When blending, blend through the vowel and hold the sound. Add the final sound(s) and spelling(s) and say the word.

PHONICS

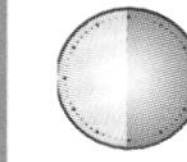

Phonics

Introduce /a/ Spelled *a* Reading 1.3, 1.4, 1.5

- Tell the students that today they will be learning about one of the special letters called vowels. Say that vowels are special because the English language has no words without a vowel.
- Turn ***Sound/Spelling Card 1—Lamb*** around. Ask students what they know about this card. If necessary, point out the red letters on the picture side of the card, and then direct attention to the colored band across the bottom of the card.
- Explain that another reason that vowels are special is that every vowel has a long sound and a short sound. Remind students that they already know that sometimes a vowel can say its own name—that sound is called the long sound.
- Explain that now they will learn the short sound of the letter *a*, which is the sound they hear in the middle of the word *lamb*. Say that whenever a card shows the short sound of a vowel, the card has a green band.
- Remind the students that the picture on the card is a clue to help them remember the letter sound and that the bottom of the card shows the spelling of the sound in words.
- Tell the students to listen for the /a/ sound and think about how the picture of the lamb will remind them of the sound. Then read the Lamb story:

  I'm Pam the Lamb, I am.
  This is how I tell my Mommy where I am: /a/ /a/ /a/ /a/ /a/.
  I'm Pam the Lamb, I am.
  This is how I tell my Daddy where I am: /a/ /a/ /a/ /a/ /a/.
  I'm Pam the Lamb, I am.
  That young ram is my brother Sam.
  This is how I tell my brother where I am: /a/ /a/ /a/ /a/ /a/.
  I'm Pam the Lamb; I'm happy where I am.
  Can you help me tell my family where I am?
  (Have students respond:) /a/ /a/ /a/ /a/ /a/.
- Have the students recite the Lamb story a second time.

Initial *a*

- Write the letter *a* on the board. Touch the letter and say /a/.
- Have students write the letter *a* several times, either on paper or with their finger on a surface, saying /a/ each time.

Listening for /a/ and /ā/ Reading 1.3, 1.4, 1.5

- To represent the /ā/ sound, write a long, thin *Aa* pair on the extreme right side of the board. To represent the /a/ sound, write a shorter, stouter *Aa* pair on the extreme left side of the board.
- Tell the students that you will read them a list of words. For each word, they should repeat the vowel sound and point to one of the letter pairs you have written on the board. If it is the /ā/ sound, they should point to the *Aa* on the right. If it is the /a/ sound, they should point to the *Aa* on the left.

am	aim	ate	**at**	**fat**	**bat**
sat	**hat**	hate	late	lame	**lamb**
lap	**tap**	tape	grape	**trap**	**track**
take	**tack**	**back**	**bad**	**mad**	maze
haze	**has**	**had**	**fan**	**pan**	**land**

- Summarize the learning by telling students that they can use the ***Lamb Card*** to remind them of the /a/ sound. The /a/ is in the middle of the word *lamb*, and the lamb says /a/ /a/ /a/ to let others know where she is. Remind them that the green color means a short-vowel sound and then ask what sound the little lamb made. Tell the students that the bottom of the card shows the spelling of the sound in words.

Sing the "Short-Vowel Song" Reading 1.5; Listen/Speak 2.1

Teach the following song to the tune of "The Farmer in the Dell." The /a/ sound is sung to the "Heigh-ho the derry-o" line. After singing the "Short-Vowel Song" once, have students recite it together.

The short *a* is in *lamb*.
The short *a* is in *lamb*.
/a/ /a/ /a/-/a/ /a/-/a/
The short *a* is in *lamb*.

Sing the song again, asking students to suggest other words to substitute for *lamb*, such as *apples*, *cat*, or *hat*. When a student suggests a word, have him or her lead the singing.

PHONICS

Reading 1.1

Teacher Tip "SHORT-VOWEL SONG" New verses will be added for each short-vowel sound. You might want to copy each verse—omitting the slash marks that indicate the sound—onto chart paper or onto a page that can be duplicated for students to make their own short-vowel songbook.

Research in Action
Short-Vowel Sounds

Short-vowel sounds are being introduced early because regular consonant-vowel-consonant words allow simple and straightforward exercise of the basic alphabet principle: Each letter represents a sound; together the sounds make a word when blended left to right. It is very important that students grasp this basic principle from the start.

This lesson introduces the short sound of the letter *a*. Here, as with all vowel sounds, it is important to emphasize that vowels are special letters. (*Marilyn J. Adams*)

Teacher Tip NAMES AND SOUNDS OF LETTERS At the beginning, students confuse the sound and the name of the letter. When you ask for the sound and the students say the name of the letter, do not find this uncommon. With time and practice, the students do learn the difference.

Routine Card
Refer to ***Routine 2*** for the sound-by-sound blending procedure, ***Routine 4*** for the whole-word blending procedure, and ***Routine 3*** for the blending sentences procedure.

Name ______ Date ______
UNIT 1 Let's Read! • Lesson 13 *Mrs. Goose's Baby*
Sounds and Spellings

a

a a a a a a a
A A A A A A A

I am Answers will vary.
I am in a Answers will vary.

18 UNIT 1 • Lesson 13 *Vowel Sounds and Spellings* • Phonics Skills

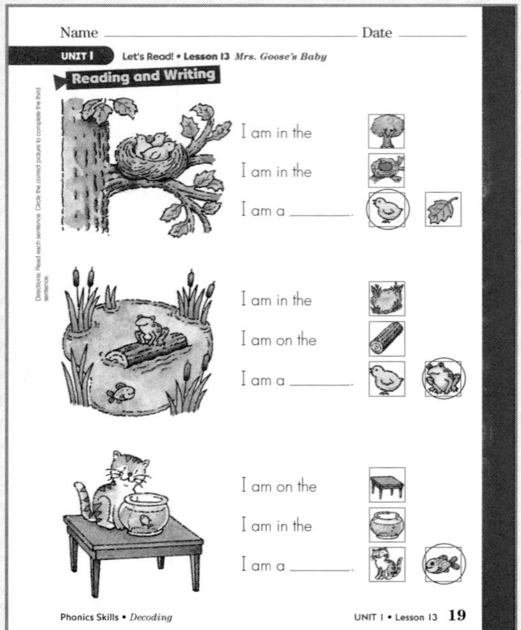

Name ______ Date ______
UNIT 1 Let's Read! • Lesson 13 *Mrs. Goose's Baby*
Reading and Writing

I am in the
I am in the
I am a ______

I am in the
I am on the
I am a ______

I am on the
I am in the
I am a ______

Phonics Skills • *Decoding* UNIT 1 • Lesson 13 19

***Phonics Skills* pp. 18–19**

PHONICS

Introducing Blending Reading 1.1, 1.3, 1.8, 1.9, 1.10 Listen/Speak 1.1

The ability to use the sounds of letters to decode written words is fundamental to learning to read. Following the introduction of each sound and spelling, students will apply it to decode written words through a process called blending. The blending students will be doing in phonics differs from the oral blending they have been practicing in Phonemic Awareness activities since Lesson 1. In phonics, students use the written letter as a guide to sounding rather than the sounds given by the teacher. Although at this point students can only blend *am* and *Sam*, this lesson introduces the blending process. This introduction is repeated in Lesson 14 of this unit. Blending procedures can be found on ***Routine Cards 2, 3,*** and in later units, ***4.***

- Ask the students which ***Sound/Spelling Cards*** they have learned so far, and review the sounds from the cards.
- Tell the students you are going to show them how these sounds can be put together to make a word.
- Write the letter *a* on the board. Touch the letter and say the /a/ sound. Have students say the sound with you as you touch the letter again.
- Write the letter *m* after the *a*, touch the letter, and say the /m/ sound. Have the students repeat the sound as you touch the letter again.
- Tell the students that you will blend the sounds together to make a word. Move your hand under the letters slowly, and pronounce each sound slowly and smoothly without stopping between sounds. Make sure your hand is under the letter that corresponds to the sound you are saying.
- Repeat, having students say the sounds with you. Make the blending motion with your hand again, but slightly faster.
- Ask what this word is. Confirm students' responses by pronouncing the word naturally as you move your hand quickly beneath the letters.
- Erase the word and have the students blend it again with you. Rewrite the letter *a*, touch it, and have them say the sound. Rewrite the letter *m*, touch it, and have students say the sound. Then blend the word with the students.
- Finally, call on a few students to make up sentences using the word *am*.

Phonics Skills Reading 1.3; Writing 1.3

- ***Phonics Skills*** page 18 reinforces the /a/ sound spelled *a*. Help the students complete the top part of the page. Have them write the letter *a* on the top line and *A* on the next line on each blank, saying the /a/ sound each time they write a letter.
- Help the students complete the second half of ***Phonics Skills*** page 18. They can fill in the first blank with their name and write a word or draw a picture to complete the second sentence. Encourage them to write legibly and space letters and words appropriately.
- On ***Phonics Skills*** page 19, help the students read the sentences and choose the correct rebus to complete the sentences.

Dictation and Spelling

Dictation Reading 1.3; Writing 1.3

Ask students to write the capital and lowercase vowels. Remind them to proofread their letters.

Spelling: /a/ Spelled *a*

- Point to the ***Sound/Spelling Card*** for /a/ ***(Lamb).*** Have students make the /a/ sound.
- Ask whether any students know how to spell some words with the /a/ sound in them. Students might be familiar with the words *an, and, am, bat, cat,* and so on. Invite them to print the words on the board.
- Encourage those students who did not provide spellings to approach the board and point to the *a* in a word. Show positive reinforcement by having the class say the /a/ sound together and then repeat the whole word.
- Remind the students of the sound/spellings that they already know (/s/ and /m/).
- Have them try to write the following words on a separate sheet of paper. Spell the first word together on the board.

am	I **am** in first grade.	**am**
me	That belongs to **me.**	**me**
an	I ate **an** egg.	**an**

- Write the words on the board and have the students correct their own papers.

PHONICS

LESSON MODELS VIDEOCASSETTE
Use the ***Lesson Models Videocassette*** at this time for an Introduction to Blending lesson model.

Reading 1.3

Teacher Tip BLENDING Students' first attempts at blending will be ragged. Do not expect mastery, but do keep working on blending sounds to make words.

UNIVERSAL ACCESS: Reading 1.3

MEETING INDIVIDUAL NEEDS

Reteach

/a/ SPELLED *a* Use ***Reteach: Phonics Skills*** pages 18 and 19 to reinforce *a* as /a/.

Challenge

PHONICS /a/ SPELLED *a* Use ***Challenge: Phonics Skills*** page 14 with students who are ready for a challenge.

Intervention Tip

VOWEL—CONSONANT—VOWEL Tell the students that when a word has only one vowel and it's between two consonants, the vowel says its short sound. Think of two consonants squeezing the vowel letter *a*, so *a* hollers "a-a-a-a." Then write *Sam* on the board for students to read.

PHONICS

Reading 1.1

Reading a Decodable Book

Core Set, Book 5: *Sam, Sam, Sam*
Phonics Focus: /a/ Spelled *a*

High-Frequency Words Reading 1.3

No high-frequency words are introduced in this book. Review the high-frequency words already in the High-Frequency Word Bank. Have students volunteer to read the ones they recognize.

Reading Recommendations Reading 1.1, 1.2, 1.3, 1.8

- No nondecodable words are in this book.
- Have the students read the title and browse the story.
- Have students read a page silently, then read the page aloud. Repeat this procedure for each page.
- Have another student reread the page before going on.
- Reread the story at least twice, calling on different students to read. Then have the entire group do a choral reading of the story.

Research in Action
Decodable Texts

Children who read stories that contain a high percentage of words with the letter-sound relationships that have been taught have significantly higher word recognition than do children who read stories that do not contain words that match their instruction. (*Connie Juel and Diane Roper/Schneider)*

Juel, Connie, and Roper/Schneider, Diane. 1985. The influence of basal readers on first grade reading. *Reading Research Quarterly, 20,* 134–152.

Informal Assessment

BLENDING Select a couple of students read *Sam, Sam, Sam* aloud to you to assess their ability to blend /a/ and /m/.

Decodable Book 5

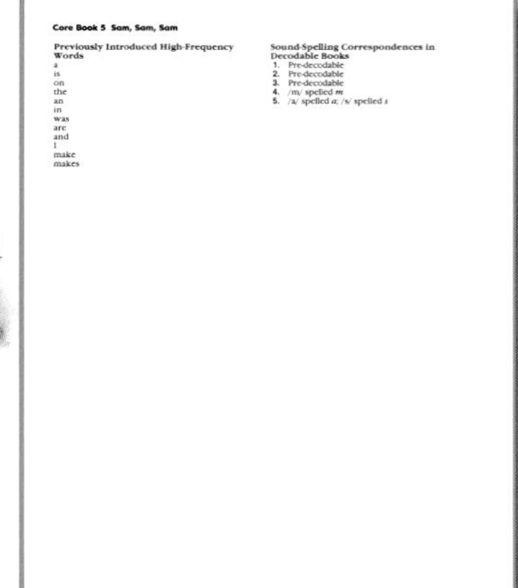
Core Book 5 Sam, Sam, Sam

Previously Introduced High-Frequency Words
a
is
on
the
an
in
was
are
and
I
make
makes

Sound-Spelling Correspondences in Decodable Books
1. Pre-decodable
2. Pre-decodable
3. Pre-decodable
4. /m/ spelled *m*
5. /a/ spelled *a*; /s/ spelled *s*

PHONICS

Responding Reading 2.2; Listen/Speak 1.2, 2.2

- Invite the students to discuss any hard words they encountered in *Sam, Sam, Sam* and how they figured out these words. Call on volunteers to retell the story.
- To make sure the students are focusing on the words in the story, rather than the pictures, ask questions such as the following, having the students answer by pointing to and reading aloud the words:

  What is the boy's name? *(The boy's name is sam.)*

  Who else is Sam? *(The girl and the dog are both named Sam.)*

Building Fluency Reading 1.16

Encourage partners to build fluency by rereading ***Decodable Book 5***, *Sam, Sam, Sam*, of the Core Set. The first time through, one partner should read the odd-numbered pages and the other the even-numbered pages. For the second reading, the partners should switch pages. After the second reading, the partners should choose one of the ***Decodable Books*** from previous lessons and continue to read to each other.

Teacher Tip **DECODABLE BOOKS** Students should keep track of their readings on a personal title sheet. Make a six-column chart for the students. The heading for the first column should be *Decodable Books,* while the headings for the remaining five columns should read *Date/Partner.* List the ***Decodable Books*** in the first column. Tell the students that each time they read one of the ***Decodables,*** they should fill in the date and/or the partner with whom they've read the book. They can read the same book up to five times. They can do this at the end of a lesson, after they have read the ***Decodable Book*** assigned for that lesson. Students can read the additional ***Decodable*** either by themselves or with a partner. This will encourage faster readers to keep reading, and it will ensure that slower readers will have the time they need to finish reading the assigned ***Decodable.***

Teacher Tip **READING ALOUD** When you read this story with the students, use lively expression so that students will start thinking about using expression.

Routine Card

Refer to ***Routine 5*** to review the procedure for reading a ***Decodable Book.***

Pages 42–45 of *Let's Read!*

First of two lessons.

Objectives

- Students will share prior knowledge about birds.
- Students will use the Table of Contents to locate information.
- Students will discuss selection vocabulary.
- Students will listen and respond to the selection.
- Students will discuss what they learned from the selection.
- Students will talk about speech balloons.
- Students will distinguish different kinds of shapes.

Materials

- Big Book *Let's Read!*, pp. 42–45

SELECTION INTRODUCTION

Reading 3.2

About the Author/Illustrator

CHARLOTTE VOAKE, born in England, is primarily a respected illustrator of children's books. Reading aloud to her daughter inspired her to retell and illustrate her own books. One of her best-received works was *The Three Little Pigs and Other Favourite Nursery Stories.*

Other Books by Charlotte Voake

Over the Moon: A Book of Nursery Rhymes, *Tom's Cat*

Selection Summary

Genre: Fiction

This is a delightful story about a goose who finds an egg, cares for it, and becomes a loving, adoptive parent who does her best for her slightly unusual offspring.

This story should provide a way for students to become acquainted with the literary genre of fiction.

The elements of fiction are listed below. Fiction may have one or more of these elements.

- The story is about things that did not really happen.
- The author invents the action in the story.
- The author's imagination is the most important thing in a work of fiction.

Inquiry Connections

Continuing the theme *Let's Read!*'s variety and exposure to text, "Mrs. Goose's Baby" is different from many of the selections encountered so far. Students will be exposed to comprehension strategies and comprehension skills that will keep them actively involved for the surprise ending. Key concepts to be explored will be similarities and differences among individuals.

Direct the students to the Concept/Question Board. Encourage them to post any questions or ideas they have about the unit. They may want to include a drawing of a goose or geese.

- Make sure the students put their names or initials on anything they post on the Board.
- Tell them that they can post something on the Board any day. Be sure to have students discuss what they put on the Board with the class.

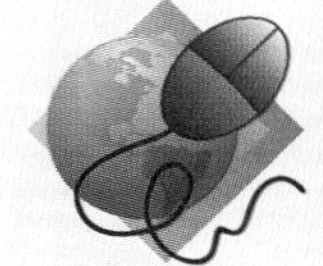

www.sra4kids.com
Web Connection
Remind students to look for additional animal stories by using Web connections that are available at the Reading link of the SRA Web page.

UNIVERSAL ACCESS: MEETING INDIVIDUAL NEEDS

ELL Support

USING ILLUSTRATIONS FOR UNDERSTANDING
Before reading the selection, go over the illustrations with the English-language learners. Associating the words in the text with the illustrations helps the English-language learners think of English words without translating them.

ELL Support

For ELD strategies, use the ***English-Language Development Guide,*** Unit 1, Lesson 13.

Intervention Support

For intervention strategies, use the ***Intervention Guide,*** Unit 1, Lesson 13.

Routine Card
Refer to ***Routine 11*** for the procedure for reading the selection.

Teacher Tip COMPREHENSION Good readers constantly evaluate their understanding of what they read. Stop often to make sure you and the students are doing this.

Reading 2.6

Teacher Tip ACTIVATE PRIOR KNOWLEDGE Inform the students that good readers typically activate what they already know about a topic before reading something new about the topic. Tell students that they should get into the habit of thinking about the topic of an upcoming selection and activating relevant background knowledge.

Build Background

Activate Prior Knowledge Reading 2.6

Ask students to think about the title "Mrs. Goose's Baby" and to figure out what they might know already that would help them understand the story.

Background Information

- Explain that in real life, birds sometimes hatch eggs that have been left alone by the mother.
- Point out that when baby birds hatch, they often think the first thing they see is their mother.

Preview and Prepare

Browse Reading 1.2

- Display *Let's Read!*, open to the Table of Contents. Tell students that you are going to read them a story called "Mrs. Goose's Baby." Invite volunteers to find the selection on the Table of Contents and to turn to the page where it begins.
- Remind students that good readers browse before they read.
- Flip through the first four pages of the story in the ***Big Book.*** Allow students to get a feel for the setting of the story—but do not give away the ending.
- Before reading the selection to the students, read the Focus Questions on the first page of the selection together. Briefly discuss the questions and tell the students to keep these questions in mind as you read.

Set Purposes

Tell students that reading can have many purposes. Suggest that their purpose for reading this story is to find out what is special about Mrs. Goose's baby.

Selection Vocabulary Reading 1.3, 1.14

- Write the following word on the board and pronounce it:

  pecking
- Ask the students whether they ever have seen a chicken or another bird poking its beak at the ground. Let students know that this is pecking. It is how birds use their beaks to get food. Baby birds also use their beaks to peck their way out of the shell and into the world.
- This is a good opportunity to help students with other words with *-ing* endings. Invite them to say *-ing* words as you write them on the board.

Reading Recommendations

- We suggest that you read the selection in two lessons, today reading pages 42–45, pausing only to model the simple reading strategies.
- In rereadings, invite students to summarize each page by looking at the illustrations before you read the page.

Using Comprehension Strategies  Reading 2.5

Explain strategy use to students by saying that good readers are always active when they read: They ask questions, form images, summarize, and make predictions to help them understand what is happening in a selection. During the reading of this section of "Mrs. Goose's Baby," you will model the use of the following reading strategy:

- **Predicting** causes readers to analyze information given about story events and characters in the context of how it may logically connect to the story's conclusion.

Introduce the Predicting strategy by telling students that good readers often pause as they read to think about, or predict, what is going to happen next. They can get clues for their predictions by looking at the illustrations or by searching through the text on the page for hints of what might happen next. Sometimes the title of a story will suggest an ending. Students also might use what they already know about a subject to predict the plot of a story about that subject. Point out that good readers always come back to their prediction to see whether it was confirmed. Say, too, that even good readers make predictions that don't happen.

Building Comprehension Skills 

In this selection, "Mrs. Goose's Baby," the students will apply the following comprehension skill:

- **Comparing and Contrasting** skills allow readers to deepen their understanding of a text by noticing similarities and differences between stories, characters, settings, events, and so on.

Explain to the students that one way we learn about new things is by finding out how they are similar to and different from what we know.

- To illustrate, draw a triangle and a square on the board. Ask students to compare the two. How are they alike? *(They are shapes. They have straight lines.)*
- Now ask the students to contrast the two. How are they different? *(They are different shapes—one's a triangle, one's a square. One has three sides; one has four sides.)*

Routine Card
Refer to ***Routine 10*** for the Selection Vocabulary procedure.

Teacher Tip HIGH FREQUENCY WORDS The following high-frequency words appear in the selection: *an, a, in, on, the, and,* and *was.* Point to these words in the High-Frequency Word Bank, have students read them, and encourage them to read these words with you when you encounter them in the reading.

Reading 2.4; Listen/Speak 1.2

UNIVERSAL ACCESS: MEETING INDIVIDUAL NEEDS

ELL Tip

PRETEACH THE SELECTION For students who are learning English or who might need extra help, you might want to read this selection a day or so before it is read by the class. As you read, give students the opportunity to discuss the selection and to clarify any vocabulary words or questions they have about it.

Teacher Tip COMPARING AND CONTRASTING An extended lesson on Comparing and Contrasting can be found on page T277. This lesson is intended to give extra practice with comparing and contrasting.

COMPREHENSION

Comprehension Strategies

Introducing Strategy Use

Tell students that another strategy readers use is predicting. When readers predict, they pause while reading to think about what is going to happen next, based on information from prior knowledge and the context of the selection. To use this strategy effectively, readers need to return to their predictions to see if what they predicted is confirmed or not. Sometimes readers will be able to confirm their predictions about what will happen next by identifying key words, or signpost words such as first, next, then, after, finally, and so on.

Teacher Modeling

1 Predicting *Mrs. Goose's baby seems very different from Mrs. Goose. As she is growing up, she looks different, too. I wonder why this is. I predict that Mrs. Goose is going to find out something funny about her baby. Predicting is a good strategy because it keeps you involved in reading. As we read on, I can check my predictions. Do you have any predictions about the baby?*

Phonemic Awareness Reading 1.4, 1.7

INITIAL CONSONANT SOUNDS Remind students how changing just the beginning sound can make a whole new word. Invite students to join you in making new words from several words in the story. Have students take turns erasing and replacing initial sounds with other consonants you suggest. Explain that the new words could be nonsense words. Use the following words and write them on the board: *nest, ran, soon, sat, look,* and *found.*

Teacher Tip **PREDICTING** Tell the students that a prediction is not a wild guess. They have to think about the story and the clues in the story to make good predictions.

Comprehension Skills

COMPREHENSION

Comparing and Contrasting

Explain to the students that when we say how things are alike, we compare them; when we say how they are different, we contrast them.

Have the students think about Mrs. Goose and her baby. Encourage them to think of one way in which they are alike and one way in which they are different.

Universal Access: Meeting Individual Needs

Intervention Tip

CONTRASTING Begin by asking how things are different because difference is often more obvious.

Teacher Tip **READING FOR ENJOYMENT** Remind students that they should spend at least 20 minutes reading after school.

Discussing the Selection

- Have the students discuss what they liked about the selection.
- Have the students look at the illustration of Mrs. Goose and her fluffy, yellow baby. Ask them to describe how Mrs. Goose and her baby are alike and how they are different.
- Ask students what they think Mrs. Goose thinks of her baby.
- Ask students whether the story makes them want to learn more about birds.

Review Selection Vocabulary

Have students review the selection vocabulary word for this lesson. Remind them that they discussed the meaning of this word at the beginning of the lesson. Have them add this and any other interesting words that they clarified while reading to the Vocabulary Words section of their Writer's Notebooks. Encourage students to refer to the vocabulary words throughout the unit. The word from this selection is

pecking

- Have the students use the word in oral sentences. Help them expand their sentences by asking who, what, where, when, why, and how questions.
- Ask the students to draw a picture that represents the word.

Encourage students to refer to the vocabulary words throughout the unit.

Print and Book Awareness

Speech Balloons Reading 3.2

- Point out the speech balloons in the story. Ask where students have seen speech balloons before, such as in the newspaper comic strips. Tell the students that in a previous selection there was an illustration that included a thought cloud. Ask the students whether they can remember where that was *("The Purple Cow," pages 6–7)*. Tell the students that a speech balloon is similar, but that words in it are spoken by the character.
- Explain that in illustrations, this is how the artist lets us know that the characters are speaking. The words in the speech balloons are the characters' words.

Teacher Tip SPEECH BALLOONS Suggest that they might like to use speech balloons in their own writing.

Supporting the Reading

Comprehension Skill: Comparing and Contrasting

Encourage the students to compare and contrast themselves with family members or friends. Have them draw pictures of themselves standing next to the individuals they choose to compare and contrast themselves with in their Writer's Notebooks. Help the students label the features or traits in their pictures that are alike and different.

Listening, Speaking, Viewing: Dramatization

- Explain to students that they are going to retell part of "Mrs. Goose's Baby" by using their actions instead of words.
- Ask for volunteers or let students pair up to play the parts of Mrs. Goose and her baby.
- Reread the first few pages of the ***Big Book,*** allowing students to discover ways to pretend they are sitting on eggs, pecking their ways out of shells, or growing bigger and bigger.
- After going through the first scene, ask volunteers to choose their favorite scenes in the story to dramatize before the class.

Objectives

- Students will use their alphabet book.
- Students will apply concepts and ideas through a curricular connection.

Materials

- Class alphabet book
- Reading
- Transparency 39

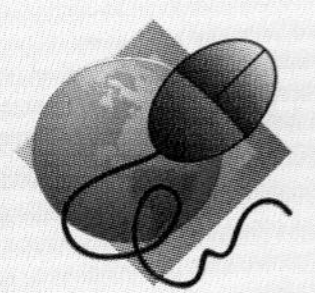

www.sra4kids.com
Web Connection
Help the students look for additional information about poems and rhymes by using the Web connections that are available at the Reading link of the SRA Web page.

INVESTIGATION

Supporting the Investigation

Investigating Concepts Beyond the Text

Remind students about the alphabet book they are working on for this unit.

- Remind the students that they have read several rhymes in this unit. Ask the students to think of rhymes that they enjoy. What are they about? Name the letters they begin with. Then find the letters in the alphabet book and add this information to the book.
- Have the students take turns naming letters, finding the pages in the alphabet book for those letters, and sharing them with the class.

Math Connection

Alike but Different

Purpose: To use informal language to categorize different shapes; to identify the attributes, such as color and size, that are used to classify the shapes.

- Ask the students to remember the previous discussion about comparing and contrasting Mrs. Goose and her baby.
- Explain to them that even though Mrs. Goose and her baby are birds, they are different sizes and different colors. Use the Venn diagram on ***Reading Transparency 39*** to compare and contrast Mrs. Goose and her baby.
- Tell them that the same forms can have different colors, and the same colors can be repeated in different forms.
- Have the students cut out three different-sized squares and two different-sized triangles from construction paper.
- Tell them to glue the shapes onto the white paper to make a design or an animal.

INVESTIGATION

Teacher Tip MATERIALS for this Math Connection you will need two different colors of construction paper, white paper, scissors, glue, and ***Reading Transparency 39.***

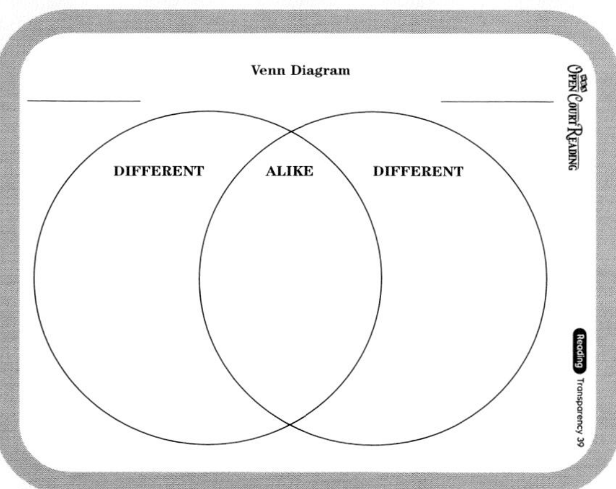

Reading Transparency 39

Objectives

Word Analysis Vocabulary
- **Vocabulary Strategies: Context Clues.** Using words from "Mrs. Goose's Baby," identify helpful context clues as a way to infer meaning of unfamiliar vocabulary.

Writing Process Strategies
- **Introduction to the Writing Process.** Building on the theme Let's Read!, learn strategies for drafting and understand that writing is a process that involves drafting.

English Language Conventions
- **Mechanics: Capital Letters.** Building on the Phonics lesson, develop the understanding that sentences begin with capital letters and end with periods.

Materials

- Big Book Let's Read!, pp. 42–45

Universal Access: Meeting Individual Needs

Reteach, Challenge, English-Language Development and ***Intervention*** lessons are available to support the language arts instruction in this lesson.

OVERVIEW

Language Arts Overview

Word Analysis

Vocabulary The Vocabulary activity focuses on vocabulary from "Mrs. Goose's Baby" to learn how to use context clues to infer meaning as a way of understanding vocabulary. In this lesson, the focus will be on reviewing setting and circumstance to infer meanings. This lesson is an introduction to using context clues, which will be practiced again and again as students learn to read.

Vocabulary Skill Words

fluffy **pecking***

**Also Selection Vocabulary*

Writing Process Strategies

The Writing Process Strategies lesson introduces students to the writing process by providing an overview of drafting. Teachers modeling drafting can have a strong influence on the way beginning writers go about it. In this lesson students will summarize by explaining to the teacher how to draft.

English Language Conventions

Grammar, Usage, and Mechanics **Capital Letters.** The English Language Conventions support the reading and writing skills development in this lesson. This lesson applies the conventions of capitalizing and punctuating sentences in writing.

Word Analysis

Vocabulary

Context Clues Reading 2.4, 3.2

Teach

- Write the following sentences on the board: *Mrs. Goose's baby was very small. She was fluffy and yellow.* Explain that if students don't know the word *fluffy*, they have some clues in the other sentences that could tell them something about it.
- Ask the students what clues they have for the meaning of the word *fluffy*. *(The baby is yellow and babies are usually soft.)*

Guided Practice

- Write the following sentences on the board from "Mrs. Goose's Baby": *Soon the egg started to crack open. The little bird inside was pecking at the shell.*"
- Have the students explain as if to a younger person what the word *pecking* means from the context clues in the poem. *(A little bird can do it from the inside of a shell.)*
- Conclude by explaining that context clues help students understand the meanings of unknown words.

Writing Process Strategies

Introduction to the Writing Process

Write Writing 1.0, 2.1

Teach

- Explain that after writers have a plan, it is time to write their ideas into sentences.
- Review the sample drafts you wrote about fish and favorite foods.
- Review the prewriting plan students made about their pets in Lesson 9.

Guided Practice

- Have the students explain to you how to write a draft about their pets. Follow their directions, asking questions about why they are choosing to have you write one sentence or another. Encourage them to direct you to write your ideas down without stopping to check spelling, capitalization, or punctuation at this point.
- Conclude by emphasizing the importance of getting your ideas on paper.

English Language Conventions

Grammar, Usage, and Mechanics

Capital Letters Eng. Lang. Conv. 1.1, 1.5, 1.6, 1.7

Teach

Review that sentences begin with capital letters and many end with periods.

Independent Practice in Writing

- Have students write two sentences about themselves. If necessary, provide them with models by writing some sample sentences on the board.
- Remind them to use a capital letter at the beginning of each sentence and a period at the end.

Informal Assessment

Read students' sentences, checking for capital letters at the beginning and periods at the end. If students are having trouble, refer to the blending and dictation sentences in the Phonics exercises.

Objectives

- Students will attend to initial and final consonant sounds.
- Students will associate the /t/ sound with the letter *t* in words.
- Students will blend letter sounds to read words.
- Students will read a ***Decodable Book***

Materials

- Lion Puppet
- Sound/Spelling Cards
- Sound/Spelling Card Stories Audiocassette/CD
- Routine Cards 1, 2, 3, 5, 8.
- Phonics Skills, pp. 20–21
- Letter Cards
- High-Frequency Word Cards
- Decodable Book 1, 6

Reading 1.6

Teacher Tip RHYMING WORDS Encourage the students to create lists of rhyming words using the rimes from the Consonant Riddle Game.

Universal Access: Meeting Individual Needs

ELL Support

For ELD strategies, use the ***English-Language Development Guide,*** Unit 1, Lesson 14.

Intervention Support

For intervention strategies, use the ***Intervention Guide,*** Unit 1, Lesson 14.

Warming Up

Use one or both of the following activities to focus students' attention and to review some of the concepts that they have been learning.

Consonant Riddle Game Reading 1.3, 1.4

Have the students answer the following riddles:

What starts with /m/ and rhymes with *fan?*

What starts with /t/ and rhymes with *pop?*

What starts with /s/ and rhymes with *eat?*

What starts with /t/ and rhymes with *able?*

What starts with /m/ and rhymes with *fiddle?*

What starts with /k/ and rhymes with *lake?*

What starts with /b/ and rhymes with *lake?*

Sing the "Short-Vowel Song" Reading 1.5; Listen/Speak 2.1

Review the /a/ sound by singing the "Short-Vowel Song" taught in Lesson 13. Have small groups make up their own verses by replacing the word *lamb* with another /a/ word, and then sing the verse for the group.

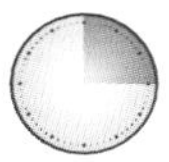

Phonemic Awareness Reading 1.4

Oral Blending

Initial Consonant Sounds Reading 1.4

- Write the letters *m* and *s* on opposite sides of the board. Tell the students that you are going to say some words and that they should listen for the beginning sound. Have the class repeat the initial sound and point to the letter for each word or give them the ***Letter Cards*** *s* and *m*. The students should hold up the beginning sound they hear.
- Begin with these words:

say	so	mow	moo
sat	sail	math	man
mom	make	sap	same
marble	muffin	simple	some
sofa	sesame	monster	moon

Segmentation

Dropping Final Consonants Reading 1.4, 1.9

- Take out the puppet and continue the game as started in the previous lessons. The puppet is leaving out the final consonant sound, and students must say what it is.

Teacher:	much
Puppet:	mu
Students:	/ch/
Teacher:	tease
Puppet:	tea
Students:	/z/

- Have the students supply the missing phoneme for the puppet as you work through the following words:

tee /n/	bea /ch/	bea /n/	stea /m/	tra /s/
trai /n/	ta /p/	ta /k/	broo /m/	brui /z/
brai /d/	gree /t/	gree /d/	twea /k/	twee /t/
stree /t/	strea /m/			

UNIVERSAL ACCESS: Reading 1.8
MEETING INDIVIDUAL NEEDS

Reteach

INITIAL CONSONANT SOUNDS Review blending initial consonant sounds with groups of students who need additional practice during Workshop.

Reading 1.9

Informal Assessment

FINAL CONSONANT SOUNDS Observe five or six students for their ability to segment final consonant sounds. Do this monitoring for the next five lessons until you have observed all students. Record your observations in the Teacher Observation Log in the ***Program Assessment Teacher's Edition.***

SOUND/SPELLING CARD STORIES PHONICS Use the ***Sound/Spelling Card Stories*** for practice with the /t/ sound. Have students silently repeat the words that are said on the cassette.

Routine Card

Refer to ***Routine 1*** to review the procedure for introducing sounds and spellings.

Informal Assessment

PHONICS Have the students make their pointer fingers go up and down each time they hear a word with the /t/ sound in the Timer story.

PHONICS

Phonics

Introduce /t/ Spelled *t* Reading 1.1, 1.3, 1.4, 1.10

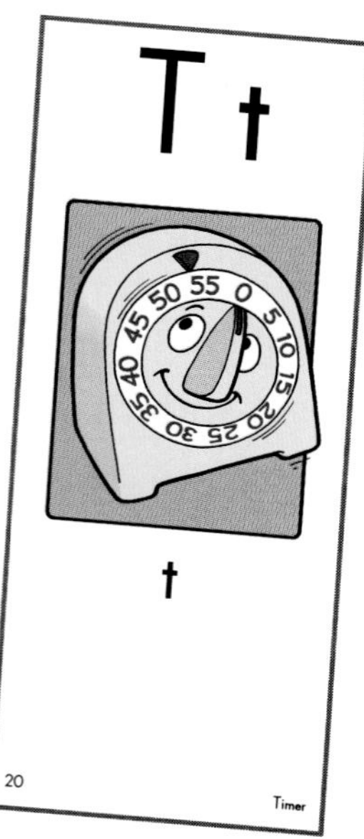

- Turn ***Sound/Spelling Card 20—Timer*** around and introduce the /t/ sound and spelling, following the steps outlined here.
- Point out the letters at the top of the card. Remind the students that the picture is a clue to help them remember the letter sound and the bottom of the card shows the spelling of the sound in words.
- Read the Timer story, asking students to listen for the /t/ sound and to think about how the picture will remind them of the sound.

When Tom Tuttle cooks, he uses his timer.

Tom Tuttle's timer ticks like this: /t/ /t/ /t/ /t/ /t/ /t/ /t/.

Tonight Tom Tuttle wants tomatoes on toast.

Tom turns on the oven.

Tom puts tomatoes on toast in the oven.

Tom sets the timer.

The timer will *Ding!* when Tom's toast and tomatoes are done.

Until the timer dings, it ticks: /t/ /t/ /t/ /t/ /t/ /t/ /t/.

Tomatoes on toast take ten minutes: /t/ /t/ /t/ /t/ /t/ /t/ /t/.

Tom can hardly wait: /t/ /t/ /t/ /t/ /t/ /t/ /t/.

He taps out the time: /t/ /t/ /t/ /t/ /t/ /t/ /t/.

What is the sound of Tom Tuttle's ticking timer?

(Have students join in:) /t/ /t/ /t/ /t/ /t/ /t/ /t/.

Ding! Time for dinner, Tom Tuttle!

- Write the letter *t* on the board and say the /t/ sound.
- Have the students write the letter on scrap paper, or use their index finger to write on a surface or in the air. Tell them to say /t/ each time they write the letter.
- Tell the students that you will say some words. Ask them to signal if they hear /t/ at the beginning of the word. Otherwise, they should remain silent.

tea	sea	**two**	new	**turtle**
tight	right	**table**	snail	**tickle**
shop	**tale**	pickle	**tambourine**	**tornado**

- Ask the students to suggest some words that begin with /t/.
- Have the students listen for the /t/ sound at the end of the next group of words. They should give the thumbs-up or thumbs-down sign as you pronounce the words.

am	**at**	**hat**	ham	**hot**
hop	shop	**shot**	**pot**	**rot**
root	room	boom	**boot**	**bite**
bait	bake	lake	**late**	fix
night	home	nice	**fit**	**light**

- Ask the students to suggest some words that end with /t/.
- Remind the students that the name of the card is ***Timer,*** the sound is /t/, and the spelling is *t*. Say that the word *timer* begins with /t/ and it says /t/ /t/ /t/ as it ticks.

PHONICS

Teacher Tip SIGNAL If you show the students the action associated with the card, the students can use the action to signal whether they hear the sound. Have them move just their pointer fingers back and forth, left and right to represent the hands of a timer.

PHONICS

Universal Access: Meeting Individual Needs

ELL Tip

WORD MEANING Make sure the English-language learners know the meanings of the words in the activities. Use pictures, photos, objects, stick drawings, pantomime, or the ***English-Language Development Glossary.***

Routine Card
Refer to **Routine 2** for the sound-by-sound blending procedure. **Routine 3** for the blending sentences procedure.

LESSON MODELS VIDEOCASSETTE
Use the ***Lesson Models Videocassette*** at this time for a Blending Words and Sentences lesson model.

Blending Reading 1.1, 1.3, 1.8, 1.9, 1.11

The blending procedure was introduced in Lesson 13. For your convenience, it is reviewed here. Introduce each word in the wordlines through this basic procedure. The words, sentences, and special points that should be made throughout the blending lesson are provided after the example.

Each blending activity consists of two or more lines of individual words and one or more complete sentences. Here are the words and sentence for this lesson:

Line 1:	am	at	
Line 2:	at	mat	sat
Line 3:	mats	mast	Sam
Sentence 1:	Sam sat on the mat.		

About the Words and Sentences Reading 1.1, 1.3, 1.8, 1.9, 1.11

Explain to the students that they now will be using the sounds and spellings they have learned so they can read and write whole words. Putting the spellings together to make words is called blending.

Line 1: eview the ***Sound/Spelling Cards*** that have been introduced. Then blend the word *am*.

- Write the letter *a*, touch it, and prompt students to say the /a/ sound.
- Write an *m* next to the *a*. Touch the *m* and have students say /m/.
- Tell the students to listen as you blend the sounds. Then demonstrate blending by moving your hand slowly and smoothly under the letters and pronouncing the sounds continuously, moving from /a/ to /m/ without a break.
- As you make the smooth blending motion, be sure that your hand is pointing to the letter that corresponds to the sound you are saying at that moment. As you make the smooth, blending transition from one sound to the next, your hand should be moving from left to right beneath the two letters.
- Have the students join you in saying the sounds as you move your hand slowly beneath the letters again.
- Ask the students to blend the word, modeling as necessary. Listen to make sure that they are pronouncing the sounds without a break.
- Have the students pronounce the word naturally. It is important for students to realize that blending results in a word.

- To confirm the response, have a student use the word in a sentence.

Line 2: Repeat the process in Line 1 with the second word, *at*. Proceed to Line 2, quickly writing and sounding the spellings for the word *at*. Ask students whether they know what the word is. If necessary, point out that it is the same as the word in Line 1. For the word *mat*, write and blend as follows:

- Write *m*, say /m/.
- Write *a*, say /a/.
- Blend /ma/.
- Write *t*, say /t/.
- Blend /ma/ /t/, then say *mat*.
- This "blending through the vowel" will encourage smoother blending. Students will need to hold fewer sounds in mind, and there will be fewer sound distortions.

Line 3: Blend the words in Line 3 in the same manner as in Lines 1 and 2.

- When all the words are blended, point to them in random order and have students read them.

Sentence 1: After you have blended the individual words, write today's sentence on the board *(Sam sat on the mat.)*, sounding and blending each word as described above. Underline the words *on* and *the*. Frame each word, one at a time with your hands. Ask how students know where one word stops and the next one begins. *(There is a space between words.)* Beginning with this lesson, words that students are unable to decode—because they are irregular or they contain sounds and spellings that students haven't learned yet—are underlined.

- As you write the sentences on the board, underline each high-frequency word, explaining to students that these words should not be sounded out. Provide help reading these words as necessary.
- Have students join you in reading the sentence, blending the words *Sam*, *sat*, and *mat* as you come to each one. Have the sentence reread with a natural intonation. Reread the sentence several times: whole class, boys, girls, several individuals.
- Before writing the sentence, write *on* and *the* on the board and pronounce them. Explain to students that the *t* in *the* does not make the /t/ sound. Say the word *the* again and have students repeat the word several times. Tell student that *on* and *the* are words they will use often. Underline them and have students use *on* and *the* in sentences.
- Discuss with students that you began the sentence with a capital letter and ended it with a period. Explain that all sentences begin with capital letters and end with some kind of punctuation mark.

PHONICS

Blending 1.8

Teacher Tip BLENDING At this point in the year, some students might not seem to understand blending. The continued use of the routine will support these students and provide critical practice.

Research in Action

Blending

Learning to recognize new words by blending together their letters and spelling patterns is one of the most critical steps in becoming a reader.

Some students have more difficulty learning to blend than others, so you should not be concerned if only a few students seem to catch on at first. However, the clarity with which you introduce and guide the blending process is extremely important because it will strongly influence the success with which all of your students will learn to blend. Make sure that every student is attempting the blending exercises, even though at this stage many of them can only do it imitatively. You will probably need to lead early blending exercises, but encourage students to take over as soon as they can. *(Marilyn J. Adams)*

UNIVERSAL ACCESS:
MEETING INDIVIDUAL NEEDS

Reteach

/t/ SPELLED t PHONICS Students who need more help with this sound/spelling can complete ***Reteach: Phonics Skills*** pages 20–21 during Workshop.

Challenge

/t/ SPELLED t PHONICS Use ***Challenge: Phonics Skills*** page 15 with students who are ready for a challenge.

PHONICS

Developing Oral Language

- Have one or more students extend the words by using them in a sentence. To help, you might ask them Where?, Why?, When?, or How? Be sure that when the students add to sentences, they say the entire new sentence and not just its extension.

Phonics Skills Reading 1.3

Phonics Skills pages 20–21 provide additional practice with /t/ spelled *t*.

- Point out the picture of the timer at the top of the page and review the /t/ sound. Have students complete the first two lines by writing letter *t* or *T* on each blank and saying /t/ each time they write a letter. Then read the words at the bottom of the page with the students, and have them write the words in the spaces provided.
- On page 21, tell the students to say the name of each picture aloud. If the name begins with /t/, write *t* in the first space. If the name of the picture ends with /t/, write *t* in the second space. *(The names of the pictures are table, hat, ten, ant, cat, kite, toothbrush, and tent.)*

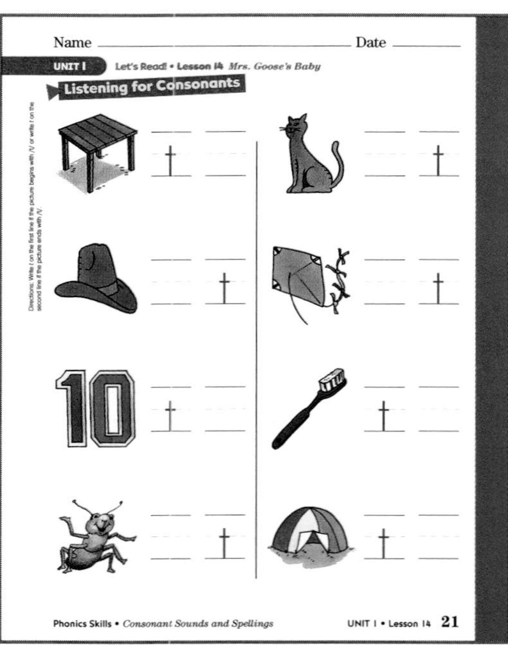

Phonics Skills pp. 20–21

Dictation and Spelling

Dictation: Word Building Game

Reading 1.1, 1.3, 1.4, 1.8, 1.9; Eng. Lang. Conv. 1.8

For the Word Building Game, students use their individual ***Letter Cards*** to build the words. (As an alternative they can use pencil and paper.) You will write on the board.

- Students will need their *a*, *m*, *s*, and *t* ***Letter Cards.*** The list for the Word Building Game is *am*, *at*, *sat*, *mat*, and *mast*.
- Say the word *am*. (Use it in a sentence if you want.) Have students repeat the word. Say the word slowly, sound by sound. Tell the students to find the ***Sound/Spelling Cards*** to locate the letters and spell the sounds. Touch the ***Lamb Card*** and have students say /a/, then touch the ***Monkey Card*** and have students say /m/. Write the word on the board while the students use their ***Letter Cards*** to spell it. Have the students compare their words with your word and proofread as needed. Have the students blend and read the word with you.
- Students can change *am* to make a different word. Say the word *at*. Segment the sounds of the word and have students find the ***Sound/Spelling Cards*** that correspond with the sounds. Point out that the first sound is the same as the first sound of *at*. Point to the ***Timer Card*** and have students say /t/ with you. Write *at* under *am* on the board and have students change the cards to spell *at*. Have students compare their words to yours and proofread as needed. Blend and read the word with students.
- Continue this procedure with the remaining words.

Spelling: /t/ Spelled *t*

- Point to the ***Sound/Spelling Card*** for /t/ ***(Timer).*** Have students make the /t/ sound.
- Have students name some common things that contain the /t/ sound. Examples might include *light*, *cat*, *bat*, *toy*, *feet*, and *boat*. Write a few of the student responses on the board.
- Have a few students go to the board and circle the *t* in each word.
- Read the following words and sentences. Have students attempt to spell each word on a separate sheet of paper. Remind them to think of the sound/spellings they already know.

at	You are **at** school.	**at**
mat	Wipe your shoes on the **mat.**	**mat**
sat	The cat **sat** on the mat.	**sat**
to	I'm going **to** the store.	**to**

- Write the words on the board and have students correct their own papers.

LESSON MODELS VIDEOCASSETTE
Use the ***Lesson Models Videocassette*** at this time for a Word Building Game lesson model.

Readin 1.3

Teacher Tip SENTENCES Encourage the students to use each of the words they made in a sentence.

Routine Card
Refer to ***Routine 8*** for the Word Building Game procedure.

Universal Access: Meeting Individual Needs

ELL Tip

/T/ SOUND You may find it helpful to show the students that the sound is made with the tongue behind the teeth.

PHONICS

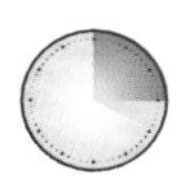

Reading a Decodable Book

Reading 1.1

Core Set, Book 6: *Matt and Sam*
Phonics Focus: /t/ spelled *t*

High-Frequency Words

Reading 1.3

No high-frequency words are introduced in this book. Review the high-frequency words already in the High-Frequency Word Bank. Have students volunteer to read the ones they recognize.

Reading Recommendations

Reading 1.1, 1.2, 1.3, 1.8

- No nondecodable words are in this book.
- Have the students read the title and browse the story.
- Have students read a page silently, then read the page aloud. Repeat this procedure for each page.
- Have another student reread the page before going on.
- Reread the story at least twice, calling on different students to read. Then have the entire group do a choral reading of the story.

Teacher Tip **RESPONDING** Watch for students who can't find the answers and work with them during Workshop.

Decodable Book 6

Sam

6

Sam sat.

7

Sam sat on a mat.

8

Core Book 6 Matt and Sam

Previously Introduced High-Frequency Words

a
is
on
the
an
in
was
are
and
I
make
makes

Sound-Spelling Correspondences in Decodable Books

1. Pre-decodable
2. Pre-decodable
3. Pre-decodable
4. /m/ spelled *m*
5. /a/ spelled *a*; /s/ spelled *s*
6. /t/ spelled *t*

PHONICS

Responding Reading 2.2; Listen/Speak 1.2, 2.2

- Invite the students to discuss any hard words they encountered in *Matt and Sam* and how they figured out these words. Call on volunteers to retell the story.
- To make sure the students are focusing on the words in the story, ask questions such as the following, having the students answer by pointing to and reading aloud the words:

  Who is Matt? *(Matt is a dog.)*
  Who did Matt sit on? *(Matt sat on Sam.)*
  Who is Sam? *(Sam is a boy.)*
  Where did Sam sit? *(Sam sat on a mat.)*

Building Fluency Reading 1.16

Encourage partners to build fluency by rereading ***Decodable Book 5,*** *Matt and Sam,* of the Core Set. The first time through, one partner should read the odd-numbered pages and the other the even-numbered pages. For the second reading, the partners should switch pages. After the second reading, the partners should choose one of the ***Decodable Books*** from previous lessons and continue to read to each other. If students need extra practice with /t/ spelled *t,* have the students read ***Decodable Book 1,*** *On a Mat,* of the Practice Set.

Teacher Tip READING ALOUD When you read this story with the students, use lively expression so that students will begin thinking about using expression.

Informal Assessment

BLENDING Select a couple of students to read *Matt and Sam* aloud to you so you can assess their ability to blend /a/ and /t/.

Routine Card

Refer to ***Routine 5*** to review the procedure for reading a ***Decodable Book.***

Pages 46–53 of *Let's Read!*

Second of two lessons.

Objectives

- Students will listen and respond to pages 46–53 of "Mrs. Goose's Baby."
- Students will listen for /m/ and /s/.
- Students will use the compare and contrast comprehension skill.
- Students will use basic conversation strategies.
- Students will use drama to express themselves.

Materials

- Big Book *Let's Read!, pp. 46–53*
- Comprehension and Language Arts Skills, pp. 14–15

Routine Card

Refer to *Routine 11* for the procedure for reading the selection.

UNIVERSAL ACCESS: MEETING INDIVIDUAL NEEDS

ELL Tip

READING ALOUD To encourage English-language learners to practice using English, have the class read the selection aloud in a choral reading. Then divide the class into two groups. Have one group read the narration and the other group read the dialogue balloons.

Build Background

Activate Prior Knowledge

- Have students retell what they remember from reading the first part of this selection.

Preview and Prepare

Browse

Encourage the students to browse pages 46–53, and tell what they find interesting.

Set Purposes

Review with the students the purpose(s) set for reading "Mrs. Goose's Baby" in the previous lesson.

Selection Vocabulary

Write the following words on the board, read them, and use them in sentences.

shore **smooth**

- Tell the students that a shore is the edge of a beach next to water. Ask the students whether they've ever been to a shore. Encourage the students to use *shore* in a sentence.
- Tell the students that something that is smooth is not rough. Invite the students to name some objects that are smooth *(apple, tabletop, ball, and so on).* Encourage the students to use *smooth* in a sentence.

Reading Recommendations

- Read pages 46–53, pausing only to model simple reading strategies.
- Invite students to summarize a page by looking at the illustrations before you read the page itself.

Using Comprehension Strategies  Reading 2.5

During the first reading of this section of "Mrs. Goose's Baby," you will model the use of the following reading strategies:

Visualizing helps readers picture in their minds what is going on in a selection to gain a clearer understanding.

Predicting causes readers to analyze information given about story events and characters in the context of how it may logically connect to the story's conclusion.

As you read these pages, pause to remind students how good readers use these strategies to help them better understand what they read.

Building Comprehension Skills 

Students will continue to apply the comprehension skill Compare and Contrast to "Mrs. Goose's Baby." Before continuing the story, ask students what they think Mrs. Goose's baby will look like when it's grown up. Encourage them to remember clues from the first part of the story.

Routine Card
Refer to ***Routine 10*** for the Selection Vocabulary procedure.

Teacher Tip HIGH-FREQUENCY WORDS The following high-frequency words appear in the selection: *the, and, in,* and *was.* Point to these words in the High-Frequency Word Bank, have students read them, and encourage them to read these words with you when you encounter them in the reading.

UNIVERSAL ACCESS:
MEETING INDIVIDUAL NEEDS

ELL Support

For ELD strategies, use the ***English-Language Development Guide,*** Unit 1, Lesson 14.

Intervention Support

For intervention strategies, use the ***Intervention Guide,*** Unit 1, Lesson 14.

Teacher Tip COMPREHENSION STRATEGIES Let the students know that good readers are using Visualizing and Predicting all the time. Students should use these strategies whenever they read.

Teacher Tip COMPARING AND CONTRASTING An extended lesson on Comparing and Contrasting can be found on page T299. This lesson is intended to give exta practice with comparing and contrasting.

COMPREHENSION

Comprehension Strategies

Teacher Modeling

2 Visualizing Invite students to close their eyes and imagine exactly what the two creatures must have looked like. Ask volunteers to tell what they saw in their own minds as page 48 was read. *Do the two birds appear to be much the same, like baby zebras and their mothers, or much different?*

Phonemic Awareness Reading 1.4

INITIAL CONSONANT SOUNDS Write *t* on the board. Recall the sound for *t* with students. Remind them that they have listened for the sound at the beginning of words. Reread pages 46–49, encouraging the students to signal when they hear a word that begins with /t/. *(Words that begin with* t *include* to, teach, toes.*)*

Teacher Tip **LISTENING FOR SOUNDS** You may also wish to have students listen for /t/ at the end of words.

Comprehension Skills

Comparing and Contrasting

Have students look at the illustrations and help them notice that Mrs. Goose and her baby have feathers but their feathers aren't the same colors.

Universal Access: Meeting Individual Needs

Intervention Tip

COMPARE AND CONTRAST If students are having difficulty recognizing the similarities and differences between Mrs. Goose and her baby, make a chart to compare and contrast them.

COMPREHENSION

Comprehension Strategies

Introducing Strategy Use

Modeling

3 Confirming Predictions *Remember that I predicted Mrs. Goose would find out something funny about her baby? Here's the answer to my question. The baby bird looks different because it's a chicken, not a goose. That's pretty funny. It doesn't tell whether Mrs. Goose will still like the baby, but I'm sure she will. She's taken such good care of it. Sometimes answers aren't stated directly in the story. You have to think about what's happened in the story and other things you know.*

Phonemic Awareness

Reread pages 50–53, and have the students signal when they hear /t/ at the end of a word. *(Words include* kept, eat.*)*

Teacher Tip **READING FOR ENJOYMENT** Remind students they should spend at least 20 minutes reading after school.

Comprehension Skills

Comparing and Contrasting

Have students discuss what they learned about the differences between geese and chickens.

Teacher Tip **RESPONDING IN CLASS** Encourage students to use the appropriate signal before responding.

COMPREHENSION

Science/Social Studies Connection Center

Refer to the Science/Social Studies Connection Center for an activity about what babies look like growing up.

Teacher Tip VOCABULARY Read all the words in the *Let's Read!* Word Bank, and encourage the students to review what they mean by using the words in sentences or using actions to describe them.

Discussing the Selection

Reading 2.2; Listen/Speak 1.2, 1.4, 1.5

- Ask students the following questions about the selection:

  Who is the story about? *(a goose and a chicken)*
  What kind of animal is Mrs. Goose's Baby? *(a chicken.)*
  Where does this story take place? *(Using the illustrations, it looks like it takes place on a farm.)*
  When did Mrs. Goose's Baby cuddle up to Mrs. Goose? *(at night)*
  Why didn't Mrs. Goose's baby not eat grass or go swimming in the pond? *(Mrs. Goose's baby was a chicken and chickens don't eat grass and don't swim in ponds.)*
- Ask students how Mrs. Goose takes care of her baby. Do you think it matters to her that she and her baby are different? How do you know?
- What does the illustration of Mrs. Goose's baby in different sizes tell you about the baby? *(The illustration shows the reader that the baby is growing.)* Encourage students to ask questions, raise their hands when they want to speak, take turns, and stay on the topic of discussion.
- Ask the students how they think Mrs. Goose got a baby chicken instead of a baby goose, or gosling. *(Mrs. Goose found an egg. She didn't lay it herself).* Who do the students think laid the egg? *(A chicken must have laid the egg.)*
- Ask students whether they were surprised by the ending. Did they figure it out before the last page that the baby was a chicken? What clues helped them figure it out? *(The baby didn't honk; the baby was brown and Mrs. Goose was white, and so on.)*
- Invite students to think about topics such as the following: How do you think Mrs. Goose and her baby get along? (Students should recognize that at the end of the story, Mrs. Goose and her baby seem very happy together.) What do you think the farmer thought about Mrs. Goose and her baby? *(Students' answers will vary.)*
- With the students, refer back to the Focus Questions for the selection. Have all the questions been answered? If not, answer them now.

Have the students record their responses to the selection in the Response Journal section of their Writer's Notebooks by drawing pictures of Mrs. Goose and her baby. Help the students label their drawings.

Review Selection Vocabulary

Have students review the selection vocabulary words for this lesson. Remind them that they discussed the meanings of these words at the beginning of the lesson. Have the add these and any other interesting words that they clarified while reading to the vocabulary words section of their Writer's Notebooks. The words from this selection are

shore **smooth**

- Have the students use the words in oral sentences. Help the students expand their sentences by asking who, what, where, when, why, and how questions.

Print and Book Awareness

Speech Balloons

- Invite the students to look at the speech balloons on page 50. Encourage them to describe how the method the artist uses to display Mrs. Goose's words lets the reader know what is happening.
- Ask students why the word *Honk* gets larger. This increase lets the reader know that Mrs. Goose probably is shouting at the dog.

Supporting the Reading

Comprehension Skill: Comparing and Contrasting

Use ***Comprehension and Language Arts Skills*** pages 14 and 15 for added practice with compare and contrast.

Name ______ Date ______

UNIT 1 Let's Read! • Lesson 14 *Mrs. Goose's Baby*

Comparing and Contrasting

(A) D

A (D)

A (D)

A (D)

(A) D

A (D)

14 UNIT 1 • Lesson 14 Comprehension and Language Arts Skills

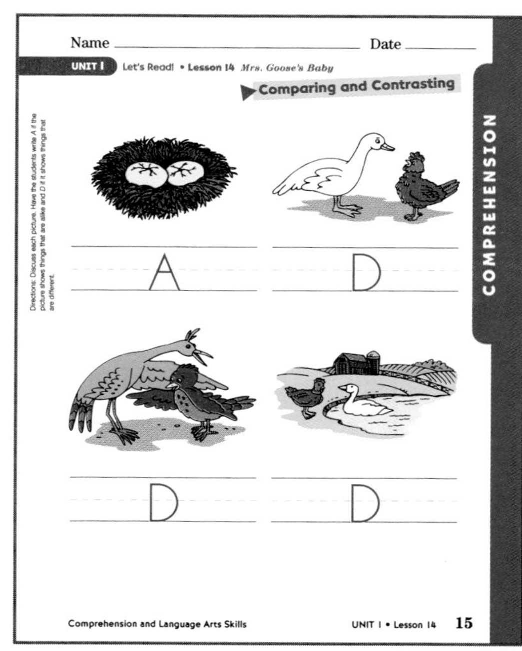

Name ______ Date ______

UNIT 1 Let's Read! • Lesson 14 *Mrs. Goose's Baby*

Comparing and Contrasting

A D

D D

COMPREHENSION

Comprehension and Language Arts Skills UNIT 1 • Lesson 14 15

Comprehension and Language Arts Skills pp. 14–15

Purposes for Reading

Remind students that before reading the story, they talked about what is special about Mrs. Goose's baby. Ask students to describe what they think is special about Mrs. Goose's baby.

Universal Access: Meeting Individual Needs

Reteach

For additional practice with comparing and contrasting, have students complete ***Reteach: Comprehension and Language Arts Skills*** pp. 8–9.

Challenge

For a challenge with comparing and contrasting, have students complete ***Challenge:*** Comprehension and Language Arts Skills page 8.

Objectives

- Students will continue sharing and working on their alphabet book.
- Students will apply concepts and ideas through a curricular connection.

Materials

- Class alphabet book

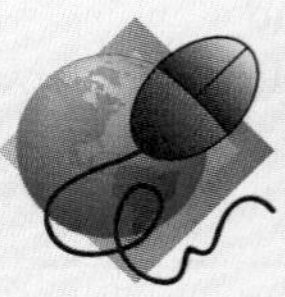

www.sra4kids.com
Web Connection
Help the students look for additional information about poems and rhymes by using the Web connections that are available at the Reading link of the SRA Web page.

INVESTIGATION

Supporting the Investigation

Investigating Concepts Beyond the Text

Remind students about the alphabet book they are working on for this unit.

- Invite the students to continue sharing their pages of the alphabet book as they move through the alphabet.
- Comment on any words used and on how students have organized their pages.

Drama Connection

Talk Without Speaking

Purpose: To have students assume roles that exhibit concentration and contribute to the action of classroom dramatizations based on personal experience and heritage, imagination, literature, and history

- Remind the students of the previous discussion on print awareness. Have students explain what they now know about speech balloons and large print used for emphasis. Be sure they realize that when the word *Honk* got larger in "Mrs. Goose's Baby," the reader understands how loudly Mrs. Goose is shouting and her mood.
- Tell the students that actors on the stage express their ideas and emotions through their body gestures and facial expressions. Students can use their bodies in the same way.
- Read the following activities to the class. Have students work with a partner, using only actions and facial expressions to do the activities. Do not allow words or sounds.
  1. You want to say "no" without speaking. What actions can you make?
  2. How many ways can you say "yes" without speaking?
  3. What actions say "I don't know"?
  4. Your class is going to the zoo. How do you act when you feel excited?

Objectives

Word Analysis Vocabulary

- **Vocabulary Strategies: Context Clues.** Using words from "Mrs. Goose's Baby," identify helpful context clues as a way to infer meaning of unfamiliar vocabulary.

Writing Process Strategies

- **Introduction to the Writing Process.** Building on the theme Let's Read!, learn strategies for drafting and understand that writing is a process that involves drafting.

English Language Conventions

Listening, Speaking, Viewing

- **Language: Informal and Formal Language.** Using the selection "Mrs. Goose's Baby," distinguish between informal and formal language.

Materials

- Big Book Let's Read!, pp. 42–53
- Writing Folder
- Writer's Workbook p. 3

UNIVERSAL ACCESS: MEETING INDIVIDUAL NEEDS

Reteach, Challenge, English-Language Development and ***Intervention*** lessons are available to support the language arts instruction in this lesson.

Research in Action

Language

Children, their parents, and others in the immediate community share vocabulary, grammar, dialect, and accent. After about five years of age, the community exerts more influence on the shape of a child's language than the parents do (but the language children develop is still referred to as the *home language*). As a result, when parents from the Northwest move to the South, they generally do not begin speaking with a Southern dialect and accent, but their children normally do. . . . (*James D. Williams.* Preparing to Teach Writing: Research, Theory, and Practice)

OVERVIEW

Language Arts Overview

Word Analysis

Context Clues The Vocabulary activity in this lesson focuses on vocabulary from "Mrs. Goose's Baby" to draw attention to context clues. Check to see that students grasp the concept of using context clues to infer meaning of unfamiliar words. If particular students have not participated in class discussions, follow up on their progress by assessing their ability to recognize words in a sentence that offer meaningful hints for an unfamiliar word. Refer back to previous lessons as needed.

Vocabulary Skill Words

pond **cuddled**

Writing Process Strategies

The Writing Process Strategies lesson introduces students to the writing process by providing an overview of drafting. Teachers modeling drafting can have a strong influence on the way beginning writers go about it. In this lesson students will apply the drafting instruction by beginning to draft their autobiographies.

English Language Conventions

Listening, Speaking, Viewing **Language: Informal and Formal Language** This lesson provides an introduction to the differences between formal and informal language in students' speech. Families send many children to school speaking a home language and expect them to learn standard English, the language of government, science, business, technology, and education. This lesson provides an opportunity to review classsroom rules for the types of language that will be acceptable in your classroom.

Word Analysis

Vocabulary

Context Clues Reading 2.4, 3.2

Teach

- Write the following sentences from "Mrs. Goose's Baby" on the board: *Mrs. Goose took her baby to the pond to teach her how to swim. But her baby just sat on the shore.*
- Ask the students what clues they have for the meaning of the word *pond*. *(You can swim in it. It has a shore.)*

Guided Practice

- Write the following sentence on the board from "Mrs. Goose's Baby." *The baby followed Mrs. Goose everywhere and cuddled up to her at night.*"
- Have the students explain what the word *cuddled* means from the context clues in the poem.
- Conclude by explaining that context clues help students understand the meanings of unknown words.

Writing Process Strategies

Introduction to the Writing Process

Write for Autobiography Writing 2.1

Teach

- Have the students review the web they made about themselves in ***Writer's Workbook*** page 3.
- Explain that they have a plan for their autobiographies, and now it is time to write their ideas into sentences quickly.

Independent Practice

- Have students use their webs to write their autobiography drafts on a sheet of paper.
- Explain that they can change their plans at any time before or while they are drafting.
- Have the students keep their drafts in their ***Writing Folders.***
- Conclude by emphasizing the importance of getting your ideas on paper.

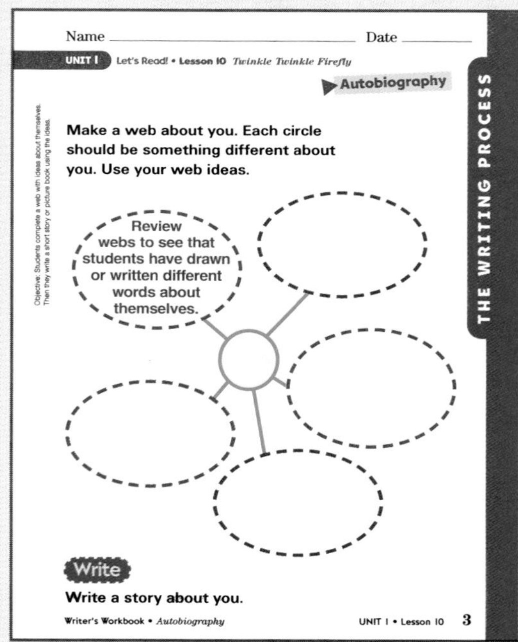

Name ______ Date ______

UNIT 1 Let's Read! • Lesson 10 *Twinkle Twinkle Firefly*

Autobiography

THE WRITING PROCESS

Make a web about you. Each circle should be something different about you. Use your web ideas.

Review webs to see that students have drawn or written different words about themselves.

Write

Write a story about you.

Writer's Workbook • *Autobiography* UNIT 1 • Lesson 10 3

***Writer's Workbook* p. 3**

English Language Conventions

Listening, Speaking, Viewing

Language: Informal and Formal Language

Listen/Speak 1.0

Teach

- Explain to the students that today they are going to practice school language. In the story "Mrs. Goose's Baby," the speech balloons show how the mother and baby speak to each other at home.
- Explain that in school there are several rules for language. These may include:
  - Showing respect for other students by not calling anyone mean names
  - Refusing to let someone play with you
  - Not using bad words
  - Showing respect for school staff by calling them by their titles
  - Not talking back to the teacher or each other
  - Using please and thank you

Guided Practice

- Form a circle and invite students to introduce the next person using school language.
- **Teacher Model:** Begin by saying, *My name is ___, and I'd like to introduce ___ to the class.* Have the person you introduced repeat the phrase, introducing the person next in line.
- Repeat until the last person introduces you.
- Close by explaining that the language of school may or may not be the same as your home language. It is all right to speak differently at home and at school.

Informal Assessment

Note students' ability to use school language appropriately in the classroom and in other parts of the school, such as special classes, in the cafeteria, library, or playground.

1 Preparing to Read

Babybuggy

Objectives

- Students will blend sounds orally to form words.
- Students will segment final consonant sounds.
- Students will associate the /h/ sound with the letter *h* in words.
- Students will blend sounds to read words.
- Students will read a ***Decodable Book.***

Materials

- Lion Puppet
- Sound/Spelling Card Stories Audiocassette/CD
- Sound/Spelling Cards
- Routine Card 1, 5, 8
- Letter Cards
- Phonics Skills, pp. 22–23
- High-Frequency Word Cards
- Decodable Books 2, 7

Teacher Tip LETTER CARDS You may wish to have the students use their *m* and *s* cards for the Consonant Discrimination Game.

UNIVERSAL ACCESS:
MEETING INDIVIDUAL NEEDS

ELL Support

For ELD strategies, use the ***English-Language Development Guide,*** Unit 1, Lesson 15.

Intervention Support

For intervention strategies, use the ***Intervention Guide,*** Unit 1, Lesson 15.

Warming Up

Use one or both of the following activities to focus students' attention for the learning that follows.

Consonant Discrimination Game Reading 1.3, 1.4

- Write the letter *m* on one side of the board and the letter *s* on the other side. Touch each letter and have the students say the /m/ and /s/ sounds.
- Clarify the difference between individual letters and words. Explain that each letter represents a sound that is a part of a word.
- Explain that you are going to say some words that begin with those sounds. If a word begins with the /m/ sound, they should point to the letter *m* on the board; if they hear the /s/ sound, they should point to the letter *s*.

man	said	sad	map	mom
see	me	mask	sack	music

The Sounds Like Game Reading 1.3, 1.4

Explain to the students that in this consonant riddle game, they have to replace the *final* sound. Have them answer these riddles.

What starts like *tape* but ends with /k/?
What starts like *rope* but ends with /z/?
What starts like *boom* but ends with /t/?
What starts like *suit* but ends with /p/?
What starts like *flame* but ends with /k/?
What starts like *same* but ends with /l/?
What starts like *mom* but ends with /p/?

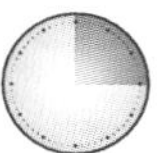

Phonemic Awareness

Oral Blending

One-Syllable Words Reading 1.8, 1.9

- Explain to the students that you are going to tell them a story and that you might need their help blending some of the words.
- Use the following story and questions:

The old brown Frog sat in the /s/ /u/ /n/.
Where did the Frog sit? *(in the sun)*
His pal Toad hid under a /r/ /o/ /k/.
Where did Toad hide? *(under a rock)*
Toad told Frog that the sun would turn him into /m/ /u/ /sh/.
What would Frog turn into? *(mush)*
Frog told Toad that he looked like a gopher's next /m/ /ē/ /l/.
What did Toad look like? *(a gopher's next meal)*
Suddenly it began to /r/ /ā/ /n/.
What did it begin to do? *(rain)*
Frog and Toad played together in the /m/ /u/ /d/.
Where did they play? *(in the mud)*

Segmentation

Restoring Final Consonant Sounds Reading 1.4, 1.9

- Continue final consonant segmentation, but this time ask the students to correct the puppet. Bring out the puppet and continue the game you started in the previous lesson.

Teacher:	seed	
Puppet:	see	
Students:	/d/	seed
Teacher:	teeth	
Puppet:	tee	
Students:	/th/	teeth

- Have the students correct the puppet. Prompt them, if necessary, by asking "What's the whole word? What sound did the puppet leave out?"

Teacher:	loud
Puppet:	lou
Students:	no, *loud!* /d/, /d/, *loud!*

Use the following words:

cloud	lane	seat	seem	brake	brain
train	treat	teach	tease	reach	read

- Divide the students into partners, and have one speak for the puppet while the other gives the puppet words and corrects the answers. After a few moments, have students switch roles.

Research in Action

The final step in oral blending is to blend individual phonemes and recognize the word they form. Success with this activity will help students master what is for many the most difficult step in learning to read. To ease the task, phonemes are presented in story context, which aids in identifying the meaningful word. Also, the first words chosen for oral blending use sounds that are easy to blend. *(Marilyn J. Adams)*

Reading 1.8, 1.9

Universal Access: Meeting Individual Needs

Reteach

PHONEMIC AWARENESS During Workshop, review oral blending and segmentation with groups of students who need extra help.

Teacher Tip MODEL FOR STUDENTS Demonstrate the third puppet activity using two students before having them try it with partners.

SOUND/SPELLING CARD STORIES
PHONICS Use the ***Sound/Spelling Card Stories*** for practice with the /h/ sound. Have students respond by clapping their hands together for each word they hear that starts with the /h/ sound.

UNIVERSAL ACCESS:
MEETING INDIVIDUAL NEEDS

ELL Tip

VOCABULARY Make sure the English-language learners know the meanings of words used in the activities. Use pictures or photos, objects, board stick drawings, pantomime, or the ***English-Language Development Glossary.***

Routine Card
Refer to ***Routine 1*** for an introduction to the sounds and spellings procedure.

LESSON MODELS VIDEOCASSETTE
Use the ***Lesson Models Videocassette*** at this time for a lesson model that shows how to blend *h_*.

PHONICS

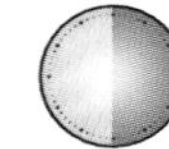

Phonics

Introduce /h/ Spelled *h_* Reading 1.1, 1.3, 1.4, 1.10

- Turn ***Sound/Spelling Card 8—Hound*** around, and tell the students that they will be learning the sound of the letter *h*.
- Read the Hound story that follows:

  Harry the Hound hurries around.
  Can you hear Harry's hurrying hound sound?
  This is the sound Harry's breathing makes when he hurries:
  /h/ /h/ /h/ /h/ /h/ /h/.
  When Harry the Hound sees a hare hop by,
  He tears down the hill, and his four feet fly.
  Hurry, Harry, hurry! /h/ /h/ /h/ /h/ /h/ /h/.
  How Harry the Hound loves to hunt and chase!
  He hurls himself from place to place.
  Hurry, Harry, hurry! /h/ /h/ /h/ /h/ /h/ /h/.
  When Harry the Hound sees a big skunk roam,
  He howls for help and heads for home.
  What sound does Harry make when he hurries?
  (Have students answer:) /h/ /h/ /h/ /h/ /h/ /h/.

- Write the letter *h* on the board and say /h/. Point out the blank line after the letter *h* at the bottom of the card and explain that this line shows that the *h* makes its sound only when it comes at the beginning of a word or syllable.
- Give the students an opportunity to write the spelling on scrap paper or use their index finger to write on a surface or in the air. Have them say /h/ each time they write the letter. When the students write the spelling, have them include the blank line when they say the spelling—say h-blank.
- Tell the students that you will say a number of words and that they should repeat each word. Ask them to signal by raising their hand if they hear the /h/ sound at the beginning of the word and to remain silent if they do not.

hat	**hit**	**hot**	not	**hop**
top	**hip**	rip	**hide**	side
hope	**heap**	deep	roam	**home**
house	mouse	kite	bold	**happy**
hair	**hungry**	tape	**hammock**	**hurry**

- Have the students say some words including their names that begin with the /h/ sound.
- Conclude the activity by reviewing the ***Hound Card*** with the students. The name of the card is ***Hound,*** the sound is /h/, and the spelling is *h_*.

Phonics

Blending Reading 1.1, 1.3, 1.8, 1.9, 1.11

Review the ***Sound/Spelling Cards*** that have been introduced by touching each card and having students say the sound. Then write and blend the following words and sentences with students:

Line 1:	at	hat	sat
Line 2:	am	ham	Sam
Line 3:	as	has	
Sentence:	Matt has a hat.		

About the Words and Sentences Reading 1.1, 1.3, 1.8, 1.9, 1.11

Line 1: Write, touch, and have the students say the sound for each spelling in the word *at*. Signal students to blend by moving your hand under the word. Then have them say the word naturally.

- Have the word used in a sentence and have the sentence extended by asking questions such as where, when, and how.
- For the word *hat*, write each letter, touch it, and have students say each sound. Blend the sounds successively in the following manner: after writing and sounding /h/ /a/ *(ha)*, make the blending motion and have the students blend through the vowel (/ha/).
- Write *t*, have the students say the /t/ sound, make the blending motion under the word, and have students blend *hat*. To encourage natural pronunciation ask, "What's the word?"
- Have the word used in a sentence and have the sentence extended.
- Blend *sat* in the same way. Discuss how the words in the line are alike. If necessary, call attention to the repeated spelling pattern *-at*. Quickly have all the words in the line reread.

Line 2: Follow the procedure outlined above to build each word letter by letter as students say each sound and blend the words.

Line 3: Point out that a final *s* often makes a sound like a *z*.

Sentence: Before writing the sentence, introduce the high-frequency words *has* and *a* by writing them on the board and pronouncing them. Explain to students that *a* does not make the /a/ sound because it does not follow the rules. Say the word *a* again and have students repeat the word several times. Write *has* on the board and pronounce it. Explain to students that the *s* in *has* makes the /z/ sound. Say the word *has* again and have students repeat the word several times. Tell students that *has* and *a* are words they will see many times in their reading. Underline them and have students use *has* and *a* in sentences.

PHONICS

Reading 1.8

Universal Access: Meeting Individual Needs

Intervention Tip

BLENDING During Workshop, repeat the blending activity with individuals or small groups of students who need additional practice. If students have difficulty extending sentences, help them by asking *when, how, why,* and *who* questions.

ELL Tip

/H/ SOUND Have the students put their hands in front of their mouths. When they make the /h/ sound, they can feel a puff of air on their hands. When you introduce /h/, be sure to present the spelling as *h_*. The blank indicates the *h* is /h/ only at the beginning of a word or syllable.

ELL Tip

SILENT *H* IN SPANISH In Spanish, the *h* is silent. Help students make the /h/ sound by pretending they are the *hurrying hound* that is out of breath—/h/, /h/, /h/. Blend words beginning with *h_* sound by sound so the students focus on the sound of the *h_* spelling. Have them hold their hands in front of their mouths to feel the stream of breath made when /h/ is spoken.

Reading 1.8

Teacher Tip BLENDING In the first blending lessons, have all the words used in sentences; as more words are included in the blending exercise, you probably will want to select some words to be used in sentences.

Reading 1.8

Informal Assessment

During the lesson, observe six or seven students per day by calling on them individually to determine if they can blend initial consonant sounds orally. Do this each day until you have checked every student. Record you observations in the Teacher Observation Log in the ***Program Assessment Teacher's Edition.***

UNIVERSAL ACCESS:
MEETING INDIVIDUAL NEEDS

Reteach

/h/ SPELLED h Use ***Reteach: Phonics Skills*** pages 22 and 23 for additional practice.

Challenge

/h/ SPELLED h Use ***Challenge: Phonics Skills*** page 16 with students who are ready for a challenge.

Name ______ Date ______

UNIT I Let's Read! • Lesson 15 *Babybuggy*

Sounds and Spellings

h_

h h h h h h h h h

H H H H H H H

Completing Sentences

A tam is a hat.

Matt has a ham.

22 UNIT I • Lesson 15 *Consonant Sounds and Spellings* • Phonics Skills

Name ______ Date ______

UNIT I Let's Read! • Lesson 15 *Babybuggy*

Listening for Consonants

h h

h

h h

Phonics Skills • *Consonant Sounds and Spellings* UNIT I • Lesson 15 23

Phonics Skills pp. 22–23

PHONICS

- Write today's sentence on the board *(Matt has a hat.)*, sounding and blending each word as described above. Frame each word, one at a time, with your hands.
- Ask how students know where one word stops and the next one begins. *(There is a space between words.)*
- Then help the students tell how they know where a sentence begins and where it ends. *(The first word has a capital letter; it ends with a punctuation mark.)*
- After all the words in the sentence have been read, have the sentence reread in a natural and fluent manner.
- Ask the students to tell what was special at the beginning *(a capital letter)* and at the end *(a period)*.

Developing Oral Language Reading 1.1, 1.3

To review the words, point to them in random order and have students read them. Ask the students to find and erase the word for each of the following clues.

You might put this meat in a sandwich. *(ham)*

You wear this on your head. *(hat)*

It's a name. *(Sam)*

Phonics Skills Reading 1.3, 1.8

- ***Phonics Skills*** pages 22–23 reinforce the /h/ sound spelled *h*__. Help the students complete the first page at this time. They will practice writing *h* on the first line and *H* on the second. At the bottom of the page, have them say the name of each picture. Then blend the sounds in each word to read the sentences, writing the name of each picture in the blank.
- On page 23, have the students write *h* under each picture whose name begins with the /h/ sound. *(The names of the pictures are: hand, house, ant, mouse, turtle, hat, table, helicopter, and hamburger.)*

Dictation and Spelling

Dictation: Word Building Game Reading 1.1, 1.3, 1.4, 1.8, 1.9; Eng. Lang. Conv. 1.8

- Students will need the ***Letter Cards*** *a*, *h*, *m*, and *t*. The list of words for this Word Building Game follows:

  at
  am
  ham
  hat
  mat

- Say the word *at*. Have the students repeat the word. Pronounce the word slowly, sound by sound, blending the sounds into the word, and have students find the corresponding ***Sound/Spelling Card.*** Have students spell the word using their ***Letter Cards*** while you write it on the board. Students should compare their words to yours and proofread as necessary. Blend and read the word and then point to each letter and spell the word.
- Follow the same procedure for the words *am* and *ham*, focusing on the new sounds. Model the spelling at the board.

Spelling: /h/ Spelled *h_* Reading 1.3

- Point to the ***Sound/Spelling Card*** for the /h/ sound ***(Hound).*** Have students make the /h/ sound.
- Write the following sentence fragment on the board:

  Harry Hopkins likes to read about . . .

- Have the students suggest words that begin with the /h/ sound to finish the sentence (*hammers*, *houses*, *hogs*, *helicopters*, *horses*, and so on). Write a few of their suggestions on the board.
- Have a few students come up and underline the letter *h* in each word.
- Read the following words and sentences and have students spell the words on a separate sheet of paper.

at	You are **at** school.	**at**
hat	Henry wears a **hat.**	**hat**
her	Give the pencil to **her.**	**her**
ham	I like to eat **ham.**	**ham**

- Write the words on the board and have students correct their own papers.

PHONICS

Routine Card
Refer to ***Routine 8*** for the dictation and spelling procedures.

Reading 1.3

Teacher Tip DICTATION As an extension, have the students use each word in a sentence.

PHONICS

Reading a Decodable Book Reading 1.1

Core Set, Book 7: *A Hat*

Phonics Focus: /h/ Spelled *h*

High-Frequency Words Reading 1.3

No high-frequency words are introduced in this book. Review the high-frequency words already in the High-Frequency Word Bank. Have students volunteer to read the ones they recognize.

Reading Recommendations Reading 1.1, 1.2, 1.3, 1.8

- No nondecodable words are in this book.
- Have the students read the title and browse the story.
- Have students read a page silently, then read the page aloud. Repeat this procedure for each page.
- Have another student reread the page before going on.
- Reread the story at least twice, calling on different students to read. Then have the entire group do a choral reading of the story.
- As students read, have them blend the sounds to read the words *Matt*, *has*, *hat*,and *ham*.

Teacher Tip **DECODABLE BOOKS** Students should keep track of their readings on a personal title sheet. Make a six-column chart for the students. The heading for the first column should be ***Decodable Books,*** while the headings for the remaining five columns should read *Date/Partner.* List the ***Decodable Books*** in the first column. Tell the students that each time they read one of the ***Decodables,*** they should fill in the date and/or the partner with whom they've read the book. They can read the same book up to five times. They can do this at the end of a lesson, after they have read the ***Decodable Book*** assigned for that lesson. Students can read the additional ***Decodable*** either by themselves or with a partner. This will encourage faster readers to keep reading, and it will ensure that slower readers will have the time they need to finish reading the assigned ***Decodable.***

Decodable Book 7

Responding Reading 2.2; Listen/Speak 1.2, 2.2

- Invite the students to discuss any hard words they encountered in *A Hat* and how they figured out these words. Call on volunteers to retell the story.
- To make sure the students are focusing on the story, ask questions such as the following, having the students answer by pointing to and reading aloud the words.

  What does Matt have? *(Matt has a hat.)*

  What is in the hat? *(In the hat is a bird.)*

  Where is the ham? *(In the hat is a ham.)*

  Where is the rabbit? *(In the hat is a rabbit.)*

Building Fluency Reading 1.16

Encourage partners to build fluency by rereading ***Decodable Book 7,*** *A Hat*, of the Core Set. The first time through, one partner should read the odd-numbered pages and the other the even-numbered pages. For the second reading, the partners should switch pages. After the second reading, the partners should choose one of the ***Decodable Books*** from previous lessons and continue to read to each other. If students need extra practice with /h/ spelled *h* have them read ***Decodable Book 2,*** *Tam Has Ham*, of the Practice Set.

Informal Assessment

MONITORING Observe five or six students as they read *The Hat.* Continue this observation over the next several days until you have observed all students. Note students who seem to understand the concepts of picture and word; observe their left-to-right tracking and whether they can recognize a word that is out of position. Record your observations in the Teacher Observation Log in the ***Program Assessment Teacher's Edition.***

Teacher Tip **RESPONDING** Watch for students who can't find the answers and work with them during Workshop.

Routine Card
Refer to ***Routine 5*** for reading ***Decodable Books.***

Pages 54–55 of *Let's Read!*

Objectives

- Students will share prior knowledge about rhyme.
- Students will listen and respond to the selection.
- Students will substitute initial consonant sounds orally.
- Students will illustrate individual words.
- Students will talk about the parts of a poem.
- Students will discuss words that describe the weather.

Materials

- Big Book *Let's Read!*, pp. 54–55
- Home Connection, p. 7

SELECTION INTRODUCTION

About the Author Reading 3.2

Jane Yolen, who lives in Hatfield, Massachusetts, has written more than 100 books for children and young people. She was a founding member of the Western New England Storytellers Guild and the Bay State Writers' Guild, and she has actively supported new writers of children's books by holding regular writers' workshops.

Other Books by Jane Yolen

Owl Moon, illustrated by John Schoenherr (Caldecott Medal); Commander Toad series for early readers

About the Illustrator Reading 3.2

Rex Schneider is an author, illustrator, and filmmaker. He primarily illustrates for children's literature. He was named a Children's Choice by the International Reading Association for authoring and illustrating *The Wide-Mouthed Frog.*

Other Books Illustrated by Rex Schneider

That's Not All!; I'm Nobody, Who Are You?; Jog, Frog, Jog

Selection Summary

Genre: Poetry

Students will delight in hearing and reciting the silly words in this poem about a baby ladybug and its funny adventures.

The elements of poetry are listed below. Poetry may have one or more of these elements.

- Sentences are sometimes broken into parts. Each part is on a line of its own.
- Words that rhyme are often used.
- The lines of a poem often have rhythm or meter.
- Some words may be repeated.

Inquiry Connections

In this selection of the ***Big Book,*** the students will listen to a silly rhyme about ladybugs.

Key concepts explored are

- the elements of poetry.
- matching oral words to printed words.
- becoming more aware of print.

Direct the students to the Concept/Question Board. Encourage them to post any questions or ideas they have about the unit. They may want to include a drawing or poem about ladybugs or other kinds of bugs.

- Make sure the students put their names or initials on anything they post on the Board.
- Tell them that they can post something on the Board any day. Be sure to have students discuss what they put on the Board with the class.

Concept/Question Board

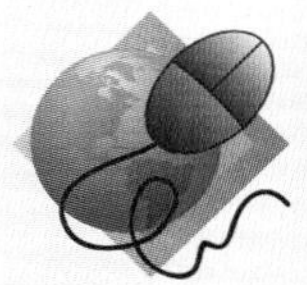

www.sra4kids.com
Web Connection
Remind students to look for additional information about ladybugs by using Web connections that are available at the Reading link of the **SRA** Web page.

UNIVERSAL ACCESS:
MEETING INDIVIDUAL NEEDS

ELL Support

For ELD strategies, use the ***English-Language Development Guide,*** Unit 1, Lesson 15.

Intervention Support

For intervention strategies, use the ***Intervention Guide,*** Unit 1, Lesson 15.

Routine Card
Refer to ***Routine 11*** for the procedure for reading the selection.

Reading 2.6

Teacher Tip ACTIVATE PRIOR KNOWLEDGE Tell the students that good readers typically activate what they already know about a topic before reading something new about the topic.

Build Background

Activate Prior Knowledge

- Tell the students that this rhyme has lots of funny-sounding words. Ask whether they remember other rhymes with funny-sounding words. As necessary, help them recall the nonsense words in "Hey, Diddle, Diddle."
- Have students look at the first illustration, and ask whether anyone can identify this "bug." The spots on her wings should help students recognize a ladybug.

Preview and Prepare

Browse

- Remind the students that good readers browse before they read.
- Display pages 54–55 of *Let's Read!* and read the title of the rhyme. Point to and read the names of the author and the illustrator.
- Allow the students to discuss what they notice about the poem. If they comment on the illustrations only, ask them what they notice about the print. They also might identify some high-frequency words they have learned already.
- Before reading the selection to the students, read the Focus Questions on the first page of the selection together. Briefly discuss the questions, and tell the students to keep these questions in mind as you read.

Set Purposes

Explain to the students that readers sometimes read poems for fun. Suggest to students that the poem "Babybuggy" is about having fun with rhyming words and playing with the word *buggy*. Have students distinguish which words in the poem rhyme and which ones do not.

Selection Vocabulary

This poem is full of made-up words that offer students many opportunities for word play and for creating their own silly words. Discuss with the students the word *buggy.* Tell them that this word is used to describe things that the bugs have in the story.

Reading Recommendations

Read Aloud

- Give an animated reading of the poem without pausing.
- Reread the poem and invite students to chime in on all the words that end in *-uggy.*

Using Comprehension Strategies Listen/Speak 1.2

Comprehension strategy instruction allows students to become aware of what good readers do when they read. Good readers constantly check their understanding as they are reading and ask themselves questions. Skilled readers also recognize when they are having problems understanding a selection and stop to use various comprehension strategies to help them make sense of what they are reading.

During the reading of this selection, you will model the use of the following comprehension strategy:

- **Asking Questions** helps readers focus their attention on what they are reading, and engages them in a deeper understanding of themes, concepts, and ideas.

Building Comprehension Strategies

During the reading of "Babybuggy," have the students decide whether it is real or fantasy.

Routine Card
Refer to ***Routine 10*** for the Selection Vocabulary procedure.

Teacher Tip HIGH-FREQUENCY WORDS The following high-frequency words appear in the selection: *a, on,* and *the.* Point to these words in the High-Frequency Word Bank, have students read them, and encourage them to read these words with you when you encounter them in the reading.

UNIVERSAL ACCESS:
MEETING INDIVIDUAL NEEDS

ELL Tip

PRETEACH Before reading a selection, talk to the English-language learners about the illustrations in it. Associating the words in the text with the illustrations helps the English-language learners learn English words.

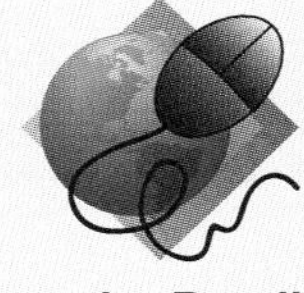

www.sra4kids.com
Web Connection
Remind students to look for additional funny poems by using Web connections that are available at the Reading link of the SRA Web page.

Teacher Tip COMPREHENSION Skilled readers constantly evaluate their understanding of what they read. Stop often to make sure you and the students are doing this.

Teacher Tip ASKING QUESTIONS An extended lesson on Asking Questions can be found on page T319. This lesson is intended to give extra practice with asking questions.

COMPREHENSION

Comprehension Strategies

Teacher Modeling

Asking Questions *We will understand what we read if we ask questions. By looking at pages 54 and 55, what questions can you ask about the poem?* (Answers will vary; accept all reasonable answers.)

Phonemic Awareness Reading 1.4

INITIAL CONSONANT SOUNDS Invite students to join you in making new words by changing the first sounds in the following words from the poem: *gives, him, big, wait, pull, silly,* and *baby.* Suggest that the initial sound replacement for each word might make a real word or a nonsense word. List students' suggestions on the board under *Real* or *Nonsense.*

Teacher Tip READING FOR ENJOYMENT Remind students that they should spend at least 20 minutes reading after school.

Focus Questions What words rhyme with buggy? What do you think is a babybuggy?

Babybuggy

Jane Yolen
illustrated by
Rex Schneider

Ladybuggy's
babybuggy
rides inside
a buggysnuggie.

When he cries,
Ms. Ladybuggy
gives him a big
buggyhuggy.

54

Comprehension Skills

Reality and Fantasy

Tell the students that one way we can better understand a selection is by figuring out whether it could really happen or not. Remind the students that they figured out that "The Chase" could not really happen. Have the students retell what clues told them that "The Chase" was not real. Then discuss whether "Babybuggy" is real or not. *(No, it is not real because animals cannot talk and they do not wear clothes.)*

UNIVERSAL ACCESS: MEETING INDIVIDUAL NEEDS

Challenge

INDEPENDENT READING Some students will be ready to read, but others will benefit from turning pages and thinking about pictures and stories. Provide a selection of trade books for students to choose from. If your class is using the small version of *Let's Read!,* encourage students to read on their own during Workshop.

California Theme Connection
Reading/Language Arts

Read California Cheer!
Hey all you reading fans
Stand up and clap your hands (clap, clap, clap)
Hey all you reading fans
Stand up and stomp your feet (stomp, stomp, stomp)
Clap your hands (clap, clap, clap)
Stomp your feet (stomp, stomp, stomp)
READ California, read, read, **read!**

Discuss with students how the Read California Cheer will get them excited about reading.

COMPREHENSION

Writing 1.1

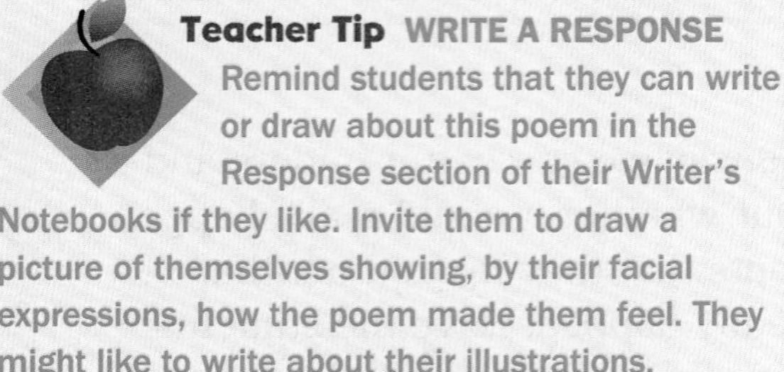

Teacher Tip WRITE A RESPONSE Remind students that they can write or draw about this poem in the Response section of their Writer's Notebooks if they like. Invite them to draw a picture of themselves showing, by their facial expressions, how the poem made them feel. They might like to write about their illustrations.

Discussing the Selection

Reading 1.3; Listen/Speak 1.4, 1.5

- Ask the students what words they thought were silly or made up in this selection. Then discuss what normal words the silly words came from (for example, *buggymuggy* came from *bug* and *mug*). If necessary, reread the lines to remind students of the silly words. Encourage the students to use basic conversation strategies such as asking questions, taking turns, raising a hand to speak, and staying on the topic of discussion.
- Ask the students to look at the picture of the ladybug taking a bath. Have them discuss how this fun picture helps them understand the main idea of the text.
- Ask the students to think about the following questions:

  What might happen if the baby pulled the buggypluggy? Can you think of a sound the water might make? *(Students' responses will vary.)*
- Ask the students to describe how this poem made them feel differently about ladybugs. Compare their feelings about ladybugs to their feelings about some of the other animals featured in earlier selections.
- With students, refer back to the Focus Questions for the selection. Have all the questions been answered? If not, answer them now.

Have the students record their responses to the selection in the Response Journal Section of their Writer's Notebooks by drawing pictures. Help the students label their drawings.

Review Selection Vocabulary

As students dictate, write a list of words that rhyme with *buggy* on the board. Briefly discuss what the words mean. Invite students to illustrate their favorite *-uggy* word.

Print and Book Awareness

Illustration/Text Relationship

- Ask the students what they notice about how the lines of "Babybuggy" are grouped. Tell them that the lines are in groups, called stanzas, of four lines each.
- Ask the students why they think the lines are divided up like this, and help them understand that each stanza shares something new about Babybuggy.
- Point out the humorous way the illustrator of "Babybuggy" dealt with the ladybug's three pairs of legs; for example, Ms. Ladybuggy is using one pair of legs to hold a book while another pair is holding a broom. Mention that beetles, like all insects, have six legs.

Supporting the Reading

Comprehension Strategy: Asking Questions Listen/Speak 1.2

Remind the students that they asked questions when they listen to "Babybuggy." Encourage them to look again at pages 54–55 to see whether there are any more questions they'd like to discuss.

Purposes for Reading

Remind the students that before reading the poem, they talked about having fun with rhyming words and exploring an imaginary world. Ask students how this poem served these two purposes.

Home Connection

Distribute ***Home Connection*** page 7, which provides an art activity for students to do with their family in remembrance of *Let's Read!*'s last selections. This letter also is available in Spanish on page 8.

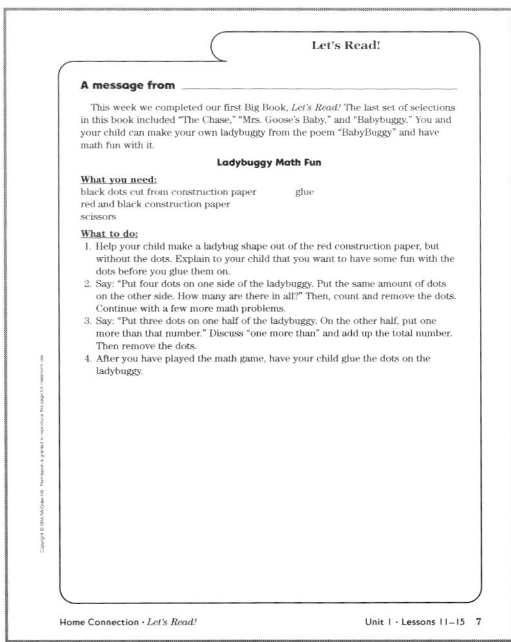

Let's Read!

A message from ____________

This week we completed our first Big Book, *Let's Read!* The last set of selections in this book included "The Chase," "Mrs. Goose's Baby," and "Babybuggy." You and your child can make your own ladybuggy from the poem "BabyBuggy" and have math fun with it.

Ladybuggy Math Fun

What you need:
black dots cut from construction paper
glue
red and black construction paper
scissors

What to do:
1. Help your child make a ladybug shape out of the red construction paper, but without the dots. Explain to your child that you want to have some fun with the dots before you glue them on.
2. Say: "Put four dots on one side of the ladybuggy. Put the same amount of dots on the other side. How many are there in all?" Then, count and remove the dots. Continue with a few more math problems.
3. Say: "Put three dots on one half of the ladybuggy. On the other half, put one more than that number." Discuss "one more than" and add up the total number. Then remove the dots.
4. After you have played the math game, have your child glue the dots on the ladybuggy.

Home Connection • *Let's Read!* Unit 1 • Lessons 11–15 7

Home Connection p. 7

Objectives

- Students will complete their alphabet book.
- Students will generate rhyming words.

Materials

- Class alphabet book

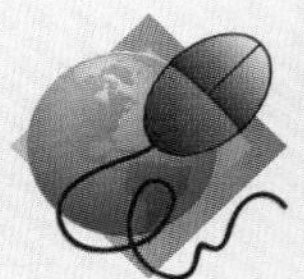

www.sra4kids.com
Web Connection
Help the students look for additional information about poems and rhymes by using the Web connections that are available at the Reading link of the SRA Web page.

INVESTIGATION

Supporting the Investigations

Investigating Concepts Beyond the Text

Remind the students about the alphabet book they are working on for this unit.

- Remind the students that they have read several rhyming poems in this unit. Review one or two. Then ask students to complete this rhyming couplet.

  Come with me and take a look.

  Come and read this alphabet _____.

- Add this couplet to the beginning of the alphabet book.
- Share the completed alphabet book again and then add it to the class library.

Concept/Question Board

Ask students to look at the Concept/Question Board

- Are there any questions on the Board that they can answer now?
- Have students read and think about posted questions, articles, pictures, and other materials that interest them and provide answers to their questions or provoke new questions.
- Remind students that they will continue to utilize the Concept/Question Board in the next unit.

INVESTIGATION

Teacher Tip MATERIALS For this Language Arts Connection, you will need rhyming cards.

Language Arts Connection

Making Rhymes Reading 1.6; Listen/Speak 2.1

Purpose: To practice rhyming through the use of well-known melodies and to learn the difference between rhyming and non-rhyming words

- Recall with students the rhyming words *tree* and *sea* in their selection. Then hold up pairs of rhyming cards. Name the first object pictured and a verb. For example, holding up a picture of a duck and a truck, prompt: Have you ever seen a duck driving a ________ ?
- After several rhymes are made using the cards, prompt for rhymes without using cards; for example: Yesterday I saw some ants doing a _______ .
- Here is a list of pairs from which you could build rhyming cards, including unpictured words in parentheses to use without cards.

  fish, dish (wish)

  cat, bat, hat, (flat, sat)

  bug, mug, rug, (hug)

  snake, cake, rake (ache)

  goat, boat, coat, (float)

  flea, knee, key, (see)
- Ask students to try to think of new rhyming words to go with the well-known melodies such as "Twinkle, Twinkle, Little Star" or "Mary Had a Little Lamb." After singing both songs, ask students which song they prefer. Explain that they don't have to think of new words for the whole song; for example, "Twinkle, Twinkle, Little Car."

Objectives

Word Analysis Vocabulary

- **Vocabulary Strategies: Context Clues.** Using words from "Babybuggy," identify helpful context clues as a way to infer meaning of unfamiliar vocabulary.

Writing Process Strategies

- **Introduction to the Writing Process.** Building on the theme Let's Read!, learn strategies for drafting and understand that writing is a process that involves drafting.

English Language Conventions

- **Penmanship: Letters Are Lines.** To extend the letter formation instruction in Phonics and Fluency and understand that letters are made of different types of lines.

Materials

- ***Big Book Let's Read!*** pp. 54–55
- ***Writer's Workbook,*** p. 3

UNIVERSAL ACCESS:
MEETING INDIVIDUAL NEEDS

Reteach, Challenge, English-Language Development and ***Intervention*** lessons are available to support the language arts instruction in this lesson.

Research in Action

Research has shown that students need to encounter a word about twelve times before they know it well enough to improve their comprehension.—*Michael Pressley.*

OVERVIEW

Word Analysis

Vocabulary **Context Clues.** The Vocabulary activity in this lesson reviews the concept of context clues using vocabulary in "Babybuggy." Students should have a basic understanding of inferring meaning of an unfamiliar word from helpful clues embedded in the context of its surrounding sentences. Remind students that using context clues can help them in other curricular areas by enabling them to secure meaning for unknown vocabulary.

Vocabulary Skill Words

ladybug **snug** **hug** **mug** **rug** **tub** **plug**

Writing Process Strategies

The Writing Process Strategies lesson introduces students to the writing process by providing an overview of drafting. Teachers modeling drafting can have a strong influence on the way beginning writers go about it. In this lesson students will apply the drafting instruction by beginning to draft their autobiographies.

English Language Conventions

Penmanship **The Letters are Lines.** This lesson reinforces the letter formation instruction in Phonics and Fluency by teaching students that letters are made of vertical, horizontal, curved, and slanted lines. The instruction in this lesson presents a ball-and-stick model of manuscript handwriting. Continuous stroke models are available in the Appendix of the ***Teacher's Edition.***

Word Analysis

Vocabulary

Context Clues Reading 2.4, 3.2

Teach

- Have students help you make a list of all the rhyming words in "Babybuggy" on the board: *ladybuggy, babybuggy, buggysnuggie, buggyhuggy, buggymuggy, buggyruggy, buggytubby, buggypluggy.*
- Have students look for the key word in each nonsense word that is the clue to the meaning *(bug, snug, hug, mug, rug, tub, plug).* Explain that sometimes the meanings of words are right in the words themselves.

Guided Practice

- Ask students what all the key words have in common. *(They all have to do with being home.)* Explain that even if they didn't understand one of the words, they could figure it out with help from the others.
- Conclude by explaining that context clues help students understand the meanings of unknown words.

Informal Assessment

Check to see which students are beginning to use context clues and which may need help.

Writing Process Strategies

Introduction to the Writing Process

Write for Autobiography Writing 2.1

Teach

- Have students review the webs they made about themselves in ***Writer's Workbook*** page 3.
- Have them review the drafts that they started the previous day. Explain that they made a plan for their autobiographies and now it is time to finish writing their ideas.

Independent Practice

- Have students complete their autobiography drafts.
- Explain that they can change their plans at any time before or while they are drafting.
- Conclude by emphasizing the importance of getting your ideas on paper.

English Language Conventions

Penmanship Writing 1.3

Letters Are Lines

Teach

- Tell students again how we use different types of lines to write letters of the alphabet. These lines are called curved lines, vertical lines, horizontal lines, and slanted lines.
- Ask students to think about the letters they practiced in Phonics and Fluency. Tell them that those letters are all made of the four types of lines, and we are going to look at those letters today.
- **Teacher Model:** Draw a curved, horizontal, vertical, and slanted line on the board to show how these lines look and are formed.

Guided Practice

- Write the letters *I, J, K,* and *L* on the board. Tell the students you need their help finding the lines again.
- Tell students that they first need to find all the vertical lines. Invite a student to come to the board to find and trace the vertical lines (in *I, J, K,* and *L*).
- Ask them to help you find any slanted lines. Invite another student to come to the board to find and trace the slanted lines (in *K*).
- Tell students that you need all the horizontal lines. Invite a student to come to the board to find and trace the horizontal lines (in *I* and *L*).
- Tell the students there is one more line missing. Ask if anyone can find the curved line. Invite a student to come to the board to find and trace the curved line (in *J*).
- Have students practice drawing vertical lines on a sheet of first-grade paper.

Informal Assessment

As students practice writing vertical lines, observe how they hold their pencils and how much control they have in making each stroke.

INVESTIGATION WRAP-UP

Review the Concepts

After you have finished sharing the class Alphabet Book, lead the students in a discussion about the unit activity. Ask the students which part of the activity they enjoyed the most. Which part was the most challenging? Which part was the most interesting?

Review with the students the following key concepts:

- Letters have corresponding sounds.
- Written English is a code system.
- Skilled readers have certain behaviors to help them understand the text.

Tips for Reviewing the Concepts

- If necessary, remind the students of the questions they raised throughout the unit and ask them to discuss each one.
- Students' ideas should determine the discussion.
- Remind the students that they can make their own alphabet book even though they have completed the unit.

Evaluating the Unit

- Have students conduct an evaluation of the unit selections, identifying those selections they found most interesting and those they found least interesting.
- Have students evaluate the different activities in which they participated throughout the unit. Which activities did they find the most enjoyable and informative?
- Invite students to make suggestions about other ideas they would like to learn more about regarding poetry or the alphabet, possibly beginning with any questions left on the Concept/Question Board.

Concept/Question Board

Self-Evaluation

In order for the students to evaluate their experience with the units investigation, ask them the following questions:

- How did you feel about working on the investigation?
- Would you say this investigation was easy, difficult, or somewhere in between?
- What was the hardest part of the investigation?
- What was the easiest?
- What was the most interesting thing you learned?
- What did you discover about the way you learn?
- What are some other ways you could learn more in later investigations?

Formal Assessment Options

Use these summative assessments along with your informal observations to assess student progress.

Written Assessments

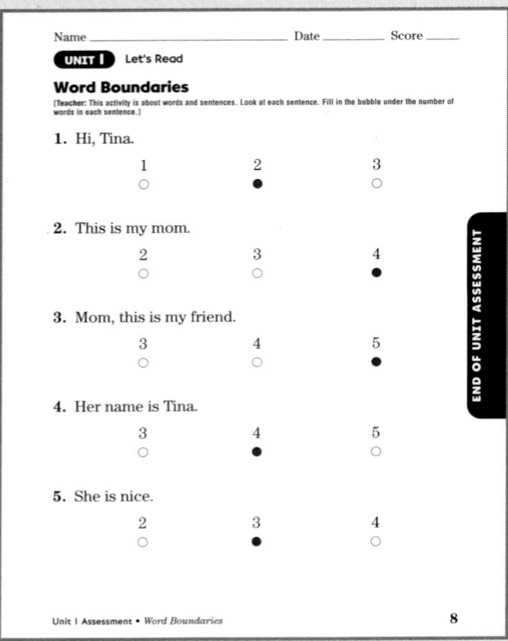

Name ______________ Date ________ Score _____

UNIT I Let's Read

Word Boundaries

[**Teacher:** This activity is about words and sentences. Look at each sentence. Fill in the bubble under the number of words in each sentence.]

1. Hi, Tina.
   1 2 3
2. This is my mom.
   2 3 4
3. Mom, this is my friend.
   3 4 5
4. Her name is Tina.
   3 4 5
5. She is nice.
   2 3 4

END OF UNIT ASSESSMENT

Unit I Assessment • *Word Boundaries* 8

Units 1–6 Assessment p. 8

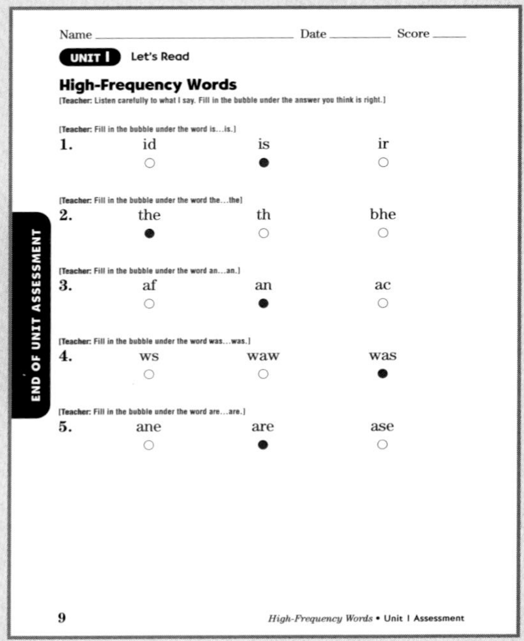

Name ______________ Date ________ Score _____

UNIT I Let's Read

High-Frequency Words

[**Teacher:** Listen carefully to what I say. Fill in the bubble under the answer you think is right.]

[**Teacher:** Fill in the bubble under the word is...is.]
1. id is ir

[**Teacher:** Fill in the bubble under the word the...the]
2. the th bhe

[**Teacher:** Fill in the bubble under the word an...an.]
3. af an ac

[**Teacher:** Fill in the bubble under the word was...was.]
4. ws waw was

[**Teacher:** Fill in the bubble under the word are...are.]
5. ane are ase

END OF UNIT ASSESSMENT

9 *High-Frequency Words* • Unit I Assessment

Units 1–6 Assessment p. 9

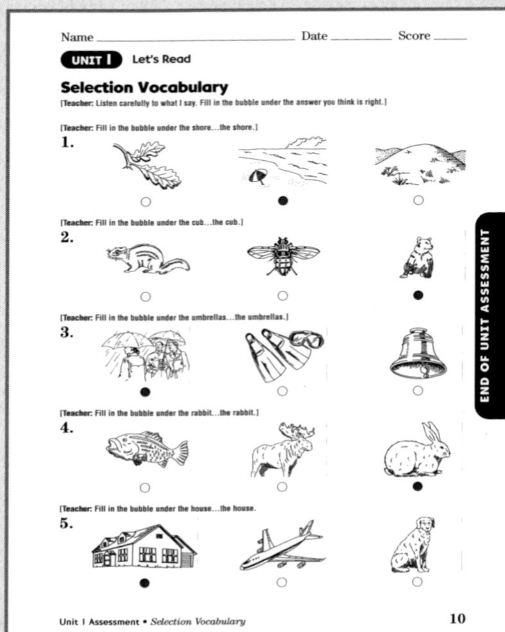

Name ______________ Date ________ Score _____

UNIT I Let's Read

Selection Vocabulary

[**Teacher:** Listen carefully to what I say. Fill in the bubble under the answer you think is right.]

[**Teacher:** Fill in the bubble under the shore...the shore.]
1.

[**Teacher:** Fill in the bubble under the cub...the cub.]
2.

[**Teacher:** Fill in the bubble under the umbrellas...the umbrellas.]
3.

[**Teacher:** Fill in the bubble under the rabbit...the rabbit.]
4.

[**Teacher:** Fill in the bubble under the house...the house.
5.

END OF UNIT ASSESSMENT

Unit I Assessment • *Selection Vocabulary* 10

Units 1–6 Assessment p. 10

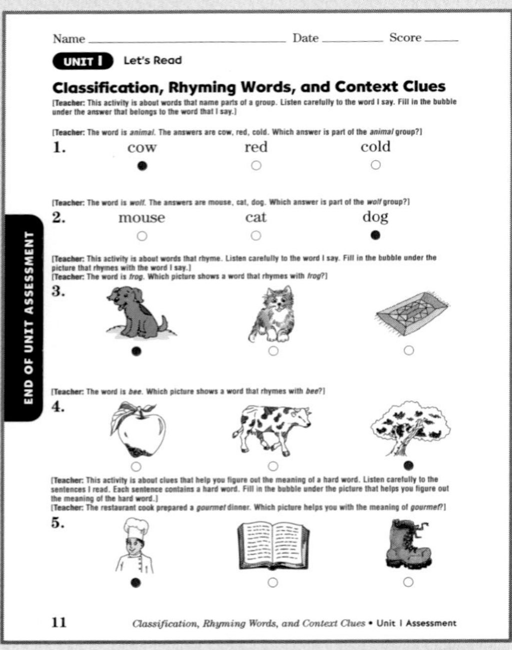

Name ______________ Date ________ Score _____

UNIT I Let's Read

Classification, Rhyming Words, and Context Clues

[**Teacher:** This activity is about words that name parts of a group. Listen carefully to the word I say. Fill in the bubble under the answer that belongs to the word that I say.]

[**Teacher:** The word is *animal*. The answers are cow, red, cold. Which answer is part of the *animal* group?]
1. cow red cold

[**Teacher:** The word is *wolf*. The answers are mouse, cat, dog. Which answer is part of the *wolf* group?]
2. mouse cat dog

[**Teacher:** This activity is about words that rhyme. Listen carefully to the word I say. Fill in the bubble under the picture that rhymes with the word I say.]
[**Teacher:** The word is *frog*. Which picture shows a word that rhymes with *frog*?]
3.

[**Teacher:** The word is *bee*. Which picture shows a word that rhymes with *bee*?]
4.

[**Teacher:** This activity is about clues that help you figure out the meaning of a hard word. Listen carefully to the sentences I read. Each sentence contains a hard word. Fill in the bubble under the picture that helps you figure out the meaning of the hard word.]
[**Teacher:** The restaurant cook prepared a *gourmet* dinner. Which picture helps you with the meaning of *gourmet*?]
5.

END OF UNIT ASSESSMENT

11 *Classification, Rhyming Words, and Context Clues* • Unit I Assessment

Units 1–6 Assessment p. 11

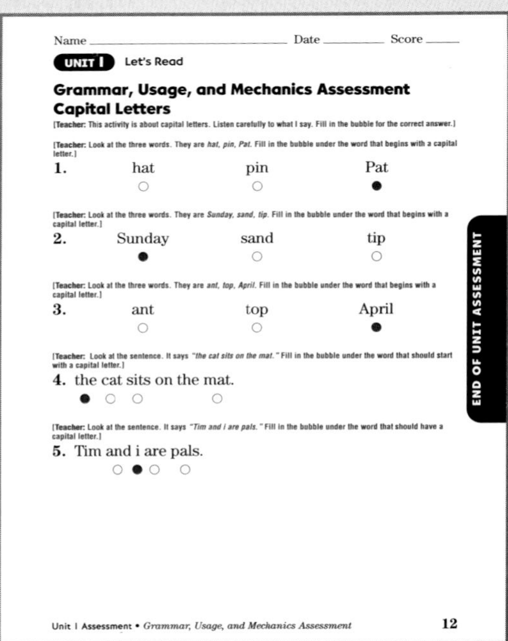

Name ______________ Date ________ Score _____

UNIT I Let's Read

Grammar, Usage, and Mechanics Assessment
Capital Letters

[**Teacher:** This activity is about capital letters. Listen carefully to what I say. Fill in the bubble for the correct answer.]

[**Teacher:** Look at the three words. They are *hat, pin, Pat*. Fill in the bubble under the word that begins with a capital letter.]
1. hat pin Pat

[**Teacher:** Look at the three words. They are *Sunday, sand, tip*. Fill in the bubble under the word that begins with a capital letter.]
2. Sunday sand tip

[**Teacher:** Look at the three words. They are *ant, top, April*. Fill in the bubble under the word that begins with a capital letter.]
3. ant top April

[**Teacher:** Look at the sentence. It says *"the cat sits on the mat."* Fill in the bubble under the word that should start with a capital letter.]
4. the cat sits on the mat.

[**Teacher:** Look at the sentence. It says *"Tim and i are pals."* Fill in the bubble under the word that should have a capital letter.]
5. Tim and i are pals.

END OF UNIT ASSESSMENT

Unit I Assessment • *Grammar, Usage, and Mechanics Assessment* 12

Units 1–6 Assessment p. 12

Oral Assessments

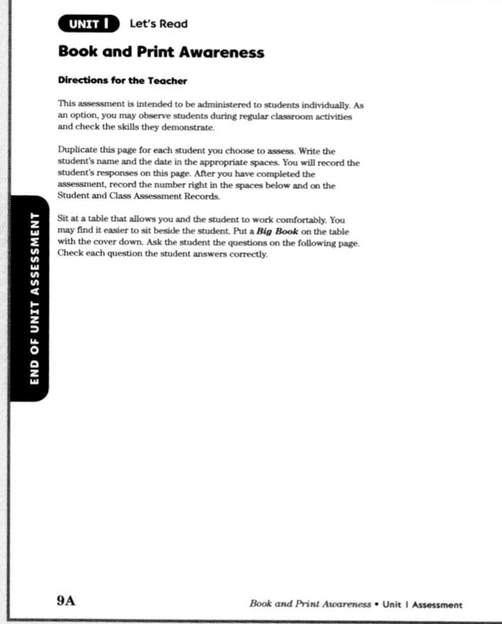

UNIT 1 Let's Read

Book and Print Awareness

Directions for the Teacher

This assessment is intended to be administered to students individually. As an option, you may observe students during regular classroom activities and check the skills they demonstrate.

Duplicate this page for each student you choose to assess. Write the student's name and the date in the appropriate spaces. You will record the student's responses on this page. After you have completed the assessment, record the number right in the spaces below and on the Student and Class Assessment Records.

Sit at a table that allows you and the student to work comfortably. You may find it easier to sit beside the student. Put a ***Big Book*** on the table with the cover down. Ask the student the questions on the following page. Check each question the student answers correctly.

END OF UNIT ASSESSMENT

9A *Book and Print Awareness* • Unit 1 Assessment

***Units 1–6 Assessment, Teacher's Edition* p. 9A**

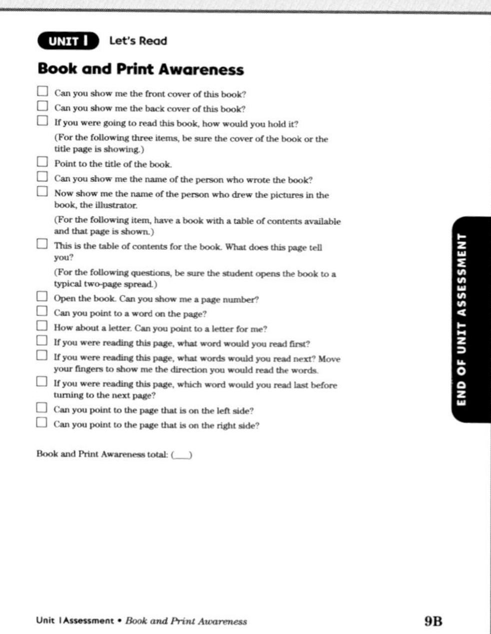

UNIT 1 Let's Read

Book and Print Awareness

- ☐ Can you show me the front cover of this book?
- ☐ Can you show me the back cover of this book?
- ☐ If you were going to read this book, how would you hold it?

(For the following three items, be sure the cover of the book or the title page is showing.)

- ☐ Point to the title of the book.
- ☐ Can you show me the name of the person who wrote the book?
- ☐ Now show me the name of the person who drew the pictures in the book, the illustrator.

(For the following item, have a book with a table of contents available and that page is shown.)

- ☐ This is the table of contents for the book. What does this page tell you?

(For the following questions, be sure the student opens the book to a typical two-page spread.)

- ☐ Open the book. Can you show me a page number?
- ☐ Can you point to a word on the page?
- ☐ How about a letter. Can you point to a letter for me?
- ☐ If you were reading this page, what word would you read first?
- ☐ If you were reading this page, what words would you read next? Move your fingers to show me the direction you would read the words.
- ☐ If you were reading this page, which word would you read last before turning to the next page?
- ☐ Can you point to the page that is on the left side?
- ☐ Can you point to the page that is on the right side?

Book and Print Awareness total: (___)

END OF UNIT ASSESSMENT

Unit 1 Assessment • *Book and Print Awareness* 9B

***Unit 1–6 Assessment, Teacher's Edition* p. 9B**

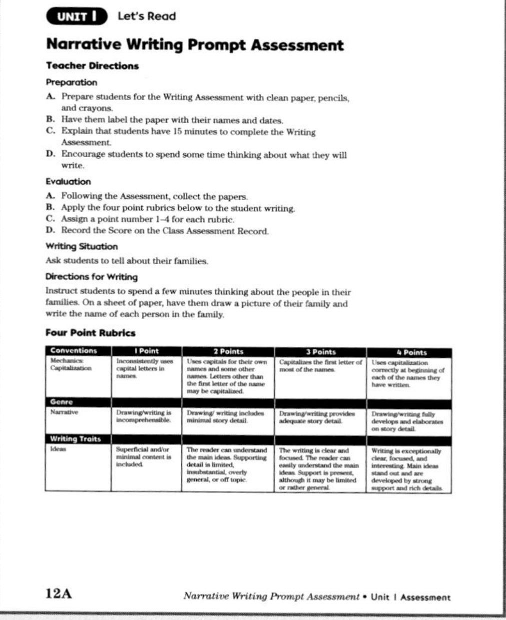

UNIT 1 Let's Read

Narrative Writing Prompt Assessment

Teacher Directions

Preparation

A. Prepare students for the Writing Assessment with clean paper, pencils, and crayons.
B. Have them label the paper with their names and dates.
C. Explain that students have 15 minutes to complete the Writing Assessment.
D. Encourage students to spend some time thinking about what they will write.

Evaluation

A. Following the Assessment, collect the papers.
B. Apply the four point rubrics below to the student writing.
C. Assign a point number 1–4 for each rubric.
D. Record the Score on the Class Assessment Record.

Writing Situation

Ask students to tell about their families.

Directions for Writing

Instruct students to spend a few minutes thinking about the people in their families. On a sheet of paper, have them draw a picture of their family and write the name of each person in the family.

Four Point Rubrics

Conventions	1 Point	2 Points	3 Points	4 Points
Mechanics: Capitalization	Inconsistently uses capital letters in names.	Uses capitals for their own names and some other names. Letters other than the first letter of the name may be capitalized.	Capitalizes the first letter of most of the names.	Uses capitalization correctly at beginning of each of the names they have written.
Genre				
Narrative	Drawing/writing is incomprehensible.	Drawing/ writing includes minimal story detail.	Drawing/writing provides adequate story detail.	Drawing/writing fully develops and elaborates on story detail.
Writing Traits				
Ideas	Superficial and/or minimal content is included.	The reader can understand the main ideas. Supporting detail is limited, insubstantial, overly general, or off topic.	The writing is clear and focused. The reader can easily understand the main ideas. Support is present, although it may be limited or rather general.	Writing is exceptionally clear, focused, and interesting. Main ideas stand out and are developed by strong support and rich details.

12A *Narrative Writing Prompt Assessment* • Unit 1 Assessment

***Unit 1–6 Assessment, Teacher's Edition* p. 12A**

Notes

Use this page to record lessons or elements that work well or need to be adjusted for future reference.

Lessons that work well.

Lessons that need adjustments.

Notes

Use this page to record lessons or elements that work well or need to be adjusted for future reference.

Lessons that work well.

Lessons that need adjustments.

Use this page to record lessons or elements that work well
or need to be adjusted for future reference.

Lessons that work well.

Lessons that need adjustments.

Notes

Use this page to record lessons or elements that work well
or need to be adjusted for future reference.

Lessons that work well.

Lessons that need adjustments.

Notes

Use this page to record lessons or elements that work well or need to be adjusted for future reference.

Lessons that work well.

Lessons that need adjustments.

Use this page to record lessons or elements that work well or need to be adjusted for future reference.

Lessons that work well.

Lessons that need adjustments.

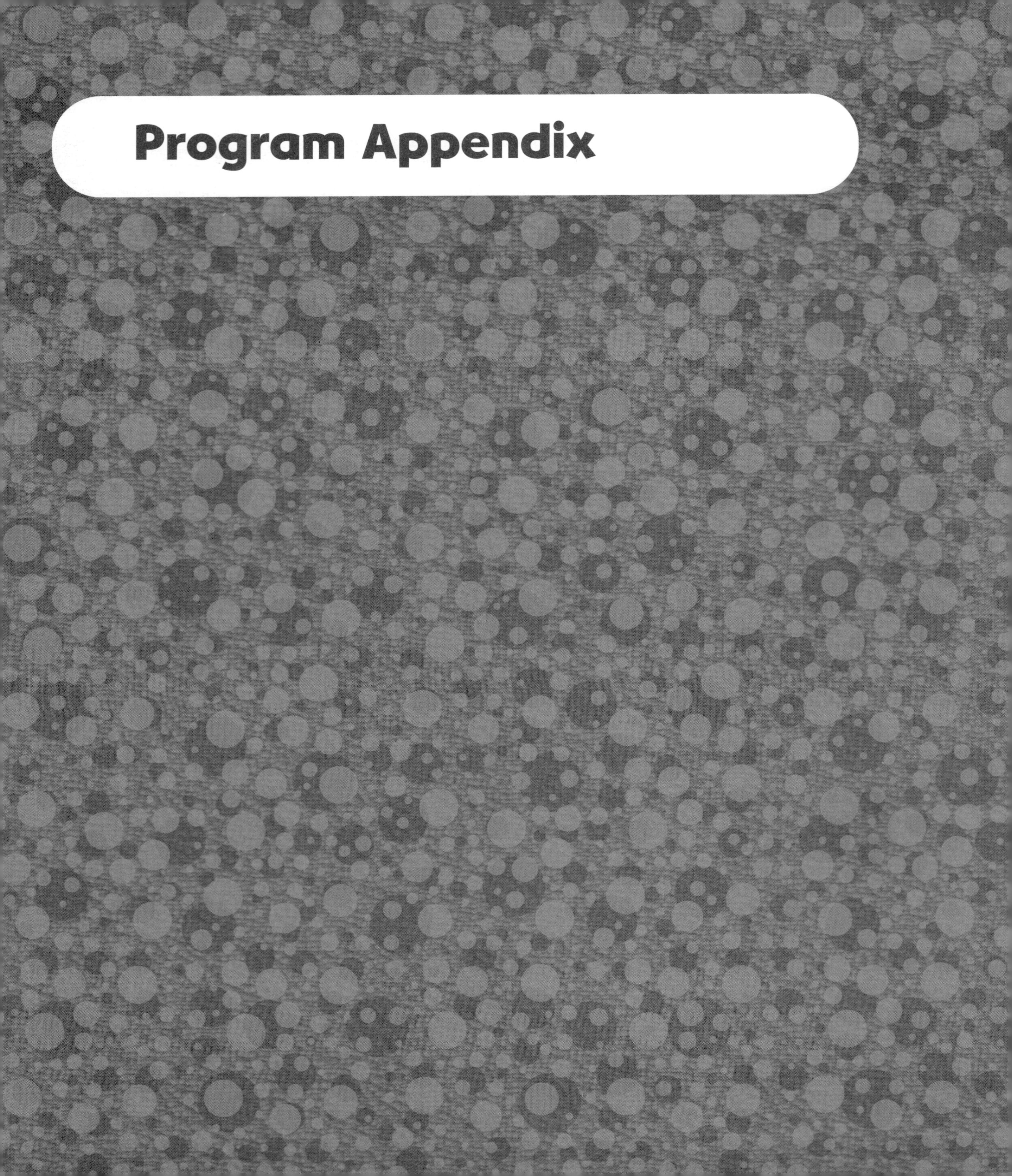

Program Appendix

The Program Assessment includes a step-by-step explanation of procedures for research-based, effective practices in reading instruction that are repeatedly used throughout ***SRA/Open Court Reading.*** These practices may also be used in other instructional materials.

Table of Contents

Effective Teaching Practices

Teacher References

Reading Materials and Techniques

PROGRAM APPENDIX

Different reading materials and techniques are appropriate at different stages of reading development. The purpose of this section is to discuss different types of reading materials and how they may be used most effectively.

Reading Big Books

Purpose

Many students come from homes where they are read to often, but a significant number of other students have not had this valuable experience. Big Books (Levels K and 1) offer all students crucial opportunities to confirm and expand their knowledge about print and reading. They are especially useful for shared reading experiences in the early grades.

The benefits of reading Big Books include engaging even nonreaders in:

- unlocking the books' messages.
- developing print awareness.
- participating in good reading behaviors.
- observing what a good reader does: remarking on the illustrations and the title, asking questions about the content and what might happen, making predictions, and clarifying words and ideas.
- promoting the insight that a given word is spelled the same way every time it occurs as high-frequency words are pointed out.
- reinforcing the correspondence between spoken and written words and spelling patterns.
- enjoying the illustrations and connecting them to the text to help students learn to explore books for enjoyment and information.
- interpreting and responding to literature and expository text before they can read themselves.

Procedure for Reading Big Books

During the first reading of the Big Books, you will model reading behaviors and comprehension strategies similar to those that will later be taught formally. During the second reading, you will address print awareness and teach comprehension skills such as classifying and categorizing or sequencing, which help the reader organize information. In addition, you will teach skills such as making inferences and drawing conclusions, which help the reader focus on the deeper meaning of the text. At first, teachers should expect to do all of the reading but should not prevent students from trying to read on their own or from reading words they already know.

- **Activate Prior Knowledge.** Read the title of the selection and the author's and illustrator's names. At the beginning of each Big Book, read the title of the book and discuss what the whole book is about before going on to reading the first selection.
- **Discuss Prior Knowledge.** Initiate a brief discussion of any prior knowledge the students have that might help them understand the selection.
- **Browse the Selection.** Ask students to tell what they think the story might be about just from looking at the illustrations. This conversation should be brief so that the students can move on to a prereading discussion of print awareness.

Big Books offer all students crucial opportunities to confirm and expand their knowledge about print and reading.

- **Develop Print Awareness.** The focus of browsing the Big Books is to develop awareness of print. Urge students to tell what words or letters they recognize rather than what they expect the selection to be about.

  To develop print awareness, have students look through the selection page by page and comment on whatever they notice in the text. Some students may know some of the words, while others may only recognize specific letters or sounds. The key is to get the students to look at the print separately from the illustrations even before they have heard the actual text content. This process isolates print awareness so that it is not influenced by content. It also gives you a clearer idea of what your students do or do not know about print.
- **Read Aloud.** Read the selection aloud expressively. The reading enables the students simply to hear and enjoy the text as it is read through once. With this reading, you will model behaviors and comprehension strategies that all students will need to develop to become successful readers—for example, asking questions; clarifying unfamiliar words, first by using the pictures and later by using context; or predicting what might happen next.
- **Reread.** Read the selection expressively again. During the second reading of the stories, you will focus on teaching comprehension skills. Also, to develop print awareness, point to each word as it is read, thus demonstrating that text proceeds from left to right and from top to bottom and helping advance the idea that words are individual spoken and written units. Invite the students to identify the rhyming words in a poem or chime in on repetitive parts of text as you point to the words. Or students can read with you on this second reading, depending on the text.
- **Discuss Print.** Return to print awareness by encouraging discussion of anything the students noticed about the words. Young students should begin to realize that you are reading separate words that are separated by spaces. Later, students will begin to see that each word is made up of a group of letters. The students should be encouraged to discuss anything related to the print. For example, you might ask students to point to a word or count the number of words on a line. Or you might connect the words to the illustrations by pointing to a word and saying it and then asking the students to find a picture of that word.
- **Responding.** Responding to a selection is a way of insuring comprehension. Invite students to tell about the story by asking them what they like about the poem or story or calling on a student to explain in his or her own words what the poem or story tells about. Call on others to add to the telling as needed. For nonfiction selections, this discussion might include asking students what they learned about the topic and what they thought was most interesting.

Tips for Using Big Books

- Make sure the entire group is able to see the book clearly while you are reading.
- If some students are able to read or predict words, encourage them to do so during the rereading.
- Encourage students to present and use their knowledge of print.
- Allow students to look at the Big Books whenever they wish.
- Provide small versions of the Big Books for students to browse through and try to read at their leisure.
- The reader of the Big Book should try to be part of the collaborative group of learners rather than the leader.

Using the Pre-Decodable Books

Purpose

Pre-Decodable Books play an important role in students' early literacy development by providing them with meaningful "reading" experiences before they are actually reading on their own and by expanding their awareness of the forms and uses of print. By following along as you read aloud a **Pre-Decodable Book,** students learn about the left-to-right and top-to-bottom progression of print on a page, the clues that indicate the beginnings and endings of sentences, the connections between pictures and words, and important book conventions, such as front and back covers, authors' and illustrators' names, title pages, and page numbers.

The **Pre-Decodable Books** provide students with opportunities to apply their growing knowledge of letter names, shapes, and sounds, and to become familiar with individual words.

Through retelling the story in a **Pre-Decodable Book,** predicting or wondering about what will happen, and asking and responding to questions about the book, students not only learn about the relationship between spoken and written language, they learn to think about what they have read.

About the Pre-Decodable Books

Each **Pre-Decodable Book** contains a story that engages students' interest as it provides them with opportunities to practice what they are learning in their lessons. These "Pre-Decodable" stories each contain several high-frequency words that most students already have in their spoken vocabularies and that are a basic part of all meaningful stories. Learning to identify high-frequency words quickly, accurately, and effortlessly is a critical part of students' development as fluent, independent readers. In addition, each book contains words that familiarize students with key letter patterns, or *phonograms.* Because many words can be made from a few major phonograms, becoming aware of them is an important step in learning to read. The inside back cover of each **Pre-Decodable Book** contains a list of high-frequency words.

How to Read the Pre-Decodable Books

- Before reading a **Pre-Decodable Book,** take time to familiarize students with any new **high-frequency words** in the book and to review previously introduced words. To reinforce the idea that it is important to know these words because they are used so often in print, always point out the words in context. For example, focus students' attention on the words in Big Book selections or on signs and posters around the classroom.
- Give each student a copy of the book. Tell students that you will read the book together. Hold up your book. Read the title. If the title has a rebus picture, point to it and tell the students what it is. Then point to the word beneath it and explain that the picture represents that word. Point to and read the names of the author and illustrator, reminding students that an author writes a book and an illustrator draws the pictures. Page through the book, pointing to and naming the rebus pictures. Have the students say the name of each rebus. To avoid confusion, always *tell* them the *exact* word that a rebus represents. *Don't encourage them to guess at its meaning.*
- Allow students time to browse through the book on their own, commenting on what they see in the illustrations and making predictions about what they think the book will be about. Encourage them to comment on anything special they notice about the story, the illustrations, or the words in the book.
- Help the students to find page 3. Read the book aloud without stopping. As you read, move your hand beneath the words to show the progression of print. Pause at each rebus as you say the word it represents, pointing first to the rebus, then to the word beneath it.
- Reread the book. This time, ask the students to point to and read the high-frequency words.
- Tell the students to follow along in their books as you read the story again. Read the title aloud, and then have the students read it with you. Reread page 3. Point to each rebus picture and ask a volunteer to "read" it. Point to the word beneath the picture and remind students that the picture shows what the word is. Continue through each page of the book, calling on volunteers to "read" and stopping as necessary to clarify and help students with words.
- After reading, answer any questions the students might have about the book. Encourage them to discuss the illustrations and to explain what is happening in each one.

Reading Decodables and Building Fluency

Purpose

The most urgent task of early reading instruction is to make written thoughts intelligible to students. This requires a balanced approach that includes systematic instruction in phonics as well as experiences with authentic literature. Thus, from the very beginning, ***Open Court Reading*** includes the reading of literature. At the beginning of first grade, when students are learning phonics and blending as a tool to access words, the teacher reads aloud. During this time students are working on using comprehension strategies and skills and discussing stories. As students learn the code and blend words, recognize critical sight words, and develop some level of fluency, they take more responsibility for the actual reading of the text.

This program has a systematic instruction in phonics that allows the students to begin reading independently. This instruction is supported by ***Open Court Reading*** **Decodable Books.**

Practice

The ***Open Court Reading*** **Decodable Books** are designed to help the students apply, review, and reinforce their expanding knowledge of sound/spelling correspondences. Each story supports instruction in new phonic elements and incorporates elements and words that have been learned earlier. There are eight page and sixteen page **Decodable Books.** Grade K has eight-page **Decodable Books.** In Grade 1 the eight-page books focus on the new element introduced in the lesson, while the sixteen-page books review and reinforce the elements that have been taught since the last sixteen-page book. They review sounds from several lessons and provide additional reading practice. Grades 2–3 have eight-page **Decodable Books** in Getting Started, and sixteen-page books in the first 3–4 units of the grade level. The primary purpose is to provide practice reading the words. It is important that the students also attach meaning to what they are reading. Questions are often included in the ***Teacher's Edition*** to check both understanding and attention to words.

Fluency

Fluency is the effortless ability to read or access words with seemingly little attention to decoding. It also involves grouping words into meaningful units and using expression appropriately. Fluency is critical but not sufficient for comprehension.

To become proficient readers who fully understand what they read, the whole process of decoding must become as automatic as possible. The students need to be so familiar with the

Reading Materials and Techniques (continued)

sound/spellings and with the most common nondecodable sight words that they automatically process the letters or spellings and expend most of their energy on comprehending the meaning of the text.

While fluency begins in first grade, many students will continue to need practice in building fluency in second and third grades. Initially, students can use the ***Open Court Reading* Decodable Books** in grades 2 and 3, but fluency practice should include using materials from actual literature the students are reading.

Procedure

Preparing to Read

- Introduce and write on the board any nondecodable high-frequency or story words introduced or reviewed in the story. Tell the students how to pronounce any newly introduced high-frequency words. Then point to each new word and have the students say it. Have them read any previously introduced sight word in the Word Bank last. All of the ***Open Court Reading* Decodable Books** contain high-frequency words that may not be decodable. For example, the word *said* is a very common high-frequency word that is not decodable. Including words like *said* makes the language of the story flow smoothly and naturally. The students need to be able to recognize these words quickly and smoothly.
- Read the title. At the beginning of the year, you may need to read the title of the book to the students, but as the year goes on, you should have a student read it whenever possible. The sixteen-page ***Open Court Reading* Decodable Books** contain two related chapters, each using the same sounds and spellings. In such cases, read the title of the **Decodable** book, and then point out the two individual chapter titles. Have volunteers read the title of the chapter you are about to read.
- Browse the story. Have the students look through the story, commenting on whatever they notice in the text or illustrations and telling what they think the story will tell them.

Reading the Story

After this browsing, the students will read the story a page at a time. Again, these books are designed to support the learning of sounds and spellings. The focus should not be on comprehension. Students should understand what they are reading, and they should feel free to discuss anything in the story that interests them. Any areas of confusion are discussed and clarified as they arise, as described below.

- Have the students read a page to themselves. Then call on one student to read the page aloud, or have the whole group read it aloud.
- If a student has difficulty with a word that can be blended, help her or him blend the word. Remind the student to check the **Sound/Spelling Cards** for help. If a word cannot be blended using the sound/spellings learned so far, pronounce the word for the student.
- If a student has trouble with a word or sentence, have the reader call on a classmate for help, and then continue reading after the word or sentence has been clarified. After something on a page has been clarified or discussed, have that page reread by a different student before moving on to the next page.
- Repeat this procedure for each page.
- Reread the story twice more, calling on different students to read or read it in unison. These readings should go more quickly, with fewer stops for clarification.

Responding to the Story

Once the story has been read aloud a few times, have the students respond as follows:

- Ask the students what hard words they found in the story and how they figured them out. They may mention high-frequency words they didn't recognize, words they had to blend, and words whose meaning they did not know.
- Invite the students to tell about the story, retelling it in their own words, telling what they liked about it, or telling what they found interesting or surprising. Specific suggestions to use are listed in the ***Teacher's Edition.***
- Questions are provided in the ***Teacher's Edition.*** They are designed to focus the students' attention on the words and not just the pictures. The questions require answers that cannot be guessed by looking at the pictures alone, such as a name, a bit of dialogue, or an action or object that is not pictured. Have the students point to the words, phrases, or sentences that answer the questions.

Building Fluency

Buiding fluency is essential to gaining strong comprehension. The more fluent the students become, the more they can attend to the critical business of understanding the text. Opportunities for students to build fluency may include:

- Have students "partner read" the most recent ***Open Court Reading* Decodable Book** twice, taking turns reading a page at a time. The partners should switch the second time through so they are reading different pages from the ones they read the first time. If there is time left, the partners should choose any of the previously read stories to read together. Use this time for diagnosis, having one student at a time read with you.
- Making sure that the ***Open Court Reading* Decodable Books** are readily available in the classroom.
- Reading **Decodable Books** with as many students as possible one at a time.
- Reminding the students that they may read with partners during Workshop.

The only way the students can become fluent readers is to read as much and as often as possible.

Reading the Student Anthologies

Purpose

Reading is a complex process that requires students not only to decode what they read but also to understand and respond to it. The purpose of this section is to help you identify various reading behaviors used by good readers and to encourage those behaviors in your students.

Reading Behaviors and Comprehension Strategies

There are four basic behaviors that good readers engage in during reading. These behaviors include the application of certain comprehension strategies, which are modeled while reading the Student Anthology (Levels 1–6).

Setting Reading Goals and Expectations

Good readers set reading goals and expectations before they begin reading. This behavior involves a variety of strategies that will help students prepare to read the text.

- **Activate prior knowledge.** When good readers approach a new text, they consider what they already know about the subject or what their experiences have been in reading similar material.
- **Browse the text.** To get an idea of what to expect from a text, good readers look at the title and the illustrations. They may look for potential problems, such as difficult words. When browsing a unit, have students glance quickly at each selection, looking briefly at the illustrations and the print. Have them tell what they think they might be learning about as they read the unit.
- **Decide what they expect from the text.** When reading for pleasure, good readers anticipate enjoying the story or the language. When reading to learn something, they ask themselves what they expect to find out.

Responding to Text

Good readers are active readers. They interact with text by using the following strategies:

- **Making connections.** Good readers make connections between what they read and what they already know. They pay attention to elements in the text that remind them of their own experiences.
- **Visualizing, or picturing.** Good readers visualize what is happening in the text. They form mental images as they read. They picture the setting, the characters, and the action in a story. When reading expository text, good readers picture the objects, processes, or events described. Visualizing helps readers understand descriptions of complex activities or processes.
- **Asking questions.** Good readers ask questions that may prepare them for what they will learn. If their questions are not answered in the text, they may try to find answers elsewhere and thus add even more to their store of knowledge.
- **Predicting.** Good readers predict what will happen next. When reading fiction, they make predictions about what they are reading and then confirm or revise those predictions as they go.
- **Thinking about how the text makes you feel.** Well-written fiction touches readers' emotions; it sparks ideas.

Checking Understanding

One of the most important behaviors good readers exhibit is the refusal to continue reading when something fails to make sense. Good readers continually assess their understanding of the text with strategies such as:

- **Interpreting.** As they read, good readers make inferences that help them understand and appreciate what they are reading.
- **Summing up.** Good readers sum up to check their understanding as they read. Sometimes they reread to fill in gaps in their understanding.
- **Monitoring and adjusting reading speed.** Good readers monitor their understanding of what they read. They slow down as they come to difficult words and passages. They speed up as they read easier passages.

Monitoring and Clarifying Unfamiliar Words and Passages

- **Apply decoding skills** to sound out unknown words.
- **Determine what is unclear** to find the source of the confusion.
- **Apply context clues** in text and illustrations to help them figure out the meanings of words or passages.
- **Reread the passage** to make sure the passage makes sense.
- **Check a dictionary or the glossary** to understand the meanings of words not clarified by clues or rereading.

Procedures

Modeling and Thinking Aloud

Modeling and encouraging students to think aloud as they attempt to understand text can demonstrate for everyone how reading behaviors are put into practice. The most effective models will be those that come from your own reading. Using questions such as the following as well as your students' questions and comments will make both the text and the strategic reading process more meaningful to students.

- What kinds of things did you wonder about?
- What kinds of things surprised you?
- What new information did you learn?
- What was confusing until you reread or read further?

Model comprehension strategies in a natural way, and choose questions and comments that fit the text you are reading. Present a variety of ways to respond to text.

- Pose questions that you really do wonder about.
- Identify with characters by comparing them with yourself.
- React emotionally by showing joy, sadness, amusement, or surprise.
- Show empathy with or sympathy for characters.
- Relate the text to something that has happened to you or to something you already know.
- Show interest in the text ideas.
- Question the meaning or clarity of the author's words and ideas.

Encouraging Students' Responses and Use of Strategies

Most students will typically remain silent as they try to figure out an unfamiliar word or a confusing passage. Encourage students to identify specifically what they are having difficulty with. Once the problem has been identified, ask the students to suggest a strategy for dealing with the problem. Remind students to:

- Treat problems encountered in text as interesting learning opportunities.
- Think out loud about text challenges.
- Help each other build meaning. Rather than tell what a word is, students should tell how they figured out the meanings of challenging words and passages.
- Consider reading a selection again with a partner after reading it once alone. Partner reading provides valuable practice in reading for fluency.
- Make as many connections as they can between what they are reading and what they already know.
- Visualize to clarify meanings or enjoy descriptions.
- Ask questions about what they are reading.
- Notice how the text makes them feel.

PROGRAM APPENDIX

Reading Techniques

Reading Aloud

Purpose

Adults read a variety of materials aloud to students. These include Big Books, picture books, and novels. Research has shown that students who are read to are more likely to develop the skills they need to read successfully on their own.

In every grade level of **Open Court Reading** there are opportunities for teachers to read aloud to students. At the beginning of each unit is a Read-Aloud selection tied to the unit theme. This Read-Aloud selection allows students the opportunity to think about the unit theme before reading selections on their own.

Reading aloud at any age serves multiple purposes. Reading aloud:

- Provokes students' curiosity about text.
- Conveys an awareness that text has meaning.
- Demonstrates the various reasons for reading text (to find out about the world around them, to learn useful new information and new skills, or simply for pleasure).
- Exposes students to the "language of literature," which is more complex than the language they ordinarily use and hear.
- Provides an opportunity to teach the problem-solving strategies that good readers employ. As the students observe you interacting with the text, expressing your own enthusiasm, and modeling your thinking aloud, they perceive these as valid responses and begin to respond to text in similar ways.

Procedures

The following set of general procedures for reading aloud is designed to help you maximize the effectiveness of Read-Aloud sessions.

- **Read-aloud sessions.** Set aside time each day to read aloud.
- **Introduce the story.** Tell the students that you are going to read a story aloud to them. Tell its title and briefly comment on the topic. To allow the students to anticipate what will happen in the story, be careful not to summarize.
- **Activate prior knowledge.** Ask whether anyone has already heard the story. If so, ask them to see if this version is the same as the one they have heard. If not, activate prior knowledge by saying, "First, let's talk a little about _____." If the story is being read in two (or more) parts, before reading the second part, ask the students to recall the first part.
- **Before reading.** Invite students to interrupt your reading if there are any words they do not understand or ideas they find puzzling. Throughout the reading, encourage them to do this.
- **Read the story expressively.** Occasionally react verbally to the story by showing surprise, asking questions, giving an opinion, expressing pleasure, or predicting events. Think-aloud suggestions are outlined below.
- **Use Comprehension Strategies.** While reading aloud to the students, model the use of comprehension strategies in a natural, authentic way. Remember to try to present a variety of ways to respond to text. These include visualizing, asking questions, predicting, making connections, clarifying, and summarizing.
- **Retell.** When you have finished reading the story, call on volunteers to retell it.
- **Discuss.** After reading, discuss with the students their own reactions: how the story reminded them of things that have happened to them, what they thought of the story, and what they liked best about the story.
- **Reread.** You may wish to reread the selection on subsequent occasions focusing the discussion on the unit theme.

Think-Aloud Responses

The following options for modeling thinking aloud will be useful for reading any story aloud. Choose responses that are most appropriate for the selection you are reading.

- **React emotionally** by showing joy, sadness, amusement, or surprise.
- **Ask questions** about ideas in the text. This should be done when there are points or ideas that you really do wonder about.
- **Identify with characters** by comparing them to yourself.
- **Show empathy with or sympathy for** characters.
- **Relate the text to something** you already know or something that has happened to you.
- **Show interest** in the text ideas.
- **Question the meaning and/or clarity** of the author's words and ideas.

Questions to Help Students Respond

At reasonable stopping points in reading, ask the students general questions in order to get them to express their own ideas and to focus their attention on the text.

- What do you already know about this?
- What seems really important here? Why do you think so?
- Was there anything that you didn't understand? What?
- What did you like best about this?
- What new ideas did you learn from this?
- What does this make you wonder about?

Reading Roundtable

Purpose

Adult readers discuss their reading, give opinions on it, and recommend books to each other. Reading Roundtable, an activity students may choose to participate in during **Workshop**, provides the same opportunity for students in the classroom. Sessions can be small or large. During Reading Roundtable, students share the reading they do on their own. They can discuss a book they have all read, or one person can review a book for the others and answer questions from the group.

During Reading Roundtable, students can discuss and review a variety of books:

- Full-length versions of Anthology selections.
- Classroom Library selections.
- Books that students learn about when discussing authors and illustrators.
- Books related to the investigations of unit concepts can be shared with others who might want to read them.
- Interesting articles from magazines, newspapers, and other sources.

Procedures

Encouraging Reading

- Read aloud to your students regularly. You can read Classroom Library selections or full-length versions of Student Anthology selections.
- Provide a time each day for students to read silently. This time can be as short as 10–15 minutes but should be strictly observed. You should stop what you are doing and read. Students should be allowed to choose their own reading materials during this time and record their reactions in the Response Journal section of their Writer's Notebook.
- Establish a classroom library and reading center with books from the school or local library or ask for donations of books from students, parents, and community members.
- Take your students to the school library or to the public library.

Conducting a Reading Roundtable

- When a student reviews a book others have not read, he or she can use some of the sentence starters to tell about the book. These may include, "This book is about . . . , I chose this book because. . . , What I really like/don't like about this book is . . . " and so on.
- When several students read the same book and discuss it during Reading Roundtable, they can use discussion starters. If the book is from the Classroom Library, they can discuss how it relates to the unit concepts.

Introducing Sounds and Letters

Purpose

In ***SRA/Open Court Reading***, students learn to relate sounds to letters in Kindergarten through the use of thirty-one **Alphabet Sound Cards** (Level K). In the upper grade levels, **Sound/ Spelling Cards** (Levels 1–3) are used to relate sounds and spellings. The purpose of the **Alphabet Sound Cards** is to remind the students of the sounds of the English language and their letter correspondences. These cards are a resource for the students to use to remember sound-letter associations for both reading and writing.

Each card contains the capital and small letter, and a picture that shows the sound being produced. For instance, the **Monkey** card introduces the /m/ sound and shows a monkey looking at bananas and saying */m/ /m/ /m/*. The name of the picture on each card contains the target sound at the beginning of the word for the consonants and in the middle for most of the vowels. Vowel letters are printed in red and consonants are printed in black. In addition, the picture associates a sound with an action. This action-sound association is introduced through a short, interactive poem found in the ***Teacher's Edition*** in which the pictured object or character "makes" the sound of the letter. Long vowels are represented by a tall—or "long"—picture of the letters themselves, rather than by a picture for action-sound association.

Procedures

- Display the cards 1–26 with the picture sides to the wall. Initially post the first twenty-six cards in alphabetical order so that only the alphabet letters show. The short vowel cards may be posted as they are introduced later. As you introduce the letter sound, you will turn the card to show the picture and the letter on the other side. Once the cards are posted, do not change their positions so that the students can locate the cards quickly.
- Before turning a card, point to the letter. Ask students to tell what they know about the letter. For example, they are likely to know its name and possibly its sound if the letter is one they have already worked with.
- Turn the card and show the picture. Tell the students the name of the card, and explain that it will help them to remember the sound the letter makes.
- Read the poem that goes with the letter. Read it expressively, emphasizing the words with the target sound and the isolated sound when it occurs. Have the students join in to produce the sound.
- Repeat the poem a few times, encouraging all students to say the sound along with you.
- Follow the poem with the cards for the target sound. (These are listed within the lessons.)
- Name each picture, and have students listen for the target sound at the beginning of the word. Ask students to repeat the words and the sound.
- For every letter sound, a listening activity follows the introduction of the cards. Lead the students in the "Listening for the Sound" activity to reinforce the letter sound.
- To link the sound and the letter, demonstrate how to form the capital and small letter by writing on the board or on an overhead transparency. The students practice forming the letter and saying the sound as they write.

Alphabet Sound Cards

The pictures and letters on the **Alphabet Sound Cards** also appear on the small sets of **Alphabet Sound Cards**. The Teacher's Edition specifically suggests that you use the **Individual Alphabet Sound Cards** for some activities. You may also use the small cards for review and for small-group reteaching and practice sessions. Have sets of the cards available for the students to use during **Workshop** either alone or with partners. Add each small card to the Activity Center after you have taught the lesson in which the corresponding **Alphabet Sound Card** is introduced. Here are some suggestions for activities using the **Alphabet Sound Cards**:

1. **Saying sounds from pictures.** The leader flashes pictures as the others say the sound each picture represents.
2. **Saying sounds.** The leader flashes the letters on the cards as the others say the sound that the letters represent.
3. **Naming words from pictures.** The leader flashes pictures. The others say the sound, and then say a word beginning with that sound.
4. **Writing letters from the pictures.** Working alone, a student looks at a picture and then writes the letter for the sound that picture represents.

Tips

- Throughout the beginning lessons, help students remember that vowels are special by reminding them that vowels sometimes say their names in words. For example, the picture of the *a* on the long *a* **Alphabet Sound Card** is long because the long *a* says its name. The short *a* **Alphabet Sound Card** pictures the lamb, because the lamb makes the short *a* sound, and you can hear the sound in the word, *lamb*. In the later lessons, students will use both sets of cards to help them remember that the vowels have both a short and a long sound.
- From the very beginning, encourage students to use the **Alphabet Sound Cards** as a resource to help them with their work.
- Mastery of letter recognition is the goal students should reach so that they will be prepared to link each letter with its associated sound. If students have not yet mastered the names of the letters, it is important to work with them individually in **Workshop**, or at other times during the day.
- The *Kk* card is a little tricky. A camera makes the /k/ sound when it clicks, and the word *camera* begins with the /k/ sound. However, the word *camera* is not spelled with a *k*. While you need not dwell on this, be aware that some students may be confused by the fact that the *Cc* and *Kk* cards have the same picture.
- The picture on the *Qq* card depicts ducks, *quacking ducks*. Make sure that the students consistently call them *quacking ducks*, not *ducks*, and that they focus on the /kw/ sound.

The Alphabetic Principle: How the Alphabet Works

The Alpabetic Principle

Purpose

A major emphasis in the kindergarten program is on letter recognition and attending to sounds. Students need to learn the alphabetic principle: that letters work together in a systematic way to connect spoken language to written words. This understanding is the foundation for reading. Students are not expected to master letter/sound correspondence in kindergarten, nor are they expected to blend sounds into words themselves. They are only expected to become an "expert" on their Special Letter as they learn how the alphabet works. Through this introduction to the alphabetic principle, the students will have the basic understanding required to work through the alphabet letter by letter, attaching sounds to each.

Key concepts of the Alphabetic Principle include:

- A limited number of letters combine in different ways to make many different words.
- Words are composed of sounds and letters represent those sounds.
- Anything that can be pronounced can be spelled.
- Letters and sounds can be used to identify words.
- Meaning can be obtained by using letters and sounds to figure out words.

Procedures for Kindergarten

The following steps can be used for introducing letters and sounds in Kindergarten. These steps may be adapted for students at other grades if they do not understand the alphabetic principle. The tone of these activities should be informal, fun, and fast-paced. The purpose of these activities is to familiarize the students with how the alphabet works by having them participate in group play with letters and sounds.

Introducing Letters

- Reinforce the idea that anything that can be pronounced can be spelled with the letters of the alphabet.
- Tell the students that you can spell any word. Have them give you words to spell.
- Write the words on the board, and show studentren that the words contain the letters displayed on the **Alphabet Sound Cards**.
- Have students help you spell the words by pointing to letters as you say them and then write them.
- Encourage students to spell each word letter by letter.

Letter Expert Groups

- Have **Letter Cards** (Levels K and 1) available for the following set of letters: *b, d, f, h, l, m, n, p, s, t*. You will need two or three cards for each letter. (You will not need the **Alphabet Sound Cards** until later.)
- You will be the letter expert for the vowels.
- Divide the class into groups of two or three and assign each group a letter. Give each student the appropriate **Letter Card**.
- Tell the students that they are now in their Letter Expert groups and that they are going to become experts on their Special Letter's name, shape, and sound.

Students need to learn the alphabetic principle; that letters work together in a systematic way to connect spoken language to written words. This understanding is the foundation for reading.

Making Words

- Begin each lesson with a rehearsal of each group's letter name.
- Demonstrate how letters work by writing a word in large letters on the board.
- Tell the students the experts for each letter in the word should hold up their **Letter Cards** and name the letter. One member of the group should stand in front of their letter on the board.
- Continue until all letters in the word are accounted for. Remember that you are responsible for the vowels.
- Demonstrate that you can make different words by changing a letter or by changing the letter order.

Identifying Sounds in Words

- Use the **Alphabet Sound Cards** to demonstrate that every letter has at least one sound.
- Give each student the **Alphabet Sound Card** for his or her Special Letter.
- Point out the pictures on the cards. Explain that each card has a picture of something that makes the letter's sound. The picture will help them remember the sound.
- Tell each group the sound for its letter. (Remember, you are the expert for the vowels.)
- Quickly have each group rehearse its letter's name and sound.
- Write a word on the board in large letters. Say the word first sound-by-sound and then blend the word.
- For each letter/sound in the word, have one student from each Letter Expert group come forward, stand in front of the appropriate letter, and hold their cards. Although only one member of the group may come forward with the **Letter Card** or **Alphabet Sound Card,** all students in a Special Letter group should say the name and/or sound of their letter when it occurs in words.
- Say the word again, pointing to the **Alphabet Sound Cards**.
- Ask students who are not already standing to help you hold the vowel cards.
- Vary the activity by changing one letter sound and having an expert for that letter come forward.
- End the activity for each word by saying the sounds in the words one by one and then saying the entire word. Encourage the students to participate.

Tips

- Remind the students to use the picture on the **Alphabet Sound Card** for their Special Letter to help them remember the letter's sound. The students are expected only to "master" their own Special Letter and share the information with their classmates. They are not expected to blend and read the words by themselves. These are group activities in which you work with the students to help them gain insight into the alphabet.
- Have students note that what they learn about the letters and words applies to the words they work with in Big Book selections.
- Occasionally, have students find their special letters in a Big Book selection. Play some of the letter replacement and rearrangement games with words encountered in the Big Books.

The Alpabetic Principle

Purpose

The following activities are extended to provide kindergarten students with a more thorough understanding of how sounds "work" in words. In this group of exercises the students are introduced to specific letter/sound correspondences, consonants and short vowels. The students have previously been introduced to vowels and their special characteristics. This understanding is extended by introducing students to the convention that a vowel has a short sound in addition to its long sound. With this information and a carefully structured set of activities, the students can begin to explore and understand the alphabetic principle in a straightforward and thorough manner. The students not only listen for sounds in specified positions in words; they also link sounds to their corresponding letters. The activities in this group of lessons lay the groundwork for the students to work their way through the entire alphabet, learning letter-sound associations, and to understand the purpose and the value of this learning.

Move the students quickly through these activities. Do not wait for all the students to master each letter/sound correspondence before going on. The students will have more opportunities to achieve mastery. The goal of these activities is for the students to obtain a basic understanding of the alphabetic principle.

Procedures

Introducing Consonant Letters and Sounds

- Point to the **Alphabet Sound Card** and name the letter.
- Point to the picture. Tell the students the sound of the letter and how the picture helps them to remember the sound. Repeat the sound several times.
- Tell the students you will read them a short poem or an alliterative sentence to help them remember the sound of the letter. Read the poem several times, emphasizing the words with the target sound. Have the students join in and say the sound.
- After introducing and reviewing a letter/sound correspondence, summarize the information on the **Alphabet Sound Card**.

Generating Words with the Target Sound

- Brainstorm to create a list of words that begin with the target sound. Write the words on the board or on a chart. Include any of the students' names that begin with the target sound.
- Play the *I'm Thinking of Something That Starts With* game. Begin with the target sound and add clues until the students guess the word. If the students guess a word that does not begin with the target sound, emphasize the beginning sound and ask if the word begins with the target sound.
- Silly Sentences. Make silly sentences with the students that include many words with the target sound. Encourage the students to participate by extending the sentences: *Mary mopes. Mary mopes on Monday. Mary and Michael mope on Monday in Miami.*

Listening For Initial Sound

- Give each student a **Letter Card** for the target sound, /s/.
- Point to the picture on the **Alphabet Sound Card**, and have the students give the sound, /s/.
- Tell the students to listen for the first sound in each word you say. If it is /s/, they should hold up their *s* cards. Establish a signal so that the students know when to respond.
- Read a list of words, some beginning with /s/, some beginning with other sounds.

Listening for Final Sound

The procedure for listening for the final sound of a word is the same as that for listening for the initial sound. The students may need to be reminded throughout the activity to pay attention to the *final* sound.

- Read a list of words, some ending with the target sound and some ending with other sounds. Avoid words that begin with the target sound.

Linking the Sound to the Letter

- **Word Pairs (initial sounds).** Write pairs of words on the board. One of each pair should begin with the target sound. Say the word beginning with the target sound, and ask the students to identify it. Remind them to listen for the target sound at the beginning of the word, to think about which letter makes that sound, and to find the word that begins with that letter. For example,
  Target sound: /s/
  Word pair: *fit sit*
  Which word is *sit*?
- **Word Pairs (final sounds).** Follow the same procedure used for initial sounds, and direct the students to think about the sound that they hear at the end of the word. Since it is often more difficult for the students to attend to the ending sound, you may need to lead them through several pairs of words. Remind the students to listen for the target sound and to think about which letter makes that sound.
- **Writing Letters.** Using either of the handwriting system outlined in the Program Appendix of ***SRA/Open Court Reading***, or the system in use at your school, have students practice writing capital and small letters. Remind the students of the letter sound, and have them repeat it.

Comparing Initial Consonant Sounds

This activity is exactly like **listening for initial sounds** except that the students must discriminate between two sounds. They are given **Letter Cards** for both sounds and must hold up the appropriate card when they hear the sound.

Comparing Final Consonant Sounds

This activity is exactly like listening for final sounds except that the students must discriminate between two sounds. They are given **Letter Cards** for both sounds and must hold up the appropriate card when they hear the sound.

Linking the Consonant Sound to the Letter

In this activity to help students link sounds and letters, the students will make words either by adding initial consonants to selected word parts or by adding a different final consonant to a consonant-vowel-consonant combination.

The Alphabetic Principle: How the Alphabet Works (continued)

Introducing Short Vowel Sounds

- Tell the students that the vowels are printed in red to remind them that they are special letters. (They are not special because they are printed in red.) They are special because they have more than one sound, and every word must have a vowel sound.
- Point to the long *Aa* **Alphabet Sound Card,** and remind the students that this letter is called a *vowel*. Vowels sometimes say their names in words: for example, *say, day, tray.* This vowel sound is called long *a*.
- Have the students repeat the sound.
- Sometimes vowels say different sounds. Point to the picture of the lamb on the short *Aa* card, and tell students that *a* also makes the sound heard in the middle of *lamb*. This is the short *a*. Read the short vowel poem to help the students remember the short *a*.
- Have all the students join in saying /a/ /a/ /a/.

Listening for Short Vowel Sounds Versus Long Vowel Sounds

- Tell the students that you will read words with long *a* and short *a*. Review the two sounds.
- Give the students a signal to indicate when they hear the vowel sound. You may want one signal for short *a*, such as scrunching down, and another for long *a*, such as stretching up tall.
- Continue with lists of words such as: *add, back, aid, tan, bake, tame.*

Linking the Vowel Sound to the Letter

- Writing Letters. Have students practice writing the letter and review the sound of the letter.
- In this activity to help students link sounds and letters, the students will make words either by adding initial consonants to selected word parts or by adding a different final consonant to a consonant-vowel-consonant combination. Change the beginning of the word or the word ending, but retain the vowel sound to make new words:

at	*hat*	*mat*	*pat*
ap	*map*	*tap*	*sap*
am	*Sam*	*Pam*	*ham*

Comparing Short Vowel Sounds

This activity requires students to discriminate between short vowel sounds in the middle of words. Review the vowel sounds.

- Say a word, and have the students repeat it. Establish a signal to indicate whether they hear short *a* or short *o* in the middle of the word. For example, they can hold up the appropriate **Letter Card** when they hear a sound. Sample words: *cap, cot, rat, rot, rack, rock.*
- The way in which vowel sounds—in the initial, medial, and final position—combine to make words can be observed in a large set of words that does not contain silent letters or other special spelling conventions.

Linking the Sound to the Letter

- In this activity write a word on the board, and help the students say it.
- Change the word by changing the vowel. Help the students say the new word, for example, *map, mop; hot, hat; pot, pat.*
- For a variation of this activity, write the pairs of words, and simply have the students say which word is the target word. For example, the students see *tap* and *top*. Ask which word *top* is, directing the students's attention to the vowel.

Tips

- Lead and model the exercises as necessary until the students begin to catch on and can participate with confidence.
- To keep the students focused on the various activities, have them tell you the task for each activity. For example, after telling the students to listen for final sounds, ask the students what they will be listening for.
- Actively involve the students by giving them opportunities to tell what they know rather than supplying the information for them. Do they know the letter name? Do they know the sound? Can they think of words that begin with the sound?
- Keeping the students focused on the idea that they are learning about sounds and letters so they can read these books themselves makes the lessons more relevant for the students.

Phonemic Awareness

The basic purpose of providing structured practice in phonemic awareness is to help the students hear and understand the sounds from which words are made. Before students can be expected to understand the sound/symbol correspondence that forms the base of written English, they need to have a strong working knowledge of the sound relationships that make up the spoken language. This understanding of spoken language lays the foundation for the transition to written language.

Phonemic awareness activities provide the students with easy practice in discriminating the sounds that make up words. Phonemic awareness consists of quick, gamelike activities designed to help students understand that speech is made up of distinct, identifiable sounds. The playful nature of the activities makes them appealing and engaging, while giving the students practice and support for learning about language. Once the students begin reading and writing, this experience with manipulating sounds will help them use what they know about sounds and letters to sound out and spell unfamiliar words when they read and write.

The two main formats for teaching phonemic awareness are oral blending and segmentation. These are supported by occasional discrimination activities and general wordplay. Oral blending encourages students to combine sounds to make words. Segmentation, conversely, requires them to isolate sounds from words. Other activities support discrimination, or recognition, of particular sounds. Sometimes simple songs, rhymes, or games engage students in wordplay. In these, the students manipulate words in a variety of ways. From these playful activities, the students derive serious knowledge about language.

As the students progress through different phonemic awareness activities, they will become proficient at listening for and reproducing the sounds they hear. It is essential for their progression to phonics and reading that they are able to hear the sounds and the patterns used to make up recognizable words. The phonemic awareness activities support the phonics instruction, but the activities are oral and do not focus on sound/spelling correspondences. Because the students are not expected to read the words they are experimenting with, any consonant and vowel sounds may be used, even if the students have not been formally taught the sound and its spellings.

Oral Blending

Purpose

In oral blending, the students are led through a progression of activities designed to help them hear how sounds are put together to make words.

Until students develop an awareness of the component parts of words, they have no tools with which to decode words or put letters together to form words. Oral blending helps students master these component parts of words, from syllables down to single sounds, or phonemes. Oral blending is not to be confused with the formal blending of specific sounds whose spellings the students will be taught through phonics instruction. Oral blending does not depend on the recognition of written words; it focuses instead on hearing the sounds.

Oral blending focuses on hearing sounds through a sequence that introduces the most easily distinguished word parts and then systematically moves to sound blending that contains all the challenges of phonic decoding (except letter recognition). This sequence provides support for the least-prepared student—one who comes to first grade with no concept of words or sounds within words. At the same time, the lively pace and playful nature of oral blending activities hold the interest of students who already have some familiarity with words and letters.

Oral blending prepares students for phonics instruction by developing an awareness of the separate sounds that make up speech. Oral blending activities then continue in concert with phonics instruction to reinforce and extend new learning. And, because these activities involve simply listening to and reproducing sounds, oral blending need not be restricted to the sounds students have been or will be taught in phonics.

The tone of the activities should be playful and informal and should move quickly. Although these activities will provide information about student progress, they are not diagnostic tools. Do not expect mastery. Those students who have not caught on will be helped more by varied experiences than by more drilling on the same activity.

Procedures

Following is a description of the progression of oral blending activities.

Syllable Blending

Syllables are easier to distinguish than individual sounds (phonemes), so students can quickly experience success in forming meaningful words. Tell the students that you are going to say some words in two parts. Tell them to listen carefully so that they can discover what the words are. Read each word, pronouncing each part distinctly with a definite pause between syllables broken by. . . . The lists of words that follow are arranged in sequence from easy to harder. They cover different types of cues. At any point where they fit in the sequence, include multisyllable names of students in the class.

Model

Teacher: *dino . . . saur. What's the word?*

Students: *dinosaur*

Example Words

- First part of the word cues the whole word:
  vita . . . min *vaca . . . tion*
  hippopot . . . amus *ambu . . . lance*
- Two distinct words easily combined:
  butter. . . fly *straw. . . berry*
  surf . . . board *basket . . . ball*

Phonemic Awareness (continued)

- Two distinct words, but first word could cue the wrong ending:
  tooth . . . ache tooth . . . paste
  water . . . fall water . . . melon
- First part, consonant + vowel, not enough to guess whole word:
  re . . . member re . . . frigerator
  bi . . . cycle bi . . . ology
- Identifying clues in second part:
  light . . . ning sub . . . ject in . . . sect
- Last part, consonant + vowel sound, carries essential information:
  yester . . . day rain . . . bow
  noi . . . sy pota . . . to
- Changing the final part changes the word:
  start . . . ing start . . . er start. . . ed

Initial Consonant Sounds

Initial consonant blending prepares students for consonant replacement activities that will come later. Tell the students that you will ask them to put some sounds together to make words. Pronounce each word part distinctly, and make a definite pause at the breaks indicated. When a letter is surrounded by slash marks, pronounce the letter's sound, not its name. When you see /s/, for example, you will say "ssss," not "ess." The words that follow are arranged from easy to harder. At any point where they fit in the sequence, include names of students in the class.

Model

TEACHER: /t/ . . . iger. What's the word?

STUDENTS: tiger

Example Words

- Separated consonant blend, with rest of word giving strong cue to word identity:
  /b/ . . . roccoli /k/ . . . racker
  /f/ . . . lashlight /k/ . . . reature
- Held consonant that is easy for students to hear, with rest of word giving strong cue:
  /s/ . . . innamon /l/ . . . adybug
  /s/ . . . eventeen /n/ . . . ewspaper
- Stop consonant that is harder for students to hear preceding vowel, with rest of word giving strong cue:
  /t/. . . adpole /p/ . . . iggybank
  /d/ . . . ragonfly /b/ . . . arbecue
- Single-syllable words and words in which the second part gives a weaker cue:
  /s/ . . . ing /l/ . . . augh /v/ . . . ase

Final Consonant Sounds

In this phase of oral blending, the last sound in the word is separated.

Model

TEACHER: cabba . . . /j/. What's the word?

STUDENTS: cabbage

Example Words

- Words that are easily recognized even before the final consonant is pronounced:
  bubblegu . . . /m/ Columbu . . . /s/
  crocodi . . . /l/ submari . . . /n/
- Multisyllable words that need the final consonant for recognition:
  colle . . . /j/ (college) came . . . /l/ (camel)
- Single-syllable words:
  sa . . . /d/ gra . . . /s/ snai . . . /l/

Initial Consonant Sound Replacement

This level of oral blending further develops awareness of initial consonant sounds. The activity begins with a common word, then quickly changes its initial consonant sound. Most of the words produced are nonsense words, which helps keep the focus on the sounds in the word. Note that the words are written on the board, but the students are not expected to read them. The writing is to help the students see that when the sounds change, the letters change, and vice versa.

Model

TEACHER: [Writes word on board.] This word is *magazine.* What is it?

STUDENTS: *magazine*

TEACHER: Now I'm going to change it. [Erases initial consonant.] Now it doesn't start with /m/, it's going to start with /b/. What's the new word?

STUDENTS: *bagazine*

TEACHER: That's right . . . [Writes b where m had been.] It's *bagazine.* Now I'm going to change it again. . . .

Repeat with different consonant sounds. Then do the same with other words, such as: *remember, Saturday, tomorrow, lotion,* and *million.* Continue with single-syllable words, such as: *take, big, boot, cot, seat, look, tap, ride,* and *late.* There are two stages in using written letters:

- The replacement letter is not written until *after* the new "word" has been identified.
- Later, the replacement letter is written *at the same time* the change in the initial phoneme is announced. For example, the teacher erases *d* and writes *m* while saying, "Now it doesn't start with /d/, it starts with /m/."

You may wish to alter the procedure when the consonants used have already been introduced in phonics by writing the replacement letter and having students sound out the new word. Feel free to switch between the two procedures within a single exercise. If the students are not responding orally to written spellings that have been introduced in phonics, don't force it. Proceed by saying the word before writing the letter, and wait until another time to move on to writing before pronouncing.

One-Syllable Words

The students now begin blending individual phonemes to form words. This important step can be continued well into the year. Continued repetitions of this activity will help the students realize how they can use the sound/spellings they are learning to read and write real words.

At first, the blended words are presented in a story context that helps the students identify the words. They soon recognize that they are actually decoding meaningful words. However, the context must not be so strong that the students can guess the word without listening to the phonemic cues. Any vowel sounds and irregularly spelled words may be used, since there is no writing involved.

Model

TEACHER: *When I looked out the window, I saw a /l/ /ī/ /t/. What did I see?*

STUDENTS: *A light.*

TEACHER: *Yes, I saw a light. At first I thought it was the /m/ /o͞o/ /n/. What did I think it was?*

STUDENTS: *The moon.*

TEACHER: *But it didn't really look like the moon. Suddenly I thought, maybe it's a space /sh/ /i/ /p/. What did I think it might be?*

STUDENTS: *A space ship!*

Once the students are familiar with this phase of oral blending, they can move to blending one-syllable words without the story context.

Example Words

- CVC (consonant/vowel/consonant) words beginning with easily blended consonant sounds (/sh/, /h/, /r/, /v/, /s/, /n/, /z/, /f/, /l/, /m/):
  nip nap
- CVC words beginning with any consonant:
  ten bug lip
- Add CCVC words:
  flap step
- Add CVCC words:
  most band went
- Add CCVCC words:
  stamp grand scuffs

Final Consonant Sound Replacement

Final consonant sounds are typically more difficult for students to use than initial consonants.

- Begin with multisyllable words, and move to one-syllable words.
- As with initial consonants, first write the changed consonant after students have pronounced the new word.
- Then write the consonant as they pronounce it.
- For sound/spellings introduced in phonics instruction, write the new consonant spelling, and have students identify and pronounce it.

Model

Teacher: *[Writes word on board.] This word is* teapot. *What is it?*

Students: *teapot*

Teacher: *Now I'm going to change it.* [Erases final consonant.] *Now it doesn't end with /t/, it ends with /p/. What's the word now?*

Students: *teapop*

Teacher: *That's right . . .* [Writes *p* where *t* had been.] *It's* teapop. *Now I'm going to change it again. . . .*

Example Words

- Words that are easily recognized even before the final consonant is pronounced:
  picnic picnit picnis picnil picnid
  airplane airplate airplabe airplafe
- Multisyllable words that need the final consonant for recognition:
  muffin muffil muffim muffip muffit
  amaze amate amake amale amade
- Single-syllable words:
  neat nean neap neam neaj nead neaf
  broom broot brood broof broop broon

Initial Vowel Replacement

Up to now, oral blending has concentrated on consonant sounds because they are easier to hear than vowels. As you move to vowel play, remember that the focus is still on the sounds, not the spellings. Use any vowel sounds.

Model

Teacher: [Writes word on board.] *This word is* elephant. *What is it?*

Students: *elephant*

Teacher: *Now I'm going to change it.* [Erases initial vowel.] *Now it doesn't start with /e/, it starts with /a/. What's the word now?*

Students: *alephant*

Teacher: *That's right . . .* [Writes *a* where *e* had been.] *It's alephant. Now I'm going to change it again. . . .*

Example Words

- Multisyllable words:
  angry ingry oongry ungry engry
  ivy avy oovy evy ovy oivy
- One-syllable words:
  ink ank oonk unk onk oink
  add odd idd oudd edd udd

Segmentation

Purpose

Segmentation and oral blending complement each other: Oral blending puts sounds together to make words, while segmentation separates words into sounds. Oral blending will provide valuable support for decoding when students begin reading independently.

Procedure

Syllables

The earliest segmentation activities focus on syllables, which are easier to distinguish than individual sounds, or phonemes. Start with students' names, then use other words. As with the oral blending activities, remember to move quickly through these activities. Do not hold the class back waiting for all students to catch on. Individual progress will vary, but drilling on one activity is less helpful than going on to others. Return to the same activity often. Frequent repetition is very beneficial and allows students additional opportunities to catch on.

- Say, for example, "Let's clap out Amanda's name. A-man-da."
- Have the students clap and say the syllables along with you. Count the claps.
- Tell the students that these word parts are called *syllables.* Don't try to explain; the idea will develop with practice. Once you have provided the term, simply say, "How many syllables?" after the students clap and count.
- Mix one-syllable and multisyllable words:
  fantastic tambourine good
  imaginary stand afraid

Comparative Length of Words

Unlike most phonemic awareness activities, this one involves writing on the board or on an overhead transparency. Remember, though, that the students are not expected to read what is written. They are merely noticing that words that take longer to say generally look longer when written.

- Start with students' names. Choose two names, one short and one long, with the same first initial (for example, *Joe* and *Jonathan*).
- Write the two names on the board, one above the other, so that the difference is obvious.
- Tell the students that one name is *Jonathan* and one is *Joe.* Have them pronounce and clap each name. Then, have them tell which written word they think says *Joe.*
- Move your finger under each name as they clap and say it, syllable by syllable.
- Repeat with other pairs of names and words, such as: *tea/telephone, cat/caterpillar, butterfly/bug.* Be sure not to give false clues. For example, sometimes write the longer word on top, sometimes the shorter one; sometimes ask for the shorter word, sometimes the longer; sometimes ask for the top word, sometimes the bottom; sometimes point to a word and ask the students to name it, and sometimes name the word and ask the students to point to it.

Listen for Individual Sounds

Activities using a puppet help the students listen for individual sounds in words. Use any puppet you have on hand. When you introduce the puppet, tell the students that it likes to play word games. Each new activity begins with the teacher speaking to and for the puppet until the students determine the pattern. Next, students either speak for the puppet or correct the puppet. To make sure all the students are participating, alternate randomly between having the whole group or individuals respond. The activities focus on particular parts of words, according to the following sequence:

1. **Repeating last part of word.** Use words beginning with easy-to-hear consonants, such as *f, l, m, n, r, s,* and *z.* The puppet repeats only the rime, the part of the syllable after the initial consonant.

Model

Teacher: *farm*

Puppet: *arm*

Once the pattern is established, the students respond for the puppet.

Teacher: *rope*

Students: *ope*

Example Words

Use words such as the following: *mine . . . ine soup . . . oup feet . . . eet*

2. **Restoring initial phonemes.** Now the students correct the puppet. Be sure to acknowledge the correction.

Model

Teacher: *lake*

Puppet: *ake*

Teacher: *No, lllake. You forgot the /l/.*

Teacher: *real*

Puppet: *eal*

Teacher: *What did the puppet leave off?*

Students: */r/. It's supposed to be* real.

Teacher: *That's right. The word is* real.

Example Words

Use words such as the following:
look . . . ook mouse . . . ouse sand . . . and

3. **Segmenting initial consonants.** The puppet pronounces only the initial consonant.

Phonemic Awareness (continued)

Model

Teacher: *pay*

Puppet: */p/*

Example Words

Use words such as the following:

moon . . . /m/ *nose . . . /n/* *bell . . . /b/*

4. **Restoring final consonants.** The students correct the puppet. Prompt if necessary: *"What's the word? What did the puppet leave off?"*

Model

Teacher: *run*

Puppet: *ru*

Students: *It's run! You left off the /n/.*

Teacher: *That's right. The word is* run.

Example Words

Use words such as the following:

meet. . . mee *cool . . . coo* *boot. . . boo*

5. **Isolating final consonants.** The puppet pronounces only the final consonant.

Model

Teacher: *green*

Puppet: */n/*

Example Words

Use words such as the following:

glass . . . /s/ *boom . . . /m/* *mice . . . /s/*

6. **Segmenting initial consonant blends.** The sounds in blends are emphasized.

Model

Teacher: *clap*

Puppet: *lap*

Next have students correct the puppet.

Teacher: *stain*

Puppet: *tain*

Students: *It's* stain! *You left off the /s/.*

Teacher: *That's right. The word is stain.*

Example Words

Use words such as the following:

blaze . . . laze *draw. . . raw* *proud . . . roud*

Discrimination

Purpose

Discrimination activities help students focus on particular sounds in words.

Listening for long vowel sounds is the earliest discrimination activity. Vowel sounds are necessary for decoding, but young students do not hear them easily. This is evident in students' invented spellings, where vowels are often omitted. Early in the year, the students listen for long vowel sounds, which are more easily distinguished than short vowel sounds:

- Explain to the students that vowels are special, because sometimes they say their names in words.
- Tell the students which vowel sound to listen for.
- Have them repeat the sound when they hear it in a word. For example, if the target vowel sound is long e, the students will say long e when you say *leaf* but they should not respond when you say *loaf*.
- Initially the students should listen for one long vowel sound at a time. Later they can listen for two vowel sounds. All **Example Words**, however, should contain one of the target vowels.

Procedure

Listening for short vowel sounds discrimination activities should be done once the short vowels /a/ and /i/ have been introduced. Short vowels are very useful in reading. They are generally more regular in spelling than long vowels, and they appear in many short, simple words. However, their sounds are less easily distinguished than those of long vowels. Thus, the activities focus only on /a/ and /i/. All the words provided have one or the other of these sounds. Either have the students repeat the sound of a specified vowel, or vary the activity as follows: Write an *a* on one side of the board and an *i* on the other. Ask the students to point to the *a* when they hear a word with the /a/ sound and point to the *i* when they hear a word with the /i/ sound. Use words such as the following:

bat *mat* *sat* *sit* *spit*
pit *pat* *pan* *pin* *spin*

Consonant sounds in multisyllable words. Discriminating these sounds helps students attend to consonant sounds in the middle of words.

- Say the word *rib*, and have the students repeat it. Ask where they hear the /b/ in *rib*.
- Then say *ribbon* and ask the students where they hear the /b/ in *ribbon*.
- Tell the students that you will say some words and they will repeat each word.
- After they repeat each word, ask what consonant sound they hear in the middle of that word. Use words such as the following:

famous *message* *picky*
jogger *flavor* *zipper*

Phonemic Play

Purpose

Wordplay activities help the students focus on and manipulate sounds, thus supporting the idea that words are made of specific sounds that can be taken apart, put together, or changed to make new words. Through wordplay, students gain important knowledge about language.

Procedure

Producing rhymes. Many phonemic play activities focus on producing rhymes. A familiar or easily learned rhyme or song is introduced, and the students are encouraged to substitute words or sounds. An example is "*Willaby Wallaby Woo*," in which students change the rhyming words in the couplet "*Willaby Wallaby Woo/An elephant sat on you*" so that the second line ends with a student's name and the first line ends with a rhyme beginning with W (for example, "*Willaby Wallaby Wissy/An elephant sat on Missy*").

Generate alliterative words. Students can also say as many words as they can think of that begin with a given consonant sound. This is a valuable complement to discrimination activities in which the teacher produces the words and the students identify them.

Explicit, Systematic Phonics

The purpose of phonics instruction is to teach students the association between the sounds of the language and the written symbols—spellings—that have been chosen to represent those sounds.

As with all alphabetic languages, English has a limited number of symbols—twenty-six—that are combined and recombined to make the written language. These written symbols are a visual representation of the speech sounds we use to communicate. This is simply a code. The faster the students learn the code and how it works, the faster the whole world of reading opens to them.

Students are introduced to the sounds and spellings of English in a very systematic, sequential manner. This allows them to continually build on what they learned the day before. As each sound/symbol relationship is introduced, students are introduced to and practice with words containing the target sound/spelling and then reinforce their learning through the use of engaging text specifically written for this purpose.

It can be very difficult for students to hear the individual sounds, or phonemes, that make up words. When phonics instruction is explicit—students are told the sounds associated with the different written symbols—there is no guesswork involved. They know that this sound /b/ is spelled b. Therefore, students in an SRA/Open Court Reading classroom spend time learning to discriminate individual speech sounds and then they learn the spellings of those sounds. This systematic explicit approach affords students the very best chance for early and continuing success.

Phonemic Play

Purpose

The purpose of the **Sound/Spelling Cards** (Levels 1–3) is to remind the students of the sounds of English and their spellings. The name of the picture on each card contains the target sound at the beginning for the consonants and in the middle for most vowels. In addition, the picture associates a sound with an action. This association is introduced through an interactive story in which the pictured object or character "makes" the sound. These cards are a resource for the students to use to remember sound/spelling associations for both reading and writing.

Procedure

Posting the Cards

Initially, post the first twenty-six cards face to the wall so that only the alphabet letters on the backs show. As you introduce each card, you will turn it to show the picture and the spellings on the front of the card. If, however, most of your students already have some knowledge of the letters—this is a second- or third-grade classroom and students are reviewing what they learned the year before—you may want to go ahead and place the cards with the picture and the spellings facing forward to provide support as they begin writing. Make sure that the cards are positioned so that you can touch them with your hand or with a pointer when you refer to them and so that all of the students can see them easily. The cards should be placed where the students can readily see them during reading and writing.

Special Devices

- Vowel spellings are printed in red to draw attention to them. Consonants are printed in black. The blank line in a spelling indicates that a letter will take the place of the blank in a word. For example, the replacement of the blank with *t* in the spelling *a_ e*, makes the word *ate*. The blank lines may also indicate the position of a spelling in a word or a syllable. The blank in *h_* for example, means that the spelling occurs at the beginning of a word or a syllable.
- The blanks in *_ie_* indicate that the *ie* spelling comes in the middle of a word or a syllable, while the blank in *_oy* shows that the *oy* spelling comes at the end of a word or a syllable. Uses of blanks in specific spellings are in the lessons. Please note now, however, that when you write a spelling of a sound on the board or an overhead transparency, you should include the blanks.
- The color of the background behind the spellings also has a meaning. Consonants have a white background. The colors behind vowel spellings are pronunciation clues. Short vowel spellings have a green background, which corresponds to the green box that appears before some consonant spellings. Thus, before *_ck* or *x* you will see a green box, which indicates that a short vowel always precedes that spelling. Long vowel spellings have a yellow background; other vowel spellings, such as r-controlled vowels and diphthongs, have a blue background. The color code reinforces the idea that vowels are special and have different pronunciations.

Introducing the Sound/Spelling Cards

In first grade, each sound and spelling is introduced by using a see/hear/say/write sequence. In grades two and three the same sequence is used in the review of the cards.

1. **See:** Students see the spelling or spellings on the **Sound/Spelling Card** and the board or an overhead transparency.
2. **Hear:** Students hear the sound used in words and in isolation in the story. The sound is, of course, related to the picture (and the action) shown on the **Sound/Spelling Card.**
3. **Say:** Students say the sound.
4. **Write:** Students write the spelling(s) for the sound.

There are a number of important points to remember about this technique.

- The first item written on the board or an overhead transparency is the spelling of the sound being introduced. This gives the spelling a special emphasis in the mind of the student. It is the "see" part of the sequence.
- One of the causes of blending failure is the failure to teach sounds thoroughly during introduction of the **Sound/Spelling Card** and during initial sounding and blending. To help ensure success for all students, make certain that every student is able to see the board or screen.
- After you present the sound and spelling, have several students go to the board to write the spelling. Have them say the sound as they write the spelling. After they have written the spelling of the sound, give them a chance to proofread their own work. Then give the other

Explicit, Systematic Phonics (continued)

students the opportunity to help with proofreading by noting what is good about the spelling and then suggesting how to make it better.

Sample Lesson, Using the Letter m and the Sound /m/

- Point to the **Sound/Spelling Card** and have students tell you whether it is a vowel or a consonant. Have them tell the name of the card. If they do not know it, tell them it is Monkey. Point to the *monkey* in the picture and say the word monkey, emphasizing the initial consonant sound—*mmmonkey*.
- Point to the spelling *m*. Tell students that /m/ is spelled *m*.
- If you wish make up an alliterative sentence about the Monkey or use the alliterative story that accompanies the card. (In first grade this story is printed on the page on which the card is introduced and in the Appendix. In grades two and three, the cards are printed in the Appendix of the ***Teacher's Edition.***) For example, *When Muzzie the monkey munches bananas, the sound she makes is /mmmmmm/.*
- If students had ***SRA/Open Court Reading*** before, you can ask them if they learned an action such as rubbing their tummies to help them remember the sound. If your students don't have an action they associate with the cards already, make some up with your students. They will have fun, and it will be another way for them to remember the sound/spelling relationships.
- Write *m* on the board or on an overhead transparency and say the sound. Write the letter again and ask the students to say the sound with you as they write the letter on slates, on paper, or with their index finger on a surface. Repeat this activity several times.
- Have the students listen for words beginning with /m/, indicating by some signal, such as thumbs-up or thumbs-down, whether they hear the /m/ sound and saying /m/ when they hear it in a word. Repeat with the sound in various positions in words. Encourage students to tell you and the class words with /m/ at the beginning and end as well as in the middle of words.
- Check students' learning by pointing to the card. Have students identify the sound, name the spelling, and discuss how the card can help them remember the sound.

Individual Sound/Spelling Cards

Use the **Individual Sound/Spelling Cards** for review and for small-group reteaching and practice sessions. Students can use them alone or with partners. Here are some suggestions for activities using the **Individual Sound/Spelling Cards**:

1. **Saying sounds from pictures.** The leader flashes pictures as the others say the sound each picture represents.
2. **Saying sounds.** The leader flashes the spellings on the cards as the others say the sound that the spellings represent.

The faster the students learn the code and how it works, the faster the whole world of reading opens to them.

3. **Naming spellings from pictures.** The leader flashes pictures. The others name the card, say the sound, and then name as many spellings as they can.
4. **Writing spellings from the pictures.** Working alone, a student looks at a picture and then writes as many spellings for that **Sound/Spelling Card** as he or she can remember.
5. **Saying words from pictures.** The leader presents a series of pictures. The others form words by blending the sounds represented.

Blending

Purpose

The purpose of blending is to teach the students a strategy for figuring out unfamiliar words. Initially, students will be blending sound by sound. Ultimately, the students will sound and blend only those words that they cannot read. Eventually, the blending process will become quick and comfortable for them.

Procedure

Learning the sounds and their spellings is only the first step in learning to read and write. The second step is learning to blend the sounds into words.

Blending Techniques

Blending lines are written on the board or an overhead transparency as the students watch and participate. The lines and sentences should not be written out before class begins. It is through the sound-by-sound blending of the words and the sentences that the students learn the blending process.

Sound-by-Sound Blending

- Write the spelling of the first sound in the word. Point to the spelling, and say the sound.
- Have the students say the sound with you as you say the sound again. Write the spelling of the next sound. Point to the spelling, and say the sound. Have the students say the sound with you as you say the sound again. After you have written the vowel spelling, blend through the vowel (unless the vowel is the first letter of the word), making the blending motion—a smooth sweeping of the hand beneath the sounds, linking them from left to right, for example, *ba*. As you make the blending motion, make sure that your hand is under the letter that corresponds to the sound you are saying at the moment.
- Have the students blend through the vowel. Write the spelling of the next sound. Point to the spelling and say the sound. Have the students say the sound with you as you touch the letter and say the sound again.
- Continue as described above through the word. After pronouncing the final sound in the word, make the blending motion from left to right under the word as you blend the sounds. Then have the students blend the word. Let them be the first to pronounce the word normally.
- Ask a student to read the word again and use it in a sentence. Ask another student to extend the sentence—that is, make it longer by giving more information. Help the student by asking an appropriate question about the sentence, using, for example, *How? When? Where? or Why?* Continue blending the rest of the words.

Whole-Word Blending

Once students are comfortable with sound-by-sound blending, they are ready for whole-word blending.

- Write the whole word to be blended on the board or an overhead transparency.
- Ask the students to blend the sounds as you point to them.
- Then have the students say the whole word.
- Ask the students to use the word in a sentence and then to extend the sentence.
- When all of the words have been blended, point to words randomly and ask individuals to read them.

Blending Syllables

In reading the ***Student Anthologies,*** students will often encounter multisyllabic words. Some students are intimidated by long words, yet many multisyllabic words are easily read by reading and blending the syllables rather than the individual sounds. Following a set of rules for syllables is difficult since so many of the rules have exceptions. Students need to remember that each syllable in a word contains one vowel sound.

- Have students identify the vowel sounds in the word.
- Have students blend the first syllable sound by sound if necessary or read the first syllable.
- Handle the remaining syllables the same way.
- Have students blend the syllables together to read.

Blending Sentences

Blending sentences is the logical extension of blending words. Blending sentences helps students develop fluency, which is critical to comprehension. Encourage students to reread sentences with phrasing and natural intonation.

- Write the sentence on the board or on a transparency, underlining any high-frequency sight words—words that the students cannot decode either because they are irregular or because they contain sounds or spellings that the students have not yet learned or reviewed. If the students have not read these words before, write the words on the board or an overhead transparency and introduce them before writing the sentence. These words should not be blended but read as whole words.

Building for Success

A primary cause of students's blending failure is their failure to understand how to use the **Sound/Spelling Cards**. Students need to practice sounds and spellings when the **Sound/Spelling Cards** are introduced and during initial blending. They also need to understand that if they are not sure of how to pronounce a spelling, they can check the cards.

Early blending may be frustrating. You must lead the group almost constantly. Soon, however, leaders in the group will take over. Watch to see whether any students are having trouble during the blending. Include them in small-group instruction sessions. At that time you may want to use the vowel-first procedure described below to reteach blending lines.

Extra Help

In working with small groups during **Workshop**, you may want to use some of the following suggestions to support students who need help with blending.

Vowel-First Blending

Vowel-first blending is an alternative to sound-by-sound and whole-word blending for students who need special help. Used in small-group sessions, this technique helps students who have difficulty with the other two types of blending to focus on the most important part of each word, the vowels, and to do only one thing at a time. These students are not expected to say a sound and blend it with another at virtually the same time. The steps to use in vowel-first blending follow:

Blending is the heart of phonics instruction and the key strategy students must learn to open the world of written language.

1. Across the board or on an overhead transparency, write the vowel spelling in each of the words in the line. For a short vowel, the line may look like this:
   a a a
   For a long vowel, the line may look like this:
   ee ea ea
2. Point to the spelling as the students say the sound for the spelling.
3. Begin blending around the vowels. In front of the first vowel spelling, add the spelling for the beginning sound of the word. Make the blending motion, and have the students blend through the vowel, adding a blank to indicate that the word is still incomplete. Repeat this procedure for each partial word in the line until the line looks like this:
   ma__ sa__ pa__
   see__ mea__ tea__
4. Have the students blend the partial word again as you make the blending motion and then add the spelling for the ending sound.
5. Make the blending motion, and have the students blend the completed word—for example, *mat* or *seed.*
6. Ask a student to repeat the word and use it in a sentence. Then have another student extend the sentence.
7. Repeat steps 4, 5, and 6 for each word in the line, which might look like this:
   mat sad pan
   or
   seed meat team

Tips

- In the early lessons, do blending with as much direction and dialogue as is necessary for success. Reduce your directions to a minimum as soon as possible. You have made good progress when you no longer have to say, "Sound—Sound—Blend," because the students automatically sound and blend as you write.
- Unless the line is used to introduce or to reinforce a spelling pattern, always ask a student to use a word in a sentence and then to extend the sentence immediately after you've developed the word. If the line is used to introduce or to reinforce a spelling pattern, however, ask the students to give sentences at the end of the line. Students will naturally extend sentences by adding phrases to the ends of the sentences. Encourage them to add phrases at the beginning or in the middle of the sentence.
- Use the vowel-first procedure in small group preteaching or reteaching sessions with students who are having a lot of trouble with blending. Remember that you must adapt the blending lines in the lessons to the vowel-first method.
- The sight words in the sentences cannot be blended. The students must approach them as sight words to be memorized. If students are having problems reading sight words, tell them the words. Cue marks written over the vowels may help students.
  - ✓ Straight line cue for long vowels
    EXAMPLES: *āpe, mē, fīne, sō, ūse*
  - ✓ Curved line cue for short vowels
    EXAMPLES: *căt, pĕt, wĭn, hŏt, tŭg*
  - ✓ Tent cue for variations of a and o
    EXAMPLES: *âll, ôff*
  - ✓ Dot cue for schwa sound with multiple-syllable words
    EXAMPLES: *salȧd, planėt, pencil, wagȯn*

PROGRAM APPENDIX

Explicit, Systematic Phonics (continued)

PROGRAM APPENDIX

Dictation and Spelling

Purpose

The purpose of dictation is to teach the students to spell words based on the sounds and spellings. In addition, learning dictation gives students a new strategy for reflecting on the sounds they hear in words to help them with their own writing.

As the students learn that sounds and spellings are connected to form words and that words form sentences, they begin to learn the standard spellings that will enable others to read their writing. As students learn to encode correctly, they develop their visual memory for words (spelling ability) and hence increase their writing fluency. Reinforcing the association between sounds and spellings and words through dictation gives students a spelling strategy that provides support and reassurance for writing independently. Reflecting on the sounds theyhear in words will help students develop writing fluency as they apply the strategy to writing unfamiliar words.

A dictation activity is a learning experience; it is not a test. The students should be encouraged to ask for as much help as they need. The proofreading techniques are an integral part of dictation. Students's errors lead to self-correction and, if need be, to reteaching. The dictation activities must not become a frustrating ordeal. The students should receive reinforcement and feedback.

There are two kinds of dictation: Sounds-in-Sequence Dictation and Whole-Word Dictation. The two types differ mainly in the amount of help they give the students in spelling the words. The instructions vary for each type.

Procedure

Sounds-in-Sequence Dictation

Sounds-in-Sequence Dictation gives the students the opportunity to spell words sound by sound, left to right, checking the spelling of each sound as they write. (Many students write words as they think they hear and say the words, not as the words are actually pronounced or written.)

- Pronounce the first word to be spelled. Use the word in a sentence and say the word again (word/sentence/word). Have students say the word.
- Tell students to think about the sounds they hear in the word. Ask, "What's the first sound in the word?"
- Have students say the sound.
- Point to the **Sound/Spelling Card**, and direct the students to check the card. Ask what the spelling is. The students should say the spelling and then write it.
- Proceed in this manner until the word is complete.
- Proofread. You can write the word on the board as a model, or have a student do it. Check the work by referring to the **Sound/Spelling Cards**. If a word is misspelled, have the students circle the word and write it correctly, either above the word or next to it.

Whole-Word Dictation

Whole-Word Dictation gives the students the opportunity to practice this spelling strategy with less help from the teacher.

- Pronounce the word, use the word in a sentence, and then repeat the word (word/sentence/word). Have the students repeat the word. Tell the students to think about the word. Remind the students to check the **Sound/Spelling Cards** for spellings and to write the word.
- Proofread. Write or have a volunteer write the word on the board as a model. Check the word by referring to the **Sound/Spelling Cards**.

Sentence Dictation

Writing dictated sentences. Help students apply this spelling strategy to writing sentences. Dictation supports the development of fluent and independent writing. Dictation of a sentence will also help the students apply conventions of written language, such as capitalization and punctuation.

- Say the complete sentence aloud.
- Dictate one word at a time following the procedure for Sounds-in-Sequence Dictation.

Continue this procedure for the rest of the words in the sentence. Remind the students to put a period at the end. Then proofread the sentence, sound by sound, or word by word. When sentences contain sight words, the sight words should be dictated as whole words, not sound by sound. As the students learn to write more independently, the whole sentence can be dictated word by word.

Proofreading

Whenever the students write, whether at the board or on paper, they should proofread their work. Proofreading is an important technique because it allows the students to learn by self-correction and it gives them an immediate second chance for success. It is the same skill students will use as they proofread their writing. Students should proofread by circling—not by erasing—each error. After they circle an error, they should write the correction beside the circle. This type of correction allows you and the students to see the error as well as the correct form. Students also can see what needs to be changed and how they have made their own work better.

You may want to have students use a colored pencil to circle and write in the correction. This will make it easier for them to see the changes.

Procedure for Proofreading

- Have a student write the word or sentence on the board or on an overhead transparency.
- Have students tell what is good.
- Have students identify anything that can be made better.
- If there is a mistake, have the student circle it and write it correctly.
- Have the rest of the class proofread their own work.

The Word Building Game

The major reason for developing writing alongside reading is that reading and writing are complementary communicative processes. Decoding requires that students blend the phonemes together into familiar cohesive words. Spelling requires that students segment familiar cohesive words into separate phonemes. Both help students develop an understanding of how the alphabetic principle works.

The Word Building game gives the students a chance to exercise their segmentation abilities and to practice using the sounds and spellings they are learning. The game is a fast-paced activity in which the students spell related sets of words with the teacher's guidance. (Each successive word in the list differs from the previous one by one sound.)

For the Word Building game, the students use their ***Individual Letter Cards*** (Levels K and 1) to build the words. (As an alternative they can use pencil and paper.) You will be writing at the board.

Give the students the appropriate ***Letter Cards.*** For example, if the list for the Word Building game is *am*, *at*, *mat*, they will need their *a*, *m*, and *t* ***Letter Cards.***

- Say the first word, such as *am.* (Use it in a sentence if you wish.) Have the students repeat the word. Say the word slowly, sound by sound. Tell the students to look at the ***Sound/Spelling Cards*** to find the letters that spell the sounds. Touch the first sound's card, in this case the Lamb card, and have students say the sound. Continue the process with the second sound. Write the word on the board while the students use their ***Letter Cards*** to spell it. Have students compare their words with your word, make changes as needed, and then blend and read the word with you.
- The students will then change the first word to make a different word. Say the next word in the list, (*at*). Segment the sounds of the word, and have students find the ***Sound/Spelling Cards*** that correspond. Write the new word (*at*) under the first word (*am*) on the board and have the students change their cards to spell the new word. Have them compare their words to yours and make changes as needed. Blend and read the word with the students. Continue in a like manner through the word list.

Spelling and Vocabulary Strategies

Spelling

Many people find English difficult, because English sound/spelling patterns seem to have a million exceptions. The key to becoming a good speller, however, is not just memorization. The key is recognizing and internalizing English spelling patterns. Some people do this naturally as they read and develop large vocabularies. They intuitively recognize spelling patterns and apply them appropriately. Others need explicit and direct teaching of vocabulary and spelling strategies and spelling patterns before they develop spelling consciousness.

Purpose

Spelling is a fundamental skill in written communication. Although a writer may have wonderful ideas, he or she may find it difficult to communicate those ideas without spelling skills. Learning to spell requires much exposure to text and writing. For many it requires a methodical presentation of English spelling patterns.

English Spelling Patterns

A basic understanding of English spelling patterns will help provide efficient and effective spelling instruction. Just as the goal of phonics instruction is to enable students to read fluently, the goal of spelling instruction is to enable students to write fluently so they can concentrate on ideas rather than spelling.

- **Sound Patterns** Many words are spelled the way they sound. Most consonants and short vowels are very regular. Once a student learns the sound/spelling relationships, he or she has the key to spelling many words.
- **Structural Patterns** Structural patterns are employed when adding endings to words. Examples of structural patterns include doubling the final consonant, adding *–s* or *–es* to form plurals, and dropping the final *e* before adding *–ing, -ed, -er,* or *–est.* Often these structural patterns are very regular in their application. Many students have little trouble learning these patterns.
- **Meaning Patterns** Many spelling patterns in English are *morphological;* in other words, the meaning relationship is maintained regardless of how a sound may change. Prefixes, suffixes, and root words that retain their spellings regardless of how they are pronounced are further examples of meaning patterns.
- **Foreign Language Patterns** Many English words are derived from foreign words and retain those language patterns. For example, *kindergarten* (German), *boulevard* (French), and *ballet* (French from Italian) are foreign language patterns at work in English.

Developmental Stages of Spelling

The most important finding in spelling research in the past thirty years is that students learn to spell in a predictable developmental sequence, much as they learn to read. It appears to take the average student three to six years to progress through the developmental stages and emerge as a fairly competent, mature speller.

Prephonemic The first stage is the *prephonemic* stage, characterized by random letters arranged either in continuous lines or in word-like clusters. Only the writer can "read" it, and it may be "read" differently on different days.

Semiphonemic As emergent readers learn that letters stand for sounds, they use particular letters specifically to represent the initial consonant sound and sometimes a few other very salient sounds. This marks the discovery of *phonemic awareness* that letters represent speech sounds in writing.

Phonemic When students can represent most of the sounds they hear in words, they have entered the *phonemic* stage of spelling. They spell what they hear, using everything they know about letter sounds, letter names, and familiar words. Many remedial spellers never develop beyond this stage and spell a word the way it sounds whenever they encounter a word they can't spell.

Transitional or Within Word Pattern As they are exposed to more difficult words, students discover that not all words are spelled as they sound. They learn that they must include silent letters, spell past tenses with *–ed*, include a vowel even in unstressed syllables, and remember how words look. The *transitional* stage represents the transition from primarily phonemic strategies to rule-bound spelling.

Derivational The *derivational* stage occurs as transitional spellers accumulate a large spelling vocabulary and gain control over affixes, contractions, homophones and other meaning patterns. They discover that related or derived forms of words share spelling features even if they do not sound the same. As spellers gain control over these subtle word features and spell most words correctly, they become conventional spellers.

Procedures

The spelling lessons are organized around different spelling patterns, beginning with phonetic spelling patterns and progressing to other types of spelling patterns in a logical sequence. High-frequency words and words from the literature selection with the focused pattern comprise the lesson word list. In general, the sound patterns occur in the first units at each grade, followed by structural patterns, meaning patterns, and foreign language patterns in the upper grade levels.

- As you begin each new spelling lesson, have students identify the spelling pattern and how it is like and different from other patterns.
- Give the pretest to help students focus on the lesson pattern.
- Have students proofread their own pretests immediately after the test, crossing out any misspellings and writing the correct spelling.
- Have them diagnose whether the errors they made were in the lesson pattern or in another part of the word. Help students determine where they made errors and what type of pattern they should work on to correct them.
- As students work through the spelling pages from the ***Spelling and Vocabulary Skills*** book, encourage them to practice the different spelling strategies in the exercises.

Sound Pattern Strategies

✓ **Pronunciation Strategy** As students encounter an unknown word, have them say the word carefully to hear each sound. Then have them spell each sound. (/s/ + /i/ + /t/: *sit)*

✓ **Consonant Substitution** Have students switch consonants. The vowel spelling usually remains the same. *(bat, hat, rat, flat, splat)*

✓ **Vowel Substitution** Have students switch vowels. The consonant spellings usually remain the same. (CVC: *hit, hat, hut, hot;* CVCV: *mane, mine;* CVVC: *boat, beat, bait, beet)*

✓ **Rhyming Word Strategy** Have students think of rhyming words and the rimes that spell a particular sound. Often the sound will be spelled the same way in another word. *(cub, tub, rub)*

Structural Pattern Strategies

✓ **Conventions Strategy** Have students learn the rule and exceptions for adding endings to words (dropping *y*, dropping *e*, doubling the final consonant, and so on).

✓ **Proofreading Strategy** Many spelling errors occur because of simple mistakes. Have students check their writing carefully and specifically for spelling.

✓ **Visualization Strategy** Have students think about how a word looks. Sometimes words "look" wrong because a wrong spelling pattern has been written. Have them double-check the spelling of any word that looks wrong.

Meaning Pattern Strategies

✓ **Family Strategy** When students are not sure of a spelling, have them think of how words from the same base word family are spelled. *(critic, criticize, critical; sign, signal, signature)*

Spelling and Vocabulary Strategies (continued)

✓ **Meaning Strategy** Have students determine a homophone's meaning to make sure they are using the right word. Knowing prefixes, suffixes, and base words will also help.

✓ **Compound Word Strategy** Tell students to break a compound apart and spell each word. Compounds do not follow conventions rules for adding endings. *(homework, nonetheless)*

✓ **Foreign Language Strategy** Have students think of foreign language spellings that are different from English spelling patterns. *(ballet, boulevard, sauerkraut)*

✓ **Dictionary Strategy** Ask students to look up the word in a dictionary to make sure their spelling is correct. If they do not know how to spell a word, have them try a few different spellings and look them up to see which one is correct. *(fotograph, photograph)* This develops a spelling consciousness.

Use the Final Test to determine understanding of the lesson spelling pattern and to identify any other spelling pattern problems. Encourage student understanding of spelling patterns and use of spelling strategies in all their writing to help transfer spelling skills to writing.

Vocabulary

Purpose

Strong vocabulary skills are correlated to achievement throughout school. The purpose of vocabulary strategy instruction is to teach students a range of strategies for learning, remembering, and incorporating unknown vocabulary words into their existing reading, writing, speaking, and listening vocabularies.

Procedures

The selection vocabulary instruction in the first and second part of the lesson focuses on teaching specific vocabulary necessary for understanding the literature selection more completely. The weekly vocabulary instruction in the Language Arts part of each lesson is geared toward teaching vocabulary skills and strategies to build and secure vocabulary through word relationships or develop vocabulary strategies for unknown words.

General Strategies

There is no question that having students read and reading to students are effective vocabulary instructional strategies. Most word learning occurs through exposure to words in listening and reading. Multiple exposures to words, particularly when students hear, see, say, and write words, is also effective. Word play, including meaning and dictionary games, helps to develop a word consciousness as well.

Vocabulary Skills and Strategies

Word Relationships People effectively learn new words by relating them to words they already know. An understanding of different word relationships enables students to quickly and efficiently secure new vocabulary. The weekly vocabulary lessons are organized around these types of word groups. Word relationships include:

- **Antonyms** Words with opposite or nearly opposite meanings. *(hot/cold)*
- **Synonyms** Words with similar meanings. *(cup, mug, glass)*
- **Multiple Meanings** Words that have more than one meaning. *(run, dressing, bowl)*
- **Shades of Meaning** Words that express degrees of a concept or quality. *(like, love, worship)*
- **Levels of Specificity** Words that describe at different levels of precision. *(living thing, plant, flower, daffodil)*
- **Analogies** Pairs of words that have the same relationship. *(ball is to baseball as puck is to hockey)*
- **Compound Words** Words comprised of two or more words. *(daylight)*
- **Homographs** Words that are spelled the same but have different meanings and come from different root words. *(bear, count)*
- **Homophones** Words that sound the same but have different spellings and meanings. *(mane/main, to/two/too)*
- **Base Word Families** Words that have the same base word. *(care, careless, careful, uncaring, carefree)*
- **Prefixes** An affix attached before a base word that changes the meaning of the word. *(misspell)*
- **Suffixes** An affix attached to the end of a base word that changes the meaning of the word. *(careless)*
- **Concept Vocabulary** Words that help develop understanding of a concept. *(space, sun, Earth, satellite, planet, asteroid)*
- **Classification and Categorization** Sorting words by related meanings. *(colors, shapes, animals, foods)*

Contextual Word Lists Teaching vocabulary in context is another way to secure understanding of unknown words. Grouping words by subject area such as science, social studies, math, descriptive words, new words and so on enables students to connect word meanings and build vocabulary understanding.

- **Figurative Language.** Idioms, metaphors, similes, personification, puns, and novel meanings need to be specifically taught, especially for English language learners.
- **Derivational Word Lists.** Presenting groups of words derived from particular languages or with specific roots or affixes is an effective way to reinforce meanings and spellings of foreign words and word parts.

Vocabulary Strategies for Unknown Words

Different strategies have been shown to be particularly effective for learning completely new words. These strategies are included in the ***Spelling and Vocabulary Skills*** activities.

Key Word This strategy involves providing or having students create a mnemonic clue for unknown vocabulary. For example, the word *mole* is defined in chemistry as a "gram molecule." By relating *mole* to *molecule*, students have a key to the meaning of the word.

Definitions Copying a definition from a dictionary is somewhat effective in learning new vocabulary. Combining using the word in writing and speaking adds to the effectiveness of this strategy. Requiring students to explain a word or use it in a novel sentence helps to ensure that the meaning is understood.

Context Clues Many words are learned from context, particularly with repeated exposure to words in reading and listening. Without specific instruction in consciously using context clues, however, unknown words are often ignored.

- **Syntax** How a word is used in a sentence provides some clue to its meaning.
- **External Context Clues** Hints about a word's meaning may appear in the setting, words, phrases, or sentences surrounding a word in text. Other known words in the text may be descriptive, may provide a definition (apposition), may be compared or contrasted, or may be used synonymously in context. Modeling and teaching students to use context to infer a word's meaning can help in learning unknown words.

Word Structure Examining the affixes and roots of a word may provide some clue to its meaning. Knowing the meaning of at least part of the word can provide a clue to its meaning. (For example, *unenforceable* can be broken down into meaningful word parts.)

Semantic Mapping Having students create a semantic map of an unknown word after learning its definition helps them to learn it. Have students write the new word and then list in a map or web all words they can think of that are related to it.

Semantic Feature Analysis A semantic feature analysis helps students compare and contrast similar types of words within a category to help secure unknown words. Have students chart, for example, the similarities and differences between different types of sports, including new vocabulary such as *lacrosse* and *cricket*.

Vocabulary

Purpose

Vocabulary is closely connected to comprehension. Considerable vocabulary growth occurs incidentally during reading. A clear connection exists between vocabulary development and the amount of reading a person does, and there are strong indications that vocabulary instruction is important and that understanding the meaning of key words helps with comprehension.

In ***Open Court Reading,*** vocabulary is addressed before, during, and after reading. Before reading, the teacher presents vocabulary words from the selection. Students use skills such as context clues, apposition, and structural analysis to figure out the meaning of the words. These selection vocabulary words are not only important to understanding the text but are also high utility words that can be used in discussing and writing about the unit theme.

During reading, students monitor their understanding of words and text. When they do not understand something, they stop and clarify what they have read. Students will use these same skills—context clues, apposition, structural elements, and the like—to clarify the meaning of additional words encountered while reading. Figuring out the meaning of words while reading prepares students for the demands of independent reading both in and out of school.

After reading, students review the vocabulary words that they learned before reading the selection. They also review any interesting words that they identified and discussed during reading. Students record in their Writer's Notebook both the selection vocabulary words and the interesting words they identified during their reading and are encouraged to use both sets of words in discussion and in writing.

Procedure

Before students read a selection, the teacher uses an overhead transparency to introduce the selection vocabulary to the class. The transparency contains two sentences for each selection vocabulary word. Students must use context clues, apposition, or word structure in the sentences to figure out the meaning of the underlined vocabulary words. If students cannot figure out the meaning of the word using one of these skills, they can consult the glossary or dictionary.

Below are suggestions for modeling the use of context clues, apposition, or word structure to figure out the meaning of a word.

Modeling Using Context Clues

Have students read the sentences on the transparency. Explain to students that they will use *context clues,* or other words in the sentence, to figure out the meaning of the underlined word. For example, if the word is "treacherous," the sentences might include:

1. Mrs. Frisby must undertake a treacherous journey to bring her son some medicine.
2. We took a treacherous walk near a swamp filled with crocodiles.

Have students look for clues in the sentences that might help them understand the meaning of the underlined word. Point out that a good clue in the second sentence is "near a swamp filled with crocodiles." This clue should help them understand that *treacherous* probably has something to do with danger. Guide students until they can give a reasonable definition of *treacherous.* To consolidate understanding of the word, ask another student to use the definition in a sentence.

Modeling Using Apposition

Have students read the sentences on the transparency. Explain to students that they will use *apposition* to figure out the meaning of the word. In apposition, the word is followed by the definition, which is set off by commas. For example, if the word is "abolitionist," the sentences might include the following:

1. The conductor thought he was an abolitionist, a person who wanted to end slavery.
2. John Brown was a famous abolitionist, a person who wanted to end slavery.

It should be pretty clear to students using apposition that the definition of the word *abolitionist* is "a person who wanted to end slavery."

Modeling Using Word Structure

Have students read the sentences on the transparency. Explain to students that they will use *word structure,* or parts of the selection vocabulary word, to figure out the meaning. For example, if the word is "energetic," the sentences might include:

1. The strong wind blew Ivan's ship away into uncharted seas.
2. The explorers Lewis and Clark went into uncharted territory.

Have students look at the word *uncharted* and break it into parts: the prefix *un-*, *chart,* and the suffix *–ed.* Students should know that the suffix *un-* means "not," and that the suffix *–ed* usually indicates the past tense of a verb. However, you may need to remind students about the meanings of these affixes. Ask students for the meaning of the word *chart.* Students should know that a chart could be a "map" or a "table." Guide them as they put together the definitions of the word parts, *un-* (not), *charted* (mapped or tabled). They should be able to come up with the definition "not mapped" or "unmapped" or even "unknown." Have them substitute their definition in the sentences to see if the definition makes sense. So, for instance, the first sentence would read "The strong wind blew Ivan's ship away into unmapped (or unknown) seas." Confirm with students that the new sentence makes sense, and then repeat the same process for the second sentence.

Reading Comprehension

PROGRAM APPENDIX

Everything the students learn about phonemic awareness, phonics, and decoding has one primary goal—to help them understand what they are reading. Without comprehension, there is no reading.

Reading Comprehension Strategies

Purpose

The primary aim of reading is comprehension. Without comprehension, neither intellectual nor emotional responses to reading are possible—other than the response of frustration. Good readers are problem solvers. They bring their critical faculties to bear on everything they read. Experienced readers generally understand most of what they read, but just as importantly, they recognize when they do not understand and they have at their command an assortment of strategies for monitoring and furthering their understanding.

The goal of comprehension strategy instruction is to turn responsibility for using strategies over to the students as soon as possible. Research has shown that students' comprehension and learning problems are not a matter of mental capacity but rather their inability to use strategies to help them learn. Good readers use a variety of strategies to help them make sense of the text and get the most out of what they read. Trained to use a variety of comprehension strategies, students dramatically improve their learning performance. In order to do this, the teacher models strategy use and gradually incorporates different kinds of prompts and possible student think-alouds as examples of the types of thinking students might do as they read to comprehend what they are reading.

Setting Reading Goals

Even before they begin reading and using comprehension strategies, good readers set reading goals and expectations. Readers who have set their own goals and have definite expectations about the text they are about to read are more engaged in their reading and notice more in what they read. Having determined a purpose for reading, they are better able to evaluate a text and determine whether it meets their needs. Even when the reading is assigned, the reader's engagement is enhanced when he or she has determined ahead of time what information might be gathered from the selection or how the selection might interest him or her.

Comprehension Strategies

Descriptions of strategies good readers use to comprehend the text follow.

Summarizing

Good readers sum up to check their understanding as they read. Sometimes they reread to fill in gaps in their understanding. Good readers use the strategy of summarizing to keep track of what they are reading and to focus their minds on important information. The process of putting the information in one's own words not only helps good readers remember what they have read, but also prompts them to evaluate how well they understand the information. Sometimes the summary reveals that one's understanding is incomplete, in which case it might be appropriate to reread the previous section to fill in the gaps. Good readers usually find that the strategy of summarizing is particularly helpful when they are reading long or complicated text.

Monitoring and Clarifying

Good readers constantly monitor themselves as they read in order to make sure they understand what they are reading. They note the characteristics of the text, such as whether it is difficult to read or whether some sections are more challenging or more important than others are. In addition, when good readers become aware that they do not understand, they take appropriate action, such as rereading, in order to understand the text better. As they read, good readers stay alert for problem signs such as loss of concentration, unfamiliar vocabulary, or lack of sufficient background knowledge to comprehend the text. This ability to self-monitor and identify aspects of the text that hinder comprehension is crucial to becoming a proficient reader.

Asking Questions

Good readers ask questions that may prepare them for what they will learn. If their questions are not answered in the text, they may try to find answers elsewhere and thus add even more to their store of knowledge. Certain kinds of questions occur naturally to a reader, such as clearing up confusion or wondering why something in the text is as it is. Intentional readers take this somewhat informal questioning one step further by formulating questions with the specific intent of checking their understanding. They literally test themselves by thinking of questions a teacher might ask and then by determining answers to those questions.

Predicting

Good readers predict what will happen next. When reading fiction, they make predictions about what they are reading and then confirm or revise those predictions as they go.

Making Connections

Good readers make connections between what they are reading and what they already know from past experience or previous reading.

Visualizing

Good readers visualize what is happening in the text. They form mental images as they read. They picture the setting, the characters, and the action in a story. Visualizing helps readers understand descriptions of complex activities or processes. Visualizing can also be helpful when reading expository text. When a complex process or an event is being described, the reader can follow the process or the event better by visualizing each step or episode. Sometimes an author or an editor helps the reader by providing illustrations, diagrams, or maps. If no visual aids have been provided, it may help the reader to create one.

Monitoring and Adjusting Reading Speed

Good readers understand that not all text is equal. Because of this good readers continuously monitor what they are reading and adjust their reading speed accordingly. They skim parts of the text that are not important or relevant to their reading goals and they purposely slow down when they encounter difficulty in understanding the text.

Procedures

Modeling and Thinking Aloud

One of the most effective ways to help students use and understand the strategies good readers use is to make strategic thinking public. Modeling these behaviors and encouraging students to think aloud as they attempt to understand text can demonstrate for everyone in a class how these behaviors are put into practice. Suggestions for think-alouds are provided throughout the teacher's guide.

The most effective models you can offer will be those that come from your own reading experiences. What kinds of questions did you ask yourself? What kinds of things surprised you the first time you read a story? What kinds of new information did you learn? What kinds of things were confusing until you reread or read further? Drawing on these questions and on your students' questions and comments as they read will make the strategic reading process more meaningful to the students. Below are suggestions for modeling each of the comprehension strategies.

- **Modeling Setting Reading Goals.** To model setting reading goals, engage students in the following:

- **Activate prior knowledge.** As you approach a new text, consider aloud what you already know about the subject or what your experiences have been in reading similar material.
- **Browse the text.** To get an idea of what to expect from a text, look at the title and the illustrations. Look for potential problems, such as difficult words. Have students glance quickly at each selection, looking briefly at the illustrations and the print. Have them tell what they think they might be learning about as they read the unit.
- **Decide what to expect from the text.** Anticipate enjoying the story, the language of the text, or the new information you expect to gain from the selection.

- **Modeling Summarizing.** Just as the strategy of summarizing the plot and then predicting what will happen next can enhance a student's reading of fiction, so too can the same procedure be used to the student's advantage in reading nonfiction. In expository text, it is particularly logical to stop and summarize at the end of a chapter or section before going on to the next. One way to model the valuable exercise of making predictions and at the same time expand knowledge is to summarize information learned from a piece of expository writing and then predict what the next step or category will be. Appropriate times to stop and summarize include the following:
  - when a narrative text has covered a long period of time or a number of events
  - when many facts have been presented
  - when an especially critical scene has occurred
  - when a complex process has been described
  - any time there is the potential for confusion about what has happened or what has been presented in the text
  - when returning to a selection
- **Modeling Monitoring and Clarifying.** A reader may need clarification at any point in the reading. Model this strategy by stopping at points that confuse you or that may confuse your students. Indicate that you are experiencing some confusion and need to stop and make sure you understand what is being read. Difficulty may arise from a challenging or unknown word or phrase. It may also stem from the manner in which the information is presented. Perhaps the author did not supply needed information. As you model this strategy, vary the reasons for stopping to clarify so that the students understand that good readers do not simply skip over difficult or confusing material—they stop and figure out what they don't understand
- **Modeling Asking Questions.** Learning to ask productive questions is not an easy task. Students' earliest experiences with this strategy take the form of answering teacher-generated questions. However, students should be able to move fairly quickly to asking questions like those a teacher might ask. Questions that can be answered with a simple yes or no are not typically very useful for helping them remember and understand what they have read. Many students find it helpful to ask questions beginning with *Who? What? When? Where? How?* or *Why?* As students become more accustomed to asking and answering questions, they will naturally become more adept at phrasing their questions. As their question asking becomes more sophisticated, they progress from simple questions that can be answered with explicit information in the text to questions that require making inferences based on the text.

Good readers use a variety of strategies to help them make sense of the text and get the most out of what they read.

- **Modeling Predicting.** Predicting can be appropriate at the beginning of a selection—on the basis of the titles and the illustrations—or at any point while reading a selection. At first, your modeling will take the form of speculation about what might happen next, but tell students from the start what clues in the text or illustrations helped you predict, in order to make it clear that predicting is not just guessing. When a student makes a prediction—especially a far-fetched one—ask what in the selection or in his or her own experience the prediction is based on. If the student can back up the prediction, let the prediction stand; otherwise, suggest that the student make another prediction on the basis of what he or she already knows. Often it is appropriate to sum up before making a prediction. This will help students consider what has come before as they make their predictions about what will happen next. When reading aloud, stop whenever a student's prediction has been confirmed or contradicted. Have students tell whether the prediction was correct. If students seem comfortable with the idea of making predictions but rarely do so on their own, encourage them to discuss how to find clues in the text that will help them.
- **Modeling Making Connections.** To model making connections, share with students any thoughts or memories that come to mind as you read the selection. Perhaps a character in a story reminds you of a childhood friend, allowing you to better identify with interactions between characters. Perhaps information in an article on Native-American life in the Old West reminds you of an article that you have read on the importance of the bison to Native Americans. Sharing your connections will help students become aware of the dynamic nature of reading and show them another way of being intentional, active learners.
- **Modeling Visualizing.** Model visualizing by describing the mental images that occur to you as you read. A well-described scene is relatively easy to visualize, and if no one does so voluntarily, you may want to prompt students to express their own visualizations. If the author has not provided a description of a scene, but a picture of the scene would make the story more interesting or comprehensible, you might want to model visualizing as follows: "Let's see. The author says that the street was busy, and we know that this story is set during the colonial period. From what I already know about those times, there were no cars, and the roads were different from the roads of today. The street may have been paved with cobblestones. Horses would have been pulling carriages or wagons. I can almost hear the horses' hoofs going clip-clop over the stones." Remind students that different readers may picture the same scene quite differently, which is fine. Every reader responds to a story in her or his own way.
- **Modeling Monitoring and Adjusting Reading Speed.** Just as readers need to monitor for problems, they need to be aware that different texts can be approached in different ways. For example, if reading a story or novel for enjoyment, the reader will typically read at a relaxed speed that is neither so fast as to be missing information nor as slow as they might read a textbook. If on the other hand, the reader is reading a textbook, he or she will probably decrease speed to assure understanding and make sure that all important information is read and understood. When modeling this strategy, be sure you indicate why you, as the reader, have chosen to slow down or speed up. Good readers continually monitor their speed and ability to understand throughout reading.

Reading Comprehension (continued)

Reading Aloud

At the beginning of the year, students should be encouraged to read selections aloud. This practice will help you and them understand some of the challenges posed by the text and how different students approach these challenges.

Reading aloud helps students build fluency, which in turn will aid their comprehension. Students in grades K–3 can use **Decodable Books** to build fluency, while students in grades 4–6 can use the literature from the **Student Anthologies.** Fluent second graders read between 82 and 124 words per minute with accuracy and understanding, depending on the time of the year (fall/spring).

Fluent third graders can be expected to read between 107 and 142 words per minute; fourth (125/143); fifth (126/151); sixth (127/153).

Make sure that you set aside time to hear each student read during the first few days of class—the days devoted to Getting Started are perfect for this—so that you can determine students' abilities and needs. **Workshop** is also a good time to listen to any students who do not get to read aloud while the class is reading the selection together.

If your students have not previously engaged in the sort of strategic thinking aloud that is promoted throughout the ***SRA/Open Court Reading*** program, you will have to do all or most of the modeling at first, but encourage the students to participate as soon as possible.

As the year progresses, students should continue reading aloud often, especially with particularly challenging text. Model your own use of strategies not only to help students better understand how to use strategies but also to help them understand that actively using strategies is something that good, mature readers do constantly.

Most students are unaccustomed to thinking out loud. They will typically stand mute as they try to figure out an unfamiliar word or deal with a confusing passage. When this happens, students should be encouraged to identify specifically what they are having difficulty with. A student might identify a particular word, or he or she may note that the individual words are familiar but the meaning of the passage is unclear.

Active Response

Not only are good readers active in their reading when they encounter problems, but they respond constantly to whatever they read. In this way they make the text their own. As students read they should be encouraged to:

- Make as many connections as they can between what they are reading and what they already know.
- Visualize passages to help clarify their meanings or simply to picture appealing descriptions.
- Ask questions about what they are reading. The questions that go through their minds during reading will help them to examine, and thus better understand, the text. Doing so may also interest them in pursuing their own investigations. The questions may also provide a direction for students' research or exploration.
- Summarize and make predictions as a check on how well they understand what they are reading.

Tips

- Remember that the goal of all reading strategies is comprehension. If a story or article does not make sense, the reader needs to choose whatever strategies will help make sense of it. If one strategy does not work, the reader should try another.
- Always treat problems encountered in text as interesting learning opportunities rather than something to be avoided or dreaded.
- Encourage students to think out loud about text challenges.
- Encourage students to help each other build meaning from text. Rather than telling each other what a word is or what a passage means, students should tell each other how they figured out the meanings of challenging words and passages.
- Encourage students to freely share strategies they have devised on their own. You might want to write these on a large sheet of paper and tape them to the board.
- Assure students that these are not the only strategies that can be used while reading. Any strategy that they find helpful in understanding text is a good useful strategy.
- An absence of questions does not necessarily indicate that students understand what they are reading. Be especially alert to students who never seem to ask questions. Be sure to spend tutorial time with these students occasionally and encourage them to discuss specific selections in the context of difficulties they might have encountered and how they solved them as well as their thoughts about unit concepts.
- Observing students' responses to text will enable you to ascertain not only how well they understand a particular selection but also their facility in choosing and applying appropriate strategies. Take note of the following:

✓ Whether the strategies a student uses are effective in the particular situation.

✓ Whether the student chooses from a variety of appropriate strategies or uses the same few over and over.

✓ Whether the student can explain to classmates which strategies to use in a particular situation and why.

✓ Whether the student can identify alternative resources to pursue when the strategies she or he has tried are not effective.

✓ Whether students' application of a given strategy is becoming more effective over a period of time.

Becoming familiar and comfortable with these self-monitoring techniques gives readers the confidence to tackle material that is progressively more difficult. A good, mature reader knows that he or she will know when understanding what he or she is reading is becoming a problem and can take steps to correct the situation.

Reading Comprehension Skills

Purpose

An important purpose of writing is to communicate thoughts from one person to another. The goal of instruction in reading comprehension skills is to make students aware of the logic behind the structure of a written piece. If the reader can discern the logic of the structure, he or she will be more able to understand the author's logic and gain knowledge both of the facts and the intent of the selection. By keeping the organization of a piece in mind and considering the author's purpose for writing, the reader can go beyond the actual words on the page and make inferences or draw conclusions based on what was read. Strong, mature readers utilize these "between the lines" skills to get a complete picture of what the writer is not only saying, but what the writer is trying to say.

Effective comprehension skills include:

Author's Point of View

Point of view involves identifying who is telling the story. If a character in the story is telling the story, that one character describes the action and tells what the other characters are like. This is first-person point of view. In such a story, one character will do the talking and use the pronouns *I*, *my*, *me*. All other characters' thoughts, feelings, and emotions, will be reported through this one character.

If the story is told in third-person point of view, someone outside the story who is aware of all of the characters' thoughts and feelings and actions is relating them to the reader. All of the characters are referred to by their names or the pronouns *he/she*, *him/her*, *it*.

If students stay aware of who is telling a story, they will know whether they are getting the full picture or the picture of events as seen through the eyes of only one character.

Sequence

The reader can't make any decisions about relationships or events if he or she has no idea in which order the events take place. The reader needs to pay attention to how the writer is conveying the sequence. Is it simply stated that first this happened and then that happened? Does the writer present the end of the story first and then go back and let the reader know the sequence of events? Knowing what the sequence is and how it is presented helps the reader follow the writer's line of thought.

Fact and Opinion

Learning to distinguish fact from opinion is essential to critical reading and thinking. Students learn what factors need to be present in order for a statement to be provable. They also learn that an opinion, while not provable itself, should be based on fact. Readers use this knowledge to determine for themselves the validity of the ideas presented in their reading.

Main Idea and Details

An author always has something specific to say to his or her reader. The author may state this main idea in different ways, but the reader should always be able to tell what the writing is about.

To strengthen the main point or main idea of a piece, the author provides details to help the reader understand. For example, the author may use comparison and contrast to make a point, provide examples, provide facts, give opinions, give descriptions, give reasons or causes, or give definitions. The reader needs to know what kinds of details he or she is dealing with before making a judgment about the main idea.

Compare and Contrast

Using comparison and contrast is one of the most common and easiest ways a writer uses to get his or her reader to understand a subject. Comparing and contrasting unfamiliar thoughts, ideas, or things with familiar thoughts, ideas and things gives the reader something within his or her own experience base to use in understanding.

Cause and Effect

What made this happen? Why did this character act the way he or she did? Knowing the causes of events helps the reader to see the whole story. Using this information to identify the probable outcomes (effects) of events or actions will help the reader anticipate the story or article.

Classify and Categorize

The relationships of actions, events, characters, outcomes, and such in a selection should be clear enough for the reader to see the relationships. Putting like things or ideas together can help the reader understand the relationships set up by the writer.

Author's Purpose

Everything that is written is written for a purpose. That purpose may be to entertain, to persuade, or to inform. Knowing why a piece is written—what purpose the author had for writing the piece, gives the reader an idea of what to expect and perhaps some prior idea of what the author is going to say.

If a writer is writing to entertain, then the reader can generally just relax and let the writer carry him or her away. If on the other hand, the purpose is to persuade, it will help the reader understand and keep perspective if he or she knows that the purpose is to persuade. The reader can be prepared for whatever argument the writer delivers.

Drawing Conclusions

Often, writers do not directly state everything—they take for granted their audience's ability to "read between the lines." Readers draw conclusions when they take from the text small pieces of information about a character or event and use this information to make a statement about that character or event.

Making Inferences

Readers make inferences about characters and events to understand the total picture in a story. When making inferences, readers use information from the text, along with personal experience or knowledge, to gain a deeper understanding of a story event and its implications.

Procedure

Read the Selection

First have students read the selection through using whatever strategies they need to help them to make sense of the selection. Then discuss the selection to assure that students did, indeed, understand what they read. Talk about any confusion they may have, and make any necessary clarifications.

Reread

Revisiting or rereading a selection allows the reader to note specific techniques that authors use to organize and present information in narratives and expository genres. Once students have a basic understanding of the piece, have them reread the selection in whole or in part, concentrating on selected skills. Choose examples of how the writer organized the piece to help the reader understand.

Limit this concentration on specific comprehension/writing skills to one or two that can be clearly identified in the piece. Trying to concentrate on too many things will just confuse students and make it harder for them to identify any of the organizational devices used by the writer. If a piece has many good examples of several different aspects, then go back to the piece several times over a span of days.

Write

Solidify this connection between how an author writes and reading by encouraging students to incorporate these different devices into their own writing. As they attempt to use specific organizational devices in their writing, they will get a clearer understanding of how to identify them when they are reading.

Remind students often that the purpose of any skill exercise is to give them tools to use when they are reading and writing. Unless students learn to apply the skills to their own reading—in every area of reading and study—then they are not gaining a full understanding of the purpose of the exercise.

Grammar, Usage, and Mechanics

PROGRAM APPENDIX

Writing is a complicated process. A writer uses handwriting, spelling, vocabulary, grammar, usage, genre structures, and mechanics skills with ideas to create readable text. In addition, a writer must know how to generate content, or ideas, and understand genre structures in order to effectively present ideas in writing. Many students never progress beyond producing a written text that duplicates their everyday speech patterns. Mature writers, however, take composition beyond conversation. They understand the importance of audience and purpose for writing. They organize their thoughts, eliminating those that do not advance their main ideas, and elaborating on those that do so that their readers can follow a logical progression of ideas in an essay or story. Mature writers also know and can use the conventions of grammar, usage, spelling, and mechanics. They proofread and edit for these conventions, so their readers are not distracted by errors.

Purpose

The Study of English Conventions

Over the years the study of grammar, usage, and mechanics has gone in and out of favor. In the past century much research has been done to demonstrate the effectiveness of traditional types of instruction in the conventions of English. Experience and research have shown that learning grammatical terms and completing grammar exercises have little effect on the student's practical application of these skills in the context of speaking or writing. These skills, in and of themselves, do not play a significant role in the way students use language to generate and express their ideas—for example during the prewriting and drafting phases of the writing process. In fact, emphasis on correct conventions has been shown to have a damaging effect when it is the sole focus of writing instruction. If students are evaluated only on the proper use of spelling, grammar, and punctuation, they tend to write fewer and less complex sentences.

Knowledge of English conventions is, however, vitally important in the editing and proofreading phases of the writing process. A paper riddled with mistakes in grammar, usage, or mechanics is quickly discounted. Many immature writers never revise or edit. They finish the last sentence and turn their papers in to the teacher. Mature writers employ their knowledge of English language conventions in the editing phase to refine and polish their ideas.

The study of grammar, usage, and mechanics is important for two reasons.

1. Educated people need to know and understand the structure of their language, which in large part defines their culture.
2. Knowledge of grammar gives teachers and students a common vocabulary for talking about language and makes discussions of writing tasks more efficient and clear.

Procedures

The key issue in learning grammar, usage, and mechanics is *how* to do it. On the one hand, teaching these skills in isolation from writing has been shown to be ineffective and even detrimental if too much emphasis is placed on them. On the other hand, not teaching these skills and having students write without concern for conventions is equally ineffective. The answer is to teach the skills in a context that allows students to directly apply them to a reading or writing activity. Students should be taught proper use of puctuation or subject/verb agreement at the same time they are taught to proofread for those conventions. As they learn to apply their knowledge of conventions during the final stages of the writing process, they will begin to see that *correcting* errors is an editorial, rather than a composing skill.

History of English

A basic understanding of the history and structure of the English language helps students understand the rich but complex resource they have for writing.

Old English

The English language began about AD 450 when the Angles, Jutes, and Saxons—three tribes that lived in northern Europe—invaded the British Isles. Much of their language included words that had to do with farming (*sheep, dirt, tree, earth*). Many of their words are the most frequently used words in the English language today. Because of Latin influences, English became the first of the European languages to be written down.

Middle English

In 1066 William the Conqueror invaded England and brought Norman French with him. Slowly Old English and Norman French came together, and Middle English began to appear. Today 40% of Modern English comes from French. With the introduction of the printing press English became more widespread.

Modern English

With the Renaissance and its rediscovery of classical Greek and Latin, many new words were created from Greek and Latin word elements. This continued intensively during the Early Modern English period. This rich language was used in the writings of Shakespeare and his contemporaries and profoundly influenced the nature and vocabulary of English. With dictionaries and spelling books, the English language became more standardized, although it continues to be influenced by other languages and new word and trends. These influences continue to make English a living, dynamic language.

Punctuation

Early writing had no punctuation or even spaces between words. English punctuation had its beginning in ancient Greece and Rome. Early punctuation reflected speaking, rather than reading, but after the invention of printing, by the end of the eighteenth century, most of the rules for punctuation were established, although not the same in all languages.

The Structure of English

Grammar is the sound, structure, and meaning system of language. People who speak the same language are able to communicate because they intuitively know the grammar system of that language, the rules of making meaning. All languages have grammar, and yet each language has its own grammar.

Traditional grammar study usually involves two areas:

- **Parts of speech** (nouns, verbs, adjectives, adverbs, pronouns, prepositions, conjunctions) are typically considered the content of grammar. The parts of speech involve the *form* of English words.
- **Sentence structure** (subjects, predicates, objects, clauses, phrases) is also included in grammar study. Sentence structure involves the *function* of English.

Mechanics involves the conventions of punctuation and capitalization. Punctuation helps readers understand writers' messages. Proper punctuation involves marking off sentences according to grammatical structure. In speech students can produce sentences as easily and unconsciously as they can walk, but in writing they must think about what is and what is not a sentence.

In English there are about twelve punctuation marks (period, comma, quotation marks, question mark, exclamation point, colon, semicolon, hyphen, ellipsis, parentheses, brackets, dash). Most immature writers use only three: period, comma, and question mark. The experienced writer or poet with the command of punctuation adds both flexibility and meaning to his or her sentences through his or her use of punctuation.

Usage. Language varies over time, across national and geographical boundaries, by gender, across age groups, and by socioeconomic status. When the variation occurs within a given language, the different versions of the same language are called *dialects.* Every language has a *prestige dialect* associated with education and financial success. In the United States, this *dialect* is known as Standard English and is the language of school and business.

Usage involves the word choices people make when speaking certain dialects. Word choices that are perfectly acceptable in conversation among friends may be unacceptable in writing. Usage is often the most obvious indicator of the difference between conversation and composition. Errors in word usage can make a writer seem ignorant and thus jeopardize his or her credibility not matter how valid or important his or her overall message might be. Usage depends on a student's cultural and linguistic heritage. If the dialect students have learned is not the formal language of school settings or if it is not English, students must master another dialect or language in order to write Standard English.

The English Language Conventions lessons in ***Open Court Reading*** are structured to focus on grammar and usage or mechanics skills presented in a logical sequence. A skill is introduced on the first day of the lesson with appropriate models and then practiced in reading and writing on subsequent days to ensure that skills are not taught in isolation. Encourage students to use the focused English language convention presented in each lesson as they complete each Writing Process Strategies activity. Also encourage them to reread their writing, checking for proper use of the conventions taught. With practice, students should be able to apply their knowledge of conventions to any writing they do.

Tips

- Some of the errors students make in writing are the result simply of not carefully reading their final drafts. Many errors occur because the writer's train of thought was interrupted and a sentence is not complete or a word is skipped. These may look like huge errors that a simple rereading can remedy. Most often the writer can correct these types of errors on his or her own. A major emphasis of any English composition program should be to teach the editing and proofreading phases of the writing process so students can eliminate these types of errors themselves. This involves a shift in perception—from thinking of grammar as a set of discrete skills that involve mastery of individual rules, to understanding grammar as it applies to the act of communicating in writing.
- As students learn English language conventions, they should be expected to incorporate them into their written work. A cumulative student checklist of the grammar, usage, and mechanics skills covered in a grade level appears in the back of the ***Writer's Workbook.***
- Sometimes, students write sentences that raise grammatically complex problems that require a deep understanding of English grammar. Use the **Sentence Lifting** strategies outlined in the **Writing Process Strategies** part of the Appendix to identify and discuss these more sophisticated types of errors that can include:
  - **Faulty Parallelism.** Parts of a sentence parallel in meaning are not parallel in structure.
  - **Nonsequitors.** A statement does not follow logically from something said previously.
  - **Dangling Modifiers.** A phrase or clause does not logically modify the word next to it.
  - **Awkwardness.** Sentences are not written simply.
  - **Wordiness.** Thoughts are not written in as few words as possible.
  - **Vocabulary.** Precise words are not used.

Listening, Speaking, Viewing

Some people are naturally good listeners and others have no trouble speaking in front of groups. Many people, however, need explicit instruction on how to tune in for important details and how to organize and make an oral presentation. While some people naturally critique what they read, hear, and see, there are many others who need specific guidance to develop skills for analyzing what they encounter in images and the media. The abilities to appropriately listen and speak in conversations and in groups as well as to critically evaluate the information with which they are presented, are fundamental skills that will serve students throughout their lives.

Purpose

In addition to reading and writing, listening, speaking, and viewing complete the language arts picture. Through the development of these language arts skills, students gain flexibility in communicating orally, visually, or in writing. When speaking and listening skills are neglected, many students have difficulty speaking in front of groups, organizing a speech, or distinguishing important information they hear. A top anxiety for many adults is speaking in front of groups. Much of this anxiety would not exist if listening, speaking, and viewing skills were taught from the early years.

The Listening, Speaking, Viewing instruction focuses on the literature selection or the Writing Process Strategies to provide context, reinforce other elements of the lesson, and integrate the other language arts. Many of the Listening, Speaking, Viewing skills are very similar to reading or writing skills. For example, listening for details is the same type of skill as reading for details. Preparing an oral report employs many of the same skills as preparing a written report. Learning to use these skills effectively gives students flexibility in how they approach a task.

Procedure

Listening, speaking, and viewing skills are presented with increasing sophistication throughout every grade level of ***Open Court Reading*** in the Language Arts part of each lesson. Every unit includes at least one lesson on each of following skills so that students encounter the skills again and again throughout a grade level:

- **Listening.** Listening skills involve listening comprehension and listening for different purposes, such as to identify sequence or details, to summarize or draw conclusions, or to follow directions.
- **Speaking.** Speaking skills involve conversational speech, appropriate volume, oral presentations, and using effective grammar. Speaking skills also involve using language, including using descriptive words, using figurative language, and using formal and informal language.
- **Viewing.** Viewing skills develop critical skills for understanding main ideas and messages in images, mass media, and other multimedia.
- **Interaction.** Interaction instruction focuses on a combination of listening and speaking skills. These include asking and responding to questions, nonverbal cues such as eye contact, facial expression, and posture, as well as contributing to and interacting in group settings.
- **Presenting Information.** The last Listening, Speaking, Viewing lesson in every unit usually focuses on presentation skills. These include sharing ideas, relating experiences or stories, organizing information, and preparing for speeches. These lessons often parallel the Writing Process Strategies instruction, so that students can prepare their information in written or oral form.

Tips

- Point out the parallels among the language arts skills: providing written and oral directions, telling or writing a narrative, and so on. Encourage students to see that they have choices for communicating. Discuss the similarities and differences between different forms of communication, and determine whether one is preferable in a given situation.
- Ensure that all students have opportunities to speak in small groups and whole-class situations.
- Provide and teach students to allow appropriate wait time before someone answers a question.

Writing

The ability to write with clarity and coherence is essential to students' success in school as well as in life. Communicating through writing is becoming more and more important in this age of computers. Yet, writing remains a major problem for students at all levels, as well as adults in the workplace.

Purpose

Writing is a complex process. It requires the ability to use a variety of skills (penmanship, grammar, usage, mechanics, spelling, vocabulary) fluently and appropriately at the same time one's creative and critical thinking processes create and structure an idea. Familiarity with the structures of writing and different genres, audiences and purposes is necessary to write appropriately, as well. The art of writing well also involves writer's craft, the ability to manipulate words and sentences for effect.

As strange as it may seem, the better a writer is, the *harder* he or she works at writing. The best writers are not the best because they are naturally talented. They are the best usually because they work the hardest. Good writers really do take *more* time than others in the planning and revising stages of the writing process. Poorer writers make writing look easy by writing without planning and typically build a composition sentence by sentence. They turn in their papers with little or no correction.

The goals of writing instruction have many facets:

- To model and practice writing in a variety of writing genres so that students can choose and write in an appropriate form.
- To model and practice a writing process to help students develop routines for planning their work and then revising and editing it.
- To practice using spelling, vocabulary, and English language conventions skills in writing so that students can use them fluently.
- To develop writing traits: ideas, organization, voice, word choice, sentence fluency, and presentation so that students become effective writers.

Just as the goal of phonics instruction is to teach students to read, the Writing Process Strategies instruction in ***Open Court Reading*** focuses on skills, structures, and strategies for writing. The goal of this instruction is to learn how to write, rather than to develop a particular idea. From this instruction, students will have a comprehensive bank of tools for writing, which they can then employ in the development of their Research and Inquiry investigations in each unit or in any other writing application.

Procedures

Writing Genres

There are several different genres students are typically asked to write. These usually

The best writers are not the best because they are naturally talented. They are the best usually because they work the hardest. Good writers really do take* more *time than others in the planning and revising stages of the writing process.

include many creative stories and a few reports. The only narrative writing most adults do, however, is summaries of meetings. The bulk of adult writing consists of writing reports, letters, analyses, memos, and proposals. College students, as well, typically write research reports or critiques. A literate student needs to be able to choose and write in appropriate genre.

- Narrative writing is story writing, which has a beginning, middle, and end. It includes myth, realistic fiction, historical fiction, biography, science fiction, fantasy, folktale, and legend.
- Expository writing is informational writing. It includes research reports, scientific investigation, summaries, and explanations of a process.
- Descriptive writing is observational writing that includes details. It has descriptive paragraphs that may be part of narrative or expository writing.
- Poetry writing involves particular attention to word choice and rhythm. Poetry may be free form, ballad, rhyming or a variety of other forms.
- Personal writing is functional writing to help record ideas, thoughts, or feelings or to communicate with others and may include email, journal, lists, and messages.
- Persuasive writing involves the development of a persuasive argument. It includes posters, persuasive essays, and advertisements.

In ***Open Court Reading*** the first unit of every grade teaches the writing process and traits of writing. Each subsequent unit focuses on a particular genre appropriate for the unit content. Expository and persuasive writing are typically in the units with research themes such as medicine or surviving; personal, narrative, descriptive, and poetry writing are in units with universal themes, such as friendship and courage. Exemplary models of each form of writing are included either in the literature selection, on the ***Language Arts Transparencies,*** or in the ***Language Arts Handbook.***

Each genre has its own form and function. For example:

- A personal narrative is probably best ordered as a straightforward chronological retelling of events. Dialogue may help to tell the story.
- A process description should be told in a step-by-step order. The draft should include as much information as possible; each step must be clear. If the piece needs cutting, the student can always do it later.
- A persuasive piece appeals to feelings. It requires facts as well as expert opinions.
- An interview could be written as a series of questions and answers.
- The order of details in a descriptive piece must be easy to follow—from left to right, top to bottom, or whatever order makes sense.
- A fictional story must include details describing characters, setting, and the characters' actions. Dialogue also helps to tell the story.

The goal is not to develop full-blown novels and compositions, but to experience the structures of different forms of writing.

Structures of Writing

Structures of writing involve the effective development of sentences, paragraphs, and compositions. In ***Open Court Reading*** structures of writing are taught within the context of the Writing Process Strategies activities rather than in isolation, so that students integrate their practice of writing structures as they develop different writing genres.

Writer's Craft

Writer's Craft involves the elements and choices writers make to add drama, suspense, or lightheartedness to a written work. These elements may include foreshadowing, use of figurative language, dialogue, or enhancement of setting or use of description to affect the mood and tone. In ***Open Court Reading,*** along with structures of writing, the writer's craft is pointed out in the literature selection and then taught and practiced within the context of the Writing Process Strategies activities.

Writing Traits

Writing traits are those elements and qualities in a composition that enhance the effectiveness of the writing. These include:

- Ideas/Content. Not only the quality of the idea, but the development, support, and focus of the idea makes a strong composition.

- Organization. In quality writing, the organization develops the central idea. The order and structure move the reader through the text easily. The beginning grabs the reader's attention and the conclusion adds impact.
- Voice. Voice is the overall tone of a piece of writing. Good writers choose a voice appropriate for the topic, purpose, and audience. As students develop writing skills, a unique style begins to emerge. The writing is expressive, engaging, or sincere, demonstrating a strong commitment to the topic.
- Word Choice. In quality writing words convey the intended message in an interesting, precise, and natural way appropriate to audience and purpose.
- Sentence Fluency. Sentence fluency enhances the flow and rhythm of a composition. In good writing sentence patterns are somewhat varied, contributing to ease in oral reading.
- Conventions. Good writers demonstrate consistent use and awareness of English language conventions.
- Presentation. A quality piece of writing includes an impressive presentation with attention to format, style, illustration, and clarity.

In ***Open Court Reading,*** the traits of writing are taught in the first unit and then practiced in every Writing Process Strategies activity as an integral part of the writing process.

The Writing Process

Providing a routine or process for students to follow will help them to learn a systematic approach to writing. By following the steps of the writing process, students will learn to approach everything they write with purpose and thought. They learn that although writing takes time and thought, there are steps they can take to make their writing clear, coherent, and appealing to their audience.

In ***Open Court Reading,*** the first unit of every grade provides an overview and teaching of the writing process, including strategies and examples for getting ideas, determining audience and purpose for writing, organizing writing, drafting, revising, editing, and presenting. The vehicle used to apply this instruction is a student autobiography. The autobiographies can be collected in a school portfolio to assess writing development over the course of the elementary years.

Prewriting

Purpose

Prewriting is that phase of the writing process when students think through an idea they want to write about. To improve their writing, students should think about their ideas, discuss them, and plan how they want readers to respond. It is important for students to take time before writing to plan ahead so that they can proceed from one phase of the writing process to another without spending unnecessary time making decisions that should have been made earlier. Prewriting is the most time-consuming phase of the writing process, but it may be the most important.

The goal is not to develop full-blown novels and compositions, but to familiarize and practice the structures of different forms of writing.

Procedure

Good student writers

- Listen to advice about time requirements and plan time accordingly.
- Spend time choosing, thinking about, and planning the topic.
- Spend time narrowing the topic.
- Determine the purpose for writing.
- Consider the audience and what readers already know about the topic.
- Conduct research, if necessary, before writing.
- Get information from a lot of different sources.
- Use models for different types of writing, but develop individual plans.
- Organize the resource information.
- Make a plan for writing that shows how the ideas will be organized.
- Elaborate on a plan and evaluate and alter ideas as writing proceeds.

Noting Writing Ideas

Students can make notes of writing ideas at any time, with a special time being set aside following the discussion of each reading selection. The writing ideas students get from a discussion might be concerned with the topic of the selection they just read or with an aspect of the author's style. You should keep such a list of writing ideas also, and think aloud occasionally as you make writing idea notes.

Students must make many decisions during the prewriting phase of the writing process. Most students can benefit from talking with a partner or a small group of classmates about these decisions. They may want to discuss some of the following points.

- **Genre** or format of each writing piece. Having decided to use a writing idea such as "a misunderstanding on the first day of school," the student must decide how to use it—for example, as a personal narrative, a realistic fiction story, a poem, a fantasy story, a play, a letter, and so on.
- **Audience**. Although students' writing pieces will be shared with classmates and with you, some may ultimately be intended for other audiences.
- **Writing Purpose**. Each student should write a sentence that tells the purpose of the piece he or she plans to write. The purpose statement should name the intended audience and the effect the writer hopes to have on that audience. For example, a writer may want to describe her first day in school. The intended audience is kindergarten students, and she intends her story to be humorous. Her purpose statement would read, "I want to write a funny story for other students about my first day in kindergarten."
- **Planning**. Some writers may find it helpful to brainstorm with a partner or small group to list words and phrases they might use in a piece of writing. Sometimes this list can be organized into webs of related ideas or details. This kind of prewriting activity might be particularly useful for planning a descriptive piece. For planning a comparison/contrast piece, a writer might use another kind of visual organizer, such as a Venn diagram. Students planning fiction pieces might use a story frame or plot line.

Tips

- Circulate as students make notes on writing ideas or work in small groups on prewriting activities.
- Notice which students are having difficulty coming up with writing ideas. It may help to pair these students with students who have many ideas.
- Do not worry if this phase of the process seems noisy and somewhat chaotic. Students must be allowed to let their imaginations roam in free association and to play around with words and ideas until they hit on something that seems right. They must be permitted to share ideas and help each other.
- Do not worry if, in the early sessions, the class as a whole seems to have few ideas. Through the reading and discussion of selections in the reading anthology, most students will soon have more writing ideas than they can use.

Drafting

Purpose

During the drafting phase of the writing process, students shape their planning notes into main ideas and details. They devote their time and effort to getting words down on paper. Whether students are drafting on scrap paper or on computer screens, your role is to encourage each writer to "get it all down." You must also provide a suitable writing environment with the expectation that there will be revision to the draft and to the original plan.

Good Student Writers

- Express all their ideas in the first draft.
- Stop and think about what is being written while drafting.
- Evaluate and alter ideas while drafting.
- Change or elaborate on original plans while drafting.
- Discover that they need more information about certain parts of their writing.
- Learn a lot more about the topic while drafting.

Procedure

Here are some points to share with students before they begin drafting:

- Drafting is putting your ideas down on paper for your own use. Writers do not need to worry about spelling or exact words. They just need to get their ideas down.
- Write on every other line so that you will have room to make revisions.
- Write on only one side of a page so that when you revise you can see all of your draft at once.
- As you draft, keep in mind your purpose for writing this piece and your intended audience.
- Use your plan and your notes from research to add details.

Using Word Processors for Drafting

Many students enjoy drafting on the screen of a computer more than drafting on paper. Once they have mastered the keyboard, they may find it easier to think as they write. Their first attempts look less sloppy, and they are often more willing to make changes and experiment as they draft. They will certainly find it neater to use the delete key on the word processor than to correct their mistakes by crossing out. The Basic Computer Skills instruction in the Language Arts Overview of every lesson provides instruction on using the computer.

Tips

Sometimes the hardest part of drafting is getting the first sentence down on paper. It may help a student even before she or he starts writing to begin a story in the middle or to write the word "Draft" in big letters at the top of the paper.

- If a student feels stuck during drafting, he or she may need to go back and try a different prewriting technique.
- After an initial fifteen or twenty minutes of imposed silence, some students may work better and come up with more ideas if they share as they write.
- You may find that it is difficult to get students to "loosen up" as they draft. Remember, most students have been encouraged to be neat and to erase mistakes when they write. It may help to share some of your own marked-up manuscripts with students.

Revising

Purpose

The purpose of revising is to make sure that a piece of writing expresses the writer's ideas clearly and completely. It has been said that there is no good writing, just good rewriting. A major distinction between good writers and poor writers is the amount of time and effort they put into revision. Poor writers look for spelling and grammatical errors if they do read their work.

Good Student writers

- Evaluate what has been written.
- Read the draft as a reader, not the writer.
- Identify problems with focus, giving enough information, clarity, and order.
- Think of solutions to problems and understand when solutions will and won't work.
- Recognize when and how the text needs to be reorganized.
- Eliminate sentences or paragraphs that don't fit the main idea.
- Identify ideas that need elaboration.
- Do more research if needed to support or add ideas.
- Identify and eliminate unnecessary details.
- Ask for feedback from peer and teacher conferences.
- Take advantage of classroom and outside resources.
- Check the accuracy of facts and details.
- Give credit for any ideas from other people or sources.

Procedure

Model asking questions like the following when revising various kinds of writing:

- About a narrative:
  - ✓ Does my first sentence get my readers' attention?
  - ✓ Are events in the story told in an order that makes sense?
  - ✓ Have I included dialogue to help move the story along?
  - ✓ Does the story have a clear focus?
- About a description:
  - ✓ Have I used details that appeal to the senses?
- About a comparison/contrast piece:
  - ✓ Have I made a separate paragraph for each subject discussed?
- About an explanation:
  - ✓ Will readers understand what I am saying?
  - ✓ Are the steps of the explanation in a clear order?
  - ✓ Have I made effective use of signal words?
  - ✓ Have I included enough information?
- About fiction:
  - ✓ Have I described my characters and setting?
  - ✓ Does the plot include a problem, build to a climax, and then describe the resolution of the problem?
- About persuasive writing:
  - ✓ Have I made my position clear?
  - ✓ Does my evidence support my position?
  - ✓ Have I used opinions as well as facts, and have I said whose opinions I used?
  - ✓ Have I directed my writing to my audience?

Help students understand the value of asking questions such as the following as they revise:

- About each paragraph:
  - ✓ Does each sentence belong in it?
  - ✓ Does each sentence connect smoothly with the next?
  - ✓ Does each sentence say something about the main idea?
- About each sentence:
  - ✓ Do the sentences read smoothly?
  - ✓ Have I combined sentences that were too short?
  - ✓ Have I broken sentences that were too long into two shorter sentences?
  - ✓ Have I varied the beginnings of the sentences?
- About the words:
  - ✓ Have I changed words that were repeated too often?
  - ✓ Do transition words connect ideas?

Tips

- Use the student Writing Folder to review student progress. Check first drafts against revised versions to see how each student is able to apply revision strategies.
- You may find that some students are reluctant to revise. You might then try the following:

✓ If a student doesn't see anything that needs to be changed or doesn't want to change anything, get him or her to do something to the paper—number the details in a description or the steps in a process, circle exact words, underline the best parts of the paper. Once a paper is marked, the student may not be so reluctant to change it.

✓ One reason many students do not like to revise is that they think they must recopy everything. This is not always necessary. Sometimes writers can cut and paste sections that they want to move. Or they can use carets and deletion marks to show additions and subtractions from a piece.

✓ Give an especially reluctant student a deadline by which she or he must revise a piece or lose the chance to publish it.

✓ Students will hopefully be writing in other classes and on a variety of topics. Revision techniques can be used to improve writing in any curriculum area. Stress to students the importance of focusing on their intended audience as they revise.

Proofreading

Purpose

Writing that is free of grammatical, spelling, and technical mistakes is clearer and easier for readers to understand. By proofreading their pieces, students will also notice which errors they make repeatedly and will learn not to make them in the future.

After a piece of writing has been revised for content and style, students must read it carefully line by line to make sure that it contains no errors. This activity, the fourth phase of the writing process, is called proofreading and is a critical step that must occur before a piece of writing can be published. Students can begin proofreading a piece when they feel that it has been sufficiently revised.

Good Student Writers

- Edit the work to allow the reader to understand and enjoy the words.
- Correct most errors in English language conventions.
- Use resources or seek assistance to address any uncertainties in English language conventions.

Procedure

Using What They Have Learned

Students should be expected to proofread at a level appropriate to their grade. Young authors should not be held responsible for skills they have not yet learned. Older students will be able to check for a greater variety of errors than younger students and should be expected to take greater responsibility for their proofreading. For example, students in second grade can be expected to check for and correct omitted capital letters at the beginning of sentences, but they should not necessarily be expected to understand and correct capital letters in proper nouns or in names of organizations. Older students will have mastered many more grammatical, mechanical, usage, and spelling skills and can be expected to perform accordingly. When you spot an error related to a skill beyond a student's level, make clear to the student that you do not expect her or him to be responsible for the mistake, but do explain that the error still needs to be corrected. The following suggestions may be useful as you introduce proofreading to the students and help them develop their proofreading skills.

Proofreading Checklist

Have students use a proofreading checklist similar to the one shown here to help them remember the steps for effective proofreading.

✓ Read each sentence.

✓ Does each sentence begin with a capital letter and end with correct punctuation?

✓ Do you notice any sentence fragments or run-on sentences?

✓ Are words missing from the sentence?

✓ Is any punctuation or capitalization missing from within the sentence?

✓ Do you notice any incorrect grammar or incorrect word usage in the sentence?

✓ Do you notice any misspelled words?

✓ Are the paragraphs indented?

✓ Can very long paragraphs be broken into two paragraphs?

✓ Can very short paragraphs be combined into one paragraph?

Tips

- **Proofreader's Marks** Students should use standard Proofreader's Marks to indicate the changes they wish to make. Explain to students that these marks are a kind of code used to show which alterations to make without a long explanation. Students may also be interested to know that professional writers, editors, and proofreaders use these same marks. You may want to review these marks one by one, illustrating on the board how to use them. For example, they may insert a word or a phrase by using a caret (^). If students wish to insert more text than will fit above the line, they may write in the margin or attach another sheet of paper. It may be a good idea, when such extensive corrections are made, for students to proofread their final copy carefully to make sure they have included all their alterations.
- **Sentence lifting** is a very effective method of showing students how to proofread their own work. Because students are working on their own sentences, they will be more inclined to both pay attention to what is going on and better understand the corrections that are made.

✓ Choose several pieces of student writing and look for common errors.

✓ On an overhead transparency, write several sentences. Include at least one sentence that has no errors.

✓ Tell students that you are going to concentrate on one type of error at a time. For example, first you will concentrate on spelling.

✓ Ask students to read the first sentence and point out any words they feel are spelled incorrectly. Do not erase errors. Cross them out and write the correctly spelled word above the crossed out word.

✓ Next move to a different type of error. Ask students to check for capitalization and punctuation.

✓ Continue in this way, correcting errors as you go through the sample sentences.

- **Using a Word Processor.** If the students are using a word processor to write their pieces, they may wish to run a spell check on their document. Caution them, however, that even the most sophisticated computer cannot catch every spelling error. Misuse of homophones and other words will not be caught by the computer if the misused words appear in the computer's dictionary. For example, if a student types *form* instead of *from*, the computer will not register a mistake because *form* is also a word.

Circulate as students are proofreading on their own or in pairs.

✓ Are students able to check references when they are unsure of a spelling or usage?

✓ Are students criticizing each other's work constructively?

✓ Does a student no longer omit end punctuation because he or she noticed this error repeatedly during proofreading?

✓ Note students who are having difficulty. You may wish to address these difficulties during individual conferences.

PROGRAM APPENDIX

Publishing

Purpose

Publishing is the process of bringing private writing to the reading public. The purpose of writing is to communicate. Unless students are writing in a journal, they will want to present their writing to the public. Such sharing helps students to learn about themselves and others, provides an opportunity for them to take pride in their hard work, and thus motivates them to further writing.

Publishing their work helps motivate students to improve such skills as spelling, grammar, and handwriting. Publishing can be as simple as displaying papers on a bulletin board or as elaborate as creating a class newspaper. Publishing will not—indeed should not—always require large blocks of class time. Students will wish to spend more time elaborately presenting their favorite pieces and less time on other works. If students take an inordinate amount of time to publish their work, you may want to coach them on how to speed up the process.

Good Student Writers

- Present the work in a way that makes it easy to read and understand.
- Consider format, style, illustration, as well as clarity in the presentation of the work.
- Show pride in the finished work.

Procedure

Preparing the Final Copy

When students feel that they have thoroughly proofread their pieces, they should copy the work onto another sheet of paper, using their best handwriting, or type the work on a computer or typewriter. They should then check this copy against the proofread copy to make sure that they made all the changes correctly and did not introduce any new errors. You may need to proofread and correct students' papers one final time before publishing to make sure that they have caught all errors.

Publishing Choices

In publishing, students need to decide

✓ how to prepare the piece for publication.
✓ what form the published work should take.
✓ whether to illustrate their writing with photographs, drawings, charts with captions, as necessary.
✓ where to place any art they are using.

Publishing Checklist

The following checklist will help students when they are publishing their work. (Not every question applies to every form of publishing.)

✓ Have I revised my work to make it better?
✓ Have I proofread it carefully?
✓ Have I decided upon my illustrations?
✓ Have I recopied my piece carefully and illustrated it?
✓ Have I numbered the pages?
✓ Have I made a cover that tells the title and my name?

Tips

- Read through the piece, and tell the student if any corrections still need to be made. Also make some suggestions about the best way to publish a piece if a student has trouble coming up with an idea.
- Make suggestions and give criticism as needed, but remember that students must retain ownership of their publishing. Leave final decisions about form and design of their work up to individual students.
- Remind students to think about their intended audience when they are deciding on the form for their published piece. Will the form they have selected present their ideas effectively to the people they want to reach?

Writing Seminar

Purpose

The purpose of Writing Seminar (Levels K–6) is for students to discuss their work in progress and to share ideas for improving it.

Writing Seminar is one of the activities in which students may choose to participate during Workshop. Students will meet in small groups to read and discuss one another's writing. One student reads a piece in progress. Other students comment on the writing and ask questions about the ideas behind the writing. The student whose work is being critiqued writes down the comments made by his or her classmates and decides how to use these comments to make the writing better.

Procedure

To begin the seminar, have one student writer read his or her revised draft as other students listen carefully. When the student has finished, invite other students to retell the story in their own words. If they have trouble retelling the story, the writer knows that he or she must make some ideas clearer.

Then have listeners who wish to comment raise their hands. The writer calls on each in turn. The listeners ask questions or make comments about the writing, telling, for example, what they like about it or what they might change to make it better. After several comments have been made, the writer notes any information that she or he might use. Another student then reads his or her piece.

Guidelines for Peer Conferencing

In an early session, work with students to establish guidelines for peer conferencing. You might suggest rules such as the following:

✓ Listen quietly while someone else is speaking.
✓ Think carefully before you comment on another person's work.
✓ Make your comments specific.
✓ Comment on something that you like about the piece before you comment on something that needs to be improved.
✓ Discuss your work quietly so as not to disturb the rest of the class.

Modeling Seminar Behavior

You may need to model meaningful comments and questions. For example:

✓ What was your favorite part?
✓ I like the part where (or when)
✓ I like the way you describe
✓ What happened after . . . ?
✓ I'd like to know more about
✓ Why did ________ happen?
✓ What do you think is the most important part?

Teacher Conferencing

During Writing Seminar, you will want to schedule individual conferences with students to help them evaluate their writing so that they can recognize problems and find ways to solve them. Teacher conferences are useful during all phases of the writing process, but they are crucial during the revising phase. Conferences give you an opportunity to observe students as they evaluate their writing, solve problems, make decisions about their work, and take responsibility for the development and completion of their work. The basic procedure for conferences is:

- Have the student read his or her work aloud.
- Review any feedback the student has received so far.
- Identify positive elements of the work.
- Use one or more of these strategies to help the student improve his or her work.
  ✓ Have students explain how they got their ideas.
  ✓ Have students think aloud about how they will address the feedback they have received.
  ✓ Ask students to help you understand any confusion you may have about their writing.
  ✓ Have the student add, delete, or rearrange something in the work and ask how it affects the whole piece.
  ✓ Think aloud while you do a part of what the student was asked to do. Ask the student to compare what you did to what he or she did.
  ✓ Have the student prescribe as if to a younger student how to revise the work.

- Ask two or three questions to guide students through revising (see below).
- Conclude by having the student state a plan for continuing work on the piece.

Writing Conference Questions

Ideas

- Who is your audience?
- What is your purpose for writing?
- How does the reader know the purpose?
- Is there enough information about the topic?
- Do you like one part of your work more than the rest? Why?
- Is your main idea clear?
- Is there a better way to express this idea?
- Is this a good topic sentence?
- Is your introduction engaging?
- Are any important details left out?
- Are any not-so-important details left in?
- Do you use specific details and examples?
- Are your ideas accurate and, if necessary, supported by research?
- Does your conclusion sum up or restate your purpose for writing?
- What might be another way to end the work?

Organization

- Is the writing organized in a way that makes the most sense based on the main idea?
- Is the structure clear for the reader? Is there a clear beginning, middle, and end?
- Are there smooth transitions from one part to the next?
- Are supporting details ordered in the most logical way?
- Can you combine any smaller paragraphs or separate larger ones?

Voice

- Do you sound confident and knowledgeable?
- Does the voice you use reflect the purpose of your writing? Does your writing sound funny or serious when you want it to be?
- Is your voice appropriate for your audience?
- Do you sound interested in the subject?
- Have you confidently stated your opinion? Have you used the pronoun "I" if appropriate?
- Does your writing sound like you?
- Is your voice too formal or informal?
- Will this writing get a strong response from the reader?
- Does your writing make the reader care about your topic?

Word Choice

- Do you use the same word/phrase repeatedly?
- Could you say the same thing with different words?
- Have you defined words your audience may not understand?
- Have you used precise words to describe or explain?
- Is there a better word to express this idea?
- Have you used your own words when summarizing information from another text?
- Do you use time and order words such as *first, next, then,* and *last* to help the reader understand when events take place?

Sentence Fluency

- Are your sentences clear and to the point?
- Have you used different kinds and lengths of sentences to effectively present your ideas?
- Could any of your sentences be combined?
- Is there a rhythm to your sentences?
- Does each sentence introduce a new idea or a new piece of information?
- Do some sentences repeat what has already been stated? If so, cut or change them.
- Have you used transition words such as *in contrast, however,* and *on the other hand* to move smoothly from one subject to the other?
- Have you used transitional phrases, such as *according to, in addition to,* or *at the same time* to link sentences?
- Have you used conjunctions such as *and, but,* and *or* to combine short, choppy sentences?

Tips

- Completed pieces as well as works in progress can be shared during Writing Seminar.
- Concentrate on one phase of the writing process at a time.
- Remember to keep conferences brief and to the point. If you are calling the conference, prepare your comments in advance. Be sure that you confer regularly with every student if only to check that each one is continuing to write, revise, and publish.
- During teacher conferences, you might use the following responses to student writing.
  ✓ To open communication with the writer:
    - How is the writing going?
    - Tell me about your piece.
    - How did you get your ideas?

  ✓ To give encouragement:
    - I like the part where . . . .
    - I like the way you open your piece by . . . .
    - I like your description of . . . .

  ✓ To get the writer to clarify meaning:
    - I wonder about . . . .
    - What happened after . . . .
    - Why did . . . ?

  ✓ To get the writer to think about direction and about writing strategies:
    - What do you plan to do with your piece?
    - How will you go about doing that?
    - What could I do to help you?
- As you confer with students, also recognize growth—evidence in the text that a student has applied what he or she learned in earlier conferences to another piece of writing.
- Some cues to look for when evaluating a student's growth as a writer include:
  ✓ The writer identifies problems.
  ✓ The writer thinks of solutions to a problem.
  ✓ The writer recognizes when and how the text needs to be reorganized.
  ✓ The writer identifies ideas in the text that need elaboration.
  ✓ The writer makes thoughtful changes and pays attention to detail.
  ✓ The writer takes advantage of peer and teacher conferences, books, and other resources to improve his or her writing.

Teaching Strategies for Writing

The teacher's role in writing instruction is critical. Certain strategies have been shown to be particularly effective in teaching writing.

Teacher Modeling Students learn best when they have good models. Models for the forms of writing appear in the literature selections, ***Transparencies,*** and ***Language Arts Handbook.*** The Writing Process Strategies include instruction and models for all phases of the writing process. Teachers can also model the writing process for students every time they write.

Feedback. The most effective writing instruction is the feedback good teachers give to individual student work. Unfortunately many teachers simply mark errors in spelling, grammar, usage, and mechanics. The conference questions, the Writing Routine Card, and the ***Writer's Workbook*** provide questions that teachers can consider to offer constructive and meaningful feedback to students.

Clear Assignments. A well-written assignment makes clear to students what they are supposed to do, how they are supposed to do it, who the students are writing for, and what constitutes a successful response. When students have this information, they can plan, organize, and produce more effective work.

Instruction. Having students write a lot does not make them good writers. Few people become good writers, no matter how much they write. For many, the effect of years of practice is simply to produce increasingly fluent bad writing. Students need specific instruction and practice on different forms of writing and on different phases of the writing process, which they receive with instruction, modeling, practice, and feedback.

Classroom Discussion

PROGRAM APPENDIX

The more students are able to discuss what they are learning, voice their confusions, and compare perceptions of what they are learning, the deeper and more meaningful their learning becomes.

Purpose

It is in discussions that students are exposed to points of view different from their own, and it is through discussion that they learn how to express their thoughts and opinions coherently. Through discussion, students add to their own knowledge that of their classmates and learn to explain themselves coherently and to ask insightful questions that help them better understand what they have read and all that they are learning through their inquiry/research and explorations. The purpose of classroom discussion is to provide a sequence through which discussion can proceed.

Procedure

Reflecting on the Selection

After students have finished reading a selection, provide an opportunity for them to engage in **whole-group** discussion about the selection. Students should:

- Check to see whether the questions they asked before reading have been answered. Encourage them to discuss whether any unanswered questions should still be answered and if so have them add those questions to the Concept/Question Board.
- Discuss any new questions that have arisen because of the reading. Encourage students to decide which of these questions should go on the Concept/Question Board.
- Share what they expected to learn from reading the selection and tell whether expectations were met.
- Talk about whatever has come to mind while reading the selection. This discussion should be an informal sharing of impressions of, or opinions about, the selection; it should never take on the aspects of a question-and-answer session about the selection.
- Give students ample opportunity to ask questions and share their thoughts about the selection. Participate as an active member of the group, making your own observations about information in a selection or modeling your own appreciation of a story. Be especially aware of unusual and interesting insights suggested by students so that these insights can be recognized and discussed. To help students learn to keep the discussion student-centered, have each student choose the next speaker instead of handing the discussion back to you.

Recording Ideas

As students finish discussions about their reactions to a selection, they should be encouraged to record their thoughts, feelings, reactions, and ideas about the selection or the subject of the selection in their Writer's Notebooks. This will not only help keep the selections fresh in students' minds; it will strengthen their writing abilities and help them learn how to write about their thoughts and feelings.

Students may find that the selection gave them ideas for their own writing, or it could have reminded them of some person or incident in their own lives. Perhaps the selection answered a question that has been on their minds or raised a question they had never thought of before. Good, mature writers—especially professional writers—learn the value of recording such thoughts and impressions quickly before they fade. Students should be encouraged to do this also.

Handing Off

Handing off (Levels 1–6) is a method of turning over to students the primary responsibility for controlling discussion. Often, students who are taking responsibility for controlling a discussion tend to have all "turns" go through the teacher. The teacher is the one to whom attention is transferred when a speaker finishes, and the teacher is the one who is expected to call on the next speaker—the result being that the teacher remains the pivotal figure in the discussion.

Having the students "hand off" the discussion to other students instead of the teacher encourages them to retain complete control of the discussion and to become more actively involved in the learning process. When a student finishes his or her comments, that student should choose (hand the discussion off to) the next speaker. In this way, students maintain a discussion without relying on the teacher to decide who speaks.

When handing off is in place, the teacher's main roles are to occasionally remind students to hand off and to monitor the discussion to ensure that everyone gets a chance to contribute. The teacher may say, for example, "Remember, not just boys (or girls)," or "Try to choose someone who has not had a chance to talk yet."

In order for handing off to work effectively, a seating arrangement that allows students to see one another is essential. A circle or a semicircle is effective. In addition, all of the students need to have copies of the materials being discussed.

Actively encourage this handing-off process by letting students know that they, not you, are in control of the discussion.

If students want to remember thoughts about, or reactions to, a selection, suggest that they record these in the Writing Journal. Encourage students to record the thoughts, feelings, or reactions that are elicited by any reading they do.

Exploring Concepts within the Selection

To provide an opportunity for collaborative learning and to focus on the concepts, have students form small groups and spend time discussing what they have learned about the concepts from this selection. Topics may include new information that they have acquired or new ideas that they have had.

Students should always base their discussions on postings from the Concept/Question Board as well as on previous discussions of the concept. The small-group discussions should be ongoing throughout the unit; during this time students should continue to compare and contrast any new information with their previous ideas, opinions, and impressions about the concepts. Does this selection help confirm their ideas? Does it contradict their thinking? Has it changed their outlook?

As students discuss the concepts in small groups, circulate around the room to make sure that each group stays focused upon the selection and the concepts. After students have had some time to discuss the information and the ideas in the selection, encourage each group to formulate some statements about the concept that apply to the selection.

Sharing Ideas about Concepts

Have a representative from each group report and explain the group's ideas to the rest of the class. Then have the class formulate one or more general statements related to the unit concepts and write these statements on the Concept/Question Board. As students progress through the unit, they will gain more and more confidence in suggesting additions to the Concept/Question Board.

Visual Aids During this part of the discussion, you may find it helpful to use visual aids to aid students as they build the connections to the unit concepts. Not all units or concepts will lend themselves to this type of treatment; however, aids such as timelines, charts, graphs, or pictographs may help students see how each new selection adds to their growing knowledge of the concepts.

Encourage students to ask questions about the concepts that the selection may have raised. Have students list on the Concept/Question Board those questions that cannot be answered immediately and that they want to explore further.

Exploring Concepts across Selections

As each new selection is read, encourage students to discuss its connection with the other selections and with the unit concepts. Also encourage students to think about selections that they have read from other units and how they relate to the concepts for this unit.

Ultimately, it is this ability to make connections between past knowledge and new knowledge that allows any learner to gain insights into what is being studied. The goal of the work with concepts and the discussions is to help students to start thinking in terms of connections—how is this like what I have learned before? Does this information confirm, contradict, or add a completely different layer to that which I already know about this concept? How can the others in the class have such different ideas than I do when we just read the same selection? Why is so much written about this subject?

Learning to make connections and to delve deeper through self-generated questions gives students the tools they need to become effective, efficient, lifelong learners.

Tips

- Discussions offer a prime opportunity for you to introduce, or seed, new ideas about the concepts. New ideas can come from a variety of sources: students may draw on their own experiences or on the books or videos they are studying; you may introduce new ideas into the discussion; or you may, at times, invite experts to speak to the class.
- If students do not mention an important idea that is necessary to the understanding of some larger issue, you may "drop" that idea into the conversation and, indeed, repeat it several times to make sure that it does get picked up. This seeding may be subtle ("I think that might be important here") or quite direct ("This is a big idea, one that we will definitely need to understand and one that we will return to regularly").

Discussion is an integral part of learning.

- In order to facilitate this process for each unit, you must be aware of the unit concepts and be able to recognize and reinforce them when they arise spontaneously in discussions. If central unit concepts do not arise naturally, then, and only then, will you seed these ideas by direct modeling. The more you turn discussions over to students, the more involved they will become, and the more responsibility they will take for their own learning. Make it your goal to become a participant in, rather than the leader of, class discussions.
- Help students to see that they are responsible for carrying on the discussion. After a question is asked, always wait instead of jumping in with a comment or an explanation. Although this wait time may be uncomfortable at first, students will come to understand that the discussion is their responsibility and that you will not jump in every time there is a hesitation.
- As the year progresses, students will become more and more adept at conducting and participating in meaningful discussions about what they have read. These discussions will greatly enhance students' understanding of the concepts that they are exploring.

Discussion Starters

- I didn't know that . . . .
- Does anyone know . . . .
- I figured out that . . . .
- I liked the part where . . . .
- I'm still confused about . . . .
- This made me think . . . .
- I agree with ____________ because . . . .
- I disagree with ____________ because . . . .
- The reason I think . . . .

Inquiry and Investigation

Research and Investigation form the heart of the ***SRA/Open Court Reading*** program. In order to encourage students to understand how reading can enhance their lives and help them to become mature, educated adults, they are asked in each unit to use what they are learning in the unit as the basis for further exploration and research. The unit information is simply the base for their investigations.

There are two types of units in the ***SRA/Open Court Reading*** program—units based on universal topics of interest such as Friendship, Perseverance, and Courage and research units that provide students a very solid base of information upon which they can base their own inquiry and research. Units delving into such areas as fossils, astronomy, and medicine invite students to become true researchers by choosing definite areas of interest—problems or questions to research in small cooperative groups and then present to their classmates. In this way, students gain much more knowledge of the subject than they would have simply by reading the selections in the unit.

The selections in the units are organized so that each selection will add more information or a different perspective to students' growing bodies of knowledge.

Investigating through Reflective Activities

Purpose

The units in ***SRA/Open Court Reading*** that deal with universal topics will be explored through reflective activities. These units—such as Courage, Friendship, and Risks and Consequences—are organized to help students expand their perspectives in familiar areas. As they explore and discuss the unit concepts related to each topic, students are involved in activities that extend their experiences and offer opportunities for reflection. Such activities include writing, drama, art, interviews, debates, and panel discussions. Throughout each unit, students may be involved in a single ongoing investigative activity, or they may participate in a number of different activities. They may choose to produce a final written project or a visual aid to share with the rest of the class the new knowledge that they have gained from their reflective activities. During **Workshop** students will work individually or in collaborative groups on their investigation and/or projects.

The reflective activities will be activities of students' own choosing that allow them to explore the unit concepts more fully. They are free, of course, to make other choices or to devise activities of their own.

Procedure

Choosing an Area to Investigate

Students may work on activities alone, in pairs, or in small groups. They have the option of writing about or presenting their findings to the whole group upon completion. Before choosing a reflective activity, students should decide what concept-related question or problem they wish to explore. Generally, it is better for students to generate questions or problems after they have engaged in some discussion but before they have had a chance to consult source materials. This approach is more likely to bring forth ideas that students actually wonder about or wish to understand. Students may also look at the questions posted on the Concept/Question Board or introduce fresh ideas inspired by material they have just finished reading. Students who are working in pairs or in small groups should confer with one another before making a decision about what to explore. Some of the students may need your assistance in deciding upon, or narrowing down, a question or a problem so that it can be explored more easily. A good way to model this process for students is to make webs for a few of your own ideas on the board and to narrow these ideas down to a workable question or problem.

Organizing the Group

After a question or a problem has been chosen, the students may choose an activity that will help them to investigate that problem or question. The students' next responsibility is to decide who is going to investigate which facet of the question or the problem (when they are conducting a literature search, for example) or who is going to perform which task related to the particular reflective activity (when they are writing and performing an original playlet or puppet show, for example). Lastly, students need to decide how, or if, they want to present their findings. For instance, after conducting a literature search, some students may want to read and discuss passages from a book with a plot or theme that relates to a unit concept. Other students may prefer acting out and discussing scenes from the book.

Deciding How to Investigate

The following suggestions may help you and your students choose ways in which to pursue their investigations. You may want to post this list in the classroom so that groups have access to it as they decide what they want to investigate and how they want to proceed.

Investigation Activities

- Conduct a literature search to pursue a question or a problem. Discussion or writing may follow.
- Write and produce an original playlet or puppet show based on situations related to the concepts.
- Play a role-playing game to work out a problem related to the concepts.
- Stage a panel discussion with audience participation on a question or problem.
- Hold a debate on an issue related to the concept.
- Write an advice column dealing with problems related to the concepts.
- Write a personal-experience story related to the concepts.
- Invite experts to class. Formulate questions to ask.
- Conduct an interview with someone on a subject related to the concepts.
- Produce and carry out a survey on an issue or question related to the concept.
- Produce a picture or photo essay about the concept.

EXAMPLE: In the Heritage unit in grade 5 of ***SRA/Open Court Reading,*** students read "In Two Worlds: A Yup'ik Eskimo Family." This selection is about how three generations of Eskimos living in Alaska near the Arctic strive to adopt the best of modern ways without abandoning their traditional values. During the class discussion, some students may note that Alice and Billy Rivers want their students to learn both the new and the old ways of living. As the discussion continues, many students may conclude from the story that the older generations hope that future generations will continue to value their roots and their cultural traditions. Students then relate this story to their own heritage. Some students may share information about their customs or traditions.

Students choose some reflective activities that will help them learn more about family heritage and that will answer some of their questions about the unit concepts. Some students may be interested in interviewing family members or close family friends about their cultural traditions and heritages. These students review what they know about interviewing. They proceed by:

- Contacting in advance the person(s) they want to interview.
- Preparing a list of questions to ask.
- Preparing a list of subjects to discuss, deciding how to record the interview (by audiotape, videotape, or taking notes).
- Deciding whether to photograph the person and, if so, getting permission to do so in advance—collecting the equipment necessary for conducting the interview.

After they conduct the interviews, students decide how they wish to present the information that they have collected.

Investigating through reflective activities allows students to gain a wider perspective on a concept by relating it to their own experiences. Students quickly become aware that it is their responsibility to learn and to help their peers learn more about the unit concepts.

EXAMPLE: Another group of students in the same fifth-grade class may be more interested in planning a photo essay about one family or about a neighborhood with many families belonging to a particular culture. These students may decide to re-examine "In Two Worlds" to notice how the text and the photographs complement each other and what information is conveyed in each photograph. They may also decide to examine some photo essays listed in the unit bibliography. These students will need to make some advance preparations as well. They proceed by:

- Determining which neighborhood and which family or families to photograph.
- Contacting in advance the persons to be interviewed and photographed.
- Touring the neighborhood in advance of the photo shoot.
- Making a list of questions to ask the family or families about their heritage or about their neighborhood.
- Thinking about what information to include in their essay so that they can determine what photographs to take.
- Collecting the equipment necessary for conducting interviews and photographing subjects.

After students collect the information and take photographs, they may write and organize the photo essay and present it to the class. The teacher should remind students of the phases of the writing process, and encourage them to proofread and revise their work until they are completely pleased with it. Students can continue discussing family heritage and raising any new questions that they wish to investigate. The teacher should remind them that as they read further, they may think of a variety of ways to explore the unit concepts. The teacher should then ask students to post on the Concept/Question Board any new questions they have about family heritage. Students should sign or initial their questions so that they can identify classmates with similar interests and exchange ideas with them. The teacher should encourage students to feel free to write an answer or a note on someone else's question or to consult the board for ideas for their own explorations. From time to time, the teacher should post his or her own questions on the Concept/Question Board.

Tips

- The leveled Classroom Library contain books related to the unit concepts. Remind students that these are good sources of information and that they should consult them regularly—especially when they are investigating concept-related ideas and questions.
- Some students work better within a specified time frame. Whenever they are beginning a new activity, discuss with the students a reasonable period of time within which they will be expected to complete their investigations. Post the completion date somewhere in the classroom so that students can refer to it and pace themselves accordingly. At first, you may have to help them determine a suitable deadline, but eventually they should be able to make this judgment on their own.

Inquiry and Investigation (continued)

Investigating through Research

Purpose

Students come to school with a wealth of fascinating questions. Educators need to capitalize on this excitement for learning and natural curiosity. A classroom in which only correct answers are accepted and students are not allowed to make errors and consider alternative possibilities to questions can quickly deaden this natural curiosity and enthusiasm. The purpose of the research aspect of this program is to capitalize on students' questions and natural curiosity by using a proven structure. This structure helps students to not get lost or bogged down but at the same time to preserve the open-ended character of real research, which can lead to unexpected findings and to questions that were not originally considered.

There is a conventional approach to school research papers that can be found, with minor variations, in countless textbooks. It consists of a series of steps such as the following: select a topic, narrow the topic, collect materials, take notes, outline, and write. By following these steps, a student may produce a presentable paper, but the procedure does not constitute research in a meaningful sense and indeed gives students a distorted notion of what research is about. We see students in universities and even in graduate schools still following this procedure when they do library research papers or literature reviews; we see their dismay when their professors regard such work as mere cutting and pasting and ask them where their original contribution is.

Even elementary school students can produce works of genuine research—research that seeks answers to real questions or solutions to real problems. This skill in collecting and analyzing information is a valuable tool in the adult world in which adults, as consumers, are constantly analyzing new information and making informed decisions on the basis of this information. Preparing students for the analytic demands of adult life and teaching them how to find answers to their questions are goals of education.

Procedure

In order to make the research productive, the following important principles are embodied in this approach:

1. Research is focused on problems, not topics.
2. Conjectures—opinions based on less than complete evidence or proof—guide the research; the research does not simply produce conjectures.
3. New information is gathered to test and revise conjectures.
4. Discussion, ongoing feedback, and constructive criticism are important in all phases of the research but especially in the revising of problems and conjectures.
5. The cycle of true research is essentially endless, although presentations of findings are made from time to time; new findings give rise to new problems and conjectures and thus to new cycles of research.

Following a Process

While working with the research units, students are encouraged to follow a set pattern or cycle in order to keep their research activities focused and on track. Students may go through these steps many times before they come to the end of their research. Certainly for adult researchers, this cycle of question, conjecture, research, and reevaluate can go on for years and in some cases lifetimes.

This cycle includes:

1. **Decide on a problem or question to research.** Students should identify a question or problem that they truly wonder about or wish to understand and then form research groups with other students who have the same interests.
   - My problem or question is ___________
2. **Formulate an idea or conjecture about the research problem.** Students should think about and discuss with classmates possible answers to their research problems or questions and meet with their research groups to discuss and record their ideas or conjectures.
   - My idea/conjecture/theory about this question or problem is ___________
3. **Identify needs and make plans.** Students should identify knowledge needs related to their conjectures and meet with their research groups to determine which resources to consult and to make individual job assignments. Students should also meet periodically with the teacher, other classmates, and research groups to present preliminary findings and make revisions to their problems and conjectures on the basis of these findings.
   - I need to find out ___________
   - To do this, I will need these resources ___________
   - My role in the group is ___________
   - This is what I have learned so far ___________
   - This is what happened when we presented our findings ___________
4. **Reevaluate the problem or question based on what we have learned so far and the feedback we have received.**
   - My revised problem or question is ___________
5. **Revise the idea or conjecture.**
   - My new conjecture about this problem is ___________
6. **Identify new needs and make new plans.**
   - Based on what I found out, I still need to know ___________
   - To do this, I will need these resources ___________
   - This is what I have learned ___________
   - This is what happened when we presented our new findings ___________

Procedure for Choosing a Problem to Research

1. Discuss with students the nature of the unit. Explain to students that the unit they are reading is a research unit and that they will produce and publish in some way the results of their explorations. They are free to decide what problems or questions they wish to explore, with whom they want to work, and how they want to present their finished products. They may publish a piece of writing, produce a poster, write and perform a play, or use any other means to present the results of their investigations and research. They may work with partners or in small groups.
2. Discuss with students the schedule you have planned for their investigations: how long the project is expected to take, how much time will be available for research, when the first presentation will be due. This schedule will partly determine the nature of the problems that students should be encouraged to work on and the depth of the inquiry students will be encouraged to pursue.
3. Have students talk about things they wonder about that are related to the unit subject. For example, in the grade 3 unit, Money, students might wonder where money in the money machine comes from or how prices are determined. Conduct a free-floating discussion of questions about the unit subject.
4. Brainstorm possible questions for students to think about. It is essential that the students's own ideas and questions be the starting point of all inquiry. *Helpful hint:* For the first research unit, you might wish to generate a list of your own ideas, having students add to this list and having them choose from it.

5. Using their wonderings, model for students the difference between a research topic and a research problem or question by providing several examples. For example, have them consider the difference between the topic California and the problem, *Why do so many people move to California?* Explain to them that if they choose to research the topic California, everything they look up under the subject heading or index entry California will be related in some way to their topic. Therefore, it will be quite difficult to choose which information to record. This excess of information also creates problems in organizing their research. Clearly, then, this topic is too broad and general. Choosing a specific question or problem, one that particularly interests them, helps them narrow their exploration and advance their understanding. Some possible ideas for questions can be found in the unit introduction. Ideas can also be generated as you and your students create a web of their questions or problems related to the unit subject. For example, questions related to the subject California might include the following:
   - Why do so many people move to California?
   - How have the different groups of people living in California affected the state?
6. A good research problem or question not only requires students to consult a variety of sources but is engaging and adds to the groups' knowledge of the concepts. Furthermore, good problems generate more questions. Help students understand that the question, *Why do so many people move to California?* is an easy one to research. Many sources will contribute to an answer to the question, and all information located can be easily evaluated in terms of usefulness in answering the question. Helpful hint: Students' initial responses may indeed be topics instead of problems or questions. If so, the following questions might be helpful:
   - What aspect of the topic really interests you?
   - Can you turn that idea into a question?
7. Remember that this initial problem or question serves only as a guide for research. As students begin collecting information and collaborating with classmates, their ideas will change, and they can revise their research problem or question. Frequently, students do not sufficiently revise their problems until after they have had time to consider their conjectures and collect information.
8. As students begin formulating their research problems, have them elaborate on their reasons for wanting to research their stated problems. They should go beyond simple expressions of interest or liking and indicate what is puzzling, important, or potentially informative, and so forth, about the problems they have chosen.
9. At this stage, students' ideas will be of a very vague and limited sort. The important thing is to start them thinking about what really interests them and what value it has to them and the class.
10. Have students present their proposed problems or questions, along with reasons for their choices, and have an open discussion of how promising proposed problems are. As students present their proposed problems, ask them what new things they think they will be learning from their investigation and how that will add to the group's growing knowledge of the concepts. This constant emphasis on group knowledge building will help set a clear purpose for students' research.

Even elementary school students can produce works of genuine research—research that seeks answers to real questions or solutions to real problems.

11. Form research groups. To make it easier for students to form groups, they may record their problems on the board or on self-sticking notes. Final groups should be constituted in the way you find best for your class—by self-selection, by assignment on the basis of common interests, or by some combination of methods. Students can then meet during **Workshop** to agree on a precise statement of their research problem, the nature of their expected research contributions, and lists of related questions that may help later in assigning individual roles. They should also record any scheduling information that can be added to the planning calendar.

Using Technology

The **Research Assistant CD-ROM** (Levels 2–6), an interactive software program, supports student research by helping them organize and conduct their research.

Students using ***SRA/Open Court Reading*** have the opportunity and the wherewithal to expand their research groups nationwide and find out what other ***SRA/Open Court Reading*** students are doing with their unit investigations.

Tips

- If students are careful about the problems or questions they choose to research, they should have few problems in following through with the research. If the problem is too broad or too narrow, they will have problems.
- Have students take sufficient time in assessing their needs—both knowledge needs and physical needs in relation to their research. Careful preplanning can help the research progress smoothly with great results.
- Encourage students to reevaluate their needs often so they are not wasting time finding things they already have or ignoring needs that they haven't noticed.
- Interim presentations of material are every bit as important, if not more so, than final presentations. It is during interim presentations that students have the opportunity to rethink and reevaluate their work and change direction or decide to carry on with their planned research.

Workshop

PROGRAM APPENDIX

Every teacher and every student needs time during the day to organize, take stock of work that is done, make plans for work that needs doing, and finish up incomplete projects. In addition, time is needed for differentiating instruction and for peer conferencing.

Purpose

Workshop is the period of time each day in which students work independently or collaboratively to practice and review material taught in the lessons.

A variety of activities may occur during this time. Students may work on a specific daily assignment, complete an ongoing project, work on unit exploration activities, focus on writing, or choose from among a wide range of possibilities. With lots of guidance and encouragement, students gradually learn to make decisions about their use of time and materials and to collaborate with their peers.

A goal of **Workshop** is to get students to work independently. This is essential since **Workshop** is also the time during which the teacher can work with individuals or groups of students to reinforce learning, to provide extra help for those having difficulties, to extend learning, or to assess the progress of the class or of individuals.

Procedure

Initially, for many students, you will need to structure **Workshop** carefully. Eventually, students will automatically go to the appropriate areas, take up ongoing projects, and get the materials they will need. **Workshop** will evolve slowly from a very structured period to a time when students make choices and move freely from one activity to the next.

Adhere firmly to **Workshop** guidelines. By the time the students have completed the first few weeks of school, they should feel confident during **Workshop**. If not, continue to structure the time and limit options. For young students, early periods of **Workshop** may run no more than five to eight minutes. The time can gradually increase to fifteen minutes or longer as the students gain independence. Older students may be able to work longer and independently from the very beginning of the school year.

Introducing Workshop

Introduce **Workshop** to students by telling them that every day there will be a time when they are expected to work on activities on their own or in small groups. For young students in the beginning, you will assign the **Workshop** activities to help students learn to work on their own. Point out the shelf or area of the classroom where **Workshop** materials are stored. Tell students that when they finish working with the materials for one activity, they are to choose something else from the **Workshop** shelf. New activity materials will be added to the shelf from time to time. Make sure that the students know that they may always look at books during **Workshop**.

Tell older students that they will have an opportunity each day to work on their unit explorations, their writing and other projects. Students will be working independently and collaboratively during this time.

Guidelines

- Make sure each student knows what he or she needs to do during **Workshop**.
- Demonstrate for the whole group any activity assigned for **Workshop**; for example, teaching the students a new game, introducing new materials or projects, or explaining different areas.
- For young students, it is essential to introduce and demonstrate different activities and games before the students do them on their own. With games, you may want to have several students play while the others watch. Make sure that all the students know exactly what is expected of them.
- In the beginning, plan to circulate among the students providing encouragement and help as necessary.
- Once students are engaged in appropriate activities and can work independently, meet with those students who need your particular attention. This may include individual students or small groups.
- Let the students know that they need to ask questions and clarify assignments during **Workshop** introduction, so that you are free to work with small groups.
- Be sure that students know what they are to do when they have finished an activity and where to put their finished work.

Establish and discuss rules for **Workshop** with the students. Keep them simple and straightforward. You may want to write the finalized rules on the board or on a poster. You may want to review these rules each day at the beginning of **Workshop** for the first few lessons or so. You may also wish to revisit and revise the rules from time to time. Suggested rules include:

✓ Be polite.
✓ Share.
✓ Whisper.
✓ Take only the materials you need.
✓ Return materials.

Setting Up Your Classroom for Workshop

Carefully setting up your classroom to accommodate different **Workshop** activities will help assure that the **Workshop** period progresses smoothly and effectively. While setting up your classroom, keep the primary **Workshop** activities in mind. During **Workshop** the students will be doing independent and collaborative activities. In kindergarten and first grade, these activities may include letter recognition and phonemic awareness activities and writing or illustrating stories or projects. In addition, they will be working on individual or small group projects.

Many classrooms have centers that the students visit on a regular or rotating basis. Center time can be easily and efficiently incorporated into the **Workshop** concept. For example, the activities suggested during **Workshop** can be incorporated into reading and writing areas. Other typical classroom areas include an art center, math center, science table, play area, etc.

The following are suggestions for space and materials for use during **Workshop**:

1. **Reading Area** supplied with books and magazines. The materials in the Reading Area should be dynamic—changing with students' abilities and reflecting unit themes they are reading. You may wish to add books suggested in unit bibliographies and books from the literature collections available with each unit.
2. **Writing Area** stocked with various types and sizes of lined and unlined paper, pencils, erasers, markers, crayons, small slates, and chalk. The area should also have various **Letter Cards**, other handwriting models, and worksheets for those students who want to practice letter formation or handwriting. Students should know that this is where they come for writing supplies. In addition to the supplies described above, the Writing Area can also have supplies to encourage the students to create and write on their own:
   ✓ magazines and catalogs to cut up for pictures; stickers, paint, glue, glitter, etc. to decorate books and book covers; precut and stapled blank books for the students to write in. (Some can be plain and some cut in special shapes.)
   ✓ cardboard, tag board, construction paper, etc., for making book covers. (Provide some samples.)

✓ tape, scissors, yarn, hole punches for binding books.

✓ picture dictionaries, dictionaries, thesaurus, word lists, and other materials that may encourage independence.

3. **Listening Area** supplied with tape recorder, CD player, optional headphones, and tapes of stories, poems, and songs for the students to listen to and react to. You might also want to provide blank tapes and encourage the students to retell and record their favorite stories or make up and tell stories for their classmates to listen to on tape. You may also want to make available the Listening Library Audiocassettes/ CDs that are available with the program.
4. **Workshop Activity Center** supplied with daily Alphabet Flash Cards, individual Alphabet-Sound Card sets (Kindergarten), **Individual Sound/Spelling Cards** and **High-Frequency Word Flash Cards** (Grades 1-3), and other materials that enhance what the students are learning. Other commonly used classroom materials that enhance reading can be included (for example, plastic letters, puzzles, workbooks).

Since students will be working on their inquiry/investigations during **Workshop**, make sure there are adequate supplies to help them with their research. These might include dictionaries, encyclopedias, magazines, newspapers, and computers—preferably with Internet capability.

Workshop is the period of time each day in which students work independently or collaboratively to practice and review material taught in the lessons.

Students thrive in an environment that provides structure, repetition, and routine. Within a sound structure, the students will gain confidence and independence. This setting allows you to differentiate instruction in order to provide opportunities for flexibility and individual choice that allow students to develop their strengths, abilities, and talents to the fullest.

Suggestions for English Language Learners

Workshop affords students who are English Language Learners a wealth of opportunities for gaining proficiency in English. It also encourages them to share their backgrounds with peers. Since you will be working with all students individually and in small groups regardless of their reading ability, students who need special help with language will not feel self-conscious about working with you. In addition, working in small groups made up of students with the same interests rather than the same abilities will provide them with the opportunity to learn about language from their peers during the regular course of **Workshop** activities.

Some suggestions for meeting the special needs of students with diverse backgrounds follow:

- Preread a selection with English Language Learners to help them to identify words and ideas they wish to talk about. This will prepare them for discussions with the whole group.
- Preteach vocabulary and develop selection concepts that may be a challenge for students.
- Negotiate the meaning of selections by asking questions, checking for comprehension, and speaking with English Language Learners as much as possible.
- Draw English Language Learners into small group discussions to give them a sense that their ideas are valid and worth attention.
- Pair English Language Learners with native English speakers to share their experiences and provide new knowledge to other students.
- Have English Language Learners draw or dictate to you or another student a description of a new idea they may have during **Workshop** activities.

Workshop Management Tips

Use the following **Workshop** management tips to ensure that **Workshop** runs smoothly. Note that these suggestions for a unit/lesson may not exactly correspond to a particular unit/lesson in a given grade level.

Unit 1, Lesson 1 Introduce **Workshop** to students. Make sure they know where materials are located. Post the rules on the board or other prominent place in the classroom. Keep **Workshop** time short (less than thirty minutes) and very directed during the first few weeks until students can work independently.

Unit 1, Lesson 2 Discuss using small groups for pre/reteaching purposes and how you will indicate who will be in the groups. Start by forming one small group randomly and having other students do something specific such as a writing assignment. When you have finished with the small group, send them to do independent work. Call another small group of students to work with you. Continue this each day until students are accustomed to forming groups and working independently.

Unit 1, Lesson 3 Reading Roundtable is a student-formed and student-run book discussion. Encourage students participating in Reading Roundtable to choose a book that they all will read and discuss. Several different Reading Roundtable groups may form on the basis of the books students choose.

Unit 1, Lesson 4 For the first few weeks of the school year, make sure each student has a plan for using **Workshop** time.

Unit 1, Lesson 5 Allot time for presentation and discussion of research activities. Use a whole **Workshop** day and have all groups present their findings, or split the presentations over several days, depending on the small-group needs of your class.

Unit 1, Lesson 6 Review how students have used **Workshop** during this unit. Have they used their time well? Do they have the materials they need? Discuss suggestions for improving their use of this time. Take a few minutes at the beginning of each **Workshop** to make sure students know what they will be doing.

Unit 2, Lesson 1 Form small extra-practice groups with the more advanced students from time to time, as they also need special attention.

Unit 2, Lesson 2 To keep the whole class informed about the independent research being done, every other day or so invite a research group to explain what it is doing, how the research is going, and any problems they are encountering.

Workshop (continued)

Workshop

Unit 2, Lesson 3 Discuss the use of **Workshop** time for doing inquiry and research projects. Introduce students to the activities provided for use with this unit at **www.sra4kids.com.**

Unit 2, Lesson 4 Make sure small extra-practice groups are formed based on your observations of students' work on the different daily lessons. Small groups should be fluid and based on demonstrated need rather than becoming static and unchanging.

Unit 2, Lesson 5 One purpose of **Workshop** is to help students learn independence and responsibility. Assign students to monitor **Workshop** materials. They should alert you whenever materials are running low or missing, and they can be responsible for checking on return dates of library books and making sure the books are either returned or renewed.

Unit 2, Lesson 6 Students sometimes have difficulty starting discussions in Reading Roundtable. Try some of these discussion starters with students, and print them on a poster paper for student use.

I didn't know that . . .	I liked the part where . . .
Does anyone know . . .	I'm still confused by . . .
I figured out that . . .	This made me think . . .

I agree/disagree with ____________ because . . .

Unit 3, Lesson 1 By this time students should be accustomed to the routines, rules, expectations, and usage of **Workshop** time and be moving smoothly from small teacher-led groups to independent work. Monitor small groups occasionally to see that they are on task and making progress on their activities.

Unit 3, Lesson 2 Make a practice of reading aloud to students. All students enjoy being read to, no matter their age or grade. Encourage them to discuss the shared reading in Reading Roundtable groups and to bring books and read them aloud to their classmates.

Unit 3, Lesson 3 Encourage cooperation and collaboration by providing students with opportunities to engage in small groups.

Unit 3, Lesson 4 Spend a few minutes each day circulating around the room and monitoring what students are doing independently or in small groups. Students can then share any questions or problems they are having with you on a timely basis.

Unit 3, Lesson 5 Take note of different small groups. Make sure that quieter students are able to participate in the discussions. Often the stronger, more confident students dominate such discussions. Encourage them to give all participants a chance to share their ideas.

Unit 3, Lesson 6 If students are not productive during **Workshop**, keep them in the small group you are working with until they can successfully benefit from independent work. Discuss strategies they could use to become more independent.

Unit 4, Lesson 1 Different students can monitor **Workshop** materials and alert you when materials or supplies are running low or missing and can check that library books are either returned or renewed.

Unit 4, Lesson 2 From time to time, join a Reading Roundtable group, and take part in their discussion. Make sure students lead the discussion.

Unit 4, Lesson 3 Encourage responsibility and independence by reminding students to show respect for each other and the materials provided.

Unit 4, Lesson 4 Be sure students discuss during Reading Roundtable what they like or dislike about a book, why they wanted to read it, and how the book either lived up to their expectations or disappointed them. Discussions should not be about basic comprehension but should help students think more deeply about the ideas presented in a book.

Unit 4, Lesson 5 Make sure students continue to use the activities provided for use with this unit at **www.sra4kids.com.**

Unit 4, Lesson 6 If students are not productive in **Workshop**, keep them in the small group you are working with until they can successfully benefit from independent work. Discuss strategies they could use to become more independent.

Unit 5, Lesson 1 Students often make great tutors for other students. They are uniquely qualified to understand problems that others might be having. Encourage students to pair up during **Workshop** to help each other with their daily lessons.

Unit 5, Lesson 2 Form small extra-practice groups with the more advanced students from time to time, as they also need special attention.

Unit 5, Lesson 3 In order to keep the whole class informed about the independent research being done, every other day or so, invite a research/investigation group to explain what it is doing, how the research is going, and any problems they are encountering.

Unit 5, Lesson 4 Most of the authors of the student anthology selections are well known and have written many, many pieces of fine literature. Encourage students who enjoy the anthology selections to find other books by the same author. Encourage them to think about and discuss what about that particular author's work attracts them.

Unit 5, Lesson 5 Share your impressions of books from the ***Leveled Classroom Library*** or other reading during Reading Roundtable. Note which students initiate sharing and which are reluctant to share.

Unit 5, Lesson 6 Review with students the time they have used in **Workshop**. Have they used their time well? Do they have the materials they need? Discuss suggestions for improving the use of this time.

Unit 6, Lesson 1 Spend a few minutes each day circulating around the room and monitoring what students are doing independently or in small groups. Students can share any questions or problems they are having with you on a timely basis.

Unit 6, Lesson 2 Students should be accustomed to the routines, rules, expectations, and usage of **Workshop** time and be moving smoothly from small teacher-led groups to independent work. Make sure to monitor small groups occasionally to see that they are on task and making progress with their activities.

Unit 6, Lesson 3 Make sure students continue to use the activities provided for use with this unit at **www.sra4kids.com.**

Unit 6, Lesson 4 Allot time for presentation and discussion of research activities. You may want to use a whole **Workshop** day and have all groups present their findings or split the presentations over several days, depending on the urgency of the small-group instruction your class needs.

Unit 6, Lesson 5 Students often make great tutors for other students. The fact that they too are just learning the materials makes them uniquely qualified to understand problems that others might be having. Encourage students to pair up during **Workshop** to help each other on their daily lessons.

Unit 6, Lesson 6 If the reading selection is an excerpt from a longer piece, encourage students to read the book from which the excerpt is taken and discuss how the excerpt fits into the larger work.

Assessment can be one of your most effective teaching tools if it is used with the purpose of informing instruction and highlighting areas that need special attention.

Purpose

Assessment is a tool the teacher uses to monitor students' progress and to detect students' strengths and weaknesses. Evaluation of student learning is addressed in two ways: Informal Assessment and Formal Assessment. Informal, observational assessment, or a quick check of students' written work is presented in the Teacher's Edition in the form of assessment suggestions. Formal Assessment consists of performance assessment (both reading and writing) and objective tests (multiple choice and essay).

Procedure

Informal Assessment

Observation

Observing students as they go about their regular classwork is probably the single most effective way to learn in depth your students' strengths and areas of need. The more students become accustomed to you jotting down informal notes about their work, the more it will become just another part of classroom life that they accept and take little note of. This gives you the opportunity to assess their progress constantly without the interference and possible drawback of formal testing situations.

In order to make informal assessment of student progress a part of your everyday classroom routine, you might want to start by preparing the materials you will need on hand.

- Enter students' names in the Teacher's Observation Log.
- Before each day's lesson begins, decide which students you will observe.
- Keep the Teacher's Observation Log available so that you can easily record your observations.
- Decide what aspect of the students's learning you wish to monitor.
- During each lesson, observe this aspect in the performances of several students.
- Record your observations.
- It may take four to five days to make sure you have observed and recorded the performance of each student. If you need more information about performance in a particular area for some of your students, you may want to observe them more than once.

Progress Assessment

Written Work

Students are writing one thing or another all day long. Each of these pieces of writing can provide you with valuable information about your students' progress. Four very helpful resources that students will work in daily are the ***Comprehension and Language Arts Skills*** (Levels 1–6) and the ***Inquiry Journal*** (Levels 2–6).

- The ***Comprehension and Language Arts Skills*** include skills practice lessons that act as practice and reinforcement for the skills lessons taught during the reading of the lesson or in conjunction with the lesson. These skill pages give you a clear picture of students' understanding of the skills taught. Use them as a daily assessment of student progress in the particular skills taught through the program. In the ***Phonemic Awareness and Phonics*** (K), and ***Phonics*** (1), students practice each of the skills taught in the program.
- The ***Inquiry Journal*** can give you invaluable information on how students are progressing in many different areas. In the ***Inquiry Journal,*** students
  - ✓ Record what they know about the concepts and what they learn. You will be able to monitor their growing ability to make connections and use their prior knowledge to help them understand new concepts.
  - ✓ Keep a record of their research: what resources they need, what they have used, where they have looked, and what they have found. You can keep track of students' growing ability to find the resources and knowledge base they need to answer the questions they pose.
  - ✓ Keep track of their work with their collaborative groups. This will give you a good idea of students' growing ability to work with peers for a common goal—the acquisition of new knowledge.
  - ✓ Practice study and research skills that will help them in all of their schooling. You can easily keep track of how well they are learning to use such things as library resources, reference books, visual organizers, and much, much more.

Dictation

In grades 1–3, students use dictation to practice the sound/spelling associations they are learning and/or reviewing. Collect the dictation papers and look through them to see how the students are doing with writing and with proof-reading their words. Record notes on the papers and keep them in the student portfolios.

Portfolios

Portfolios are more than just a collection bin or gathering place for student projects and records. They add balance to an assessment program by providing unique benefits to teachers, students, and families.

- Portfolios help build self-confidence and increase self-esteem as students come to appreciate the value of their work. More importantly, portfolios allow students to reflect on what they know and what they need to learn. At the end of the school year, each student will be able to go through their portfolios and write about their progress.
- Portfolios provide the teacher with an authentic record of what students can do. Just as important, portfolios give students a concrete example of their own progress and development. Thus, portfolios become a valuable source of information for making instructional decisions.
- Portfolios allow families to judge student performance directly. Portfolios are an ideal starting point for discussions about a student's achievements and future goals during teacher/family conferences.

You will find that there are many opportunities to add to students' portfolios.

Assessment (continued)

Reading

- During partner reading, during **Workshop**, or at other times of the day, invite students, one at a time, to sit with you and read a story from an appropriate ***Decodable Book*** (grades 1–3) or from the ***Student Anthology.***
- As each student reads to you, follow along and make note of any recurring problems the student has while reading. Note students' ability to decode unknown words as well as any attempt—successful or not—to use strategies to clarify or otherwise make sense of what they are reading. From time to time, check students' fluency by timing their reading and noting how well they are able to sustain the oral reading without faltering.
- If the student has trouble reading a particular **Decodable Book**, encourage the student to read the story a few times on her or his own before reading it aloud to you. If the **Decodable Book** has two stories, use the alternate story to reassess the student a day or two later.
- If after practicing with a particular **Decodable Book** and reading it on his or her own a few times, a student is still experiencing difficulty, try the following:
  - Drop back two **Decodable Books.** (Continue to drop back until the student is able to read a story with no trouble.) If the student can read that book without problems, move up one book.
  - Continue the process until the student is able to read the current Decodable.

Preparing for Formal Assessment

Written Tests

- Have the students clear their desks.
- Make sure the students can hear and see clearly.
- Explain the instructions and complete one or two examples with students before each test to make sure they understand what to do.
- Give students ample time to finish each test.

Observing students as they go about their regular classwork is probably the single most effective way to learn in depth your students' strengths and areas of need.

The assessment components of ***Open Court Reading*** are designed to help teachers make appropriate instructional decisions. The variety of assessments is intended to be used continuously and formatively. That is, students should be assessed regularly as a follow-up to instructional activities, and the results of the assessment should be used to inform subsequent instruction.

Program Assessment

The Program Assessment is a series of three broad measures that are meant to be administered at the beginning of the school year, at midyear, and at the end of the year.

- The pretest gives teachers a snapshot of students' entry-level skills. This information allows the teacher to provide supplemental instruction to students who have not mastered critical skills and to offer more challenging material to students who demonstrate advanced abilities. In addition, this pretest can serve as a baseline against which to measure students' progress throughout the year.
- The midyear test reviews skills that were taught in the first half of the school year, allowing teachers to determine how well students are retaining what they have learned. In addition, the midyear test contains "anchor items" similar to those that appeared on the pretest. These items will allow teachers to measure student progress from the beginning of the year to the middle of the year.
- The posttest is a review of the content that was taught throughout the year and is a summative measure that reflects exit-level skills. The posttest also contains anchor items, so it is possible to compare students' performance on specific skills at three points in the school year.

In addition to the Pretest, Midyear Test, and Posttest, the Program Assessment also contains a Teacher Observation Log. Informal assessment is a part of the everyday classroom routine. Teachers can record information quickly on these observation sheets, and they may extend their observations over several days, until they have had a chance to observe each student's performance in a particular area.

Unit Assessments

Unit Assessments, as the name implies, reflect the instructional content and reading selections in each unit. The various measures within a unit assessment allow the teacher to see how well students have learned the skills that have recently been taught and to provide any additional instruction that is necessary.

Unit Assessments include a variety of measures that vary in form and difficulty so they are both motivating and challenging. Some of the questions are relatively easy, and most students should answer them correctly. Others are more difficult, but none are beyond the abilities of the majority of the students in a class. The skills featured on unit assessments are tied to reading success and reflect both state and national standards.

Unit Assessments include:

- Individual lesson assessments that assess the skills taught in each lesson immediately after instruction is delivered. These assessments will help you determine how well students are grasping the skills and concepts as they are taught.
- End-of-unit assessments that assess all of the skills taught throughout the unit. These assessments will help determine the students' ability and growing bank of knowledge as well as their ability to retain concepts over a limited period of time—generally six to eight weeks per unit.

Diagnostic Assessments

For the majority of the students in a class, the program assessment component of Open Court Reading will provide the teacher with all the information needed to make appropriate instructional decisions. In certain circumstances, however, it may be necessary to gather additional information in order to provide students with appropriate instruction. Some students, for example, may have specific skill deficits that prevent them from making adequate progress. Other students may enter the class after the beginning of the school year. A third situation is when the teacher might want to group students who have the same skill deficit. For these circumstances, we provide diagnostic assessments.

The diagnostic assessments offer a variety of measures that allow the teacher to identify students' strengths and weaknesses. The results of the assessment can help the teacher develop intervention strategies and choose the right supplemental instruction that will meet each student's needs. General and specific instructions are provided so that the teacher can use the diagnostic assessments efficiently without disrupting the instructional routine.

Tips

- When observing students, do not pull them aside; rather, observe students as part of the regular lesson, either with the whole class or in small groups.
- Encourage students to express any confusion they may be experiencing. The questions students ask can give you valuable insight into their progress and development.
- The more comfortable students become with standardized-test formats—usually multiple choice—the more confident you and they will be in the fact that the test is testing their knowledge of a subject rather than their test-taking skills.
- Make sure students know that the ultimate purpose of assessment is to keep track of their progress and to help them continue to do better.

Assessment

Rubrics

A rubric is an established rule or criterion. Rubrics provide criteria for different levels of performance. Rubrics established before an assignment is given are extremely helpful in evaluating the assignment. When students know what the rubrics for a particular assignment are, they can focus their energies on the key issues.

Using Comprehension Strategies Rubrics

The following rubrics can be used to gage the students' growing knowledge of the comprehension strategies and how adept they are becoming in their use. They are simply a guide. Students may and probably will develop strategies of their own. The important thing to consider is whether or not students are become strategic active readers—do they employ these and other strategies or do they continue to simply plough through text unaware of any problems they might be having. The rubrics indicate the types of behaviors strategic readers use and will help you identify in your students the growing facility your students gain in dealing with text of all sorts.

Grade 1: Comprehension Strategies Rubrics

Predicting

- The student makes predictions about what the text is about.
- The student updates predictions during reading, based on information in the text.

Visualizing

- The student visualizes ideas or scenes described in the text.

Grades 2-6: Comprehension Strategies Rubrics

Summarizing

- The student paraphrases text, reporting main ideas and a summary of what is in text.
- The student decides which parts of the text are important in his/her summary.
- The student draws conclusions from the text.
- The student makes global interpretations of the text, such as recognizing the genre.

Asking Questions

- The student asks questions about ideas or facts presented in the text and attempts to answer these questions by reading the text.

Predicting

- The student makes predictions about what the text is about.
- The student updates predictions during reading, based on information in the text.

Making Connections

- The student activates prior knowledge and related knowledge.
- The student uses prior knowledge to explain something encountered in text.
- The student connects ideas presented later in the text to ideas presented earlier in the text.
- The student notes ideas in the text that are new to him/her or conflict with what he/she thought previously.

Visualizing

- The student visualizes ideas or scenes described in the text.

Monitoring and Clarifying

- The student notes characteristics of the text, such as whether it is difficult to read or whether some sections are more challenging or more important than others are.
- The student shows awareness of whether he/she understands the text and takes appropriate action, such as rereading, in order to understand the text better.
- The student rereads to reconsider something presented earlier in the text.
- The student recognizes problems during reading, such as a loss of concentration, unfamiliar vocabulary, or lack of sufficient background knowledge to comprehend the text.

Monitoring and Adjusting Reading Speed

The student changes reading speed in reaction to text, exhibiting such behavior as

- Skimming parts of the text that are not important or relevant.
- Purposely reading more slowly because of difficulty in comprehending the text.

Research Rubrics

Throughout each unit, students engage in research and inquiry activities based on the unit concepts. They will present the findings of their research to the class. In this way they exhibit the wealth of knowledge and understanding they have gained about that particular concept. In addition to gaining knowledge about the concepts, students will be honing their research skills. With each unit, they will progress with their research in the same manner in which professional researchers do.

With each new unit of study, students should also become more and more sophisticated in their ability to formulate questions, make conjectures about those questions, recognize their own information needs, conduct research to find that information, reevaluate their questions and conjectures as new information is added to their knowledge base, and communicate their findings effectively. In addition, they will also become more and more adept at working as a team and being aware of the progress being made as individuals and as a group. The Research Rubrics will help you to assess the students' progress as researchers and as members of collaborative teams.

Formulating Research Questions and Problems

1. With help, identifies things s/he wonders about in relation to a topic.
2. Expresses curiosity about topics; with help, translates this into specific questions.
3. Poses an interesting problem or question for research; with help, refines it into a researchable question.
4. Identifies something s/he genuinely wonders about and translates it into a researchable question.

Making Conjectures

1. Offers conjectures that are mainly expressions of fact or opinion. ("I think the Anasazi lived a long time ago." "I think tigers should be protected.")
2. Offers conjectures that partially address the research question. ("I think germs make you sick because they get your body upset." "I think germs make you sick because they multiply really fast.")
3. Offers conjectures that address the research question with guesses. ("I think the Anasazi were wiped out by a meteor.")
4. Offers reasonable conjectures that address the question and that can be improved through further research.

Recognizing Information Needs

1. Identifies topics about which more needs to be learned. ("I need to learn more about the brain.")
2. Identifies information needs that are relevant though not essential to the research question. ("To understand how Leeuwenhoek invented the microscope, I need to know what size germs are.")
3. Identifies questions that are deeper than the one originally asked. (Original question: "How does the heart work?" Deeper question: "Why does blood need to circulate?")

Finding Needed Information

1. Collects information loosely related to topic.
2. Collects information clearly related to topic.
3. Collects information helpful in advancing on a research problem.
4. Collects problem-relevant information from varied sources and notices inconsistencies and missing pieces.

5. Collects useful information, paying attention to the reliability of sources and reviewing information critically.

Revising Problems and Conjectures

1. No revision.
2. Produces new problems or conjectures with little relation to earlier ones.
3. Tends to lift problems and conjectures directly from reference material.
4. Progresses to deeper, more refined problems and conjectures.

Communicating Research Progress and Results

1. Reporting is sparse and fragmentary.
2. Report is factual; communicates findings but not the thinking behind them.
3. Report provides a good picture of the research problem, of how original conjectures were modified in light of new information, and of difficulties and unresolved issues.
4. A report that not only interests and informs the audience but also draws helpful commentary from them.

Overall Assessment of Research

1. A collection of facts related in miscellaneous ways to a topic.
2. An organized collection of facts relevant to the research problem.
3. A thoughtful effort to tackle a research problem, with some indication of progress toward solving it.
4. Significant progress on a challenging problem of understanding.

Collaborative Group Work

1. Group members work on separate tasks with little interaction.
2. Work-related decisions are made by the group, but there is little interaction related to ideas.
3. Information and ideas are shared, but there is little discussion concerned with advancing understanding.
4. The group clearly progresses in its thinking beyond where individual students could have gone.

Participation in Collaborative Inquiry

1. Does not contribute ideas or information to team or class.
2. Makes contributions to Concept/Question Board or class discussions when specifically called upon to do so.
3. Occasionally contributes ideas or information to other students' inquiries.
4. Takes an active interest in the success of the whole class's knowledge-building efforts.

Writing Rubrics

Rubrics are particularly effective for writing assignments, which do not have simple right or wrong answers. The rubrics included in the Unit Assessments for writing cover different elements of the writing. They are intended to help teachers provide criteria and feedback to students.

Open Court Reading provides four-point rubrics for writing in each of four areas. This enables teachers to clearly distinguish among different levels of performance.

1. Point score indicates that a student is performing at a below basic level.
2. Point score indicates that a student's abilities are emerging.
3. Point score indicates that a student's work is adequate and achieving expectations.
4. Point score indicates that a student is exceeding expectations.

Conventions

The conventions rubrics provide criteria for evaluating a student's understanding and ability to use English language conventions, which include:

- Conventions
- Overall grammar, usage, mechanics, and spelling
- Grammar and Usage
- Mechanics: Punctuation
- Mechanics: Capitalization
- Sentence Structure
- Spelling

Genre

Genre rubrics, found in ***Unit Assessment*** enable evaluation of students' grasp of the different structures and elements of each of these different forms of writing:

- Descriptive Writing
- Expository Structure
- Genre
- Narrative
- Narrative Character
- Narrative Plot
- Narrative Setting
- Persuasive
- Personal
- Poetry

Writing Process

Writing process rubrics allow teachers to evaluate students' writing processes.

- Getting Ideas
- Prewriting—Organizing Writing
- Drafting
- Revising
- Editing
- Presentation/Publishing
- Self-Management
- Language Resources

Writing Traits

Writing traits rubrics, found in the ***Unit Assessment,*** provide criteria for different elements of written composition to identify a student's strengths and weaknesses.

- Audience
- Citing Sources
- Elaboration (supporting details and examples that develop the main idea)
- Focus
- Ideas/Content
- Organization
- Sentence Fluency
- Voice
- Word Choice

Audiovisual and Technology Resource Directory

This directory is provided for the convenience of ordering the Technology Resources listed on the Technology pages in each Unit Overview.

BFA Educational Media

468 Park Avenue South
New York, NY 10016
800-221-1274

Coronet/MTI

108 Wilmot Road
Deerfield, IL 60015
800-777-8100

Dorling Kindersley

95 Madison Avenue
New York, NY 10016
212-213-4800
FAX: 212-213-5240
www.dk-fl.co.uk

Great Plains National Instructional Television Library

University of Nebraska
6001 Dodge Street
Omaha, NE 68182
402-554-2800
http://www.gpn.unl.edu

Grolier Incorporated

Sherman Turnpike
Danbury, CT 06816
800-285-4534
Fax: 203-797-3130
www.grolier.com

Innovative Educators

P.O. Box 520
Montezuma, GA 31063
1-888-252-KIDS
FAX: 888-536-8553
http://www.innovative-educators.com

Library Video Company

P.O. Box 580
Wynnewood, PA 19096
FAX: 610-645-4040
http://www.libraryvideo.com

Live Oak Media

P.O. Box 652
Pine Plains, NY 12567
800-788-1121
FAX: 866-398-1070
http://www.liveoakmedia.com

Macmillan/McGraw-Hill School Division

220 East Danieldale Road
De Soto, TX 75115-9960
800-442-9685
www.mhschool.com

MCA Video MCA Records/Universal Studios

100 Universal City Plaza
Universal City, CA 91608
www.mcarecords.com

Mindscape, Inc.

88 Rowland Way
Novato, California 94945
415-895-2000
Fax: 415-895-2102
www.mindscape.com

Multicom Publishing

Multimedia 2000
2017 Eighth Avenue, 3rd Floor
Seattle, WA 98101
206-622-5530
Fax: 206-622-4380
www.multicom.com

Orange Cherry New Media

P.O. Box 505
Pound Ridge, NY 10576
914-764-4104
Fax: 914-764-0104
Email: nmsh@cloud9.net

Paramount

780 N. Gower
Hollywood, CA 90038
800-699-1085
http://homevideo.paramount.com

Queue, Inc.

338 Commerce Drive
Fairfield, CT 06432
800-232-2224
Fax: 203-336-2481
QUEUEINC@aol.com

Scholastic

555 Broadway
New York, NY 10012
800-SCHOLASTIC
http://www.scholastic.com

Sony Wonder

Sony Corporation of America
212-833-6800
http://www.sony.com

SRA/McGraw-Hill

220 East Danieldale Road
De Soto, TX 75115-9960
888-SRA-4543
www.sra4kids.com

Tom Snyder Productions

80 Coolidge Hill Road
Watertown, MA 02472
800-342-0236
Fax 617-926-6222
www.teachtsp.com/index.shtml

Scope and Sequence

PROGRAM APPENDIX

Reading

	Level						
	K	1	2	3	4	5	6
Print/Book Awareness (Recognize and understand the conventions of print and books)							
Capitalization			✔				
Constancy of Words						✔	
End Punctuation	✔						
Follow Left-to-right, Top-to-bottom	✔	✔					
Letter Recognition and Formation	✔	✔					
Page Numbering		✔					
Picture/Text Relationship	✔						
Quotation Marks	✔		✔			✔	
Relationship Between Spoken and Printed Language		✔					
Sentence Recognition						✔	
Table of Contents		✔					
Word Length	✔						
Word Boundaries		✔					
Phonemic Awareness (Recognize discrete sounds in words)							
Oral Blending: Words/Word Parts	✔	✔	✔				
Oral Blending: Initial Consonants/Blends	✔	✔	✔	✔			
Oral Blending: Final Consonants		✔		✔			
Oral Blending: Initial Vowels		✔					
Oral Blending: Syllables		✔			✔		
Oral Blending: Vowel Replacement					✔		
Segmentation: Initial Consonants/Blends		✔	✔	✔		✔	
Segmentation: Final Consonants		✔	✔	✔			
Segmentation: Words/Word Parts	✔		✔	✔	✔	✔	
Rhyming	✔	✔			✔	✔	
How the Alphabet Works							
Letter Knowledge	✔	✔		✔			
Letter Order (Alphabetic Order)	✔	✔					
Letter Sounds	✔	✔		✔	✔		
Sounds in Words	✔	✔		✔	✔		
Phonics (Associate sounds and spellings to read words)							
Blending Sounds into Words		✔					
Consonant Clusters		✔		✔			
Consonant Digraphs		✔		✔	✔		
Consonant Sounds and Spellings		✔	✔	✔			
Phonograms		✔		✔			✔
Syllables		✔			✔		
Vowel Diphthongs		✔		✔			✔
Vowels: Long Sounds and Spellings	✔	✔	✔	✔	✔	✔	✔
Vowels: r-controlled		✔	✔	✔	✔	✔	✔
Vowels: Short Sounds and Spellings	✔	✔	✔	✔	✔	✔	✔

Shaded box: Skills, strategies, and other teaching opportunities ✔ Formal, progress, or informal testing opportunities

Reading (continued)

	Level K	1	2	3	4	5	6
Comprehension Strategies							
Asking Questions/Answering Questions		✔	✔	✔	✔	✔	✔
Making Connections		✔	✔	✔	✔	✔	✔
Monitoring and Clarifying		✔	✔	✔	✔	✔	✔
Monitoring and Adjusting Reading Speed			✔	✔	✔	✔	✔
Predicting/Confirming Predictions	✔	✔	✔	✔	✔	✔	✔
Summarizing		✔	✔	✔	✔	✔	✔
Visualizing		✔	✔	✔	✔	✔	✔
Comprehension Skills							
Author's Point of View			✔	✔	✔	✔	✔
Author's Purpose			✔	✔	✔	✔	✔
Cause and Effect	✔	✔	✔	✔	✔	✔	✔
Classify and Categorize	✔	✔	✔	✔	✔	✔	✔
Compare and Contrast	✔	✔	✔	✔	✔	✔	✔
Drawing Conclusions	✔	✔	✔	✔	✔	✔	✔
Fact and Opinion		✔	✔	✔	✔	✔	✔
Main Idea and Details	✔	✔	✔	✔	✔	✔	✔
Making Inferences		✔	✔	✔	✔	✔	✔
Reality/Fantasy	✔	✔		✔	✔	✔	✔
Sequence		✔	✔	✔	✔	✔	✔
Vocabulary							
Antonyms	✔	✔	✔	✔	✔	✔	✔
Comparatives/Superlatives		✔	✔	✔	✔	✔	✔
Compound Words	✔	✔	✔	✔	✔	✔	✔
Connecting Words (Transition Words)						✔	✔
Context Clues		✔	✔	✔	✔	✔	✔
Contractions			✔	✔	✔	✔	
Homographs				✔	✔	✔	
Greek and Latin Roots				✔			
High-Frequency Words	✔	✔	✔	✔	✔	✔	✔
Figurative Language						✔	
Homophones/Homonyms		✔	✔	✔	✔	✔	✔
Idioms					✔	✔	✔
Inflectional Endings			✔	✔	✔	✔	✔
Irregular Plurals				✔		✔	✔
Multiple Meaning Words			✔	✔	✔	✔	✔
Multisyllabic Words			✔	✔		✔	
Position Words	✔	✔				✔	
Prefixes			✔	✔	✔	✔	✔
Question Words		✔					
Base or Root Words		✔	✔	✔	✔	✔	✔
Selection Vocabulary	✔	✔	✔	✔	✔	✔	✔
Suffixes		✔	✔	✔	✔	✔	✔
Synonyms		✔	✔	✔	✔	✔	✔
Time and Order Words (Creating Sequence)				✔	✔	✔	✔
Utility Words (Colors, Classroom Objects, etc.)	✔	✔					
Word Families			✔	✔	✔	✔	✔

Scope and Sequence (continued)

PROGRAM APPENDIX

Inquiry and Research

Study Skills	K	1	2	3	4	5	6
Charts, Graphs, and Diagrams/Visual Aids						✔	✔
Collaborative Inquiry			✔	✔	✔	✔	✔
Communicating Research Progress Results			✔	✔	✔	✔	✔
Compile Notes						✔	✔
Conducting an Interview							✔
Finding Needed Information			✔	✔	✔	✔	✔
Follow Directions							
Formulate Questions for Inquiry and Research			✔			✔	✔
Give Reports					✔	✔	✔
Make Outlines						✔	✔
Making Conjectures			✔	✔	✔	✔	✔
Maps and Globes					✔		✔
Note Taking					✔	✔	✔
Parts of a Book					✔		
Planning Investigation			✔	✔	✔	✔	✔
Recognizing Information Needs			✔	✔	✔	✔	✔
Revising Questions and Conjectures			✔	✔	✔	✔	✔
Summarize and Organize Information					✔	✔	✔
Time Lines					✔	✔	✔
Use Appropriate Resources (Media Source, Reference Books, Experts, Internet)					✔	✔	✔
Using a Dictionary/Glossary		✔			✔	✔	✔
Using a Media Center/Library					✔		✔
Using a Thesaurus			✔	✔	✔	✔	✔
Using an Encyclopedia					✔		✔
Using Newspapers and Magazines		✔			✔		✔
Using Technology							

Skills, strategies, and other teaching opportunities

✔ Formal, progress, or informal testing opportunities

Language Arts

Writing/Composition

	Level K	1	2	3	4	5	6
Approaches							
Collaborative Writing		✔					
Group Writing							
Process							
Brainstorming/Prewriting		✔		✔	✔	✔	
Drafting		✔		✔	✔	✔	
Revising		✔		✔	✔	✔	
Proofreading		✔		✔	✔	✔	
Publishing		✔		✔	✔	✔	
Forms							
Biography/Autobiography		✔	✔	✔	✔	✔	✔
Business Letter				✔	✔	✔	✔
Describe a Process		✔	✔	✔	✔		✔
Descriptive Writing		✔	✔	✔	✔	✔	✔
Expository/Informational Text		✔	✔	✔	✔	✔	✔
Folklore (Folktales, Fairy Tales, Tall Tales, Legends, Myths)			✔	✔	✔		
Friendly Letter		✔	✔	✔	✔	✔	✔
Historical Fiction						✔	✔
Journal Writing		✔	✔	✔	✔	✔	✔
Narrative		✔	✔	✔	✔	✔	✔
Personal Writing		✔	✔	✔	✔	✔	✔
Persuasive Writing		✔	✔	✔	✔	✔	✔
Play/Dramatization				✔	✔	✔	✔
Poetry		✔	✔	✔	✔	✔	✔
Realistic Story				✔			
Writer's Craft							
Characterization			✔	✔	✔	✔	✔
Descriptive Writing		✔	✔	✔	✔	✔	✔
Dialogue		✔	✔	✔	✔	✔	✔
Effective Beginnings			✔		✔	✔	✔
Effective Endings			✔		✔	✔	✔
Event Sequence		✔	✔	✔		✔	✔
Figurative Language	✔		✔	✔	✔	✔	✔
Identifying Thoughts and Feelings	✔		✔	✔	✔	✔	✔
Mood and Tone				✔	✔	✔	✔
Plot (Problem/Solutions)	✔	✔	✔	✔	✔	✔	✔
Point of View				✔	✔	✔	
Rhyme	✔	✔	✔	✔	✔	✔	
Sensory Details				✔		✔	✔
Sentence Variety				✔		✔	✔
Sentence Elaboration				✔		✔	✔
Setting	✔		✔	✔		✔	✔
Suspense and Surprise			✔		✔	✔	
Topic Sentences			✔	✔	✔	✔	✔
Using Comparisons						✔	
Purposes							
Determining Purposes for Writing	✔	✔				✔	

PROGRAM APPENDIX

Scope and Sequence (continued)

Language Arts

Grammar

	Level K	1	2	3	4	5	6
Parts of Speech							
Adjectives	✔	✔	✔		✔	✔	✔
Adverbs			✔	✔	✔	✔	✔
Conjunctions			✔	✔	✔	✔	✔
Nouns	✔	✔	✔	✔	✔	✔	✔
Prepositions	✔			✔	✔	✔	✔
Pronouns	✔	✔	✔	✔	✔	✔	✔
Verbs	✔	✔	✔	✔	✔	✔	✔
Sentences							
Fragments					✔		✔
Parts (Subjects/Predicates)		✔	✔	✔	✔	✔	✔
Subject/Verb Agreement	✔	✔	✔	✔	✔	✔	✔
Structure (Simple, Compound, Complex)				✔	✔	✔	✔
Types (Declarative, Interrogative, Exclamatory, Imperatives	✔	✔	✔	✔	✔	✔	✔
Verb Tenses	✔	✔	✔	✔	✔	✔	✔
Verbs (Action, Helping, Linking, Regular/Irregular)	✔	✔	✔	✔	✔	✔	✔
Usage							
Adjectives	✔	✔	✔	✔	✔	✔	✔
Adverbs			✔	✔	✔	✔	✔
Articles	✔	✔	✔	✔	✔	✔	✔
Nouns	✔	✔	✔	✔	✔	✔	✔
Pronouns	✔	✔	✔	✔	✔	✔	✔
Verbs	✔	✔	✔	✔	✔	✔	✔
Mechanics							
Capitalization (Sentence, Proper Nouns, Titles, Direct Address, Pronoun I)	✔	✔	✔	✔	✔	✔	✔
Punctuation (End punctuation, comma use, quotation marks, apostrophe, colon, semicolon, hyphen, parentheses)	✔	✔	✔	✔	✔	✔	✔
Spelling							
Contractions		✔	✔	✔		✔	
Inflectional Endings			✔	✔	✔	✔	
Irregular Plurals			✔	✔	✔	✔	✔
Long Vowel Patterns		✔	✔	✔	✔	✔	✔
Multisyllabic Words			✔	✔		✔	
Phonograms		✔	✔	✔			✔
r-controlled Vowel Spellings		✔	✔	✔	✔	✔	✔
Short Vowel Spellings		✔	✔	✔	✔	✔	✔
Silent Letters				✔			
Sound/Letter Relationships		✔	✔	✔			
Special Spelling Patterns (*-ough, -augh, -all, -al, -alk, -ion,-sion, -tion*)		✔	✔	✔	✔	✔	✔
Listening/Speaking/Viewing							
Listening/Speaking							
Analyze/Evaluate Intent and Content of Speaker's Message		✔	✔	✔	✔	✔	✔
Ask and Answer Questions	✔	✔	✔	✔	✔	✔	✔

[ ] Skills, strategies, and other teaching opportunities ✔ Formal, progress, or informal testing opportunities

Language Arts (continued)

	Level K	1	2	3	4	5	6
Listening/Speaking (continued)							
Determine Purposes for Listening			✔	✔	✔		
Follow Directions	✔	✔	✔	✔	✔	✔	✔
Learn about Different Cultures through Discussion					✔	✔	✔
Listen for Poetic Language (Rhythm/Rhyme)	✔	✔	✔	✔			
Participate in Group Discussions		✔	✔	✔	✔		✔
Respond to Speaker		✔	✔	✔	✔		✔
Use nonverbal communication techniques	✔	✔	✔	✔	✔	✔	✔
Speaking							
Describe Ideas and Feelings	✔	✔	✔	✔	✔		✔
Give Directions					✔	✔	✔
Learn about Different Cultures through Discussion				✔	✔	✔	✔
Participate in Group Discussions	✔	✔	✔	✔	✔	✔	✔
Present Oral Reports			✔	✔	✔	✔	✔
Read Fluently with Expression, Phrasing and Intonation			✔	✔	✔	✔	✔
Read Orally		✔	✔	✔	✔	✔	✔
Share Information	✔	✔	✔	✔	✔	✔	✔
Speak clearly at appropriate volume	✔	✔	✔	✔	✔	✔	✔
Summarize/Retell Stories		✔	✔	✔	✔	✔	✔
Understand formal and informal language	✔	✔	✔	✔	✔	✔	✔
Use Appropriate Vocabulary for Audience		✔	✔	✔	✔	✔	✔
Use elements of grammar in speech				✔	✔	✔	✔
Viewing							
Analyze purposes and techniques of the media				✔	✔	✔	✔
Appreciate/Interpret Artists' Techniques							
Compare Visual and Written Material on the Same Subject	✔				✔		
Gather Information from Visual Images	✔	✔	✔	✔	✔	✔	✔
View Critically		✔	✔	✔	✔	✔	✔
View Culturally Rich Materials	✔	✔	✔		✔	✔	✔
Penmanship							
Cursive Letters			✔				
Manuscript Letters	✔	✔					
Numbers	✔	✔					

Unit Themes

	LEVEL K	LEVEL 1	LEVEL 2
Unit 1	School	Let's Read!	Sharing Stories
Unit 2	Shadows	Animals	Kindness
Unit 3	Finding Friends	Things That Go	Look Again
Unit 4	The Wind	Our Neighborhood at Work	Fossils
Unit 5	Stick to It	Weather	Courage
Unit 6	Red, White, and Blue	Journeys	Our Country and Its People
Unit 7	Teamwork	Keep Trying	
Unit 8	By the Sea	Games	
Unit 9		Being Afraid	
Unit 10		Homes	

LEVEL 3	LEVEL 4	LEVEL 5	LEVEL 6
Friendship	Risks and Consequences	Cooperation and Competition	Perseverance
City Wildlife	Dollars and Sense	Astronomy	Ancient Civilizations
Imagination	From Mystery to Medicine	Heritage	Taking a Stand
Money	Survival	Making a New Nation	Beyond the Notes
Storytelling	Communication	Going West	Ecology
Country Life	A Changing America	Journeys and Quests	A Question of Value

Leveled Classroom Library Selections

PROGRAM APPENDIX

LEVEL K	LEVEL 1	LEVEL 2	LEVEL 3
Unit 1 School: *Mouse View: What the Class Pet Saw; The 100th Day of School; Billy and the Big New School; Vera's First Day of School; Bea and Mr. Jones; The Kissing Hand* **Unit 2 Shadows:** *Footprints and Shadows; Shadows Are About; I Have a Friend; My Shadow; What Makes Day and Night?; Sun Up, Sun Down* **Unit 3 Finding Friends:** *My Friends; Yo! Yes!; Will You Be My Friend?; George and Martha One Fine Day; Friends; May I Bring a Friend?* **Unit 4 The Wind:** *The Wind Blew; One Windy Wednesday; The Sun, the Wind, and the Rain; What Makes the Wind?; Millicent and the Wind; Feel the Wind* **Unit 5 Stick to It:** *The Carrot Seed; Leo the Late Bloomer; You'll Soon Grow into Them; JoJo's Flying Side Kick; Paul Bunyan: A Tall Tale; Liang and the Magic Paintbrush* **Unit 6 Red, White, and Blue:** *The Pledge of Allegiance; Night, America; This Land Is Your Land; Happy Birthday, America; The Flag We Love; Mr. Lincoln's Whiskers* **Unit 7 Teamwork:** *Can I Help?; Animal Orchestra; Tippy Bear Hunts for Honey; Helping Out; Stone Soup; The Great Trash Bash* **Unit 8 By the Sea:** *Oceans; In the Ocean; Tacky the Penguin; Fish Faces; The Seashore Book; Commotion in the Ocean*	**Unit 1 Let's Read!:** *America: My Land Your Land Our Land; I Read Signs; Miss Malarkey Doesn't Live in Room 10; The Old Woman Who Loved to Read; A Cake for Herbie; More Than Anything Else* **Unit 2 Animals:** *Sweet Dreams: How Animals Sleep; Moo Moo, Brown Cow; Here Is the African Savanna; Is Your Mama a Llama?; A Pinky is a Baby Mouse; Wolf Watch* **Unit 3 Things That Go:** *I Spy a Freight Train; Wheels Around; This Plane; This Is the Way We Go to School; The Listening Walk; Firehorse Max* **Unit 4 Our Neighborhood at Work:** *Communities; Night Shift Daddy; My Town; One Afternoon; Career Day; Mommy Works, Daddy Works* **Unit 5 Weather:** *Snow; Snowballs; Rain; Red Rubber Boot Day; Twister; Snow Is Falling* **Unit 6 Journeys:** *Rosie's Walk; The Train Ride; Amelia's Fantastic Flight; I'm Not Moving, Mama!; Ferryboat Ride!; The Josefina Story Quilt* **Unit 7 Keep Trying:** *Flap Your Wings and Try; The Chick and the Duckling; One Stuck Duck; One Fine Day; The Purple Coat; The Story of a Blue Bird* **Unit 8 Games:** *This Is Baseball; Take Me Out to the Ballgame; What's What? A Guessing Game; Leon and Bob; Moongame; James and the Rain* **Unit 9 Being Afraid:** *Sheila Rae, the Brave; Henry and Mudge and the Bedtime Thumps; First Day Jitters; Let's Go Home Little Bear; Can't You Sleep, Little Bear?; Feelings* **Unit 10 Homes:** *My House, Mi Casa: A Book in Two Languages; To Market, To Market; The Someday House; Homeplace; The Little House; Livingstone Mouse*	**Unit 1 Sharing Stories:** *Just Like Me; Mouse Tales; The Wednesday Surprise; Dear Annie; Jeremiah Learns to Read; Painted Words* **Unit 2 Kindness:** *Abe Lincoln's Hat; Jamaica's Find; The Bat in the Boot; The Giving Tree; Uncle Willie and the Soup Kitchen; A Chair for My Mother* **Unit 3 Look Again:** *The Trek; Who's Hiding There?; The Mixed Up Chameleon; A Color of His Own; What Do You Do When Something Wants to Eat You?; Hiding Out* **Unit 4 Fossils:** *Dinosaur Babies; The Day of the Dinosaur; A Boy Wants a Dinosaur; If the Dinosaurs Came Back; Archaeologists Dig for Clues; How Big Were the Dinosaurs?* **Unit 5 Courage:** *White Dynamite and Curly Kid; What's Under My Bed?; Ruth Law Thrills a Nation; Jamaica and the Substitute Teacher; Birdie's Lighthouse; The Buffalo Jump* **Unit 6 Our Country and Its People:** *Dancing with the Indians; A Picnic in October; Amelia's Road; Dragon Parade; The Lotus Seed; Dumpling Soup*	**Unit 1 Friendship:** *Charlotte's Web; Stevie; Best Friends; Amigo; The Mountain that loved a Bird; Alex Is My Friend* **Unit 2 City Wildlife:** *Wild in the City; Come Back Salmon: How a Group of Dedicated Kids Adopted Pigeon Creek and Brought it Back to Life; Farewell to Shady Glade; Coyotes in the Crosswalk: True Tales of Animal Life in the Wilds of the City; The City Kid's Field Guide; Birds, Nests, and Eggs* **Unit 3 Imagination:** *Behind the Couch; My Life with the Wave; Maria's Comet; Frederick; How I Spent My Summer Vacation; Crocodile's Masterpiece* **Unit 4 Money:** *Lemonade for Sale; Round and Round the Money Goes; Saturday Sancocho; The Treasure; Our Money; Screen of Frogs* **Unit 5 Storytelling:** *Tell Me a Story, Mama; The Worry Stone; May'naise Sandwiches & Sunshine Tea; One Grain of Rice; A Storyteller's Story; Firetalking* **Unit 6 Country Life:** *The Raft; Night in the Country; Mowing; Winter Wheat; A River Ran Wild; Unseen Rainbows, Silent Songs: The World Beyond Human Senses*

LEVEL 4

Unit 1 Risks and Consequences: *The Big Balloon Race; A Day's Work; Poppy; Sarah, Plain and Tall; The Landry News; From the Mixed-Up Files of Mrs. Basil E. Frankweiler*

Unit 2 Dollars and Sense: *Max Malone Makes a Million; What's Cooking, Jenny Archer?; The Toothpaste Millionaire; Brainstorm! The Stories of Twenty American Kid Inventors; Odd Jobs; Better Than a Lemonade Stand!*

Unit 3 From Mystery to Medicine: *Germs Make Me Sick!; Pasteur's Fight Against Microbes; Marie Curie and the Discovery of Radium; Kids to the Rescue! First Aid Techniques for Kids; The First Woman Doctor; Fever: 1793*

Unit 4 Survival: *Harry the Poisonous Centipede; My Grandmother's Journey; Whichaway; Frozen Fire; Island of the Blue Dolphins; The Voyage of the Frog*

Unit 5 Communication: *Prairie Dogs Kiss and Lobsters Wave: How Animals Say Hello; Burton and Stanley; Dear Mr. Henshaw; The Chimpanzee Family Book; The Cat's Elbow and Other Secret Languages; Julie's Wolf Pack*

Unit 6 A Changing America: *Sleds on Boston Common: A Story of the American Revolution; The Discovery of the Americas; Stranded at Plimouth Plantation, 1626; If You Traveled West in a Covered Wagon; The Louisiana Purchase; Gold Rush! The Young Prospector's Guide to Striking it Rich*

LEVEL 5

Unit 1 Cooperation and Competition: *The Big Bike Race; The Kid Who Ran For President; The Wheel on the School; Iditarod Dream: Dusty and His Sled Dogs Compete in Alaska's Jr. Iditarod; The View From Saturday; A World in Our Hands: In Honor of the 50th Anniversary of the United Nations*

Unit 2 Astronomy: *The Planets; Comets, Meteors, and Asteroids; Adventure in Space: The Flight to Fix the Hubble; The Young Astronomer; Edwin Hubble: American Astronomer; Tales of the Shimmering Sky: Ten Global Folktales with Activities*

Unit 3 Heritage: *Appalachia: The Voices of Sleeping Birds; This Land Is My Land; Going Back Home: An American Artist Returns to the South; In the Year of the Boar and Jackie Robinson; The Great Ancestor Hunt: The Fun of Finding Out Who You Are; Do People Grow on Family Trees?*

Unit 4 Making a New Nation: *Samuel's Choice; Toliver's Secret; Johnny Tremain; A Young Patriot: The American Revolution as Experienced by One Boy; Mr. Revere and I; Come All You Brave Soldiers: Blacks in the Revolutionary War*

Unit 5 Going West: *Boom Town; Striking It Rich: The Story of the California Gold; Black-Eyed Susan; By the Great Horn Spoon!; Children of the Wild West; Caddie Woodlawn*

Unit 6 Journeys and Quests: *Alicia's Treasure; Grass Sandals: The Travels of Basho; El Güero; Coast to Coast; Orphan Train Rider: One Boy's True Story; Call It Courage*

LEVEL 6

Unit 1 Perseverance: *The Most Beautiful Place in the World; Wilma Unlimited: How Wilma Rudolph Became the World's Fastest Woman; Littlejim's Dream; The Circuit: Stories from the Life of a Migrant Child; Where the Lilies Bloom; The Wright Brothers: How They Invented the Airplane*

Unit 2 Ancient Civilizations: *Androcles and the Lion; Ancient Romans at a Glance; Painters of the Caves; Pyramids!; Dig This! How Archaeologists Uncover Our Past; Religions of the World*

Unit 3 Taking a Stand: *Aunt Harriet's Underground Railroad in the Sky; Jane Addams: Pioneer Social Worker; Number the Stars; Run Away Home; Kids at Work: Lewis Hine and the Crusade Against Child Labor; Red Scarf Girl: A Memoir of the Cultural Revolution*

Unit 4 Beyond the Notes: *The Jazz Man; A Mouse Called Wolf; Play Me a Story: Nine Tales about Musical Instruments; The Sea King's Daughter: A Russian Legend; Dragonsong; Music*

Unit 5 Ecology: *The Great Kapok Tree; Lifetimes; Elephant Woman: Cynthia Moss Explores the World of Elephants; The Missing 'Gator of Gumbo Limbo; Ecology for Every Kid: Easy Activities that Make Learning Science Fun; The Most Beautiful Roof in the World*

Unit 6 A Question of Value: *Abuelita's Heart; The Golden Bracelet; Lily's Crossing; The Black Pearl; The Monkey Thief; Wringer*

Glossary

PROGRAM APPENDIX

This glossary includes linguistic, grammatical, comprehension, and literary terms that may be helpful in understanding reading instruction.

acronym a word formed from the initial letter of words in a phrase, **scuba (self-contained underwater breathing apparatus)**.

acrostic a kind of puzzle in which lines of a poem are arranged so that words or phrases are formed when certain letters from each line are used in a sequence.

adjective a word or group of words that modifies a noun.

adventure story a narrative that features the unknown or unexpected with elements of excitement, danger, and risk.

adverb a word or group of words that modifies a verb, adjective, or other adverb.

affective domain the psychological field of emotional activity.

affix a word part, either a prefix or a suffix, that changes the meaning or function of a word root or stem.

affricate a speech sound that starts as a stop but ends as a fricative, the /ch/ in **catch**.

agreement the correspondence of syntactically related words; subjects and predicates are in agreement when both are singular or plural.

alliteration the repetition of the initial sounds in neighboring words or stressed syllables.

alphabet the complete set of letters representing speech sounds used in writing a language.

alphabet book a book for helping young children learn the alphabet by pairing letters with pictures whose sounds they represent.

alphabetic principle the principle that there is an association between sounds and the letters that represent them in alphabetic writing systems.

alveolar a consonant speech sound made when the tongue and the ridge of the upper and lower jaw stop to constrict the air flow, as /t/.

anagram a word or phase whose letters form other words or phrases when rearranged, for example, **add** and **dad**.

analogy a likeness or similarity.

analytic phonics also deductive phonics, a whole-to-part approach to phonics in which a student is taught a number of sight words and then phonetic generalizations that can be applied to other words.

antonym a word that is opposite in meaning to another word.

appositive a word that restates or modifies a preceding noun. For example, **my daughter**, **Charlotte**.

aspirate an unvoiced speech sound produced by a puff of air, as /h/ in **heart**.

aspirated stop a stop consonant sound released with a puff of air, as /k/, /p/, and /t/.

auditory discrimination the ability to hear phonetic likenesses and differences in phonemes and words.

author's purpose the motive or reason for which an author writes, includes to entertain, inform, persuade.

automaticity fluent processing of information, requiring little effort or attention.

auxiliary verb a verb that precedes another verb to express time, mood, or voice, includes verbs such as **has**, **is**, **will**.

ballad a narrative poem, composed of short verses to be sung or recited, usually containing elements of drama and often tragic in tone.

base word a word to which affixes may be added to create related words.

blank verse unrhymed verse, especially unrhymed iambic pentameter.

blend the joining of the sounds of two or more letters with little change in those sounds, for example /spr/ in **spring**, also **consonant blend** or **consonant cluster**.

blending to combine the sounds represented by letters to sound out or pronounce a word, contrast with **oral blending**.

breve the symbol placed above a vowel to indicate that it is a short vowel.

browse to skim through or look over in search of something of interest.

canon in literature, the body of major works that a culture considers important at a given time.

case a grammatical category that indicates the syntactic/semantic role of a noun phrase in a sentence.

cause-effect relationship a stated or implied association between an outcome and the conditions that brought it about, also the comprehension skill associated with recognizing this type of relationship as an organizing principle in text.

chapter book a book long enough to be divided into chapters, but not long or complex enough to be considered a novel.

characterization the way in which an author presents a character in a story, including describing words, actions, thoughts, and impressions of that character.

choral reading oral group reading to develop oral fluency by modeling.

cinquain a stanza of five lines, specifically one that has successive lines of two, four, six, eight, and two syllables.

cipher a system for writing in code.

clarifying a comprehension strategy in which the reader rereads text, uses a dictionary, uses decoding skills, or uses context clues to comprehend something that is unclear.

clause a group of words with a subject and a predicate used to form a part of or a whole sentence, a dependent clause modifies an independent clause, which can stand alone as a complete sentence.

collaborative learning learning by working together in small groups.

command a sentence that asks for action and usually ends with a period.

common noun in contrast to **proper noun**, a noun that denotes a class rather than a unique or specific thing.

comprehension the understanding of what is written or said.

comprehension skill a skill that aids in understanding text, including identifying **author's purpose**, **comprehending cause and effect relationships**, **comparing and contrasting** items and events, **drawing conclusions**, distinguishing **fact from opinion**, identifying **main ideas**, making **inferences**, distinguishing **reality from fantasy**, and understanding **sequence**.

comprehension strategy a sequence of steps for understanding text, includes asking questions, clarifying, making connections, predicting, summarizing, and visualizing.

conjugation the complete set of all possible inflected forms of a verb.

conjunction a part of speech used to connect words, phrases, clauses, or sentences, including the words **and, but, or**.

consonant a speech sound, and the alphabet letter that represents that sound, made by partial or complete closure of part of the vocal tract, which obstructs air flow and causes audible friction.

context clue information from the immediate text that helps identify a word.

contraction a short version of a written or spoken expression in which letters are omitted, for example, **can't**.

convention an accepted practice in spoken or written language, usually referring to spelling, mechanics, or grammar rules.

cooperative learning a classroom organization that allows students to work together to achieve their individual goals.

creative writing prose and poetic forms of writing that express the writer's thoughts and feelings imaginatively.

cuing system any of the various sources of information that help to identify an unrecognizable word in reading, including phonetic, semantic, and syntactical information.

cumulative tale a story, such as The Gingerbread Man, in which details are repeated until the climax.

dangling modifier usually a participle that because of its placement in a sentence modifies the wrong object.

decodable text text materials controlled to include a majority of words whose sound/spelling relationships are known by the reader.

decode to analyze spoken or graphic symbols for meaning.

diacritical mark a mark, such as a breve or macron, added to a letter or graphic character, to indicate a specific pronunciation.

dialect a regional variety of a particular language with phonological, grammatical, and lexical patterns that distinguish it from other varieties.

dialogue a piece of writing written as conversation, usually punctuated by quotation marks.

digraph two letters that represent one speech sound, for example /sh/ or /ch/.

diphthong a vowel sound produced when the tongue glides from one vowel sound toward another in the same syllable, for example /oi/ or /ou/.

direct object the person or thing that receives the action of a verb in a sentence, for example, the word **cake** in this sentence: **Madeline baked a cake**.

drafting the process of writing ideas in rough form to record them.

drama a story in the form of a play, written to be performed.

edit in the writing process, to revise or correct a manuscript.

emergent literacy the development of the association of meaning and print that continues until a child reaches the stage of conventional reading and writing.

emergent reading a child's early interaction with books and print before the ability to decode text.

encode to change a message into symbols, for example, to change speech into writing.

epic a long narrative poem, usually about a hero.

exclamatory sentence a sentence that shows strong emotion and ends with an exclamation mark.

expository writing or **exposition** a composition in writing that explains an event or process.

fable a short tale that teaches a moral.

fantasy a highly imaginative story about characters, places, and events that do not exist.

fiction imaginative narrative designed to entertain rather than to explain, persuade, or describe.

figure of speech the expressive, nonliteral use of language usually through metaphor, simile, or personification.

fluency freedom from word-identification problems that hinder comprehension in reading.

folktale a narrative form of genre such as an epic, myth, or fable that is well-known through repeated storytellings.

foreshadowing giving clues to upcoming events in a story.

free verse verse with irregular metrical pattern.

freewriting writing that is not limited in form, style, content, or purpose, designed to encourage students to write.

genre a classification of literary works, including tragedy, comedy, novel, essay, short story, mystery, realistic fiction, poetry.

grammar the study of the classes of words, their inflections, and their functions and relations in sentences; includes phonological, morphological, syntactic, and semantic descriptions of a language.

grapheme a written or printed representation of a phoneme, such as **c** for /k/.

guided reading reading instruction in which the teacher provides the structure and purpose for reading and responding to the material read.

handing off a method of turning over to the students the primary responsibility for controlling discussion.

indirect object in a sentence, the person or thing to or for whom an action is done, for example, the word **dog** in this sentence: **Madeline gave the dog a treat**.

inference a conclusion based on facts, data, or evidence.

infinitive the base form of a verb, usually with the infinitive marker, for example, **to go**.

inflectional ending an ending that expresses a plural or possessive form of a noun, the tense of a verb, or the comparative or superlative form of an adjective or adverb.

interrogative word a word that marks a clause or sentence as a question, including **interrogative pronouns who**, **what**, **which**, **where**.

intervention a strategy or program designed to supplement or substitute instruction, especially for those students who fall behind.

invented spelling the result of an attempt to spell a word based on the writer's knowledge of the spelling system and how it works, often with overemphasis on sound/symbol relationships.

irony a figure of speech in which the literal meaning of the words is the opposite of their intended meaning.

journal a written record of daily events or responses.

juvenile book a book written for children or adolescents.

legend a traditional tale handed down from generation to generation.

leitmotif a repeated expression, event, or idea used to unify a work of art such as writing.

letter one of a set of graphic symbols that forms an alphabet and used alone or in combination to represent a phoneme, also **grapheme**.

linguistics the study of the nature and structure of language and communication.

literary elements the elements of a story such as **setting**, **plot**, and **characterization** that create the structure of a narrative.

macron a diacritical mark placed above a vowel to indicate a long vowel sound.

main idea the central thought or chief topic of a passage.

mechanics the conventions of capitalization and punctuation.

metacognition awareness and knowledge of one's mental processes or thinking about what one is thinking about.

metaphor a figure of speech in which a comparison is implied but not stated, for example, **She is a jewel**.

miscue a deviation from text during oral reading in an attempt to make sense of the text.

modeling an instructional technique in which the teacher serves as an example of behavior.

mood the literary element that conveys the emotional atmosphere of a story.

morpheme a meaningful linguistic unit that cannot be divided into smaller units, for example, **word**; **a bound morpheme** is a morpheme that cannot stand alone as an independent word, for example, the prefix **re-**; a **free morpheme** can stand alone, for example, **dog**.

myth a story designed to explain the mysteries of life.

narrative writing or **narration** a composition in writing that tells a story or gives an account of an event.

nonfiction prose designed to explain, argue, or describe rather than to entertain with a factual emphasis, includes biography and autobiography.

noun a part of speech that denotes persons, places, things, qualities, or acts.

novel an extended fictional prose narration.

onomatopoeia the use of a word whose sound suggests its meaning, for example, **purr**.

oral blending the ability to fuse discrete phonemes into recognizable words; oral blending puts sounds together to make a word, **see also segmentation**.

orthography correct or standardized spelling according to established usage in a language.

oxymoron a figure of speech in which contrasting or contradictory words are brought together for emphasis.

paragraph a subdivision of a written composition that consists of one or more sentences, deals with one point, or gives the words of one speaker, usually beginning with an indented line.

participle a verb form used as an adjective, for example, **the skating party**.

personification a figure of speech in which animals, ideas, or things take on human characteristics.

persuasive writing a composition intended to persuade the reader to adopt the writer's point of view.

phoneme the smallest sound unit of speech, for example, the /k/ in **book**.

phonemic awareness the ability to recognize that spoken words are made up of discrete sounds and that those sounds can be manipulated.

phonetic spelling the respelling of entry words in a dictionary according to a pronunciation key.

phonetics the study of speech sounds.

phonics a way of teaching reading that addresses sound/symbol relationships, especially in beginning instruction.

phonogram a letter or symbol that represents a phonetic sound.

Glossary (continued)

plot the literary element that provides the structure of the action of a story, which may include rising action, climax, and falling action leading to a resolution or denouement.

plural a grammatical form of a word that refers to more than one in number; an **irregular plural** is one that does not follow normal patterns for inflectional endings.

poetic license the liberty taken by writers to ignore conventions.

poetry a metrical form of composition in which language is chosen and arranged to create a powerful response through meaning, sound, or rhythm.

possessive showing ownership either through the use of an adjective, an adjectival pronoun, or the possessive form of a noun.

predicate the part of the sentence that expresses something about the subject and includes the verb phrase; a **complete predicate** includes the principal verb in a sentence and all its modifiers or subordinate parts.

predicting a comprehension strategy in which the reader attempts to figure out what will happen and then confirms predictions as the text is read.

prefix an affix attached before a base word that changes the meaning of the word.

preposition a part of speech in the class of function words, such as **of**, **on**, **at**, that precede noun phrases to create prepositional phrases.

prewriting the planning stage of the writing process in which the writer formulates ideas, gathers information, and considers ways to organize them.

print awareness in emergent literacy, a child's growing recognition of conventions and characteristics of written language, including reading from left to right and top to bottom in English, and that words are separated by spaces.

pronoun a part of speech used as a substitute for a noun or noun phrase.

proofreading the act of reading with the intent to correct, clarify, or improve text.

pseudonym an assumed name used by an author, a pen name or nom de plume.

publishing the process of preparing written material for presentation.

punctuation graphic marks such as comma, period, quotation marks, and brackets used to clarify meaning and give speech characteristics to written language.

question an interrogative sentence that asks a question and ends with a question mark.

realistic fiction a story that attempts to portray characters and events as they actually are.

rebus the use of a picture or symbol to suggest a word or syllable.

revise in the writing process, to change or correct a manuscript to make its message more clear.

rhyme identical or very similar recurring final sounds in words, often at the ends of lines of poetry.

rime a vowel and any following consonants of a syllable.

segmentation the ability to break words into individual sounds; **see also oral blending**.

semantic mapping a graphic display of a group of words that are meaningfully related to support vocabulary instruction.

semantics the study of meaning in language, including the meanings of words, phrases, sentences, and texts.

sentence a grammatical unit that expresses a statement, question, or command; a **simple sentence** is a sentence with one subject and one predicate; a **compound sentence** is a sentence with two or more independent clauses usually separated by a comma and conjunction, but no dependent clause; a **complex sentence** is a sentence with one independent and one or more dependent clauses.

sentence combining a teaching technique in which complex sentence chunks and paragraphs are built from basic sentences.

sentence lifting the process of using sentences from children's writing to illustrate what is wrong or right to develop children's editing and proofreading skills.

sequence the order of elements or events.

setting the literary element that includes the time, place, and physical and psychological background in which a story takes place.

sight word a word that is taught to be read as a whole word, usually words that are phonetically irregular.

simile a figure of speech in which a comparison of two things that are unlike is directly stated usually with the words **like** or **as**, for example, **She is like a jewel**.

spelling the process of representing language by means of a writing system.

statement a sentence that tells something and ends with a period.

study skills a general term for the techniques and strategies that help readers comprehend text with the intent to remember, includes following directions, organizing, locating, and using graphic aids.

style the characteristics of a work that reflect the author's particular way of writing.

subject the main topic of a sentence to which a predicate refers, including the principal noun; a **complete subject** includes the principal noun in a sentence and all its modifiers..

suffix an affix attached at the end of a base word that changes the meaning of the word.

summarizing a comprehension strategy in which the reader constructs a brief statement that contains the essential ideas of a passage.

syllable a minimal unit of sequential speech sounds comprised of a vowel sound or a vowel-sound combination.

symbolism the use of one thing to represent something else in order to represent an idea in a concrete way.

synonym a word that means the same as another word.

syntax the grammatical pattern or structure of word order in sentences, clauses, and phrases.

tense the way in which verbs indicate past, present, and future time of action.

text structure the various patterns of ideas that are built into the organization of a written work.

theme a major idea or proposition that provides an organizing concept through which by study, students gain depth of understanding.

topic sentence a sentence intended to express the main idea of a paragraph or passage.

tragedy a literary work, often a play, in which the main character suffers conflicts and which presents a serious theme and has an unfortunate ending.

usage the way in which a native language or dialect is used by the members of the community.

verb a word that expresses an action or state that occurs in a predicate of a sentence; an **irregular verb** is a verb that does not follow normal patterns of inflectional endings that reflect past, present, or future verb tense.

visualizing a comprehension strategy in which the reader constructs a mental picture of a character, setting, or process.

vowel a voiced speech sound and the alphabet letter that represents that sound, made without stoppage or friction of the air flow as it passes through the vocal tract.

vowel digraph a spelling pattern in which two or more letters represent a single vowel sound.

word calling proficiency in decoding with little or no attention to word meaning.

writing also **composition** the process or result of organizing ideas in writing to form a clear message, includes persuasive, expository, narrative, and descriptive forms.

writing process the many aspects of the complex act of producing a piece of writing, including prewriting, drafting, revising, proofreading, and publishing.

Alphabet Song

Purpose

To teach the names of the letters in their proper order

About the Song

There are several versions of the Alphabet Song. The children may never have heard the version used in this program, and may insist that the version they already know is the "correct" one. You might explain that this is the classroom version and the one you prefer. Have them listen as you play and/or sing it.

In some versions, the alphabet letters are sung faster and with different pauses. The last two lines of the song may also differ. In this version, all letters except W are sung slowly. The first rhyme of the song is sacrificed, but each letter is pronounced distinctly and the song is more instructive for children than the traditional version.

Instruction

After listening to this version of the song two or three times, most of the children should be able to join in and sing along. The best way to teach this version of the Alphabet Song (especially if the children already know the more traditional version), is to teach it in steps: the first phrase, *A* to *G;* then the second phrase, *H* through *N;* then the next two phrases, *O* through *T;* then two more phrases, *U* through *Z;* and finally the last two rhyming phrases.

If the ***Sound/Spelling Cards*** are on the wall, help children make the connection between the names for the letters and their written symbols by touching each letter as you and the children sing the song. You might want to make a chart of the letters.

You or the children can then lead the song, touching each letter on the chart as it is sung. (Using small letters on the chart will help the children learn to recognize these.)

a b c d e f g
h i j k l m n
o p q
r s t
u v w
x y z

Songs and Games (continued)

Alphabet Rap

In addition to the traditional Alphabet Song, the children might enjoy singing this Alphabet Rap. You might want to point to the letters on the ***Sound/ Spelling Cards*** as you recite their names, or copy the words onto a chart.

This ***A B C***
is just for me,
And ***D E F***
is next you see,
G H I J
comes after that,
K L M N
I've got down pat.
O P Q R
S T U V
are all that's left,
'cept ***W***
X Y and ***Z***.

Sing Your Way to ____ Game

The "Sing Your Way to ___ Game" provides students with a way of finding the name of any letter they might have forgotten. You can use the Lion Puppet to help introduce this activity. Use the Lion Puppet at your discretion for later lessons.

- Have the Lion Puppet point to the letter of the alphabet for the lesson you are teaching. Do not have the puppet name the letter. Ask students to sing the "Alphabet Song" with you until you reach this letter and then to stop. When the class stops, have the Lion Puppet ask, "What is the letter?"
- Have the Lion Puppet point to other letters that have already been introduced. Ask students to sing the "Alphabet Song" with you to the letter indicated and then to stop. Then have the puppet ask for the letter name.
- Point to the letter of the alphabet for the lesson you are teaching, but do not name it. Ask a student to sing his or her way to the letter and then to stop. The students should sing the "Alphabet Song," pointing to each letter and stopping as he or she comes to the letter you have indicated.
- Ask other students to sing their way to other letters that have already been introduced. Remind them that they can sing their way to any letter of the alphabet by stopping when they reach the name of that letter.

Apples and Bananas

Purpose

To help the children listen for and repeat the long vowel sounds

About the Song

"Apples and Bananas" is a vowel replacement song. It requires the children to consciously control vowel sounds in words while leaving the consonants unchanged.

Instruction

The song "Apples and Bananas" is a repeated couplet, as you see in the first verse. In the second verse, some vowels are replaced with long *a:*

I like to ate, ate, ate

ayples and baynaynays.

I like to ate, ate, ate

ayples and baynaynays.

In the next verse, the same vowels are replaced with long *e:*

I like to eat, eat, eat

eeples and beeneenees.

I like to eat, eat, eat

eeples and beeneenees.

Continue in the same way with the remaining verses, replacing the vowel each time with long *i*, long *o*, and finally, long *u*.

If you sing slowly, it will be easy for the children to make these vowel replacements. As you start to sing the new verse yourself, the children will most likely join right in. You may find that it is helpful to announce the new verse. For example: "And now /ō/!"

Later, you may want to let volunteers lead the class. Write the letters *a*, *e*, *i*, *o*, *u* on the chalkboard and let the leader touch any letter at random to tell the children how to sing the next verse.

Apples and Bananas

Did You Ever?

Purpose

To provide an opportunity for children to have fun with rhyming words and to make up rhyming verses of their own

Instruction

Write the words for the song on the board or provide a song sheet for each child. Explain that the lines enclosed within quotation marks can change with each verse they sing. Then list those two-line changes on the board or include them on the song sheet.

After learning the song, the children may enjoy making up additional verses. They probably should not do so the first time they sing the song.

In further verses, the lines within quotation marks change. Some suggested variations follow:

"Did you ever see a goose
Riding a moose?"

"Did you ever see a cat
Wearing a hat?"

"Did you ever see a duck
Driving a truck?"

"Did you ever see a bear
Curling her hair?"

When the children are familiar with the song and the rhyme pattern of the changing lines, suggest that they make up their own rhyming lines. You might first generate a list of animals that have not yet appeared in the verses. The children may suggest pig, bird, snake, and so on. Then ask the children to think of words that rhyme with the animal's name, such as *pig* and *wig*. Finally, they can make up a verse, such as, "Did you ever see a pig/Wearing a wig?"

Scrambled Sentences

Purpose

To provide practice constructing sentences

Materials

- index cards
- business-sized envelopes

Preparing Materials

Using sentences that children have blended in recent lessons, write each word of each sentence on a separate index card. Include the capital letter on the first word and the period on the last word. Place the words for one sentence in an envelope. Prepare several envelopes in this way. You may want to write the complete sentence on the inside of the envelope flap for the children to use to check their work.

How to Play the Game

A child arranges the words in an envelope to make a sensible sentence. This game can be an individual activity, or small groups of children can do the activity as a game, if they wish, competing to see who can unscramble his or her sentence the fastest. Have players write the sentence they make and then read the sentence to their classmates.

Variations

The following are variations of the Scrambled Sentences game.

- Use sentences from stories the children have read.
- Children may work in groups or alone to create their own scrambled sentences. Provide index cards on which they can write words, and envelopes in which they can place the cards. Remind them to use capital letters and periods in their sentences and to write the complete sentence on the inside flap of each envelope.

Spelling Activities

Purpose

To reinforce the children's phonics skills through spelling

Picture Spelling Game

Materials

- index cards or other small blank cards
- magazines, stickers, and other picture sources
- glue or paste
- marking pens

Preparing Materials

On one side of each index card, print an appropriate spelling word. On the other side of the card, draw or paste a picture as a clue to the word. Make as many cards as you feel are appropriate. Add to the set of cards as the children learn new words.

How to Play the Game

The Picture Spelling game can be played alone or with a partner. The picture-word cards are stacked in a pile or spread out with the pictures facing up. One player chooses a picture card, prints the word that names the picture on a blank sheet of paper, and then checks the spelling by turning the card over. If the game is played with a partner, one player can show a picture to a partner and have him or her spell the word aloud.

Spelling Challenge

How to Play the Game

Divide the class into teams of three or four children each. Explain that you will write a spelling of a sound on the chalkboard. Give the teams one minute to think of words that contain that spelling. When the time is up, call on each team in turn to say and to spell its words. Write the words on the board as each is spelled and award a point for each correct spelling. The team with the most points wins the game. (Remind the teams to whisper as they brainstorm words so that the other teams won't hear their words.)

Compound Word Puzzles

Materials

- posterboard or heavy construction paper
- scissors
- marking pen
- a large envelope

Preparing Materials

From posterboard or heavy construction paper, cut 2-by-6-inch strips. Print a compound word on each strip, leaving some space between the two parts of each word. You might begin with the words listed below and then add or replace the compound word cards as the year goes by. Cut each strip in half between the word parts, using a different curved or zigzag line for each strip (see illustration). Store all of the puzzle pieces in an envelope.

nearby	**nighttime**	**cornbread**
seaweed	**playground**	**hairbrush**
firefly	**notebook**	**haircut**
bathtub	**mailbox**	**footprint**

How to Play the Game

A child spills the puzzle pieces onto a work area, turns them face up, and reads each card. When the child thinks that two words can form a compound word, he or she tries to fit the puzzle pieces together. If the two pieces fit together exactly, a correct compound word is formed.

Yoo-oo Owls

Materials

- construction paper
- marking pens

Preparing Materials

This can be an individual or a whole-class activity. For individual work, prepare a blackline master for each child. For a whole-class activity, prepare a bulletin board display. On a bulletin board or on a blackline master, draw the outlines of two large trees. On the trunk of one tree, draw an owl for /o͞o/. Explain to students that the owl hoots by saying /o͞o/, /o͞o/, /o͞o/. On the trunk of the other tree, draw a big red letter *U*, like the one on the ***Sound/Spelling Card*** for /ū/ (see illustration).

How to Play the Game

Ask the children to make leaves for each tree. For the blackline master, have the children draw leaves on each tree and print an /o͞o/ word or a /ū/ word, as appropriate, on each leaf. For the bulletin board display, you might want to have a supply of leaf shapes cut from construction paper. Have the children print an /o͞o/ word or a /ū/ word on each leaf and then place it on the appropriate tree on the bulletin board.

Puzzle Word Game

Materials

- Letter Cards

How to Play the Game

The Puzzle Word game may be an individual, partner, or group activity. Choose a word from a ***Student Anthology*** or ***Big Book*** selection that the children have read recently—for example, *bridge* from "The Three Billy Goats Gruff." (The word must be one with no double letters, since the children will be using their ***Letter Cards*** to unscramble the word.) On the chalkboard, write the letters of the word *bridge* in mixed-up order—for example *i g d r e b*. Have the children take out their ***Letter Cards*** for those six letters and place them on the work area in front of them. They should use those six ***Letter Cards***, moving them around, to spell as many words as they can. The words may be of varying lengths, and the letters may be reused to spell different words. However, the letters may not be used more than once in a single word. For example, the children may spell the words *big*, *red*, *rid*, *bed*, *dig*, *ride*, and *bid*, but not the word *did*. Remind the children that they can refer to the ***Sound/Spelling Cards*** to help them spell words. Have them write down each new word they spell. Tell the children that all of the letters will make a special word from the selection "The Three Billy Goats Gruff." They may look through the story if they wish.

At the end of the time limit you set, which can be as long as all day or as short as ten minutes, have the children share their lists of words.

Penmanship

Open Court Reading develops handwriting skills through weekly Penmanship lessons. The instruction for these lessons appears in the Language Arts part of the lesson in every grade level. The purpose of these lessons is to develop important handwriting skills necessary for producing legible, properly spaced documents. Penmanship practice reinforces the vocabulary in the lesson selection.

In addition to the board, the overhead projector can be a very effective device for teaching penmanship. Students can move their pencils at the same time the teacher forms letters on the transparency. It also helps to recite the descriptions or chants that go with each letter.

Penmanship in Levels K to 2

Beginning in kindergarten, the Penmanship lessons expand on the sound/spelling instruction by introducing letters the students study in Sounds and Letters. Students learn that those letters are made of four basic lines: curved lines, horizontal lines, vertical lines, and slanted lines.

Next, students learn letter and number formation. The students practice letter formation by writing the letter being studied and then words from the literature selection that contain the particular letter. This instruction continues in Level 1 and is tied to the letter formation instruction in Phonics and Fluency.

Manuscript Handwriting Models

The lessons present ball and stick models of manuscript handwriting, while the Appendix offers an alternative method with continuous stroke models.

Hand and Paper Positioning

The **hand and paper positioning** models are for teachers' reference and enhance the written instruction of positioning lessons. The diagrams give teachers a visual aid so that they may better understand and demonstrate an effective technique of positioning.

A right-handed student should hold the pencil loosely about one inch above the point, between the thumb and middle finger. A left-handed student should hold the pencil the same way, but up to one half inch farther away from the point. The index fingers of both writers should rest lightly on the top of the pencil. The wrist should be level and just slightly raised from the desk.

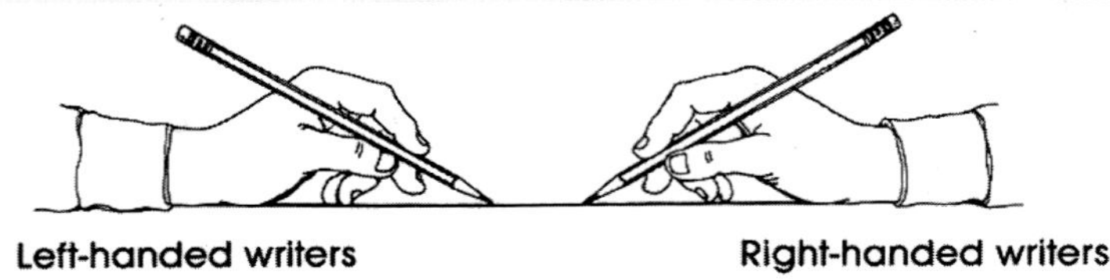

For both kinds of writers, the paper should lie straight in front of the student with the edges parallel to the edges of the desk. A left-handed writer may find it easier to slant the paper slightly to the right and parallel to the left forearm. A right-handed writer's writing hand should be kept well below the writing. The left hand should hold down the paper.

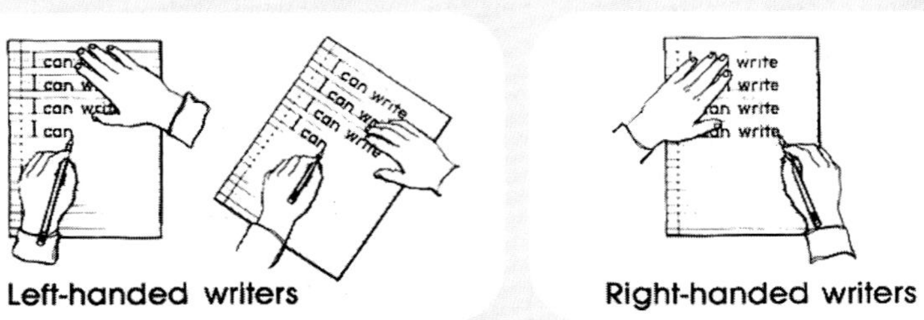

Ball and Stick Handwriting Models

The **ball and stick** models of manuscript handwriting provide teachers with a systematic method for teaching children to form uppercase and lowercase letters of the alphabet. The dots on the letters indicate starting points for the students. The numbered arrows show the students in what order and what direction the line they are drawing should go to form the particular letter. Teachers may use the chants to describe the letter step by step as he or she models the formation on the board. Students may also recite the chants in unison as they practice the formation, whether they are writing the letter or tracing it on the board.

Ball and Stick Handwriting Models

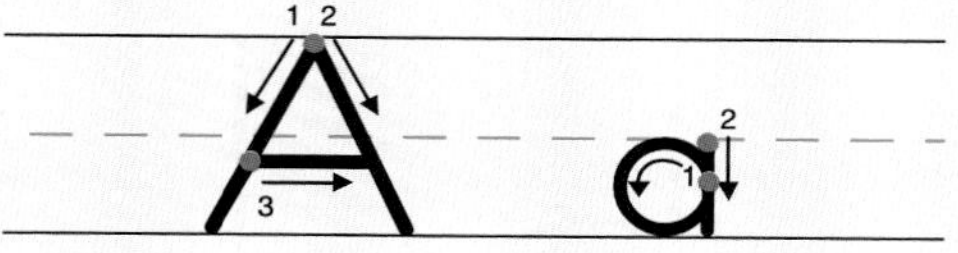

A Starting point, slanting down left
Starting point, slanting down right
Starting point, across the middle: capital *A*

a Starting point, around left all the way
Starting point, straight down, touching the circle: small *a*

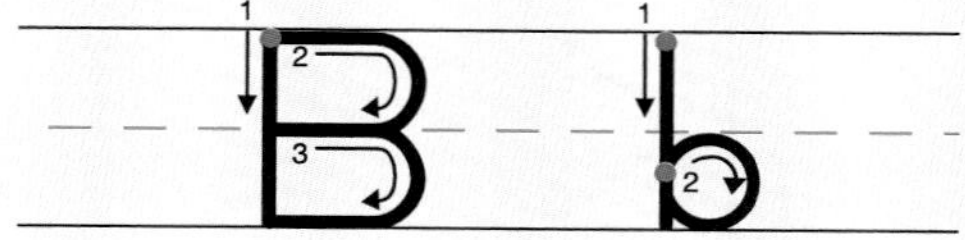

B Starting point, straight down
Starting point, around right and in at the middle, around right and in at the bottom: capital *B*

b Starting point, straight down, back up, around right all the way: small *b*

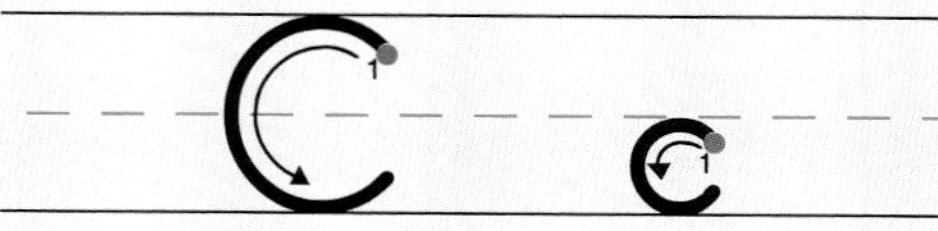

C Starting point, around left to stopping place: capital *C*

c Starting point, around left to stopping place: small *c*

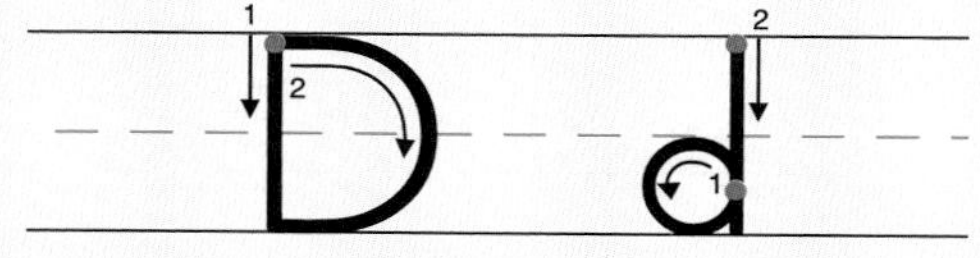

D Starting point, straight down
Starting point, around right and in at the bottom: capital *D*

d Starting point, around left all the way
Starting point, straight down, touching the circle: small *d*

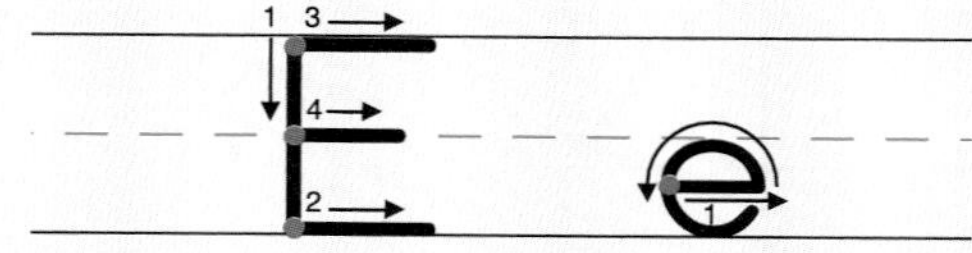

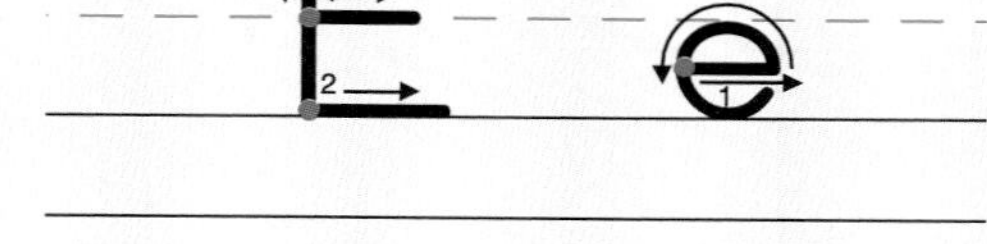

E Starting point, straight down
Starting point, straight out
Starting point, straight out
Starting point, straight out: capital *E*

e Starting point, straight out up and around to the left, curving down and around to the right: small *e*

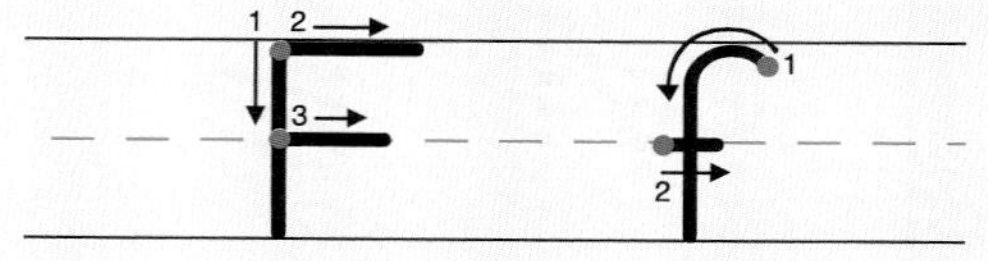

F Starting point, straight down
Starting point, straight out
Starting point, straight out: capital *F*

f Starting point, around left and straight down
Starting point, straight across: small *f*

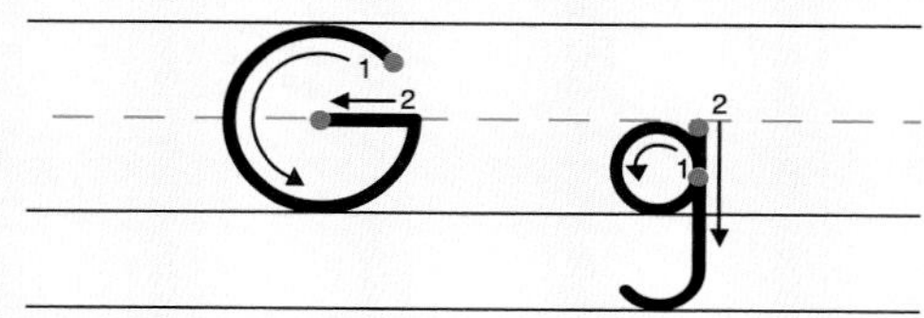

G Starting point, around left, curving up and around
Straight in: capital *G*

g Starting point, around left all the way
Starting point, straight down, touching the circle, around left to stopping place: small *g*

H Starting point, straight down
Starting point, straight down
Starting point, across the middle: capital *H*

h Starting point, straight down, back up, around right, and straight down: small *h*

I Starting point, across
Starting point, straight down
Starting point, across: capital *I*

i Starting point, straight down
Dot exactly above: small *i*

Penmanship (continued)

Ball and Stick Handwriting Models

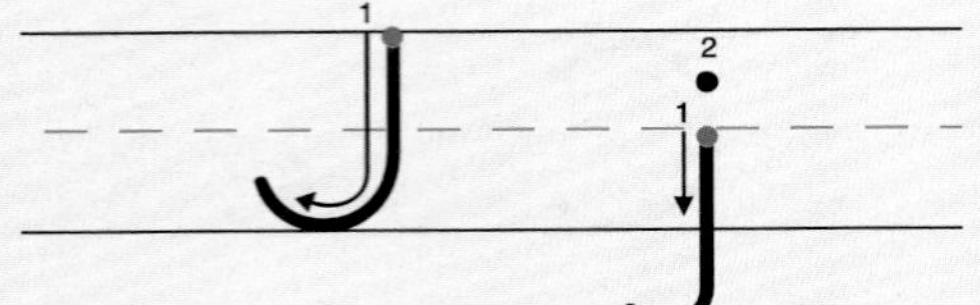

J Starting point, straight down, around left to stopping place: capital *J*

j Starting point, straight down, around left to stopping place Dot exactly above: small *j*

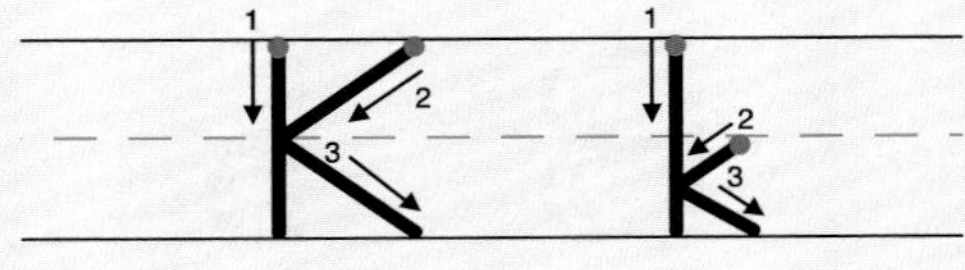

K Starting point, straight down Starting point, slanting down left touching the line, slanting down right: capital *K*

k Starting point, straight down Starting point, slanting down left, touching the line, slanting down right: small *k*

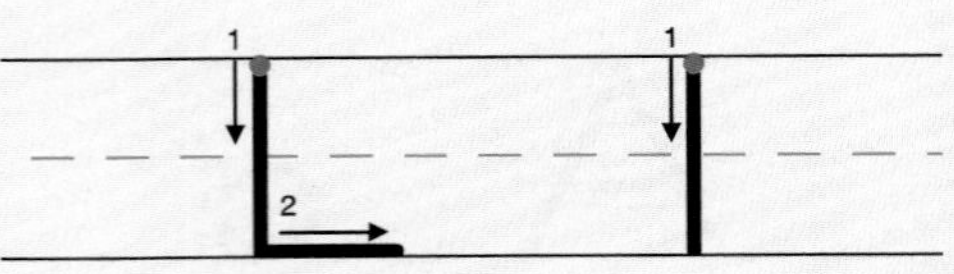

L Starting point, straight down, straight out: capital *L*

l Starting point, straight down: small *l*

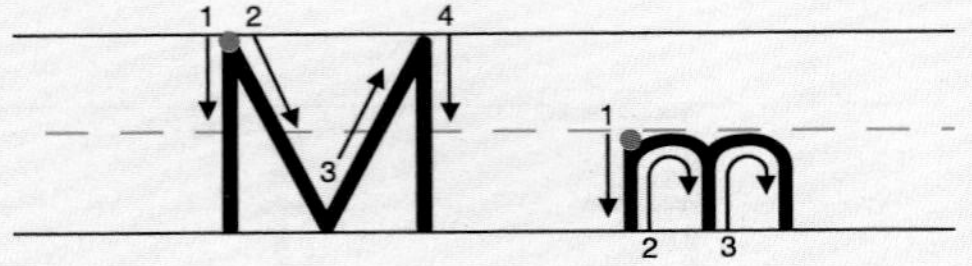

M Starting point, straight down Starting point, slanting down right to the point, slanting back up to the right, straight down: capital *M*

m Starting point, straight down, back up, around right, straight down, back up, around right, straight down: small *m*

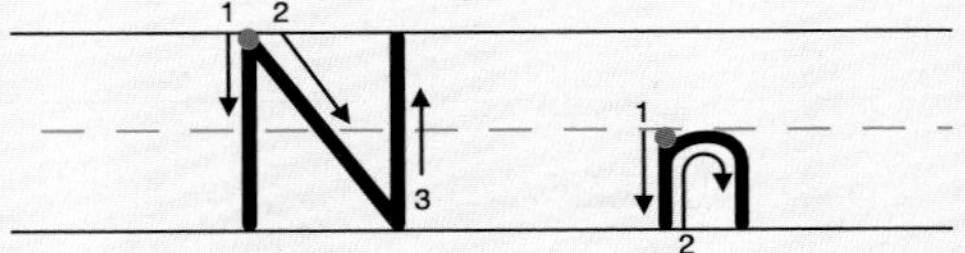

N Starting point, straight down Starting point, slanting down right, straight back up: capital *N*

n Starting point, straight down, back up, around right, straight down: small *n*

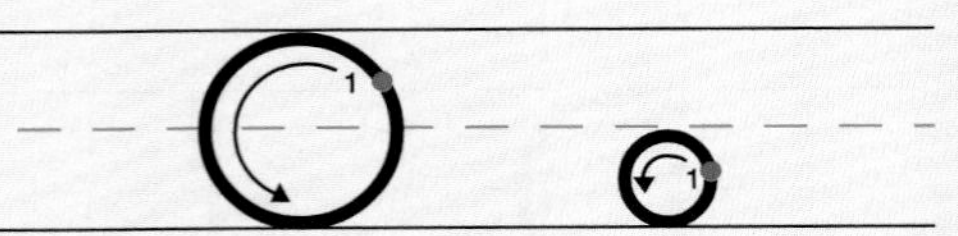

O Starting point, around left all the way: capital *O*

o Starting point, around left all the way: small *o*

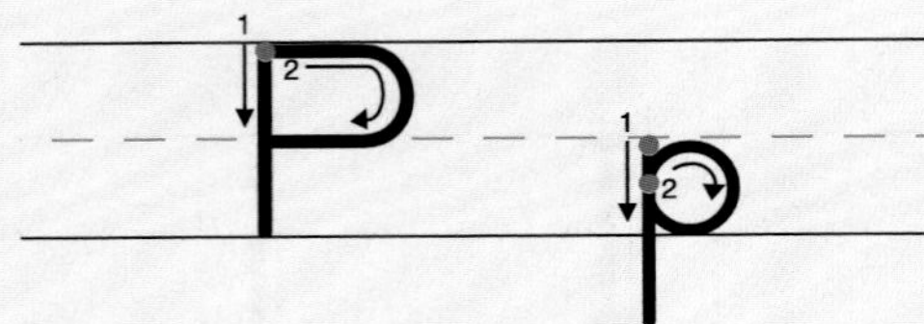

P Starting point, straight down Starting point, around right and in at the middle: capital *P*

p Starting point, straight down Starting point, around right all the way, touching the line: small *p*

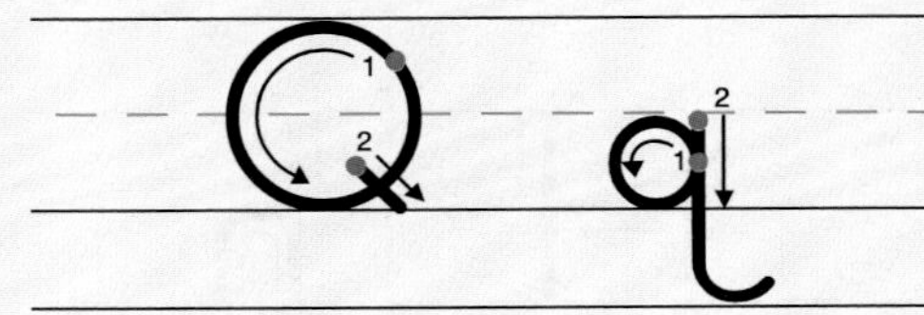

Q Starting point, around left all the way Starting point, slanting down right: capital *Q*

q Starting point, around left all the way Starting point, straight down, touching the circle, curving up right to stopping place: small *q*

R Starting point, straight down Starting point, around right and in at the middle, touching the line, slanting down right: capital *R*

r Starting point, straight down, back up, curving around right to stopping place: small *r*

Ball and Stick Handwriting Models

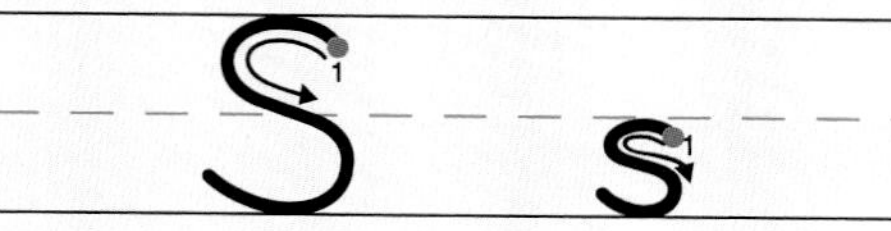

S Starting point, around left, curving right and down around right, curving left and up: capital *S*

s Starting point, around left, curving right and down around right, curving left and up to stopping place: small s

T Starting point, straight across
Starting point, straight down: capital *T*

t Starting point, straight down
Starting point, across short: small *t*

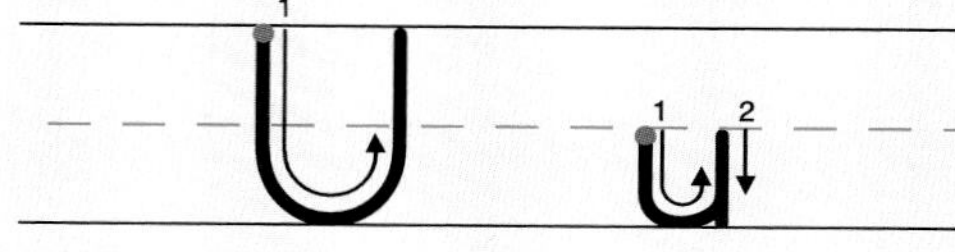

U Starting point, straight down, curving around right and up, straight up: capital *U*

u Starting point, straight down, curving around right and up, straight up, straight back down: small *u*

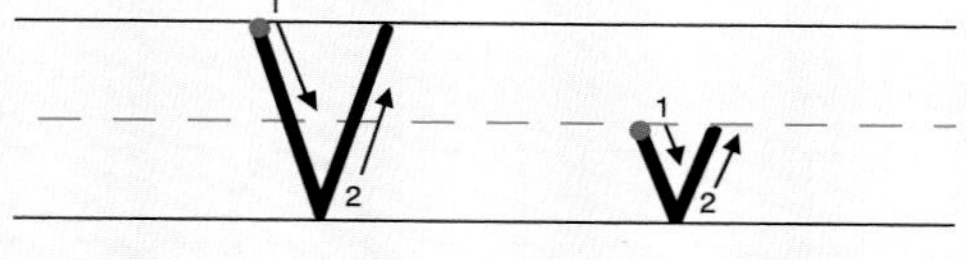

V Starting point, slanting down right, slanting up right: capital *V*

v Starting point, slanting down right, slanting up right: small *v*

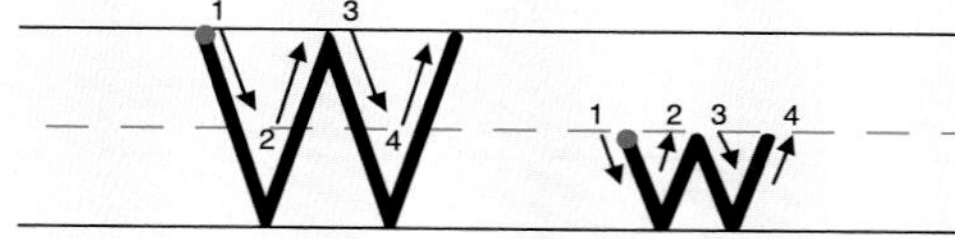

W Starting point, slanting down right, slanting up right, slanting down right, slanting up right: capital *W*

w Starting point, slanting down right, slanting up right, slanting down right, slanting up right: small *w*

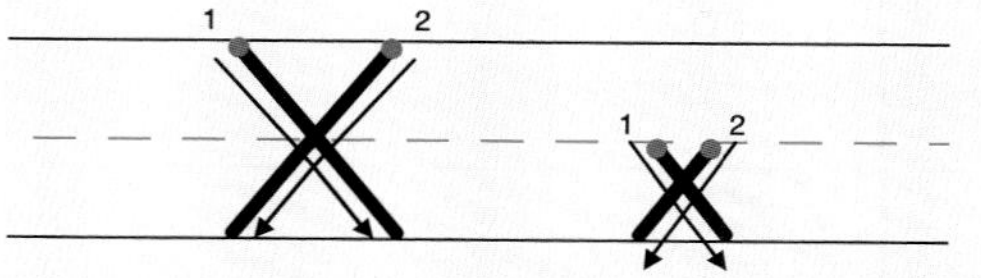

X Starting point, slanting down right
Starting point, slanting down left: capital *X*

x Starting point, slanting down right
Starting point, slanting down left: small *x*

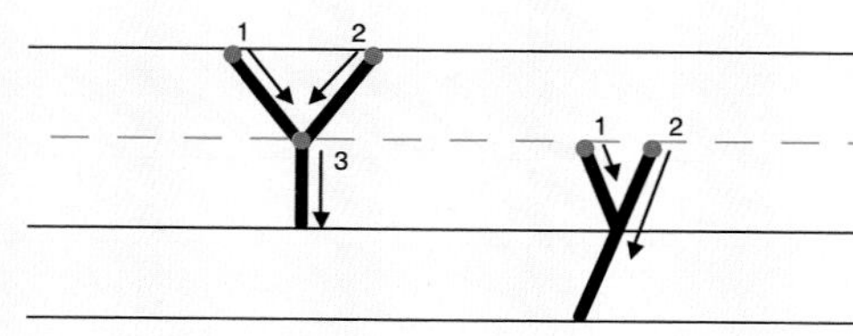

Y Starting point, slanting down right, stop
Starting point, slanting down left, stop
Starting point, straight down: capital *Y*

y Starting point, slanting down right
Starting point, slanting down left, connecting the lines: small *y*

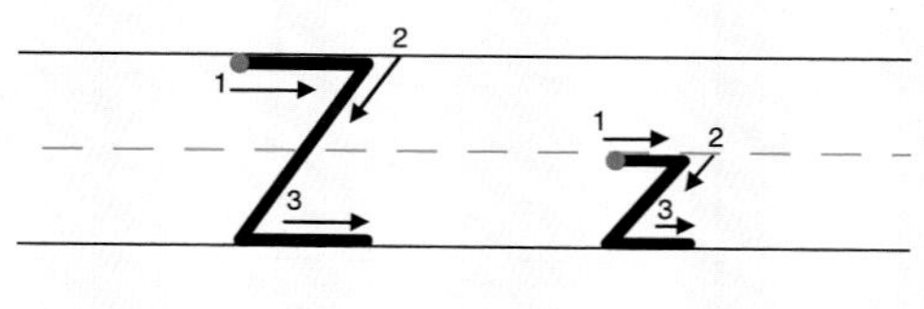

Z Starting point, straight across, slanting down left, straight across: capital *Z*

z Starting point, straight across, slanting down left, straight across: small *z*

Penmanship (continued)

Continuous Stroke Handwriting Models

Continuous stroke models of manuscript handwriting provide teachers with an alternative to the ball and stick method. The purpose of these models is geared toward teaching the students to write letters without lifting their pencils.

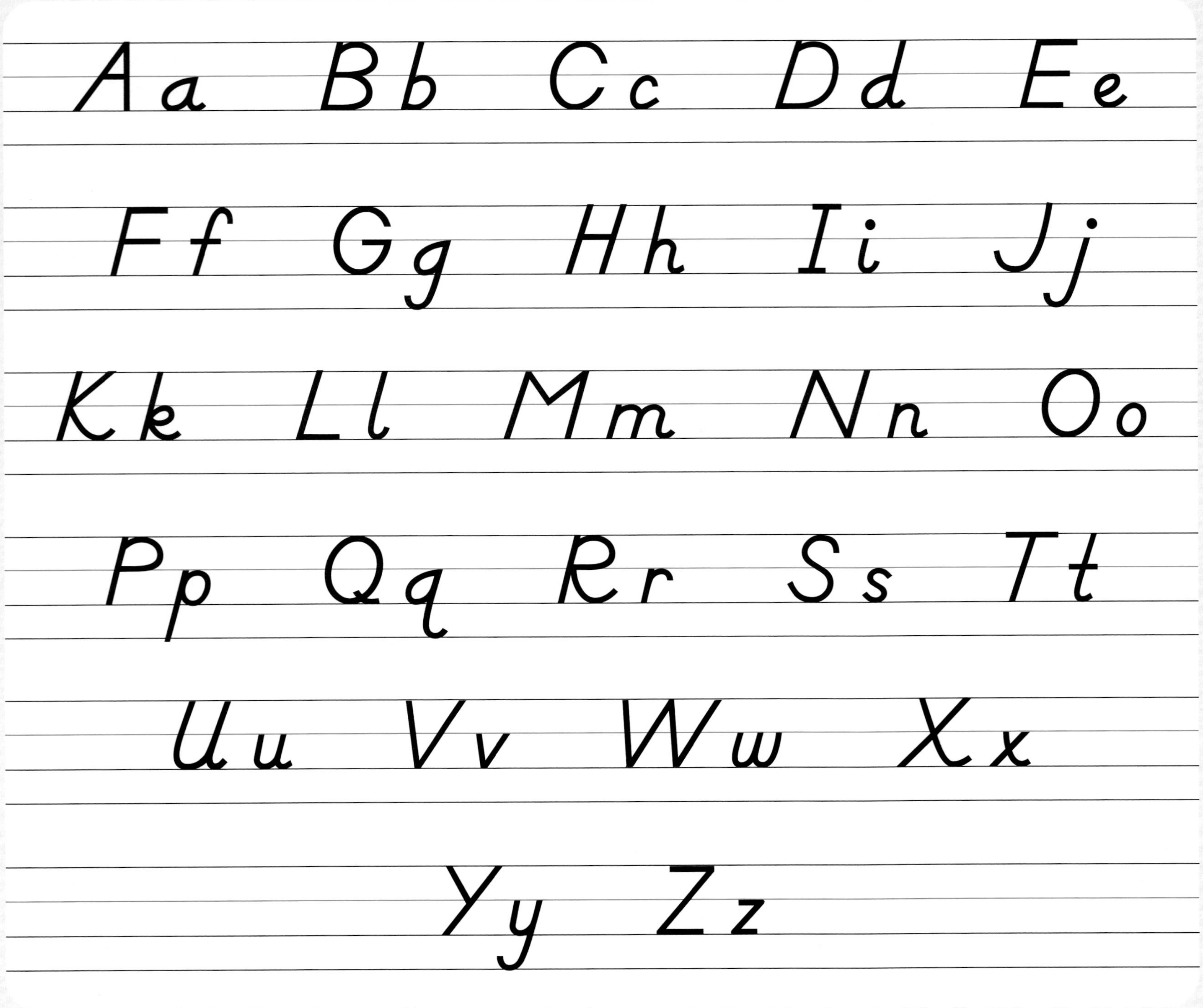

Aa Bb Cc Dd Ee

Ff Gg Hh Ii Jj

Kk Ll Mm Nn Oo

Pp Qq Rr Ss Tt

Uu Vv Ww Xx

Yy Zz

Numbers

1 Starting point, straight down: *1*

2 Starting point, around right, slanting left and straight across right: *2*

3 Starting point, around right, in at the middle, around right: *3*

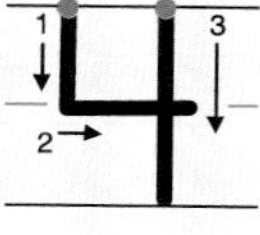

4 Starting point, straight down
Straight across right
Starting point, straight down, crossing line: *4*

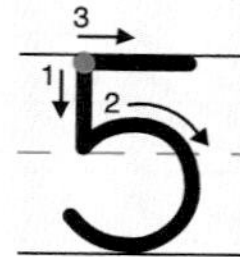

5 Starting point, curving around right and up
Starting point, straight across right: *5*

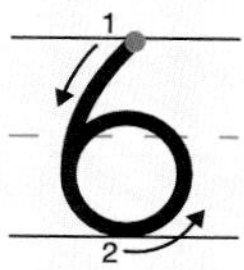

6 Starting point, slanting left, around the bottom curving up around right and into the curve: *6*

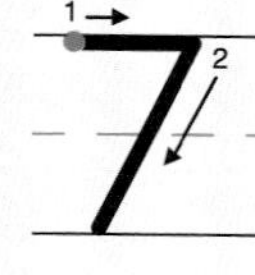

7 Starting point, straight across right, slanting down left: *7*

8 Starting point, curving left, curving down and around right, slanting up right to starting point: *8*

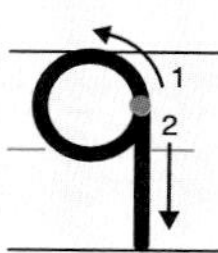

9 Starting point, curving around left all the way, straight down: *9*

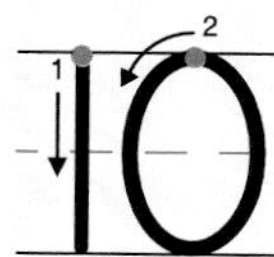

10 Starting point, straight down
Starting point, curving left all the way around to starting point: *10*

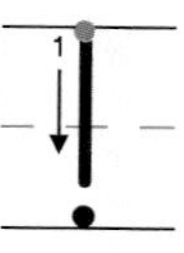

! Starting point, straight down
Dot exactly below: exclamation point

? Starting point, curving around right, straight down
Dot exactly below: question mark

Introduction to Sounds

LEVEL APPENDIX

LESSON	LETTERS AND SOUND/SPELLING	DECODABLE BOOKS CORE SET	DECODABLE BOOKS PRACTICE SET
Unit 1			
LESSON 1	Aa, Bb		
LESSON 2	Cc, Dd		
LESSON 3	Ee, Ff, Gg	Pre-Decodable Book 1: *A Table*	
LESSON 4	Hh, Ii, Jj		
LESSON 5	Kk, Ll, Mm	Pre-Decodable Book 2: *The Egg*	
LESSON 6	Nn, Oo, Pp		
LESSON 7	Qq, Rr, Ss	Pre-Decodable Book 3: *The Baby* (pp. 3–8)	
LESSON 8	Tt, Uu, Vv		
LESSON 9	Ww, Xx	Pre-Decodable Book 3: *The Baby* (pp. 9–16)	
LESSON 10	Yy, Zz		
LESSON 11	Review of capital and lowercase letters; /s/ spelled *s*		
LESSON 12	Pre-decodable; /m/ spelled *m*	Pre-Decodable Book 4: *Mom and I*	
LESSON 13	/a/ spelled *a*	Decodable Book 5: *Sam, Sam, Sam*	
LESSON 14	/t/ spelled *t*	Decodable Book 6: *Matt and Sam*	Decodable Book 1: *On a Mat*
LESSON 15	/h/ spelled *h_*	Decodable Book 7: *A Hat*	Decodable Book 2: *Tam Has Ham*
Unit 2			
LESSON 1	/p/ spelled *p*	Decodable Book 8: *The Map*	Decodable Book 3: *Pam and Hap*
LESSON 2	/i/ spelled *i*	Decodable Book 9: *Hip*	Decodable Book 4: *Tim Hit It*
LESSON 3	/n/ spelled *n*	Decodable Book 10: *Snap the Ant*	Decodable Book 5: *Nat*
LESSON 4	/l/ spelled *l*	Decodable Book 11: *Lil's Hat*	Decodable Book 6: *Pals*
	special spellings: *ll, all*	Decodable Book 12: *A Mill on a Hill*	Decodable Book 7: *Pam's Hill*
LESSON 5	Review	Decodable Book 13: *Nan's Family*	
LESSON 6	/d/ spelled *d*	Decodable Book 14: *Dan Spins*	Decodable Book 8: *Dad's Mitt*
LESSON 7	/o/ spelled *o*	Decodable Book 15: *The Spot*	Decodable Book 9: *Tom and Pop*
LESSON 8	/b/ spelled *b*	Decodable Book 16: *Bob at Bat*	Decodable Book 10: *Bop!*
LESSON 9	/k/ spelled *c*	Decodable Book 17: *The Cab*	Decodable Book 11: *Cal's Cap*
LESSON 10	Review	Decodable Book 18: *Sis the Cat*	
LESSON 11	/k/ spelled ■*ck*	Decodable Book 19: *Picnic*	Decodable Book 12: *The Snack*
LESSON 12	/r/ spelled *r*	Decodable Book 20: *Nat's Nap*	Decodable Book 13: *Rick and Rob*
LESSON 13	/u/ spelled *u*	Decodable Book 21: *Ron on the Run*	Decodable Book 14: *Ann Hunts for Nuts*
LESSON 14	/g/ spelled *g*	Decodable Book 22: *The Bug*	Decodable Book 15: *Stuck!*
LESSON 15	Review: /a/, /i/, /u/, /k/ spelled ■*ck*, /r/, /u/, /g/	Decodable Book 23: *Sinbad the Pig*	
Unit 3			
LESSON 1	/j/ spelled *j*	Decodable Book 24: *Jan and Jack*	Decodable Book 16: *Just Jam*
	/j/ spelled ■*dge*	Decodable Book 25: *The Badge*	Decodable Book 17: *Madge*
LESSON 2	/f/ spelled *f*	Decodable Book 26: *Brad's Ram*	Decodable Book 18: *Fran's Fudge*
	special spelling: /or/ spelled *or*	Decodable Book 27: *Boris, Doris, and Norm*	Decodable Book 19: *The Horn*
LESSON 3	/e/ spelled *e*	Decodable Book 28: *Jen's Pen*	Decodable Book 20: *Big Ted Is Best*
	/d/, /t/ spelled *ed*	Decodable Book 29: *Best Mom*	Decodable Book 21: *Fred and Jen Jumped*
LESSON 4	special spelling: /f/ spelled *ff*; Review: short vowels; /j/ spelled *j*, ■*dge*; /f/ spelled *f*, *ff*	Decodable Book 30: *Jeff's Job*	Decodable Book 22: *Fred*
LESSON 5	/ks/ spelled ■*x*	Decodable Book 31: *A Fox and His Box*	Decodable Book 23: *Max Can Fix It*
LESSON 6	/z/ spelled *z*	Decodable Book 32: *Zack the One Man Band*	Decodable Book 24: *Liz*
	/z/ spelled *zz*	Decodable Book 33: *Bizz Buzz*	Decodable Book 25: *Fuzz on a Cuff*
	/z/ spelled *_s*	Decodable Book 34: *Dogs and Cats*	Decodable Book 26: *Don and Jim*

Introduction to Sounds (continued)

LESSON	LETTERS AND SOUND/SPELLING	DECODABLE BOOKS CORE SET	DECODABLE BOOKS PRACTICE SET
LESSON 7	special spelling: /e/ spelled *_ea_*	Decodable Book 35: *Jen Dreamt*	Decodable Book 27: *Zip the Tug*
	/s/ spelled *ss*	Decodable Book 36: *Run and Pass*	Decodable Book 28: *Ross's Mess*
	Review: /z/ spelled *z, zz, _s;* /e/ spelled *_ea_*		
LESSON 8	/sh/ spelled *sh,* es ending	Decodable Book 37: *Trash*	Decodable Book 29: *Trish's Ship*
LESSON 9	/th/ spelled *th*	Decodable Book 38: *Seth's Bath*	Decodable Book 30: *Beth Gets a Snack*
	Schwa	Decodable Book 39: *The Children Get a Rabbit*	Decodable Book 31: *The Animal in the Closet*
LESSON 10	Review: /sh/, /th/	Decodable Book 40: *Panda Band*	
LESSON 11	/ch/ spelled *ch*	Decodable Book 41: *Chuck's Chest*	Decodable Book 32: *Lunch on the Porch*
	/ch/ spelled ■*tch*	Decodable Book 42: *Patch Gets the Ball*	Decodable Book 33: *Patch Helps*
LESSON 12	/ar/ spelled *ar*	Decodable Book 43: *Grab a Star*	Decodable Book 34: *At the Farm*
LESSON 13	special spelling: /m/ spelled *mb;*	Decodable Book 44: *A Lamb on a Limb*	Decodable Book 35: *Lora Lamb*
LESSON 14	/w/ spelled *w_*	Decodable Book 45: *Wendell's Pets*	Decodable Book 36: *Wes Gets Wet*
	/hw/ spelled *wh_*	Decodable Book 46: *The Whiz*	Decodable Book 37: *Wilma's Cat*
LESSON 15	/er/ spelled *er*	Decodable Book 47: *Garden Sisters*	Decodable Book 38: *Chandler Gets Under*
	/er/ spelled *ir*	Decodable Book 48: *Whir and Stir*	Decodable Book 39: *Brenda and the Bird*
	/er/ spelled *ur*	Decodable Book 49: *A Blur with Fur*	Decodable Book 40: *Curt the Surfer*
Unit 4			
LESSON 1	Review: short vowel sounds; /ch/, /ar/, /w/, /hw/, /er/	Decodable Book 50: *Chirp and Scat*	
	/l/ spelled *le*	Decodable Book 51: *Little Pat*	Decodable Book 41: *Turtle's Bundle*
	/l/ spelled *el*	Decodable Book 52: *Just a Nickel*	Decodable Book 42: *Satchel's Nickel*
LESSON 2	/k/ spelled *k*	Decodable Book 53: *Kim's Trip*	Decodable Book 43: *Breakfast in Bed*
LESSON 3	/ng/ spelled ■*ng*	Decodable Book 54: *Hank the Crank*	Decodable Book 44: *Ding Dong*
LESSON 4	/kw/ spelled *qu_*	Decodable Book 55: *Quinn's Pond*	Decodable Book 45: *The Squirrel Plan*
LESSON 5	/y/ spelled *y_*	Decodable Book 56: *The Stand*	Decodable Book 46: *Beth's Yak*
LESSON 6	Review: /k/ spelled *k;* /ng/ spelled *_ng;* /kw/ spelled *qu_;* /y/ spelled *y_*	Decodable Book 57: *The King of Purple*	
LESSON 7	/ā/ spelled *a*	Decodable Book 58: *Mason's Big Hat*	Decodable Book 47: *Mabel's Bread*
	/ā/ spelled *a_e*	Decodable Book 59: *Gull and Crane*	Decodable Book 48: *Monster Cake*
LESSON 8	/s/ spelled *ce*	Decodable Book 60: *Lance's Dragon*	Decodable Book 49: *Just Ten Cents*
	/s/ spelled *ci_*	Decodable Book 61: *A Stencil and a Pencil*	Decodable Book 50: *Cilla's Fun*
LESSON 9	Review of Sounds		
LESSON 10	/ī/ spelled *i*	Decodable Book 62: *The Pilot*	Decodable Book 51: *Brian's Spiders*
	/ī/ spelled *i_e*	Decodable Book 63: *Spice Cake*	Decodable Book 52: *Brice Likes Limes*
LESSON 11	/ō/ spelled *o*	Decodable Book 64: *Bo and Mo*	Decodable Book 53: *Old Gold*
	/ō/ spelled *o_e*	Decodable Book 65: *The Cold Troll*	Decodable Book 54: *Simone Awoke!*
LESSON 12	Review: /ā/ spelled *a, a_e;* /ī/ spelled *i, i_e;* /ō/ spelled *o, o_e;* and /s/ spelled *ci_, ce*	Decodable Book 66: *Rose Takes a Hike*	
LESSON 13	Review of Sounds		
LESSON 14	/v/ spelled *v*	Decodable Book 67: *At the Vet*	Decodable Book 55: *Bev Travels*
LESSON 15	/ū/ spelled *u*	Decodable Book 68: *Music*	Decodable Book 56: *Hubert's Bugle*
	/ū/ spelled *u_e*	Decodable Book 69: *Muse the Mule*	Decodable Book 57: *Pam Is Not Amused*
Unit 5			
LESSON 1	/j/ spelled *ge*	Decodable Book 70: *Gem Gets a Bath*	Decodable Book 58: *Marge's Barge*
	/j/ spelled *gi_*	Decodable Book 71: *Magic Pages*	Decodable Book 59: *Gingerbread Magic*

Introduction to Sounds (continued)

LESSON	LETTERS AND SOUND/SPELLING	DECODABLE BOOKS CORE SET	DECODABLE BOOKS PRACTICE SET
LESSON 2	/ē/ spelled *e*	Decodable Book 72: *A Gift for Me*	Decodable Book 60: *No Regrets*
	/ē/ spelled *e_e*	Decodable Book 73: *Pete and Steve Compete*	Decodable Book 61: *The Play*
LESSON 3	Review: /v/ spelled *v;* /ū/ spelled *u, u_e;* /j/ spelled *ge, gi_;* /ē/ spelled *e, e_e*	Decodable Book 74: *Steve Sells Vans*	
LESSON 4	Review of Sounds		
LESSON 5	/ē/ spelled *ee*	Decodable Book 75: *The Bee and the Deer*	Decodable Book 62: *I Can't Sleep*
	/ē/ spelled *ea*	Decodable Book 76: *Dragons Don't Get Colds*	Decodable Book 63: *The Clean Kitchen*
LESSON 6	/ē/ spelled *_y*	Decodable Book 77: *The City Bus*	Decodable Book 64: *Smith City Cubs Win*
	/ē/ spelled *_ie_*	Decodable Book 78: *Nellie and Charlie*	Decodable Book 65: *The Game Pieces*
LESSON 7	Long vowels followed by r		
LESSON 8	/ā/ spelled *ai_*	Decodable Book 79: *Craig Sails*	Decodable Book 66: *The Train*
	/ā/ spelled *_ay*	Decodable Book 80: *No Way*	Decodable Book 67: *A Gray, Rainy Day*
LESSON 9	/ī/ spelled *igh*	Decodable Book 81: *The Opossum at Night*	Decodable Book 68: *City Lights at Night*
LESSON 10	Review: /ē/ spelled *ee, ea, _y,_ ie_;* /ā/ spelled *ai_, _ay;* /ī/ spelled *igh*	Decodable Book 82: *The King Who Was Late*	
LESSON 11	/ī/ spelled *_y*	Decodable Book 83: *Why, Bly?*	Decodable Book 69: *Sly and Ty*
	/ī/ spelled *_ie*	Decodable Book 84: *Dean's Pies*	Decodable Book 70: *The Best Pie*
LESSON 12	/ō/ spelled *_oe*	Decodable Book 85: *The Farmer and the Doe*	Decodable Book 71: *Joe Oboe*
LESSON 13	/ō/ spelled *oa_*	Decodable Book 86: *Load the Boat*	Decodable Book 72: *Joan's Boat*
	/ō/ spelled *_ow*	Decodable Book 87: *It Will Not Snow*	Decodable Book 73: *Sam and Dad Bowl*
LESSON 14	/ū/ spelled *_ew*	Decodable Book 88: *Mew, Mew*	Decodable Book 74: *Dad's Chair*
	/ū/ spelled *_ue*	Decodable Book 89: *Who Will Rescue the Cat?*	Decodable Book 75: *Mark's Dream*
LESSON 15	Review: /ī/ spelled *_y, _ie;* /ō/ spelled *_oe, oa_, _ow;* /ū/ spelled *_ew, _ue*	Decodable Book 90: *I Will Be a Firefighter*	
Unit 6			
LESSON 1	/o͞o/ spelled *oo*	Decodable Book 91: *Leo the Lion*	Decodable Book 76: *Jayce Helps*
	/o͞o/ spelled *_ue*	Decodable Book 92: *Sue's Clues*	Decodable Book 77: *A Bluebird for Sue*
	/o͞o/ spelled *u_e*	Decodable Book 93: *Flute Music*	Decodable Book 78: *What Tune?*
	/o͞o/ spelled *_ew*	Decodable Book 94: *The TV Crew*	Decodable Book 79: *A Space Crew*
	/o͞o/ spelled *u*	Decodable Book 95: *Ruby Tells the Truth*	Decodable Book 80: *Ruth and Ruby*
LESSON 2	/oo/ spelled *oo*	Decodable Book 96: *Who Took My Book?*	Decodable Book 81: *The Best Cook*
LESSON 3	Review /oo/		
LESSON 4	/ow/ spelled *ow*	Decodable Book 97: *A Clown Comes to Town*	Decodable Book 82: *Maggy's Flower*
LESSON 5	/ow/ spelled *ou_*	Decodable Book 98: *Max the Grouch*	Decodable Book 83: *Nicky Gets a Hit*
LESSON 6	Review: /o͞o/ spelled *oo;* /oo/ spelled *oo;* /ow/ spelled *ow, ou_*	Decodable Book 99: *Our Town Garden*	
LESSON 7	/aw/ spelled *au_*	Decodable Book 100: *Paul and the Crab*	Decodable Book 84: *Too Much Help*
	/aw/ spelled *aw*	Decodable Book 101: *Gramps Likes to Draw*	Decodable Book 85: *Awful the Hawk*
LESSON 8	Review: /ow/ spelled *ou_, ow;* /aw/ spelled *au_, aw*		
LESSON 9	/n/ spelled *kn_*	Decodable Book 102: *The Knight Who Did Not Know*	Decodable Book 86: *Grammy's Knot*
LESSON 10	Review: /oo/, /o͞o/,/n/ spelled *kn_*		
LESSON 11			
LESSON 12	/oi/ spelled *oi*	Decodable Book 103: *The Choice*	Decodable Book 87: *Cooking Supper*
	/oi/ spelled *_oy*	Decodable Book 104: *Roy and Big Boy*	Decodable Book 88: *Joy's Jobs*

Introduction to Sounds (continued)

LESSON	LETTERS AND SOUND/SPELLING	DECODABLE BOOKS CORE SET	DECODABLE BOOKS PRACTICE SET
LESSON 13	/r/ spelled *wr_*	Decodable Book 105: *Little Wren's Surprise*	Decodable Book 89: *Thank-You Note*
	/er/ spelled *or*	Decodable Book 106: *Bookworm*	Decodable Book 90: *Jobs in the World*
	/er/ spelled *ar*	Decodable Book 107: *Oscar the Bear*	Decodable Book 91: *Edgar*
LESSON 14	/f/ spelled *ph*	Decodable Book 108: *A Photo for Fred*	Decodable Book 92: *A Phantom Frog*
LESSON 15	Review: /aw/ spelled *au_, aw;* /oi/ spelled *oi, _oy;* /r/ spelled *wr_;* /f/ spelled *ph*	Decodable Book 109: *The Secret Sauce*	
Unit 7			
LESSON 1			
LESSON 2			
LESSON 3			
LESSON 4			
LESSON 5			
LESSON 6			
LESSON 7			
LESSON 8			
LESSON 9	General Review	Decodable Book 110: *The Everybody Club*	
Unit 8			
LESSON 1	/aw/ spelled *augh*	Decodable Book 111: *Naughty Max*	Decodable Book 93: *The Spider's Daughter*
LESSON 2	/aw/ spelled *ough*	Decodable Book 112: *Bob Thought*	Decodable Book 94: *Thoughtful Gifts*
LESSON 3			
LESSON 4			
LESSON 5			
LESSON 6			
LESSON 7			
LESSON 8	General Review	Decodable Book 113: *Superhero to the Rescue*	
Unit 9			
LESSON 1			
LESSON 2			
LESSON 3			
LESSON 4			
LESSON 5			
LESSON 6			
LESSON 7			
LESSON 8			
LESSON 9			
LESSON 10			
LESSON 11	General Review	Decodable Book 114: *Andy Lee*	
Unit 10			
LESSON 1			
LESSON 2			
LESSON 3	/er/ spelled *ear*	Decodable Book 115: *Earnest's Search*	Decodable Book 95: *Pearl's Flowers*
LESSON 4			
LESSON 5			
LESSON 6			
LESSON 7	Long e spelled *_ey*	Decodable Book 116: *The Silly Monkey*	Decodable Book 96: *Dudley the Donkey*
LESSON 8	/shun/ spelled *tion,* /yun/ spelled *ion*	Decodable Book 117: *Tony and Dom Go West*	Decodable Book 97: *The Skipper*
LESSON 9			
LESSON 10	General Review	Decodable Book 118: *How the Rabbit Caught the Tiger*	

Sound/Spelling Card Stories

Card 1: /a/ Lamb

I'm Pam the Lamb, I am.
This is how I tell my Mommy where I am: /a/ /a/ /a/ /a/ /a/.

I'm Pam the Lamb, I am.
This is how I tell my Daddy where I am: /a/ /a/ /a/ /a/ /a/.

I'm Pam the Lamb, I am.
That young ram is my brother Sam.
This is how I tell my brother where I am: /a/ /a/ /a/ /a/ /a/.

I'm Pam the Lamb; I'm happy where I am.
Can you help me tell my family where I am? *(Have the children respond.)* /a/ /a/ /a/ /a/ /a/

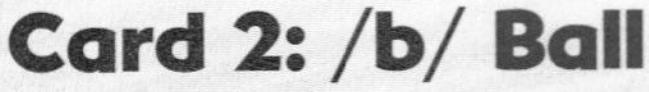

Card 2: /b/ Ball

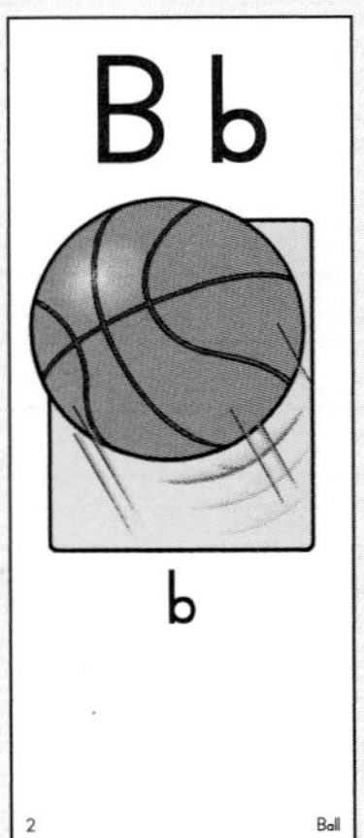

Bobby loved to bounce his basketball.
He bounced it all day long.
This is the sound the ball made: /b/ /b/ /b/ /b/ /b/.

One day, while Bobby was bouncing his basketball,
Bonnie came by on her bike.

Bonnie said, "Hi, Bobby. I have a little bitty ball.
May I bounce my ball with you?"

Bobby said, "Sure!" and Bonnie bounced her little bitty ball.
What sound do you think Bonnie's ball made?
(Encourage a very soft reply.) /b/ /b/ /b/ /b/ /b/

Soon Betsy came by. "Hi, Bobby. Hi, Bonnie," she said.
"I have a great big beach ball. May I bounce my ball with you?"

Bobby and Bonnie said, "Sure!" and Betsy bounced her big beach ball.
What sound do you think the beach ball made?
(Encourage a louder, slower reply.) /b/ /b/ /b/ /b/ /b/

(Designate three groups, one for each ball sound.)
Now when Bobby, Bonnie, and Betsy bounce their balls together, this is the sound you hear:
(Have all three groups make their sounds in a chorus.)
/b/ /b/ /b/ /b/ /b/

Card 3: /k/ Camera

Carlos has a new camera. When he takes pictures, his camera makes a clicking sound like this: /k/ /k/ /k/ /k/ /k/.

In the garden, Carlos takes pictures of caterpillars crawling on cabbage: /k/ /k/ /k/ /k/ /k/.
At the zoo, Carlos takes pictures of a camel, a duck, and a kangaroo: /k/ /k/ /k/.
In the park, Carlos takes pictures of his cousin flying a kite: /k/ /k/ /k/ /k/ /k/.
In his room, Carlos takes pictures of his cute kitten, Cozy: /k/ /k/ /k/ /k/ /k/.

Can you help Carlos take pictures with his camera?
(Have the children join in.) /k/ /k/ /k/ /k/ /k/ /k/ /k/

Card 4: /d/ Dinosaur

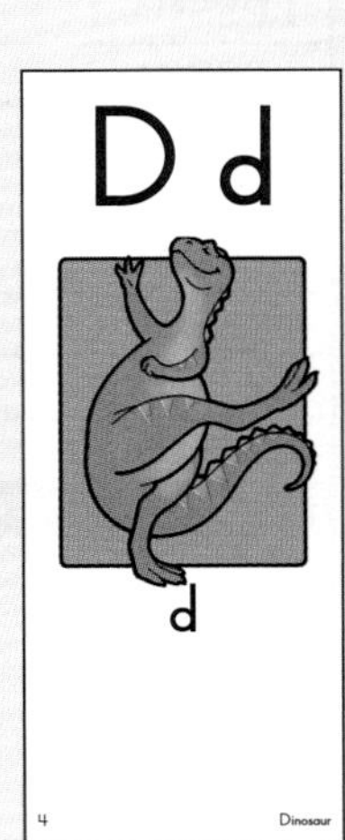

Dinah the Dinosaur loves to dance.
She dances whenever she gets the chance.
Whenever that dinosaur dips and whirls,
This is the sound of her dancing twirls:
/d/ /d/ /d/ /d/ /d/ /d/!

Dinah the Dinosaur dances all day.
From dawn to dark, she dances away.
And when Dinah dances, her dinosaur feet
make a thundering, thudding, extremely loud beat:
(loudly, with an exaggerated rhythm)
/d/ /d/ /d/ /d/ /d/ /d/!

Now if you were a dinosaur just like Dinah,
you would certainly dance just as finely as she.
And if you were a Dino, and you had a chance,
what sound would your feet make when you did a dance?
(Have the children join in.) /d/ /d/ /d/ /d/ /d/ /d/

Card 5: /e/ Hen

Jem's pet hen likes to peck, peck, peck.
She pecks at a speck on the new red deck.
This is how her pecking sounds:
/e/ /e/ /e/ /e/ /e/.

Jem's pet hen pecks at corn in her pen.
She pecks ten kernels, then pecks again.
This is how her pecking sounds:
/e/ /e/ /e/ /e/ /e/.

Jem's hen pecks at a cracked egg shell.
She's helping a chick get out, alive and well.
This is how her pecking sounds:
/e/ /e/ /e/ /e/ /e/.

Can you help Jem's hen peck?
(Have children say:) /e/ /e/ /e/ /e/ /e/.

Card 6: /f/ Fan

/f/ /f/ /f/ /f/ /f/—What's that funny sound?
It's Franny the Fan going round and round,
and this is the sound that old fan makes:
/f/ /f/ /f/ /f/ /f/.

When it gets too hot, you see,
Franny cools the family: /f/ /f/ /f/ /f/ /f/.
She fans Father's face
and Foxy's fur
and Felicity's feet.
Hear the Fan whir: /f/ /f/ /f/ /f/ /f/.

Can you make Franny the Fan go fast?
(Have the children say quickly:)
/f/ /f/ /f/ /f/ /f/.
Faster? /f/ /f/ /f/ /f/ /f/
Fastest? /f/ /f/ /f/ /f/ /f/

Card 7: /g/ Gopher

Gary's a gopher.
He loves to gulp down food.
/g/ /g/ /g/ /g/ /g/, gulps the gopher.

Gary the Gopher gulps down grass
because it tastes so good.
/g/ /g/ /g/ /g/ /g/, gulps the gopher.

Gary the Gopher gulps down grapes—
gobs and gobs of grapes.
/g/ /g/ /g/ /g/ /g/, gulps the gopher.

Gary the Gopher gobbles green beans
and says once more,
/g/ /g/ /g/ /g/ /g/. He's such a hungry gopher!

Gary the Gopher gobbles in the garden
until everything is gone.

What sound does Gary the Gopher make?
(Ask the children to join in.) /g/ /g/ /g/ /g/ /g/

Card 8: /h/ Hound

Harry the Hound dog hurries around.
Can you hear Harry's hurrying hound-
dog sound?
This is the sound Harry's breathing
makes when he hurries:
/h/ /h/ /h/ /h/ /h/ /h/!

When Harry the Hound dog sees a
hare hop by,
he tears down the hill, and his four
feet fly.
Hurry, Harry, hurry! /h/ /h/ /h/ /h/ /h/ /h/!

How Harry the Hound dog loves to hunt
and chase!
He hurls himself from place to place.
Hurry, Harry, hurry! /h/ /h/ /h/ /h/ /h/ /h/!

When Harry the Hound dog sees a big skunk roam,
He howls for help and heads for home.

What sound does Harry make when he hurries?
(Have the children answer.) /h/ /h/ /h/ /h/ /h/ /h/

Sound/Spelling Card Stories (continued)

Card 9: /i/ Pig

This is Pickles the Pig.
If you tickle Pickles, she gets the giggles.
This is the sound of her giggling:
/i/ /i/ /i/ /i/ /i/.

Tickle Pickles the Pig under her chin.
Listen! She's giggling: /i/ /i/ /i/ /i/ /i/.
Wiggle a finger in Pickles' ribs.
Listen! She's giggling: /i/ /i/ /i/ /i/ /i/.

Give Pickles the Pig a wink,
and what do you think? First comes a grin.
Then listen!
She's giggling again: /i/ /i/ /i/ /i/ /i/.

Quick! Tickle Pickles the Pig. What will
she say? *(Have the children join in.)* /i/ /i/ /i/ /i/ /i/

Card 10: /j/ Jump

When Jenny jumps her jump rope,
it sounds like this: /j/ /j/ /j/ /j/ /j/.
When Jackson jumps his jump rope,
it sounds like this: /j/ /j/ /j/ /j/ /j/.

The judges generally agree
that Jenny jumps most rapidly:
(quickly) /j/ /j/ /j/ /j/ /j/.

When Jenny jumps, she jumps to this jingle:
"Jump, jump, jump so quick.
Whenever I jump, I like to kick."
/j/ /j/ /j/ /j/ /j/

The Judges generally agree
that Jackson jumps most quietly:
(quietly) /j/ /j/ /j/ /j/ /j/.

When Jackson jumps, he jumps to this jingle:
"Jump, jump, nice and quiet.
See what happens when you try it." /j/ /j/ /j/ /j/ /j/

(to the children) Jump rope like Jenny.
(quickly) /j/ /j/ /j/ /j/ /j/
(to the children) Jump rope like Jackson.
(quietly) /j/ /j/ /j/ /j/ /j/

Card 11: /k/ Camera

Carlos has a new camera. When he
takes pictures,
His camera makes a clicking sound like this:
/k/ /k/ /k/ /k/ /k/.

In the garden, Carlos takes pictures of
caterpillars crawling on cabbage:
/k/ /k/ /k/ /k/ /k/.
At the zoo, Carlos takes pictures of a camel,
a duck, and a kangaroo:
/k/ /k/ /k/.
In the park, Carlos takes pictures of his
cousin flying a kite: /k/ /k/ /k/ /k/ /k/
In his room, Carlos takes pictures of his
cute kitten, Cozy. /k/ /k/ /k/ /k/ /k/

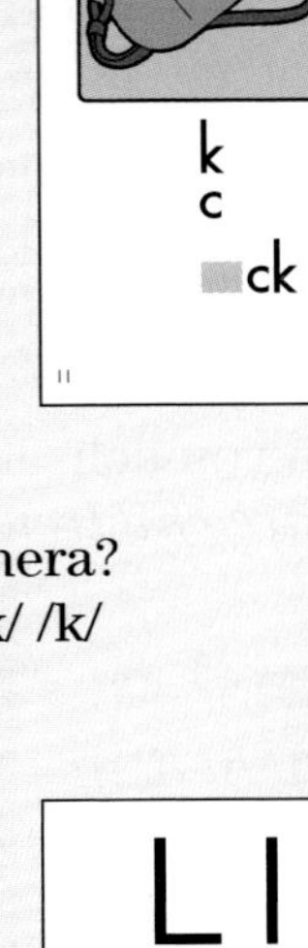

Can you help Carlos take pictures with his camera?
(Have the children join in.) /k/ /k/ /k/ /k/ /k/ /k/ /k/

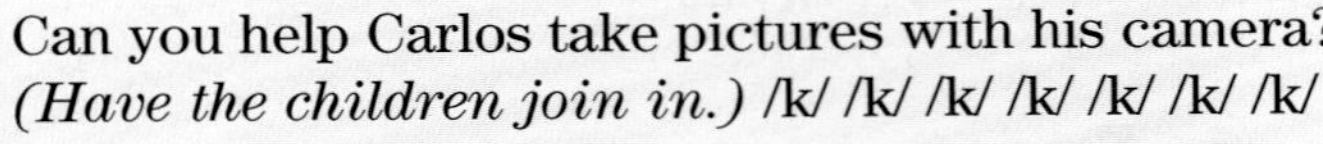

Card 12: /l/ Lion

Look! It's Leon the Lion.
Leon loves to lap water from lakes,
and this is the sound the lapping lion
makes: /l/ /l/ /l/ /l/ /l/.

Let's join Leon. Quick!
Take a little lick: /l/ /l/ /l/ /l/ /l/.

Are you a thirsty lass or lad?
Then lap until you don't feel bad:
/l/ /l/ /l/ /l/ /l/.

What sound do you make when you lap
like Leon the Lion?
(Have the children say:) /l/ /l/ /l/ /l/ /l/.

Card 13: /m/ Monkey

For Muzzy the Monkey, bananas
are yummy.
She munches so many, they fill up
her tummy.
When she eats, she says:
/m/ /m/ /m/ /m/ /m/!

Bananas for breakfast, bananas
for lunch.
Mash them up, mush them up,
Munch, munch, munch, munch!
What does Muzzy the Monkey say?
(Have the children say:) /m/ /m/ /m/ /m/ /m/.

Bananas at bedtime? I have a hunch
Muzzy will mash them up, mush them up,
Munch, munch, munch, munch!
Then what will Muzzy the Monkey say?
(Have the children say:) /m/ /m/ /m/ /m/ /m/.

Card 14: /n/ Nose

When Norman Newsome has a cold,
his nose just won't work right.
It makes a noisy, stuffy sound
through morning, noon, and night.
When Norman has a cold, his nose goes:
/n/ /n/ /n/ /n/ /n/!

When Norman Newsome has a cold,
it's hard to just be quiet.
His nose just sniffs and snuffs
and snarls.
Norman wishes he could hide it!
Instead, his poor, sick, noisy nose just goes:
/n/ /n/ /n/ /n/ /n/!

Norman doesn't hate his nose;
It just does as it pleases!
Even when he sniffs a rose,
he nearly always sneezes.
Then Norman Newsome's nose
again goes *(Have the children say:)*
/n/ /n/ /n/ /n/ /n/.

Card 15: /o/ Fox

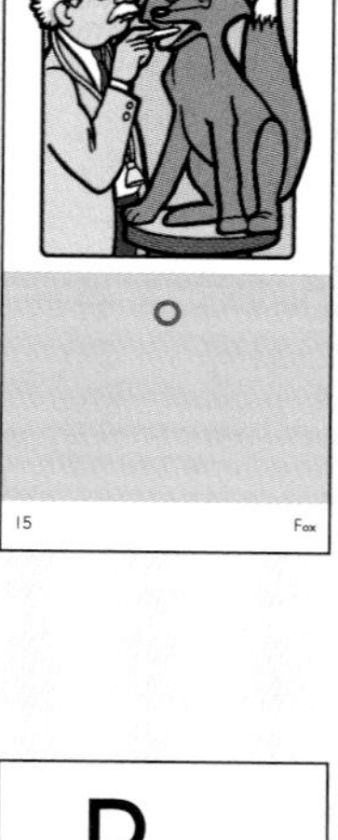

Bob the Fox did not feel well at all.
He jogged to the doctor's office.
"Say /o/ Mr. Fox! /o/ /o/ /o/."

"My head is hot, and my throat hurts a lot,"
said the fox.
"Say /o/ Mr. Fox! /o/ /o/ /o/ /o/."

"Yes, you've got a rotten cold," said
the doctor.
"Say /o/ Mr. Fox! /o/ /o/ /o/."

"Find a spot to sit in the sun," said the doctor.
"Say /o/ Mr. Fox! /o/ /o/ /o/."

He sat on a rock in the sun.
Soon he felt much better.
(with a satisfied sigh) "/o/" said Mr. Fox.
/o/ /o/ /o/

Card 16: /p/ Popcorn

Ping and Pong liked to pop corn. As
it cooked, it made this sound:
/p/ /p/ /p/ /p/ /p/ /p/ /p/.
One day Ping poured a whole package of
popcorn into the pot. It made this sound:
/p/ /p/ /p/ /p/ /p/ /p/ /p/.

The popcorn popped and popped. Ping filled
two pots, and still the popcorn popped:
/p/ /p/ /p/ /p/ /p/ /p/ /p/.
Pong filled three pails with popcorn, and still
it kept popping: /p/ /p/ /p/ /p/ /p/ /p/ /p/.

"Call all your pals," said their pop. "We'll have a party."
And the popcorn kept popping.
(Have the children say the /p/ sound very fast.)

Card 17: /kw/ Quacking ducks

Quincy the Duck couldn't quite quack
like all the other quacking ducks.
Oh, he could say /kw/ /kw/ /kw/ /kw/,
but it never seemed just right.

When Quincy tried to quack quietly *(softly)*
/kw/ /kw/ /kw/ /kw/
his quack came out loudly *(loudly)*
/kw/ /kw/ /kw/ /kw/!
When he tried to quack slowly *(slowly)*
/kw/ . . . /kw/ . . . /kw/ . . . /kw/
his quack came out quickly *(quickly)*
/kw/ /kw/ /kw/ /kw/!
Quincy just couldn't quack right!

One day Quincy was practicing quacks.
His friend Quip quacked along with him.
"Repeat after me," said Quip
(quietly) /kw/ /kw/ /kw/ /kw/.
But Quincy quacked back,
(in normal voice) /kw/ /kw/ /kw/ /kw/ /kw/!
Quincy still couldn't quack quite right.

But Quincy kept quacking. He said, "I won't quit until I quack
like the best quackers around."
Can you show Quincy how quacking ducks quack?
(Have the children join in.)
/kw/ /kw/ /kw/ /kw/ /kw/ /kw/ /kw/ /kw/

Card 18: /r/ Robot

Little Rosie Robot just runs and runs and runs.
She races round and round to get her chores
all done.
Here's how Rosie sounds when she's working:
/r/ /r/ /r/ /r/ /r/!

Rosie can rake around your roses.
Here comes that running robot!
/r/ /r/ /r/ /r/ /r/!

Rosie can repair your wrecked radio.
Here comes that racing robot!
(softly) /r/ /r/ /r/ /r/ /r/

Rosie can mend your round red rug.
Here comes that roaring robot!
(loudly) /r/ /r/ /r/ /r/ /r/!

Rosie rarely does anything wrong.
But there are two things that Rosie can't
do: rest and relax.
Here comes that roaring robot!
What does she say?
(Have the children call out the answer:)
/r/ /r/ /r/ /r/ /r/.

Sound/Spelling Card Stories (continued)

Card 19: /s/ Sausages

Sue and Sammy had a nice place in the city.
On Saturday, Sue and Sammy decided to have sausages for supper.
Sammy put seven sausages in a skillet. /s/ /s/ /s/ /s/ /s/ /s/ /s/

Soon the smell of sausages filled the air.
/s/ /s/ /s/ /s/ /s/, sizzled the sausages.

"Pull up a seat, Sue," said Sammy.
"The sausages are almost ready to serve."
/s/ /s/ /s/ /s/ /s/, sizzled the sausages.

Ss
s
ce
ci_

Sue and Sammy ate the delicious sausages.
Soon they wanted more, so Sam put six more sausages in the frying pan.
/s/ /s/ /s/ /s/ /s/ /s/, sizzled the sausages.

If you were cooking sausages with Sammy and Sue,
What sound would the sausages make as they sizzled?
(Have the children join in:) /s/ /s/ /s/ /s/ /s/ /s/.

Card 20: /t/ Timer

When Tom Tuttle cooks, he uses his timer.
Tom Tuttle's timer ticks like this:
/t/ /t/ /t/ /t/ /t/ /t/ /t/

Tonight Tom Tuttle wants tomatoes on toast.
Tom turns on the oven.
Tom puts tomatoes on toast in the oven.
Tom sets the timer.
The timer will Ding! when Tom's toast and tomatoes are done.
Until the timer dings, it ticks: /t/ /t/ /t/ /t/ /t/ /t/ /t/.

Tomatoes on toast take ten minutes.
/t/ /t/ /t/ /t/ /t/ /t/ /t/
Tom can hardly wait. /t/ /t/ /t/ /t/ /t/ /t/ /t/
He taps out the time: /t/ /t/ /t/ /t/ /t/ /t/ /t/.

What is the sound of Tom Tuttle's ticking timer?
(Have the children join in.) /t/ /t/ /t/ /t/ /t/ /t/ /t/
Ding! Time for dinner, Tom Tuttle!

Card 21: /u/ Tug

Tubby the Tugboat can huff and puff
and push and pull to move big stuff.
/u/ /u/ /u/ /u/ /u/ /u/ /u/
That's the sound of Tubby the Tug.

If a boat is stuck and will not budge,
Tubby the Tugboat can give it a nudge. /u/ /u/ /u/ /u/ /u/ /u/ /u/
It's Tubby the Trusty Tug.

If a ship is caught in mud and muck,
Tubby the Tugboat can get it unstuck.
/u/ /u/ /u/ /u/ /u/ /u/ /u/
It's Tubby the Trusty Tug.

Can you help Tubby push and pull?
(Have the children join in.)
/u/ /u/ /u/ /u/ /u/ /u/ /u/

Card 22: /v/ Vacuum

Vinny the Vacuum is cleaning again.
Before visitors visit, he always begins.
This is the sound of his very loud voice:
/v/ /v/ /v/ /v/ /v/!
If only that Vinny could clean without noise!

Vinny sucks up the crumbs baby Vicki dropped.
/v/ /v/ /v/ /v/ /v/!
He visits nearly everywhere except the tabletop.
/v/ /v/ /v/ /v/ /v/!
Three vine leaves, two vitamins, part of a vase—
all vanish when Vinny goes over the place! /v/ /v/ /v/ /v/ /v/

As Vinny vacuums the velvety rug
a van full of visitors starts to drive up.
But Vinny's not done with the very last room!
Will you help Vinny the Vacuum vacuum?
(Ask groups of children to say /v/ in a round to make the continuous sound of a vacuum cleaner.)

Card 23: /w/ Washer

Willie the Washer washed white clothes all week.
When he washed, he went:
/w/ /w/ /w/ /w/ /w/ /w/ /w/.

All winter, Willie worked well.
/w/ /w/ /w/ /w/ /w/ /w/ /w/
But last Wednesday, Willie was weak. *(softly)*
/w/ /w/ /w/ /w/ /w/ /w/ /w/
This week, he got worse. *(slower and slower)*
/w/. . . /w/. . . /w/. . .
Poor Willie was worn out. *(slowly)* /w/

Then a worker came and fixed Willie's wires.
Willie felt wonderful. *(more loudly)*
/w/ /w/ /w/ /w/ /w/ /w/ /w/!
Now Willie can wash and wash wildly!
(quickly) /w/ /w/ /w/ /w/ /w/ /w/ /w/!

How does Willie the Washer sound now when he washes?
(Have the children join in.) /w/ /w/ /w/ /w/ /w/ /w/ /w/
Can you wash just like Willie?
(Children together:) /w/ /w/ /w/ /w/ /w/ /w/ /w/.

Card 24: /ks/ Exit

Rex is called the Exiting X;
he runs to guard the door.
To get past Rex, make the sound of X:
/ks/ /ks/ /ks/ /ks/.
That is what Rex expects!

The ox knows the sound of X,
so she says /ks/ /ks/ /ks/ /ks/
and gets past Rex.

The fox knows the sound of X,
so he says /ks/ /ks/ /ks/ /ks/
and gets past Rex.

Can you say /ks/ /ks/ /ks/ /ks/
and get past Rex the Exiting X?
(Have the children respond:) /ks/ /ks/ /ks/ /ks/!
Did we get past Rex?
(Have the children say:) Yes!

Card 25: /y/ Yaks

Yolanda and Yoshiko are yaks.
They don't yell.
They don't yelp.
They don't yodel.
They don't yawn.
These young yaks just yak.
Yakety-yak, yakety-yak!
Can you hear the sound they make?
/y/ /y/ /y/ /y/ /y/ /y/ /y/.

Yolanda and Yoshiko yak in the yard.
/y/ /y/ /y/ /y/ /y/ /y/ /y/
They yak on their yellow yacht.
/y/ /y/ /y/ /y/ /y/ /y/ /y/
They yak in the yam patch.
/y/ /y/ /y/ /y/ /y/ /y/ /y/
These yaks yak all year!
/y/ /y/ /y/ /y/ /y/ /y/ /y/

Do you think these yaks like to yak?
(Have the children answer:) Yes!
(Ask the children to yak like Yolanda and Yoshiko.)

Card 26: /z/ Zipper

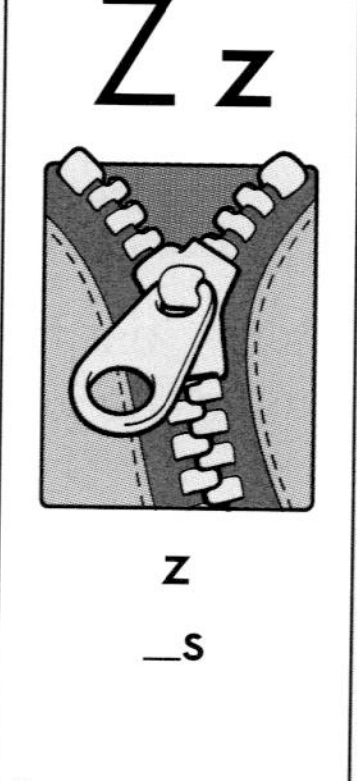

Zack's jacket has a big long zipper.
The zipper zips like this: /z/ /z/ /z/ /z/.

When little Zack goes out to play,
he zips the zipper up this way:
/z/ /z/ /z/ /z/.
Later, when he comes back in,
Zack zips the zipper down again:
/z/ /z/ /z/ /z/.

Can you help Zack zip his jacket zipper?
(Have the children join in.) /z/ /z/ /z/ /z/

Card 27: /ar/ Armadillo

Arthur Armadillo likes to whistle,
hum, and sing.
But when he gets a head cold,
his voice won't do a thing.

To sing and still sound charming—
and not sound so alarming—
Arthur has thought up the thing
of very often gargling.

Then Arthur Armadillo sounds like this:
/ar/ /ar/ /ar/ /ar/ /ar/.

Arthur gargles in the park. /ar/ /ar/ /ar/
/ar/ /ar/
He gargles in the dark. /ar/ /ar/ /ar/ /ar/ /ar/
He gargles on the farm. /ar/ /ar/ /ar/ /ar/ /ar/
He gargles in the barn. /ar/ /ar/ /ar/ ar/ /ar/
Arthur is great at gargling! /ar/ /ar/ /ar/ /ar/ /ar/

What does Arthur Armadillo's gargling sound like?
(Have the children respond.) /ar/ /ar/ /ar/ /ar/ /ar/

Card 28: /hw/ Whales

Look! It's Whitney the Whispering Whale!
Listen to her whisper: /hw/ /hw/ /hw/ /hw/ /hw/.

When Whitney meets with other whales,
she entertains them, telling tales.
She whispers: /hw/ /hw/ /hw/ /hw/ /hw/.
She's Whitney the Whispering Whale.

What ocean wonders does Whitney relate?
Does she whisper of whirlpools or whales
that are great?
We're only people, so we'll never guess.
She's Whitney the Whispering Whale!
/hw/ /hw/ /hw/.

wh_

28 Whales

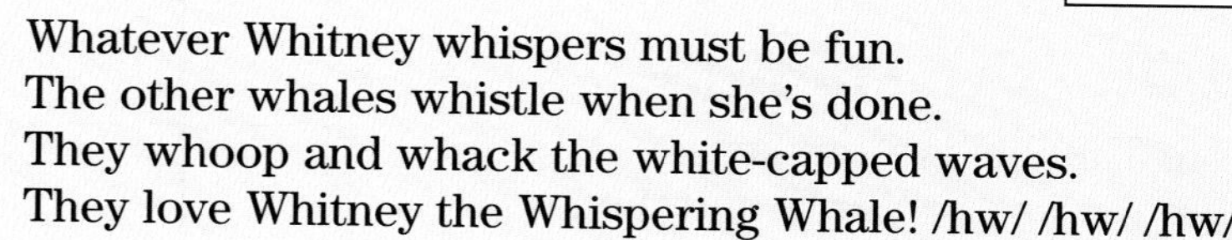

Whatever Whitney whispers must be fun.
The other whales whistle when she's done.
They whoop and whack the white-capped waves.
They love Whitney the Whispering Whale! /hw/ /hw/ /hw/.

If you were Whitney, what sounds would you whisper
to your whale friends as they gathered to listen?
(Have the children whisper:) /hw/ /hw/ /hw/ /hw/ /hw/.

Sound/Spelling Card Stories (continued)

Card 29: /er/ Bird

Bertie the Bird is the oddest bird
that anyone has ever heard.
He doesn't caw like a crow or a gull,
or tweet like a robin or a wren.
Instead, he makes a chirping sound—
over and over again!
/er/ /er/ /er/ /er/ /er/ /er/!

Bert can't fly, since his wings are too short.
He arranges his feathers in curls.
He admits, "I've short wings and I don't really sing,
But I still am an interesting bird!"
/er/ /er/ /er/ /er/ /er/ /er/

Can you chirp like Bertie the Bird?
(Have children say:) /er/ /er/ /er/, /er/ /er/ /er/!

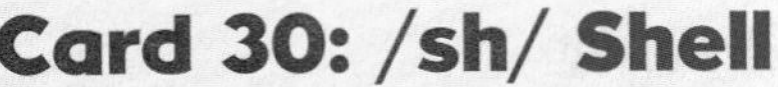

Card 30: /sh/ Shell

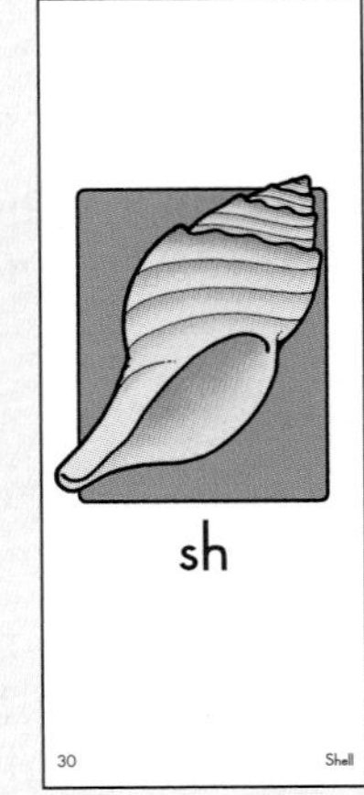

Sheila and Sharon went to the seashore.
They saw lots of shells.
Sheila rushed from shell to shell.
Sharon held a shell to Sheila's ear.

"Do you hear anything?" asked Sharon.
"Yes, it sounds like the ocean crashing on
the shore," shouted Sheila,
"/sh/ /sh/ /sh/ /sh/ /sh/."

"Let's try different shaped shells," said Sharon.
She found a big shell. It made a loud /sh/
/sh/ /sh/ /sh/.
Sheila found a small shell. It made a soft /sh/ /sh/ /sh/ /sh/.
They found a thin shell. It made a high /sh/ /sh/ /sh/ /sh/.
They found a fat shell. It made a deep /sh/ /sh/ /sh/ /sh/.

Sheila and Sharon listened to lots of shells. But no matter
What the size and shape, what do you think Sheila and Sharon
Heard in every shell?
(Have the children join in.) /sh/ /sh/ /sh/ /sh/

Card 31: /th/ Thimble

Theodore Thimble is a thinker.
Theodore thinks and thinks and thinks.
And when he thinks, he rubs his head.
/th/ /th/ /th/ /th/ /th/ /th/ /th/ /th/ /th/

Theodore thinks of thumbs—
Thin thumbs
Thick thumbs
All different kinds of thumbs.
/th/ /th/ /th/ /th/ /th/ /th/ /th/ /th/ /th/

Theodore thinks of thread—
Red thread
Blue thread
All different color thread.
/th/ /th/ /th/ /th/ /th/ /th/ /th/ /th/ /th/

Thread and thumb
Thumb and thread
These are the thoughts
In Theodore's head.
/th/ /th/ /th/ /th/ /th/ /th/ /th/ /th/ /th/

Card 32: /ch/ Chipmunk

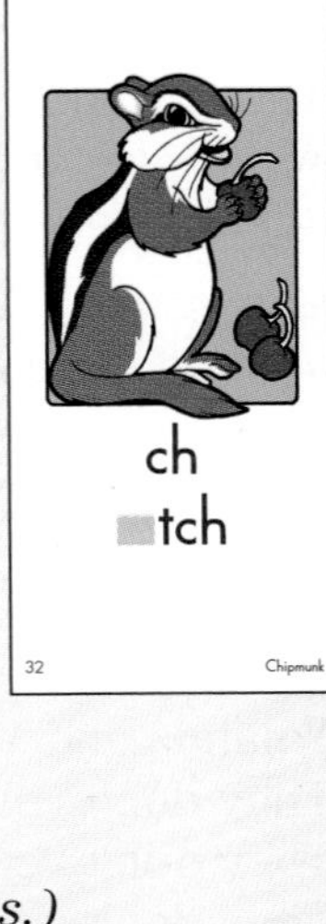

Chipper the chipmunk is cheerful and chubby.
He chats and he chatters all day.
/ch/ /ch/ /ch/ /ch/ /ch/ /ch/
He sits on a chimney.
Can you hear him chat?
He chats and he chatters this way:
/ch/ /ch/ /ch/ /ch/ /ch/ /ch/.

Chipper stuffs cherries into his cheek.
Then he chatters /ch/ /ch/ /ch/ /ch/ /ch/ /ch/.
Chipper likes chestnuts and acorns to eat.
Then he chatters /ch/ /ch/ /ch/ /ch/ /ch/ /ch/.

Can you children chatter like Chipper?
(Have the children answer.)
/ch/ /ch/ /ch/ /ch/ /ch/ /ch/

Now chat with the chipmunk child beside you.
(Ask partners to have chipmumk conversations.)
/ch/ /ch/ /ch/ /ch/ /ch/ /ch/

Card 38: /ng/ Gong

The young king has slept much
too long.
Let's go and awaken the king with
a gong.

A pinging gong? It makes a quiet song:
(softly) /ng/ /ng/ /ng/ /ng/ /ng/.

That gong is wrong.
(softly) /ng/ /ng/ /ng/ /ng/
We need a louder gong!

A dinging gong? It makes this song:
(a bit louder) /ng/ /ng/ /ng/ /ng/ /ng/ /ng/.

That, too, is wrong.
(as before) /ng/ /ng/ /ng/ /ng/
We need an even louder gong!

A clanging gong?
It makes this song: *(loudly)* /ng/ /ng/ /ng/ /ng/ /ng/!

That's just the thing! /ng/ /ng/ /ng/ /ng/ /ng/!
That's the gong we needed all along!

Now, which gong should we bring to awaken the King?
(Have children make the /ng/ sound loud enough to wake the king.) /ng/ /ng/ /ng/ /ng/ /ng/

Note: Cards 33 through 37 are long vowel cards and do not have corresponding stories.

Card 39: /ow/ Cow

Wow! Can you see poor Brownie
the Cow?
She got stung by a bee and look at
her now!
She jumps up and down with an
/ow/ /ow/ /ow/ /ow/.

Poor Brownie found that a big buzzing sound
meant bees all around—in the air, on the ground.
Just one little bee gave Brownie a sting.
Now you can hear poor Brownie sing:
/ow/ /ow/ /ow/ /ow/.

Now if you were a cow and a bee found you
You'd probably jump and shout out too!
(Have the children join in.) /ow/ /ow/ /ow/ /ow/

Card 40: /aw/ Hawk

Hazel the Hawk never cooks her food;
Instead, she eats it raw.
And when she thinks of dinnertime
She caws: /aw/ /aw/ /aw/ /aw/.

Hazel the Hawk likes rabbits and mice
and catches them with her claws.
In August, she flies high above the fields
and spies them below, in the straw.
Sometimes she even snatches a snake!
And when she's caught one, she caws:
/aw/ /aw/ /aw/ /aw/.

If you were a hawk thinking of dinnertime,
what do you think you'd say?
(Have the children answer.) /aw/ /aw/ /aw/ /aw/

Card 41: /o͞o/ Goo

/o͞o/ /o͞o/ /o͞o/ /o͞o/
What can be making that sound?
Could it be a new flute playing a tune?
No. It's goo!
/o͞o/ /o͞o/ /o͞o/ /o͞o/
The goo is oozing all over my hand.
/o͞o/ /o͞o/ /o͞o/ /o͞o/
The goo is oozing on my boots.
/o͞o/ /o͞o/ /o͞o/ /o͞o/
The goo is oozing off the roof.
The goo is oozing everywhere!
/o͞o/ /o͞o/ /o͞o/ /o͞o/
The goo is as sticky as glue.
It is as thick as stew.
/o͞o/ /o͞o/ /o͞o/ /o͞o/
Soon the goo will fill the school!
/o͞o/ /o͞o/ /o͞o/ /o͞o/

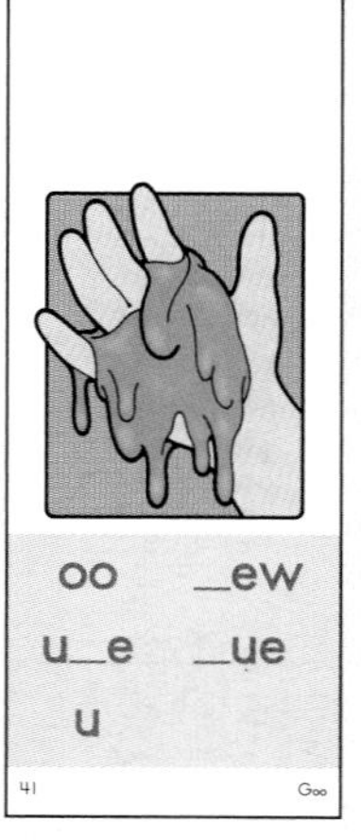

Soon the goo will reach the moon!
/o͞o/ /o͞o/ /o͞o/ /o͞o/
What sound does the oozing goo make?
(Have the children join in.) /o͞o/ /o͞o/ /o͞o/ /o͞o/

Card 42: /o͝o/ Foot

Mr. Hood took off his shoes and socks
And went out walking in the wood.
He kicked a rock and hurt his foot.
/o͝o/ /o͝o/ /o͝o/ /o͝o/
"Look, look!" said Mr. Hood. "There's a
babbling, bubbling brook. I'll walk
in the brook, so I won't hurt my foot."
So he stepped in the water, and guess what?
/o͝o/ /o͝o/ /o͝o/ /o͝o/
Mr. Hood stepped on a hook!
/o͝o/ /o͝o/ /o͝o/ /o͝o/
Mr. Hood stood. He shook his foot.
/o͝o/ /o͝o/ /o͝o/ /o͝o/
"This isn't good," said Mr. Hood.
"I think I'll go home and read a book.
At least that won't hurt my foot."
(Have the children join in.) /o͝o/ /o͝o/ /o͝o/ /o͝o/

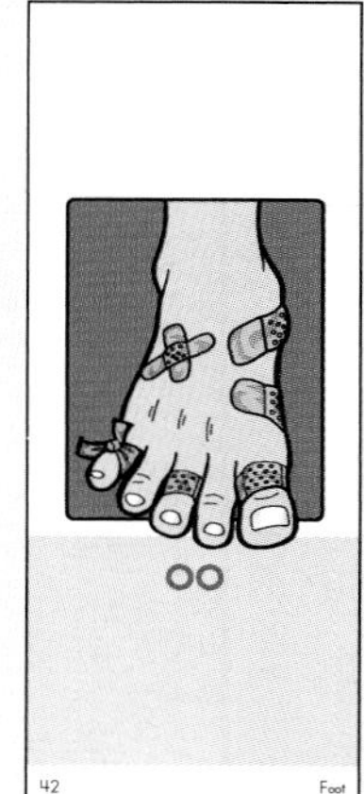

Card 43: /oi/ Coil

Boing! Boing! Boing! Boing!
Roy the Coil is a bouncing toy,
and this is the sound of his bounce:
/oi/ /oi/ /oi/ /oi/ /oi/.

Doing! Doing! Doing! Doing!
Roy the Coil just dances for joy.
This is the sound of his dance:
/oi/ /oi/ /oi/ /oi/ /oi/.

Ke-boing! Ke-boing!
Roy the Coil springs over a boy.
What springing sound does he make?
(Have the children join in.)
/oi/ /oi/ /oi/ /oi/ /oi/

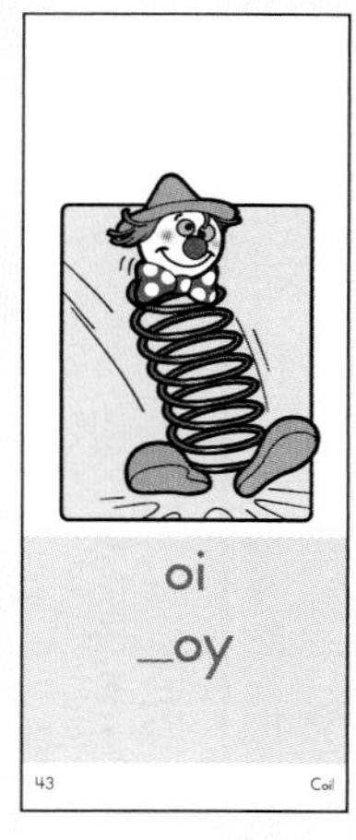

High-Frequency Word List

a
about
after
again
all
always
am
an
and
any
are
around
as
ask
at
ate
away
be
because
been
before
best
better
big
black
blue
both
bring
brown
but
buy
by
call
came
can
carry
clean
cold
come
could
cut
did
do
does
done
don't
down
draw
drink
eat
eight
every
fall
far
fast
find
first
five
fly
for
found
four
from
full
funny
gave
get
give
go
goes
going
good
got
green
grow
had
has
have
he
help
her
here
him
his
hold
hot
how
hurt
I
if
in
into
is
it
its
jump
just
keep
kind
know
laugh
let
light
like
little
live
long
look
made
make
many
may
me
much
must
my
myself
never
new
no
not
now
of
off
old
on
once
one
only
open
or
our
out
over
own
pick
play
please
pretty
pull
put
ran
read
red
ride
right
round
run
said
saw
say
see
seven
shall
she
show
sing
sit
six
sleep
small
so
some
soon
start
stop
take
tell
ten
thank
that
the
their
them
then
there
these
they
think
this
those
three
to
today
together
too
try
two
under
up
upon
us
use
very
walk
want
warm
was
wash
we
well
went
were
what
when
where
which
white
who
why
will
wish
with
work
would
write
yellow
yes
you
your

Index

A

INDEX

INDEX

B

C

INDEX

INDEX

G

H

INDEX

I

J

K

L

INDEX

INDEX

M

INDEX

N

P

INDEX

Q

R

INDEX

S

INDEX

T

U

V

INDEX

INDEX

Notes

Use this page to record lessons or elements that work well or need to be adjusted for future reference.

Lessons that work well.

Lessons that need adjustments.

Notes

Use this page to record lessons or elements that work well
or need to be adjusted for future reference.

Lessons that work well.

Lessons that need adjustments.

Notes

Use this page to record lessons or elements that work well or need to be adjusted for future reference.

Lessons that work well.

Lessons that need adjustments.

Use this page to record lessons or elements that work well
or need to be adjusted for future reference.

Lessons that work well.

Lessons that need adjustments.

Notes

Use this page to record lessons or elements that work well or need to be adjusted for future reference.

Lessons that work well.

Lessons that need adjustments.

Notes

Use this page to record lessons or elements that work well or need to be adjusted for future reference.

Lessons that work well.

Lessons that need adjustments.

California Resources

The following pages provide a list of California museums, zoos, historical sites, and nature preserves that could be helpful as students do research or seek further information about topics they've studied. Some sites may be physically close enough for classes or students to visit. Other sites farther away may be accessible to students via the Internet. While we have reviewed these sites for accuracy and appropriateness, Web sites do change. Teachers should plan to review the content of each site before allowing students to visit.

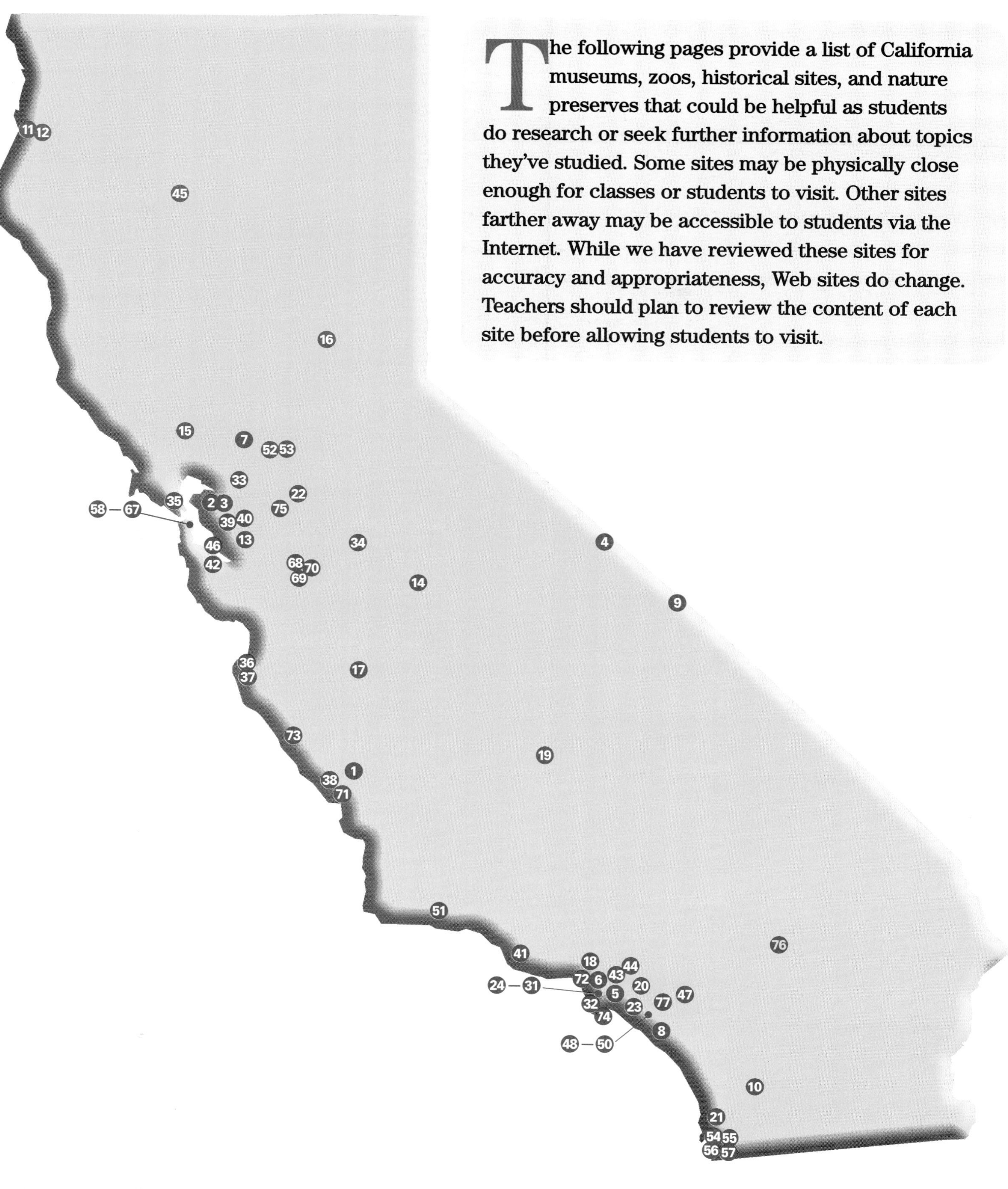

California Resources

CALIFORNIA RESOURCES

Atascadero
1 Charles Paddock Zoo
9305 Pismo
Atascadero, CA 93422
Phone: (805) 461-5080
http://www.atascadero.org/zoo/

Berkeley
2 Habitot Children's Museum
1563 Solano Avenue #326
Berkeley, CA 94707
Phone: (510) 647-1111
http://www.habitot.org/habitot/home.htm

3 Lawrence Hall of Science
1 Centennial Drive
Berkeley, CA 94720
Phone: (510) 642-5132
http://www.lhs.berkeley.edu/

Bishop
4 Inyo National Forest's Bristlecone Pines
873 N. Main St.
Bishop, CA 93514
Phone: (760) 873-2500
http://www.r5.fs.fed.us/inyo

Buena Park
5 Movieland Wax Museum
7711 Beach Boulevard
Buena Park, CA 90620
Phone: (714) 522-1154
http://www.movielandwaxmuseum.com/

Culver City
6 Museum of Jurassic Technology
9341 Venice Boulevard
Culver City, CA 90232
Phone: (310) 836-6131
http://www.mjt.org/

Davis
7 Explorit Science Center
3141 Fifth Street
Davis, CA 95617-1288
Phone: (530) 756-0191
http://www.dcn.davis.ca.us/go/explorit/

Dana Point
8 Doheny State Beach Interpretive Center
25300 Dana Point Harbor Drive
Dana Point, CA 92629
Phone: (949) 496-6172
http://www.dohenystatebeach.org/

Death Valley
9 Death Valley National Park
P.O. Box 579
Death Valley, CA 92328
Phone: (760) 786-2331
http://www.nps.gov/deva/index.htm

Escondido
10 San Diego Wild Animal Park
15500 San Pasqual Valley Road
Escondido, CA 92027-7017
Phone: (760) 747-8702
http://www.sandiegozoo.org/wap/visitor_info.html

Eureka
11 Redwood Discovery Museum
3rd & F Street, Old Town
P.O. Box 3456
Eureka, CA 95502
Phone: (707) 443-9694
http://www.northcoast.com/~discover/

12 Sequoia Park Zoological Society
3414 W Street
Eureka, CA 95503
Phone: (707) 442-6552
http://www.eurekawebs.com/zoo/

Fremont
13 Ardenwood Historic Farm
34600 Ardenwood Boulevard
Fremont, CA 94555
Phone: (510) 791-4196
http://www.stanford.edu/~wellis/ardenwd/

Fresno
14 Chaffee Zoological Gardens of Fresno
894 West Belmont Avenue
Fresno, CA 93728
Phone: (559) 498-2671
http://www.chaffeezoo.org/

Glen Ellen
15 Jonathan Bailey Home & Park
13421 E Camilla Street
Whittier, CA 90601
Phone: (562) 698-3534
http://www.whittierbiz.com/info/bailey.htm

Grass Valley
16 Grass Valley Museum
410 S. Church Street
Grass Valley, CA 95945
Phone: (530) 273-5509
http://www.ncgold.com/Museum_Parks/GVmuseum.html

Hanford
17 Fort Roosevelt Science Center
870 West Davis Road
Hanford, CA 93232
Phone: (559) 582-8970
http://www.ccwr.org/region4.html

Hollywood
18 Hollywood Studio Museum
7021 Hollywood Boulevard
Hollywood, CA 90028-6044
Phone: (323) 465-7900
http://www.seeing-stars.com/Museums/HollywoodEntertainment.shtml

Kernville
19 The Kern Valley Museum
49 Big Blue Road
Kernville, CA 93238
Phone: (760) 376-6683
http://www.kernvalley.com/news/museum.htm

La Habra
20 Children's Museum at La Habra
301 South Euclid Street
La Habra, CA 90631
Phone: (562) 905-9793
http://www.lhcm.org/

La Jolla
21 Stephen Birch Aquarium at Scripps
2300 Expedition Way
La Jolla, CA 92037
Phone: (858) 534-3474
http://www.artcom.com/Museum/vs/sz/92093-02.htm

Lodi
22 Micke Grove Zoo
11793 N. Micke Grove Road
Lodi, CA 95240
Phone: (209) 953-8840
http://www.mgzoo.com/

Long Beach
23 Long Beach Aquarium of the Pacific
100 Aquarium Way
Long Beach, CA 90802
Phone: (562) 590-3100
http://www.aquariumofpacific.org/

Los Angeles
24 El Pueblo de Los Angeles
622 N Main Street
Los Angeles, CA 90012
Phone: (213) 628-3562
http://www.cityofla.org/elp/guide/elpueblo.htm

25 La Brea Tar Pits
5801 Wilshire Boulevard
Los Angeles, CA 90036
Phone: (323) 934-7243
http://www.tarpits.org/

26 California African American Museum
600 State Drive
Los Angeles, CA 90037
Phone: (213) 744-7432
http://www.caam.ca.gov/

27 National History Museum of Los Angeles County
900 Exposition Boulevard
Los Angeles, CA 90007
Phone: (213) 763-3466
http://www.nhm.org/

28 Museum of Tolerance
Simon Wiesenthal Plaza
9786 West Pico Blvd
Los Angeles, CA 90035
Phone: (310) 553-8403
http://www.wiesenthal.com/mot/index.cfm

29 J. Paul Getty Museum
1200 Getty Center drive
Los Angeles, CA 90049-1687
Phone: (310) 440-7330
http://www.getty.edu/museum/

30 California Science Center
700 State Drive
Los Angeles, CA 90037
Phone: (323) 724-3623
http://www.casciencecectr.org/

31 Los Angeles Zoo
5333 Zoo Drive
Los Angeles, CA 90027-1498
Phone: (323) 644-6400
http://www.lazoo.org/

Manhattan Beach
32 Roundhouse Marine Studies Lab & Aquarium/Museum
P.O. Box 1
Manhattan Beach, CA 90266
Phone: (310) 379-8117
http://www.commpages.com/roundhouse/

Martinez
33 Martinez Museum
1005 Excobar Street
Martinez, CA
Phone: (510) 228-8160
http://www.artcom.com/museums/nv/mr/94553.htm

Merced
34 Yosemite Wildlife Museum
2040 Yosemite Parkway
Merced, CA 95340
Phone: (209) 383-1052
http://www.caohwy.com/y/yosewimu.htm

Mill Valley
35 Muir Woods National Monument
Mill Valley, CA 94941-2696
Phone: (415) 556-2766
http://www.nps.gov/muwo/index.htm

Monterey
36 MY Museum
601 Wave Street, Suite100
Monterey, CA 93940
Phone: (831) 649-6444
http://www.mymuseum.org/

37 Monterey Bay Aquarium
886 Cannery Row
Monterey, CA 93940-1085
Phone: (831) 648-4800
http://www.mbayaq.org/

Morro Bay
38 Morro Bay Aquarium
595 Embarcadero
Morro Bay, CA 93442
Phone: (805) 772-7647
http://www.morrobay.com/MorroBayAquarium/

Oakland
39 Chabot Space & Science Center
10000 Skyline Boulevard
Oakland, CA 94619
Phone: (510) 336-7300
http://www.chabotspace.org

40 Oakland Zoo in Knowland Park
9777 Golf links Road
Oakland, CA 94605
Phone: (510) 632-9525
http://www.oaklandzoo.org/

Oxnard

41 Gull Wings Children's Museum
418 W 4th St
Oxnard, CA 93030
Phone: (805) 483-3005
http://www.caohwy.com/g/guwichmu.htm

Palo Alto

42 Palo Alto Junior Museum & Zoo
1451 Middlefield Road
Palo Alto, CA 94301
Phone: (650) 329-2111
http://www.city.palo-alto.ca.us/ross/museum.html

Pasadena

43 Norton Simon Museum
411 west Colorado Boulevard
Pasadena, CA 91105
Phone: (626) 449-6840
http://www.nortonsimon.org/

44 Kidspace Museum
390 South El Molino Avenue
Pasadena, CA 91101
Phone: (626) 449-9144
http://cwire.com/orgs/kidspace.Museum/

Redding

45 Carter House Natural Science Museum
P.O. Box 990185
Redding, CA 96099-0185
Phone: (916) 243-5457
http://library.thinkquest.org/2899/basics.html

Redwood City

46 Marine Science Institute
500 Discovery Parkway
Redwood City, CA 94063-4715
Phone: (650) 364-2760
http://www.sfbaymsi.org/

Riverside

47 Riverside Youth Museum /KidZone
3800 Main Street
Riverside, CA 92501
Phone: (909) 683-3800
http://www.kidzone.org/

Santa Ana

48 The Bowers Kidseum
2002 North Main Street
Santa Ana, CA 92706
Phone: (714) 567-3600
http://www.kidseum.org/link1.htm

49 Discovery Science Center
2500 North Main Street
Santa Ana, CA 92705
Phone: (714) 542-2823
http://www.discoverycube.org/home.htm

50 Santa Ana Zoo
1801 East Chestnut Avenue
Santa Ana, CA 92701
Phone: (714) 835-7484
http://www.santaanazoo.org/

Santa Barbara

51 Santa Barbara Zoological Gardens
500 Ninos Drive
Santa Barbara, CA 93103
Phone: (805) 962-6310
http://www.santabarbarazoo.org/

Sacramento

52 California State Railroad Museum
111 "I" Street
Sacramento, CA 95814-2265
Phone: (916) 445-6645
http://www.csrmf.org/

53 Sacramento Zoo
3930 West Land Park Drive
Sacramento, CA 95822
Phone: (916) 264-5888
http://www.saczoo.com/

San Diego

54 Cabrillo National Monument
1800 Cabrillo Memorial Drive
San Diego, CA 92106-3601
Phone: (619) 224-4140
http://www.nps.gov/cabr/index.htm

55 San Diego Natural History Museum
P.O. Box 121390
San Diego, CA 92112-1390
Phone: (619) 232-3821
http://www.sdnhm.org/

56 Reuben H. Fleet Science Center
1875 El Prado Balboa Park
San Diego, CA 92163-3303
Phone: (619) 238-1233
http://www.rhfleet.org/

57 San Diego Zoo
2920 Zoo Drive
San Diego, CA 92101
Phone: (619) 234-3153
http://www.sandiegozoo.org/

San Francisco

58 Alcatraz Island
Fort Mason, Building 201-Alcatraz
San Francisco, CA 94123
Phone: (415) 705-1045
http://www.nps.gov/alca/index.htm

59 William Penn Mott Jr. Visitor Center
Building 102, Montgomery Street
San Francisco, CA 94129
Phone: (415) 561-4323
http://www.nps.gov/prsf/index.htm

60 M.H. de Young Memorial Museum
75 Tea Garden Drive
San Francisco, CA 94118
Phone: (415) 863-3330
http://www.thinker.org/deyoung/features/ndy-home.html

61 Museum of the City of San Francisco
945 Taraval Street
San Francisco, CA 94116
Phone: (415) 928-0289
http://www.sfmuseum.org/

62 The Randall Museum
199 Museum Way
San Francisco, CA 94114
Phone: (415) 554-9600
http://www.randall.mus.ca.us/

63 California Indian Museum & Cultural Center
P.O. Box 29908 Presidio Station
San Francisco, CA 94129
Phone: (415) 561-3992
http://cimcc.indian.com/

64 Steinhart Aquarium California Academy of Sciences
55 Concourse Drive
Golden Gate Park
San Francisco, CA 94118
Phone: (415) 750-7145
http://www.calacademy.org/aquarium

65 Exploratorium
3601 Lyon Street
San Francisco, CA 94123
Phone: (425) 397-5673
http://www.exploratorium.edu/

66 San Francisco Zoo
1 Zoo Road
San Francisco, CA 94132-1098
Phone: (415) 753-7080
http://www.sfzoo.com/

67 Fort Point National Historic Site
Long Avenue & Marine Drive
San Francisco, CA 94129
Phone: (415) 556-1693
http://www.nps.gov/fopo/index.htm

San Jose

68 Children's Discovery Museum
180 Woz Way
San Jose, CA 95110
Phone: (408) 298-5437
http://www.cdm.org/

69 History Museums of San Jose
1650 Senter Road
San Jose, CA 95112
Phone: (408) 287-2290
http://www.sjhistory.org/

70 Happy Hollow Park & Zoo
1300 Senter Road
San Jose, CA 95112
Phone: (408) 295-8383
http://www.happyhollowparkandzoo.org/

San Luis Obispo

71 San Luis Obispo Children's Museum
1010 Nipomo Street
San Luis Obispo, CA 93401-3870
Phone: (805) 544-5437
http://www.slonet.org/~slokids/

Santa Monica

72 UCLA Ocean Discovery Center
1600 Ocean Front Walk
Santa Monica, CA 90401
Phone: (310) 393-6149
http://www.odc.ucla.edu/

San Simeon

73 Hearst Castle
750 Hearst Castle Road
San Simeon, CA 93452-9741
Phone: (805) 927-2020
http://www.sansimeonsbest.com/hearstcastle/

San Pedro

74 Cabrillo Marine Aquarium
3720 Stephen White Drive
San Pedro, CA 90731
Phone: (310) 548-7562
http://www.cabrilloaq.org/

Stockton

75 Children's Music of Stockton
402 W. Weber Ave
Stockton, CA 95203
Phone: (209) 465-4386
http://www.sonnet.com/usr/children/

76 Twentynine Palms
Joshua Tree National Park
74485 National Park Drive
Twentynine Palms, CA 92277
Phone: (760) 367-5500
http://www.desertusa.com/jtree/jtmain.html

Whittier

77 Jonathan Bailey Home & Park
13421 E Camilla Street
Whittier, CA 90601
Phone: (562) 698-3534
http://www.whittierbiz.com/info/bailey.htm

Phonetic Problems Linked to Students' First Language

The following table focuses on some of the main pronunciation problems English-Language Learners from eight language groups may encounter while learning English. The purpose of this table is to help teachers decide which steps to take in order to address chronic pronunciation problems. The table is by no means exhaustive and is meant to serve only as a guide. It shows pronunciation variances that students may make while learning English. For example, a student whose first language is Spanish may say something like *cot* when trying to pronounce the word *cat*. An empty cell indicates that the English sound listed poses no particular problem for students from the given language group.

English Element	Spanish	Vietnamese
/a/ *cat*	/o/ *cot*	/o/ *cot*
/ē/ *tea*		
/e/ *bet*	/ā/ *bait*	/a/ *bat*
/i/ *ship*	/ē/ *sheep*	/ē/ *sheep*
/ō/ *cloak*		
/o/ *clock*	/ô/ *clawk*	
/u/ *cup*	/o/ *cop*, /o͞o/ *coop*	
/o͝o/ *pull*	/o͞o/ *pool*	/o͞o/ *pool*
/ə/	Nonexistent. Replaced by another vowel sound.	
/b/ *bad*		
/f/ *fan*		
/j/ *jar*	/h/ *har*, /y/ *yar*	/z/ *zar*
/n/ *need*		
/r/ *rock, terrible*	Rolled or trilled.	
/v/ *vet*	/b/ *bet*, /f/ *fet*	
/w/ *week*	/v/ *veek*, /o͞o/ *ooeek*	
/z/ *zoo*	/s/ *soo*	
/zh/ *measure*	/z/ *meazure*	
/th/ *think*	/s/ *sink*, /t/ *tink*	/s/ *sink*, /t/ *tink*
/t͟h/ *though*	/d/ *doe*	/d/ *doe*, /z/ *zoh*
/sh/ *shoe*	/ch/ *chew*	/s/ *sue*, /ch/ *chew*
Initial /s/ *stop*	Adds /e/ *estop*	
Final consonants /f/, /th/, etc. *life, path...*		Final consonants unpronounced. *lie, pa...*
Final /p/, /t/, /k/ *tip, sit, sick*		
Final /s/ after consonants. *cats, rocks*		None. *cat, rock*
Final /v/ *love*		/b/ *lub*, /p/ *lup*
Final consonant blends	Rare. One or more sounds dropped	None. One or more sounds dropped.
Polysyllabic words		None. All words monosyllabic.
Intonation of sentences		None. Tone of individual words changes meaning.

[1] The sound contrasts for Hmong are based on information about Thai-Lao/English contrasts.

[2] The sound contrasts for Haitian Creole are based on information about French/English contrasts.

Hmong[1]	Cantonese	Tagalog	Haitian Creole[2] (French)	Portuguese	Khmer
/o/ *cot*		/o/ *cot*	/o/ *cot*	/o/ *cot*	/u/ *cut*, /e/ *yet*
/ü/ like French tu			/i/ *ti*		
	All vowel sounds will vary, depending on the consonant sounds combined with them.	/ā/ *bait*		/ā/ *bait*	
		/ē/ *sheep*	/ē/ *sheep*	/ē/ *sheep*	/ē/ *sheep*
/o/ *clock*					/o/ *clock*
		/ô/ *clawk*		/ō/ *cloak*	
		/o/ *cop*	/ä/ *(father) cap*	/a/ *cap*, /ä/ *(father) cäp*	
		/o͞o/ *pool*	/o͞o/ *pool*	/o͞o/ *pool*	
Nonexistent. Replaced by another vowel sound.		Nonexistent. Replaced by another vowel sound.		Sound difficult, especially at the beginning of the word.	Nonexistent. Replaced by another vowel sound.
/p/ *pad*				May sound close to /y/.	
		/p/ *pan*			Sound difficult. May be dropped.
		/y/ *yar*	/zh/ *zher* (as in *measure*) *zher*	/y/ *yar*	/ch/ *char*
	/l/ *leed*				
	/l/ *lock*, *tellable*		Pronounced as uvular r.	Pronounced too far back, close to /h/.	
	/f/ *fet*	/b/ *bet*, /f/ *fet*		/w/ *wet*, /b/ *bet*	/w/ *wet*, /b/ *bet*
/h/ *heek*		/v/ *veek*, /o͞o/ *ooeek*			
/s/ *soo*	/s/ *soo*	/s/ *soo*		/s/ *soo*	/s/ *soo*
	/z/ *meazure*, /sh/ *meashur*	/z/ *meazure*		/z/ *meazure*, /s/ *meassure*	/j/ *meajure*
/t/ *tink*	/t/ *tink*	/t/ *tink*	/s/ *sink*	/s/ *sink*, /t/ *tink*	/t/ *tink*
/d/ *doe*	/d/ *doe*	/d/ *doe*	/z/ *zoe*	/d/ *doe*	/d/ *doe*
	/s/ *sue*			/ch/ *chew*	/ch/ *chew*
				Adds /e/ *estop*	May sound close to /h/.
Many final consonants dropped. *lifuh, pathuh*	Many final consonants dropped or vocalized.				Difficult. Often dropped
/b/ *tib*, /d/ *sid*, /g/ *sig*	Often dropped or vocalized. *situh*		Not aspirated. Confusion with *b*, *d*, and *g*.		Often dropped.
None. *cat, rock*	None. *cat, rock*	None. *cat, rock*			
Often dropped.	Often dropped.				Often dropped.
None. One or more sounds dropped.	None. One or more sounds dropped.			Rare. One or more sounds dropped.	None. One or more sounds dropped
Rare. Most words monosyllabic.	Rare. Most words monosyllabic				
None. Tone of individual words changes meaning.	None. Tone of individual words changes meaning.				

CALIFORNIA RESOURCES

Correlation to California Reading/Language Arts Standards Grade K

Reading

	Unit 1	Unit 2	Unit 3
1.0 Word Analysis, Fluency, and Systematic Vocabulary Development Students know about letters, words, and sounds. They apply this knowledge to read simple sentences.			
Concepts About Print			
1.1 Identify the front cover, back cover, and title page of a book.	T237		
1.2 Follow words from left to right and from top to bottom on the printed page.	T28, T48–T59, T68–T79, T85, T93, T110, T111, T116–T125, T132, T133, T136–T141, T153, T162, T196–T197, T204–T205	T25, T37, T42–T49, T55, T64, T67, T76, T92, T95, T100–T109, T115, T118–T123, T129, T141, T162, T165, T170–T171	T40–T49, T51, T100–T115, T118, T124–T131, T138–T145, T228–T243, T246, T282
1.3 Understand that printed materials provide information.	T37, T39, T59, T61, T81, T97, T125, T127, T197, T199, T221, T241, T275, T277, T295, T333	T33, T45, T49, T51, T61, T63, T75, T83, T109, T111, T116, T125, T137, T145, T153, T171, T181, T183, T195, T243	T33, T65, T75, T115, T131, T133, T147, T155, T163, T183, T191, T197, T205, T213, T243, T281, T289
1.4 Recognize that sentences in print are made up of separate words.	T97, T159, T169, T177, T205, T241, T255, T333	T33, T35, T51–T52, T63–T65, T76, T83, T93, T111, T112, T126, T137, T146, T153, T162, T173, T175, T183, T195	T45, T52, T79, T83, T113, T163, T213, T289
1.5 Distinguish letters from words.	T323	T33, T51, T63, T103, T111–T112, T125–T126, T137–T138, T146, T153, T183, T195, T245, T261, T278, T293	T94, T120, T135, T150
1.6 Recognize and name all uppercase and lowercase letters of the alphabet.	T53, T55, T62, T69, T108, T110, T123, T130, T132, T137, T139, T146–T149, T153, T160, T170–T171, T190, T204, T214	T24–T25, T37, T43, T55, T66, T67, T78, T95, T103, T107, T112, T114–T116, T125–T126, T128–T129, T138, T141	T25, T35, T41, T47, T52, T53, T70–T71, T94, T101, T109, T120, T158, T206, T208, T233, T282, T284–T285
Phonemic Awareness			
1.7 Track (move sequentially from sound to sound) and represent the number, sameness/difference, and order of two and three isolated phonemes (e.g., /f, s, *th*/, /j, *d*, *j*/).			
1.8 Track (move sequentially from sound to sound) and represent changes in simple syllables and words with two and three sounds as one sound is added, substituted, omitted, shifted, or repeated (e.g., vowel-consonant, consonant-vowel, or consonant-vowel-consonant).			
1.9 Blend vowel-consonant sounds orally to make words or syllables.			T23, T35, T53, T69, T77, T149, T261, T275, T283
1.10 Identify and produce rhyming words in response to an oral prompt.	T65, T85, T91, T93, T107, T111, T129, T133, T145, T149, T159, T163, T169, T187, T191, T201, T213, T223, T227, T233	T34, T52, T64, T76, T92, T112, T126, T138, T146, T184, T196, T204, T220, T262, T278, T286	T22, T52, T68, T76, T148, T172, T184, T192, T198, T206, T260, T274, T282, T285
1.11 Distinguish orally stated one-syllable words and separate into beginning or ending sounds.			
1.12 Track auditorily each word in a sentence and each syllable in a word.	T145, T159, T169	T65, T76–T77, T79	T22, T76, T93, T119, T135, T149, T157, T173, T185, T193, T198–T199, T207, T222–T223, T246–T247, T285
1.13 Count the number of sounds in syllables and syllables in words.			T157, T173, T185, T193, T199, T207, T223
Decoding and Word Recognition			
1.14 Match all consonant and short-vowel sounds to appropriate letters.			
1.15 Read simple one-syllable and high-frequency words (i.e., sight words).	T173, T236–T237, T328	T130, T149, T180–T181, T207–T208, T289	T43, T78–T80, T109, T158–T159, T208, T233, T282, T284
1.16 Understand that as letters of words change, so do the sounds (i.e., the alphabetic principle).			T185, T193, T200, T209

Unit 4	Unit 5	Unit 6	Unit 7	Unit 8
		T31, T40	T31, T296	T33
T44–T55, T116–T127, T136–T139, T148–T151, T160–T163, T192–T193, T222, T248–T262	T42–T49, T58–T65, T100–T109, T151, T196, T226–T239, T248–T255, T266–T271, T284	T42–T51, T70, T106–T117, T162, T180, T186–T187, T196–T197, T220, T242–T256, T296, T306	T31, T42–T53, T110–T123, T126, T172, T190, T196–T197, T206–T207, T230, T252–T270, T314, T326	T33, T44–T55, T92, T114–T127, T174, T194–T195, T204–T205, T224, T244–T259, T301
T33, T35, T47, T57, T77, T87, T97, T114, T127, T129, T141, T153, T163, T165, T175, T195, T205, T213, T221, T231	T33, T43, T51, T67, T83, T105, T107, T111, T121, T137, T145, T175, T193, T201, T227, T233, T264	T33, T45, T53, T65, T109, T111, T147, T167, T199, T301	T43, T45, T51, T53, T115, T119, T121, T123	T35, T57, T77, T87, T129, T145, T159, T169, T179, T197, T207, T213, T221, T229, T291, T299, T307
T53, T97, T117, T141, T175, T231, T255, T315	T47, T83, T101, T124, T137, T155, T193, T201–T202, T209, T289	T89, T119, T133, T147, T167, T180, T207, T220, T225, T259, T273, T291, T311	T33, T93, T119, T126, T177, T199, T229, T307	T77, T97, T145, T159, T169, T174, T179, T197, T207, T213, T221, T229, T261, T275, T291, T307
T35, T49, T281	T52	T53		
T35, T49, T57, T77, T87, T92, T97, T129, T141, T153, T165, T170, T175, T199, T206, T226, T282, T310	T24, T55, T114, T126, T178, T186, T188, T231, T244	T22, T24, T33, T36, T49, T51, T53, T56–T57, T65, T68, T85, T100, T113, T115, T122, T150–T151, T178	T24, T45, T47, T59, T74, T89, T104, T111, T113, T117, T126, T146, T160, T161, T197, T202, T212, T220, T228, T246	T39, T53, T60, T108, T123, T127, T132, T245, T261, T275, T281, T291
	T139, T147, T165, T187, T219	T23, T70	T23, T35, T57, T71, T74, T87, T103, T127	
T93, T156, T199, T227	T197, T276	T23, T38, T67, T83, T99, T121, T135, T149, T158–T159, T162, T177, T180, T191, T201, T216–T217, T220, T235, T261	T23, T35, T57, T59, T71, T74, T87, T103, T127, T145, T159, T169, T189, T226, T244, T314, T325	T23, T25, T37, T39, T59, T61, T78–T79, T81, T90, T92, T107, T131, T147, T161, T239, T262, T264, T277, T293
T23, T37, T59, T79, T89, T107, T131, T143, T155, T156, T167, T185, T197, T199, T207, T215, T223, T227, T241, T267	T139–T140, T147–T148, T151, T165, T187, T195, T197, T219, T262–T263, T276, T285	T70, T158, T162, T180, T209, T216, T220, T296, T306	T23–T24, T35, T57, T71, T74, T87, T103, T127, T145, T159, T169, T172, T190, T227, T230, T244, T245, T247, T275	T23, T25, T37, T39, T59, T61, T79, T81, T89, T91–T92, T107, T109, T131, T133, T147, T149, T161, T163
T22, T58, T78, T93, T106, T130, T142, T154, T166, T171, T184, T193, T196, T214, T222, T306	T22, T52, T68, T76, T92, T112, T138, T146, T164, T173, T242, T274, T282	T34, T54, T66, T82, T98, T107, T109, T113, T162, T176, T190, T208, T266, T274, T292, T296, T302	T22, T33, T69, T85, T93, T102, T143, T168, T210, T225, T244, T310, T322, T326	T38, T60, T88, T92, T109, T130, T146, T162, T170, T195, T198, T208, T238, T262, T273, T281, T283, T285, T287, T292
T26, T38, T39, T60, T80, T111, T119, T121, T132–T133, T144–T145, T156–T157, T168–T169, T186–T187, T217, T224–T225	T22–T23, T25, T34–T37, T53–T55, T68–T71, T77–T78, T93, T107, T113–T115, T124–T127, T138, T166–T167	T23–T25, T34–T37, T54–T57, T66–T69, T82–T85, T122–T123, T135–T137, T148–T150, T159–T162, T178–T179	T24–T25, T34, T36–T37, T56, T58, T88, T105, T128–T129, T144, T158, T160–T161, T170–T172, T187–T188, T201–T203	T24, T38, T60, T80, T108, T131–T132, T148, T162, T172, T188, T199, T208, T214–T215, T222, T238, T276, T292, T300
T58, T166, T171, T306	T76	T220	T22, T34, T119, T126, T200	T36, T174
T58, T166, T171			T22, T34–T35, T57, T71, T87	T36
T26, T27, T38, T39, T47, T60–T61, T80, T90–T91, T109, T110, T111, T119, T121, T132–T133, T145, T156, T157	T22–T25, T34–T37, T52, T54–T55, T68–T71, T77–T79, T93–T95, T107, T113–T115, T124–T127, T138, T140	T22–T25, T24–T37, T55–T57, T67–T70, T83–T85, T100–T101, T120, T122–T123, T134, T136–T137, T148, T150–T151	T23–T25, T35–T37, T57–T59, T71–T74, T87–T89, T103–T105, T127–T129, T145–T147, T159–T161, T169–T172	T22–T25, T37, T39, T59–T61, T78–T81, T90–T91, T107–T108, T131–T133, T147–T148, T160–T162, T172, T174
T49, T92–T93, T121, T170, T226, T249, T298, T310–T311	T56, T103, T128, T151, T196–T197, T262–T263, T276, T285	T70, T148, T162, T180, T220, T234, T296, T306	T24, T43, T45, T49, T70, T74, T86, T113, T161, T172, T186, T190, T200, T230, T255, T261, T314, T326	T22, T60, T78, T81, T91–T92, T109, T130, T133, T149, T163, T173–T174, T188–T189, T198, T200, T208–T209, T214
T199	T197, T276	T23, T35, T55, T67, T83, T158, T162, T200, T218, T220, T296, T306	T23, T35, T57, T59, T71, T87, T103, T127, T145, T159, T169, T189, T325	T22, T25, T39, T61, T78, T81, T90, T107, T147, T161, T172, T239, T262, T264, T277, T293, T301

CALIFORNIA RESOURCES

Correlation to California Reading/Language Arts Standards Grade K

Reading

	Unit 1	Unit 2	Unit 3
Vocabulary and Concept Development			
1.17 Identify and sort common words in basic categories (e.g., colors, shapes, foods).	T39, T61, T81, T89, T97, T106, T111, T127–T128, T143–T144, T157, T199, T211–T212, T221–T222, T239, T277–T278	T93, T111, T125, T137, T145, T153, T201, T245, T261, T277, T285, T293	T33, T51, T67, T75, T83, T117, T133, T147, T155, T163, T183, T191, T197, T245, T259, T273, T281, T289
1.18 Describe common objects and events in both general and specific language.	T30, T39, T61, T81, T89, T97, T106, T110, T113, T132, T148, T162, T167, T177, T204, T219, T227, T229, T277, T295	T29, T33, T51, T56, T68, T81, T98, T111, T125, T130, T137, T143, T145, T151, T153, T168, T173, T183, T190, T201	T29, T31, T33, T37–T38, T51, T67, T75, T83, T177, T195, T203
2.0 Reading Comprehension Students identify the basic facts and ideas in what they have read, heard, or viewed. They use comprehension strategies (e.g., generating and responding to questions, comparing new information to what is already known). The selections in *Recommended Readings in Literature, Kindergarten Through Grade Eight* (California Department of Education, 1996) illustrate the quality and complexity of the materials to be read by students.			
Structural Features of Informational Materials			
2.1 Locate the title, table of contents, name of author, and name of illustrator.	T81, T227, T283	T178, T262	T122, T136, T209
Comprehension and Analysis of Grade-Level-Appropriate Text			
2.2 Use pictures and context to make predictions about story content.	T39, T46, T61, T81, T89, T97, T127, T143, T157, T167, T177, T199, T211, T221, T231, T241, T277	T33, T51, T63, T75, T83, T98, T168, T195, T203, T211, T282	T31, T38, T98, T197, T205, T213, T226
2.3 Connect to life experiences the information and events in texts.	T36, T39, T61, T81, T89, T97, T127, T141, T143, T155, T157, T167, T173, T177, T199, T211, T221, T231, T241, T271	T33, T51, T63, T75, T83, T97, T111, T125, T137, T145, T149, T153, T173, T183, T195, T203, T211, T245, T261, T277	T33, T51, T67, T75, T83, T153, T181, T183, T186, T189, T191, T278, T286
2.4 Retell familiar stories.	T87, T155, T164, T237, T320–T321	T135, T142, T207, T283	T54, T80, T136, T159, T191, T210, T271
2.5 Ask and answer questions about essential elements of a text.	T36, T59, T71, T73, T79, T87, T119, T125, T137, T139, T141, T153, T155, T197, T209, T255, T267, T271, T273, T275	T29, T47, T49, T59, T61, T71, T73, T79–T80, T105, T107, T109, T116, T119, T121, T123, T133, T135, T142, T171	T29, T41, T49, T57, T59, T61, T63, T65, T72, T107, T111, T115, T125, T127, T129, T131, T136, T139, T141, T143
3.0 Literary Response and Analysis Students listen and respond to stories based on well-known characters, themes, plots and settings. The selections in *Recommended Readings in Literature, Kindergarten Through Grade Eight* (California Department of Education, 1996) illustrate the quality and complexity of the materials to be read by students.			
Narrative Analysis of Grade-Level-Appropriate Text			
3.1 Distinguish fantasy from realistic text.		T107, T109, T116, T130, T253, T255, T257, T259, T269, T271, T273	
3.2 Identify types of everyday print materials (e.g., storybooks, poems, newspapers, signs, labels).	T28, T199, T211, T221, T231, T241	T211	T33, T51, T83, T133, T147, T155, T163, T183, T191, T197, T213, T245, T259, T273, T281, T289
3.3 Identify characters, settings, and important events.	T87, T97, T125, T133, T150, T164, T261, T275, T295, T313, T320	T142, T282	T49, T54, T73, T136, T152, T155, T160, T229, T243, T251, T253, T255, T265, T267, T269, T271, T278

Writing

	Unit 1	Unit 2	Unit 3
1.0 Writing Strategies Students write words and brief sentences that are legible.			
Organization and Focus			
1.1 Use letters and phonetically spelled words to write about experiences, stories, people, objects, or events.			
1.2 Write consonant-vowel-consonant words (i.e., demonstrate the alphabetic principle).			
1.3 Write by moving from left to right and from top to bottom.	T331	T150, T291	T147, T197, T273

Unit 4	Unit 5	Unit 6	Unit 7	Unit 8
T35, T57, T77, T87, T97, T129, T141, T153, T165, T175, T195, T205, T213, T221, T231, T265, T281, T297, T305, T315	T33, T51, T56, T67, T75, T83, T111, T123, T137, T145, T155, T175, T185, T191, T193, T201, T209, T241, T257, T273	T33, T53, T65, T81, T89, T119, T133, T147, T157, T167, T189, T199, T207, T215, T225, T259, T273, T291, T301, T311	T35, T55, T69, T85, T93, T125, T143, T157, T167, T177, T186, T199, T209, T217, T225, T235, T273, T291, T309, T321	T35, T57, T77, T87, T97, T129, T145, T159–T160, T169, T179, T197, T207, T213, T221, T229, T261, T275, T291, T299
T33, T35, T57, T77, T87, T97, T129, T141, T153, T165, T175, T189, T195, T205, T211, T213, T219, T221, T231, T246	T26, T31, T33, T39–T40, T51, T56, T67, T75, T80, T83, T97, T111, T116, T119, T123, T137, T145, T155, T169–T170	T31, T33, T39–T40, T53, T63, T65, T81, T89, T103–T104, T119, T133, T147, T157, T167, T183, T189, T199, T205	T26, T31, T35, T40, T55, T69, T85, T93, T107–T108, T125, T143, T157, T167, T177, T199, T209, T215, T217, T223	T26, T33, T35, T41–T42, T57, T77, T87, T97, T111–T112, T129, T145, T159, T169, T179, T197, T207, T211, T213
T42, T114, T134, T146, T158, T190, T200, T270	T56, T98, T116, T264	T148, T184, T194	T31, T60, T70, T76, T148, T194, T200, T204	T78, T134, T150, T192, T202
T42, T153, T165, T175, T190, T246	T40, T51, T111, T123, T150, T193, T201, T209, T224	T40, T104, T184, T207, T215, T225, T240	T26, T40, T69, T85, T93, T108, T194, T250, T273	T26, T42, T112, T192, T242
T41, T75, T85, T129, T139, T141, T227, T245, T311	T33, T51, T67, T75, T80, T83, T175, T185, T241, T257, T263, T273, T281, T289	T33, T53, T63, T65, T70, T75, T81, T89, T117, T119, T129, T133, T145, T147, T157, T167, T187, T189, T197, T199	T35, T39, T55, T67, T83, T125, T141, T143, T157, T167, T177, T199, T207, T209, T217, T225, T235, T273, T291, T309	T31, T35, T47, T57, T77, T87, T97, T195, T197, T207, T213, T221, T229, T259, T261, T275, T291, T299, T307
T83, T85, T227, T302, T303, T311	T49, T65, T72, T135, T142, T151, T197, T255, T263, T278–T279	T155, T162, T298, T306	T163, T174, T190, T316, T318–T319, T326	T82, T84–T85, T164–T167, T294–T297, T302
T31, T51, T55, T65, T67, T69, T71, T73, T75, T82, T83, T93, T117, T123, T125, T127, T137, T139, T149, T151	T29, T49, T59, T61, T63, T65, T72, T73, T103, T109, T119, T121, T131, T133, T135, T142, T173, T180, T183, T235	T30, T51, T61, T63, T70, T75, T77, T79, T117, T127, T129, T131, T141, T143, T145, T180, T194, T257, T267, T269	T30, T39, T53, T63, T65, T67, T79, T81, T83, T123, T133, T135, T137, T139, T141, T151, T153, T155, T162, T164	T31, T41, T45, T55, T65, T67, T69, T71, T73, T75, T87, T127, T137, T139, T141, T143, T153, T155, T157, T195
T273, T275, T277, T289, T291, T293	T241, T257, T273, T281, T289		T271	T195
	T75, T81, T155, T175, T185, T289	T33, T109	T33, T69, T199, T209, T217, T235, T331	T35, T129, T145, T197, T207, T221, T262
T51, T82–T83, T263, T279, T295, T297	T45, T59, T61, T63, T65, T72–T73, T135, T155, T237, T255, T278, T286	T298, T311	T30, T163, T164, T174, T281, T283, T285, T289, T299, T307 T316–T319	T82, T84, T85, T143, T165, T166, T167, T179, T294

Unit 4	Unit 5	Unit 6	Unit 7	Unit 8
T94			T69	T77
T209, T285, T305, T315		T263, T299		T94, T159, T224, T305
T94, T209, T285, T313	T193, T289	T86, T164, T263, T299	T217, T232, T309	T94, T97, T167, T224, T305

CALIFORNIA RESOURCES

Correlation to California Reading/Language Arts Standards Grade K

Writing

	Unit 1	Unit 2	Unit 3
Penmanship			
1.4 Write uppercase and lowercase letters of the alphabet independently, attending to the form and proper spacing of the letters.	T108–T109, T130–T131, T147, T161, T189, T203, T215, T225–T226, T234, T238, T252–T253, T278, T281, T299, T317, T331	T24, T36–T37, T54, T66, T94, T114, T129, T140, T150, T164, T176–T177, T186, T198, T222, T248, T265, T281, T288	T213, T223, T277, T289

Written and Oral English Language Conventions

The standards for written and oral English language conventions have been placed between those for writing and for listening and speaking because these conventions are essential to both sets of skills.

	Unit 1	Unit 2	Unit 3
1.0 Written and Oral English Language Conventions Students write and speak with a command of standard English conventions.			
Sentence Structure			
1.1 Recognize and use complete, coherent sentences when speaking.	T41, T63, T83, T91, T113, T145, T158–T159, T169, T205–T206, T223, T233, T258, T284, T296, T329	T23, T34–T35, T77, T93, T116, T139, T147	T38, T76, T118, T157, T184, T203, T208, T222, T284
Spelling			
1.2 Spell independently by using pre-phonetic knowledge, sounds of the alphabet, and knowledge of letter names.			

Listening and Speaking

	Unit 1	Unit 2	Unit 3
1.0 Listening and Speaking Strategies Students listen and respond to oral communication. They speak in clear and coherent sentences.			
Comprehension			
1.1 Understand and follow one- and two-step oral directions.	T24, T41, T43, T46, T49, T51, T53, T55, T57, T59, T62–T63, T65–T66, T69, T71, T75, T77, T79, T82–T85	T22–T25, T34–T37, T43, T45, T52, T54–T56, T64–T67, T76–T78, T92–T95, T98, T101, T103, T107, T112	T22–T23, T25, T34–T35, T41, T43, T45, T47, T51–T53, T68–T72, T73, T76–T77, T80, T92–T94, T101
1.2 Share information and ideas, speaking audibly in complete, coherent sentences.	T89, T167, T230, T323, T330	T75, T145, T173, T183, T203, T290	T115, T181, T195, T203, T205
2.0 Speaking Applications (Genres and Their Characteristics) Students deliver brief recitations and oral presentations about familiar experiences or interests, demonstrating command of the organization and delivery strategies outlined in Listening and Speaking Standard 1.0. Using the listening and speaking strategies of kindergarten outlined in Listening and Speaking Standard 1.0, students:			
2.1 Describe people, places, things (e.g., size, color, shape), locations, and actions.	T28, T30, T36, T39, T45, T53, T61, T81, T89, T97, T106, T110, T113, T128, T132, T141, T148, T157, T162, T174	T25–T26, T29, T39–T40, T47, T51, T55–T56, T67–T68, T81, T98, T111, T116, T125, T130, T137, T143, T145	T26, T29, T31, T33, T37–T38, T51, T59, T63, T67, T75, T83, T98, T117, T122, T133, T136, T147, T153, T155
2.2 Recite short poems, rhymes, and songs.	T24–T26, T28, T40–T42, T63–T64, T82–T84, T90, T92, T94, T108, T125, T130, T146, T160, T163–T165, T188	T22, T36, T53–T54, T65–T66, T76, T78, T92, T94, T112, T114, T126–T128, T140, T142–T143, T148, T162, T164	T26, T148, T156, T172, T184, T192, T199, T282
2.3 Relate an experience or creative story in a logical sequence.	T221	T75, T203	T49, T65, T136, T152, T210, T243, T257, T278

Unit 4	Unit 5	Unit 6	Unit 7	Unit 8
T27, T35, T57, T61, T77, T81, T87, T91, T94, T97, T111, T129, T133, T141, T145, T153, T157, T165, T169, T175	T37, T71, T79, T83, T95, T127, T142, T143, T155, T179, T206, T209, T221, T261, T289	T25, T37, T69, T86, T89, T101, T123, T137, T161, T164, T167, T193, T203, T219, T225, T237, T263, T295, T299, T311	T25, T33, T37, T57, T71, T73–T74, T93, T105, T129, T171, T177, T199, T203, T213, T217, T229, T235, T331	T94, T97, T167, T179, T224, T229, T305, T307
T93, T306	T40, T56, T98, T128, T140, T148, T151, T176, T195, T197, T202, T209, T246, T262, T276, T285	T234, T260	T86, T172, T190, T230, T296, T326	T22, T25, T39, T61, T91, T92, T174, T189, T200, T209, T216, T223, T224, T239, T263, T277, T293, T301, T302
			T292	T92, T94, T264, T277
T22, T24, T26–T27, T36–T39, T42, T45, T47, T49, T53, T59–T61, T78–T81, T88–T91, T93–T95, T106	T22–T25, T30–T31, T34–T37, T43, T47, T52–T56, T67–T73, T76–T77, T79–T81, T92–T95, T98, T101	T22–T25, T34–T37, T43, T47, T49, T51, T54–T58, T66–T70, T72, T82–T85, T98–T101, T104, T107, T109	T22–T25, T34–T37, T40, T43, T45, T47, T49, T51, T53, T56–T60, T70–T74, T76, T86–T90, T102, T103	T22–T25, T36–T39, T49, T53, T55, T58–T62, T78–T81, T83–T84, T88, T90–T92, T94, T106–T109, T115
T35, T57, T75, T77, T87, T97, T165, T172, T195, T205, T213, T221, T231, T312	T111, T123, T137, T145, T155, T175, T185, T193, T201, T281	T81, T189, T199, T207, T215, T225, T259, T273, T291, T301, T311	T85, T199, T209, T215, T217, T223, T225, T235, T273, T321	T129, T145, T159, T169, T179, T197, T207, T213, T221, T229, T261, T299
T28, T33, T41, T55, T62, T94, T129, T134, T141, T146, T153, T158, T165, T172, T175, T189, T211, T219, T228, T265	T26, T31, T33, T39–T40, T51, T56, T67, T75, T80, T83, T97, T115–T116, T119, T169–T170, T191, T199, T224	T31, T33, T39, T53, T65, T81, T89, T104, T119, T133, T138, T147, T154, T157, T164, T167, T183, T197, T205, T213	T26, T31, T35, T40, T55, T67, T69, T76, T85, T93, T107–T108, T125, T143, T157, T167, T177, T193, T204, T207	T26, T33, T41–T42, T45, T47, T51, T65, T67, T69, T71, T73, T75, T85, T111–T112, T150, T191, T202, T211
T22, T25, T36, T58, T80, T85, T88, T90, T108, T143, T167–168, T196, T206, T208, T214, T224, T240, T242, T263	T36, T54, T70, T78, T112, T114, T124, T166, T186, T202, T282	T34, T68, T83, T98, T157, T192, T215, T216, T218	T22, T36, T56, T72, T74, T85, T126, T190, T200, T226, T244, T291, T326, T331	T36, T38, T78, T85, T143, T146, T157, T198, T213–T214, T221–T222, T229, T276, T300
T85, T165, T263, T295, T302, T303, T305	T65, T72, T123, T135, T143, T255, T263, T278–T279	T131, T155, T162, T298, T306	T163–T164, T174, T317–T318	T85, T143, T157, T165, T167, T294, T296, T297, T302

California Resources

CALIFORNIA RESOURCES

Correlation to California Reading/Language Arts Standards Grade 1

Reading

	Unit 1	Unit 2	Unit 3	Unit 4
1.0 Word Analysis, Fluency, and Systematic Vocabulary Development Students understand the basic features of reading. They select letter patterns and know how to translate them into spoken language by using phonics, syllabication, and word parts. They apply this knowledge to achieve fluent oral and silent reading.				
Concepts About Print				
1.1 Match oral words to printed words.	T66–T67, T102M, T128, T148, T167, T184–T186, T203, T224, T250, T265–T266, T268, T284, T286, T289–T290, T306-T310	T27–T30, T44, T46–T48, T66–T70, T88, T90–T93, T104, T108–T110, T112, T134, T138–T142, T156, T160, T162	T25, T27–T29, T44–T45, T63–T65, T79–T80, T97–T98, T123–T126, T143–T145, T157–T158, T180–T181, T195	T23–T26, T28–T29, T38, T40, T42–T44, T58, T60, T62–T64, T80–T82, T94, T96–T98, T120–T122, T139
1.2 Identify the title and author of a reading selection.	T50, T55, T70, T88, T132, T148, T152, T175, T190, T211, T250, T252, T272, T290, T310	T30, T48, T70, T92, T93, T112, T142, T164, T184, T202, T224, T228, T254, T274, T278, T296, T316, T332	T28–T29, T35, T44–T45, T48, T64–T66, T80, T82, T98, T100, T108, T124–T126, T130, T144–T146, T158, T162	T26, T28–T29, T35, T44, T64, T66, T82, T84, T98, T100, T122, T126, T144–T146, T162–T164, T180, T198–T200
1.3 Identify letters, words, and sentences.	T25, T27–T28, T30–T33, T42–T43, T45–T47, T53–T54, T56, T60–T61, T63–T64, T66–T67, T71, T73	T22–T28, T30, T40–T41, T43–T46, T48, T53, T62, T65–T68, T70, T75, T87–T90, T92–T93, T95, T104	T23–T26, T28–T29, T39–T42, T44–T45, T49, T53, T59–T61, T64–T65, T67, T71, T76–T78, T80, T83	T22–T26, T28–T29, T38–T42, T44, T48, T58–T62, T64, T67, T78–T82, T94–T98, T118–T122, T138–T139
Phonemic Awareness				
1.4 Distinguish initial, medial, and final sounds in single-syllable words.	T33, T42, T44, T46, T60–T62, T64, T72, T80–T81, T84, T90, T98–T100, T108, T124–T125, T128, T134, T142	T22–T26, T28–T29, T40–T41, T44, T46–T47, T62–T66, T69, T84–T85, T88, T91, T104–T108, T116, T135	T22–T27, T38–T40, T58–T60, T62–T63, T76–T77, T79, T94–T97, T120–T123, T132, T140–T141, T143, T155	T22–T23, T25, T39–T40, T42–T43, T58–T60, T63, T78–T81, T94–T97, T118–T119, T121, T138, T140–T141
1.5 Distinguish long- and short vowel sounds in orally stated single-syllable words (e.g., *bit/bite*).	T64, T84, T128, T166, T181, T200, T224, T264, T265, T282	T43, T159–T161, T194, T218–T219, T246, T266, T288, T291, T308–T309, T328	T22, T38, T94–T95, T140, T216, T246–T248	T23, T96, T139–T140, T158–T159, T176–T177, T193–T194, T196, T216–T217, T220, T238–T240, T256–T257, T270, T284
1.6 Create and state a series of rhyming words, including consonant blends.	T141, T144, T161, T163, T173, T175, T179, T192, T199, T215, T224, T282, T321	T68, T84, T147	T264	T61, T118, T194
1.7 Add, delete, or change target sounds to change words (e.g., change *cow* to *how; pan* to *an*).	T144, T180, T201, T208, T224–T225, T244–T245, T263	T22–T23, T40–T41, T62, T84, T104–T105, T107, T134–T135, T156, T176, T194, T195, T198, T216–T217, T266, T268	T22, T43, T94, T174, T192, T246, T264	T37, T118, T120, T192, T225, T269, T272, T283, T297
1.8 Blend two to four phonemes into recognizable words (e.g., /c/a/t/ = cat; /f/l/a/t/ = flat).	T102, T125, T148, T162–T163, T183, T192, T225, T245, T250, T262, T266, T283, T286, T289–T290, T305, T307–T308, T310	T23–T24, T26–T27, T41–T42, T44–T45, T46, T63–T64, T66–T68, T84–T86, T88, T105–T106, T108, T135	T25, T28–T29, T40, T44–T45, T60, T64–T65, T77, T80, T96, T98, T122–T126, T141, T144–T145, T158, T176	T23–T26, T28–T29, T40, T44, T60, T64, T80, T82, T96, T98, T118–T119, T121–T122, T141, T144–T145, T158
1.9 Segment single syllable words into their components (e.g., /c/a/t/ = cat; /s/p/l/a/t/ = splat; /r/i/c/h/ = rich).	T26, T43, T125, T143, T163, T167, T183, T185, T201, T203, T263, T266, T283, T286, T289, T305, T307	T23–T24, T28–T29, T41–T43, T46–T47, T63–T64, T66, T68–T69, T84, T90–T91, T106, T109–T110, T136	T43, T157, T179, T195, T235, T249, T269, T285	T25, T40, T42, T60, T62, T80–T81, T96–T97, T119, T141, T143, T159, T161, T177, T194, T196, T218, T220, T239
Decoding and Word Recognition				
1.10 Generate the sounds from all the letters and letter patterns, including consonant blends and long- and short-vowel patterns (i.e., phonograms), and blend those sounds into recognizable words.	T98, T226, T266, T284, T306	T28–T29, T47, T66, T69, T88, T91, T107, T137, T141, T163, T177, T183, T201, T223, T253, T268, T273, T295, T315	T25, T27, T40, T60, T63, T77, T79, T96–T97, T123, T141, T143, T156–T157, T179, T195, T221, T234–T235, T247	T22, T25, T40, T43, T58, T60, T63, T81, T96–T97, T118–T119, T121, T141, T143, T159, T161, T179, T194, T197
1.11 Read common, irregular sight words (e.g., *the, have, said, come, give, of*).	T65–T67, T71, T85, T101–T103, T187, T203, T286, T307	T22, T44–T45, T66, T88, T134, T180, T194, T198, T220, T250, T292, T312, T329	T67, T83, T163, T183, T199, T225, T239, T247, T255, T273	T24, T40, T58, T60, T80, T94, T96, T119, T141, T146, T165, T177, T181, T194, T216, T218, T227, T240
1.12 Use knowledge of vowel digraphs and *r*-controlled letter-sound associations to read words.			T233, T234, T281	T80, T81
1.13 Read compound words and contractions.		T198	T77, T183	T126–T127, T137, T157, T175, T177, T191, T194, T207, T251

Unit 5	Unit 6	Unit 7	Unit 8	Unit 9	Unit 10
T24-T25, T27-T29, T40-T45, T61, T63-T64, T67, T78-T79, T81, T96-T97, T100-T101, T103, T124-T125	T27-T32, T43-T46, T62, T64-T65, T79-T82, T97-T100, T122-T123, T125, T143- T147, T160, T163, T174-T175	11Z, 12A-12B, 26K-26L, 46K-46L, 66K-66L, 66O, 86A-86B, 86E, 92K-92L, 98A-98B, 99E-99F	101W-101X, 101FF, 102A-102B, 112A-112C, 112E, 124K-124L, 124O, 132A-132B, 132E, 154K-154L, 154O, 180K-180L, 180O	11W-11X, 12A-12B, 36K-36L, 38A-38B, 54K-54L, 70A-70B, 84K-84L, 90A-90B, 120K-120L, 122A-122C	137N, 137X, 138A-138B, 150A-150B, 158K-158L, 180K-180L, 200A-200B, 206K-206L, 206N, 220A-220B, 220D, 236K-236L
T28-T29, T35, T44-T45, T48, T64, T66, T82, T100-T102, T128-T129, T132, T148, T152, T163, T178, T194, T224	T28- T32, T46, T50, T82, T100, T130, T136, T146-T148, T164, T178, T180, T196, T222, T238-T239, T242, T258, T260	12C, 26M, 46M, 66M, 86C, 92M	101DD, 124M, 132C, 154M, 180M	11DD, 12C, 36M, 38E, 54M, 70C, 84M, 90C, 120M, 120, 122E	
T22-T25, T28-T29, T38-T42, T44-T45, T60-T64, T78-T79, T81, T94-T97, T100-T101, T108, T122-T125	T26-T32, T42-T46, T51, T57, T62-T65, T67, T78-T82, T85, T96-T98, T100, T113, T122-T123, T125-T126	11Z, 12A-12B, 26K-26L, 46K-46L, 66K-66L, 86A-86B, 92K-92L, 98A-98B, 99E-99F	101W-101X, 102A-102D, 112A, 112, 124K-124L, 132A-132B, 135, 154K-154L, 180K-180L, 195I-195J	11W-11X, 12A-12B, 35D, 36K-36L, 38A-38B, 54K-54L, 70A-70B, 84K-84L, 90A-90B, 92, 120K, 122A	137N, 137X, 138A-138B, 150A-150B, 158K-158L, 180K-180L, 200A-200B, 206K-206L, 220A-220B, 236K-236L, 261I-261J
T22, T24, T27, T38, T40, T42-T43, T60-T61, T63, T79, T81, T94-T96, T124-T125, T143, T145, T158-T159	T27, T42-T45, T63, T65, T78-T79, T81, T96-T97, T99, T122, T125, T142-T143, T145, T160, T163, T190, T192	12A-12B, 26K, 46K-46L, 66K, 86A-86B, 92K, 99F	101W, 101FF, 102A-102B, 111E-111F, 112A-112B, 123E-123F, 124K-124L, 129F, 132A, 153E-153H, 179F-179J	11W, 12A, 36K, 38A, 54K, 70A, 84K, 90A, 121, 122A, 135G	137W, 137FF, 149E-149F, 150A, 157E, 158K, 180K, 197F-197G, 206K, 220A, 236K, 261I
T38-T39, T41, T60, T63, T78, T81, T96, T122, T142-T143, T145, T161, T174, T177, T191, T218, T245, T262, T287	T44, T62-T65, T78, T122, T160, T174, T192-T193, T296	11Z, 12A-12B, 26K-26L, 46K, 66L, 86A-86B, 98A-98B, 99E	112A, 129F, 132A, 153E-153H, 154K, 179F-179J, 195F-195K, 195Q-195R	11W, 12A, 36K, 38A, 38D, 38L, 54K, 90A, 120K, 122A-122B	137W, 206K, 236K, 261I
T45, T142, T191, T276	T62, T141, T159, T173, T179, T189, T207, T277		127B	36, 120M	261J
T22, T93, T142-T143, T190, T221, T287, T304	T45, T81, T90, T141, T159, T173, T189, T190, T207, T254	11Z	112A, 123E	54L	
T24, T26, T28-T29, T40-T41, T44-T45, T61, T64, T79, T94, T96, T100-T101, T123-T124, T128-T129, T143	T28-T32, T43-T46, T64, T78-T79, T81-T82, T97, T100, T122-T123, T143-T144, T146-T147, T160, T175, T178	12A, 26K-26L, 46K, 66K, 86A, 92K, 98A, 99E	101W, 102A, 112A, 124K, 132A, 154K, 180K, 195I	11W, 12A, 36K, 38A, 38B, 54K, 70A, 84K, 90A, 120K, 135G	137W, 138A, 138B, 150A, 158K, 180K, 200A, 206K, 236K, 261I
T41-T42, T63, T79, T81, T96-T97, T123-T125, T144-T145, T160-T161, T176-T177, T192, T220, T264-T265	T27, T45, T65, T79, T81, T98-T99, T145, T163, T177, T192, T219, T257, T278, T297-T298	12B, 46L, 66L, 86B, 92L, 98A-98B, 99F	101X, 102B, 112B, 124L, 132B, 154L, 180K-180L, 195J	11X, 12B, 36L, 38B, 54L, 70B, 84L, 90B, 120K-120L, 122C, 135H	137X, 138B, 180L, 200B, 206L, 220B, 236L, 260J
T27, T43, T63, T81, T123, T145, T161, T176-T177, T190, T220, T242, T245, T265, T287, T307	T27, T44-T45, T64-T65, T81, T99, T125, T144-T145, T177, T193, T219, T257, T279, T299	11Z, 12A, 26K, 46K, 66K-66L, 86A, 92K, 98A-98B, 99E	101W, 101FF, 102A, 111E-111F, 112A, 112D-123F, 124K, 124M, 129F, 132A, 153E-153H, 154N, 179F-179I, 180K-180L, 180N	12A, 36K, 38A, 54L, 70A, 84K, 90A, 120K, 122A, 135G	137W, 137FF, 138A, 149E-149F, 150A, 157E-157F, 180K, 197F-197G, 200A, 206K, 220A-220B, 236K, 261I
T160, T246, T264		11Z, 12A, 12E, 26K, 46K-46L, 66O, 86A, 92K, 92O, 99E	124O, 132A, 132F, 153K, 154P, 180K, 180P, 195I	11W, 12A, 36K, 120K, 135G-135H	150B, 206N, 261I-261J
T96, T124, T143-T145, T159-T160, T191, T242, T264	T78, T97-T98, T144, T160-T161, T235, T255		101FF, 111E-111F, 123E-123F, 129F, 153E-153H, 195F-195I, 195Q-195R	11W, 84K-84L, 120K, 122A-122B, 135H	137FF, 149E-149F, 157E-157F, 158K, 179F-179G, 179I-179J, 197F-197G, 206K, 220A, 260I
T51, T88, T176, T278	T44, T234	46K, 99E	120-121, 134-135, 139-140, 169	11W, 90A, 135G	193, 197G, 200A, 201, 236K

CALIFORNIA RESOURCES

Correlation to California Reading/Language Arts Standards — Grade 1

Reading	Unit 1	Unit 2	Unit 3	Unit 4
1.14 Read inflectional forms (e.g., *-s, -ed, -ing*) and root words (e.g., *look, looked, looking*).	T272	T44, T178, T250	T156, T218, T282	T24, T227, T261
1.15 Read common word families (e.g., *-ite, -ate*).		T44, T140, T180		T256
1.16 Read aloud with fluency in a manner that sounds like natural speech.	T103, T149, T251, T269, T291, T311	T31, T49, T71, T113, T143, T165, T185, T203, T225, T230, T249, T255, T271, T275, T292, T297, T317, T333	T29, T45, T65, T81, T99, T125, T127, T145, T159, T176, T181, T193, T197, T223, T237, T251, T287, T289	T27, T29, T40, T45, T60, T65, T80, T83, T96
Vocabulary and Concept Development				
1.17 Classify grade-appropriate categories of words (e.g., concrete collections of animals, foods, toys).	T41, T51, T59, T79, T97, T115, T159, T171	T39, T61, T83, T103, T125, T155, T175, T193, T215, T237, T263, T265, T287, T307, T325, T341	T37, T49, T51, T53, T57, T67, T69, T75, T83, T85, T87, T93, T101, T103, T105, T111, T131, T139, T147, T149	T30, T57, T69, T71, T77, T87, T93, T103, T109, T127
2.0 Reading Comprehension Students read and understand grade-level-appropriate material. They draw upon a variety of comprehension strategies as needed (e.g., generating and responding to essential questions, making predictions, comparing information from several sources). The selections in *Recommended Readings in Literature, Kindergarten Through Grade Eight* illustrate the quality and complexity of the materials to be read by students. In addition to their regular school reading, by grade four, students read one-half million words annually, including a good representation of grade-level-appropriate narrative and expository text (e.g., classic and contemporary literature, magazines, newspapers, online information). In grade one, students begin to make progress toward this goal.				
Structural Features of Informational Materials				
2.1 Identify text that uses sequence or other logical order.	T252, T257, T282		T120	T175, T191, T225, T269, T283, T291
Comprehension and Analysis of Grade-Level-Appropriate Text				
2.2 Respond to *who, what, when, where,* and *how* questions.	T38, T103, T110, T136, T149, T156, T187, T194, T241, T251, T256, T269, T291, T311	T31, T35, T49, T56, T71, T78, T92, T93, T95, T97, T113, T117, T120, T143, T165, T185, T203, T210, T225, T255	T28–T29, T33, T44–T45, T51, T61, T64–T65, T70, T72, T81, T88, T99, T107, T124–T125, T127, T134, T136	T27–T29, T45, T65, T83, T99, T123, T132, T144–T145, T152, T162, T170, T186, T198–T199, T202, T222–T223, T233
2.3 Follow one-step written instructions.			T275	
2.4 Use context to resolve ambiguities about word and sentence meanings.	T54, T191, T195, T233, T243, T261, T273, T281, T303, T323	T147, T151, T229, T233, T279, T299, T319	T131, T135, T147	T70, T247, T248, T262, T263
2.5 Confirm predictions about what will happen next in a text by identifying key words (i.e., signpost words).	T273, T293	T205	T67, T68, T83, T84, T101	
2.6 Relate prior knowledge to textual information.	T50, T70, T88, T110, T132, T152, T170, T190, T206, T232, T272, T314	T94, T114, T186, T206–T207, T229, T257, T279, T298–T299, T318–T319, T321	T30, T47–T50, T83, T86, T89, T101, T104, T106, T130–T131, T146–T147, T162, T198, T224, T238, T254, T272	T48, T66, T84, T126, T146, T164
2.7 Retell the central ideas of simple expository or narrative passages.	T257	T52, T58, T147, T149, T152, T169, T171, T207, T229, T231, T257, T259, T261–T262, T299, T303, T319	T66, T82, T100, T146, T163, T183, T187, T199, T225, T238–T239	T66, T72, T132, T152, T170, T186, T202, T232, T250, T264, T278
3.0 Literary Response and Analysis Students read and respond to a wide variety of significant works of children's literature. They distinguish between the structural features of the text and the literary terms or elements (e.g., theme, plot, setting, characters). The selections in *Recommended Readings in Literature, Kindergarten Through Grade Eight* illustrate the quality and complexity of the materials to be read by students.				
Narrative Analysis of Grade-Level-Appropriate Text				
3.1 Identify and describe the elements of plot, setting, and character(s) in a story, as well as the story's beginning, middle, and ending.	T136, T233, T235, T237–T238, T256, T257, T299		T66	T133
3.2 Describe the roles of authors and illustrators and their contributions to print materials.	T55, T57, T86, T95, T104, T150, T168, T188, T204, T211, T230, T243, T261, T270, T277, T281, T299, T303, T312, T323	T50, T72, T205, T227, T276	T46, T82, T129, T161, T182, T253	T225
3.3 Recollect, talk, and write about books read during the school year.			T290	

Unit 5	Unit 6	Unit 7	Unit 8	Unit 9	Unit 10
T124, T177, T191, T220–T221, T242, T305	T44, T217-T219, T236, T297	12A-12B, 66K	112A, 124K	120K, 122A, 135G	138A, 150A
	T141, T159, T173, T189, T207	12B, 99F			
T29, T41, T61, T65, T79, T96, T101, T124, T129, T144, T160, T163, T176, T179, T191, T195, T220, T225, T242, T247	T33, T37, T281	11Z, 12A, 26K, 46K, 66K, 86A, 92K, 96A, 98A, 99E-99F	102E, 124K, 132A, 153K, 154L, 180K, 195I	11W, 12A, 12W, 36K, 36N, 38A-38B, 38G, 54K, 54O, 70E, 84K, 84O, 90B, 90E, 120K, 120N, 122G, 135H	138E, 150B, 150E, 158O, 180O, 200E, 206N, 206Q, 220D, 220G, 236O, 260J
T37, T59, T77, T113, T201, T239, T254, T261, T283, T303, T315	T41, T61, T71, T77, T95, T113, T141, T159, T173, T189, T207, T233, T253, T275, T295	23B	111E-111F, 113, 121B, 127B, 151B, 153E-153G, 177B, 193B, 195H	39, 41, 43, 45, 47	138F, 139, 145, 149E-149F, 157E-157F, 179H
T253, T275	T197, T203, T265		103, 105, 107, 180O, 181, 195M	51E	149D, 150C, 236M, 246
T28-T29, T44-T45, T65, T100-T101, T108, T128-T129, T162-T163, T179, T195, T224-T225, T247, T268-T269, T288	T29-T31, T33, T37, T47, T56, T71-T72, T83, T89-T90, T92, T100, T108, T127, T136, T138, T146-T147, T154	11DD, 13, 22, 25, 43, 43A, 63, 63A, 81A, 89A, 95A	109, 121, 127, 130, 151, 177, 193	33, 51, 81	137BB, 147, 203
					149,157,205
T37, T73, T93, T103, T113, T141, T150, T157, T173, T181, T189, T204, T229, T251, T273	T51, T85, T131, T149, T165, T181, T197, T223, T233, T242, T253, T275, T285, T295, T307	66O	132E, 148, 155, 161	12F, 25, 33C, 40, 70E, 84P, 122G, 133C	150C, 150E, 155C, 158O, 180O, 206Q, 220G, 236O, 258
	T131, T149, T165, T181, T185, T197		154, 170, 180O, 185, 190	38G, 54O, 84O, 87C, 90E, 122G	158O, 206Q
T30, T66, T82, T102, T132, T197, T228, T250, T272, T292	T34, T50, T66, T84, T85, T102, T130, T131, T148-T149, T164, T165, T169, T180-T181, T196, T222, T242, T264, T284	11AA, 12C, 26M, 46M, 66M, 86C, 92M, 98C	101Y, 102G, 112C, 124M, 132C, 154M, 179G-179I, 180M, 195Q	11Y, 12C, 36M, 38E, 54M, 70C, 84M, 90C, 122E	137Y, 138C, 150C, 158M, 158O, 180M, 200C, 200E, 206O, 220E, 236M, 236O
T70, T74, T134, T153	T49, T51, T67, T69, T71, T85, T87, T89, T138, T149, T165, T181	11DD, 22-23, 23A, 26, 89C	122, 133, 135, 143, 145, 147, 149, 151C, 180O, 180, 192	28, 38G, 51C, 51E, 54O, 81E, 84O, 90E- 90F, 109, 122G	138F, 180O, 200F, 201, 203C, 220G, 247
T46, T126, T142, T148	T67	23E, 63E, 81E, 89E, 93, 95C, 95E, 97A	109C, 109E, 121A, 151E, 193F	33E, 51E, 65E, 73, 75, 77, 79, 81E, 87, 87E	217E
T46, T130, T141, T146, T152, T173, T189, T204		11P, 24, 26B, 66B, 92B, 96	110, 124B, 154B, 178, 180B, 194	34, 52, 66, 82, 88, 118, 134	137N, 137Y, 148, 156, 158B, 178, 196, 204, 206B, 218, 234, 236B, 260
			195M		251

Correlation to California Reading/Language Arts Standards — Grade 1

Writing

	Unit 1	Unit 2	Unit 3	Unit 4
1.0 Writing Strategies Students write clear and coherent sentences and paragraphs that develop a central idea. Their writing shows they consider the audience and purpose. Students progress through the stages of the writing process (e.g., prewriting, drafting, revising, editing successive versions).				
Organization and Focus				
1.1 Select a focus when writing.	T79, T97, T115, T141, T159, T161, T175, T179, T195–T196, T199, T215, T318	T125, T212, T262, T284, T304, T323	T37, T57, T75, T93, T111, T139, T148, T153, T173, T191, T207, T228, T231, T242, T245, T263, T277, T279, T295	T37, T57, T137, T157, T237, T281
1.2 Use descriptive words when writing.		T61, T83	T149, T163, T173	
Penmanship				
1.3 Print legibly and space letters, words, and sentences appropriately.	T28, T31, T33, T45, T63, T83, T84, T100, T101, T115, T127, T129, T145–T146, T165–T166, T183–T185, T203, T248	T89, T125, T221, T237, T307, T341	T111, T171, T207, T260, T284, T295	T61, T109, T160, T207, T297
2.0 Writing Applications (Genres and Their Characteristics) Students write compositions that describe and explain familiar objects, events, and experiences. Student writing demonstrates a command of standard American English and the drafting, research, and organizational strategies outlined in Writing Standard 1.0. Using the writing strategies of grade one outlined in Writing Standard 1.0, students:				
2.1 Write brief narratives (e.g., fictional, autobiographical) describing an experience.	T215, T243, T261, T281, T303, T323	T237, T287, T307, T325, T341		
2.2 Write brief expository descriptions of a real object, person, place, or event, using sensory details.			T173, T188, T207, T277, T279, T295	

Written and Oral English Language Conventions

The standards for written and oral English language conventions have been placed between those for writing and for listening and speaking because these conventions are essential to both sets of skills.

	Unit 1	Unit 2	Unit 3	Unit 4
1.0 Written and Oral English Language Conventions Students write and speak with a command of standard English conventions appropriate to this grade level.				
Sentence Structure				
1.1 Write and speak in complete, coherent sentences.	T88, T89, T92, T199, T243, T261, T281	T175, T193, T263, T285	T191	T80, T297
Grammar				
1.2 Identify and correctly use singular and plural nouns.			T139, T153, T173, T231, T241, T245, T263	
1.3 Identify and correctly use contractions (e.g., *isn't, aren't, can't, won't*) and singular possessive pronouns (e.g., *my/mine, his/her, hers, your/s*) in writing and speaking.	T126			
Punctuation				
1.4 Distinguish between declarative, exclamatory, and interrogative sentences.		T155, T175, T193, T265, T287, T307	T187	T137, T157, T175, T269
1.5 Use a period, exclamation point, or question mark at the end of sentences.	T243, T261, T281	T155, T175, T193, T287, T292, T307, T312	T27, T62, T97, T143, T179, T187, T221, T249, T285	T137, T157, T175, T237, T255, T269
1.6 Use knowledge of the basic rules of punctuation and capitalization when writing.	T141, T161, T179, T243, T281	T175, T193, T307	T62, T97, T143, T179, T221, T249, T285	T77, T109, T175, T207, T269, T297

Unit 5	Unit 6	Unit 7	Unit 8	Unit 9	Unit 10
T37, T59, T141, T189, T229, T261	T41, T61, T110, T141, T159, T186, T233, T253, T275		109F, 111E, 121A, 123F, 129F, 153E, 153H, 179F-179G, 179J, 195F-195G, 195R	117E	137FF, 149E, 179F-179G, 197F-197G, 259F
T37, T57, T59, T77, T129, T239, T261, T276, T283, T303			111F, 153F-153G, 179H-179I, 195H	51E, 121B	149F, 179I
T113, T173, T204, T283, T315	T113, T207		123F, 153H, 179J, 195R		157F, 179J
				117D	
T77, T129, T204	T77, T95, T173, T186, T189, T295	98D	123E, 153F-153G, 179H-179I, 195H, 195Q		
T57, T175, T189, T239, T315	T275	26O, 66O, 86E	129F, 153E-153F, 153H, 195H, 195Q-195R	117O, 121B	149E, 157F, 179I
			179F-179H, 195G-195H		179F-179H, 197F-197G
	T72	26O	101FF, 111E-111F, 195F, 195H	115	
T75, T113, T315	T113, T184, T202, T207, T307		111F, 123F, 153G-153H, 179J, 195F, 195H, 195R		
T75, T108, T113, T315	T41, T61, T72, T77, T106, T113, T136, T141, T154, T159, T168, T173, T184, T202, T207, T233, T253, T270, T290, T307		111F, 153H, 179J, 195R	133E	157F

CALIFORNIA RESOURCES

Correlation to California Reading/Language Arts Standards — Grade 1

Written and Oral English Language Conventions

	Unit 1	Unit 2	Unit 3	Unit 4
Capitalization				
1.7 Capitalize the first word of a sentence, names of people, and the pronoun *I*.	T41, T59, T79, T243, T261, T281	T155, T175, T180, T287, T307	T27, T62, T97, T143, T157, T179, T195, T221, T235, T249, T269, T285	T37, T57, T77, T237, T255, T269
Spelling				
1.8 Spell three- and four-letter short-vowel words and grade-level-appropriate sight words correctly.	T65, T101, T129, T147, T167, T185, T203, T289	T46, T68, T84, T90, T104, T109–T110, T134, T140, T156, T162, T176, T183, T194, T200, T215–T216, T219, T222, T246	T27, T43, T62, T79, T143, T157, T179, T195, T221, T235, T249, T269, T285	T42, T62, T81, T97, T121, T143, T161, T179, T196, T220, T273, T288

Listening and Speaking

	Unit 1	Unit 2	Unit 3	Unit 4
1.0 Listening and Speaking Strategies Students listen critically and respond appropriately to oral communication. They speak in a manner that guides the listener to understand important ideas by using proper phrasing, pitch, and modulation.				
Comprehension				
1.1 Listen attentively.	T25, T32, T43, T97, T137, T156, T182, T248, T266	T23, T25, T42–T43, T86, T106, T113, T157, T203, T298, T319, T325, T337–T338	T23, T37, T93	T37, T78, T138
1.2 Ask questions for clarification and understanding.	T54, T71, T75, T92, T103, T107, T111, T149, T171, T175, T187, T210, T233, T251, T269, T291, T298, T311, T319	T31, T49, T71, T75, T92, T93, T99–T100, T106, T122, T143, T150, T152, T165, T172, T185, T210, T215, T225, T232	T28, T29, T44–T45, T52, T62, T64–T65, T81, T99, T124–T125, T127, T144–T145, T159, T163, T169, T180–T181	T27–T29, T45, T65, T67, T83, T99, T123, T144–T145, T147, T162, T165, T191, T198–T199, T222–T223, T227, T242
1.3 Give, restate, and follow simple two-step directions.	T97		T275	
Organization and Delivery of Oral Communication				
1.4 Stay on the topic when speaking.	T74, T92, T156, T298, T318	T258		T227
1.5 Use descriptive words when speaking about people, places, things, and events.	T110, T154, T156, T210, T298, T318	T103, T155, T171, T193, T198, T215, T237, T265, T287, T307	T279	T93
2.0 Speaking Applications (Genres and Their Characteristics) Students deliver brief recitations and oral presentations about familiar experiences or interests that are organized around a coherent thesis statement. Student speaking demonstrates a command of standard American English and the organizational and delivery strategies outlined in Listening and Speaking Standard 1.0. Using the speaking strategies of grade one outlined in Listening and Speaking Standard 1.0, students:				
2.1 Recite poems, rhymes, songs, and stories.	T24, T27, T39, T42, T45, T60, T63, T80, T85, T98, T106, T108, T113, T124, T142, T144, T153, T162, T177, T180	T22, T40, T44, T62, T84, T104, T176, T194, T216, T218, T291, T308	T120, T140, T192, T216, T255	T22, T23, T139, T192–T193, T217, T237, T251, T255, T283, T285, T291
2.2 Retell stories using basic story grammar and relating the sequence of story events by answering *who, what, when, where, why,* and *how* questions.	T103, T149, T187, T251, T269, T291, T311	T31, T42, T49, T63, T71, T86, T92, T93, T95, T113, T136, T143, T157, T165, T185, T203, T225, T255, T275, T297	T28–T29, T44–T45, T64–T65, T81, T99, T124, T125, T127, T136, T144–T145, T159, T180–T181, T187, T197, T199	T27–T29, T45, T65, T83, T99, T123, T144–T145, T162, T198–T199, T222–T223, T242, T275, T290–T291
2.3 Relate an important life event or personal experience in a simple sequence.	T152, T206	T52, T228, T278		T226, T260–T261, T283
2.4 Provide descriptions with careful attention to sensory detail.	T90, T154, T210			

Unit 5	Unit 6	Unit 7	Unit 8	Unit 9	Unit 10
T75, T108, T113, T234, T315	T72, T113, T154, T207, T270, T290, T307		123F, 153H, 179J, 195R		157F
T26, T42, T97, T113, T125, T177, T192, T245, T265, T287, T307	T65, T96, T113, T142, T145, T163, T177, T207, T276, T298	12B, 46L, 66L, 86B, 92L, 98B, 99F	101X, 123F, 124L, 132B, 154L, 179J, 180L, 195J, 195R	11X-11Y, 12B, 36L, 38C, 54L, 70B, 84L, 90B, 120L, 122C-122D, 135H	137X, 138B, 150B, 150L, 179J, 180L, 200B, 206L, 220B, 236L, 260J
T37, T57, T69, T75, T85, T93, T105, T139, T255, T275, T277	T41, T100, T281, T301	83D, 98D	101Y, 111E, 123E	11Y, 90C, 107, 120M	137Y, 149E, 157E, 259E
T28-T29, T44-T45, T49, T57, T65, T70, T72, T75, T86, T88-T101, T128, T139, T152, T162-T163, T179, T181	T28-T31, T33, T47, T51, T56, T58, T67, T72, T74, T83, T85, T87, T90, T100, T102, T108, T136, T138, T146	11DD, 43A, 63A, 81A, 89A, 92M, 95A	110, 111C, 112C, 112E, 112, 120, 123E, 188	33A, 51A, 81A, 87A, 90C, 100	137BB, 155A, 177A, 195A, 200E, 203A, 217A, 233A, 259A
T77, T122		92K	107, 127B		203E
	T295		195D, 195Q		261M
T74			111E-111F, 119, 123E, 153E-153F, 179I	90C, 96, 98	179I, 230, 233E, 261M
T39, T124, T276, T284	T78, T142, T191, T234-T235	98D	125, 127	37B, 92, 107, 121	177E
T28-T29, T44-T45, T65, T100-T101, T128, T162-T163, T179, T195, T224-T225, T247, T268-T269, T288-T289, T309	T28-T31, T33, T47, T83, T92, T127, T146-T147, T179, T238-T239, T259-T261, T281, T295, T301-T302	23A	102, 106, 108-109, 109A, 109C, 121, 132E, 151, 177E, 193, 195M, 195Q	33, 37, 51, 65, 81, 87A, 135I	217E
		86C, 98C		14, 54O, 65C, 70E, 120	
		81F	119, 121E, 124, 127, 179I	21, 39, 45	233E

CALIFORNIA RESOURCES

Correlation to California Reading/Language Arts Standards Grade 2

Reading

	Unit 1	Unit 2
1.0 Word Analysis, Fluency, and Systematic Vocabulary Development Students understand the basic features of reading. They select letter patterns and know how to translate them into spoken language by using phonics, syllabication, and word parts. They apply this knowledge to achieve fluent oral and silent reading.		
Decoding and Word Recognition		
1.1 Recognize and use knowledge of spelling patterns (e.g. diphthongs, special vowel spellings) when reading.	14, 14K, 14N, 14P-14Q, 15-19, 21, 26L, 26N, 26-41, 46L, 46N, 46Q, 47-51, 62, 62N, 62P	108L, 108N, 108P, 108-116, 120L, 120N, 120-121, 123-124, 126-130, 132, 135, 138L-138N, 138, 140, 142
1.2 Apply knowledge of basic syllabication rules when reading (e.g. vowel-consonant-vowel= *su/per*; vowel-consonant/consonant-vowel = *sup/per*).	14K, 14M-14N, 14P-14Q, 15-19, 21, 26K, 26M-26N, 26P, 26-35, 37-40, 46K, 46M-46N, 46Q	108K, 108M-108N, 108P, 108-111, 113, 115, 116, 120M-120N, 120-121, 124, 126-127, 129, 132, 138K, 138M
1.3 Decode two-syllable nonsense words and regular multisyllable words.	14K, 14M-14N, 14P, 15-19, 21, 26K, 26M-26N, 26, 29-30, 32-33, 35, 37-40, 46K, 46M	108K, 108M, 108P, 108-111, 113, 115-116, 120K, 120M-120N, 120P, 120-121, 124, 126-127, 129, 132, 138K
1.4 Recognize common abbreviations (e.g., *Jan., Sun., Mr., St.*).		
1.5 Identify and correctly use regular plurals (e.g., *-s, -es, -ies*) and irregular plurals (e.g., *fly/flies, wife/wives*).	84K, 84-85, 87-90, 93-94, 97, 101, 103	120K, 124, 126, 128-130, 156K, 156, 161-162, 170, 172
1.6 Read aloud fluently and accurately and with appropriate intonation and expression.	14N, 14Q, 26N, 26Q, 41, 45A, 46N, 46Q, 57, 62N, 62Q, 81A, 84N, 84Q	108L, 108N, 108Q, 120L, 120N, 120Q, 138L, 138N, 156L, 156N, 180L, 180N, 180Q, 200L, 200N, 222L, 222N
Vocabulary and Concept Development		
1.7 Understand and explain common antonyms and synonyms.	62N, 105H	
1.8 Use knowledge of individual words in unknown compound words to predict their meaning.	14M, 26K, 26P, 26, 29-30, 39-40, 46K, 61I, 62P	180K, 180, 188, 190, 192, 200K, 200-201, 205-206, 209, 213, 216, 222K, 222-223, 225, 233
1.9 Know the meaning of simple prefixes and suffixes. (e.g. *over-, un-, -ing, -ly*).	26P, 46K, 46P, 47, 49-51, 62K, 62P, 62-63, 65, 69-72, 76-77	108K-108L, 108P, 109-112, 114-116, 117B, 120K, 120P, 121, 123, 127, 135, 138K, 138P, 138, 140, 143-144
1.10 Identify simple multiple-meaning words.	14N, 26N, 46N, 62N, 84N	
2.0 Reading Comprehension Students read and understand grade-level-appropriate material. They draw upon a variety of comprehension strategies as needed (e.g., generating and responding to essential questions, making predictions, comparing information from several sources). The selections in *Recommended Readings in Literature, Kindergarten Through Grade Eight* illustrate the quality and complexity of the materials to be read by students. In addition to their regular school reading, by grade four, students read one-half million words annually, including a good representation of grade-level-appropriate narrative and expository text (e.g., classic and contemporary literature, magazines, newspapers, online information). In grade two, students continue to make progress toward this goal.		
Structural Features of Informational Materials		
2.1 Use titles, table of contents, and chapter headings to locate information in expository text.	43D	
Comprehension and Analysis of Grade-Level-Appropriate Text		
2.2 State the purpose in reading (i.e., tell what information is sought).	14P, 26P, 46P, 62P, 84P	108P, 108R, 120P, 120R, 138P, 138R, 156P, 156R, 180P, 180R, 200P, 200R, 222P, 222R
2.3 Use knowledge of the author's purpose(s) to comprehend informational text.	15, 17, 19, 21	
2.4 Ask clarifying questions about essential textual elements of exposition (e.g., *why, what if, how*).		153C, 155G-155I, 208, 222
2.5 Restate facts and details in the text to clarify and organize ideas.	27, 29, 31, 33, 35, 37, 39, 41	15, 108Q, 110, 114, 117E, 121, 123, 131, 133, 161-165, 167, 169, 174, 201, 203, 205, 207-209, 211
2.6 Recognize cause-and-effect relationships in a text.		147, 149, 151, 153, 223, 225, 227, 229, 231, 233
2.7 Interpret information from diagrams, charts, and graphs.		153E, 177D, 233F
2.8 Follow two-step written instructions.		117B, 155D

Unit 3	Unit 4	Unit 5	Unit 6
238N, 238P, 238Q, 238-248, 252L, 252N, 252P, 252-258, 260, 262, 268N, 268P, 268, 270-272, 274-275, 277	14L, 14O, 14-19, 21, 23, 26-27, 30K-30L, 30O, 30-32, 34, 37, 42L, 42N-42O, 42, 47	122L, 122N-122O, 122, 148N, 160N, 160, 178L, 178N, 178, 196L, 196N-196O, 196, 212L, 212N, 212	248L, 248, 250-256, 258, 260-263, 268L, 268, 270-274, 276-280, 284L, 284-293, 298L, 298-302, 305
238D, 238K-238Q, 238-242, 244-246, 248, 252K-252N, 252P, 252-254, 260, 268K, 268M, 268P, 268-269, 278	14K-14L, 14N-14O, 14-15, 17, 19-21, 24-25, 27, 30K-30L, 30N-30O, 30, 33-34, 37	122K, 122N-122O, 122, 148K, 148N, 148, 160K-160L, 160N, 160, 178K-178L, 178N, 196K-196L, 196N-196O, 212K-212L	248K-248L, 248, 251-256, 258, 260-263, 268K-268L, 270-274, 276-277, 279-280, 284K-284L, 284-288
238K-238N, 238P, 238-242, 244-246, 248, 252K-252N, 252-254, 259-261, 268K, 268P, 268-269, 278-284	14K-14L, 14N, 14-15, 17, 19-22, 24-25, 27, 27B, 30K-30L, 30N, 30, 33-34, 37, 42K	122K, 122N, 122, 148K, 148N, 148, 160K, 160N, 160, 178K, 178N, 178, 196K, 196N, 196, 212K, 212N, 212	248L, 248K, 248, 251-258, 260-263, 268K-268L, 268, 270-277, 279-280, 284K-284L, 284-288, 290-293
	113	178K	362K
256, 334K, 334-335, 337-343, 346, 349, 351-353, 355, 357	42K, 42-43, 45-46, 50-51, 119D	178K, 212K	248K, 298K, 298-302, 305-307, 309
238L, 238N, 249, 252N, 252Q, 262, 268N, 268Q, 296L, 296N, 296Q, 314L, 314N, 314Q, 334L, 334N, 334Q, 356	14L, 14O, 30L, 30O, 42L, 42O, 64L, 64O, 82L, 82O, 92L, 92O, 119D	122L, 122O, 148L, 148O, 155, 160L, 160O, 178L, 178O, 196L, 196O, 212L, 212O	248L, 248O, 268L, 284L, 284O, 298L, 298O, 316L, 316O, 336L, 362L
252N, 291B	39G-39J, 40, 79G-79I, 82L, 89B, 91G, 117B, 119H, 119J	145G-145H, 145J, 148L, 155G, 155J, 160L, 178L, 212K	362K
251I, 265G-265J, 268P, 293G-293J, 296P, 314P, 334K-334L, 334P, 334, 336, 342, 344, 347, 349-350, 354, 359H	14K, 14, 18-19, 27, 30K, 30, 33, 37, 37B, 42N, 64N, 82K, 82N, 92N	148N, 160L, 178O, 196N, 212K, 212N	254, 258, 284K, 297G-297I, 362K, 362, 365
238K, 241, 244, 246, 252D, 254, 268M, 313G-313J, 314D, 333G-333J, 334M, 339, 359G, 359I	14K-14L, 14-15, 17, 21, 23, 26, 27B, 37B, 42K, 42N, 46, 48, 54, 64K, 64N, 64, 66, 68	122K, 148K, 148N, 178K, 178O, 195G-195J, 196K, 196N, 209G, 211H-211I, 212N	283G-283J, 248K, 248, 250, 252, 268K, 268, 270-271, 273, 316K, 316, 319-320, 326, 375I
242, 244, 296N	82K, 82, 85	160K	316K, 333G-333I
263F, 333D, 357E	61D		295F
238P, 252P, 263F, 268P, 296P, 314P, 334P	14N, 14P, 30N, 30P, 42N, 42P, 64N, 64P, 82N, 92N, 119D	122N, 148N, 160N, 178N, 178P, 196N, 196P, 212N	268N, 284N, 316N
297, 299, 301, 303	14M, 77D, 82N, 89E		257, 259, 261, 263, 265, 265D, 311D
244, 246, 318, 320, 342	16, 18, 44, 52, 100, 110	134, 164, 168, 170, 193C, 196, 198, 206, 208, 212	248, 268, 280, 284, 286, 288, 290, 295C, 304, 306, 318, 348, 352
239-241, 243-245, 247, 249, 249C, 268R, 272, 276, 282, 286, 300, 304-307, 309, 311, 315, 317, 319	14O, 15, 17, 19, 21-23, 25, 27, 31, 33, 35, 37, 37C, 43, 45-47, 49, 51, 53-55	123, 125, 127, 129, 131, 133, 135, 137, 139, 141, 143, 143E, 152, 155C, 166, 200, 203-205, 207, 209	249, 251, 253-256, 258-259, 262, 264, 278, 281C, 299, 301, 303-305, 307, 309, 311, 331E, 342, 346
281, 283, 285, 287, 289, 291	65, 67	161, 163, 165, 167, 169, 171, 173, 173C, 173D, 219, 221, 223, 225, 229, 237, 241	269, 271, 273, 275, 277, 279, 281, 281C
	57, 59	145E, 157E, 175E, 195E, 211D-211E, 245E	265E, 283E, 297E, 313E, 333E, 361E, 375E
	82D, 82P, 89C		

California Resources

CALIFORNIA RESOURCES

Correlation to California Reading/Language Arts Standards — Grade 2

Reading

	Unit 1	Unit 2
3.0 Literary Response and Analysis Students read and respond to a wide variety of significant works of children's literature. They distinguish between the structural features of the text and the literary terms or elements (e.g., theme, plot, setting, characters). The selections in *Recommended Readings in Literature, Kindergarten Through Grade Eight* illustrate the quality and complexity of the materials to be read by students.		
Narrative Analysis of Grade-Level-Appropriate Text		
3.1 Compare and contrast plots, settings, and characters presented by different authors.	41D, 43, 61, 81, 103E, 105	137, 150, 155, 197, 221, 233F, 235
3.2 Generate alternative endings to plots and identify the reason or reasons for, and the impact of, the alternatives.		136, 153D, 231, 233D
3.3 Compare and contrast different versions of the same stories that reflect different cultures.	21C	233F, 235
3.4 Identify the use of rhythm, rhyme, and alliteration in poetry.	25A, 45A, 59D	

Writing

	Unit 1	Unit 2
1.0 Writing Strategies Students write clear and coherent sentences and paragraphs that develop a central idea. Their writing shows they consider the audience and purpose. Student progress through the stages of the writing process (e.g., prewriting, drafting, revising, editing successive versions).		
Organization and Focus		
1.1 Group related ideas and maintain a consistent focus.		
Penmanship		
1.2 Create readable documents with legible handwriting.	23J, 43J, 61J, 81J, 105J	119J, 137J, 155J, 177J, 197J, 221J, 235J
Research		
1.3 Understand the purposes of various reference materials (e.g., dictionary, thesaurus, atlas).	61G, 81G–81J, 105G–105H, 105J	119D, 221I
Evaluation and Revision		
1.4 Revise original drafts to improve sequence and provide more descriptive detail.		197H
2.0 Writing Applications (Genres and Their Characteristics) Students write compositions that describe and explain familiar objects, events, and experiences. Student writing demonstrates a command of standard American English and the drafting, research, and organizational strategies outlined in Writing Standard 1.0. Using the writing strategies of grade two outlined in Writing Standard 1.0, students:		
2.1 Write brief narratives based on their experiences: a. Move through a logical sequence of events. b. Describe the setting, characters, objects, and events in detail.		
2.2 Write a friendly letter complete with the date, salutation, body, closing, and signature.		137F–137J, 155F–155J

Written and Oral English Language Conventions

The standards for written and oral English language conventions have been placed between those for writing and for listening and speaking because these conventions are essential to both sets of skills.

	Unit 1	Unit 2
1.0 Written and Oral English Language Conventions Students write and speak with a command of standard English conventions appropriate to this grade level.		
Sentence Structure		
1.1 Distinguish between complete and incomplete sentences.		
1.2 Recognize and use the correct word order in written sentences.		
Grammar		
1.3 Identify and correctly use various parts of speech, including nouns and verbs, in writing and speaking.	23F–23H, 61F–61H	

Unit 3	Unit 4	Unit 5	Unit 6
263E, 291D, 331B, 333	61, 82M, 92P	157, 175, 178P, 196G, 204, 209E, 212P, 232, 243E, 245	274, 284P, 295B, 297A, 322, 328, 331E, 333, 338, 359C, 361, 361A
329		211	281B, 331E, 373E
301, 311D	41A		311D, 315A

Unit 3	Unit 4	Unit 5	Unit 6
251H	79G, 91H		
251J, 265J, 293J, 313J, 333J, 359J	29J, 39J, 61J, 79J, 91J, 119J	145J, 157J, 175J, 195J, 211J, 245J	267J, 283J, 297J, 313J, 333J, 361J, 375J
251H	29H, 61I, 79I	175I	267J, 361J
	91I, 119I	145I, 175I, 245I	
		145F-145J, 157F-157J, 175F-175J, 211F-211J	

Unit 3	Unit 4	Unit 5	Unit 6
333F-333H			
313F-313H			
265F	61F-61H, 79F-79H, 91F-91H		

California Resources

CALIFORNIA RESOURCES

Correlation to California Reading/Language Arts Standards — Grade 2

Written and Oral English Language Conventions

	Unit 1	Unit 2
Punctuation		
1.4 Use commas in the greeting and closure of a letter and with dates and items in a series.		137F-137H, 177F-177H, 221F-221H
1.5 Use quotation marks correctly.		135E, 197F-197H
Capitalization		
1.6 Capitalize all proper nouns, words at the beginning of sentences and greetings, months and days of the week, and titles and initials of people.	23F-23H	119F-119H, 137F-137H, 138N, 155F-155H
Spelling		
1.7 Spell frequently used, irregular words correctly (e.g., *was, were, says, said, who, what, why*).		
1.8 Spell basic short-vowel, long-vowel, r-controlled, and consonant-blend patterns correctly.	23F-23J, 43F-43J, 61F-61J, 81F-81J, 105F-105J	119G-119J, 137G-137J, 155G-155J, 197G-197J, 221G-221J, 235G-235J

Listening and Speaking

	Unit 1	Unit 2
1.0 Listening and Speaking Strategies Students listen critically and respond appropriately to oral communication. They speak in a manner that guides the listener to understand important ideas by using proper phrasing, pitch, and modulation.		
Comprehension		
1.1 Determine the purpose or purposes of listening (e.g., to obtain information, to solve problems, for enjoyment).	23I, 25B, 59A, 103B	117A, 119A, 119I, 153A, 198, 199B, 235C
1.2 Ask for clarification and explanation of stories and ideas.	23A, 41A, 59A, 79A, 103A, 105I	117A, 135A, 153A, 175A, 195A, 219A, 221C, 233A, 235C
1.3 Paraphrase information that has been shared orally by others.	23A, 41A, 59A, 79A, 103A	117A, 135A, 153A, 175A, 195A, 219A, 233A
1.4 Give and follow three- and four-step oral directions.		153F
Organization and Delivery of Oral Communication		
1.5 Organize presentations to maintain a clear focus.		221C, 235C
1.6 Speak clearly and at an appropriate pace for the type of communication (e.g., informal discussion, report to class).	23A, 41A, 43I, 44, 45B, 59A, 61I, 79A, 103A	117A, 119A, 135A, 137I, 199B, 221C, 235C
1.7 Recount experiences in a logical sequence.	41F, 45B, 79	221I
1.8 Retell stories, including characters, setting, and plot.	23A, 81A	235I
1.9 Report on a topic with supportive facts and details.		221C, 235C
2.0 Speaking Applications (Genres and Their Characteristics) Students deliver brief recitations and oral presentations about familiar experiences or interests that are organized around a coherent thesis statement. Student speaking demonstrates a command of standard American English and the organizational and delivery strategies outlined in Listening and Speaking Standard 1.0. Using the speaking strategies of grade two outlined in Listening and Speaking Standard 1.0, students:		
2.1 Recount experiences or present stories: a. Move through a logical sequence of events. b. Describe story elements (e.g., characters, plot, setting).		235I
2.2 Report on a topic with facts and details, drawing from several sources of information.		235C

Unit 3	Unit 4	Unit 5	Unit 6
		195F-195H	
	29F-29J	145F-145J, 175F-175J, 245F-245J	313F-313J, 333F-333J, 361F-361J, 375F-375J
251F-251J, 265F-265J, 293F-293J, 313F-313J, 333F-333J, 359F-359J	61F-61J, 79F-79J	145F-145J	
251I, 267, 291B, 311A, 311D, 359C	29I, 37A, 41B, 62, 63B, 59F, 77A, 91A, 119C	145I, 143A, 155E, 173A, 209A, 245C	265C, 314, 315B, 333I
249A, 263A, 291A, 311A, 331A, 331I, 357A, 359C	27A, 37A, 59A, 77A, 89A, 117A, 119C	143A, 155A, 173A, 193A, 245C	331A, 359A, 361I
249A, 263A, 291A, 311A, 331A, 357A	27A, 37A, 59A, 77A, 89A, 117A	143A, 155A, 173A, 193A	267I, 331A, 359A
	91A		
313I, 333F-333J	119C	155E, 195C, 211C	375I
249A, 263A, 267B, 291A, 311A, 331A, 357A	27A, 37A, 39I, 41B, 59A, 59F, 62, 63B, 77A, 89A, 91I, 117A, 119C, 119I	143A, 155A, 157I, 173A, 193A, 243A, 245C, 245I	314, 315B
	27A, 59F, 62, 63B, 91I	129, 175I	
291D		145J, 157J, 175J, 211J, 245J	
313I-313J, 359C	119C	155E, 195C, 211C	311E-311F, 375I
		157I	311F
313I, 359C	119C	155E, 195C, 211C	313D

California Resources

CALIFORNIA RESOURCES

Correlation to California Reading/Language Arts Standards Grade 3

Reading

	Unit 1	Unit 2
1.0 Word Analysis, Fluency, and Systematic Vocabulary Development Students understand the basic features of reading. They select letter patterns and know how to translate them into spoken language by using phonics, syllabication, and word parts. They apply this knowledge to achieve fluent oral and silent reading.		
Decoding and Word Recognition		
1.1 Know and use complex word families when reading (e.g., *-ight*) to decode unfamiliar words.		126K, 136K, 166M
1.2 Decode regular multisyllabic words.	61G–61J, 94K, 94M	166K, 182K, 182M
1.3 Read aloud narrative and expository text fluently and accurately and with appropriate pacing, intonation, and expression.	19Q, 19, 28Q, 33, 48, 64Q, 82Q, 94Q	114Q, 126Q, 136Q, 148Q
Vocabulary and Concept Development		
1.4 Use knowledge of antonyms, synonyms, homophones, and homographs to determine the meanings of words.	28K, 48K, 111G, 111I, 111J	114K, 125G, 125J, 126K, 145G–145J, 148P, 181G–181J, 195G, 195H, 195I
1.5 Demonstrate knowledge of levels of specificity among grade-appropriate words and explain the importance of these relations (e.g., *dog/mammal/animal/living things*).		115, 117, 119, 121, 123, 133G–133J, 195G
1.6 Use sentence and word context to find the meaning of unknown words.	14P, 27G, 27I, 28P, 45G–45I, 48P, 82P, 91B, 94P	109B, 114P, 114Q, 123B, 136P, 148P, 161B, 163G–163J, 166P, 179B, 182P, 193B, 195G
1.7 Use a dictionary to learn the meaning and other features of unknown words.	93F	133H, 133I, 145I, 163G, 163I, 181H, 181I, 193B
1.8 Use knowledge of prefixes (e.g., *un-, re-, pre-, bi-, mis-, dis*) and suffixes (e.g., *-er, -est, -ful*) to determine the meaning of words.	28K, 48K, 82K	114K, 166K
2.0 Reading Comprehension Students read and understand grade-level-appropriate material. They draw upon a variety of comprehension strategies as needed (e.g., generating and responding to essential questions, making predictions, comparing information from several sources). The selections in *Recommended Readings in Literature, Kindergarten Through Grade Eight* illustrate the quality and complexity of the materials to be read by students. In addition to their regular school reading, by grade four, students read one-half million words annually, including a good representation of grade-level-appropriate narrative and expository text (e.g., classic and contemporary literature, magazines, newspapers, online information). In grade three, students make substantial progress toward this goal.		
Structural Features of Informational Materials		
2.1 Use titles, tables of contents, chapter headings, glossaries, and indexes to locate information in text.	93D	133D, 163D, 195D
Comprehension and Analysis of Grade-Level-Appropriate Text		
2.2 Ask questions and support answers by connecting prior knowledge with literal information found in, and inferred from, the text.	81I	198O
2.3 Demonstrate comprehension by identifying answers in the text.	25, 27J, 43, 59, 79, 91, 111H	120, 123, 126, 131, 138, 143, 145H, 150, 161, 170, 176
2.4 Recall major points in the text and make and modify predictions about forthcoming information.	79C	140, 142, 160, 161C, 178, 192
2.5 Distinguish the main idea and supporting details in expository text.	83, 85, 87, 89, 91C	161
2.6 Extract appropriate and significant information from the text, including problems and solutions.	14O, 25A, 28P, 43A, 48O, 59A, 64O, 65, 79A, 82O, 91, 94O, 95, 97, 99, 101, 103, 105, 107, 109	114, 123A, 126O, 131A, 136O, 143A, 148O, 149, 151, 154, 155, 157, 159, 161, 161A, 161C, 163A, 166O, 179, 182O
2.7 Follow simple multiple-step written instructions (e.g. how to assemble a product or play a board game).		

Unit 3	Unit 4	Unit 5	Unit 6
213F-213J, 223G, 237G, 237H, 260M, 269G, 269J	14K, 25G-25J, 35G, 35H, 35I, 38K, 48K, 58K, 72K, 93G, 94K, 105I	120K, 143G-143I, 146K, 158K, 168K, 179G, 180K	236K, 247F-247J, 250K, 261F-261J, 262K, 284K, 295H, 295I
198Q, 216Q, 224Q, 240K, 240M, 250K, 250M, 250P, 260M	48K, 58K, 72K, 72N, 94K	146K, 158K, 168K, 180K	236K, 250K, 262K, 284K
198K, 240Q, 250Q, 260Q	140, 260, 28, 380, 40, 480, 580, 93, 93H	1080, 1200, 128K, 1280, 145B, 1460, 1580, 1680, 175, 180	1980, 2040, 2160, 2360, 2500, 2620, 2840
198K, 260K	14K, 26K, 72K	108K, 120K, 127G-127J, 146K, 193G	204K, 213G-213J, 216K, 230G-230J, 233G-233J, 295G
198K, 251, 253, 255, 257, 257C		117G-117J, 147, 149, 151, 153, 193G	259C
198P, 216P, 224P, 237I, 240P, 249G-249J, 250P, 259G-259J, 260, 269H, 269I	14N, 26N, 38N, 45B, 47G-47J, 48N, 53B, 58N, 69B, 69C, 72N, 91B, 93H, 94N, 103B, 105G, 105H	108N, 120N, 125B, 127G-127I, 128N, 146N, 153B, 155G-155I, 158N, 163B, 165G-165I, 168N, 177B, 180N, 181B, 193I	204N, 211B, 216N, 236N, 245B, 247G, 247I, 250N, 259B, 262N, 281B, 284N, 293B, 295H
237D, 249G, 249I, 250P, 259D, 259G	69B, 71G, 71I, 93H, 93I, 105H, 105I	117G-117I, 125E, 127H, 143G, 155G, 155I, 163B, 165G, 165H, 180N, 193D, 193I	203G, 213H, 233H, 236N, 250N, 262N, 283G, 283I, 284N
216K, 223G-223J, 224K, 224M, 237G-237J, 240M, 250K, 269G, 269H	25G-25J, 26K, 35G-35J, 38K, 58K, 72K, 94K	120K, 128K, 143G-143J, 179G-179J, 193G, 193H, 198K	204K, 233F-233J, 236K, 250K, 262K
47D, 93A, 93D	155C, 165D, 193D		247A
216O, 240O, 249, 259	48M, 55A, 55, 58, 69A, 71, 74M, 93, 94M, 103, 105	153, 158, 163A, 179, 182, 190, 191, 191A, 193	216M, 247, 261, 266, 281, 281A, 283, 285, 287-289, 291-293, 293A, 293C, 293D, 295
211, 221, 235, 247, 249G-249I, 254, 257, 259, 267A, 269	23, 33, 45, 50, 55, 68, 69C, 74, 82, 86, 93, 103, 103A, 105	115, 125, 141, 153, 155, 160, 163A, 165, 170, 177, 177A, 179, 180, 191, 191A, 193	201, 211, 213I, 231, 245, 247, 256, 259, 261, 270, 272, 281, 281A, 283, 286, 292, 293, 293A, 295
206, 216, 218, 230, 232, 256	16, 22, 23C, 64, 80, 90, 102	110, 112, 120, 125C, 138, 140, 153, 155, 160, 163, 174, 176, 177C, 186, 190	222, 224, 226, 230, 238, 252, 254, 268, 270, 276, 290
	39, 41, 43, 45, 91	153, 155, 169, 171, 173, 175, 177	245, 263, 265, 267, 281C
198, 211A, 216O, 221A, 224O, 235A, 241, 243, 245, 247, 247A, 247C, 247D, 250O, 257A, 260O, 267A, 267C, 269D	14M, 23A, 26M, 33A, 38M, 45A, 48M, 48N, 53, 69A, 72M, 74, 75, 77, 79, 81, 83, 85, 87, 89	108M, 115A, 120M, 125A, 128M, 141A, 146M, 146, 153A, 159M, 159, 161, 163, 165V, 168M, 177A, 178A, 180M, 181, 183	198M, 201A, 204M, 211A, 216M, 231A, 236M, 240, 242, 244, 245, 250M, 259, 259A, 262M, 269, 271, 273, 275, 27
	81D	115B, 117D, 128L, 146L, 193D	204L

CALIFORNIA RESOURCES

Correlation to California Reading/Language Arts Standards Grade 3

Reading

	Unit 1	Unit 2
3.0 Literary Response and Analysis Students read and respond to a wide variety of significant works of children's literature. They distinguish between the structural features of the text and literary terms or elements (e.g., theme, plot, setting, characters). The selections in *Recommended Readings in Literature, Kindergarten Through Grade Eight* illustrate the quality and complexity of the materials to be read by students.		
Structural Features of Literature		
3.1 Distinguish common forms of literature (e.g., poetry, drama, fiction, nonfiction).	25A, 43A, 59A, 91A, 91E, 109A, 109D	123A, 131, 131E, 143A, 143E, 148O, 165A, 193A
Narrative Analysis of Grade-Level-Appropriate Text		
3.2 Comprehend basic plots of classic fairy tales, myths, folktales, legends, and fables from around the world.	109, 109A	
3.3 Determine what characters are like by what they say or do and by how the author or illustrator portrays them.	59E, 79D, 81I	123D
3.4 Determine the underlying theme or author's message in fiction and nonfiction text.	27, 45, 61, 91, 109A	125, 133, 145, 183, 185, 187, 189, 191, 193, 193A, 193C
3.5 Recognize the similarities of sounds in words and rhythmic patterns (e.g., alliteration, onomatopoeia) in a selection.		134, 135A, 135B, 165B, 193E
3.6 Identify the speaker or narrator in a selection.	25D	182O

Writing

	Unit 1	Unit 2
1.0 Writing Strategies Students write clear and coherent sentences and paragraphs that develop a central idea. Their writing shows they consider the audience and purpose. Students progress through the stages of the writing process (e.g., prewriting, drafting, revising, editing successive versions).		
Organization and Focus		
1.1 Create a single paragraph: a. Develop a topic sentence. b. Include simple supporting facts and details.	27H, 45H, 61F-61J, 81H, 93H, 111H	125F-125J, 133F-133J, 145F-145J, 163F-163J, 181F-181J, 195F-195J
Penmanship		
1.2 Write legibly in cursive or joined italic, allowing margins and correct spacing between letters in a word and words in a sentence.	27J, 45J, 61J, 81J, 93J, 111J	125J, 133J, 145J, 163J, 181J, 195J
Research		
1.3 Understand the structure and organization of various reference materials (e.g., dictionary, thesaurus, atlas, encyclopedia).	45D, 81G-81J, 93G-93J	195F, 195G-195J
Evaluation and Revision		
1.4 Revise drafts to improve the coherence and logical progression of ideas by using an established rubric.	27I, 45I, 61I, 81F-81J, 93F-93J, 111I	125F-125J, 133F-133J, 145F-145J, 163F-163J, 181F-181J, 195I
2.0 Writing Applications (Genres and Their Characteristics) Students write compositions that describe and explain familiar objects, events, and experiences. Student writing demonstrates a command of standard American English and the drafting, research, and organizational strategies outlined in Writing Standard 1.0. Using the writing strategies of grade three outlined in Writing Standard 1.0, students:		
2.1 Write narratives: a. Provide a context within which an action takes place. b. Include well-chosen details to develop the plot. c. Provide insight into why the selected incident is memorable.		
2.2 Write descriptions that use concrete sensory details to present and support unified impressions of people, places, things, or experiences.		131C, 135A, 161D
2.3 Write personal and formal letters, thank-you notes, and invitations: a. Show awareness of the knowledge and interests of the audience and establish a purpose and context. b. Include the date, proper salutation, body, closing, and signature.		

Unit 3	Unit 4	Unit 5	Unit 6
211A, 217, 221A, 221C, 235A, 247A, 247E	23A, 33A, 45A, 45D, 53A, 53E, 69A, 91E, 102A	115A, 115E, 125A, 125D, 141A, 146M, 153A, 153D, 163A, 168M, 177A, 177D, 191A	201A, 211A, 231A, 245A, 245D, 259A, 281A, 293E
257A	69, 71	115E, 117A, 177A, 177D	259E
257A	33E, 59, 61, 63, 103D	153, 153A, 177, 191	259A, 293, 293A
213, 223, 237	25, 35, 47, 49, 51, 53, 53C, 91, 103A	117, 121, 123, 125, 127, 143	203, 213, 233, 237, 239, 241, 243, 245, 293
211D	37A, 69D	167A	
261, 263, 265, 267	65, 67, 69	141E, 145A, 146O, 163E, 187, 189, 191, 191C, 199A	211E, 215A, 281E
213H, 223H, 237H, 249H, 259H, 269H	25H, 35H, 47H, 55H, 71H, 93H, 105H	117H, 117J, 127H, 143H, 155H, 155J, 165H, 179H, 193H	203H, 213H, 233H, 247H, 261H, 283H, 295H
213J, 223J, 237J, 249J, 259J, 269J	25J, 35J, 47J, 55J, 71J, 93J, 105J	117H, 127H, 143H, 143J, 155H, 165H, 165J, 179H, 193H	203H, 203J, 213H, 213J, 233H, 233J, 247H, 247J, 261H, 261J, 283H, 283J, 295H
		127H	
213I, 223I, 237I, 249I, 259I, 269I	25I, 35I, 47I, 55I, 71I, 93I, 105I	117I, 127I, 143I, 155I, 165I, 179I, 193I	203I, 213I, 233I, 247I, 261I, 283I, 295I
		117G, 117H, 127H, 143H, 155H, 165G, 179G, 193H	
213H, 237H, 267E, 269H		167A, 195A	201C
	25H, 47G, 47H, 71H		213H, 233H, 247G, 283H

CALIFORNIA RESOURCES

Correlation to California Reading/Language Arts Standards — Grade 3

Written and Oral English Language Conventions

The standards for written and oral English language conventions have been placed between those for writing and for listening and speaking because these conventions are essential to both sets of skills.

1.0 Written and Oral English Language Conventions Students write and speak with a command of standard English conventions appropriate to this grade level.	Unit 1	Unit 2
Sentence Structure		
1.1 Understand and be able to use complete and correct declarative, interrogative, imperative, and exclamatory sentences in writing and speaking.	93F–93H, 111F–111H	
Grammar		
1.2 Identify subjects and verbs that are in agreement and identify and use pronouns, adjectives, compound words, and articles correctly in writing and speaking.	45F–45H, 61F–61H, 111F–111H	
1.3 Identify and use past, present, and future verb tenses properly in writing and speaking.		
1.4 Identify and use subjects and verbs correctly in speaking and writing simple sentences.	61F–61H, 81F–81H, 111F–111H	
Punctuation		
1.5 Punctuate dates, city and state, and titles of books correctly.		
1.6 Use commas in dates, locations, and addresses and for items in a series.		133F–133H, 195F–195H
Capitalization		
1.7 Capitalize geographical names, holidays, historical periods, and special events correctly.		163F–163H, 195F–195H
Spelling		
1.8 Spell correctly one-syllable words that have blends, contractions, compounds, orthographic patterns (e.g., *qu*, consonant doubling, changing the ending of a word from *-y* to *-ies* when forming the plural), and common homophones (e.g., *hair-hare*).	27F–27J, 45F–45J, 61F–61J, 81F–81J, 93F–93J, 111F–111J	125F–125J, 133F–133J, 145F–145J, 163F–163J, 181F–181J, 195F–195J
1.9 Arrange words in alphabetical order.	61D, 61H, 111	

Listening and Speaking

1.0 Listening and Speaking Strategies Students listen critically and respond appropriately to oral communication. They speak in a manner that guides the listener to understand important ideas by using proper phrasing, pitch, and modulation.	Unit 1	Unit 2
Comprehension		
1.1 Retell, paraphrase, and explain what has been said by a speaker.	27H, 43F, 111I	125I, 125J, 145H, 161C, 181J
1.2 Connect and relate prior experiences, insights, and ideas to those of a speaker.	43F, 93I	133G, 195A
1.3 Respond to questions with appropriate elaboration.	27I, 45I, 79A, 93I	118, 133H, 163H, 181I, 195A, 195J
1.4 Identify the musical elements of literary language (e.g., rhymes, repeated sounds, instances of onomatopoeia).	47A	193E
Organization and Delivery of Oral Communication		
1.5 Organize ideas chronologically or around major points of information.	111I	195I
1.6 Provide a beginning, a middle, and an end, including concrete details that develop a central idea.		
1.7 Use clear and specific vocabulary to communicate ideas and establish the tone.		109, 133I
1.8 Clarify and enhance oral presentations through the use of appropriate props (e.g., objects, pictures, charts).		123F, 131F, 163I
1.9 Read prose and poetry aloud with fluency, rhythm, and pace, using appropriate intonation and vocal patterns to emphasize important passages of the text being read.	28Q, 46, 47B, 48Q, 109E	114Q, 126Q, 135B, 164, 165B

Unit 3	Unit 4	Unit 5	Unit 6
			233F-233H
213F-213H, 223F-223H, 237F-237H, 259F-259H, 269F-269H	35F-35H, 55F-55H, 71F-71J, 105F-105H, 105J		233F-233H, 261F-261H, 283F-283H
223F-223H, 237F-237H, 269F-269H	55G-55J, 105-105J		261F-261H
223F-223H, 237F-237H, 269F-269H	35F-35H, 71F-71H, 105F-105H	117F-117H, 193F-193H	233F-233H, 261F-261H, 283F-283H, 295F-295H
		155F-155H, 193F-193H	203F-203H, 295F-295H
			203F-203H, 247F-247H
		165F-165H, 179F-179H, 193F-193H	247F-247H, 295F-295H
213F-213J, 223F-223J, 237F-237J, 249F-249J, 259F-259J, 269F-269J	14K, 25F-25J, 35F-35J, 47F-47J, 55F-55J, 71F-71J, 93F-93J, 105F-105J	117F-117J, 127F-127J, 143F-143J, 155F-155J, 165F-165J, 179F-179J, 193F-193J	203F-203J, 204K, 213F-213J, 233F-233J, 236K, 250K, 261F-261H, 262K, 283F-283J, 284K, 295F, 295G, 295J
			233E

Unit 3	Unit 4	Unit 5	Unit 6
213G, 213H, 213J, 221F	93I, 93J	125F, 127J, 145B	203I, 203J, 211F, 213G, 215B, 249B, 295I
221F, 262, 269I	23E, 78, 93A, 103A	125F, 127J, 145F, 179J	203I, 211F, 215B, 231F
223H, 232, 249J, 259I, 262	25I, 71I	153A, 163A, 165H, 179I	215B, 261I, 283H
211B, 221E, 237I	37A	141E, 167A	211E, 215A, 233I
249O	105D	125E, 127J, 145B	203E, 213E, 233E
	93I	127J	
223I	35I, 47I	115, 127J, 195B	213I, 249A
235F, 259A	25E, 35E, 47E, 55E, 71E, 93E, 105A, 105E	115F, 117E, 125E, 125F, 127E, 141F, 143E, 155E, 165E, 179E, 191F, 193E	201F, 211E, 211F, 231F, 233A
198Q, 215B, 216Q, 224Q, 235A, 250	140, 260, 37B, 380, 480, 720, 940	1080, 119B, 1200, 1280, 143I, 145, 1460, 1580, 166, 180, 194	1980, 2040, 211E, 2160, 2360, 248, 249A, 2500, 2620, 2840

California Resources

CALIFORNIA RESOURCES

Correlation to California Reading/Language Arts Standards — Grade 3

Listening and Speaking

Listening and Speaking	Unit 1	Unit 2
Analysis and Evaluation of Oral and Media Communications		
1.10 Compare ideas and points of view expressed in broadcast and print media.		
1.11 Distinguish between the speaker's opinions and verifiable facts.		
2.0 Speaking Applications (Genres and Their Characteristics) Students deliver brief recitations and oral presentations about familiar experiences or interests that are organized around a coherent thesis statement. Student speaking demonstrates a command of standard American English and the organizational and delivery strategies outlined in Listening and Speaking Standard 1.0. Using the speaking strategies of grade three outlined in Listening and Speaking Standard 1.0, students:		
2.1 Make brief narrative presentations: a. Provide a context for an incident that is the subject of the presentation. b. Provide insight into why the selected incident is memorable. c. Include well-chosen details to develop character, setting, and plot.		
2.2 Plan and present dramatic interpretations of experiences, stories, poems, or plays with clear diction, pitch, tempo, and tone.	47B, 109D	
2.3 Make descriptive presentations that use concrete sensory details to set forth and support unified impressions of people, places, things, or experiences.		

Grade 4

Reading

Reading	Unit 1	Unit 2
1.0 Word Analysis, Fluency, and Systematic Vocabulary Development Students understand the basic features of reading. They select letter patterns and know how to translate them into spoken language by using phonics, syllabication, and word parts. They apply this knowledge to achieve fluent oral and silent reading.		
Word Recognition		
1.1 Read narrative and expository text aloud with grade-appropriate fluency and accuracy and with appropriate pacing, intonation, and expression.	200, 320, 480, 660, 820, 1000, 1160	1260, 132, 1460, 1560, 1720, 1880, 2020
Vocabulary and Concept Development		
1.2 Apply knowledge of word origins, derivations, synonyms, antonyms, and idioms to determine the meaning of words and phrases.	20K, 32K, 48K, 48N, 66K, 67, 82K, 100K, 116K	126K, 132, 132K, 135, 137, 139, 143G, 143I, 143H, 146K, 156K, 166, 171G, 171I, 171H, 172K, 176, 202K, 205G, 205H
1.3 Use knowledge of root words to determine the meaning of unknown words within a passage.	48N, 82N, 100N, 116N, 117	126N, 156N, 172N, 188N
1.4 Know common roots and affixes derived from Greek and Latin and use this knowledge to analyze the meaning of complex words (e.g., international).	20K, 32K, 32N, 48K, 48N, 53, 82K, 86, 88, 90, 91, 92, 95, 100, 100K, 102, 103, 104, 109, 111	126K, 146K, 146L, 188K
1.5 Use a thesaurus to determine related words and concepts.	97D, 97G, 97H, 97I, 123G, 123I	126N, 132N, 146N, 156N, 172N, 188N, 202N
1.6 Distinguish and interpret words with multiple meanings.	66K, 73	132K, 133, 137, 138, 140
2.0 Reading Comprehension Students read and understand grade-level-appropriate material. They draw upon a variety of comprehension strategies as needed (e.g., generating and responding to essential questions, making predictions, comparing information from several sources). The selections in *Recommended Readings in Literature, Kindergarten Through Grade Eight* illustrate the quality and complexity of the materials to be read by students. In addition to their regular school reading, students read one-half million words annually, including a good representation of grade-level-appropriate narrative and expository text (e.g., classic and contemporary literature, magazines, newspapers, online information).		
Structural Features of Informational Materials		
2.1 Identify structural patterns found in informational text (e.g., compare and contrast, cause and effect, sequential or chronological order, proposition and support) to strengthen comprehension.	82P, 83, 85, 87, 89, 91, 93, 95, 95C	126P, 127, 129, 129C, 129E, 132P, 133, 135, 137, 139, 141, 147, 149, 156P, 157, 159, 161, 163, 165, 167

Unit 3	Unit 4	Unit 5	Unit 6
249I	55I	155I, 158P, 163C	216B
	25I, 25J	141C, 141D, 158P, 163C	
		179J, 179I	249B
	37B	145B, 193I, 193J, 195B	249B, 283I
213I, 256		195C	267B

Unit 3	Unit 4	Unit 5	Unit 6
2080, 2260, 2420, 2580, 2640, 2880, 3080,	3220, 3340, 3600, 3780, 3920, 4060	4160, 4260, 4340, 4460, 4760	4840, 4920, 5020, 5220, 5320, 5420
208K, 208N, 212, 221B, 226L, 237B, 239G, 242K, 242N, 253B, 258K, 261B, 264K, 264N, 270, 272, 274, 280, 285B	331B, 333G, 333H, 333I, 334K, 335, 338, 357B, 360K, 373B, 378K, 378N, 380, 381, 383, 384, 387B, 392K, 395	416K, 426K, 434K, 443G, 443H, 443I, 446K, 460K, 476K	484K, 489B, 492, 492K, 494, 495, 497B, 502K, 502N, 505B, 508K, 517B, 522K, 529B, 532K, 532N, 533, 536, 539B
210, 212, 213, 214, 215, 216, 218, 219, 270, 272	301, 334N, 335, 338, 380, 383, 384, 406N	426, 428	484N, 502, 508N, 532N, 533, 536, 542N
208K, 212, 213, 214, 215, 216, 218, 219, 221B, 237B, 253B, 285B, 305A, 308N, 317B	331B, 357B, 373B, 387B, 389G, 389I, 389H, 401B, 411B	416K, 426K, 446K, 460K, 476K	484N, 489B, 502K, 505B, 508K, 517B, 519G, 519H, 519I, 529B, 531G, 531H, 531I 532N, 539B, 545B
226L			
288K, 296	322K	433G, 433H, 433I, 460K	542K
208P, 209, 211, 213, 215, 217, 219, 221, 243, 245, 247, 261E	335, 337, 339, 341, 351, 353, 355, 357, 407, 411C	416P, 417, 419, 421, 460P, 461, 463, 465	485, 487, 489, 489C, 523, 525, 527, 529, 529C, 529E, 533, 535, 537, 539, 539D, 543, 545, 545C

CALIFORNIA RESOURCES

Correlation to California Reading/Language Arts Standards Grade 4

Reading

	Unit 1	Unit 2
Comprehension and Analysis of Grade-Level-Appropriate Text		
2.2 Use appropriate strategies when reading for different purposes (e.g., full comprehension, location of information, personal enjoyment).	20M, 32N, 48N, 66N, 82N, 100N, 116N	126N, 128, 132N, 140, 141C, 146N, 156N, 168, 172N, 188N, 198, 202, 202N
2.3 Make and confirm predictions about text by using prior knowledge and ideas presented in the text itself, including illustrations, titles, topic sentences, important words, and foreshadowing clues.	20M, 32M, 48M, 63A, 66M, 82M, 111A, 116M, 121A	126M, 129A, 132M, 141A, 146M, 151A, 156M, 172M, 188M, 196, 199A, 199C, 202M
2.4 Evaluate new information and hypotheses by testing them against known information and ideas.		128
2.5 Compare and contrast information on the same topic after reading several passages or articles.	47A, 79B	131, 143, 143A, 146N, 153, 153A, 181, 187, 201, 201A, 205
2.6 Distinguish between cause and effect and between fact and opinion in expository text.		
2.7 Follow multiple-step instructions in a basic technical manual (e.g., how to use computer commands or video games).		
3.0 Literary Response and Analysis Students read and respond to a wide variety of significant works of children's literature. They distinguish between the structural features of the text and literary terms or elements (e.g., theme, plot, setting, characters). The selections in *Recommended Readings in Literature, Kindergarten Through Grade Eight* illustrate the quality and complexity of the materials to be read by students.		
Structural Features of Literature		
3.1 Describe the structural differences of various imaginative forms of literature, including fantasies, fables, myths, legends, and fairy tales.	29A, 45A, 48M, 63A, 63F, 66M, 77A, 116M, 121A, 121E	199D, 203A, 203D, 203F
Narrative Analysis of Grade-Level-Appropriate Text		
3.2 Identify the main events of the plot, their causes, and the influence of each event on future actions.	21, 23, 25, 29, 29A, 45A, 63A, 69, 71, 77A, 95A, 111A, 113, 121A	185, 185A, 199A, 203, 203A,
3.3 Use knowledge of the situation and setting and of a character's traits and motivations to determine the causes for that character's actions.	29E, 31, 45E, 47, 69, 71, 79, 111A, 111E, 121A, 123	143, 185A, 185C, 187, 189, 191, 197, 199, 199A, 201, 203A, 205
3.4 Compare and contrast tales from different cultures by tracing the exploits of one character type and develop theories to account for similar tales in diverse cultures (e.g., trickster tales).		199D
3.5 Define figurative language (e.g., simile, metaphor, hyperbole, personification) and identify its use in literary works.	81A, 114, 115A	199D

Writing

	Unit 1	Unit 2
1.0 Writing Strategies Students write clear, coherent sentences and paragraphs that develop a central idea. Their writing shows they consider the audience and purpose. Students progress through the stages of the writing process (e.g., prewriting, drafting, revising, editing successive versions).		
Organization and Focus		
1.1 Set a focus, an organizational structure, and a point of view based upon purpose, audience, length, and format requirements.	31F–31J, 47F–47J	131G, 143G, 153C, 153G, 171G, 187G, 201G, 205G
1.2 Create multiple-paragraph compositions: a. provide an introductory paragraph. b. Establish and support a central idea with a topic sentence at or near the beginning of the first paragraph. c. Include supporting paragraphs with simple facts, details, and explanations. d. Conclude with a paragraph that summarizes the points. e. Use correct indention.	65J, 79G–79H, 123J	131H, 153H, 187H, 201H, 205H
1.3 Use traditional structures for conveying information (e.g., chronological order, cause and effect, similarity and difference, and posing and answering a question).	65J, 79I	131G–131H, 143H, 171G–171H, 187H, 201H, 205H
Penmanship		
1.4 Write fluidly and legibly in cursive or joined italic.	31J, 47J, 65J, 79J, 97J, 113J, 123J	131J, 143J, 153J, 171J, 187J, 201J, 205J
Research and Technology		
1.5 Quote or paraphrase information sources, citing them appropriately.		187F
1.6 Locate information in reference texts by using organizational features (e.g., prefaces, appendixes).		143D

Unit 3	Unit 4	Unit 5	Unit 6
208N, 2080, 221C, 226N, 242N, 2420, 258N, 264N, 288N, 308N	322N, 334N, 360N, 378N, 392N, 406N	416N, 426N, 434M, 446N, 460N, 476N	484, 484M, 492N, 502N, 508N, 522N, 532N, 542N
208M, 221A, 226M, 237A, 242M, 248, 253A, 258M, 261A, 264M, 285A, 288M, 305A, 308M, 317A	322M, 324, 326, 328, 331A, 331C, 334M, 357A, 360M, 362, 378, 378M, 380, 382, 387A, 392M, 401A, 406M, 411A	416M, 421A, 426M, 431A, 434M, 441A, 446, 446M, 448, 452, 457A, 460M, 471A, 476M, 479A	484M, 489A, 492M, 497A, 502M, 505A, 508M, 517A, 522M, 529A, 532M, 539A, 542M, 545A
216, 230, 261F		430	
285E, 319	372, 389, 389A, 399, 403, 413	433, 443, 459, 473, 481	493, 497, 507, 519, 531, 531A, 541, 547, 547A
259, 261, 261C		426P, 427, 429, 431, 431C, 460P, 461, 463, 465	
263B	389B	423B, 473B	491B, 519B
253A, 285A, 317A	331A, 357D, 373E, 387A	476A	
237, 237A, 253A, 285A, 285E, 289, 291, 317A, 317D	331A, 331D, 357A, 367, 369, 371, 373, 373A, 380, 384, 387A, 387D, 401A		517A
237, 237A, 237C, 239, 253A, 285A, 285E, 319	331A, 331D, 367, 371	447, 449, 451, 469, 471, 471C	505D, 517A
	331D		
255G, 319G, 319H	348, 360K, 362, 375G, 375H, 377A, 413G, 413H	473G, 473H, 473I, 475A	
223G-223H, 263G-263H	333F-333G, 359F-359G, 375F-375G, 389F-389G, 403F-403G, 413F-413G	423G, 433G, 443G-443H, 459G, 473G, 481G-481H	491G, 499G, 507G, 519G, 531G, 541G, 547G
	333H, 359H, 375H, 389H, 403H	459H, 473H	541H
305C	333H, 403H	423H, 433G-433H, 443G, 453G-453H, 473G-473H, 481G-481H	541H, 547H
223J, 239J, 255J, 263J, 287J, 307J, 319J	333J, 359J, 375J, 389J, 403J, 413J	423J, 433J, 443J, 459J, 473J, 481J	491J, 499J, 507J, 519J, 531J, 541J, 547J
		473G-473H	
	375D		531D

California Resources

CALIFORNIA RESOURCES

Correlation to California Reading/Language Arts Standards Grade 4

Writing

Writing	Unit 1	Unit 2
1.7 Use various reference materials (e.g., dictionary, thesaurus, card catalog, encyclopedia, online information) as an aid to writing.	79C, 95E, 113J	131D, 187F
1.8 Understand the organization of almanacs, newspapers, and periodicals and how to use those print materials.		
1.9 Demonstrate basic keyboarding skills and familiarity with computer terminology (e.g., cursor, software, memory, disk drive, hard drive).	31E, 47E, 65E, 79E, 97E, 113E, 123E	131E, 143E, 153E, 171E, 187E, 201E, 205E
Evaluation and Revision		
1.10 Edit and revise selected drafts to improve coherence and progression by adding, deleting, consolidating, and rearranging text.	97J, 113J	131J, 143J, 153J, 171J, 187J, 201J, 205J
2.0 Writing Applications (Genres and Their Characteristics) Students write compositions that describe and explain familiar objects, events, and experiences. Student writing demonstrates a command of standard American English and the drafting, research, and organizational strategies outlined in Writing Standard 1.0. Using the writing strategies of grade four outlined in Writing Standard 1.0, students:		
2.1 Write narratives: a. Relate ideas, observations, or recollections of an event or experience. b. Provide a context to enable the reader to imagine the world of the event or experience. c. Use concrete sensory details. d. Provide insight into why the selected event or experience is memorable.	77C	
2.2 Write responses to literature: a. Demonstrate an understanding of the literary work. b. Support judgments through references to both the text and prior knowledge.	45D, 121E	205H
2.3 Write information reports: a. Frame a central question about an issue or situation. b. Include facts and details for focus. c. Draw from more than one source of information (e.g., speakers, books, newspapers, other media sources).	95E	187H
2.4 Write summaries that contain the main ideas of the reading selection and the most significant details.		143H, 187D

Written and Oral English Language Conventions

The standards for written and oral English Language conventions have been placed between those for writing and for listening and speaking because these conventions are essential to both sets of skills.

1.0 Written and Oral English Language Conventions	Unit 1	Unit 2
1.0 Written and Oral English Language Conventions Students write and speak with a command of standard English conventions appropriate to this grade level.		
Sentence Structure		
1.1 Use simple and compound sentences in writing and speaking.	97F–97H, 113F–113H	131F–131H
1.2 Combine short, related sentences with appositives, participial phrases, adjectives, adverbs, and prepositional phrases.		
Grammar		
1.3 Identify and use regular and irregular verbs, adverbs, prepositions, and coordinating conjunctions in writing and speaking.		131F-131H
Punctuation		
1.4 Use parentheses, commas in direct quotations, and apostrophes in the possessive case of nouns and in contractions.	47F-47H, 77E	171F-171H, 185D, 201F-201H, 205F-205H
1.5 Use underlining, quotation marks, or italics to identify titles of documents.		187F-187H, 205F-205H
Capitalization		
1.6 Capitalize names of magazines, newspapers, works of art, musical compositions, organizations, and the first word in quotations when appropriate.	77E	143F-143H, 185D, 205F-205H
Spelling		
1.7 Spell correctly roots, inflections, suffixes and prefixes, and syllable constructions.	79I	201H, 201G, 201I, 131G, 131H, 131I, 433H, 443H, 459H, 481H

Unit 3	Unit 4	Unit 5	Unit 6
221E, 223B, 223E, 239E, 253F, 255E, 263E, 287D, 287E, 307E, 319E	331E, 333D, 375D, 389D, 411F	459G, 473G	489F, 499I, 505F, 507I, 519D, 531D, 531I, 539E, 545F
	375D		
223I-223J, 263I-263J	333I-333J, 359I-35J, 375I-375J, 389I-389J, 403I-403J, 413I-413J	423I-423J, 433I-433J, 443I-443J, 459I-459J, 473I-473J, 481I-481J	491I-491J, 499I-499J, 507I-507J, 519I-519J, 531I-531J, 541I-541J, 547I-547J
263G-263J	333G-333H		487E
255G-255J			497D

Unit 3	Unit 4	Unit 5	Unit 6
255F-255H, 263D, 263F-263H, 287F-287H, 319F-319H	375F-375H		519F-519H, 547F-547H
		433H	507F-507H, 547F-547H
239F-23H, 255F-255H, 307F-307H, 319F-319H	375F-375H, 389F-389H, 403F-403H, 413F-413H		491F-491H, 507F-507H, 519F-519H, 531F-531H, 541F-541H, 547F-547H
223F-234H, 319F-319H			499F-499H, 547F-547H
			499F-499H, 547F-547H
		423H, 473H, 481H	531G, 531H, 519G, 519H, 519I

CALIFORNIA RESOURCES

Correlation to California Reading/Language Arts Standards — Grade 4

Listening and Speaking

	Unit 1	Unit 2
1.0 Listening and Speaking Strategies Students listen critically and respond appropriately to oral communication. They speak in a manner that guides the listener to understand important ideas by using proper phrasing, pitch, and modulation.		
Comprehension		
1.1 Ask thoughtful questions and respond to relevant questions with appropriate elaboration in oral settings.	19P, 29A, 45A, 95A, 111A, 121A, 123A	129A, 141A, 151A, 169A, 185A, 187I, 199A
1.2 Summarize major ideas and supporting evidence presented in spoken messages and formal presentations.	19P	131I
1.3 Identify how language usages (e.g., sayings, expressions) reflect regions and cultures.		153I
1.4 Give precise directions and instructions.		201C
Organization and Delivery of Oral Communication		
1.5 Present effective introductions and conclusions that guide and inform the listener's understanding of important ideas and evidence.	113C	201I
1.6 Use traditional structures for conveying information (e.g., cause and effect, similarity and difference, and posing and answering a question).		201C, 201I
1.7 Emphasize points in ways that help the listener or viewer to follow important ideas and concepts.	113C	205I
1.8 Use details, examples, anecdotes, or experiences to explain or clarify information.		205I
1.9 Use volume, pitch, phrasing, pace, modulation, and gestures appropriately to enhance meaning.	81B, 115B	141E, 201C
Analysis and Evaluation of Oral Media Communication		
1.10 Evaluate the role of the media in focusing attention on events and in forming opinions on issues.		171I
2.0 Speaking Applications (Genres and Their Characteristics) Students deliver brief recitations and oral presentations about familiar experiences or interests that are organized around a coherent thesis statement. Student speaking demonstrates a command of standard American English and the organizational and delivery strategies outlined in Listening and Speaking Standard 1.0. Using the speaking strategies of grade four outlined in Listening and Speaking Standard 1.0, students:		
2.1 Make narrative presentations: a. Relate ideas, observations, or recollections about an event or experience. b. Provide a context that enables the listener to imagine the circumstances of the event or experience. c. Provide insight into why the selected event or experience is memorable.	65A	
2.2 Make informational presentations: a. Frame a key question. b. Include facts and details that help listeners to focus. c. Incorporate more than one source of information (e.g., speakers, books, newspapers, television or radio reports).		205I
2.3 Deliver oral summaries of articles and books that contain the main ideas of the event or article and the most significant details.	113C	143I, 201I
2.4 Recite brief poems (i.e., two or three stanzas), soliloquies, or dramatic dialogues, using clear diction, tempo, volume, and phrasing.	81B, 115B	201I

Unit 3	Unit 4	Unit 5	Unit 6
221A, 223I, 237A, 253A, 261A, 285A, 287I, 305A, 307C	331A, 357A, 387A, 403I, 411A, 413C	421A, 423I, 431A, 441A, 457A, 471A, 481C	489A, 497A, 505A, 517A, 529A, 531I, 539A, 541I, 545A
307C, 319C	413C	481C	547C
287G, 287I, 287H, 255I	307E, 409		
	375A, 413I	481C	
319D		473C	547D
319D		481C	547D
307C, 319C		459C	541C, 547D
	389C	473C	
239I, 307I, 319C, 319I		459C, 473I	499I, 541C, 547D
	389I	423C, 459I	536, 542
319D	333I, 389C	473C	
307C, 319D	389C	473C	547I
287B, 307C		459C	541C
241B	391B	425B, 475B	491I, 521B

California Resources

Correlation to California Reading/Language Arts Standards — Grade 5

Reading

Reading	Unit 1	Unit 2
1.0 Word Analysis, Fluency, and Systematic Vocabulary Development Students use their knowledge of word origins and word relationships, as well as historical and literary context clues, to determine the meaning of specialized vocabulary and to understand the precise meaning of grade-level-appropriate words.		
Word Recognition		
1.1 Read aloud narrative and expository text fluently and accurately and with appropriate pacing, intonation, and expression.	200, 360, 46, 480, 580, 660, 860	1020, 1200, 1280, 1400, 1520, 1660
Vocabulary and Concept Development		
1.2 Use word origins to determine the meaning of unknown words.	200, 33B, 43B	
1.3 Understand and explain frequently used synonyms, antonyms, and homographs.	36K, 36L, 85G–85J, 86K, 86L, 99H	111B, 117B, 125B, 127G–127J, 152K, 152L, 166K, 166L
1.4 Know abstract, derived roots and affixes from Greek and Latin and use this knowledge to analyze the meaning of complex words (e.g., *controversial*).	20K	114K, 114L, 119G–119J, 137G–137J, 151G–151J, 161H, 177H
1.5 Understand and explain the figurative and metaphorical use of words in context.		165
2.0 Reading Comprehension Students read and understand grade-level-appropriate material. They describe and connect the essential ideas, arguments, and perspectives of the text by using their knowledge of text structure, organization, and purpose. The selections in *Recommended Readings in Literature, Kindergarten Through Grade Eight* illustrate the quality and complexity of the materials to be read by students. In addition, by grade eight, students read one million words annually on their own, including a good representation of grade-level-appropriate narrative and expository text (e.g., classic and contemporary literature, magazines, newspapers, online information). In grade five, students make progress toward this goal.		
Structural Features of Informational Materials		
2.1 Understand how text features (e.g., format, graphics, sequence, diagrams, illustrations, charts, maps) make information accessible and usable.	59, 63C, 63D, 99D	113D, 113E, 117C, 119D, 119E, 127E, 135E, 137E, 151E, 161E, 177E
2.2 Analyze text that is organized in sequential or chronological order.	61, 63, 63C, 63D	
Comprehension and Analysis of Grade-Level-Appropriate Text		
2.3 Discern main ideas and concepts presented in texts, identifying and assessing evidence that supports those ideas.	97	111, 113, 115, 117, 125, 129, 131, 135, 135C, 151, 159, 161, 167, 169, 171, 173, 175
2.4 Draw inferences, conclusions, or generalizations about text and support them with textual evidence and prior knowledge.	21, 33C, 37, 39, 41, 43, 43C, 43D, 45, 53, 55, 63, 65, 83, 85, 99	103, 105, 107, 109, 111, 121, 123, 125, 149
2.5 Distinguish facts, supported inferences, and opinions in text.		153
3.0 Literary Response and Analysis Students read and respond to historically or culturally significant works of literature. They begin to find ways to clarify the ideas and make connections between literary works. The selections in *Recommended Readings in Literature, Kindergarten Through Grade Eight* illustrate the quality and complexity of the materials to be read by students.		
Structural Features of Literature		
3.1 Identify and analyze the characteristics of poetry, drama, fiction, and nonfiction and explain the appropriateness of the literary forms chosen by an author for a specific purpose.	47A, 53E, 97C	111D, 117D, 125D, 163A, 165A, 175D
Narrative Analysis of Grade-Level-Appropriate Text		
3.2 Identify the main problem or conflict of the plot and explain how it is resolved.	63E, 83E	
3.3 Contrast the actions, motives (e.g., loyalty, selfishness, conscientiousness), and appearances of characters in a work of fiction and discuss the importance of the contrasts to the plot or theme.	33E	
3.4 Understand that *theme* refers to the meaning or moral of a selection and recognize themes (whether implied or stated directly) in sample works.		
3.5 Describe the function and effects of common literary devices (e.g., imagery, metaphor, symbolism).	47A, 47B	159E, 163A, 165A
Literary Criticism		
3.6 Evaluate the meaning of archetypal patterns and symbols that are found in myth and tradition by using literature from different eras and cultures.		125D
3.7 Evaluate the author's use of various techniques (e.g., appeal of characters in a picture book, logic and credibility of plots and settings, use of figurative language) to influence readers' perspectives.	87, 97E, 53C	

Unit 3	Unit 4	Unit 5	Unit 6
1920, 2120, 2280, 2480, 2780	2880, 309, 3160, 3320, 3660	3900, 4060, 4460, 4620, 4960	5100, 5400, 541B, 5420, 5660, 626, 627B
223B	305B, 332K, 366K, 366L, 379G, 379H, 379J	390L, 430K, 430L	510K, 522K, 537B, 565G, 565H, 565J
180K, 180L, 192K, 248K, 248L, 277G–277K, 278K	315G–315J, 350K, 387I	427G–427J, 430L, 446K, 446L, 462K	602K
223B	288K, 305B, 332K, 366K, 366L, 379I	390L, 430K, 430L	510K, 522K, 537B, 539G, 539H, 542K, 565G–565J, 625H
	296, 329D, 331G–331J	473G, 473I, 473J, 507H	521G–521J, 601G, 601I, 601J
193, 209D	305E, 307E, 311, 315E, 331D, 331E, 347E, 365E, 379E, 387E	405D, 431, 435, 441, 441C, 441D, 495D, 507D	511, 513, 515, 517, 519, 519C, 565D
	311, 331D	433, 435, 437, 439, 441, 441C, 441D, 507D	511, 513, 515, 517, 519, 519C
193, 195, 197, 207, 279, 281, 283	305A, 307, 315, 345A, 347, 385A	403A, 405, 407, 409, 411, 413, 415, 417, 419, 421, 423, 425, 425A, 425C, 425D, 427, 441, 441A, 443, 461	521, 537, 539, 543, 547, 549, 551, 557, 561, 563, 565, 583, 601, 603, 605, 607, 609, 611, 613, 615
207, 209, 213, 215, 217, 219, 221, 223, 225, 231, 235, 237,	305, 307, 313, 315, 329, 331, 345, 347, 351, 353, 355, 357,	391, 393, 395, 397, 399, 401, 403, 403C, 403D, 405, 425,	519, 521, 537, 539, 563, 565, 581, 583, 591, 593, 595, 597,
	367, 369, 371, 373, 375, 377, 377A	403E, 475, 477, 479, 481, 483, 485, 487, 489, 491, 493C, 493D	545, 553, 555, 559
187, 189, 189C, 211A, 247A	309A, 313D, 345E	425E, 429A, 459D, 493E, 505E	519E, 537D, 541A, 569, 573, 577, 581, 581C, 627A
275D		471E	
		441E	599D, 625D
207E	345, 385	403, 425, 429, 441, 459, 471, 493, 505	623D, 625D
243E, 247A	331H–331J	429A, 429B, 473G, 473I, 473J	521G–521J, 601G, 601I, 601J
211A, 243E			519E
187, 275D, 283D	329D, 377E, 379A	469, 471	581E

CALIFORNIA RESOURCES

Correlation to California Reading/Language Arts Standards — Grade 5

Writing

	Unit 1	Unit 2
1.0 Writing Strategies Students write clear, coherent, and focused essays. The writing exhibits the students' awareness of the audience and purpose. Essays contain formal introduction, supporting evidence, and conclusions. Students progress through the stages of the writing process as needed.		
Organization and Focus		
1.1 Create multiple-paragraph narrative compositions: a. Establish and develop a situation or plot. b. Describe the setting. c. Present an ending.	55F, 55I	
1.2 Create multiple-paragraph expository compositions: a. Establish a topic, important ideas, or events in sequence or chronological order. b. Provide details and transitional expressions that link one paragraph to another in a clear line of thought. c. Offer a concluding paragraph that summarizes important ideas and details.	55H	113F, 113H, 113I, 119G, 137G, 137H, 137J, 151J,
Research and Technology		
1.3 Use organizational features of printed text (e.g., citations, end notes, bibliographic references) to locate relevant information.		151D, 151H
1.4 Create simple documents by using electronic media and employing organizational features (e.g., passwords, entry and pull-down menus, word searches, the thesaurus, spell checks).	99G	113E, 119E, 127E, 137E, 151E, 161E, 177E, 177H,
1.5 Use a thesaurus to identify alternative word choices and meanings.		
Evaluation and Revision		
1.6 Edit and revise manuscripts to improve the meaning and focus of writing by adding, deleting, consolidating, clarifying, and rearranging words and sentences.	55G, 65F-65J, 85F-85J	137I, 161F-161H, 177I
2.0 Writing Applications (Genres and Their Characteristics) Students write narrative, expository, persuasive, and descriptive texts of at least 500 to 700 words in each genre. Student writing demonstrates a command of standard American English and the research, organizational, and drafting strategies outlined in Writing Standard 1.0.Using the writing strategies of grade three outlined in Writing Standard 1.0, stude		
2.1 Write narratives: a) Establish a plot, point of view, setting, and conflict. b. Show, rather than tell, the events of the story.		
2.2 Write responses to literature: a. Demonstrate an understanding of a literary work. b. Support judgments through references to the text and to prior knowledge. c. Develop interpretations that exhibit careful reading and understanding.		119H-119J, 127H, 127I, 177H
2.3 Write research reports about important ideas, issues, or events by using the following guidelines: a. Frame questions that direct the investigation. b. Establish a controlling idea or topic. c. Develop the topic with simple facts, details, examples, and explanations.		151I, 161H
2.4 Write persuasive letters or compositions: a. State a clear position in support of a proposal. b. Support a position with relevant evidence. c. Follow a simple organizational pattern. d. Address reader concerns.		

Written and Oral English Language Conventions

The standards for written and oral English language conventions have been placed between those for writing and for listening and speaking because these conventions are essential to both sets of skills.

	Unit 1	Unit 2
1.0 Written and Oral English Language Conventions Students write and speak with a command of standard English conventions appropriate to this grade level.		
Sentence Structure		
1.1 Identify and correctly use prepositional phrases, appositives, and independent and dependent clauses; use transitions and conjunctions to connect ideas.	85J, 99H	
Grammar		
1.2 Identify and correctly use verbs that are often misused (e.g., *lie/lay, sit/set, rise/raise*), modifiers, and pronouns.	45F, 45G, 45H	
Punctuation		
1.3 Use a colon to separate hours and minutes and to introduce a list; use quotation marks around the exact words of a speaker and titles of poems, songs, short stories, and so forth.		161F-161H, 177F, 177H

Unit 3	Unit 4	Unit 5	Unit 6
			521H-521J, 539H, 565H, 583H, 601H, 625H
209F, 209H	365F, 365G, 379F-379I, 387G, 387J	461H, 507H	
	305E	443D	
		405E, 427E , 427I, 427J, 443E, 461E, 473E, 495D, 495E, 507E	521E, 539E, 565E, 583E, 601E, 625E
	315H, 387I	427H	541A
191J, 209J, 225I, 225J, 245J, 277J, 285J	347I, 365I, 387H-387I	443I, 443J, 461I, 461J, 473I, 473J, 495I, 495J, 507I, 507J	521I, 539I, 565I, 583I, 601I, 625I
211A			521H, 521J, 539H, 539J, 565H, 565J, 583H, 583J, 601H, 601J, 625H, 625J
		403D	
207F	305F		563C
	347G, 365G, 365H, 379I, 379J, 385E	505F	

Unit 3	Unit 4	Unit 5	Unit 6
225F-225H, 285F-285H	307F, 331H, 387F, 387H	405F-405H, 473F-473H, 495F-495H, 507F-507H	565F-565H, 583F-583H, 601F-601H, 625F-625H
191F, 191G, 209F, 209G, 285F, 285G	331F-331H		583F-583H; 625G
	363E		539F-539H, 563D, 601F-601H

CALIFORNIA RESOURCES

Correlation to California Reading/Language Arts Standards Grade 5

Written and Oral English Language Conventions

Standard	Unit 1	Unit 2
Capitalization		
1.4 Use correct capitalization.	35F-35H, 65F-65J, 85F-85H, 99F-99H	113F-113H, 119F-119H, 177F-177H
Spelling		
1.5 Spell roots, suffixes, prefixes, contractions, and syllable constructions correctly.	35F-35J, 45F-45J, 55F-55J, 65F-65J, 85F-85J, 99F-99J	113F-113J, 119F-119J, 127F-127J, 137F-137J, 151F-151J, 161F-161J, 177F-177J

Listening and Speaking

Standard	Unit 1	Unit 2
1.0 Listening and Speaking Strategies Students deliver focused, coherent presentations that convey ideas clearly and relate to the background and interests of the audience. They evaluate the content of oral communication.		
Comprehension		
1.1 Ask questions that seek information not already discussed.	65I, 85I, 99C	151I, 177C
1.2 Interpret a speaker's verbal and nonverbal messages, purposes, and perspectives.	99A	
1.3 Make inferences or draw conclusions based on an oral report.	35I, 99C	113I, 177C
Organization and Delivery of Oral Communication		
1.4 Select a focus, organizational structure, and point of view for an oral presentation.	45C, 85C	119C, 151C, 161C, 161I
1.5 Clarify and support spoken ideas with evidence and examples.	85A	161I
1.6 Engage the audience with appropriate verbal cues, facial expressions, and gestures.	99C	163B, 165B, 177C
Analysis and Evaluation of Oral and Media Communications		
1.7 Identify, analyze, and critique persuasive techniques (e.g., promises, dares, flattery, glittering generalities); identify logical fallacies used in oral presentations and media messages.	99A	137I
1.8 Analyze media as sources for information, entertainment, persuasion, interpretation of events, and transmission of culture.		137I
2.0 Speaking Applications (Genres and Their Characteristics) Students deliver well-organized formal presentations employing traditional rhetorical strategies (e.g., narration, exposition, persuasion, description). Student speaking demonstrate a command of standard American English and the organizational and delivery strategies outlined in Listening and Speaking Standard 1.0. Using the speaking strategies of grade three outlined in Listening and Speaking Standard 1.0, students:		
2.1 Deliver narrative presentations: a. Establish a situation, plot, point of view, and setting with descriptive words and phrases. b. Show, rather than tell, the listener what happened.		
2.2 Deliver informative presentations about an important idea, issue, or events by using the following means: a. Frame questions to direct the investigation. b. Establish a controlling idea or topic. c. Develop the topic with simple facts, details, examples, and explanations.		119D, 161I, 161J
2.3 Deliver oral responses to literature: a. Summarize significant events. b. Articulate an understanding of several ideas or images communicated by the literary work. c. Use examples or textual evidence from the work to support conclusions.		127J, 177I

Unit 3	Unit 4	Unit 5	Unit 6
		443F-443H, 461F-461H	539F-539H
191F-191J, 209F-209J, 225F-225J, 245F-245J, 277F-277J, 285F-285J	307F-307J, 315F-315J, 331F-331J, 347F-347J, 365F-365J, 379F-379J, 387F-387J	405F-405J, 427F-427J, 443F-443J, 461F-461J, 473F-473J, 495F-495J, 507F-507J	521F-521J, 539F-539J, 565F-565J, 583F-583J, 601F-601J, 625F-625J
285C		507C	565I, 625C
191I, 277I		429B	601I
285C		405I, 507C	625C
209C, 277C	315C, 365C, 387I	427C, 473C, 495C	539C, 601C
285I	387I		
277I, 285C	309B	507C	601I, 625C
	307D, 307I, 347I		
245I	307A, 307D, 347I	461I	
211B			625I, 625J
191C	307C, 363F	405C	521C
247B, 285I			566G

Correlation to California Reading/Language Arts Standards — Grade 6

Reading	Unit 1	Unit 2
1.0 Word Analysis, Fluency, and Systematic Vocabulary Development Students use their knowledge of word origins and word relationships, as well as historical and literary context clues, to determine the meaning of specialized vocabulary and to understand the precise meaning of grade-level appropriate words.		
Word Recognition		
1.1 Read aloud narrative and expository text fluently and accurately and with appropriate pacing, intonation, and expression.	320, 500, 640, 760, 920	1140, 1360, 1620, 1740, 1960
Vocabulary and Concept Development		
1. 2 Identify and interpret figurative language and words with multiple meanings.	64, 66	
1.3 Recognize the origins and meanings of frequently used foreign words in English and use these words accurately in speaking and writing.		161G–161J, 196K, 213D, 242K
1.4 Monitor expository text for unknown words or words with novel meanings by using word, sentence, and paragraph clues to determine meaning.		193C
1.5 Understand and explain "shades of meaning" in related words (e.g., *softly* and *quietly*).		216K
2.0 Reading Comprehension (Focus on Informational Materials) Students read and understand grade-level-appropriate material. They describe and connect the essential ideas, arguments, and perspectives of the text by using their knowledge of text structure, organization, and purpose. The selections in Recommended Readings in Literature, Kindergarten Through Grade Eight illustrate the quality and complexity of the materials to be read by students. In addition, by grade eight, students read one million words annually on their own, including a good representation of grade-level-appropriate nar and expository text (e.g., classic and contemporary literature, magazines, newspapers, online information). In grade six, students continue to make progress toward this goal.		
Structural Features of Informational Materials		
2.1 Identify the structural features of popular media (e.g., newspapers, magazines, online information) and use the features to obtain information.		
2.2 Analyze text that uses the compare-and-contrast organizational pattern.		169E, 215A, 239A
Comprehension and Analysis of Grade-Level-Appropriate Text		
2.3 Connect and clarify main ideas by identifying their relationships to other sources and related topics.		114, 136P, 161A, 168, 171A, 174M, 174, 177, 182, 185, 191, 195A, 215A, 215D, 239A, 263A
2.4 Clarify an understanding of texts by creating outlines, logical notes, summaries, or reports.	89D	122, 129, 132, 158, 159C, 161A, 161D, 164, 192, 198, 201, 202, 209, 213C, 215A, 215D, 216M, 224, 228, 236
2.5 Follow multiple-step instructions for preparing applications (e.g., for a public library card, bank savings account, sports club, league membership).		
Expository Critique		
2.6 Determine the adequacy and appropriateness of the evidence for an author's conclusions.		
2.7 Make reasonable assertions about a text through accurate, supporting citations.	77, 79, 81, 83, 85, 87, 87C	145, 147, 149, 151, 153, 159, 174, 193D, 243, 245, 247, 249
2.8 Note instances of unsupported inferences, fallacious reasoning, persuasion, and propaganda in text.		225
3.0 Literary Response and Analysis Students read and respond to historically or culturally significant works of literature that reflect and enhance their studies of history and socia science. They clarify the ideas and connect them to other literary works. The selections in *Recommended Readings in Literature, Kindergarten Through Grade Eight* illustrate the quality and complexity of the materials to be read by students.		
Structural Features of Literature		
3.1 Identify the forms of fiction and describe the major characteristics of each form.	107E	

Unit 3	Unit 4	Unit 5	Unit 6
2660, 2820, 2920, 3060, 3120, 3280, 3400	3540, 3860, 4020, 4320, 4400, 4620, 4920		6000, 6240
282K, 291G-291J, 307E-307F, 309G-309J, 313	421G-421J, 432K, 437G-437J, 440K, 461G-461J		570K, 621E, 623G-623J, 624K
292K, 306K	356	381E, 533F-533J, 567F-567J	584K, 624K, 624L, 633C
292M, 313, 314, 318, 323, 325C	386M	381E, 432, 472M, 492M, 521G-521J, 522M, 536M	
306K		551G-551J	608K
291D, 303D	383D	489E, 507E, 521D, 521E, 533D, 533E, 551E, 567E	623D
309A			
294, 298, 303A, 309A, 327A, 332, 339A, 349F, 351A	399A, 421A, 437A, 459E, 459F, 461A, 469A	489A, 489C, 507A, 519F, 521A, 526, 531E, 533A, 538, 539, 541, 542, 546, 548, 551A, 552, 567A	583A, 599A, 603E, 605A, 621F, 623A, 624, 635A, 651A
278, 300, 301C, 301D, 301E, 301F, 307F, 325D, 327D, 328, 337E, 349C, 349D, 351A	412, 414, 418, 421A, 437A, 461A, 462M, 469A	381C, 381F, 472, 482, 486, 505E, 507A, 511, 513, 515, 516, 518, 519C, 519F, 521A, 523, 525, 527, 529, 531	599A, 605A, 623A, 632, 633D, 635D
351F-351J			
	437A	473, 475, 477, 479, 481, 483, 485, 487, 507A, 521A	627, 629, 631, 633
336	355, 356, 357, 358, 359, 361, 363, 364, 365, 367, 369, 371	487C, 494, 498, 501, 502, 503, 505, 543, 545, 547, 549	
		487C, 567A	651D
	397D, 435E	565D	581F, 597D, 603D, 649F

CALIFORNIA RESOURCES

Correlation to California Reading/Language Arts Standards Grade 6

Reading

	Unit 1	Unit 2
Narrative Analysis of Grade-Level-Appropriate Text		
3.2 Analyze the effect of the qualities of the character (e.g., courage or cowardice, ambition or laziness) on the plot and the resolution of the conflict.		116
3.3 Analyze the influence of setting on the problem and its resolution.		
3.4 Define how tone or meaning is conveyed in poetry through word choice, figurative language, sentence structure, line length, punctuation, rhythm, repetition, and rhyme.		
3.5 Identify the speaker and recognize the difference between first- and third-person narration (e.g., autobiography compared with biography).	29E	217, 219
3.6 Identify and analyze features of themes conveyed through characters, actions, and images.		
3.7 Explain the effects of common literary devices (e.g., symbolism, imagery, metaphor) in a variety of fictional and nonfictional texts.		
Literary Criticism		
3.8 Critique the credibility of characterization and the degree to which a plot is contrived or realistic (e.g., compare use of fact and fantasy in historical fiction).		

Writing

	Unit 1	Unit 2
1.0 Writing Strategies Students write clear, coherent, and focused essays. The writing exhibits students' awareness of the audience and purpose. Essays contain formal introductions, supporting evidenc and conclusions. Students progress through the stages of the writing process as needed.		
Organization and Focus		
1.1 Choose the form of writing (e.g., personal letter, letter to the editor, review, poem, report, narrative) that best suits the intended purpose.	49F–49J	215C
1.2 Create multiple-paragraph expository compositions: a. Engage the interest of the reader and state a clear purpose. b. Develop the topic with supporting details and precise verbs, nouns, and adjectives to paint a visual image in the mind of the reader. c. Conclude with a detailed summary linked to the purpose of the composition.	49H, 73J	161G–161I, 171G, 215I, 239F, 239G, 263G, 263H
1.3 Use a variety of effective and coherent organizational patterns, including comparison and contrast; organization by categories; and arrangement by spatial order, order of importance, or climactic order.	49G–49J, 63G, 63J, 73I	135A, 135G, 161G, 161H, 171G, 195G, 195H, 215C, 215I, 239A, 263G
Research and Technology		
1.4 Use organizational features of electronic text (e.g., bulletin boards, databases, keyword searches, e-mail addresses) to locate information.		195C
1.5 Compose documents with appropriate formatting by using word-processing skills and principles of design (e.g., margins, tabs, spacing, columns, page orientation).	109I	239J
Evaluation and Revision		
1.6 Revise writing to improve the organization and consistency of ideas within and between paragraphs.	73H–73J	135I, 161I, 171I, 195I, 239C, 239G, 239H, 263I
2.0 Writing Applications (Genres and Their Characteristics) Students write narrative, expository, persuasive, and descriptive texts of at least 500 to 700 words in each genre. Student writing demonstrates a command of standard American English and the research, organizational, and drafting strategies outlined in Writing Standard 1.0. Using the writing strategies of grade six outlined in Writing Standard 1.0, studer		
2.1 Write narratives: a. Establish and develop a plot and setting and present a point of view that is appropriate to the stories. b. Include sensory details and concrete language to develop plot and character. c. Use a range of narrative devices (e.g., dialogue, suspense).		
2.2 Write expository compositions (e.g., description, explanation, comparison and contrast, problem and solution): a. State the thesis or purpose. b. Explain the situation. c. Follow an organizational pattern appropriate to the type of composition. d. Offer persuasive evidence to validate arguments and conclusions as needed.		161H, 195H, 239D, 263H, 263I

Unit 3	Unit 4	Unit 5	Unit 6
349E			581E, 605A, 617, 619, 633D, 651A
349E	397C	519E	
	385A, 439B	491A, 533A	
301D, 307C	435E, 439A, 439B		
274, 289E, 349D, 349E	435E		571, 573, 575, 579, 581, 581C, 605A, 621C, 625, 635A, 651A
266, 279D, 309G–309H	385A, 397C, 435E	491A, 533A	617, 621E
237E, 279C	459D		597D

Unit 3	Unit 4	Unit 5	Unit 6
279C, 291D, 303A, 307F, 309A, 327G	399C, 399D, 437C, 459D, 461C, 469A, 469F	487F, 489A, 491A, 507A, 551A	583C, 597D, 599A, 621C, 623C, 623D
281G, 309I	437C		583G–583I, 599I, 623C
281H, 291G, 291H, 303H, 303I, 309G, 339G, 339H	383G, 383H, 399G, 399I, 421A, 421G, 421H, 429G, 459D, 461G, 469G	489G–489I, 491A, 507A, 507G–507H, 521G, 549E, 551A, 551G–551I, 567C	583G, 583H, 597D, 599G, 599H, 605C, 605G, 605H, 635G, 635H, 651G, 651H
301D, 351D	459F	487F, 521C, 521D, 551F	623C
	437J	533J, 567C	623D
281I, 291I, 303J, 309I, 339C, 339I, 351C	383I, 399I, 421I, 437G, 437H, 461C, 469C, 469I	489I, 507I, 521I, 533I, 551C, 567C, 567G–567H	583I, 599I, 605I, 623I, 635C, 635I, 651C, 651I
	383H, 397D, 399H, 399I, 421H, 421I, 429G–429J, 437F, 437H, 461F–461I, 469H		
339C		489A, 533C	

CALIFORNIA RESOURCES

Correlation to California Reading/Language Arts Standards Grade 6

Writing

Writing	Unit 1	Unit 2
2.3 Write research reports: a. Pose relevant questions with a scope narrow enough to be thoroughly covered. b. Support the main idea or ideas with facts, details, examples, and explanations from multiple authoritative sources (e.g., speakers, periodicals, online information searches). c. Include a bibliography.		171C, 161C, 195C, 239I
2.4 Write responses to literature: a. Develop an interpretation exhibiting careful reading, understanding, and insight. b. Organize the interpretation around several clear ideas, premises, or images. c. Develop and justify the interpretation through sustained use of examples and textual evidence.		
2.5 Write persuasive compositions: a. State a clear position on a proposition or proposal. b. Support the position with organized and relevant evidence. c. Anticipate and address reader concerns and counterarguments.		

Written and Oral English Language Conventions

The standards for written and oral English Language conventions have been placed between those for writing and for listening and speaking because these conventions are essential to both sets of skills.

1.0 Written and Oral English Language Conventions Students write and speak with a command of standard English conventions appropriate to this grade level.	Unit 1	Unit 2
Sentence Structure		
1.1 Use simple, compound, and compound-complex sentences; use effective coordination and subordination of ideas to express complete thoughts.	73H	216L
Grammar		
1.2 Identify and properly use indefinite pronouns and present perfect, past perfect, and future perfect verb tenses; ensure that verbs agree with compound subjects.	73H, 89I, 109F, 109H	
Punctuation		
1.3 Use colons after the salutation in business letters, semicolons to connect independent clauses, and commas when linking two clauses with a conjunction in compound sentences.		
Capitalization		
1.4 Use correct capitalization.	89G, 89I, 109F, 109H	
Spelling		
1.5 Spell frequently misspelled words correctly (e.g., *their, they're, there*).	31F-31J, 49F-49J, 63F-63J, 73F-73J, 89F-89J, 109F-109J	135F-135J, 161F-161J, 171F-171J, 195F-195J, 215F-215J, 239F-239J, 263F-263J

Listening and Speaking

1.0 Listening and Speaking Strategies Students deliver focused, coherent presentations that convey ideas clearly and relate to the background and interests of the audience. They evaluate the content of oral communication.	Unit 1	Unit 2
Comprehension		
1.1 Relate the speaker's verbal communication (e.g., word choice, pitch, feeling, tone) to the nonverbal message (e.g., posture, gesture).		
1.2 Identify the tone, mood, and emotion conveyed in the oral communication.	31I	
1.3 Restate and execute multiple-step oral instructions and directions.		
Organization and Delivery of Oral Communication		
1.4 Select a focus, an organizational structure, and a point of view, matching the purpose, message, occasion, and vocal modulation to the audience.		
1.5 Emphasize salient points to assist the listener in following the main ideas and concepts.		213C, 239I, 263I
1.6 Support opinions with detailed evidence and with visual or media displays that use appropriate technology.		135E, 161E, 171E, 195E, 215E, 239E, 239I, 263E, 263I

Unit 3	Unit 4	Unit 5	Unit 6
339C, 351D	383C, 397F, 421A, 437C, 461C	521C, 533C, 551C, 567C, 567I	605C
307E	459D	551A	597D
		487C, 489H, 489I, 507G–507H, 521G, 551F–551J, 567F–567G	

291F–291H, 327F–327H, 351F–351H	383I		605F–605H, 651F–651H
	399F–399H, 469G, 469H		623F–623H, 635F–635H, 651F–651H
327F–327H, 351G, 351H	429G, 461G, 469F, 469H		605F–605H, 623F–623H, 651F–651H
			583F–583H, 651F–651H
281F–281J, 291F–291J, 303F–303J, 309F–309J, 327F–327J, 339F–339J, 351F–351J	383F–383J, 399F–399J, 421F–421J, 429F–429J, 437F–437J, 461F–461J, 469F–469J	489F–489J, 507F–507J, 521F–521J, 533F–533J, 551F–551J, 567F–567J	583F–583J, 599F–599J, 605F–605J, 623F–623J, 635F–635J, 651F–651J

301F, 309A	439A	491B	635I, 651C
281I, 301F, 307E, 309A, 309D	439A	491B, 535B	583C, 651C
	383I		
307E, 309D, 339C	399A, 437C, 461C, 461I, 469C, 469D	521A, 533C, 549F, 551C, 567C	599A, 623C, 635A, 651C, 651I
301E, 307E	399A, 437I, 439A, 461C, 469C	531C, 531E, 551C, 567C, 567I	635A, 651C, 651I
281E, 291E, 303E, 309E, 327E, 339C, 339E, 339I, 351E	383E, 399A, 399E, 421E, 429E, 437E, 461C, 461E, 469C, 469E	531E, 551C, 567C	635A, 635D, 651C

Correlation to California Reading/Language Arts Standards Grade 6

Writing	Unit 1	Unit 2
1.7 Use effective rate, volume, pitch, and tone and align nonverbal elements to sustain audience interest and attention.	49I	161I
Analysis and Evaluation of Oral and Media Communications		
1.8 Analyze the use of rhetorical devices (e.g., cadence, repetitive patterns, use of onomatopoeia) for intent and effect.		
1.9 Identify persuasive and propaganda techniques used in television and identify false and misleading information.		
2.0 Speaking Applications (Genres and Their Characteristics) Students deliver well-organized formal presentations employing traditional rhetorical strategies (e.g., narration, exposition, persuasion, description). Student speaking demonstrates a command of standard American English and the organizational and delivery strategies outlined in Listening and Speaking Standard 1.0. Using the speaking strategies of grade six outlined in Listening and Speaking Standard 1.0, students:		
2.1 Deliver narrative presentations: a. Establish a context, plot, and point of view. b. Include sensory details and concrete language to develop the plot and character. c. Use a range of narrative devices (e.g., dialogue, tension, or suspense).		239I, 239J
2.2 Deliver informative presentations: a. Pose relevant questions sufficiently limited in scope to be completely and thoroughly answered. b. Develop the topic with facts, details, examples, and explanations from multiple authoritative sources (e.g., speakers, periodicals, online information).		161C, 195C, 239C, 239I, 263I
2.3 Deliver oral responses to literature: a. Develop an interpretation exhibiting careful reading, understanding, and insight. b. Organize the selected interpretation around several clear ideas, premises, or images. c. Develop and justify the selected interpretation through sustained use of examples and textual evidence.		177I
2.4 Deliver persuasive presentations: a. Provide a clear statement of the position. b. Include relevant evidence. c. Offer a logical sequence of information. d. Engage the listener and foster acceptance of the proposition or proposal.		
2.5 Deliver presentations on problems and solutions: a. Theorize on the causes and effects of each problem and establish connections between the defined problem and at least one solution. b. Offer persuasive evidence to validate the definition of the problem and the proposed solutions.		

Unit 3	Unit 4	Unit 5	Unit 6
291I, 303I, 307E, 309A	399I, 439A	491B, 535B, 551C, 551I, 567C	635D, 635I, 651C
309A	439A		605I
	429I	489I, 505D, 533I	
351I	437I, 469I		
339C, 351C, 351I	421C, 469C	489E, 507A, 507E, 521E, 533E, 551E, 567E	
			651I
		567I	
339C		507I	

Notes

Use this page to record lessons or elements that work well or need to be adjusted for future reference.

Lessons that work well.

Lessons that need adjustments.

Notes

Use this page to record lessons or elements that work well or need to be adjusted for future reference.

Lessons that work well.

Lessons that need adjustments.

Notes

Use this page to record lessons or elements that work well or need to be adjusted for future reference.

Lessons that work well.

Lessons that need adjustments.

Notes

Use this page to record lessons or elements that work well
or need to be adjusted for future reference.

Lessons that work well.

Lessons that need adjustments.

Notes

Use this page to record lessons or elements that work well or need to be adjusted for future reference.

Lessons that work well.

Lessons that need adjustments.

Notes

Use this page to record lessons or elements that work well or need to be adjusted for future reference.

Lessons that work well.

Lessons that need adjustments.

Notes

Use this page to record lessons or elements that work well
or need to be adjusted for future reference.

Lessons that work well.

Lessons that need adjustments.